Web Design with
HTML5 & CSS3

COMPREHENSIVE

MINNICK

Eighth Edition

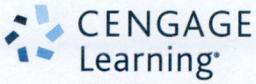
CENGAGE
Learning®

Australia • Brazil • Mexico • Singapore • United Kingdom • United States

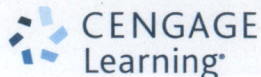

Web Design with HTML5 and CSS3, Comprehensive, Eighth Edition
Jessica Minnick

Product Director: Kathleen McMahon

Product Team Manager: Kristin McNary

Senior Content Developers: Kate Mason and Marjorie Hunt

Marketing Director: Michelle McTighe

Senior Content Project Manager: Matthew Hutchinson

Art Director: Heather Marshall, Lumina Datamatics, Inc.

Manufacturing Planner: Julio Esperas

IP Analyst: Amber Hill

Senior IP Project Manager: Kathryn Kucharek

Production Service: Lumina Datamatics, Inc.

Compositor: Lumina Datamatics, Inc.

Cover Images:
Background image: iStockPhoto.com/ virusowy
Computers: iStockPhoto.com/scyther5

Unless otherwise stated, all screenshots courtesy of Microsoft Corporation. Microsoft is either a registered trademark or a trademark of Microsoft Corporation in the United States and/ or other countries. Cengage Learning is an independent entity from the Microsoft Corporation, and not affiliated with Microsoft in any manner.

For product information and technology assistance, contact us at
Cengage Learning Customer & Sales Support, 1-800-354-9706

For permission to use material from this text or product, submit all requests online at **cengage.com/permissions**
Further permissions questions can be emailed to **permissionrequest@cengage.com**

Library of Congress Control Number: 2015958528

Student Edition:
ISBN: 978-1-305-57816-6

Cengage Learning
20 Channel Center Street
Boston, MA 02210
USA

Cengage Learning is a leading provider of customized learning solutions with employees residing in nearly 40 different countries and sales in more than 125 countries around the world. Find your local representative at **www.cengage.com**.

Cengage Learning products are represented in Canada by Nelson Education, Ltd.

For your course and learning solutions, visit **www.cengage.com**

Purchase any of our products at your local college store or at our preferred online store **www.cengagebrain.com**

Trademarks:
Some of the product names and company names used in this book have been used for identification purposes only and may be trademarks or registered trademarks of their respective manufacturers and sellers.

Printed in the United States of America
Print Number: 01 Print Year: 2016

Web Design with
HTML5 & CSS3

COMPREHENSIVE Eighth Edition

Contents

Appendices

Preface

The Shelly Cashman Series® offers the finest textbooks in computer education. We are proud that our previous web design and development books have been so well received. With each new edition of our HTML and CSS books, we make significant improvements based on web technology and comments made by instructors and students. For *Web Design with HTML5 and CSS3, Eighth Edition*, the Shelly Cashman Series development team carefully reviewed our pedagogy and analyzed its effectiveness in teaching today's student. Contemporary students read less, but need to retain more. As they develop and perform skills, students must know how to apply the skills to different settings. Today's students need to be continually engaged and challenged to retain what they're learning.

With this web design book, we continue our commitment to focusing on the user and how they learn best.

Objectives of This Textbook

Web Design with HTML5 and CSS3, Eighth Edition, is intended for a first course that offers an introduction to HTML, CSS, and responsive web design techniques. No experience with webpage development or computer programming is required. The objectives of this book are:

- To teach the fundamentals of how to plan and organize the webpages for a new website

- To thoroughly apply two fundamental webpage technologies to realistic case studies: HTML for structure and CSS for style and layout

- To provide an exercise-oriented approach that reinforces learning by doing

- To introduce students to new web technologies and trends, including responsive web design and mobile-first design strategies

- To demonstrate current techniques for incorporating audio and video and for encouraging interactivity through social media and JavaScript

- To promote curiosity and independent exploration of web resources

- To support current, professional webpage development best practices

- To encourage independent study and support distance learners

The Shelly Cashman Approach

Proven Pedagogy with an Emphasis on Project Planning

Each chapter presents a practical problem to be solved, within a project planning framework. The project orientation is strengthened by the use of the Roadmap, which provides a visual guide for the project. Step-by-step instructions with supporting screens guide students through the steps. Instructional steps are supported by the Q&A, Other Ways, Experimental Steps, and BTW features.

Visually Engaging Book That Maintains Student Interest

The step-by-step tasks with supporting figures create a rich visual experience for the student. Callouts on the screens that present both explanatory and navigational information provide students with information they need when they need to know it.

Supporting Reference Materials (Appendices)

The appendices provide additional information about the details of HTML and CSS so that students can quickly look up information about web design terms, HTML elements, attributes, and valid values as well as CSS properties and values.

End-of-Chapter Student Activities

Extensive end-of-chapter activities provide a variety of reinforcement opportunities for students where they can apply and expand their skills. To complete some of these assignments, you will be required to use the Data Files for Students. Visit www .cengagebrain.com for detailed access instructions or contact your instructor for information about accessing the required files.

New to This Edition

Fresh, Industry-Leading Website Design Practices

For this edition, the development team made a huge leap forward in bringing up-to-date, forward-thinking website development practices into focus and application.

Semantic Wireframe

The webpage development process starts with a semantic wireframe, which uses the structural elements new to HTML5 to efficiently organize the regions of a webpage.

Focus on Responsive Design, Fluid Layouts, and Mobile-First Web Development

Design a single website that responds to the screen displays of desktop and laptop computers, tablets, smartphones, and other mobile devices.

HTML5 and CSS3 Features

The chapter project and exercises incorporate the latest additions to HTML and CSS, including new HTML5 elements, CSS3 properties, and syntax recommended by the World Wide Web Consortium (W3C). Every chapter validates documents using online tools for HTML5 and CSS3.

All New Projects

This edition contains a wealth of contemporary projects that logically build in complexity and probe for understanding. Our goal is not only to help you teach valid HTML and CSS, but to reveal deeper conceptual issues essential to the field of web development. Using the technologies of today's web developers results in websites that are worthy candidates for an electronic portfolio.

Professional Best Practices

With the advent of today's powerful content management systems and website builder tools, do you still need to learn how to create HTML and CSS files from scratch in a text editor? Professionals in the field answer that question with a united, enthusiastic yes! Mastering these technologies is essential to all web-related careers.

Instructor Resources

The Instructor Resources include both teaching and testing aids and can be accessed via www.cengage.com/login.

Instructor's Manual Includes lecture notes summarizing the chapter sections, figures, and boxed elements found in every chapter, teacher tips, classroom activities, lab activities, and quick quizzes in Microsoft® Word® files.

Syllabus Easily customizable sample syllabus covers policies, assignments, exams, and other course information.

Figure Files Illustrations for every figure in the textbook in electronic form.

PowerPoint Presentations A multimedia lecture presentation system that provides slides for each chapter. Presentations are based on chapter objectives.

Data Files for Students Includes all the files that are required by students to complete the exercises.

Solutions to Exercises Includes solutions for all end-of-chapter exercises and chapter reinforcement exercises.

Test Bank & Test Engine Test banks include questions for every chapter, featuring objective-based and critical thinking question types. Cengage Learning Testing Powered by Cognero is a flexible, online system that allows you to:

- author, edit, and manage test bank content from multiple Cengage Learning solutions
- create multiple test versions in an instant
- deliver tests from your LMS, your classroom, or wherever you want

Learn Online

CengageBrain.com is the premier destination for purchasing or renting Cengage Learning textbooks, eBooks, eChapters, and study tools at a significant discount (eBooks up to 50% off Print). In addition, CengageBrain.com provides direct access to all digital products including eBooks, eChapters, and digital solutions, regardless of where purchased.

course|notes™
quick reference guide

CourseNotes

CourseNotes are six-panel quick reference cards that reinforce the most important and widely used features of a software application in a visual and user-friendly format. CourseNotes serve as a great reference tool during and after the student completes the course. CourseNotes are available for software applications such as Microsoft Office 2013, Windows 8, and HTML. Topic-based CourseNotes, including Best Practices in Social Networking, Hot Topics in Technology, and Leverage the Internet for Your Career Search, are also available. Visit www.cengagebrain.com to learn more!

Textbook Walk-Through

The Shelly Cashman Series Pedagogy: Project-Based — Step-by-Step — Variety of Assessments

Roadmaps provide a visual guide to each project, showing the students where they are in the process of creating each project.

Step-by-step instructions now provide a context beyond point-and-click. Each step provides information on why students are performing each task, or what will occur as a result.

Q&A boxes anticipate questions students may have when working through the steps and provide additional information about what they are doing right where they need it.

Figure 10–3

Figure 10–4

Roadmap

In this chapter, you will learn how to create the webpages shown in Figures 10–1, 10–2, 10–3, and 10–4. The following roadmap identifies general activities you will perform as you progress through this chapter:

1. INSERT SOCIAL MEDIA ICONS and LINKS.
2. STYLE SOCIAL MEDIA ICONS.
3. CREATE JAVASCRIPT ALERT MESSAGE.
4. CREATE EXTERNAL JAVASCRIPT FILE.
5. CALL JAVASCRIPT FUNCTIONS.

At the beginning of step instructions throughout the chapter, you will see an abbreviated form of this roadmap. The abbreviated roadmap uses colors to indicate chapter progress: gray means the chapter is beyond that activity, blue means the task being shown is covered in that activity, and black means that activity is yet to be covered. For example, the following abbreviated roadmap indicates the chapter would be showing a task in the 2 STYLE SOCIAL MEDIA ICONS activity.

2

- Save your changes and refresh classes.html in your browser (Figure 8–23).

Q&A Why does the border appear only around the sides of the table?
The style rule you created applies to the table only. You will style the th and td elements in subsequent steps.

table border

table is centered on the page

table width is 100% within the main element

Figure 8–23

3

- In the styles.css file, tap or click at the end of Line 276, if necessary, and then press the ENTER key twice to insert new Lines 277 and 278.

- On Line 278, type /* Style specifies border and padding for th and td elements */ to insert a new comment.

- Press the ENTER key to insert a new Line 279, and then type th, td { to insert a new selector.

- Press the ENTER key to insert a new Line 280, increase the indent, and then type border: 0.1em solid #000000; to insert a new property and value.

- Press the ENTER key to insert a new Line 281, and then type padding: 1em; to insert a new property and value.

- Press the ENTER key to insert a new Line 282, decrease the indent, and then type } to insert a closing brace (Figure 8–24).

comment

Line 278

```
276  /* Style specifies border and padding for th and td elements */
279  th, td {
280      border: 0.1em solid #000000;
281      padding: 1em;
282  }
```

style rule for th and td elements

Figure 8–24

Q&A What is the result of the new style?
The style applies a thin (0.1em) solid black (#000000) border and 1em of padding to all sides of the table header and the table data elements.

Explanatory callouts summarize what is happening on screen.

Navigational callouts in red show students where to tap or click.

❷

- Press the ENTER key to insert a new Line 71, and then type `<source src="media/ffc_aud.ogg" type="audio/ogg">` to insert a source element.

```
69    <audio autoplay controls>
70        <source src="media/ffc_aud.mp3" type=""audio/mp3">
71        <source src="media/ffc_aud.ogg" type="audio/ogg">
72        <source src=" media/ffc_aud.wav" type="audio/wav">
73        <p>Your browser does not support the audio tag.</p>
74    </audio>
```

Line 71 → (points to line 71)
paragraph element → (points to line 73)
source elements → (points to lines 71, 72)
closing audio tag → (points to line 74)

Figure 9–14

- Press the ENTER key to insert a new Line 72, and then type `<source src=" media/ffc_aud.wav" type="audio/wav">` to insert a source element.
- Press the ENTER key to insert a new Line 73, and then type `<p>Your browser does not support the audio tag.</p>` to insert a paragraph element.
- Press the ENTER key to insert a new Line 74, decrease the indent, and then type `</audio>` to insert a closing audio tag (Figure 9–14).

Q&A Why do I need to include three source elements?
To accommodate all major browsers, you specify three audio source files, MP3, Ogg, and WAV. These are the three file formats supported by the audio element.

Will the webpage display the paragraph element?
The webpage displays the paragraph element only if the browser does not support the `audio` element.

❸

- Save your change, open index.html in your browser, adjust the window to the size of a desktop viewport, and then scroll down to view the audio controls (Figure 9–15).

index.html page in desktop viewport

Start Today!

audio element
controls

Figure 9–15

© Rob Marmion/Shutterstock.com,
© faysal/Shutterstock.com, © Millefiore
Images/Shutterstock.com

Experiment

- The loop attribute automatically replays the audio file after it is finished. To see how this works, add the loop attribute to the audio tag, save your changes, and then refresh index.html in your browser.
- Remove the controls attribute from the audio element to view the page without controls, save your changes, and then refresh index.html in your browser.
- Remove the loop attribute, add the controls attribute to the audio tag, and then save your changes.

Q&A A message appears at the bottom of my window, "Internet Explorer restricted this webpage from running scripts or ActiveX controls." How should I proceed?
Tap or click the Allow blocked content button to play the audio file and display the audio controls.

My controls do not look like the controls in Figure 9–15. Why?
Figure 9–15 shows the controls in Internet Explorer 11. If you are using a different browser, your controls will look different.

Break Point: If you want to take a break, this is a good place to do so. You can exit the text editor now. To resume at a later time, run your text editor, open the file called about.html, and continue following the steps from this location forward.

Experiment Steps within the step-by-step instructions encourage students to explore, experiment, and take advantage of web technologies. These steps are not necessary to complete the projects, but are designed to increase confidence and problem-solving skills.

CONSIDER THIS

Can I redesign a desktop-only website for multiplatform displa
Yes. If your audience is accustomed to the desktop-only website, retrofitting t
makes sense because the site remains familiar to users. You also avoid buildin
vantage of design decisions such as color scheme and use media you have al
content and number of pages, redesigning may be a time-consuming process

Wireframe

Before web designers actually start crea
they sketch the design using a wireframe. A w
clearly identifies the location of main webpag
organization logo, content areas, and images.
your webpages, use lines and boxes as shown
plenty of white space within your design to i
distinguish among the areas on the webpage. A
active white space and passive white space. A
that is intentionally left blank. Typically, the g
the design of an asymmetrical page. **Passive**
areas. Passive white space helps a user focus on one part of the page. Proper use of white
space makes webpage content easy to read and brings focus to page elements.

tabs or buttons with short
text links for navigating site
appealing graphic or text — Logo — Navigation
passive white space
heading or advertisement — Banner
passive white space
Image — Article — content related to main content
headings and main written content — Text area — active white space
Image
legal matter and contact details — Footer

© 2016 Cengage Learning®

Figure 1–12

Site Map

A **site map** is a planning tool that lists or displays all the pages on a website and indicates how they are related to each other. In other words, a site map shows the structure of a website. Begin defining the structure of a website by identifying the information to provide and then organize that information into divisions using the organizing method that makes the most sense for the content. For example, if the website offers three types of products for sale, organize the site by product category. If the website provides training, organize the site in a step-by-step sequence.

Next, arrange the webpages according to a logical structure. A website can use several types of structures, including linear, hierarchical, and webbed. Each structure connects the webpages in a different way to define how users navigate the site and view

---

Consider This boxes pose thought-provoking questions with answers throughout each chapter, promoting critical thought along with immediate feedback.

Textbook Walk-Through

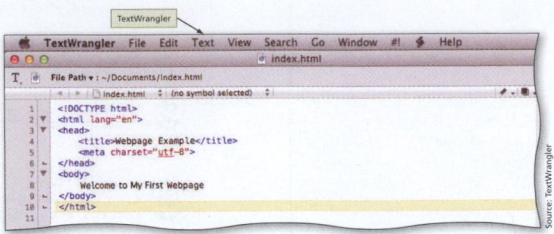

TextWrangler

Figure 1–43

Source: TextWrangler

Chapter Summary

In this chapter, you learned about the Internet, the web, and associated technologies, including web servers and web browsers. You learned the essential role of HTML in creating webpages and reviewed tools used to create HTML documents. You also learned how to create a basic HTML webpage. The items listed below include all the new concepts and skills you have learned in this chapter, with the tasks grouped by activity.

Creating a Basic Webpage
Start Notepad++ and Create a Blank Document (HTML 30)
Add Basic HTML Tags to a Document (HTML 31)
Add a Title and Text to a Webpage (HTML 32)
Save a Webpage (HTML 33)
View a Webpage in a Browser (HTML 34)

Exploring the Internet
Describe the Internet (HTML 3)
Describe the World Wide Web (HTML 4)
Define Protocols (HTML 6)
Discuss Web Browsers (HTML 7)
Identify Types of Websites (HTML 9)

Planning a Website
Identify the Purpose and Audience of the Website (HTML 11–12)

Design for Multiplatform Display (HTML 13)
Describe a Wireframe and a Site Map (HTML 14)
Consider Graphics, Navigation, Typography, and Color (HTML 17–19)
Design for Accessibility (HTML 20)

Understanding the Basics of HTML
Define Hypertext Markup Language (HTML 21)
Describe HTML Elements (HTML 21)
List Useful HTML Practices (HTML 22)
Identify Technologies Related to HTML (HTML 23)
Explain the Role of Other Web Programming Languages (HTML 23)

Using Web Authoring Tools
Identify Text Editors (HTML 24)
Download and Install a Text Editor (HTML 27)
Describe WYSIWYG Editors (HTML 27)

What decisions will you need to make when creating your next webpage?
Use these guidelines as you complete the assignments in this chapter and create your own webpages outside of this class.

1. Plan the website.
   a. Identify the purpose of the website.
   b. Identify the users of the website.
   c. Recognize the computing environments of the users.
   d. Design a wireframe and a site map.
2. Choose the design components.
   a. Identify possible graphics for the website.
   b. Determine the types of navigation tools and typography to use.
   c. Select a color scheme.
   d. Consider accessibility.

CONSIDER THIS

Continued >

Responsive Design Part 1: D

How should you submit solutions to questions in the assignment
Every assignment in this book contains one or more questions identified wit
require you to think beyond the assigned presentation. Present your solution
required by your instructor. Possible formats may include one or more of the
contains the answer; present your answer to the class; discuss your answer
dio or video using a webcam, smartphone, or portable media player; or pos

Apply Your Knowledge

Reinforce the skills and apply the concepts you learned in

Styling for Responsive Design

Instructions: In this exercise, you will use your text editor to ap
responsive design principles to an existing webpage. You will m
images flexible, change the layout to a fluid layout, and add a vi
meta tag. The completed webpage is shown in Figure 5–55. You
also use professional web development practices to indent, spac
comment, and validate your code.

Perform the following tasks:

1. Open apply05.html in your browser to view the webpage. Adjust the browser window to view the fixed layout.

2. Open apply05.html in your text editor and modify the comment at the top of the page to include your name and today's date.

3. Remove the width and height attributes from the image elements and save your changes.

4. Open the styles05.css file from the apply\css folder. Modify the comment at the top of the styles05.css page to include your name and today's date.

5. In the styles05.css file, add a max-width property with a value of 100% to the img selector.

6. Locate the #container selector and change the width value to use a relative measurement and take up the full width of the page.

7. Save the styles05.css file and refresh the apply05.html file in your browser. Resize the browser to make sure that a fluid layout has been applied and that the images are flexible.

8. In apply05.html, add the following meta tag within the head section of the document:

```
<meta name="viewport" content="width=device-width, initial-scale=1">
```

9. Save your changes to apply05.html and open the file in Google Chrome.

10. Use the developer tools in Google Chrome to view the page in an emulator.

11. Select a device and refresh the page. The page should look similar to Figure 5–55.

12. Validate your HTML document using the W3C validator found at validator.w3.org and fix any errors that are identified.

13. Validate your CSS file using the W3C validator found at http://jigsaw.w3.org/css-validator/ and fix any errors that are identified.

14. Submit the apply05.html and styles05.css files in a format specified by your instructor. Your instructor may also ask you to submit the images folder used with apply05.html.

15. In step 5, you changed the value to use a percentage (%) measurement. Explain how the percentage unit of measurement makes a fluid layout more flexible as compared to px.

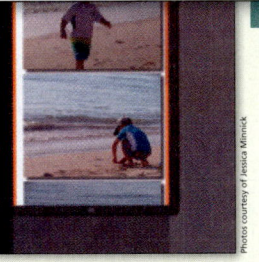

Figure 5–55

Photos courtesy of Jessica Minnick

Extend Your Knowledge

Extend the skills you learned in this chapter and experiment with new skills. You may need to use additional resources to complete the assignment.

Learning More About Google Webmaster Guidelines
Instructions: In this exercise, you research information about Google webmaster guidelines and summarize your findings.

Perform the following tasks:
1. Use your browser to search for Google Webmaster Guidelines.
2. Read the information and use your word processor to summarize your findings.
3. Include the following information in your response.
   a. Identify at least three design guidelines.
   b. Identify at least three technical guidelines.
   c. Identify at least five things to avoid.
4. Name your file `extend_11` and submit it in a format specified by your instructor.
5. 🌐 In this exercise, you learned more about Google webmaster guidelines. Research Bing webmaster guidelines and identify three of its guidelines that coincide with the Google guidelines.

Analyze, Correct, Improve

Analyze a website, correct all errors, and improve it.

Improving SEO for a Webpage
Instructions: Work with the analyze11.html file in the analyze folder and the analyze11styles.css file from analyze/css folder from the Data Files for Students. The analyze11.html webpage needs a page title, a meta description, and an h1 tag. The alt text on the page also needs to be improved. Use Figure 11–24 as a guide to correct these files.

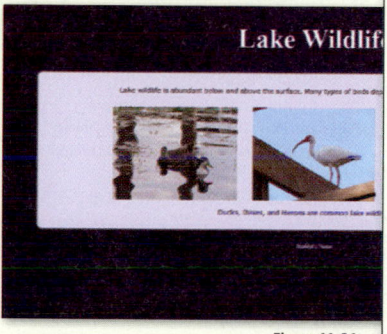

Figure 11–24

Analyze, Correct, Improve
projects call on students to analyze a file, discover errors in it, fix the errors, and then improve the file using the skills they learned in the chapter.

Extend Your Knowledge projects at the end of each chapter allow students to extend and expand on the skills learned within the chapter. Students use critical thinking to experiment with new skills to complete each project.

Analyze, Correct, Improve

Analyze an external style sheet, correct all errors, and improve it.

Changing a Nonresponsive Page into a Responsive Page
Instructions: Work with the responsive05.html file in the analyze folder and the responsivestyles05.css file in the analyze\css folder from the Data Files for Students. Several responsive web design resources are listed on the responsive05 webpage, but the HTML document and the style sheet are not coded for responsive design as shown in Figure 5–57. Use Figure 5–58 as a guide to correct these files. You will also use professional web development best practices to comment, indent, space, and validate your work.

Figure 5–57 ◄ **Figure 5–58**

1. **Correct**
   a. Open the responsive05.html file in your editor from the Data Files for Students and then modify the comment at the top of the page to include your name and today's date.
   b. Open the responsivestyles05.css file in your editor from the Data Files for Students and then modify and correct the comment at the top of the document to include your name and today's date.
   c. View responsive05.html in your browser and resize the page to recreate the problems with a nonresponsive webpage as shown in Figure 5–56. The content and images are cut off as the browser width decreases.
   d. In the responsive05.html file, add the viewport meta tag right above the closing </head> tag:

```
<meta name="viewport" content="width=device-width, initial-scale=1">
```

Continued >

Textbook Walk-Through

In the Labs

Labs 1 and 2, which increase in difficulty, require you to create webpages based on what you learned in the chapter; Lab 3 requires you to dive deeper into a topic covered in the chapter.

Lab 1: Adding Video to the New Harvest Food Bank Website

Problem: You volunteer at a local food bank called New Harvest Food Bank that collects community food donations and provides food and other services to those in need. You have already created a responsive website but now need to add a video to the home page to attract volunteers. You also need to format the video on the page. Create and style the video as shown in Figure 9–27.

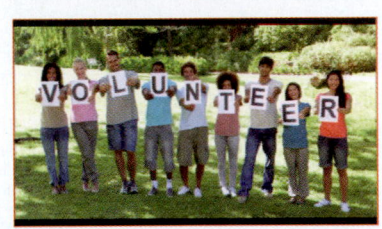

Figure 9–27

In the Lab Three in-depth assignments in each chapter require students to apply the chapter concepts and techniques to solve problems. One Lab is devoted to special topics in web development.

3. Using the web server documentation provided by your instructor or school, fill out the right column of the table to identify the pieces of information needed to publish your webpages. A sample solution is provided in webpublishing.docx that applies to students at Johnson County Community College in Overland Park, Kansas.

4. Use the web to research three inexpensive web server alternatives.

5. Open the webserveralternatives.docx document from the Data Files for Students.

6. Using the information you found in Step 4, complete the table in the webserveralternatives. docx document to compare three web server alternatives. You may be asked to share and compare this information with the rest of the class.

7. Confirm if and how your instructor wants you to publish your webpages, as well as how your work will be submitted for grading purposes.

8. ✿ Some web hosting companies offer *free* web hosting services. However, all businesses need to generate revenue in order to survive. Using your favorite search engine, identify three ways *free* web hosting companies generate revenue.

following tasks:

folder from the Data Files for Students to your lab1 folder.

r and then open the index.html document in the lab1 folder and update top of the page to include today's date.

ent of the index.html document, insert a `video` element with ontrols attributes.

g three source files within the `video` element and insert the appropriate value for each source.

```
nteer.mp4"
nteer.ogg"
nteer.webm"
```

ement below the source elements with text that states `Your browser t the video element.`

ent in a `div` element and include a `class="video"` attribute and

✿ Consider This: Your Turn

Apply your creative thinking and problem-solving skills to design and implement a solution.

Note: To complete this assignment, you will be required to use the Data Files for Students. Visit www.cengage.com/ct/studentdownload for detailed instructions or contact your instructor for information about accessing the required files.

1. Design and Create a Personal Portfolio Website

Personal

Part 1: As in almost every field, the job market for the best jobs in web development are competitive. One way to give yourself a big edge in a job search is to create an appropriate personal portfolio website to showcase your skills. Plan the website by completing the table in the portfolio.docx document in the Data Files for Students. Answer the questions with thoughtful, realistic responses. Be sure to sketch the wireframe for your home page on the last page. Submit your assignment in the format specified by your instructor.

Part 2: ✿ What do you want this website to accomplish?

2. Design and Create a Website for a Web Development and Consulting Business

Professional

Part 1: When you are finished with college, you plan to join a web development and consulting firm to gain experience in the field. Your long-term goal is to start and own a web development and consulting firm. You decide to begin by designing a website you would eventually like to build for the firm. Start planning the website by completing the table in the webdevelopment.docx document in the Data Files for Students. Answer the questions with thoughtful, realistic responses. Be sure to sketch the wireframe for your home page on the last page. Submit your assignment in the format specified by your instructor.

Part 2: ✿ What are some general characteristics of any successful small business that you want this website to portray? What are some characteristics of a successful web development consulting firm that you want this website to portray?

Continued >

Consider This: Your Turn exercises call on students to apply creative-thinking and problem-solving skills to design and implement a solution.

1 Introduction to the Internet and Web Design

Objectives

You will have mastered the material in this chapter when you can:

- Define the Internet and associated key terms
- Recognize Internet protocols
- Discuss web browsers and identify their main features
- Describe the types and purposes of websites
- Plan a website for a target audience
- Define a wireframe and a site map
- Explain how websites use graphics, navigation tools, typography, and color

- Design for accessibility and multiplatform display
- Define Hypertext Markup Language (HTML) and HTML elements
- Recognize HTML versions and web programming languages
- Identify web authoring tools
- Download and use a web authoring tool
- Create and view a basic HTML webpage

1 | Introduction to the Internet and Web Design

Introduction

Today, millions of people worldwide have access to the Internet, the world's largest network. Billions of webpages providing information on any subject you can imagine are currently available on the web. People use the Internet to search for information, to communicate with others around the world, and to seek entertainment. Students use the Internet to register for classes, pay tuition, and find out final grades. Businesses and other organizations rely on the Internet and the web to sell products and services. Hypertext Markup Language (HTML) and Cascading Style Sheets (CSS) are two of the technologies that make this possible.

The most recent version of HTML is called HTML5. Before exploring the details of creating webpages with HTML5 and CSS, it is useful to look at how these technologies relate to the development of the Internet and the web. In this chapter, you learn some basics about the Internet and the web, and the rules both follow to allow computers to communicate with each other. You review types of websites and learn how to properly plan a website so that it is appealing and useful to your target audience. You also explore web browsers, HTML, and its associated key terms. Lastly, you create a basic webpage using a text editor.

Project — Create a Basic Webpage

People and organizations create webpages to attract attention to information such as products, services, multimedia, news, and research. Although webpages display content including text, drawings, photos, animations, videos, and links to other webpages, they are created as documents containing only text.

The project in this chapter follows general guidelines and uses a text editor to create the webpage shown in Figure 1–1. Figure 1–1a shows the **code**, meaningful combinations of text and symbols that a web browser interprets to display the webpage shown in Figure 1–1b. The content includes two lines of text. Other parts of the code indicate that one line of text should be displayed as the webpage title, which appears in the browser on a webpage tab. Code also specifies that the other line of text should appear as a paragraph of body text.

(a) HTML code in index.html

(b) Webpage in Internet Explorer

Figure 1–1

Source: Notepad++

Roadmap

In this chapter, you learn how to create the webpage shown in Figure 1–1. The following roadmap identifies general activities you perform as you progress through this chapter:

1. **RUN** a **TEXT EDITOR** and **CREATE** a **BLANK DOCUMENT**.
2. **ENTER HTML TAGS** in the document.
3. **ADD TEXT** to the webpage.
4. **SAVE** the **WEBPAGE** as an HTML document.
5. **VIEW** the **WEBPAGE** in a browser.

At the beginning of step instructions throughout the chapter, you see an abbreviated form of this roadmap. The abbreviated roadmap uses colors to indicate chapter progress: gray means the chapter is beyond that activity; blue means the task being shown is covered in that activity; and black means that activity is yet to be covered. For example, the following abbreviated roadmap indicates the chapter would be showing a task in the 4 SAVE WEBPAGE activity.

1 RUN TEXT EDITOR & CREATE BLANK DOCUMENT | 2 ENTER HTML TAGS
3 ADD TEXT | **4 SAVE WEBPAGE** | 5 VIEW WEBPAGE

Use the abbreviated roadmap as a progress guide while you read or step through the instructions in this chapter.

Exploring the Internet

Every day, millions of people use a computer to connect to the Internet. The **Internet** is a worldwide collection of computers linked together for use by businesses, governments, educational institutions, other organizations, and individuals using modems, phone lines, television cables, satellite links, fiber-optic connections, radio waves, and other communications devices and media (Figure 1–2).

© nmedia/Shutterstock.com

Figure 1–2

The Internet was developed in the 1960s by the Department of Defense Advanced Research Projects Agency (ARPA). ARPANET (as the Internet was originally called) had only four nodes and sent its first message in 1969. A **node** is any device, such as a computer, tablet, or smartphone, connected to a **network**, which is a collection of two or more computers linked together to share resources and information. The Internet has billions of nodes on millions of networks. The **Internet of Things** is a term used to describe the ever-growing number of devices connecting to a network, including televisions and appliances. Today, high-, medium-, and low-speed data lines connect networks. These **data lines** allow data (including text, graphical images, audio, and video) to move from one computer to another. The **Internet backbone** is a collection of high-speed data lines that link major computer systems located around the world. An **Internet service provider (ISP)** is a company that has a permanent connection to the Internet backbone. ISPs use high- or medium-speed data lines to allow personal and business computer users to connect to the backbone for access to the Internet. A home Internet connection is generally provided through a cable or fiber-optic line that connects to an ISP.

Billions of people in most countries around the world connect to the Internet using computers in their homes, offices, schools, and public locations such as libraries. In fact, the Internet was designed to be a place in which people could share information and collaborate. Users with computers connected to the Internet can access a variety of popular services, including email, social networking, and the web.

World Wide Web

Many people use the terms Internet and World Wide Web interchangeably, but these terms have different meanings. The Internet is the infrastructure, or the physical networks of computers. The **World Wide Web**, also called the **web**, is the service that provides access to information stored on web servers, the high-capacity, high-performance computers that power the web. The web consists of a collection of linked files known as **webpages**, or pages for short. Because the web supports text, graphics, audio, and video, a webpage can display any of these multimedia elements in a browser.

A **website**, or site for short, is a related collection of webpages created and maintained by a person, company, educational institution, or other organization, such as the U.S. Department of Education (Figure 1–3). Each website contains a **home page**, which is the main page and the first document users see when they access the website. The home page typically provides information about the website's purpose and content, often by including a list of links to other webpages on the website.

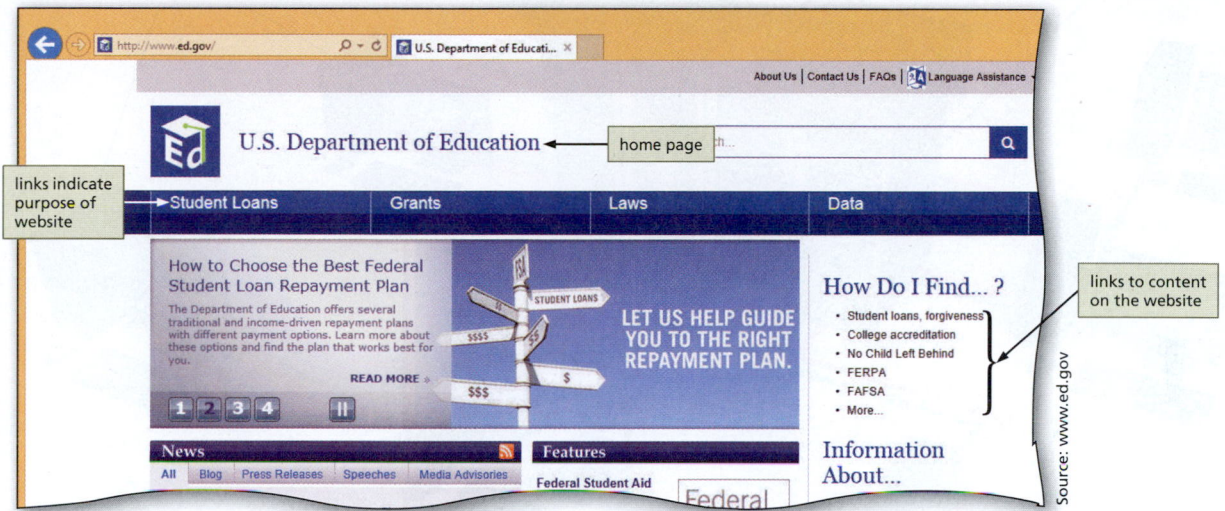

Figure 1–3

Hyperlinks are an essential part of the web. A **hyperlink**, more commonly called a **link**, is an element that connects one webpage to another webpage on the same server or to any other web server in the world. Tapping or clicking a link allows you to move quickly from one webpage to another without being concerned about where the webpages reside. You can also tap or click links to move to a different section of the same webpage.

With hyperlinks, you do not necessarily have to view information in a linear way. Instead, you can tap or click the available links to view the information in a variety of ways, as described later in this chapter. Many webpage components, including text, graphics, and animations, can serve as links. Figure 1–4 shows examples of several webpage components used as hyperlinks.

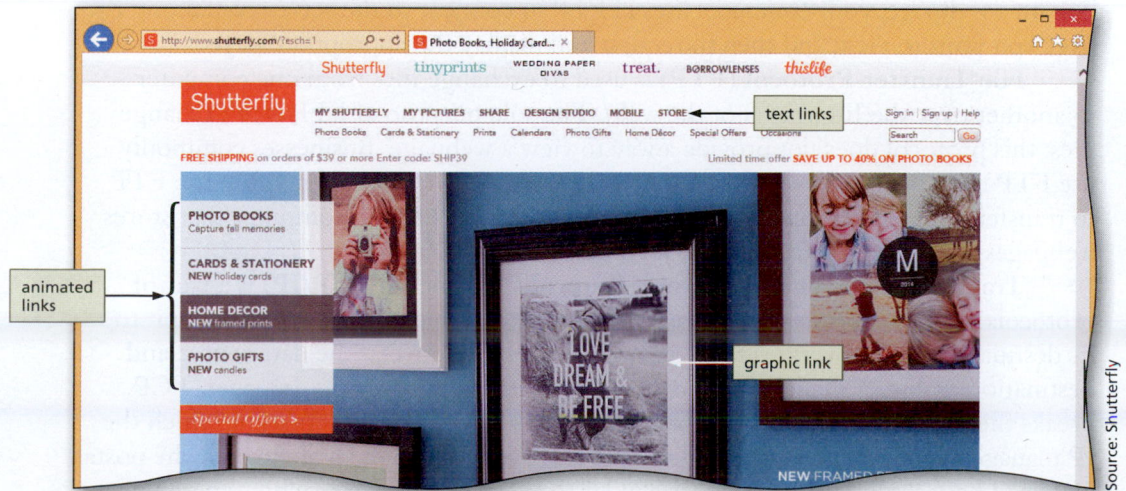

Figure 1–4

Protocols

A computer is also referred to as a client workstation. Client workstations connect to the Internet through the use of a protocol. A **protocol** is a set of rules that defines how a client workstation can communicate with a server. A client workstation uses a protocol to request a connection to a server. The **server** is the host computer that stores resources and files for websites (Figure 1–5).

Figure 1–5

Hypertext Transfer Protocol (HTTP) is the fundamental protocol used on the web to exchange and transfer webpages. HTTP is a set of rules for exchanging text, graphics, audio, video, and other multimedia files on the web. When you tap or click a link on a webpage, your computer uses HTTP to connect to the server containing the page you want to view, and then to request and display the appropriate page.

File Transfer Protocol (FTP) is used to exchange files from one computer to another over the Internet (not the web). The sole purpose of FTP is to exchange files; this protocol does not provide a way to view a webpage. Businesses commonly use FTP to exchange files with vendors and suppliers. Web designers often use FTP to transfer updated website content to a web hosting server, the computer that stores webpages and other related content for a website.

Transmission Control Protocol/Internet Protocol (TCP/IP) is a pair of protocols used to transfer data efficiently over the Internet by properly routing it to its destination. TCP oversees the network connection between the data source and destination and micromanages the data. When data is sent over the Internet, TCP breaks the data into packets. Each packet contains addressing information, which the IP manages. One way to better understand TCP/IP is through an analogy of the postal system. The tasks TCP performs are similar to those workers or machines perform when handling a bundle of packages in a post office. In this analogy, the packages are addressed to one destination, but are too large to send as a single bundle. TCP breaks up the bundle into manageable pieces and then sends them out for delivery. When each piece arrives at the destination, TCP reassembles the bundle of packages.

Internet Protocol (IP) ensures data is sent to the correct location. In the postal system analogy, the IP part of TCP/IP refers to the street address and zip code to route a piece of mail. Just as people have a unique mailing address, every client workstation and server on the Internet has a unique IP address. An example of an IP address is 192.168.1.5. Every website has a unique IP address, which makes it easy for computers to find websites. However, most people have difficulty remembering and using IP addresses to access websites. The **Domain Name System (DNS)** was created to resolve this issue. The DNS associates an IP address with a domain name. For example, the DNS associates the IP address 204.79.197.200 with the domain name bing.com.

Web Browsers

To access a website and display a webpage, a computer, tablet, or mobile device must have a web browser. A **web browser**, also called a **browser**, is a program that interprets and displays webpages so you can view and interact with them. Computing devices such as smartphones, tablets, laptops, and desktops include their own default browser, but you also have the option to download and use the browser of your choice. Microsoft Internet Explorer, Mozilla Firefox, Google Chrome, Apple Safari, and Opera (Figure 1–6) are popular browsers. You use a browser to locate websites, to link from one webpage to another, to add a favorite or bookmark a webpage, and to choose security settings.

(a) Internet Explorer

(b) Google Chrome

(d) Opera

(c) Mozilla Firefox

(e) Apple Safari

Source: Google

Source: Opera

Source: Mozilla

Source: Apple

Figure 1–6

Besides varying by publisher, browsers vary by version. Most browsers do not display webpages identically. In fact, older versions of some browsers do not support the most recent HTML5 standards. As you are designing your website, you must view it using various browsers to ensure that it looks and functions as you intended.

Internet Explorer (Figure 1-7) is the default browser provided with the Windows 8.1 operating system and provides tools for visiting webpages and an array of options to customize settings. As with all browsers, you can use Internet Explorer to enter a website address in the address bar to display a particular webpage, designate a specific webpage or set of webpage tabs to display when you run the browser, and bookmark frequently visited websites as favorites for easy access. Important features of Internet Explorer are summarized in Table 1–1.

Figure 1–7

Table 1–1 Features of Internet Explorer 11

Feature	Description
Address bar	Displays the website address of the webpage you are viewing
Webpage tab	Displays the title of the webpage; you can open multiple tabs to view multiple webpages
Home button	Opens the browser's designated home page or default webpage, which can be customized on the General tab of the Internet Options dialog box
Favorites button	Allows you to save and view your favorite webpages
Tools button	Provides access to print, zoom, and safety features and lets you view downloads and manage add-ons
Document window	Displays the current webpage content

CONSIDER THIS

What is the difference between a website's home page and a web browser's home page?
A website's home page is the default page displayed when you enter a web address such as www.cengage.com into the address bar of a browser. As mentioned earlier, this type of home page is the introductory page of a website and provides links to access other parts of the site. A browser also has a home page, which appears when you open a browser or tap or click the Home button in the browser window. You can specify any webpage as the default home page of a browser.

A web address, or **Uniform Resource Locator (URL)**, is the address of a document or other file accessible on the Internet and identifies the network location of a website, such as www.bing.com. To access a website using a browser, you type the webpage's URL in the browser's address bar (Figure 1–8).

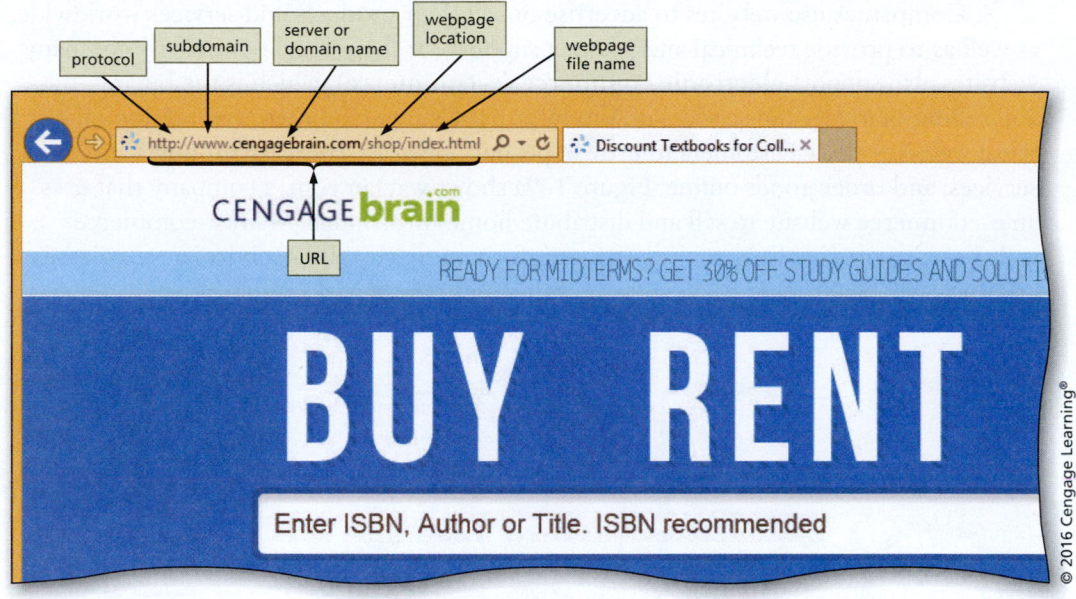

Figure 1–8

© 2016 Cengage Learning®

The URL in Figure 1–8 indicates to the browser to use the HTTP communications protocol to locate the index.html webpage in the shop folder on the cengagebrain.com server or domain. A **domain** is an area of the Internet a particular organization or person manages. In this case, cengagebrain.com is the name of the domain, with the .com indicating it is registered as a commercial enterprise. The www part of the URL is short for World Wide Web and is a common subdomain used in a URL. The www is not required and can be omitted or replaced with another meaningful name for the subdomain. You can find webpage URLs in a wide range of places, including school catalogs, business cards, product packaging, and advertisements.

How do you use a subdomain within a URL?

A subdomain further identifies an area of content. For example, the URL support.microsoft.com indicates that support is a subdomain name used in the microsoft.com domain or server. This subdomain contains helpful information to support Microsoft products.

CONSIDER THIS

Types of Websites

An **Internet site** is another term for a website that is generally available to anyone with an Internet connection. Other types of websites include intranets and extranets, which also use Internet technology, but limit access to specified groups. An **intranet** is a private network that uses Internet technologies to share company information among employees. An intranet is contained within an organization's network, which makes it private and available only to those who need access. Organizations often distribute documents such as policy and procedure manuals, employee directories, company newsletters, product catalogs, and training manuals on an intranet.

An **extranet** is a private network that uses Internet technologies to share business information with select corporate partners or key customers. Companies and other organizations can use an extranet to share product manuals, training modules, inventory status, and order information. An extranet might also allow retailers to purchase inventory directly from their suppliers or to pay bills online.

Companies use websites to advertise or sell their products and services worldwide, as well as to provide technical and product support for their customers. Many company websites also support **electronic commerce (e-commerce)**, which is the buying and selling of goods and services on the Internet. Using e-commerce technologies, these websites allow customers to browse product catalogs, compare products and services, and order goods online. Figure 1–9a shows wayfair.com, a company that uses an e-commerce website to sell and distribute home furnishings. Many e-commerce websites also provide links to order status information, customer service, news releases, and customer feedback tools to solicit comments from their customers.

(a) Wayfair

(b) LMS

(c) Facebook

(c) Blog

Figure 1–9

Colleges, universities, and other schools use websites to distribute information about areas of study, provide course information, and register students for classes online. Many educational institutions use a **Learning Management System (LMS)** to simplify course management. An LMS is a web-based software application designed to facilitate online learning. Instructors use the LMS to communicate announcements, post questions on reading material, list contact information, and provide access to lecture slides and videos. Students use the LMS to find information related to their courses, including project instructions and grades. Many LMS tools allow instructors to write their own webpage content that provides further information for their students. For example, the LMS webpage in Figure 1–9b is an HTML page written by an instructor to provide an assignment schedule to students.

While organizations create commercial and academic websites, individuals might create personal websites to share information with family and friends. Families and other groups can exchange photographs, video and audio clips, stories, schedules, or other information through websites. Many individual websites allow password protection, which creates a safer environment for sharing information. Another popular type of website is a social media site, such as Facebook, Twitter, or LinkedIn (Figure 1–9c). These websites encourage their users to share information, pictures, videos, and job-related skills. Many business websites also include links to their social media pages.

People use search engine websites to research topics. Popular search engine sites include Google, Bing, and Yahoo!. A news website provides information about current events. Another type of common website is a blog, which is short for weblog. A single person or small group creates and oversees a blog, which typically reflects the author's point of view on a particular topic (Figure 1–9d).

Planning a Website

When visiting a physical retail store, visitors are more likely to make a purchase if the store is clean and well organized and offers quality products and services. Likewise, computer users have several expectations when visiting a website. They expect the website to load quickly in the browser. If a website takes more than a few seconds to load, a visitor is likely to leave and find another site, possibly belonging to a competitor. Website visitors also expect an attractive design and color scheme that enhances the experience of visiting the site and makes it easy to read and view information. They expect a clear navigation system that helps them quickly find the products, services, or information they are seeking. A poor design, distracting color scheme, or confusing website navigation tools also prompt visitors to switch to another website. An attractive, useful, and well-organized website is not created by accident. Building a successful website starts with a solid strategic plan.

Web designers begin planning activities by meeting with key business personnel to ask several important questions to understand the purpose of the website and the goals of the business. If you are a web designer working as a consultant or contractor, you meet with your clients to plan the website. If you are a web designer providing services within an organization, you meet with decision makers and others who are sponsoring the web design project. In either case, you begin by identifying the purpose of the website and goals of the business to help shape the design and type of website you are developing.

Purpose of the Website

The purpose of a commercial business website is related to the goal of selling products or services. A business can take a direct approach and use a website to sell products and services through e-commerce or through information that prompts website users to visit a physical location such as a store or restaurant. As an alternative, a business can take an indirect approach and use a website to generate leads to potential customers, promote the expertise of the business, raise the public profile of the business, or inform and educate its customers. Each purpose demands a different type of website and design. For example, if the purpose of a website is to serve as an online store, the website should allow easy access to product information, reviews, and e-commerce tools. If the purpose of the website is to build a company's reputation, the website should feature articles about the company, its employees, and its products and integrate with social media sites such as Facebook.

Every business needs to have a mission statement that clearly addresses the purpose and goal of the business. For example, the mission statement of a bank might be "Our mission is to provide world-class service while helping our customers achieve their financial goals." The business website should promote the mission statement. Web designers often ask their clients for a copy of the mission statement and use it as the foundation for the website plan. The more you know about the purpose of the website, the more likely you are to be successful with a web development project.

Target Audience

In addition to understanding the website's purpose, you should understand the people who will use the website, also known as the target audience. Knowing the makeup of your target audience — including age, gender, general demographic background, and level of computer literacy — helps you design a website appropriate for them. Figure 1–10 shows the website for Michaels, an arts and crafts store. Its target audience includes creative people who enjoy making decorations and other items. The home page displays an image customized for the year-end holiday season and offers special savings to further entice its target audience to make a purchase. The simple navigation bar near the top of the page makes it easy for a customer to shop, discover a new project, or find inspiration. A search tool above the navigation bar provides quick access to products. Knowing the information that your target audience is searching for means you can design the site to focus on that information, which enhances the shopping and purchasing experience of your audience.

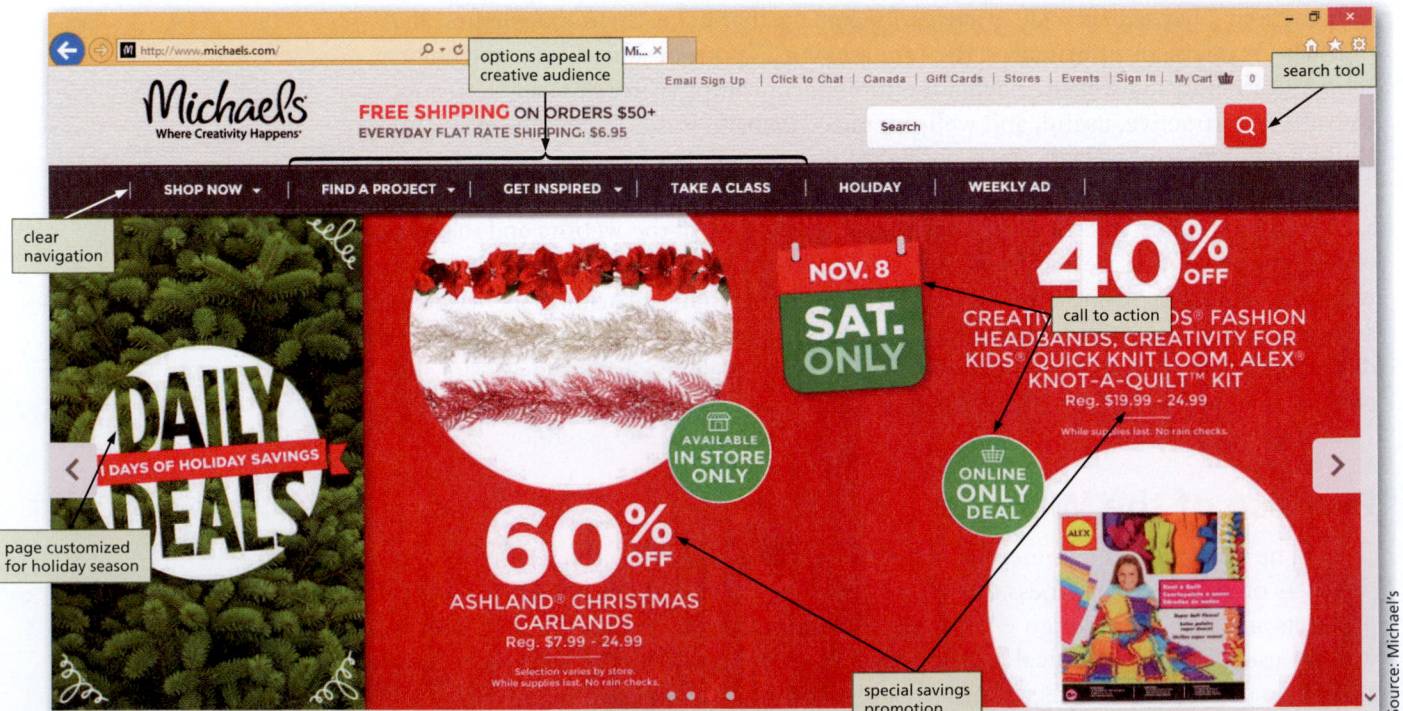

Figure 1–10

Multiplatform Display

Today, users can access a website with computing devices ranging from desktop computers to laptops, tablets, and smartphones. In fact, people are rapidly increasing their use of a tablet or smartphone to access websites. According to Pew Research, the number of mobile (or smartphone) Internet users increased by 100 percent from 2009 to 2014. Today, more than 55 percent of Americans own a smartphone, and more than 50 percent of smartphone owners use their phone to access the Internet. In addition, more than 30 percent of those who access the Internet do so exclusively with their smartphones. These trends are only expected to increase. Yet most webpages are designed for a large display screen on a desktop or laptop and do not translate well to the smaller screen of a tablet or smartphone. This problem leads to another question web developers must ask: "How do I consistently reach the people in my target audience when they are using so many difference devices?" The solution is to use **responsive design**, which allows you to create one website that provides an optimal viewing experience across a range of devices. The website itself responds and adapts to the size of screen on the visitor's device. For example, Figure 1–11 shows the responsive design of angieslist.com in desktop, tablet, and mobile screen sizes. Chapter 5 provides much more information about responsive design.

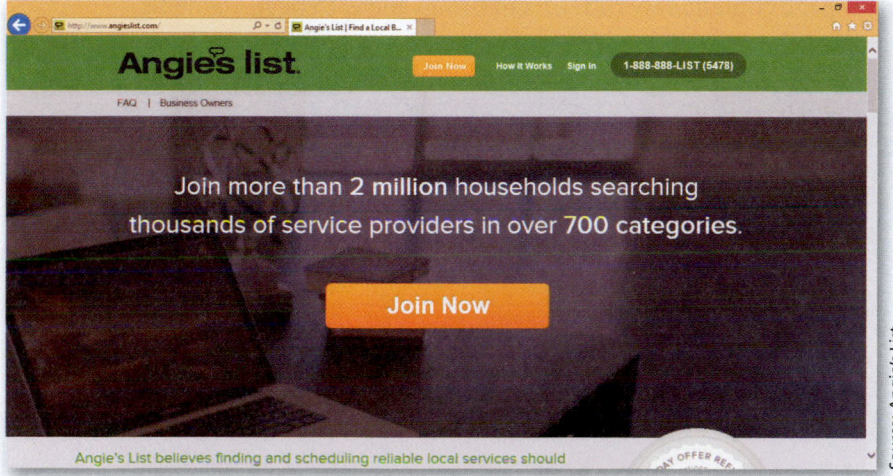

Source: Angie's List

(a) Desktop Display

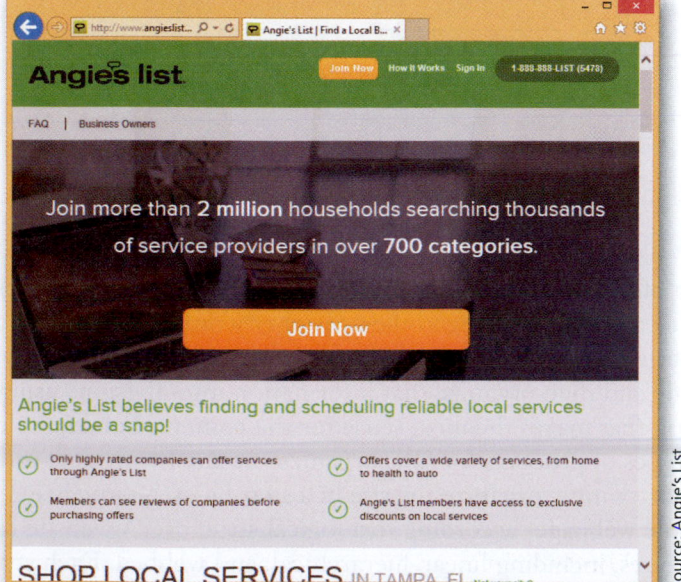

Source: Angie's List

(b) Tablet Display

Source: Angie's List

(c) Mobile Display

Figure 1–11

Can I redesign a desktop-only website for multiplatform display?

Yes. If your audience is accustomed to the desktop-only website, retrofitting the website for tablet and mobile display screens makes sense because the site remains familiar to users. You also avoid building a new site from scratch and you can take advantage of design decisions such as color scheme and use media you have already acquired. However, depending on the site content and number of pages, redesigning may be a time-consuming process.

Wireframe

Before web designers actually start creating the first webpage for a website, they sketch the design using a wireframe. A **wireframe** is a simple, visual guide that clearly identifies the location of main webpage elements, such as the navigation area, organization logo, content areas, and images. When you create a wireframe sketch for your webpages, use lines and boxes as shown in Figure 1–12. Also be sure to incorporate plenty of white space within your design to improve readability and to clearly distinguish among the areas on the webpage. You can use two types of white space: active white space and passive white space. **Active white space** is an area on the page that is intentionally left blank. Typically, the goal of active white space is to help balance the design of an asymmetrical page. **Passive white space** is the space between content areas. Passive white space helps a user focus on one part of the page. Proper use of white space makes webpage content easy to read and brings focus to page elements.

Figure 1–12

Site Map

A **site map** is a planning tool that lists or displays all the pages on a website and indicates how they are related to each other. In other words, a site map shows the structure of a website. Begin defining the structure of a website by identifying the information to provide and then organize that information into divisions using the organizing method that makes the most sense for the content. For example, if the website offers three types of products for sale, organize the site by product category. If the website provides training, organize the site in a step-by-step sequence.

Next, arrange the webpages according to a logical structure. A website can use several types of structures, including linear, hierarchical, and webbed. Each structure connects the webpages in a different way to define how users navigate the site and view the webpages. You should select a structure for the website based on how you want users to navigate the site and view the content.

A **linear** website structure connects webpages in a straight line, as shown in Figure 1–13. Each page includes a link to the next webpage and another link to the previous webpage. A linear website structure is appropriate if visitors should view the webpages in a specific order, as in the case of training material in which users need to complete Training module 1 before attempting Training module 2. If the information on the first webpage is necessary for understanding information on the second webpage, you should use a linear structure.

Linear structure

Figure 1–13

In a variation of a linear website structure, each page can include a link to the home page of the website, as shown in Figure 1–14. For some websites, moving from one page to the next page is still important, but you also want to provide users with easy access to the home page at any time. To meet these goals, you provide links from each page to the previous, next, and home pages. In this way, users do not have to tap or click the previous link multiple times to get back to the home page. The home page also includes links to all the pages in the site so users can quickly return to a page.

Linear structure with home page links

Figure 1–14

A **hierarchical** website connects webpages in a treelike structure, as shown in Figure 1–15. This structure works well on a site with a main index or table of contents page that links to all other webpages. With this structure, the main index page displays general information and secondary pages include more detailed information. Notice how logically the information in Figure 1–15 is organized. A webpage visitor can go from the home page to any of the three modules. In addition, the visitor can easily find the first page of Training module 3 by way of the Training module 3 link. One of the inherent problems with this structure and the two linear structures, however, is the inability to move easily from one section of pages to another. As an example, to move from Training module 1, page 2, to Training module 3, visitors must tap or click a link to return to Training module 1, introduction, tap or click another link to return to the home page, and then tap or click the Training module 3 link. This is moderately annoying for a site with two webpages, but think what it would be like if Training module 1 had 100 webpages.

Hierarchical structure

Figure 1–15

To circumvent the problems with the hierarchical model, you can use a webbed model. A **webbed** website structure has no set organization, as shown in Figure 1–16. Visitors can move easily between pages, even if the pages are located in different sections of the website. A webbed structure works best on sites with information that does not need to be read in a specific order and pages that provide many navigation options. The web itself uses a webbed structure, so users can navigate among webpages in any order they choose. With this model, you most often provide a link to the home page from each page. Many websites use a graphical image (usually the organization's logo) in the upper-left corner of each webpage as the home page link. You will use that technique later in the book.

Webbed structure

Figure 1–16

Most websites use a combination of linear, hierarchical, and webbed structures. Some information on the website might be organized hierarchically from an index page, other information might be accessible from all areas of the site, and still other information might be organized in a linear structure to be read in a specific order. Using a combination of the three structures is appropriate if it helps users navigate the site easily. The goal is to get the right information to the users in the most efficient way possible.

Graphics

Graphics add visual appeal to a webpage and enhance the visitor's perception of your products and services. Be sure to use appropriate graphics on your site, those that communicate your brand, products, and services. For example, the website for Pret A Manger shown in Figure 1–17 displays a new product that serves as the focal point on the website. The graphic communicates to the user that the new dish is fresh and hot, right out of the oven. The smaller graphics below the primary graphic offer additional visual stimulation and provide an aesthetically pleasing balance to the page. These graphics are simple, yet effective in catching the user's attention.

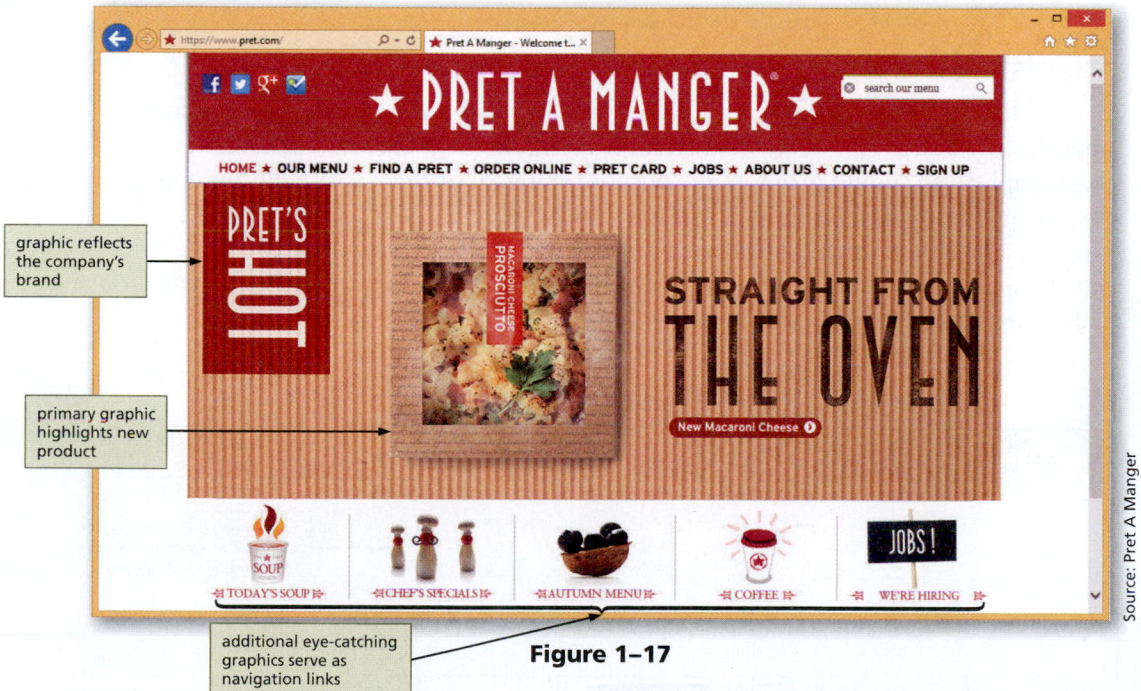

graphic reflects the company's brand

primary graphic highlights new product

additional eye-catching graphics serve as navigation links

Source: Pret A Manger

Figure 1–17

Navigation

As mentioned previously, the navigation of your website should be clear and concise. Each webpage should have a designated navigation area with links to other pages in the site, as shown in Figure 1–18. The navigation area should be prominent and easy to use. Incorporating a search box near the navigation area provides another avenue for customers to find the item they want.

navigation links

search box

Figure 1–18

Source: Sketchers

Typography

The use of effective typography, or fonts and font styles, enhances the visual appeal of a website. Above all, the text must be legible or the website is useless. Typography also should promote the purpose and goal of the website. For example, review the wedding photography website shown in Figure 1–19. The style of the text conveys an attitude of practical elegance mixed with fun. The typography of the title at the top of the page is elegant and whimsical, while the typography of the navigation links is uncluttered and easy to read.

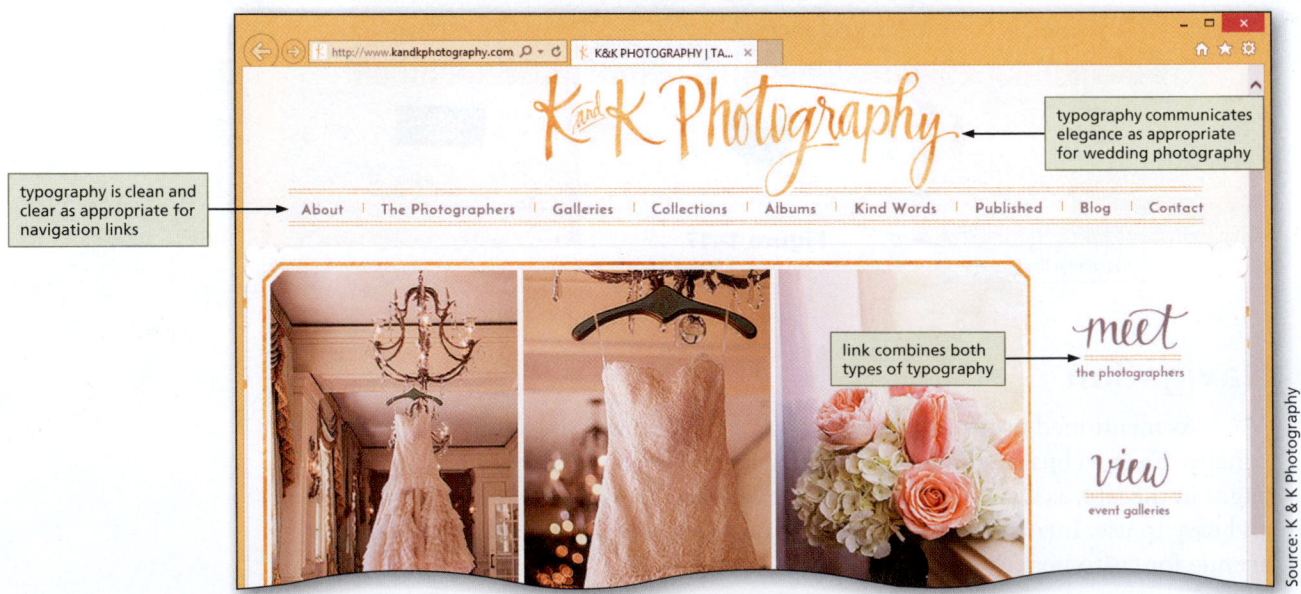

typography communicates elegance as appropriate for wedding photography

typography is clean and clear as appropriate for navigation links

link combines both types of typography

Figure 1–19

Source: K & K Photography

Color

All websites use color, even if the colors are black and white. Select a limited number of coordinated colors that help promote your purpose and brand. The combination of colors, also called a color scheme, contributes to the appeal and legibility of the website. Font and background colors must provide high color contrast for readability, so use dark text on a light background or light text on a dark background. Likewise, avoid a color combination such as a primary red background with yellow text, which is hard on the eyes. Aim to strike a balance among the background color, text color, and the color that represents your brand. Many successful color schemes have one main color, such as medium blue, and add at least one lighter and darker shade of the same color, such as sky blue and navy. Even a single shade can serve as a color scheme. Figure 1–20 displays the home page for the grocery store Publix. The store's logo is green. The site reinforces its brand by integrating the same shade of green throughout the site.

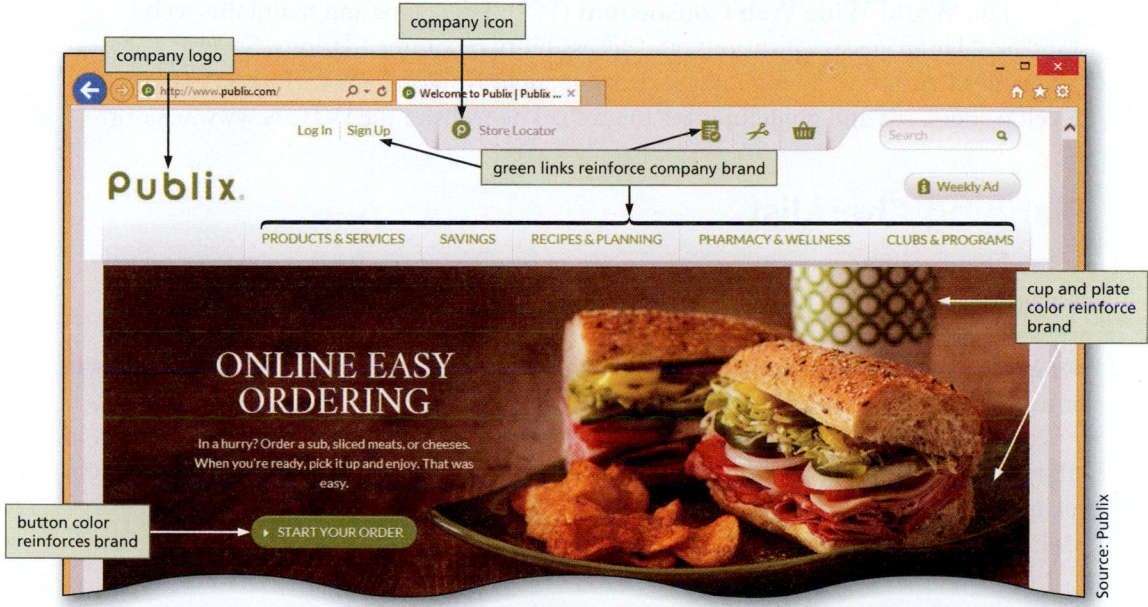

Figure 1–20

Colors convey meanings. For example, green is associated with things that are friendly, fresh, and healthy. Table 1–2 lists colors and their common meanings.

| Table 1–2 Common Color Meanings | |
Color	Common Meaning
Red	Love, romance, anger, energy
Blue	Trust, loyalty, integrity, honesty, dependability
Green	Freshness, friendliness, health, safety, strength
Yellow	Warmth, cheer, joy, excitement, humor
Orange	Energy, warmth, health
Brown	Nature, wholesomeness, simplicity, friendliness
Black	Elegance, tradition, sophistication, formality
White	Purity, honesty, sincerity, cleanliness

Accessibility

Finally, address accessibility and localization issues. A web designer should create pages for viewing by a diverse audience, including people with physical impairments and global users. Consider the software used by those with physical impairments to work with some web features. For instance, for each graphic you include on the website, always include alternative text so people with sight limitations can use screen-reading software to identify the visual content. To support an international audience, use generic icons that can be understood globally, avoid slang expressions in the content, and build simple pages that load quickly over low-speed connections.

In 1998, the Rehabilitation Act was amended with Section 508, which requires that any information technology created or bought by a government agency be accessible to persons with disabilities. Information technology includes websites, which means web designers must consider users with visual, auditory, motor, and cognitive disabilities in their website designs. Visit www.section508.gov for more information.

The **World Wide Web Consortium (W3C)** develops and maintains web standards, language specifications, and accessibility recommendations. Several companies that use web technologies participate in work groups with the W3C to develop standards and guidelines for the web. The website for W3C is www.w3.org.

BTW
W3C
The mission of the W3C is "to lead the World Wide Web to its full potential by developing protocols and guidelines that ensure the long-term growth of the Web." Information about the membership process is available at www.w3.org /consortium/membership.

Planning Checklist

The planning items just discussed are only a few of the basic webpage design issues that you need to consider when developing a website. A more sophisticated website requires additional design considerations and research of the business, its competition, and a complete business analysis. Throughout this book, design issues will be addressed as they relate to the chapter project.

The rest of the chapters in this book employ professional web design practices in addition to the development of webpages. You will learn many design and development techniques, including how to add links, styles, layout, graphics, tables, forms, and multimedia to your webpages.

Table 1–3 serves as a checklist of items to consider when planning a website.

Table 1–3 Checklist for Planning a Website	
Topic	**Web Designer Questions**
Purpose of the website	What is the purpose and goal of the website? What is the organization's mission statement?
Target audience	Describe the target audience (age, gender, demographics). What information is most pertinent to the users?
Multiplatform display	Will you design for display on multiple platforms or focus only on a desktop or mobile design?
Site map	How many webpages will be included in the website? How will the webpages be organized? What type of website structure is appropriate for the content?
Wireframe	What features will be displayed on each webpage?
Graphics	What graphics will you use on the website?
Color	What colors will you use within the site to enhance the purpose and brand?
Typography	What font styles will you use within the website?
Accessibility	How will the website accommodate people with disabilities?

Break Point: If you want to take a break, this is a good place to do so. To resume at a later time, continue reading the text from this location forward.

Understanding the Basics of HTML

Webpages are created using **Hypertext Markup Language (HTML)**, which is an authoring language used to create documents for the web. HTML consists of a set of special instructions called **tags** to define the structure and layout of content in a webpage. A browser reads the HTML tags to determine how to display the webpage content on a screen. Because the HTML tags define or "mark up" the content on the webpage, HTML is considered a **markup language** rather than a traditional programming language. HTML has evolved through several versions from the initial public release of HTML 1.0 in 1989 to the current version, HTML5. Each version has expanded the capabilities of the language.

HTML Elements and Attributes

A webpage is a text file that contains both content and HTML tags and is saved as an HTML document. HTML tags mark the text to define how it should appear when viewed in a browser. HTML includes dozens of tags that describe the structure of webpages and create links to other content. For instance, the HTML tags <nav> and </nav> mark the start and end of a navigation area, while <html> and </html> indicate the start and end of a webpage. An **HTML element** consists of everything from the start tag to the end tag, including content, and represents a distinct part of a webpage such as a paragraph or heading. For example, <title> Webpage Example </title> is an HTML element that sets the title of a webpage. In common usage, when web designers say "Use a p element to define a paragraph," or something similar, they mean to use a starting <p> tag to mark the beginning of the paragraph and an ending </p> tag to mark the end of the paragraph.

You can enhance HTML elements by using **attributes**, which define additional characteristics, or properties, of the element such as the width and height of an image. An attribute includes a name, such as width, and can also include a value, such as 300px, which sets the width of an element in pixels. Attributes are included within the element's start tag. Figure 1–21 shows the anatomy of HTML elements in Notepad++, which uses color coding to distinguish parts of the code. For example, Notepad++ displays tags in blue, attribute names in red, attribute values in purple, and content in black.

BTW

Lowercase HTML Tags
Although most browsers interpret a tag such as <nav> the same way it interprets <NAV>, the convention for HTML5 is to use all lowercase tags. Using lowercase tags means your HTML documents conform to the current W3C standard.

Figure 1–21

HTML combines tags and descriptive attributes that define how a document should appear in a web browser. HTML elements include headings, paragraphs, hyperlinks, lists, and images. Most HTML elements have a start tag and an end tag and follow the same rules, or **syntax**, which determine how the elements should be written so they are interpreted correctly by the browser. These HTML elements are called **paired** tags and use the syntax *<start tag> content </end tag>*, which has the following meaning:

- HTML elements begin with a start tag, or opening tag, such as <title>.
- HTML elements finish with an end tag, or closing tag, such as </title>.
- Content is inserted between the start and end tags. In Figure 1–21, the content for the title tags is Webpage Example.

Some HTML elements are void of content. They are called **empty**, or **void**, tags. Examples of empty tags are <br> for a line break and <hr> for a horizontal line, or rule. The syntax for empty tags is *<tag>*.

Figure 1–22 shows the HTML code and content needed to create the webpage shown in Figure 1–23.

Figure 1–22

Figure 1–23

Technologies Related to HTML

Several technologies, listed as follows, have been developed since the introduction of HTML to extend its capabilities. These technologies also use tags to mark up content in a text document.

- **XML** — The W3C introduced **XML (Extensible Markup Language)** in 1998 to exchange and transport data. It does not replace HTML, but rather, can work with HTML by transporting web data obtained through an HTML webpage.

- **XHTML** — **XHTML (Extensible Hypertext Markup Language)** is a rewritten version of HTML using XML and was developed in 2000. Its primary benefit is that it is more widely accepted on mobile device platforms.

- **DHTML** — **DHTML (Dynamic Hypertext Markup Language)** is a term that refers to a combination of web technologies, such as HTML, CSS, and JavaScript to create interactive and dynamic webpage content. DHTML was introduced in the mid-1990s.

HTML5

With its debut in 2008, HTML5 is the most recent version of HTML. HTML5 introduces several new elements such as header, nav, main, and footer to better define the areas of a webpage. They are classified as structural elements because they define the structure of a webpage. These new elements also are considered semantic HTML elements because they provide meaning about the content of the tags. (The term *semantic* refers to the meaning of words or ideas.) For example, <header> is a semantic tag because it defines content that appears at the top of a webpage. The name and purpose of the <header> tag reflect its meaning. On the other hand, <b>, for bold, is not a semantic tag because it defines only how content should look, not what it means.

HTML5 also provides a more flexible approach to web development. For instance, with HTML5, you can incorporate audio and video with the use of <audio> and <video> tags. These new features reduce the need for browser plugins, which are small programs that let webpages play sounds or videos, for example. This book shows HTML5 tags and attributes that are currently supported by modern browsers.

Understanding the Role of Other Web Programming Languages

In addition to HTML, web developers use other web programming languages such as JavaScript and PHP to add interactivity and functionality. Although you can create websites without these languages, they are useful when you need to include features beyond the scope of HTML. You should be aware of these languages as you begin learning about web development.

JavaScript

JavaScript is a popular scripting language used to create interactivity within a web browser. Common uses for JavaScript include creating popup windows and alert messages, displaying the current date, and validating form data. JavaScript is a **client-side scripting language**, which means that the browser processes it on the client computer. Webpages that contain JavaScript are named with an .htm or .html extension, just like a webpage without JavaScript.

jQuery

jQuery is a library of JavaScript programs designed for easy integration onto a webpage. jQuery makes it easy for web developers to add JavaScript to a webpage. The jQuery Foundation (https://jquery.org) is a group of web developers that work together to create open-source projects. Their mission is to "improve the open web, making it accessible for everyone, through the development and support of open-source software, and collaboration with the development community."

PHP

PHP (Hypertext Preprocessor) is an open-source scripting language often used for common tasks such as writing to or querying a database located on a central server. PHP is a **server-side scripting language**, which means that the PHP script is processed at the server. The result of the PHP script is often an HTML webpage that is sent back to the client. Pages that contain PHP scripts must have file names that end with the file extension .php.

ASP

ASP (Active Server Pages) is a server-side scripting technology from Microsoft used to accomplish many of the same server-side processing tasks as PHP. Pages that contain ASP scripts must have file names that end with the file extension .asp.

Using Web Authoring Tools

You can create webpages using HTML with a simple text editor, such as Notepad, Notepad++, Sublime, Programmer's Notepad, TextEdit, and TextWrangler. Notepad comes installed with the Windows operating system, and TextEdit comes installed with the Mac OS X operating system. TextWrangler also runs only on Mac OS X, while the other text editors run on Windows. A **text editor** is a program that allows you to enter, change, save, and print text, which includes HTML tags. Text editors do not typically have many advanced features, but they do allow you to develop HTML documents easily. An HTML editor or code editor is a program that provides basic text-editing functions, as well as more advanced features such as color-coding for various HTML tags, menus to insert HTML tags, and a spelling checker. HTML is **platform independent**, meaning you can create, or code, an HTML file in Windows or Mac and then view it on any browser.

Text Editors

Notepad++ is a free, open-source text editor. You can use it to create files in several markup, scripting, and programming languages, including HTML, CSS, JavaScript, PHP, Java, C#, and Visual Basic. Notepad++ runs on Windows computers; go to http://notepad-plus-plus.org to download the program. Figure 1–24 displays the Notepad++ user interface.

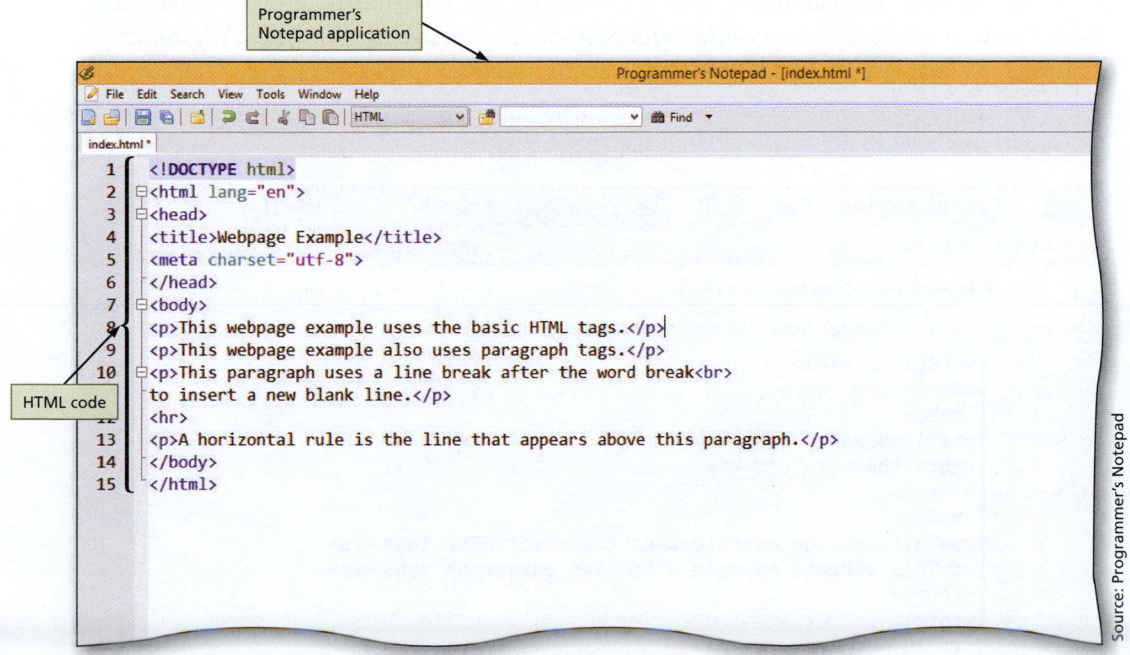

Notepad++
application

HTML code

```
 1  <!DOCTYPE html>
 2  <html lang="en">
 3  <head>
 4  <title>Webpage Example</title>
 5  <meta charset="utf-8">
 6  </head>
 7  <body>
 8  <p>This webpage example uses the basic HTML tags.</p>
 9  <p>This webpage example also uses paragraph tags.</p>
10  <p>This paragraph uses a line break after the word break<br>
11  to insert a new blank line.</p>
12  <hr>
13  <p>A horizontal rule is the line that appears above this paragraph.</p>
14  </body>
15  </html>
```

Courtesy of Notepad++

Figure 1–24

Programmer's Notepad is another free, open-source text editor you can use to create webpages. Like Notepad++, you can use Programmer's Notepad to create files in several markup, scripting, and programming languages as well. Programmer's Notepad runs on Windows; go to www.pnotepad.org to download the program. Figure 1–25 displays the Programmer's Notepad user interface.

Programmer's
Notepad application

```
 1  <!DOCTYPE html>
 2  <html lang="en">
 3  <head>
 4  <title>Webpage Example</title>
 5  <meta charset="utf-8">
 6  </head>
 7  <body>
 8  <p>This webpage example uses the basic HTML tags.</p>
 9  <p>This webpage example also uses paragraph tags.</p>
10  <p>This paragraph uses a line break after the word break<br>
    to insert a new blank line.</p>
    <hr>
13  <p>A horizontal rule is the line that appears above this paragraph.</p>
14  </body>
15  </html>
```

HTML code

Source: Programmer's Notepad

Figure 1–25

Sublime is a cross-platform text editor you can use on the Windows, Mac OS X, or Linux operating system. With Sublime, you can create files in several formats, including HTML and CSS. Go to www.sublimetext.com to find a free trial version of the software and one with a license for purchase. Figure 1–26 displays the Sublime user interface.

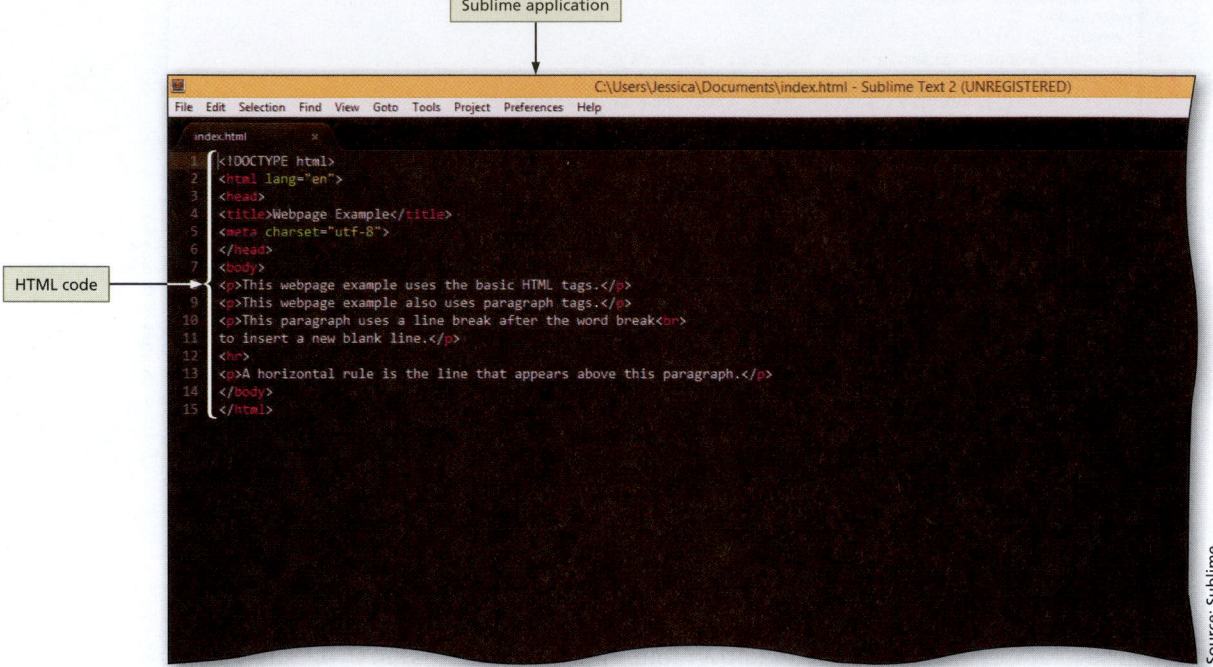

Figure 1–26

TextWrangler is a free, open-source text editor available for Mac OS X 10.6.8 or a later version. You can use it to create files in many formats, including HTML and CSS. Go to www.barebones.com/products/textwrangler to download TextWrangler. Figure 1–27 displays the TextWrangler user interface.

Figure 1–27

To Download and Install a Text Editor

Before you can create your first webpage, you must select a text editor that you will use to create your webpages. Begin by asking whether your instructor has a preferred text editor to use in the course. If not, use a text editor provided by your operating system (such as Notepad or TextEdit) or download one of the HTML text editors previously discussed. If you want to download and install an HTML text editor, you would perform the following steps.

1. Use your browser to access the website for Notepad++, Programmer's Notepad, Sublime, or TextWrangler.

   - Notepad++: http://notepad-plus-plus.org
   - Programmer's Notepad: www.pnotepad.org
   - Sublime: www.sublimetext.com
   - TextWrangler (Mac OS X only): www.barebones.com/products/textwrangler

2. Navigate the text editor's website to locate the download link.

3. Tap or click the link to download the software.

4. When the download is complete, open the downloaded file to begin the installation.

5. Follow the instructions in the setup wizard to complete the installation.

6. Run the text editor when finished.

WYSIWYG Editors

Many popular software applications also provide features that enable you to develop webpages easily. Microsoft Word and Excel, for example, have a Save As Web Page option that converts a document into an HTML file by automatically adding HTML tags to the document. Using Microsoft Access, you can create a webpage that allows you to view data from a database. Adobe Acrobat also has an export feature that creates HTML files. While these programs provide the capability to save as a webpage, they do not substitute the use of a text editor or a WYSIWYG editor. **WYSIWYG** stands for What You See Is What You Get. WYSIWYG editors provide a graphical user interface to design a webpage, as opposed to the blank page provided in a text editor used to write code. The WYSIWYG editor allows you to drag HTML elements onto the page while the editor writes the code for you. While these editors can be useful in developing webpages, understanding the code means you have the control and flexibility to create webpages that meet your needs.

Adobe Dreamweaver is a popular WYSIWYG editor used by many people and businesses around the world for web development. Several types of web file formats can be developed with Dreamweaver, including HTML, CSS, JavaScript, and PHP. Dreamweaver can be installed on a computer running Windows or Mac OS X. Dreamweaver provides several views for working with a webpage file, including Design view, Code view, Split view, and Live view. Design view shows the design of the webpage, while Code view is similar to a text editor. Split view provides a side-by-side view of the webpage design and code. Live view mimics a browser display. Figure 1–28 shows an example of Dreamweaver in Split view. Dreamweaver is part of Adobe Creative Cloud and is available for purchase as a monthly or annual subscription. Visit www.adobe.com for more information about Adobe Dreamweaver Creative Cloud.

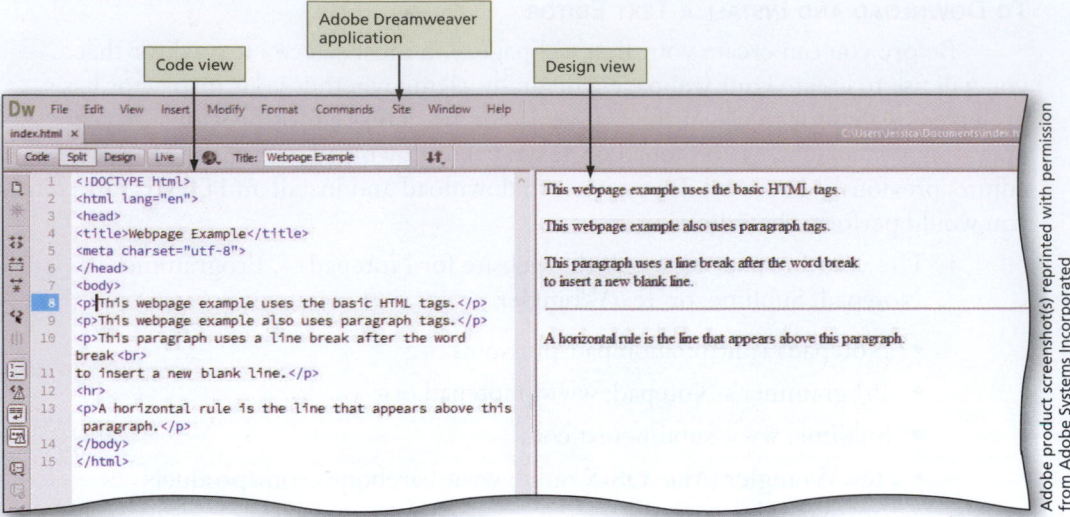

Figure 1–28

Microsoft Expression Web 4 is a WYSIWYG webpage editor from Microsoft. Expression Web 4 is the final version of the software and is shown in Figure 1–29. Expression Web is available as a free download on the Microsoft website. To replace Expression Web, Microsoft is currently directing customers to use its Visual Studio Express 2013 for Web; however, this is a text editor and not a WYSIWYG editor. Visual Studio Express 2013 for Web is shown in Figure 1–30.

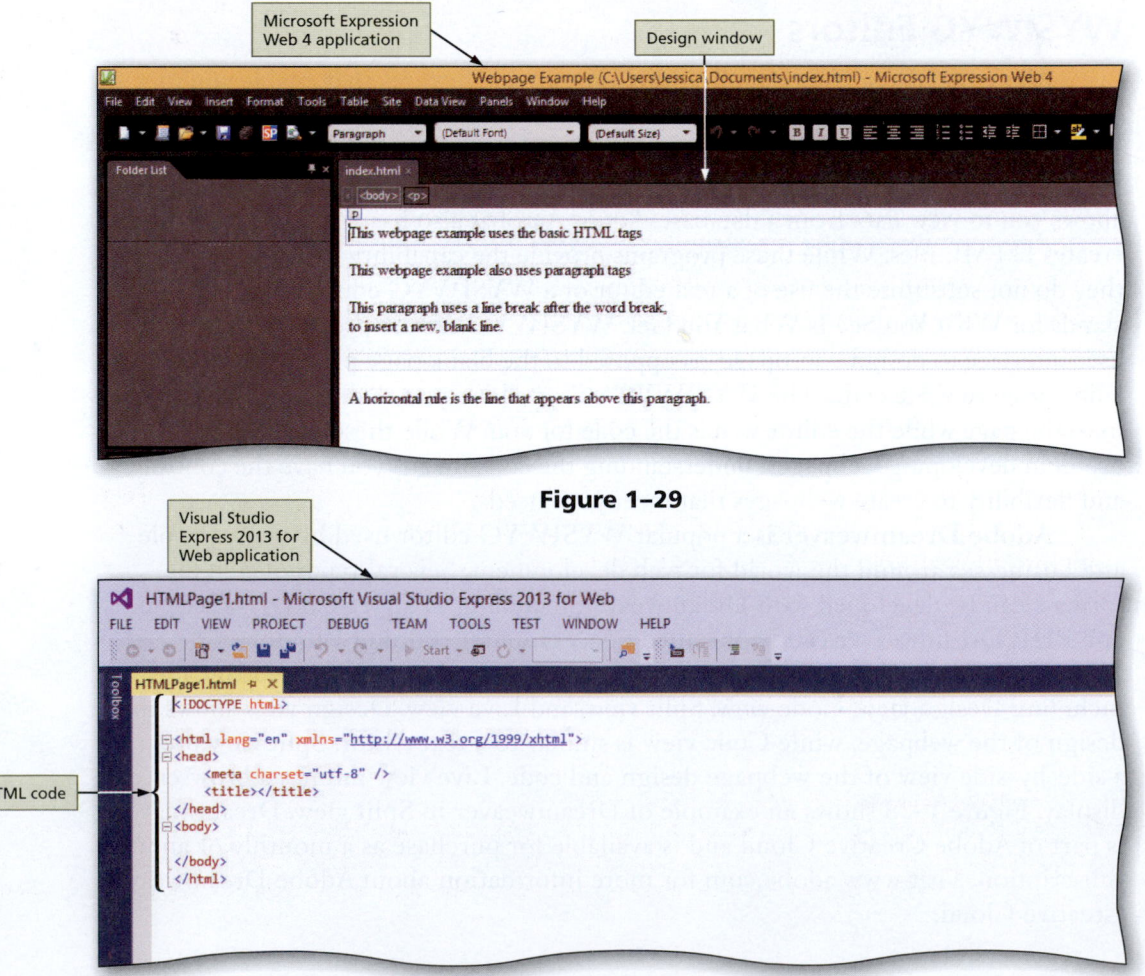

Figure 1–29

Figure 1–30

Creating a Basic Webpage

Every HTML webpage includes the basic HTML tags shown in Figure 1–31.

Figure 1–31

The numbers on the left represent line numbers for each line of HTML code. Line 1 shows the tag for declaring an HTML5 webpage. All HTML5 webpages must begin with the HTML element **<!DOCTYPE html>**. This is the first line of HTML code for all of your HTML webpages.

Line 2 shows the HTML tag needed to begin an HTML document. The basic opening tag is **<html>** and the closing tag is **</html>**, which always appears on the last line of the webpage. The lang="en" contained within the opening html tag is an attribute that defines the type of language used (English).

Line 3 shows the head tag, which contains the webpage title and other information about the webpage. The opening head tag is **<head>** and the closing tag is **</head>**.

Line 4 shows the webpage title tags, **<title>** and **</title>**. The text contained between these tags is displayed within the web browser tab. The title tags belong within the opening and closing head tags. To make the head section easier to read, web developers customarily indent the tags in the head section, such as the title and meta tags.

Line 5 shows the meta tag. A **meta** tag contains information about the data on the webpage. In this instance, the meta tag designates the type of character set the browser should use, charset="utf-8". The charset is an attribute within the meta tag that specifies the character encoding to be used for the webpage. The **Unicode Transformation Format (UTF)** is a compressed format that allows computers to display and manipulate text. When the browser encounters this meta tag, it displays the webpage properly. UTF-8 is standard for HTML5 pages and is the preferred encoding standard for email and other applications. The encoding chosen is also important when validating the webpage, which you will do in Chapter 2. Note that the meta tag is a single tag element without opening and closing tags making it an empty element. The meta tag belongs within the opening and closing head tags.

Lines 7 and 8 show the **<body>** and **</body>** tags. All text, images, links, and other content displayed on the webpage are included within the <body> and </body> tags.

BTW

<!DOCTYPE> Statement
Because the web includes billions of documents, a browser refers to the HTML version and type in the <!DOCTYPE> statement to display a webpage correctly. Previous versions of HTML had complicated <!DOCTYPE> statements.

Do I have to indent certain lines of HTML code?

Indenting lines of code is not required, but it helps improve the readability of the webpage. In Figure 1–31, Lines 4 and 5 are indented to clearly show the tags contained in the <head> and </head> tags. If the code included elements between the <body> and </body> tags, those lines could also be indented to make them easier to read. Using indents is a good web design practice.

CONSIDER THIS

Now that you have learned the basic HTML tag elements, it is time to create your first webpage. The following steps use Notepad++ to create an HTML document. You may complete these steps using a text editor other than Notepad++, but your screens will not match those in the book and your line numbers may vary slightly.

To Start Notepad++ and Create a Blank Document

1 RUN TEXT EDITOR & CREATE BLANK DOCUMENT | 2 ENTER HTML TAGS
3 ADD TEXT | 4 SAVE WEBPAGE | 5 VIEW WEBPAGE

The following steps start Notepad++ based on a typical installation in Windows 8.1. **Why?** *Before you can create a webpage, you must open a text editor.* You may need to ask your instructor how to download, install, and start Notepad++ for your computer.

1

- Open the Charms bar in Windows 8.1 and then tap or click the Search charm on the Charms bar to display the Search menu.

- Type **Notepad++** in the Search text box and watch the search results appear in the Apps list (Figure 1–32).

Figure 1–32

2

- Tap or click Notepad++ in the search results to start Notepad++ and display a new blank page.

- If the Notepad++ window is not maximized, tap or click the Maximize button next to the Close button on the title bar to maximize the window (Figure 1–33).

Note: To help you locate screen elements that are referenced in the step instructions, such as buttons and commands, this book uses red boxes to point to these screen elements.

Source: Notepad++

Figure 1–33

Other Ways

1. Double-tap or double-click Notepad++ icon on desktop

CONSIDER THIS

How do I use the touch keyboard with a touch screen?
To display the on-screen touch keyboard, tap the Touch Keyboard button on the Windows taskbar. When finished using the touch keyboard, tap the X button on the touch keyboard to close the keyboard.

To Add Basic HTML Tags to a Document

1 RUN TEXT EDITOR & CREATE BLANK DOCUMENT | 2 ENTER HTML TAGS
3 ADD TEXT | 4 SAVE WEBPAGE | 5 VIEW WEBPAGE

Create your first webpage beginning with the required minimum HTML tags. *Why? An HTML webpage requires several basic HTML tags so it can be displayed properly on a web browser.* The following steps add the required HTML tags to a document.

- On Line 1, type `<!DOCTYPE html>` to declare an HTML5 document.

- Press the ENTER key and then type `<html lang="en">` to add the opening html tag on Line 2.

- Press the ENTER key and then type `<head>` to add the opening head tag on Line 3 (Figure 1–34).

Q&A Why is the text "lang" underlined with a wavy red line?
The wavy red line indicates a possible spelling error. Because "lang" is the correct spelling for the language attribute, you can ignore this error.

```
1  <!DOCTYPE html>
2  <html lang="en">
3  <head>
```
line numbers → | HTML tags

Source: Notepad++

Figure 1–34

- Press the ENTER key and enter the lines of code as listed in Table 1–4 to add the remaining basic HTML tags (Figure 1–35).

Q&A How should I move from one line to another in the document?
Press the ENTER key after each line to continue to the next line.

Should I indent any lines of code?
Yes. Indent Lines 4 and 5 by pressing the TAB key. Press the SHIFT+TAB keys to return the insertion point to the left margin.

```
1  <!DOCTYPE html>
2  <html lang="en">
3  <head>
4      <title></title>
5      <meta charset="utf-8">
6  </head>
7  <body>
8  </body>
9  </html>
```
remaining HTML tags

Source: Notepad++

Figure 1–35

Table 1–4 HTML Tags	
Line Number	HTML Tag
4	<title></title>
5	<meta charset="utf-8">
6	</head>
7	<body>
8	</body>
9	</html>

To Add a Title and Text to a Webpage

1 RUN TEXT EDITOR & CREATE BLANK DOCUMENT | 2 ENTER HTML TAGS
3 ADD TEXT | 4 SAVE WEBPAGE | 5 VIEW WEBPAGE

Now that you have added required HTML tags, you are ready to designate a title and add content to the page. *Why? A webpage title appears on the browser tab and usually displays the name of the webpage. After titling a webpage, you add content to the body section.* The following steps add a title and content to the webpage.

- Place the insertion point between the opening and closing title tags to prepare to enter a webpage title.
- Type **My First Webpage** to add a webpage title (Figure 1–36).

Figure 1–36

Source: Notepad++

2

- Place the insertion point after the opening body tag and press the ENTER key to add a new line.
- Press the TAB key to indent the line.
- Type **Welcome to My First Webpage** to add content to the webpage (Figure 1–37).

Figure 1–37

Source: Notepad++

To Save a Webpage

After creating a webpage, you must save it as an HTML file. ***Why? A text editor can be used to create many types of files; therefore, you must specify that this is an HTML file so a browser can display it as a webpage.*** The following steps save the document as an HTML file.

1
- Tap or click File on the menu bar to display the File menu options.
- Tap or click Save As on the File menu to display the Save As dialog box (Figure 1–38).

Figure 1–38

Source: Notepad++

2
- Tap or click the Save in list box and then navigate to your Documents folder.

Q&A Can I save the file in another location on my hard drive or on my flash drive?
Yes. If your instructor specified a different location, use that instead of the Documents folder. You learn about managing website files in Chapter 2.

- In the File name text box, delete the existing text and then type **index** to name the file.

Q&A Why am I using index as the file name?
The file name *index* is the standard name of a home page.

Why am I using all lowercase letters for the file name?
The current convention in web development is to use all lowercase letters for folder and file names.

- Tap or click the Save as type list box and then tap or click Hyper Text Markup Language file to select the HTML file type (Figure 1–39).

Figure 1–39

Source: Notepad++

3
- Tap or click the Save button to save the HTML document.

Other Ways

1. Press CTRL+S

To View a Webpage in a Browser

After saving an HTML document, you can view it as a webpage in a web browser. *Why? A web browser reads the HTML code and displays the webpage content.* The following steps display a webpage in a browser.

- Tap or click Run on the menu bar to display the Run menu options.

- Tap or click Launch in IE to run Internet Explorer and display the webpage (Figure 1–40).

Q&A Why are the HTML tags not displayed in the browser?
The browser interprets the HTML code and displays only the content that appears within the tags, not the tags themselves.

Why is the content not indented in the browser when I indented it in the text editor?
The browser ignores indents, spaces, and extra blank lines inserted in the HTML file to improve readability.

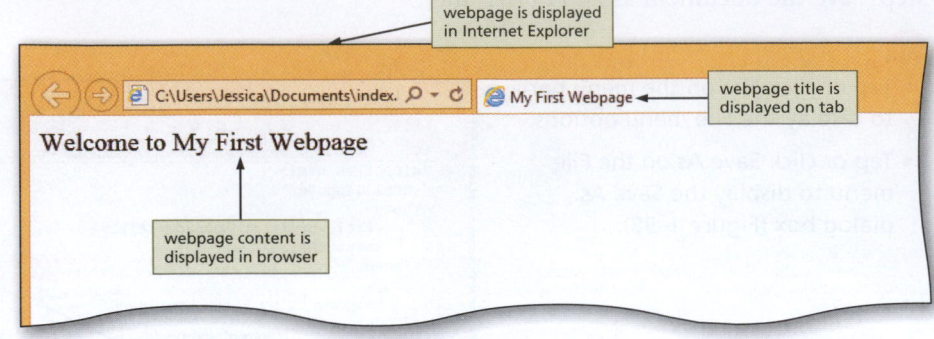

Figure 1–40

Using a Different Text Editor

If you completed the previous steps with a text editor other than Notepad++, your screen will look similar to Figure 1–41 for Programmer's Notepad, to Figure 1–42 for Sublime, and to Figure 1–43 for TextWrangler.

Figure 1–41

Figure 1–42

TextWrangler

Figure 1–43

Chapter Summary

In this chapter, you learned about the Internet, the web, and associated technologies, including web servers and web browsers. You learned the essential role of HTML in creating webpages and reviewed tools used to create HTML documents. You also learned how to create a basic HTML webpage. The items listed below include all the new concepts and skills you have learned in this chapter, with the tasks grouped by activity.

Creating a Basic Webpage
Start Notepad++ and Create a Blank Document (HTML 30)
Add Basic HTML Tags to a Document (HTML 31)
Add a Title and Text to a Webpage (HTML 32)
Save a Webpage (HTML 33)
View a Webpage in a Browser (HTML 34)

Exploring the Internet
Describe the Internet (HTML 3)
Describe the World Wide Web (HTML 4)
Define Protocols (HTML 6)
Discuss Web Browsers (HTML 7)
Identify Types of Websites (HTML 9)

Planning a Website
Identify the Purpose and Audience of the Website (HTML 11–12)

Design for Multiplatform Display (HTML 13)
Describe a Wireframe and a Site Map (HTML 14)
Consider Graphics, Navigation, Typography, and Color (HTML 17–19)
Design for Accessibility (HTML 20)

Understanding the Basics of HTML
Define Hypertext Markup Language (HTML 21)
Describe HTML Elements (HTML 21)
List Useful HTML Practices (HTML 22)
Identify Technologies Related to HTML (HTML 23)
Explain the Role of Other Web Programming Languages (HTML 23)

Using Web Authoring Tools
Identify Text Editors (HTML 24)
Download and Install a Text Editor (HTML 27)
Describe WYSIWYG Editors (HTML 27)

What decisions will you need to make when creating your next webpage?

Use these guidelines as you complete the assignments in this chapter and create your own webpages outside of this class.

1. Plan the website.

    a. Identify the purpose of the website.

    b. Identify the users of the website.

    c. Recognize the computing environments of the users.

    d. Design a wireframe and a site map.

2. Choose the design components.

    a. Identify possible graphics for the website.

    b. Determine the types of navigation tools and typography to use.

    c. Select a color scheme.

    d. Consider accessibility.

CONSIDER THIS

Continued >

STUDENT ASSIGNMENTS

CONSIDER THIS *continued*

3. Select a webpage authoring tool.

    a. Review available authoring tools.

    b. Determine an authoring tool to use to create the webpages.

4. Create a basic HTML webpage.

    a. Insert the basic HTML tags.

    b. Indent some elements to improve readability.

    c. Add content to the webpage.

    d. Save the file as an HTML document.

    e. Display the webpage in a browser.

CONSIDER THIS

How should you submit solutions to questions in the assignments identified with a symbol?

Every assignment in this book contains one or more questions identified with a ✳ symbol. These questions require you to think beyond the assigned presentation. Present your solutions to the questions in the format required by your instructor. Possible formats may include one or more of these options: write the answer; create a document that contains the answer; present your answer to the class; discuss your answer in a group; record the answer as audio or video using a webcam, smartphone, or portable media player; or post answers on a blog, wiki, or website.

Apply Your Knowledge

Reinforce the skills and apply the concepts you learned in this chapter.

Creating a Basic HTML Webpage

Instructions: The page shown in Figure 1–44 contains the required HTML5 tags for all webpages. In your HTML editor, you will enter these required HTML tags and save the file as an HTML document that can serve as the model, or template, for other HTML documents. You will make a copy of the HTML template and insert the paragraph content to create and personalize a page to introduce yourself, your major, and your goals for the class. The figures in this exercise use Notepad++ (Windows) and TextWrangler (Mac) as HTML editors, but you can complete the exercises in this book using any HTML editor such as Sublime, Programmer's Notepad, KompZer, HTML Kit, CoffeeCup, Aptana, UltraEdit, or Microsoft WebMatrix, to mention a few.

Perform the following tasks:

1. Open your HTML editor, and enter the required HTML tags as shown in Figure 1–44. In this figure, the tags within the <head> section are indented to visually separate the <head> section from the <body> section. Adding spaces, indents, or extra blank lines to an HTML document does not change the way the page looks in the browser. Professional webpage developers use indents and blank space to make the code easier to read and maintain.

```
new 0

 1  <!DOCTYPE html>
 2  <html lang="en">
 3  <head>
 4      <title></title>
 5      <meta charset="utf-8">
 6  </head>
 7  <body>
 8
 9
10  </body>
11  </html>
```

Source: Notepad++

Figure 1–44

2. Save the file as a Hyper Text Markup Language file with the name `template01` in the chapter01\apply folder provided with the Data Files for Students. (*Hint*: If you are using TextWrangler, enter the entire file name and extension of `template01.html` to save the file as an HTML file). Both Notepad++ and TextWrangler save HTML files with an html file name extension and apply color coding.

3. Tap or click the opening <html> tag. Examine the HTML document shown in Figure 1–45, which displays the code in Notepad++. In a Word document, answer the following questions:

   a. In what color does Notepad++ display HTML tags?

   b. What color are HTML attributes?

   c. What color are HTML attribute values?

   d. When you tap or click the start or end tag of a set of paired tags, what background color is used to highlight the pair?

Figure 1–45

4. Examine the HTML document shown in Figure 1–46, which displays the code in TextWrangler. In a Word document, answer the following questions:

   a. In what color does TextWrangler display HTML tags?

   b. What color are HTML attributes?

   c. What color are HTML attribute values?

   d. In what background color is the current line highlighted?

Figure 1–46

Continued >

Apply Your Knowledge *continued*

If you are using a plain text editor such as Notepad (Windows) or TextEdit (Mac), all of the code and content is black, as shown in Figure 1–47.

```
template01.html - Notepad
File   Edit   Format   View   Help
<!DOCTYPE html>
<html lang="en">
<head>
        <title></title>
        <meta charset="utf-8">
</head>
<body>


</body>
</html>
```

Figure 1–47

5. Delete the closing quotation mark in the <meta charset="utf-8"> tag and observe how the colors change on the screen. In a Word document, explain how the colors changed on the screen. Replace the missing quotation mark. Observing how the colors work in your HTML editor helps you productively find and correct errors.

6. Save the template01.html file with the name **intro.html** in the chapter01\apply folder provided with the Data Files for Students. Given all HTML5 pages start with the same required tags, a productive way to create a new file is to open the template01.html file and then save it with a new name as a starting point for the new page.

7. Enter the paragraph tags, horizontal rule tags, and content as shown in Figure 1–48 (Notepad++) and Figure 1–49 (TextWrangler). Modify the content within the paragraph <p> … </p> tags to introduce yourself in this page. Use indents as desired to make the page easy to read.

```
intro.html
 1     <!DOCTYPE html>
 2    <html lang="en">
 3    <head>
 4        <title>Introduction</title>
 5        <meta charset="utf-8">
 6    </head>
 7    <body>
 8        <p>Insert your name</p>
 9        <p>Insert the current date</p>
10        <p>Insert the name of the course</p>
11        <p>Insert your instructor's name</p>
12        <hr>
13
14        <p>Insert the degree or certificate you are working toward<p>
15        <p>Insert any relevant work experience or webpage development experience</p>
16        <p>Insert a fun fact about yourself</p>
17        <hr>
18
19        <p>Insert any questions you have at this time.</p>
20
21    </body>
22    </html>
23
24
25
```

Source: Notepad++

Figure 1–48

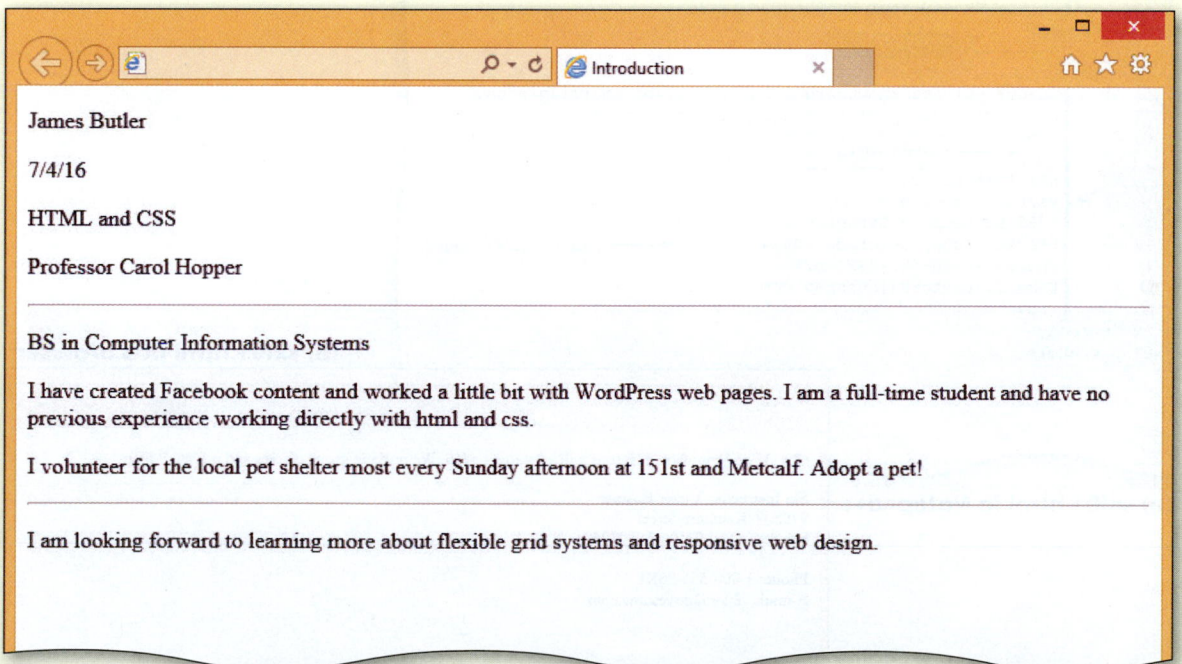

```
1    <!DOCTYPE html>
2  ▼ <html lang="en">
3  ▼ <head>
4    <title></title>
5    <meta charset="utf-8">
6  └ </head>
7  ▼ <body>
8        <p>Insert your name</p>
9        <p>Insert the current date</p>
10 └     <p>Insert the name of the course</p>
11 └     <p>Insert your instructor's name</p>
12       <hr>
13
14       <p>Insert the degree or certificate you are working toward</p>
15       <p>Insert any relevant work experience or webpage development experience</p>
16       <p>Insert a fun fact about yourself</p>
17       <hr>
18
19       <p>Insert any questions you have at this time.</p>
20
21   </body>
22   </html>
23
```

Source: TextWrangler

Figure 1–49

8. Save intro.html and then open the file in a current browser. A sample solution is shown in Figure 1–50.

James Butler

7/4/16

HTML and CSS

Professor Carol Hopper
_____

BS in Computer Information Systems

I have created Facebook content and worked a little bit with WordPress web pages. I am a full-time student and have no previous experience working directly with html and css.

I volunteer for the local pet shelter most every Sunday afternoon at 151st and Metcalf. Adopt a pet!
_____

I am looking forward to learning more about flexible grid systems and responsive web design.

Figure 1–50

9. Submit the files you created in this exercise in a format specified by your instructor. You may be asked to electronically submit the files as an email attachment or drop-box attachment. You may be asked to publish the pages to a web server. See Lab 3 in this chapter and Chapter 12 for more information on publishing pages to web servers.

10. ✳ In Step 2, you saved a text file as an HTML file. At that point, an HTML editor will provide color-coded visual support. Identify three different ways that the color supports productive web development skills. Also, identify the HTML editor you are using, and note three different color codes applied by that editor.

Extend Your Knowledge

Extend the skills you learned in this chapter and experiment with new skills. You may need to use additional resources to complete the assignment.

Adding Comments to an HTML Document

Note: To complete this assignment, you will be required to use the Data Files for Students. Visit www.cengage.com/ct/studentdownload for detailed instructions or contact your instructor for information about accessing the required files.

Instructions: Open your HTML editor and then open the extend01.html file provided in the Data Files for Students. Add the HTML tags, text, indents, blank lines, and comments as instructed. Save the page as **ski01.html** in the same location and view it in a browser. Figure 1–51a shows the completed HTML document in Notepad++ and Figure 1–51b shows the completed webpage in a browser.

(a) ski01.html in Notepad++

(b) ski01.html in a browser

Source: Notepad++

Figure 1–51

Perform the following tasks:

1. HTML comments are inserted into a webpage using special tags with the following syntax:

   <!-- comment goes here -->

   A comment may be placed anywhere in the HTML document after the opening <!DOCTYPE html> statement and may be one or more lines long as needed. The only requirement is that the comment opens with the same four characters <!--, and ends with the same three characters, -->. In ski01.html, enter a comment after the opening <!DOCTYPE html> declaration statement that includes your name and the current date as shown in Figure 1–51a.

2. Enter the remaining tags and text shown in Figure 1–51a without any indents or blank lines. Save the file and open it in a browser. In a Word document named **ski01.docx**, answer these questions:

   a. How do HTML comments appear on the webpage when it is opened in a browser?

   b. How does the content within the <p> … </p> tags appear in a browser?

3. Return to your HTML editor and add blank lines and indents as shown in Figure 1–51a. Save the HTML file and refresh it in your browser to see the changes. In your Word document, answer these questions:

   a. What is the purpose of adding extra lines and indents in the HTML editor?

   b. How do the extra lines and indents change the way the webpage appears in the browser?

4. Add <p>, </p>, and <br> tags as shown in Figure 1–51a so that the content is rendered in the browser on multiple lines. In your Word document, answer these questions:

   a. What is the purpose of adding the <p> and </p> tags?

   b. What is the purpose of adding the <br> tags?

5. Save the HTML file and refresh it in your browser to see the changes. Compare Figure 1–51a and Figure 1–51b. In your Word document, identify how the following two lines use white space in the HTML editor and compare that to how the browser reads and displays the same line.

   a. "Our ski and snowboard…"

   b. "Phone: 1-800…"

6. Submit your assignment in the format specified by your instructor.

7. ✳ What would happen if webpage developers did not use comments, indents, and white space? Identify a potential problem associated with each.

Analyze, Correct, Improve

Analyze a webpage, correct all errors, and improve it.

Correcting HTML Errors

Note: To complete this assignment, you will be required to use the Data Files for Students. Visit www.cengage.com/ct/studentdownload for detailed instructions or contact your instructor for information about accessing the required files.

Instructions: Open your HTML editor and then open the analyze01.html file provided in the Data Files for Students. This document lists 10 HTML5 best practices in its body section. You will follow these 10 guidelines to correct the webpage as instructed. Save the page as **practices01.html** in the same location and view it in a browser. Figure 1–52a shows the completed HTML document in Notepad++ and Figure 1–52b shows the completed webpage in a browser.

Continued >

Analyze, Correct, and Improve *continued*

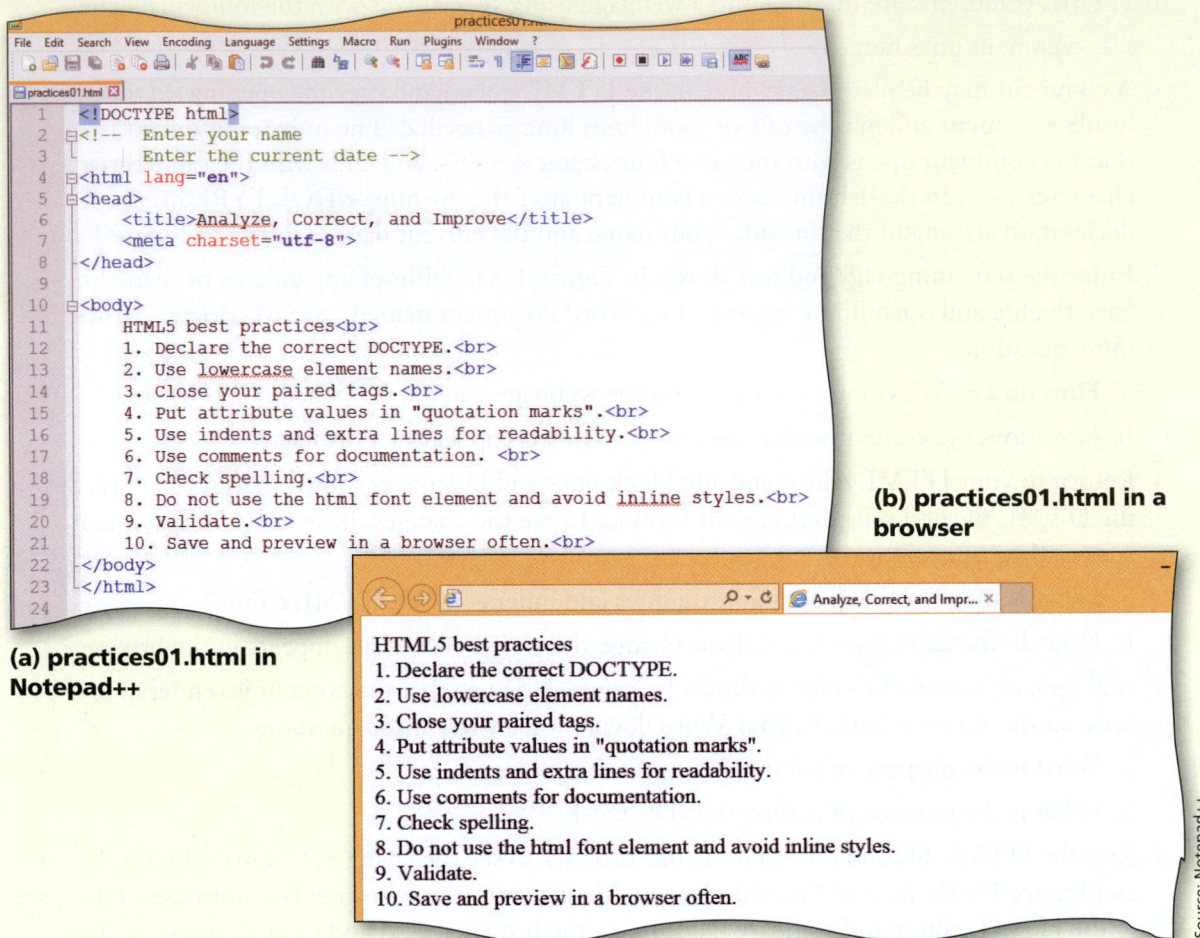

(a) practices01.html in Notepad++

(b) practices01.html in a browser

Source: Notepad++

Figure 1–52

1. **Correct**

   a. Replace the existing HTML4 DOCTYPE statement with the correct DOCTYPE statement for an HTML5 webpage.

   b. Go through the page and change all uppercase element and attribute names in the tags to lowercase.

   c. Go through the page and make sure all paired elements end with a closing slash (/) such as </title> or </head>.

   d. Go through the page and make sure all attribute values are surrounded by "quotation marks".

   e. Go through the page and add indents and extra lines for readability.

   f. Check the comments to make sure they start with <!-- and end with -->. Change the generic text in the comment to include *your* name and the current date.

   g. Select the content within the <body> . . . </body> tags and then check the spelling. Your HTML editor may have a spelling checker, or you may need to copy and paste the content into another program with a spelling checker such as Word. Fix any spelling errors you find.

   h. By completing Steps a–g, you have followed HTML5 best practices 1–7. You will learn about styles and validation in future chapters. Skip ahead to best practice 10 to save and view your webpage in a browser.

2. Improve

    a. In future chapters you will learn how to create an ordered list that automatically numbers each item in the list. For now, add a <br> tag after "HTML5 best practices" and after each item in the list to place the title and each item on the list on its own line.

    b. Save and preview the webpage.

    c. Submit your assignment in the format specified by your instructor.

3. ✳ Which error identified in Steps 1a–1g was the most difficult to find and correct? Use specific HTML terminology in your answer.

In the Labs

Labs 1 and 2, which increase in difficulty, require you to create webpages based on what you learned in the chapter. Lab 3 requires you to dive deeper into a topic covered in the chapter.

Lab 1: Creating a Webpage from a Template and Using Placeholder Text

Problem: You work for a local but rapidly growing gardening supply company that specializes in products to support food self-sufficiency. The company has identified a small number of extremely successful products that they want to market through a website and have hired you to get started. Create the webpage shown in Figure 1–53b that identifies the type of content you want to include on the company's home page. In later chapters, you will replace the placeholders with actual text and images.

(a) cityfarmer.html in Notepad++

(b) cityfarmer.html in a browser

Source: Notepad++

Figure 1–53

Continued >

In the Labs *continued*

Instructions: Perform the following tasks:

1. If you created the template01.html file in the Apply Your Knowledge exercise in this chapter, open template01.html and then save it with the name `cityfarmer.html` in the chapter01\ lab1 folder provided with the Data Files for Students.

   If you did not create the template01.html file, enter the required HTML tags as shown in Figure 1–53a and then save the file with the name `cityfarmer.html` in the chapter01\ lab1 folder provided with the Data Files for Students.

2. Enter the text `City Farmer Home Page` within the <title> … </title> tags.

3. Within the body section, add the following content using six sets of paragraph tags. At this point, the content consists of six placeholder paragraphs that you will replace with actual webpage content in a later chapter.

   ```
   <p>Clear Navigation Bar</p>

   <p>Company Description and Featured Products</p>

   <p>How to Contact Us</p>

   <p>News and Events</p>

   <p>Customer Interaction - Call to Action</p>

   <p>Home Page Images</p>
   ```

4. Add an <hr> tag after each of the closing paragraph tags to insert a horizontal line after each paragraph.

5. Indent the code and content within the head and body sections to make each section distinct and readable.

6. Add a comment after the opening <!DOCTYPE html> statement that contains your name and the current date.

7. Check the spelling of the text within the title and body tags, as shown in Figure 1–53a.

8. Save the page and then open it in a browser, as shown in Figure 1–53b.

9. Submit your assignment in the format specified by your instructor.

10. ✳ The term *placeholder* refers to any area of a webpage that you want to reserve for a particular purpose. A webpage developer will often use text or image placeholders when designing webpages, especially if actual content is not yet available. Using your favorite search engine, search to find three different reasons to use webpage placeholders.

Lab 2: **Creating a Webpage from a Template**

Problem: You are part of a philanthropic group of motorcyclists who participate in community events and parades to raise cancer awareness. Your group is called Cycle Out Cancer, and the director has asked you to help create a website for the group. Create the webpage shown in Figure 1–54b, which identifies the type of content to include on the organization's home page. In later chapters, you will replace the placeholders with actual text and images.

```
1   <!DOCTYPE html>
2   <html lang="en">
3   <head>
4       <title>Cycle Out Cancer Home Page</title>
5       <meta charset="utf-8">
6   </head>
7   <body>
8       <p>1 Headline: Cycle Out Cancer </p>
9       <p>2 Sub-headline: We Ride So Others May Live</p>
10      <p>3 Benefits: Explain how we make a difference to this world.</p>
11      <p>4 Call-to-Action: Links to email, Facebook, Twitter, and other ways to contact us.</p>
12      <p>5 Features: Include pictures, maps, and descriptions of planned rides.</p>
13      <p>6 Cancer Survivors: Include quotes from lives we've touched.</p>
14      <p>7 Website Navigation System</p>
15      <p>8 Images </p>
16      <p>9 Resources</p>
17      <p>Your Name<br>
18          University of Oklahoma<br>
19          12345 College Blvd<br>
20          Norman, OK 73072<br>
21      </p>
22
23  </body>
24  </html>
25
26
```

(a) cycle.html in Notepad++

(b) cycle.html in a browser

1 Headline: Cycle Out Cancer

2 Sub-headline: We Ride So Others May Live

3 Benefits: Explain how we make a difference to this world.

4 Call-to-Action: Links to email, Facebook, Twitter, and other ways to contact us.

5 Features: Include pictures, maps, and descriptions of planned rides.

6 Cancer Survivors: Include quotes from lives we've touched.

7 Website Navigation System

8 Images

9 Resources

Your Name
University of Oklahoma
12345 College Blvd
Norman, OK 73072

Source: Notepad++

Figure 1–54

Instructions: Perform the following tasks:

1. If you created the template01.html file in the Apply Your Knowledge exercise in this chapter, open template01.html and then save it with the name `cycle.html` in the chapter01\lab2 folder provided with the Data Files for Students.

   If you did not create the template01.html file, enter the required HTML tags as shown in Figure 1–54a and then save the file with the name `cycle.html` in the chapter01\lab2 folder provided with the Data Files for Students.

2. Enter the text `Cycle Out Cancer Home Page` within the <title> … </title> tags.

3. Within the body section, add the following content using 10 sets of paragraph tags. At this point, the content consists of 10 placeholder paragraphs that you will replace with actual webpage content in later chapters.

```
<p>1 Headline: Cycle Out Cancer</p>

<p>2 Sub-headline: We Ride So Others May Live</p>

<p>3 Benefits: Explain how we make a difference to this world.</p>

<p>4 Call-to-Action: Links to email, Facebook, Twitter, and other
ways to contact us.</p>

<p>5 Features: Include pictures, maps, and descriptions of planned
rides.</p>
```

Continued >

In the Labs *continued*

```
<p>6 Cancer Survivors: Include quotes from lives we've touched.</p>
<p>7 Website Navigation System</p>
<p>8 Images</p>
<p>9 Resources</p>
<p>10 Address</p>
```

4. Replace the "10 Address" placeholder text with *your* name and the address of your school. Include a <br> tag at the end of each line so that each line of the address appears on its own line as shown in Figure 1–54a. The entire address should be surrounded by only one set of <p> … </p> tags.

5. Indent the code and content within the head and body sections to make each section distinct and readable.

6. Check the spelling of the text within the title and body tags.

7. Save the page and then open it in a browser as shown in Figure 1–54b.

8. Submit your assignment in the format specified by your instructor.

9. ✳ The term *Call to Action* (CTA) refers to anything that urges the reader of a webpage to take an immediate action. The CTA on a webpage is often a button or hyperlink. Using your favorite search engine, identify five reasons you might use a CTA and then provide five techniques for drawing attention to your CTAs.

Lab 3: Expand Your World
Publishing to a Website

Note: To complete this assignment, you will be required to use the Data Files for Students. Visit www.cengage.com/ct/studentdownload for detailed instructions or contact your instructor for information about accessing the required files.

Problem: If you want your webpages to be viewed by anyone connected to the Internet, you must store the pages on a web server. Transferring webpage files from your local computer to a web server is called publishing. Once your webpages are published on the web server, the server creates an http:// address that allows others to find and view your pages using any browser connected to the Internet.

Several key pieces of information and permissions need to be in place before you can successfully publish your webpages to a web server. This exercise will help you find and record the information you need to publish your webpages to your school's web server. If your school does not provide free web server space to students, this exercise will help you find free or inexpensive web server space where you can publish your webpages. (*Note:* Always check with your instructor regarding whether your webpages are to be published. Each school is set up differently, but this exercise helps you collect the necessary information.)

Instructions:
1. Ask your instructor if you are going to publish your webpages to a school web server and if any supporting documentation is available.

2. Open the webpublishing.docx document from the Data Files for Students.

3. Using the web server documentation provided by your instructor or school, fill out the right column of the table to identify the pieces of information needed to publish your webpages. A sample solution is provided in webpublishing.docx that applies to students at Johnson County Community College in Overland Park, Kansas.

4. Use the web to research three inexpensive web server alternatives.

5. Open the webserveralternatives.docx document from the Data Files for Students.

6. Using the information you found in Step 4, complete the table in the webserveralternatives. docx document to compare three web server alternatives. You may be asked to share and compare this information with the rest of the class.

7. Confirm if and how your instructor wants you to publish your webpages, as well as how your work will be submitted for grading purposes.

8. ✸ Some web hosting companies offer *free* web hosting services. However, all businesses need to generate revenue in order to survive. Using your favorite search engine, identify three ways *free* web hosting companies generate revenue.

✸ Consider This: Your Turn

Apply your creative thinking and problem-solving skills to design and implement a solution.

Note: To complete this assignment, you will be required to use the Data Files for Students. Visit www.cengage.com/ct/studentdownload for detailed instructions or contact your instructor for information about accessing the required files.

1. Design and Create a Personal Portfolio Website

Personal

Part 1: As in almost every field, the job market for the best jobs in web development are competitive. One way to give yourself a big edge in a job search is to create an appropriate personal portfolio website to showcase your skills. Plan the website by completing the table in the portfolio.docx document in the Data Files for Students. Answer the questions with thoughtful, realistic responses. Be sure to sketch the wireframe for your home page on the last page. Submit your assignment in the format specified by your instructor.

Part 2: ✸ What do you want this website to accomplish?

2. Design and Create a Website for a Web Development and Consulting Business

Professional

Part 1: When you are finished with college, you plan to join a web development and consulting firm to gain experience in the field. Your long-term goal is to start and own a web development and consulting firm. You decide to begin by designing a website you would eventually like to build for the firm. Start planning the website by completing the table in the webdevelopment.docx document in the Data Files for Students. Answer the questions with thoughtful, realistic responses. Be sure to sketch the wireframe for your home page on the last page. Submit your assignment in the format specified by your instructor.

Part 2: ✸ What are some general characteristics of any successful small business that you want this website to portray? What are some characteristics of a successful web development consulting firm that you want this website to portray?

Continued >

Consider This: Your Turn *continued*

3. Design and Create a Website for the Dog Hall of Fame

Research and Collaboration

Part 1: Dogs add an enormous amount of joy and happiness to a family. Some dogs guard and protect. Others fetch, herd, search, or hunt. Almost all pets provide loving companionship and unconditional acceptance. Because dogs play such a major role in the lives of their owners, your class has been approached by a retired veterinarian to help him build a website, the "Dog Hall of Fame," that honors three special dogs each year. The three award categories will include working dog, hero dog, and companion dog.

Your first order of business is to organize a group of three or four peers in your class to plan the website by completing the table in the doghalloffame.docx document in the Data Files for Students. Answer the questions with thoughtful, realistic responses. Be sure to sketch the wireframe for your home page on the last page. Submit your assignment in the format specified by your instructor.

Part 2: ✳ You made several decisions while planning the website for this assignment. Which two or three of the questions did you find the most difficult to answer and why? What additional information would be helpful in planning this website?

2 Building a Webpage Template with HTML5

Objectives

You will have mastered the material in this chapter when you can:

- Explain how to manage website files

- Describe and use HTML5 semantic elements

- Determine the elements to use when setting the structure of a webpage

- Design and build a semantic wireframe

- Create a webpage template

- Insert comments in an HTML document

- Add static content to a webpage template

- Insert symbol codes and other character entities

- Describe the benefits of validating web documents

- Validate an HTML template

- Create a home page from an HTML template

- Add unique content to a webpage

2 | Building a Webpage Template with HTML5

Introduction

Building a website from scratch involves a lot of time and planning, which is one reason that professional web design services are in high demand. Some web designers have their own business and provide their services on contract to clients, who are people or other businesses that want to build or redesign a website. Other web designers work in larger organizations and provide their services to people within the organization, who are called stakeholders. As an introduction to basic website design and development, this book provides a foundation on which to build your web design skills.

As discussed in Chapter 1, before you start building a website, you must plan it, which includes meeting with the clients or stakeholders to discover their needs, the purpose of the website, and their target audience. After developing a plan, you can start constructing the website by creating an HTML document and then adding the required basic HTML elements so visitors can display the webpage in a browser. Next, include HTML5 elements to define the specific sections or areas of the webpage. This initial HTML document can serve as the template for the site. A **template** is a predefined webpage that contains a specific HTML structure to be used by all pages within the website. This chapter focuses on how to build a webpage template with HTML5 elements and then use that template to create a home page.

Project — Plan and Build a Website

A local fitness center called Forward Fitness Club opened recently and needs a website to help promote its business. The business owner wants the website to showcase the club's equipment, group fitness classes, nutrition information, and contact information. The owner hired you to plan and design the Forward Fitness Club website.

The project in this chapter follows generally accepted guidelines for planning and building the webpage template shown in Figure 2–1a to produce the home page shown in Figure 2–1b. The template contains code and text including the document title, header, navigation area, and footer, which is repeated on each page of the Forward Fitness Club website. The template also includes comments to remind the web designer about the purpose of each section.

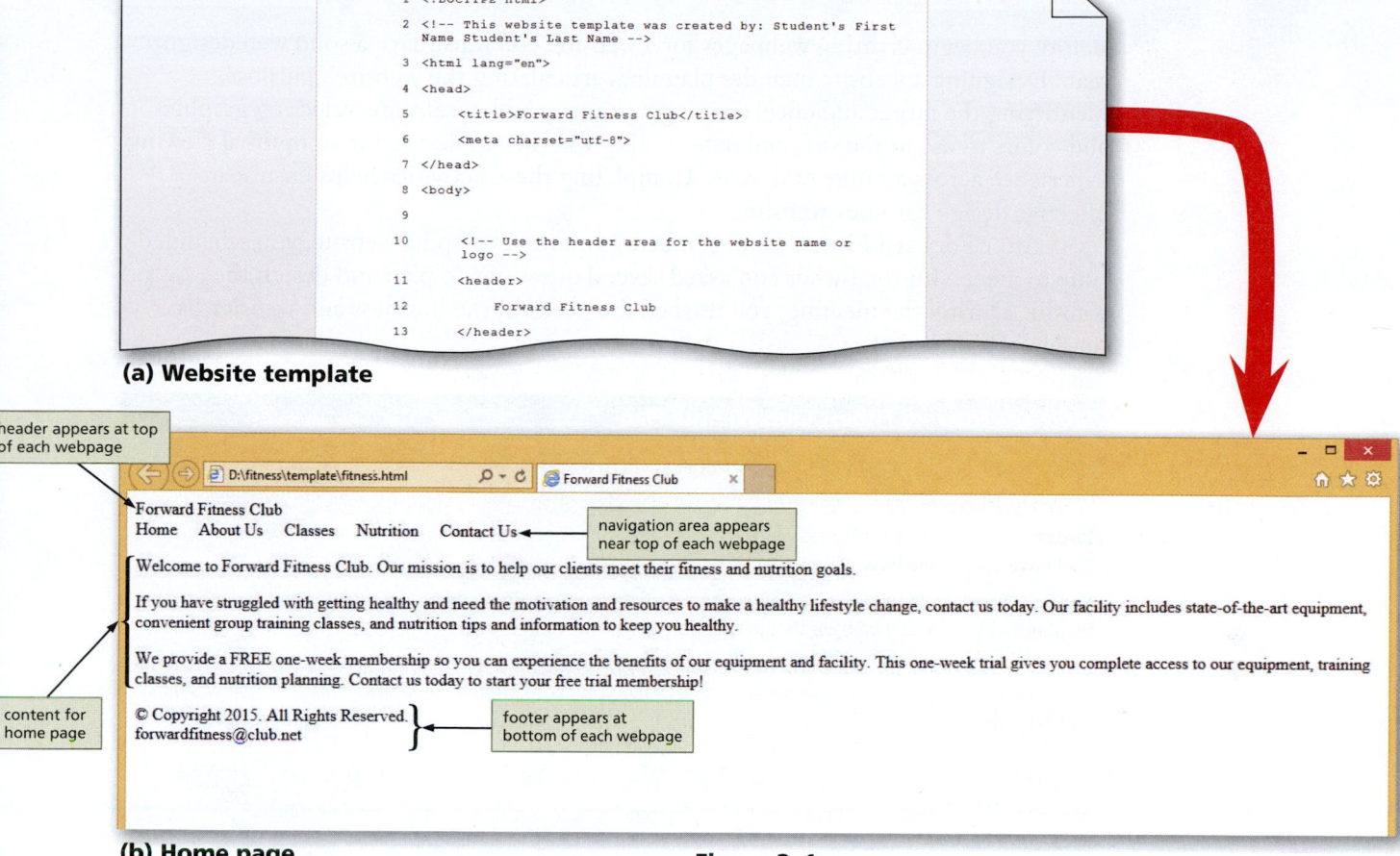

(a) Website template

header appears at top
of each webpage

navigation area appears
near top of each webpage

content for
home page

footer appears at
bottom of each webpage

(b) Home page

Figure 2–1

Roadmap

In this chapter, you will learn how to create the webpage shown in Figure 2–1. The following roadmap identifies general activities you will perform as you progress through this chapter:

1. CREATE WEBSITE FOLDERS to organize files.
2. CREATE a TEMPLATE.
3. ENTER HTML5 SEMANTIC ELEMENTS in the document.
4. ADD COMMENTS AND CONTENT to the document.
5. VALIDATE the DOCUMENT.
6. CREATE AND VIEW the HOME PAGE.

At the beginning of step instructions throughout the chapter, you will see an abbreviated form of this roadmap. The abbreviated roadmap uses colors to indicate chapter progress: gray means the chapter is beyond that activity; blue means the task being shown is covered in that activity, and black means that activity is yet to be covered. For example, the following abbreviated roadmap indicates the chapter would be showing a task in the 4 ADD COMMENTS & CONTENT activity.

1 CREATE WEBSITE FOLDERS | 2 CREATE TEMPLATE | 3 ENTER HTML5 SEMANTIC ELEMENTS
4 ADD COMMENTS & CONTENT | 5 VALIDATE DOCUMENT | 6 CREATE & VIEW HOME PAGE

Use this abbreviated roadmap as a progress guide while you read or step through the instructions in this chapter.

Designing a Website

Before you begin creating webpages for a website, you must have a solid web design plan. Designing a website includes planning, articulating the website's purpose, identifying the target audience, creating a site map and wireframe, selecting graphics and colors to use in the site, and determining whether to design for an optimal viewing experience across a range of devices. Completing these activities helps ensure an effective design for your website.

After Forward Fitness Club contacted you to develop its website, you scheduled time to meet with the owner and asked several questions to plan and design the website. During the meeting, you learned the needs of the business and website, as outlined in Table 2–1.

Table 2–1 Forward Fitness Club Website Plan	
Purpose of the Website	To promote fitness services and gain new clients. The Forward Fitness Club mission: to facilitate a healthy lifestyle and help our clients meet their fitness and nutrition goals.
Target Audience	Forward Fitness Club customers are adults between the ages of 18 and 50 within the local community.
Multiplatform Display	Forward Fitness Club recognizes the growth in smartphone and tablet usage and wants a single website that provides an optimal viewing experience regardless of whether visitors are using a desktop, laptop, tablet, or smartphone.
Wireframe and Site Map	The initial website will consist of five webpages arranged in a hierarchal structure with links to the home page on every page. Each webpage will include a header area, navigation area, main content area, and footer area.
Graphics	Forward Fitness Club wants to display its fitness equipment and logo to help with local branding. Photos of the facility, members, and staff will increase visual appeal.
Color	Forward Fitness Club wants to use its logo colors, green and yellow, to promote health, strength, and a bright future.
Typography	To make the content easy to read, the website will use a serif font style for paragraphs, lists, and other body content, while providing contrast by using a sans serif font style for headings.
Accessibility	Standard accessibility attributes, such as alternative text for graphics, will be used to address accessibility. See Appendix D for an accessibility reference list.

Site Map

Recall that a site map indicates how the pages in a website relate to each other. To create a site map, you first need to know how many pages to include in the website. The owner of Forward Fitness Club has many ideas for the website, including some ambitious ones. To keep the website simple for now while allowing room for growth, you and the owner agree that the initial website will have a total of five webpages titled Home, About Us, Classes, Nutrition, and Contact Us. Because each page will contain links to all pages and accommodate future growth, the website will use a modified hierarchal structure. The webpages will include the following content:

- Home page: Introduces the fitness center and its mission statement
- About Us page: Showcases the facility's equipment and services
- Classes page: Includes a schedule of available group training and fitness classes
- Nutrition page: Provides nutrition tips and simple meal plans
- Contact Us page: Provides a phone number, email address, physical address, and form for potential clients to request additional information about the fitness center's services

Figure 2–2 depicts the site map for the Forward Fitness Club website.

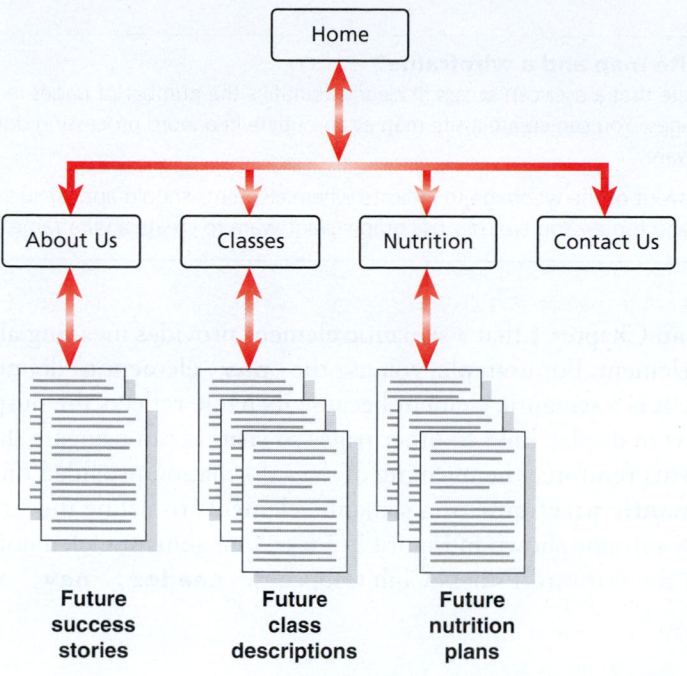

Figure 2–2

Wireframe

In addition to the site map for the Forward Fitness Club website, you have sketched out a webpage wireframe. Recall that a wireframe depicts the layout of a webpage, including its major content areas. Forward Fitness Club wants to promote its brand by including its logo, so each page will contain a designated area called the header for the logo. The header is located at the top of a webpage and identifies the site, often by displaying the business name or logo. For easy navigation, each page also will have a horizontal list of links to the other pages in the site. These page links will appear below the header in the navigation area. The primary page content, or the main content area, will follow the navigation area and will contain information that applies to the page, including headings, paragraphs of text, and images. Lastly, the footer will be located below the primary page content and will contain copyright and contact information. Figure 2–3 shows the proposed wireframe with these major content areas.

Figure 2–3

What is the difference between a site map and a wireframe?

A site map lists all the webpages in a website that a user can access. It clearly identifies the number of pages in the website and shows how each page is linked to other pages. You can create a site map as an outline in a word processing document or as an image using flowcharting or graphics software.

In contrast, a wireframe shows the visual layout of the webpage to indicate where elements should appear such as the logo, search box, navigation bar, main content, and footer. You typically use graphics software to create a wireframe.

Recall from Chapter 1 that a semantic element provides meaning about the content of the element. For example, you use the `nav` element to define the navigation area. It is a semantic element because its name reflects the purpose of its content, which is to display links to other pages so visitors can navigate the website. Semantic elements reinforce the meaning of the information provided on the webpage. A **semantic wireframe** uses semantic elements to define the structure of a webpage. The wireframe shown in Figure 2–3 uses four semantic elements to define the structure of the Forward Fitness Club webpages: `header, nav, main,` and `footer`.

File Management

Websites use several types of files, including HTML files, image files, media such as audio and video files, and CSS files, which you learn about in Chapter 4. Even a simple website might use hundreds of files. Therefore, each site must follow a systematic method to organize its files. Before you begin to create your first HTML page, start by creating a folder and subfolders to contain and organize your website files as shown in Figure 2–4.

Figure 2–4

The main folder (also called the **root folder**) for the Forward Fitness Club website is the fitness folder. It contains all of the files and other folders for the website. The css folder will contain CSS files, which you create in Chapter 4 to format a webpage and its elements. The images folder will contain the Forward Fitness Club logo, photos, and other images to display on the webpages. The media folder will contain audio and video files, which you add in Chapter 9. The template folder contains the template document for the site's webpages, which you create in this chapter.

To Create a Website Folder and Subfolders

The following steps, which assume Windows 8.1 is running, create a folder and subfolders for the fitness website. *Why? Before you can create a website, you should create a folder for the website files.* You may need to ask your instructor whether you should create the website folder on a portable storage device, such as a USB flash drive.

- If necessary, tap or click the Desktop tile on the Windows 8.1 Start screen to display the desktop.

- Tap or click the File Explorer app button on the taskbar to display the File Explorer window.

- Navigate to the desired location for the website folder, such as the Documents folder or your USB flash drive, to prepare to create a new folder.

- Tap or click the New folder button on the Quick Access toolbar to create a new folder.

- Type **fitness** and then press the ENTER key to name the folder (Figure 2–5).

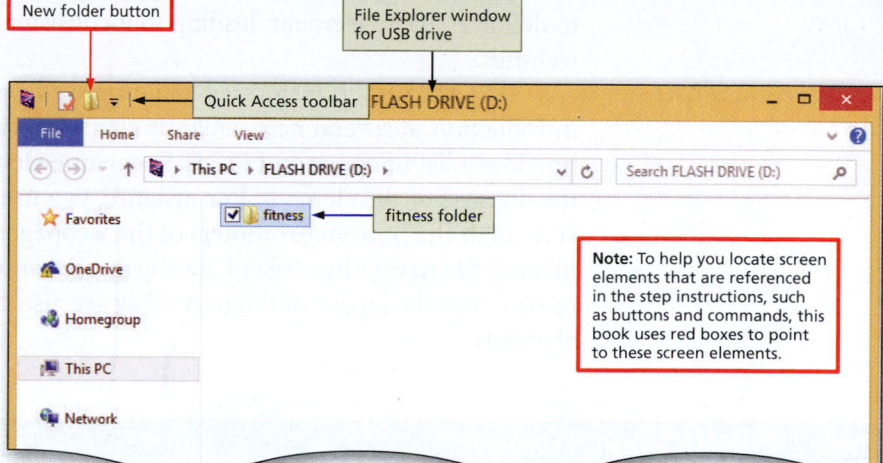

Figure 2–5

Note: To help you locate screen elements that are referenced in the step instructions, such as buttons and commands, this book uses red boxes to point to these screen elements.

2

- Double-tap or double-click the fitness folder to open it.

- Tap or click the New folder button on the Quick Access toolbar to create a new folder.

- Name the new folder **css**.

- Tap or click the New folder button on the Quick Access toolbar to create a new folder.

- Name the new folder **images**.

- Tap or click the New folder button on the Quick Access toolbar to create a new folder.

- Name the new folder **media**.

- Tap or click the New folder button on the Quick Access toolbar to create a new folder.

- Name the new folder **template** (Figure 2–6).

Figure 2–6

Other Ways

1 Tap or click New folder button (Home tab | New group) 2 Press CTRL+SHIFT+N 3 Press and hold or right-click blank spot in window, tap or click New, tap or click Folder

Using HTML5 Semantic Elements

As you learned in Chapter 1, you begin a new HTML document by adding the basic required HTML elements to it, such as the **html, head,** and **body** elements. Within the **body** element, you next add HTML elements that define the structure of the page. HTML 4.01 introduced the **div** element (with the <div> and </div> tags) to divide a page into separate sections. Each **div** element has a unique name to distinguish it from other **div** elements on the page. For example, you might use a **div** element named header for the header area and another **div** element named nav for the navigation area. However, webpage authors can use any name they like to define a **div** element, leading to inconsistency among naming conventions for websites.

HTML5 has transformed and improved website development with the introduction of several new semantic elements with standardized names. Table 2–2 provides a list of common HTML5 semantic elements. The name of each tag reflects the purpose of the element. For instance, you use the **footer** element to display content at the bottom (or footer) of the webpage. You use the **nav** element to identify the navigation area of a webpage. Because many of the semantic elements help to structure the layout of the page, they are also called structural elements or layout elements.

Table 2–2 HTML5 Semantic Elements	
Element	**Description**
<header>…</header>	Indicates the header information on the webpage. Header content typically consists of a business name or logo and is commonly positioned immediately after the opening <body> tag.
<nav>…</nav>	Indicates the start and end of a navigation area within the webpage. The **nav** element contains hyperlinks to other webpages within a website and is commonly positioned immediately after the closing </header> tag.
<main>…</main>	Indicates the start and end of the main content area of a webpage. Contains the primary content of the webpage. Only one main element can appear on a page.
<footer>…</footer>	Indicates the start and end of the footer area of a webpage. Contains the footer content of the webpage.
<section>…</section>	Indicates the start and end of a section area of a webpage. Contains a specific grouping of content on the webpage.
<article>…</article>	Indicates the start and end of an article area of a webpage. Contains content such as forum or blog posts.
<aside>…</aside>	Indicates the start and end of an aside area of a webpage. Contains information about nearby content and is typically displayed as a sidebar.

Professional web designers debate whether to use the **div** element or the **main** element to define the main content area of a webpage. Those who favor the **div** element argue that it has widespread browser support. The W3C introduced the **main** element after other semantic elements, and not all browsers or text editors recognize it yet.

Web designers who favor the **main** element do so because **main** is a semantic element while **div** is not. In other words, the name of the **main** element describes its purpose and function. The **div** element relies on its id attribute to provide meaning.

After discussing the pros and cons of the **main** and **div** elements with the owner of the Forward Fitness Club, you decide to use the **main** element for the fitness website. Because it is a new site that does not have to incorporate webpages created with earlier versions of HTML, it will use the new HTML5 structural elements, including `header, nav, main,` and `footer`, to lay out the webpages. Although the `div` element achieves the same results in layout, the future of web development includes using the new HTML5 layout tags, and Forward Fitness wants to create a foundation for this future. Using the semantic HTML5 elements standardizes naming conventions, making webpages more universal, accessible, and meaningful to search engines.

Header Element

The `header` element structurally defines the header area of a webpage. The `header` element starts with a <header> tag and ends with a </header> tag. Content placed between these tags appears on the webpage as part of the `header` element. Web designers often place a business name or logo within the `header` element.

Nav Element

The nav element structurally defines the navigation area of a webpage. The `nav` element starts with a <nav> tag and ends with a </nav> tag. The `nav` element usually includes links to other pages within the website.

Main Element

The `main` element structurally defines the `main` content area of a webpage. The main element starts with a <main> tag and ends with a </main> tag. Each page can have only one `main` element because its content should be unique to each page. At the time this book was written, all major browsers supported the `main` element, with the exception of Internet Explorer 11 and earlier versions. While Internet Explorer 11 will display content within the `main` element, it does not fully support the element. For example, Internet Explorer 11 might not correctly display formatting applied to the `main` element.

Footer Element

The `footer` element structurally defines the bottom, or footer area, of a webpage. The footer element starts with a <footer> tag and ends with a </footer> tag. Common content found within a webpage footer includes copyright information, contact information, and page links.

Figure 2–7 identifies the relationship between a coded webpage template with `header`, `nav`, `main`, and `footer` elements and the conceptual wireframe design of a webpage.

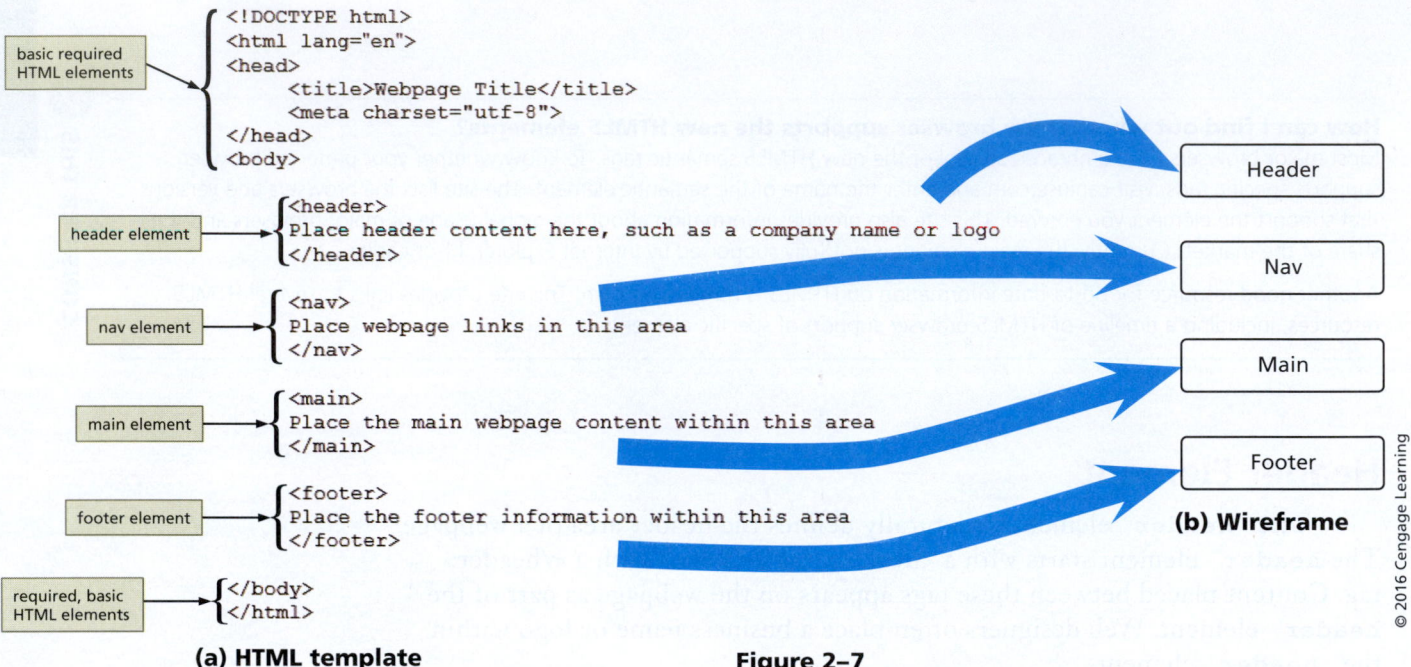

(a) HTML template   **Figure 2–7**

© 2016 Cengage Learning

Creating a Webpage Template

A hallmark of a well-designed website is that its webpages have the same look and feel. In other words, most pages have the same layout and all the pages share the same color scheme, typography, and style of graphics. In addition, elements work the same way on each page. For example, the navigation bar appears in the same position on each page and uses the same colors, fonts, and font styles. Visitors select a link on the navigation bar the same way, such as by tapping or clicking a page name. The selected link then appears in a contrasting color.

To make sure the webpages in a site share a standard layout, you can create a template, an HTML document that contains elements that should appear on each page. Instead of creating a webpage from scratch, open the template document in a text editor and save it using the name of the new webpage. You can then concentrate on adding content for that particular page rather than re-creating the basic required HTML elements and the structural elements.

For the fitness website, you can create a template that includes the basic required HTML elements (the DOCTYPE declaration and the `html`, `head`, `title`, `meta`, and `body` elements) and the four HTML structural semantic elements identified in the webpage wireframe shown in Figure 2–3: `header`, `nav`, `main`, and `footer`.

BTW

Saving Your Work
It is a good idea to save your HTML file periodically as you are working to avoid the risk of losing your work.

To Create a Webpage Template Document

To create a webpage template, you create an HTML document with the HTML elements that define the webpage structure. Use your preferred text editor to create the template or ask your instructor which text editor to use. The following steps create a basic webpage template.

 1

- Open your text editor, tap or click File on the menu bar, and then tap or click New if you need to open a new blank document.
- Tap or click File on the menu bar and then tap or click Save As to display the Save As dialog box.
- Navigate to your fitness folder and then double-tap or double-click the template folder to open it.
- In the File name box, type **fitness** to name the file.

Q&A Why is the new file named fitness instead of index?
Fitness is the name of the template file you use to create webpages for this website. Use index as the file name for the home page.

- Tap or click the Save as type button and then tap or click Hyper Text Markup Language to select the file format.
- Tap or click the Save button to save the template in the template folder.
- On Line 1 of the text editor, type **<!DOCTYPE html>** to define a new HTML5 document (Figure 2–8).

Q&A Why does the <!DOCTYPE html> text appear in bold and red in Figure 2–8?
Throughout the book, the new text you add to a file in the current step is shown in bold and red in the accompanying figure.

Figure 2–8

 2

- Press the ENTER key to add Line 2 and then type **<html lang="en">** to add a starting <html> tag that defines the language as English.

- Press the ENTER key to add Line 3 and then type **<head>** to add a starting <head> tag (Figure 2–9).

Figure 2–9

3

- Add the following HTML elements, also shown in bold and red in Figure 2–10, to complete the template, using the SPACEBAR or TAB key to indent Lines 4 and 5 and using the SHIFT+TAB keys to stop indenting.

```
<title></title>
<meta charset="utf-8">
</head>
<body>
</body>
</html>
```

Figure 2–10

4

- Save your changes.

To Add HTML5 Semantic Elements to a Webpage Template

The wireframe in Figure 2–3 defines four areas to display content for the website. To define these content areas, insert the following HTML5 tags between the <body> and </body> tags: <header> </header>, <nav> </nav>, <main> </main>, and <footer> </footer>. Recall that the HTML5 **header** element defines the header area of the webpage. The **nav** element defines the navigation area of the webpage. The **main** element defines the primary content area of the webpage. The **footer** element defines the footer area of the webpage. The following steps insert HTML5 structural elements within the body tags.

- Place your insertion point after the beginning <body> tag and press the ENTER key twice to insert new Lines 8 and 9.

- On Line 9, press the TAB key and then type **<header>** to add a starting header tag.

- Press the ENTER key to insert a new Line 10 and then type **</header>** to add an ending header tag (Figure 2–11).

Figure 2–11

Q&A Why is Line 8 blank?
Line 8 is intentionally left blank to improve readability. As you add more HTML elements to a page, including white space helps to clearly identify the areas of a page. Using blank lines between HTML elements is a good design practice.

Will the blank line be noticeable when the page is displayed in a browser?
No. Browsers ignore blank lines when interpreting the code on the page.

2

- Add the following HTML5 tags, also shown in bold and red in Figure 2–12, to complete the wireframe, indenting each line and inserting a blank line after each ending tag.

```
<nav>
</nav>
(blank line)
<main>
</main>
(blank line)
<footer>
</footer>
```

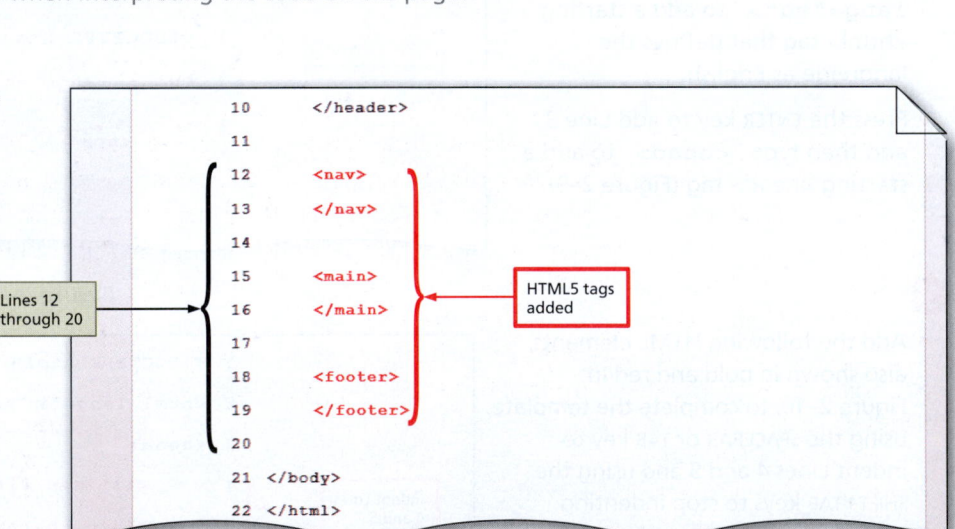

Figure 2–12

3

- Save your changes.

Q&A In Notepad++, why are the **main** tags not blue like the **header, nav,** and **footer** tags?
Because the **main** element is not completely supported by the current version of Internet Explorer (Internet Explorer 11), one of the most widely used browsers, the **main** element is not color-coded. However, Notepad++ still recognizes the main tags and pairs them together when you tap or click a tag.

To Add a Title to a Webpage Template

Recall that when a webpage is displayed in a browser, the browser tab displays the document title. To add a document title, type the title text between the starting and ending title tags. The following steps add a webpage title to a template.

1

- Place your insertion point after the beginning <title> tag and type **Forward Fitness Club** to add a webpage title.

2

- Save your changes and then view the page in a browser to display the webpage title (Figure 2–13).

Q&A How do I display the webpage in a browser?

Recall from Chapter 1 that you can use a command in your HTML text editor to display a webpage. For example, in Notepad++, you can tap or click Run on the menu bar and then tap or click Launch in IE.

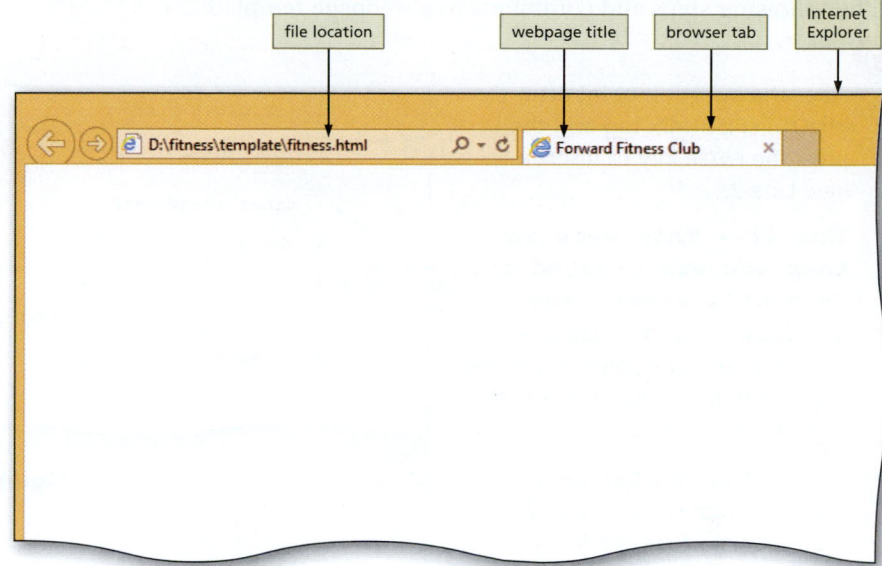

Why is the webpage blank when displayed in a browser?

You are creating a webpage template that will be used to create pages for the website. The subsequent webpages will contain content, but you have not added any content yet.

Figure 2–13

Comments

As you create a webpage template, include comments about the HTML elements you use to define the areas within the webpage. Comments can provide additional information about these areas and the type of information they include, which is especially helpful if you stop working on a partially completed page and then return to it later. Add a comment before a tag using the following syntax:

`<!-- Place your comment here -->`

The comment syntax uses the angle brackets, similar to the HTML tags. The next character is an exclamation mark followed by two dashes (--). Add the comment text after the first set of dashes. For example, you use comments to give instructions on how to use the template or to identify the author of the website. Close the comment by adding two dashes, followed by a closing angle bracket.

If you are using Notepad++, the text you enter scrolls continuously to the right unless you turn on the word wrap feature. **Word wrap** causes text lines to break at the right edge of the window and appear on a new line, so all entered text is visible in the Notepad++ window. When word wrap is enabled, a paragraph of text is assigned a single logical line number even though it may be displayed on multiple physical lines in Notepad++. Word wrap does not affect the way text prints.

BTW

Auto-Fill and Highlighting Features

If you are using Notepad++ or Sublime, you can use the auto-fill feature by starting to type the name of a tag and letting the text editor complete the tag for you. If you are using Notepad++, tap or click the starting <body> tag to highlight the starting and ending tags so you can easily identify them.

BTW

Turning on Word Wrap

To turn on word wrap in Notepad++, select View on the menu bar and then select Word wrap.

To Add Comments to a Webpage Template

When you create a webpage template, including comments provides additional information about how to use the sections of the webpage. You can also use a comment to identify that you are the author of the webpage. *Why? When creating a new webpage from a template, comments provide insight on the type of information to include.* The following steps add comments to a webpage template.

1

- Place the insertion point after the <!DOCTYPE html> tag and then press the ENTER key to insert a new Line 2.

- Type `<!-- This website template was created by: *Student's First Name Student's Last Name* -->` on Line 2 to add a comment at the beginning of the document that identifies the author (Figure 2–14).

Figure 2–14

Q&A Should I type "Student's First Name Student's Last Name"?
No. Type your first and last names to identify yourself as the author of the template.

My comment is shown on two lines. Is that okay?
Yes. If your text editor is using word wrap and your document window is not maximized, your comment might wrap to the next line. Note, however, that it is still numbered as Line 2.

2

- Place the insertion point on the blank Line 9 and press the ENTER key to insert a new Line 10.

- On Line 10, press the TAB key and then type `<!-- Use the header area for the website name or logo -->` to add a comment identifying the type of information to include in the header area (Figure 2–15).

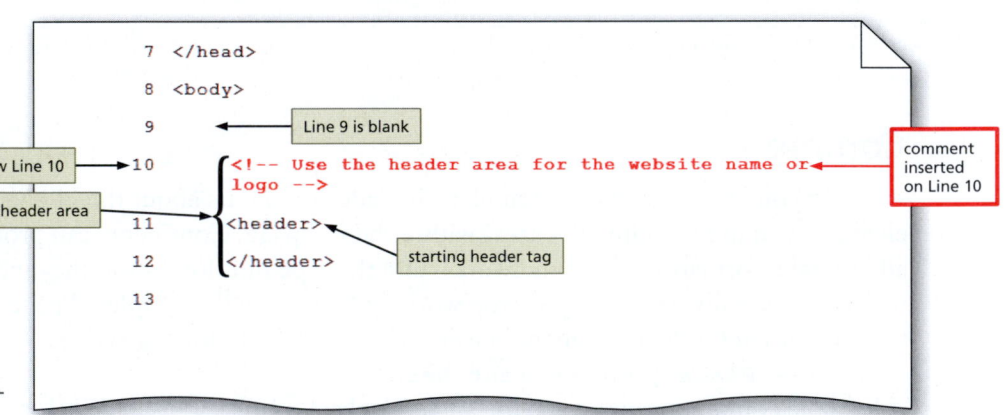

Figure 2–15

Q&A Do the blank lines affect the HTML elements?
No. inserting blank lines before or after HTML elements does not affect the structure of the webpage.

3

- Place the insertion point on the blank Line 13 and press the ENTER key to insert a new Line 14.

- On Line 14, type `<!-- Use the nav area to add hyperlinks to other pages within the website -->` to add a comment above the navigation area (Figure 2–16).

Figure 2–16

4

- Place the insertion point on the blank Line 17 and press the ENTER key to insert a new Line 18.

- On Line 18, type `<!-- Use the main area to add the main content of the webpage -->` to add a comment above the main area.

- Place the insertion point on the blank Line 21 and press the ENTER key to insert a new Line 22.

- On Line 22, type `<!-- Use the footer area to add webpage footer content -->` to add a comment above the footer area (Figure 2–17).

Figure 2–17

5

- Save your changes.

> **Break Point:** If you want to take a break, this is a good place to do so. You can exit the text editor now. To resume at a later time, run your text editor, open the file called fitness.html, and continue following the steps from this location forward.

Webpage Content

After inserting the HTML tags and comments for a webpage template, add static content or content that will appear on every webpage, such as the business name or logo, the webpage links, and the footer information. Content is the text or other item that is displayed in a browser. Place content between the starting and ending tags. Following is an example of content added between header tags:

```
<header>Forward Fitness Club</header>
```

For the Forward Fitness Club website, the header area contains the business name, which will appear at the top of every page. (In Chapter 3, you replace the text with a graphic logo.) Other tags that contain static content include the nav area, which contains links to all pages within the website and will remain the same on each page. In addition, the footer area, which contains the copyright notice and an email address, will remain the same throughout the website.

Adding static content to a template saves time. Remember that the template will be used to create the webpages for the website. Because this content is meant to be displayed on each page, add it to the template once rather than to each page many times.

To Add Content to the Header Section

Now that the webpage template structure is complete, you can add static content that will appear on each webpage within the website. The header of each webpage in the fitness website should display the name of the business, Forward Fitness Club. For now, you enter the business name as text. In Chapter 3, you insert an image that displays the business logo, including a graphic and the business name. The following steps add content to the header area of a webpage template.

1

- Place the insertion point after the beginning <header> tag and press the ENTER key to insert a new Line 12.

2

- On Line 12, press the TAB key and then type **Forward Fitness Club** to add the business name to the webpage template (Figure 2–18).

Q&A Do I have to place the content on the line between the beginning and ending <header> tags?

No. This HTML element can also be written on one line as <header>Forward Fitness Club</header>. In Step 2, you place the header content on a separate line for improved readability.

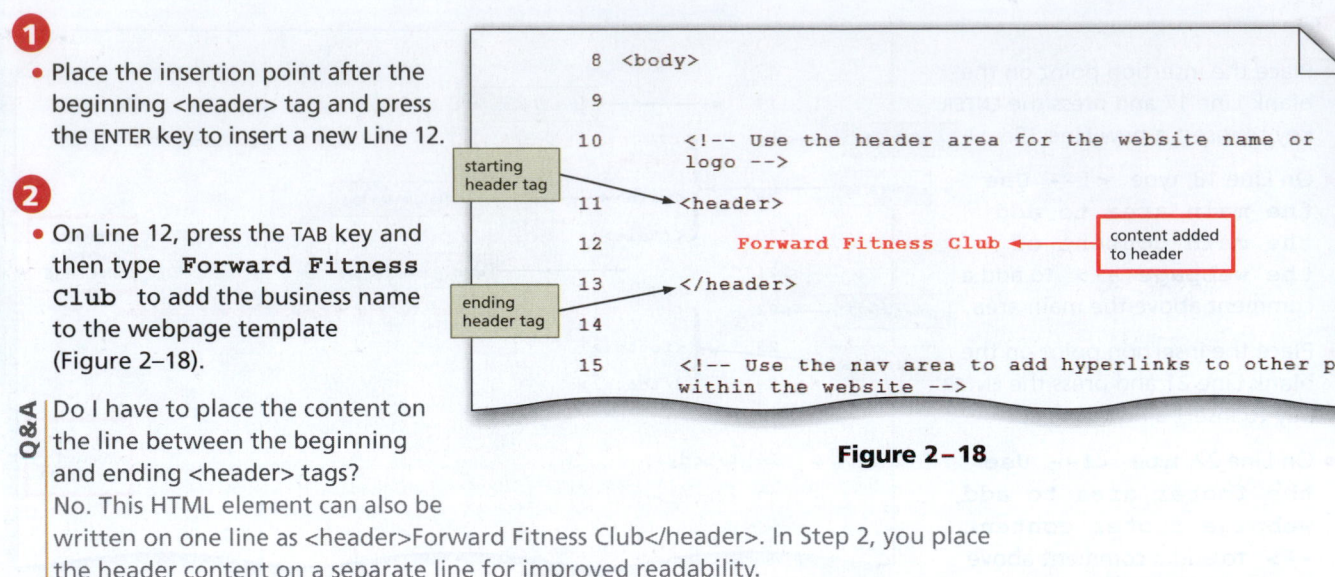

Figure 2–18

Using Symbol Entities

When adding content to a webpage, you often need to insert symbols, such as a copyright symbol, ©. Some symbols such as less than (<) or greater than (>) are reserved for other uses, such as signifying the start and end of HTML tags. Other symbols such as © or € are not included on standard keyboards. Rather than inserting reserved symbols directly or avoiding other special symbols, you can insert a symbol on an HTML webpage by typing its HTML entity name or entity number. Inserting an **HTML character entity** in the code displays a reserved HTML character on the webpage. All character entities start with an ampersand (&) and end with a semicolon (;) to signal to the browser that everything in between is an entity representing a symbol. An **entity name** is an abbreviated name, and an **entity number** is a combination of the pound sign (#) and a numeric code. For example, the entity name for the copyright symbol is **©** and the entity number for the copyright symbol is **©**. You can use either an entity's name or number in your HTML code. An entity name is easier to remember than an entity number, though more browsers support entity numbers than names.

Table 2–3 lists common symbols along with their entity names and numbers.

Table 2–3 Common Symbol Entities			
Character	**Description**	**Entity Name**	**Entity Number**
©	Copyright symbol	&copy;	&#169;
®	Registered trademark	&reg;	&#174;
€	Euro	&euro;	&#8364;
&	Ampersand	&amp;	&#38;
<	Less than	&lt;	&#60;
>	Greater than	&gt;	&#62;
	Nonbreaking space		

A commonly used character is a nonbreaking space ** **, which forces browsers to display a blank space. You can insert indents, extra spaces, and paragraph breaks to make HTML code easier to read and maintain. When a browser displays the webpage, however, it ignores this extra white space, treating multiple spaces, indents, and paragraph breaks as a single space. For example, when you press the TAB key or use the SPACEBAR to indent header tags and content in the HTML code, a browser displays the header content on the left margin of the webpage with no indent. Likewise, if you insert two spaces between the page names in the nav area, a browser removes the extra spaces when it displays the webpage so only one space appears between the page names. What can you do if you want to display the extra spaces in a browser? You use the nonbreaking space character entity as in the following code:

```
Home     About Us
```

What is the purpose of the UTF-8 character set?
Computers can read many types of character sets. The Unicode Consortium developed Unicode Transformation Format (UTF)-8 to create a standard character set. The UTF-8 has been widely accepted and is the preferred character set for several types of web programming languages, such as HTML, JavaScript, and XML.

To Add Text and Nonbreaking Spaces to the Nav Section

1 CREATE WEBSITE FOLDERS | 2 CREATE TEMPLATE | 3 ENTER HTML5 SEMANTIC ELEMENTS
4 ADD COMMENTS & CONTENT | 5 VALIDATE DOCUMENT | 6 CREATE & VIEW HOME PAGE

Next, between the beginning and ending nav tags, add the name of the links to the other pages. *Why? The nav area is designed to contain hyperlinks to other pages within the website.* To insert two spaces between each page name, use the nonbreaking space character entity ` `. The following steps add content to the nav area of a webpage template.

1

- Place the insertion point after the beginning <nav> tag and press the ENTER key to insert a new Line 17.

- On Line 17, press the TAB key and then type **Home** to add the first webpage link name.

- Press the SPACEBAR once and then type **   ** to add two nonbreaking spaces (Figure 2–19).

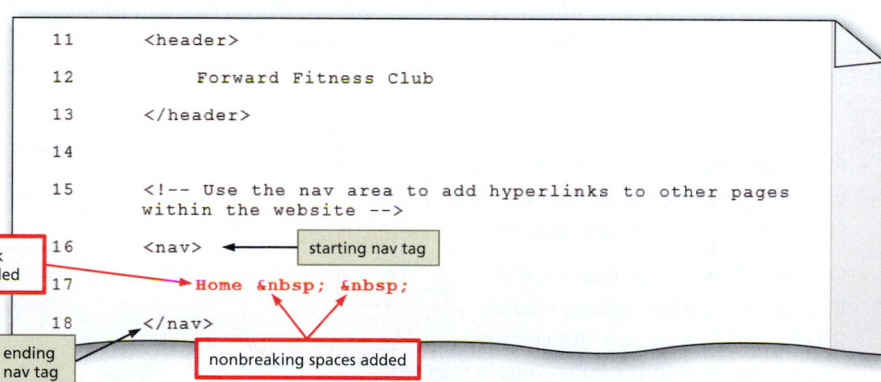

```
11        <header>
12              Forward Fitness Club
13        </header>
14
15        <!-- Use the nav area to add hyperlinks to other pages
          within the website -->
16        <nav>        ← starting nav tag
17              Home    
18        </nav>
```

Home link name added

nonbreaking spaces added

ending nav tag

Figure 2–19

Do I have to place the link names on the line between the beginning and ending <nav> tags?
No. This HTML element can also be written on one line as `<nav>Home    </nav>`. In this case, you place the name of the link on a separate line to improve readability.

2

- Press the ENTER key to insert a new Line 18.
- On Line 18, type **About Us** to add the second webpage link name.
- Press the SPACEBAR once and then type **   ** to add two nonbreaking spaces (Figure 2–20).

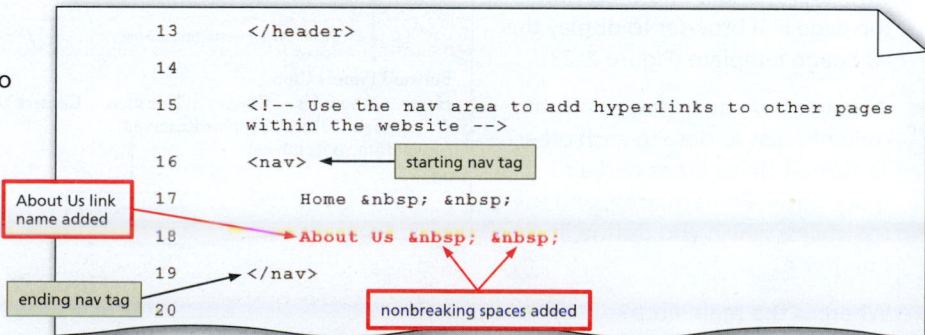

```
13        </header>
14
15        <!-- Use the nav area to add hyperlinks to other pages
          within the website -->
16        <nav>        ← starting nav tag
17              Home    
18        About Us    
19        </nav>
20
```

About Us link name added

nonbreaking spaces added

ending nav tag

Figure 2–20

3

- Press the ENTER key to insert a new Line 19, type `Classes` to add the third webpage link name, press the SPACEBAR, and then type `   ` to add two nonbreaking spaces.

- Press the ENTER key to insert a new Line 20, type `Nutrition` to add the fourth webpage link name, press the SPACEBAR, and then type `   ` to add two nonbreaking spaces.

- Press the ENTER key to insert a new Line 21 and then type `Contact Us` to add the fifth webpage link name (Figure 2–21).

Figure 2–21

4

- Save your changes.

To Add Content and a Symbol to the Footer Section

1 CREATE WEBSITE FOLDERS | 2 CREATE TEMPLATE | 3 ENTER HTML5 SEMANTIC ELEMENTS
4 ADD COMMENTS & CONTENT | 5 VALIDATE DOCUMENT | 6 CREATE & VIEW HOME PAGE

The footer section of the website contains a copyright symbol and an email address. ***Why?*** *Legal notices and contact information usually appear in the footer of a webpage. You add this content to the footer in the template file so that the content appears on all webpages in the website.* The following steps add content to the footer area of a webpage template.

1

- Place the insertion point after the beginning `<footer>` tag and press the ENTER key to insert a new Line 30.

- On Line 30, press the TAB key and then type `&copy; Copyright 2015. All Rights Reserved.` to add the copyright symbol and additional copyright information.

- Type `<br>` to insert a line break.

- Press the ENTER key to insert a new Line 31 and then type `forwardfitness@club.net` to add an email address to the footer section (Figure 2–22).

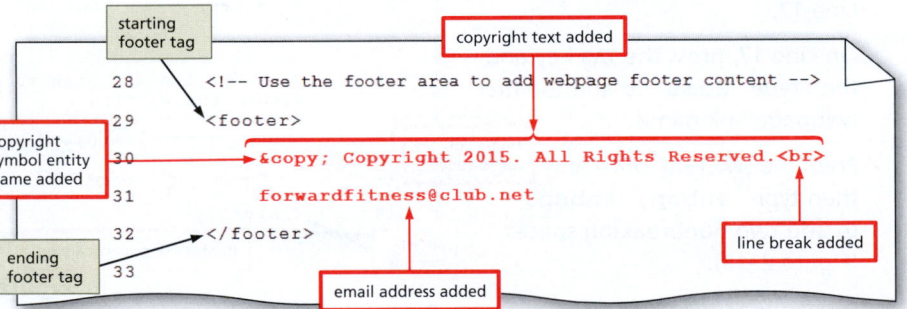

Figure 2–22

2

- Save your changes and then view the page in a browser to display the webpage template (Figure 2–23).

Q&A

Why are the header, nav, and footer content areas so close to each other?
To format these areas and add space between each area, you use CSS styles, which you define in Chapter 4.

Figure 2–23

Where is the main area?
The main area is located after the navigation area and before the footer. Because the main area does not currently have any content, it is not displayed in the browser.

Validating HTML Documents

After creating an HTML file, you **validate** the document to verify the validity of the HTML code. When you validate an HTML document, you confirm that all of the code is correct and follows the established rules set by the W3C, the organization that sets the standards for HTML. The W3C recommends validating all HTML documents and making validation part of your webpage testing.

Many validation services are available on the web; you can use any of them to make sure that your HTML code follows standards and is free of errors. Some check only for errors, while others flag errors and suggest how to correct them. The W3C has a free online validator that checks for errors, indicates where they are located, and suggests corrections. Keep in mind that a validator looks for coding errors; it cannot make sure that browsers will display the webpage as you intend. To test the design of a webpage, you must display it in all of the popular browsers.

This book uses the online W3C Markup Validation Service (validator.w3.org). This validator checks the markup validity of web documents in HTML and XHTML, along with some other markup languages. The validator scans the DOCTYPE statement to see which version of HTML or XHTML you are using, and then checks to see if the code is valid for that version. You **upload** your HTML file to the validator, which means you transfer a copy of the document to the validation website. The validator reviews each line of code and locates any errors.

If the validator detects an error in your HTML code, it displays a warning such as "Errors found while checking this document as HTML5!" The W3C validator displays this warning in red in the header bar. A Result line below the header bar shows the number of errors in the document. You can scroll down the page or tap or click the Jump To: Validation Output link to see detailed comments on each error.

BTW

Common Validation Errors
Common validation errors include not spelling tags or attributes correctly and using uppercase letters (except for DOCTYPE). A single coding error can cause many lines of errors during validation.

BTW

Byte-Order Mark (BOM) Warning
In a common result, the validator finds a BOM in a file encoded for UTF-8. This is a warning rather than an error and does not need to be corrected. However, you can adjust the preferences in your text editor to use UTF-8 without BOM to avoid this warning.

To Validate the Webpage Template

1 CREATE WEBSITE FOLDERS | 2 CREATE TEMPLATE | 3 ENTER HTML5 SEMANTIC ELEMENTS
4 ADD COMMENTS & CONTENT | 5 VALIDATE DOCUMENT | 6 CREATE & VIEW HOME PAGE

Before you use the webpage template to create the necessary webpages for the fitness website, run the template through the W3C validator to check the document for errors. *Why? If the document has any errors, validating gives you a chance to identify and correct them before using the template to create a webpage.* The following steps validate an HTML document.

1
- Open your browser and type **http://validator.w3.org/** in the address bar to display the W3C Markup Validation Service page.

- Tap or click the Validate by File Upload tab to display the Validate by File Upload information.

- Tap or click the Browse button to display the Choose File to Upload dialog box.

Q&A I do not see a Browse button, but I do have a Choose File button. Should I select the Choose File button instead?
Yes. The button names and other options may vary slightly depending on your browser.

- Navigate to your webpage template folder to find the fitness.html file (Figure 2–24).

Figure 2–24

Source: validator.w3.org

2

- Tap or click the fitness.html document to select it.

- Tap or click the Open button to upload the selected file to the W3C validator.

- Tap or click the Check button to send the document through the validator and display the validation results page (Figure 2–25).

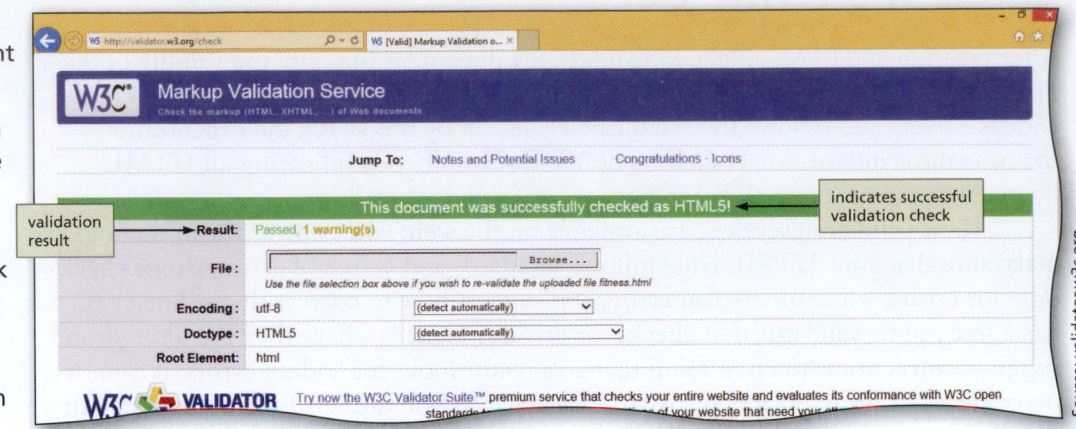

Figure 2–25

Q&A

Why does the result show "Passed, 1 warning"?

The warning advises you that the validator checked the file with an experimental feature, the HTML5 conformance check. This message means the document does not contain errors and no corrections are necessary. You can scroll down to display the Notes and Potential Issues section, which explains this warning.

My results show errors. How do I correct them?

Scroll down the page to display the Notes and Potential Issues section. Review the errors listed below the validation output. Any line number that contains an error is shown in this section.

To Validate an HTML Document with Errors

1 CREATE WEBSITE FOLDERS | 2 CREATE TEMPLATE | 3 ENTER HTML5 SEMANTIC ELEMENTS
4 ADD COMMENTS & CONTENT | **5 VALIDATE DOCUMENT** | **6 CREATE & VIEW HOME PAGE**

If the webpage template was created successfully, you should not receive any errors, but you can review what the validator provides when a document with errors is uploaded to the validator. *Why? When errors are detected on a webpage, the validator provides information about the location of the error so you can identify and correct them.* The following steps insert an error in the fitness document and then validate the document with the W3C validator.

1

- Return to the fitness document in your text editor and delete html on Line 1 to remove "html" from the DOCTYPE declaration.

- Save your changes and then return to the W3C Markup Validation Service page in your browser to display the W3C validator.

- If necessary, tap or click the Validate by File Upload tab to display the Validate by File Upload information.

- Tap or click the Browse button to display the Choose File to Upload dialog box.

- Navigate to the template folder in the fitness folder, select the fitness.html file, and then tap or click the Open button to upload the file.

- Scroll down to display the Revalidate button (Figure 2–26).

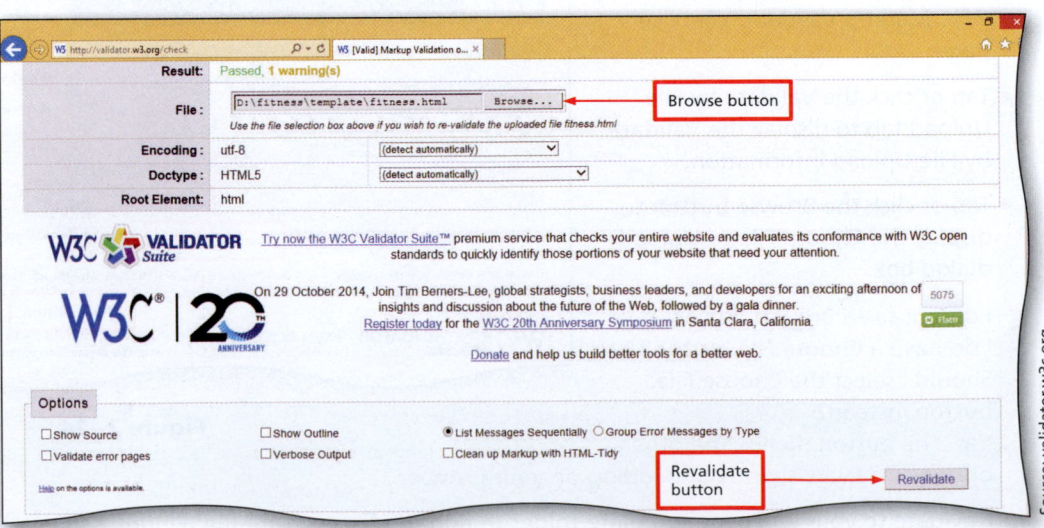

Figure 2–26

2

- Tap or click the Revalidate button to send the revised document through the validator and display the validation results (Figure 2–27).

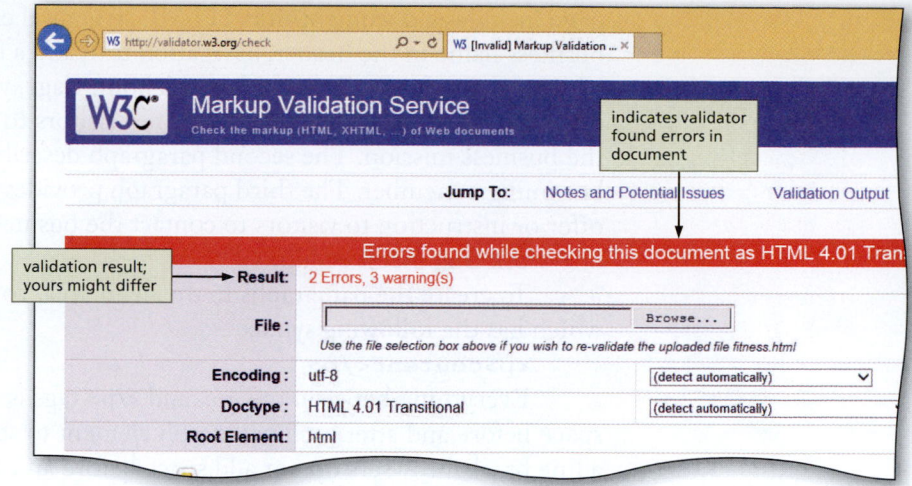

Figure 2–27

3

- Scroll down to display the Validation Output Errors.

- Review the errors and note the line numbers of the errors in the document (Figure 2–28).

4

- Return to your text editor and type **html** after the <!DOCTYPE declaration on Line 1 to correct the error.

- Save your changes and validate the document again to confirm it does not contain any errors.

Figure 2–28

Creating a Home Page Using a Webpage Template

After creating a template for a website, you can save time by using the template to create the webpages in the site. The advantage of starting with a template is that it includes content and HTML elements that appear on every page. By opening the template and then saving it with a new name that corresponds to a page on the site, you save time, ensure consistency across the website, and avoid having to re-create repeating elements such as navigation bars. In the new webpage document, you can focus on developing the parts that are unique to that page.

Now that you have created a template for the Forward Fitness Club website, use it to create the website home page. Recall from Chapter 1 that the home page of a website is usually named index.html. Website home pages use this name for a practical reason. If someone uses a browser to enter a URL that includes the site's domain but does not end with a file name, the browser looks for and displays the index.html page automatically.

When you create the Forward Fitness Club home page from a template, the page includes a document title, HTML structural elements to organize the page, the business name in the header, navigation text, and a copyright notice and business email address in the footer. To complete the home page, you add three paragraphs to the main area. The first paragraph welcomes visitors to Forward Fitness Club and restates the business mission. The second paragraph describes the facility and the benefits of becoming a member. The third paragraph provides a strong call to action, which is an offer or instruction to visitors to contact the business to take advantage of a free one-week trial membership.

To create the paragraphs in the main area, you use the paragraph (<p>) element, which has the following syntax:

```
<p>content</p>
```

Everything between the <p> and </p> tags is a single paragraph. Browsers add space before and after each paragraph element to separate paragraphs. In contrast, for a line break, browsers do not add space before and after the <br> tag.

To Create a Home Page Using a Webpage Template and Add Content

1 CREATE WEBSITE FOLDERS | 2 CREATE TEMPLATE | 3 ENTER HTML5 SEMANTIC ELEMENTS
4 ADD COMMENTS & CONTENT | 5 VALIDATE DOCUMENT | **6 CREATE & VIEW HOME PAGE**

Create the Forward Fitness Club home page by opening the webpage template and then saving the page with a new name in the root fitness folder. *Why? Using a template saves time in coding because the basic wireframe for the page is already established in the template. As a document for one of the main pages of the site, the home page belongs in the root folder.* You use the fitness template to create all the webpages for the website. The following steps create the home page for the fitness website using the webpage template.

1

- Tap or click File on the menu bar and then tap or click Save As to display the Save As dialog box.

- Tap or click the Up One Level button to display the contents of the fitness folder.

- In the File name text box, type **index** to name the file.

- Tap or click the Save button to save the index file in the fitness folder.

- Place your insertion point after the beginning <main> tag and press the ENTER key twice to insert two new lines, in this case, Lines 26 and 27.

- On Line 27, press the TAB key and then type **<p>Welcome to Forward Fitness Club. Our mission is to help our clients meet their fitness and nutrition goals.</p>** to add paragraph tags and content to the page (Figure 2–29).

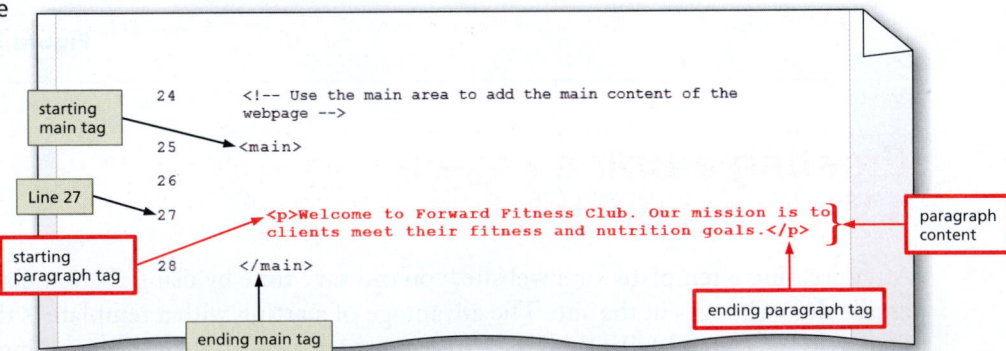

```
24    <!-- Use the main area to add the main content of the
      webpage -->
25    <main>
26
27    <p>Welcome to Forward Fitness Club. Our mission is to
      clients meet their fitness and nutrition goals.</p>
28    </main>
```

starting main tag

Line 27

starting paragraph tag

ending main tag

paragraph content

ending paragraph tag

Figure 2–29

2

- Press the ENTER key two times to insert two new lines and then type `<p>If you have struggled with getting healthy and need the motivation and resources to make a healthy lifestyle change, contact us today. Our facility includes state-of-the-art equipment, convenient group training classes, and nutrition tips and information to keep you healthy.</p>` on Line 29 to add a second paragraph to the page.

- Press the ENTER key two times to insert two new lines and then type `<p>We provide a FREE one-week membership so you can experience the benefits of our equipment and facility. This one-week trial gives you complete access to our equipment, training classes, and nutrition planning. Contact us today to start your free trial!</p>` on Line 31 to add a third paragraph to the page (Figure 2–30).

```
24        <!-- Use the main area to add the main content of the
          webpage -->

25        <main>

26

27          <p>Welcome to Forward Fitness Club. Our mission is to
            clients meet their fitness and nutrition goals.</p>

28

29          <p>If you have struggled with getting healthy and
            need the motivation and resources to make a healthy
            lifestyle change, contact us today. Our facility
            includes state-of-the-art equipment, convenient group
            training classes, and nutrition tips and information
            to keep you healthy.</p>

30

31          <p>We provide a FREE, one-week membership to
            experience the benefits of our equipment and
            facility. This one-week trial gives you complete
            access to our equipment, training classes, and
            nutrition planning. Contact us today to start your
            free trial!</p>

32        </main>
```

Line 29 — starting paragraph tags — Line 31 — content for second paragraph — ending paragraph tag — content for third paragraph — ending paragraph tag — ending main tag

Figure 2–30

3

- Press the ENTER key to insert a new blank line above the ending `</main>` tag.

- Check the spelling of your document and save your changes.

To Display a Home Page in the Default Browser

1 CREATE WEBSITE FOLDERS | 2 CREATE TEMPLATE | 3 ENTER HTML5 SEMANTIC ELEMENTS
4 ADD COMMENTS & CONTENT | 5 VALIDATE DOCUMENT | 6 CREATE & VIEW HOME PAGE

After creating the home page or any other page of the website and adding content to it, display it in a browser to view the completed page. *Why? You should view every page you create in a browser.* Besides using a command in an HTML editor, such as the Launch in IE command on the Run menu in Notepad++, you can open an HTML file from a file viewer such as File Explorer or Finder. When you double-tap or double-click an HTML file, it opens in the default browser on your computer. If you want to open the file in a different browser, you can press and hold or right-click the HTML file, tap or click Open with, and then tap or click an alternate browser. The following steps display the Forward Fitness Club home page in the default browser.

1

- Run File Explorer and navigate to the fitness folder to display the index .html page.

- Double-tap or double-click the index.html file to display the page in the default browser on your computer (Figure 2–31).

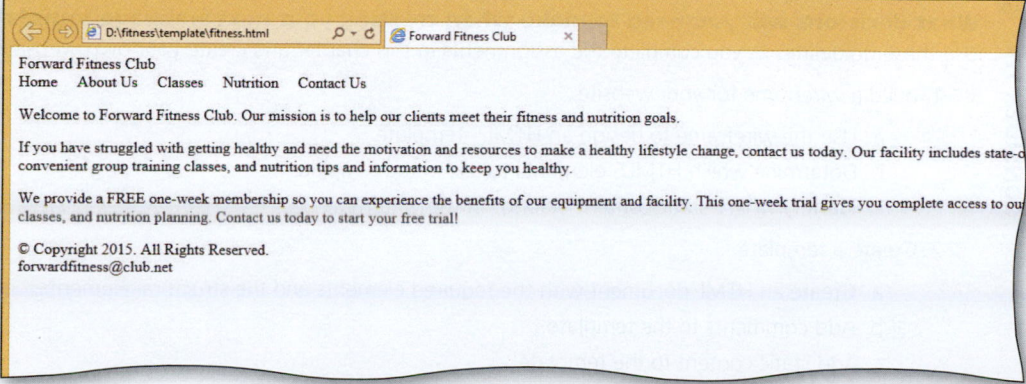

Figure 2–31

BTW
Default Browsers
You can make any browser your default browser by adjusting your browser settings. For example, in Google Chrome, tap or click the Customize button and then tap or click Settings. Tap or click Make Google Chrome the default browser.

Q&A This page lacks color and looks rather boring. Can I format this page?
Yes, you format the page in Chapter 4, when you learn about CSS.

I clicked the link names in the navigation area, but they do not work. Why not?
The link names are not currently linked to other webpages with a hyperlink. You explore links in Chapter 3.

- If spelling errors appear in the page, run the spelling checker or edit the text in your HTML text editor and then save your changes.
- Refresh the browser by tapping or clicking the Refresh button on the address bar.
- Close the browser.
- Exit the HTML text editor.

Other Ways

1 Press and hold or right-click file, tap or click Open with, tap or click browser

Chapter Summary

In this chapter, you learned how to prepare a website by organizing folders for the webpage files, using HTML5 structural elements to create a webpage template, validating the template, and then creating the home page. The items listed below include all the new concepts and skills you have learned in this chapter, with the tasks grouped by activity.

Designing a Website
Examine the Site Map (HTML 53)
Review the Wireframe (HTML 53)
Create a Website Folder and Subfolders (HTML 55)

Using HTML5 Semantic Elements
Use the Header Element (HTML 57)
Include the Nav Element (HTML 57)
Use the Main Element (HTML 57)
Insert the Footer Element (HTML 57)

Creating a Webpage Template
Create a Webpage Template Document (HTML 59)
Add HTML5 Semantic Elements to a Webpage Template (HTML 60)
Add Comments to a Webpage Template (HTML 62)

Using Symbol Entities
Add Text and Nonbreaking Spaces to the Nav Section (HTML 65)
Add Content and a Symbol to the Footer Section (HTML 66)

Validating HTML Documents
Validate the Webpage Template (HTML 67)
Validate an HTML Document with Errors (HTML 68)

Creating a Home Page
Create a Home Page Using a Webpage Template and Add Content (HTML 70)
Display a Home Page in the Default Browser (HTML 71)

CONSIDER THIS

What decisions will you need to make when creating your next webpage template?
Use these guidelines as you complete the assignments in this chapter and create your own websites outside of this class.

1. Build a wireframe for your website.

    a. Use the wireframe to design an HTML5 template.

    b. Determine which HTML5 elements to use in the template.

    c. Identify where static content belongs in the wireframe.

2. Create a template.

    a. Create an HTML document with the required elements and the structural elements.

    b. Add comments to the template.

    c. Add static content to the template.

    d. Validate your template and correct any errors.

3. Use the template to create the home page for your website.

    a. Add content to the main area and other areas that do not contain static content.

    b. Validate the home page to confirm that it does not contain any errors.

    c. View the home page in more than one browser.

    d. Identify any changes you need to make.

4. Depending on the structure of your website, determine whether you need to create additional templates to accommodate multiple wireframes.

How should you submit solutions to questions in the assignments identified with a ✳ symbol? Every assignment in this book contains one or more questions identified with a ✳ symbol. These questions require you to think beyond the assigned presentation. Present your solutions to the questions in the format required by your instructor. Possible formats may include one or more of these options: create a document that contains the answer; present your answer to the class; discuss your answer in a group; record the answer as audio or video using a webcam, smartphone, or portable media player; or post answers on a blog, wiki, or website.

Apply Your Knowledge

Reinforce the skills and apply the concepts you learned in this chapter.

Creating a Template with a Semantic Wireframe

Instructions: The page shown in Figure 2–31 contains the required HTML5 tags for all webpages as well as HTML5 structural tags for a basic, semantic wireframe. As you add content to your webpages, you should understand what each area of the wireframe represents and what type of content each section contains. In this exercise, you will use your HTML editor to enter the required HTML tags and semantic HTML5 structural tags to create a webpage template with a standard webpage wireframe. You will also use HTML comments to document where each section of the wireframe will appear on the webpage, as well as the type of content that is added to each section.

Perform the following tasks:

1. Open your HTML editor and enter the required HTML tags as shown in Lines 1–8 and Lines 25–26 in Figure 2–32. (Do not enter the comments.) Be sure to add indents as shown to make your code easy to read.

```
1   <!DOCTYPE html>
2   <html lang="en">
3   <head>
4       <title><!--Where does this content appear?
5                   What is typically contained in this section?--></title>
6       <meta charset="utf-8">
7   </head>
8   <body>
9       <header>
10          <!-- Where does this section appear on the web page?
11              What is typically contained in this section? -->
12      </header>
13      <nav>
14          <!-- Where does this section appear on the web page?
15              What is typically contained in this section? -->
16      </nav>
17      <main>
18          <!-- Where does this section appear on the web page?
19              What is typically contained in this section? -->
20      </main>
21      <footer>
22          <!-- Where does this section appear on the web page?
23              What is typically contained in this section? -->
24      </footer>
25  </body>
26  </html>
27
```

Source: Notepad++

Figure 2–32

Continued >

Apply Your Knowledge *continued*

2. Save the file as a Hyper Text Markup Language file with the name `template02.html`.

3. Using your favorite search engine, research the `title` element to answer the questions posed as a comment between the <title>…</title> tags shown in Figure 2–32.

4. Replace the comment between the <title>…</title> tags in the template02.html file with the answer to those two questions. Enter the answer as an HTML comment. A sample answer for the <title>…</title> tags is shown in Figure 2–33. Use or modify that answer for your page.

```
1   <!DOCTYPE html>
2   <html lang="en">
3   <head>
4       <title><!--Shown in the webpage tab.
5               Contains keywords for SEO, search engine optimization.--></title>
6       <meta charset="utf-8">
7   </head>
8   <body>
9       <header>
10          <!-- Shown at the top of the page.
11              Contains introductory content typically found on each page.
12              The company logo, name, and tagline often go here. -->
13      </header>
14      <nav>
15          <!-- Shown at the top of each page, right after the header.
```

Source: Notepad++

Figure 2–33

5. Open the `apply02.docx` Word document from the Data Files for Students, copy the address of the webpage you used to research the `title` element, and then paste it into the table. (A sample answer is already provided for the `title` element in the apply02 document as a guide. Replace it with the address you used.)

6. Repeat Steps 3, 4, and 5 to research the `header, nav, main,` and `footer` elements, the elements used to define the semantic wireframe.

   a. In the template02.html document, replace the questions posed as comments for the `header, nav, main,` and `footer` elements with answers to the questions. Be sure that your answers are also coded as comments.

   b. In the apply02.docx document, save the website address links used to answer each question.

7. In the template02.html document, review and check the spelling of your comments. Note that two questions are posed for each set of tags, so make sure that you have answered both questions. Also make sure that all of your answers are coded as HTML comments.

8. Validate the template02.html document using the W3C validator at validator.w3.org and fix any errors the validator identifies. Validation is complete when the validator returns the message "This document was successfully checked as HTML5!" in a green bar near the top of the webpage.

9. Submit the template02.html file in a format specified by your instructor.

10. ✳ In Steps 3, 4, 5, and 6, you researched the required `title` element as well as the semantic wireframe `header, nav, main,` and `footer` elements. Using your favorite search engine, research these questions that further explore the new semantic HTML5 elements:

   a. What is the definition of "semantic html?"

   b. What are the benefits of "semantic html?"

   c. What are the new, HTML5 semantic elements?

   d. What is the primary advantage and the primary disadvantage of using the <main> element vs. <div id="main">?

Extend Your Knowledge

Extend the skills you learned in this chapter and experiment with new skills. You may need to use additional resources to complete the assignment.

Converting an Old Template to a Semantic Wireframe

Instructions: Open your HTML editor and create the webpage with the wireframe and content shown in Figure 2–34. The starting data file contains many `div` tags that you will replace with more meaningful, semantic HTML5 elements.

Perform the following tasks:

1. Open the `ski02.html` file from the Data Files for Students and then modify the HTML code to update it to semantic HTML5 as shown in Figure 2–34. Be sure to make the following updates:

   a. Change the DOCTYPE statement. The HTML5 DOCTYPE statement is different and greatly simplified from any version of the HTML4 DOCTYPE statement.

   b. Replace the <div id="*name*">…</div> tags with their semantic HTML5 counterparts.

   c. Add all of the content including two headings in the <header>…</header> section and the <p>…</p> paragraph content in the <nav>, <main>, and <footer> sections. The company name in the <header> section should be marked up with <h1> tags. The tagline "Let it snow, let it snow, let it snow" should be marked up with <h2> tags.

   d. To mark up and duplicate the line spacing in the <main> section, insert a beginning paragraph tag before the "Ski Instructor:" text and insert an ending paragraph tag after the zip code. insert line break tags after the instructor's name and the street address. Mark up the phone and email lines each as their own paragraph. Enter a line break tag after the phone number.

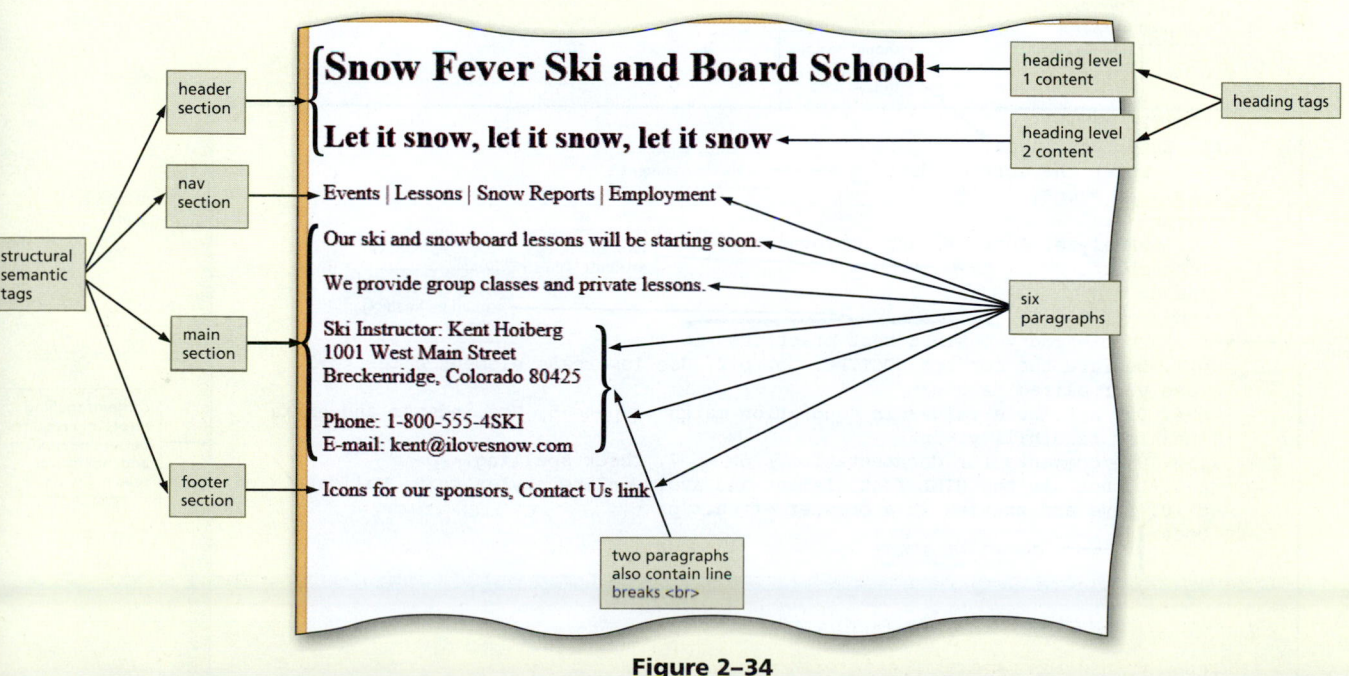

Figure 2–34

Continued >

Extend Your Knowledge *continued*

2. Save and review your work. Check the spelling of the content on the webpage.

3. Validate your webpage using the W3C validator at validator.w3.org and fix any errors that it identifies. Validation is complete when the validator returns the message "This document was successfully checked as HTML5!" in a green bar near the top of the webpage.

4. Submit the ski02.html file in a format specified by your instructor.

5. ✳ After reflecting on this exercise and using outside resources if needed, answer the following questions that further explore the appropriate use of the `div` element.

   a. What does the `div` element represent?

   b. What is the `div` element used for?

   c. Why do HTML5 webpages use fewer `div` tags than HTML4 pages?

   d. Why is the `div` element still used in HTML5?

   e. Why is the `id` attribute almost always used with the `div` element?

Analyze, Correct, Improve

Analyze a webpage, correct all errors, and improve it.

Correcting HTML Errors

Note to instructors and students: From this point forward, the exercises at the end of the chapter use <div id="main"> to identify the main content in the wireframe instead of <main> tag. Using <div id="main"> accommodates browsers that may not yet support the semantic <main> tag.

Instructions: Open your HTML editor and then open the analyze02.html file from the Data Files for Students. Ten HTML5 best practices are listed in the body section of this webpage, but the page contains many errors identified with callouts in Figure 2–35. You will use the W3C validator at validator.w3.org to find and correct the HTML errors on the webpage as instructed.

Figure 2–35

1. Correct

a. Open the `analyze02.html` file in your HTML editor.

b. Open a browser and go to the W3C validator at http://validator.w3.org.

c. Using either the Validate by File Upload or Validate by Direct Input method, validate the analyze02.html file. (*Hint*: To use the Validate by Direct Input method, tap or click that tab and then copy and paste the code from analyze02.html directly into the 'Validate by direct input' box.)

The validator returns a message that it found several errors and warnings.

d. Scroll down the validation webpage to the "Validation Output" section. The first two errors refer to Line 1, the DOCTYPE statement. Correct the DOCTYPE statement in your analyze02.html file. It should include a leading exclamation point character, as in `<!DOCTYPE html>`.

e. Save and revalidate the updated page. The validator returns a message that it found several errors and warnings. Fixing the DOCTYPE error allowed the validator to successfully read other parts of the webpage where it found more errors.

f. Scroll down the validation webpage to the "Validation Output" section. The first error identified refers to Line 2, the comment. Correct the comment statement in your analyze02 .html file. Both the opening and closing tags should include two dashes instead of one, as follows:

```
<!-- Enter your name

Enter the current date -->
```

g. Save and revalidate analyze02.html. Scroll down the validation webpage to the "Validation Output" section. The first error identified refers to Line 7, the `meta` tag. Notice that the attribute value is not properly surrounded with quotation marks on each side. Correct the attribute and value to `charset="utf-8"`

h. Save and revalidate analyze02.html. Scroll down the validation webpage to the "Validation Output" section and then read each of these errors. You will fix each of these errors in this pass.

- Delete the `<font color="red">` and `</font>` tags. The <font> tag has been deprecated (removed) from the HTML5 standard. You will style your content with Cascading Style Sheets (CSS) in upcoming chapters.

- On Lines 16 and 17, change the `<body>` and `<html>` tags into closing `</body>` and `</html>` tags.

i. Save and revalidate analyze02.html. Your validation process is complete when you see the green message "This document was successfully checked as HTML5!"

2. Improve

a. Although the webpage has been successfully validated, the HTML validator only checks for HTML issues: correct elements, attributes, and syntax. The validator does not check for readability such as white space and indents, whether tags are semantically correct, or the whether the content is spelled correctly. You will work on readability first. To make the webpage more readable in the HTML editor, press the ENTER key after every closing </p> tag to move each numbered item to its own line.

b. Indent every line within the <head>…</head> and <body>…</body> sections to make them easier to read.

Continued >

Analyze, Correct, Improve *continued*

    c. Change the <p>...</p> tags that surround the HTML5 best practices title to <h1>...</h1> tags. The <h1> (heading level 1) tag is more meaningful (semantic) for this content than the <p> (paragraph) tag.

    d. Find and correct the two spelling errors. (*Hint*: The word *lowercase* and *inline* are spelled correctly in this context.)

    e. Replace the placeholder text in the comment with your own name and the current date.

3. Submit the analyze02.html file in a format specified by your instructor.

4. ✹ After reflecting on this exercise and using outside resources if needed, answer these questions.

    a. Identify three types of errors the W3C validator helps you find and correct.

    b. Identify three types of errors that the W3C validator will *not* help you find and correct.

    c. Identify three reasons it is a good practice to validate all webpages.

In the Lab

Labs 1 and 2, which increase in difficulty, require you to create webpages based on what you learned in the chapter; Lab 3 requires you to dive deeper into a topic covered in the chapter.

Lab 1: Creating a Home Page for City Farmer

Problem: You work for a local but rapidly growing gardening supply company called City Farmer that specializes in products that support food self-sufficiency. The company has identified a small number of extremely successful products that they want to market through a website and have hired you to get started. Create the webpage shown in Figure 2–36 that contains the textual content that City Farmer wants on their home page.

Instructions: Perform the following tasks:

    1. If you created the cityfarmer.html file in the Lab 1 exercise from Chapter 1, open the file and then save it with the name `cityfarmer02.html`. If you did not create the cityfarmer.html file, enter the required HTML tags as shown in Figure 2–36 and save the file with the name `cityfarmer02.html`.

    2. Make sure the <title>...</title> tags contain the text `City Farmer Home Page`.

    3. Delete the existing content in the body section, and add the content in the <header>, <nav>, <div id="main">, and <footer> sections as shown in Figure 2–36a.

    4. Indent the code and content within the `head` and `body` sections to make each section distinct and readable.

    5. Add or modify the comment after the opening <!DOCTYPE html> statement to contain your name and the current date.

    6. Validate your code and fix any errors.

    7. Check the spelling of the text so it matches the code in Figure 2–36a, which shows the file in Notepad++ (the appearance varies if you are using a different HTML editor).

    8. Save and open the page within a browser as shown in Figure 2–36b.

    9. Submit your assignment in the format specified by your instructor.

```
1   <!DOCTYPE html>
2   <!-- Student Name and current date -->
3   <html lang="en">
4   <head>
5       <title>City Farmer Home Page</title>
6       <meta charset="utf-8">
7   </head>
8   <body>
9       <header>
10          <p>City Farmer</p> <!--Company Name-->
11          <p>...today's urban cowboy</p><!--Company tagline-->
12          <!--Add Company Logo here-->
13      </header>
14      <nav>Products  
15          Order  
16          News  
17          Events  
18      </nav>
19      <div id="main">
20          <!-- Main content will include a monthly newsletter
21          with articles, photos, and tips for the urban farmer-->
22      </div> <!--end main-->
23      <footer>
24          <p>&copy; Copyright 2015 <br> feedback@cityfarmer.com</p>
25      </footer>
26
27  </body>
28  </html>
```

b) cityfarmer02.html in browser

City Farmer

...today's urban cowboy

Products Order News Events

© Copyright 2015
feedback@cityfarmer.com

Source: Notepad++

a) cityfarmer02.html in HTML editor

Figure 2–36

10. ✳ What are the benefits of entering the wireframe HTML elements such as `header, nav, <div id="main">`, and `footer` before entering the textual content for the webpage?

Lab 2: Creating a Home Page for Cycle Out Cancer

Problem: You are part of a philanthropic group of motorcyclists who participate in community events and parades to distribute cancer awareness information. Your group is called Cycle Out Cancer and the director has asked you to help create a website for them. Create the webpage shown in Figure 2–37 that better defines the wireframe and content desired on the organization's home page. In later chapters, you'll replace the placeholders with actual text and images.

Instructions: Perform the following tasks:

1. If you created the cycle.html file in the Lab 2 exercise from Chapter 1, open the file and then save it with the name `cycle02.html`. If you did not create the cycle.html file, enter the required HTML tags as show in Figure 2–37a and save the file with the name `cycle02.html`. Be sure to modify the <main> tag as <div id="main">. Be sure to change the closing </main> tag to </div>. Given the </div> tag is not semantic, add the comment <!--end main--> after the closing </div> tag.

2. Make sure the <title>…</title> tags contain the text `Cycle Out Cancer Home Page`.

3. Modify the `body` element by adding the content in the <header>, <nav>, <div id="main">, and <footer> sections in Figure 2–37a, which shows the file in Notepad++ (the appearance varies if you are using a different HTML editor).

4. Indent the code and content within the `head` and `body` elements to make each section distinct and readable.

5. Add or modify the comment after the opening <!DOCTYPE html> statement to contain your name and the current date.

Continued >

In the Lab *continued*

6. Validate your code and fix any errors.

7. Check the spelling of the text so it matches the code shown in Figure 2–37a.

8. Save and open the page within a browser as shown in Figure 2–37b.

9. Submit your assignment in the format specified by your instructor.

```
1   <!DOCTYPE html>
2   <!-- Student Name and current date -->
3   <html lang="en">
4   <head>
5       <title>Cycle Out Cancer Home Page</title>
6       <meta charset="utf-8">
7   </head>
8   <body>
9       <header>
10          <p>Headline: Cycle Out Cancer </p>
11          <p>Sub-headline: We Ride So Others May Live</p>
12          <!--add logo-->
13      </header>
14      <nav>
15          About Us    
16          Events    
17          Cancer FAQs    
18          Contact Us    
19      </nav>
20      <div id="main">
21          <!-- Insert paragraph on how we make a difference to this world. -->
22          <!-- Insert quotes from lives we've touched -->
23          <!-- Insert photos of people, rides, events -->
24      </div> <!--end main-->
25      <footer>
26          <p>Your Name<br>
27          Your School Name<br>
28          Your School Address<br>
29          Your School City, State Zip<br>
30          </p>
31          To-Action: Links ...        ok, Twitter-->
```

a) cycle02.html in HTML editor

b) cycle02.html in browser

Headline: Cycle Out Cancer

Sub-headline: We Ride So Others May Live

About Us   Events   Cancer FAQs   Contact Us

Your Name
Your School Name
Your School Address
Your School City, State Zip

Source: Notepad++

Figure 2–37

10. ✳ It is easy to forget to check the spelling and grammar of your webpage content. But incorrectly spelled words as well as poor grammar can lead to negative impressions. What negative impressions might be created if you forget to check the spelling and grammar of the content on the webpages that you create or maintain?

Lab 3: Expand Your World
File and Folder Best Practices

Problem: Websites consist of many files such as webpages, images, and other files used to complete the website. In this chapter you were introduced to a folder organization that encouraged the use of five folders for a single website to keep the files well organized. In this exercise you'll expand your knowledge of file and folder management best practices.

Instructions:

1. Open the `filefolderbestpractices.docx` document from the Data Files for Students.

2. Using the information in this chapter as well as the web, complete the two tables by answering the questions posed in each. The first table, *File and Folder Organization*, asks questions about the types of files and the file name extensions of the files stored in the folders presented in Figure 2–4. The second table, *File and Folder Naming Conventions*, asks questions about best practices associated with file and folder names.

3. ✳ Identify three potential problems that could occur if you stored all of the files for an entire website in one folder. Identify three potential problems that could occur if you did not follow "best practice" file and folder naming conventions.

✳ Consider This: Your Turn

Apply your creative thinking and problem-solving skills to design and implement a solution.

1. Create the Home Page for Your Personal Portfolio Website

Personal

Part 1: In Chapter 1, you completed the personal portfolio website planning document to help think through the purpose, content, and organization of your personal portfolio website. In this exercise, you'll create the initial html semantic wireframe for your home page and add some content. Start by entering the basic required HTML tags in a new HTML document in your HTML editor. Include a title for the webpage that includes your name, such as Kris Lee Portfolio. Next, enter the four pairs of HTML tags to define the <header>, <nav>, <div id="main">, and <footer> sections according to your wireframe. Add a <!--end main> comment immediately after the closing </div> tag to better identify the end of the main content. Insert content in each section using the planning document you created in Chapter 1 as a guide. Customize the webpage with as much personal information for your own electronic portfolio as possible. Below the DOCTYPE declaration, insert a comment with your first and last names and the current date. Use other comments as placeholders for content that you will add in later chapters. Name the webpage `portfolio02.html`. Submit your assignment in the format specified by your instructor.

Part 2: ✳ Use your favorite search engine to find articles and images for electronic portfolios. What new ideas did you find that you want to incorporate into your own personal electronic portfolio? Include at least three links to sites that you like and your reasons for choosing those sites in your answer.

2. Create the Home Page for a Web Development and Consulting Business

Professional

Part 1: In Chapter 1, you completed the professional web consulting firm website planning document to help think through the purpose, content, and organization of your web consulting firm website. In this exercise, you'll create the initial html semantic wireframe for your home page and add some of the initial content. Start by entering the basic required HTML tags in a new HTML document in your HTML editor. Include an appropriate title for the webpage, such as the name of your business. Next, enter the four pairs of HTML tags to define the <header>, <nav>, <div id="main">, and <footer> sections according to your wireframe. Add a <!--end main> comment immediately after the closing </div> tag to better identify the end of the main content. Insert content in the header and nav sections using the planning document you created in Chapter 1 as a guide. Below the DOCTYPE declaration, insert a comment with your first and last names and the current date. Use other comments as placeholders for content that you will add in later chapters. Name the webpage `webdev02.html`. Submit your assignment in the format specified by your instructor.

Part 2: ✳ Your website will feature testimonials from satisfied customers. Contact a web development consulting firm in your area, introduce yourself as a student at your college, and ask to make an appointment to speak to a web developer in that firm. Once connected, explain that you are a student learning about web development, and ask the web developer if they could share a recent success story with you. Ask them to describe the project, the technologies and software they used to complete the project, and any other "keys to success." Substituting fictitious names, use this information to write an article on this success story to showcase it in your website.

Continued >

Consider This: Your Turn *continued*

3. Create the Home Page for the Dog Hall of Fame

Research and Collaboration

Part 1: In Chapter 1, you completed the dog hall of fame website planning document to craft the purpose, content, and organization of the website. In this exercise, each member of your team will create the initial html semantic wireframe for the home page and add some content. Start by entering the basic required HTML tags in a new HTML document in your HTML editor. Include an appropriate title for the webpage. Next, enter the four pairs of HTML tags to define the <header>, <nav>, <div id="main">, and <footer> sections according to your wireframe. Add a <!--end main> comment immediately after the closing </div> tag to better identify the end of the main content. Insert content in the header and nav sections using the planning document you created in Chapter 1 as a guide. Below the DOCTYPE declaration, insert a comment with your first and last names and the current date. Use other comments as placeholders for content that you will add in later chapters. Name the webpage `dogfame02.html`.

Part 2: ✳ Your team will require content in several areas. Assign one or more content areas to each team member to research. Ask each member to gather or create sample content to use in the website to represent the three different awards of Hero, Working, and Companion dog as described below.

- **Hero dog**: Find articles and pictures of dogs that have heroic stories. Hero dogs are ordinary dogs with extraordinary stories.

- **Working dog**: Find articles and pictures of dogs with astonishing stories in the "working dog" category. Examples include dogs who work to protect people, livestock, and property as well as dogs who hunt or track. Identify the common breeds of working dogs.

- **Companion dog**: Find articles and pictures of dogs that have amazing stories in the area of human companionship. Any dog can be a "companion" dog but examples often include dogs who provide an extraordinary benefit to someone who is suffering from health issues or other hardships.

Collect your research in a document in Word named `dogfame02.docx`. Submit your assignment in the format specified by your instructor.

3 Enhancing a Website with Links and Images

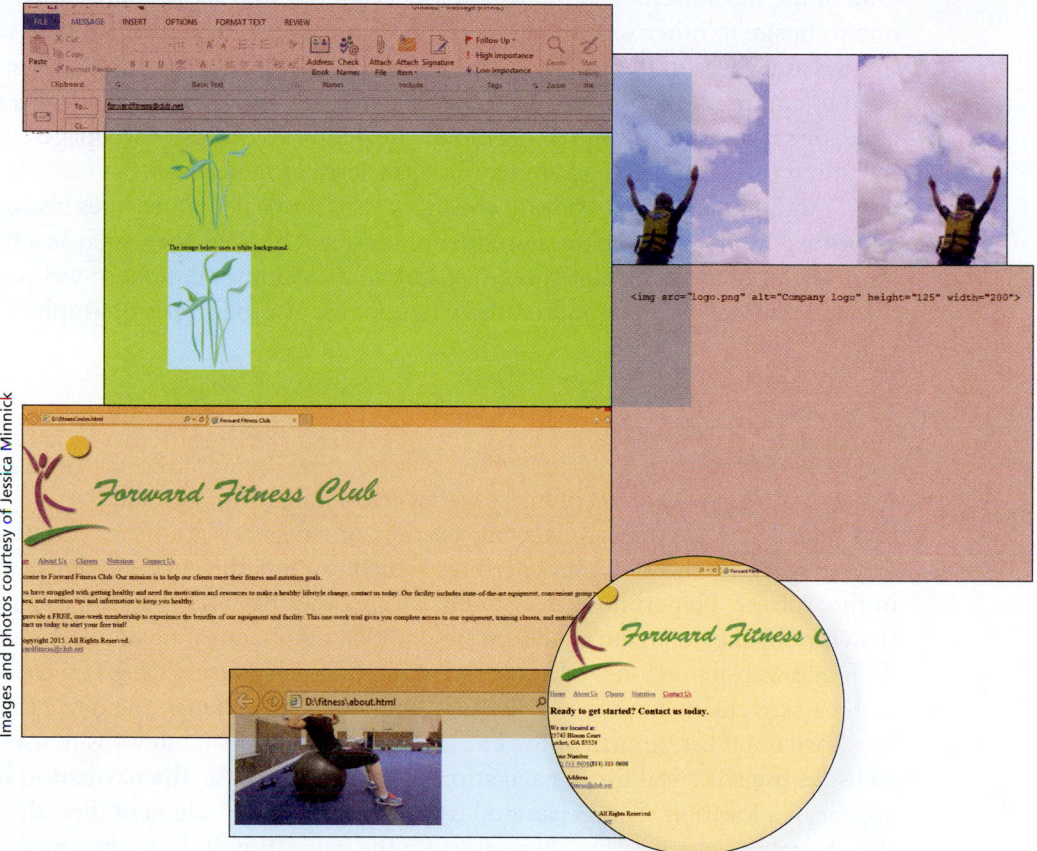

Images and photos courtesy of Jessica Minnick

Objectives

You will have mastered the material in this chapter when you can:

- Describe types of hyperlinks
- Create relative links, absolute links, email links, and telephone links
- Describe image file formats
- Describe the image tag and its attributes
- Add images to a website
- Explain div elements and attributes
- Use a div element to mark a page division

- Define the class attribute
- Describe and use HTML heading tags
- Describe the types of lists in an HTML document
- Create an unordered list and a description list
- Test and validate links on a webpage

3 | Enhancing a Website with Links and Images

Introduction

One of the most useful and important aspects of the web is the ability to connect (link) one webpage to other webpages — on the same server or on different web servers — located anywhere in the world. Using hyperlinks, a website visitor can move from one page to another, view a page on another website, start a new email message, download a file, or make a phone call from a mobile device. Many types of webpage content, including text, graphics, and animations, can serve as hyperlinks.

Adding images to a website enhances visual appeal and provides visitors with additional information about a product or service. Other images, such as a business logo, promote the company's presence and brand. Almost all modern webpages contain images, whether they are photos, drawings, logos, or other types of graphics.

Project — Add Links and Images to a Website

Because a website consists of many webpages of content, visitors need a way to open one webpage while they are viewing another, or navigate the site. As you know, visitors can navigate a website using hyperlinks, which can link the current page to other pages in the website. Hyperlinks can also link to any other page on the web, to a file other than a webpage, to an email address, to a phone number, or to a network server. A well-designed website includes a list of navigation links specifically designed to let visitors easily access the main pages on the site. Some websites arrange the navigation links in a horizontal list, similar to the one the Forward Fitness Club website uses. Other websites use a vertical list of navigation links. In either case, the navigation links should appear in a location visitors can find easily. Using a **nav** element directly below the **header** element and then inserting the navigation links in the **nav** element ensures that the links appear near the header, where visitors can access them easily. To create a link to a webpage, you insert code in an HTML document that references the webpage by its name and location. When a visitor taps or clicks the link, the browser retrieves the webpage identified in the code.

Most websites also use images to enhance the look and feel of their webpages. In fact, one reason the web is so popular is that its images create immediate visual appeal. However, recall that HTML files are simple text files. To display an image on a webpage, you insert code in an HTML document that references the name and location of the image file, similar to the way you create a hyperlink. When a visitor opens the webpage, the browser retrieves the image file identified in the code and displays it on the webpage.

In Chapter 2, you created a website template for the Forward Fitness Club. You then used the template to create the home page for the website. For this project, you edit the template to add hyperlinks to the text in the navigation area and add an image in the header area that displays the club's logo. You use the template to create two pages for the site: the About Us and Contact Us pages. Finally, you add content to the new pages, including headings, images, and links. Figure 3–1a shows the home page of the fitness site; Figure 3–1b shows the About Us page, which contains text and images; and Figure 3–1c shows the Contact Us page with the fitness club's contact information and contact links.

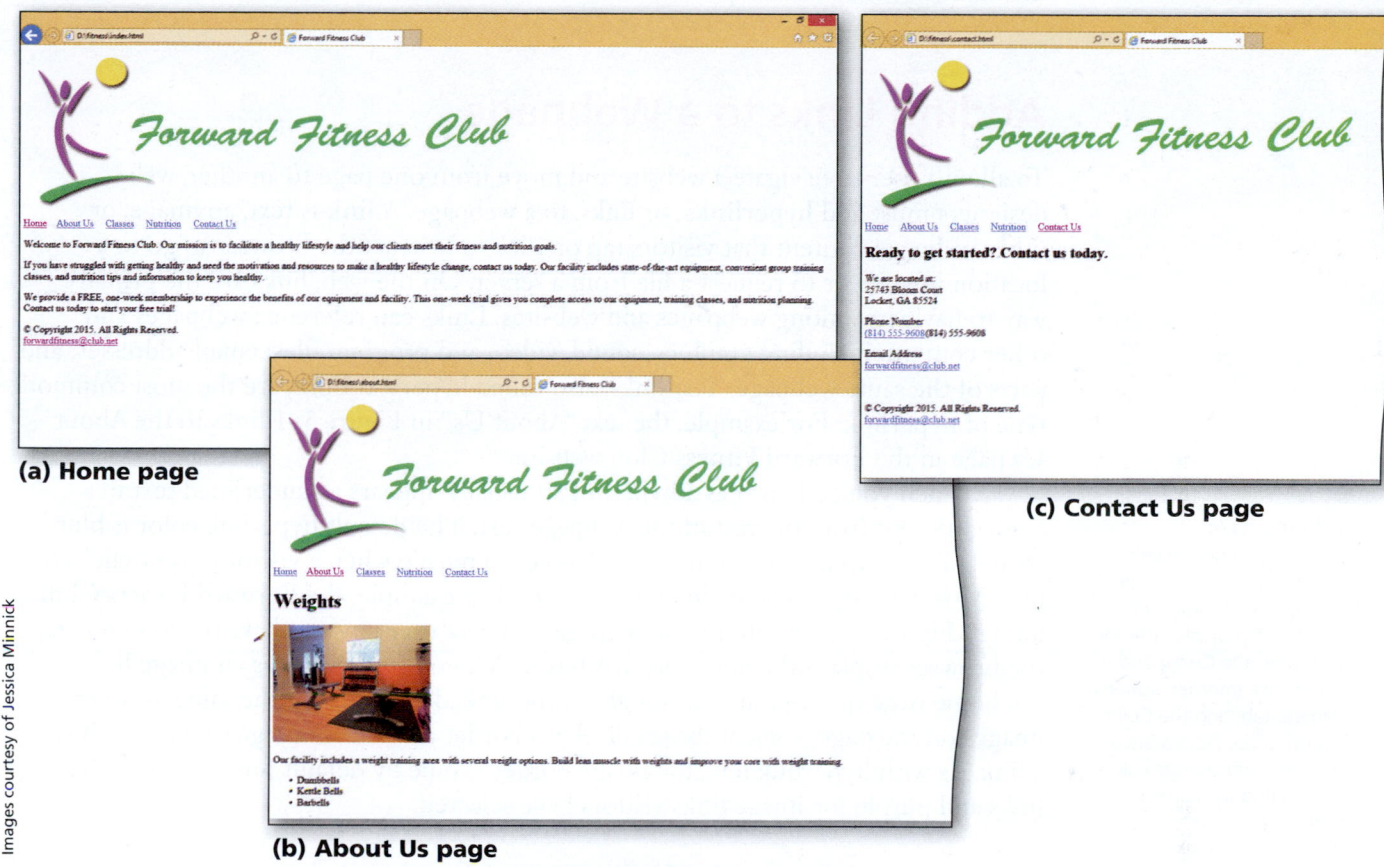

(a) Home page

(b) About Us page

(c) Contact Us page

Figure 3–1

Images courtesy of Jessica Minnick

Roadmap

In this chapter, you will learn how to create the webpages shown in Figure 3-1. The following roadmap identifies general activities you will perform as you progress through this chapter:

1. ADD HYPERLINKS to a template and to webpages.
2. ADD IMAGES to a template and to webpages.
3. ADD DIV ELEMENTS to a template.
4. ADD HEADINGS AND LISTS to webpages.
5. VIEW the WEBSITE IN a BROWSER AND TEST the webpage LINKS.
6. VALIDATE the new PAGES.

At the beginning of step instructions throughout the chapter, you will see an abbreviated form of this roadmap. The abbreviated roadmap uses colors to indicate chapter progress: gray means the chapter is beyond that activity; blue means the task being shown is covered in that activity; and black means that activity is yet to be covered. For example, the following abbreviated roadmap indicates the chapter would be showing a task in the 4 ADD HEADINGS & LISTS activity.

1 ADD HYPERLINKS | 2 ADD IMAGES | 3 ADD DIV ELEMENTS | **4 ADD HEADINGS & LISTS**
5 VIEW WEBSITE IN BROWSER & TEST LINKS | 6 VALIDATE PAGES

Use the abbreviated roadmap as a progress guide while you read or step through the instructions in this chapter.

Adding Links to a Webpage

To allow a user to navigate a website and move from one page to another, web designers must add **hyperlinks**, or links, to a webpage. A **link** is text, an image, or other webpage content that visitors tap or click to instruct the browser to go to a location in a file or to request a file from a server. On the web, links are the primary way to navigate among webpages and websites. Links can reference webpages and other content, including graphics, sound, video, and program files; email addresses; and parts of the same webpage. Text links, also called hypertext links, are the most common type of hyperlink. For example, the text "About Us" in Figure 3–1 links to the About Us page in the Forward Fitness Club website.

When you code text as a hyperlink, it usually appears as underlined text in a color different from the rest of the webpage text. The default hyperlink color is blue. By default, the font color of link text changes to purple when a visitor taps or clicks the link. Most webpages also include image links. For example, the Forward Fitness Club logo in Figure 3–1 links to the home page. When a user taps or clicks the logo image, the browser displays the home page. A business logo often serves as an image link to the home page of a website. Although a hyperlinked image looks the same as other images on the page, some websites display a border around an image to indicate it is a link. As with hyperlink text, the image border is blue by default for unvisited image links and purple for image links visitors have selected.

Anchor Element

You use an **anchor element** to create a hyperlink on a webpage. An anchor element begins with an <a> tag and ends with an </a> tag. Insert the text, image, or other webpage content you want to mark as a hyperlink between the starting and ending anchor tags. Include the **href** attribute (short for "hypertext reference") in the starting anchor tag to identify the webpage, email address, file, telephone number, or other content to access. Recall from Chapter 1 that when you use attributes in HTML code, you insert the attribute name followed by an equal sign and then insert the attribute value between quotation marks, as in *name="value"* where *name* is an attribute name such as href. The value of the **href** attribute is the content to link to, such as a file or a URL. Figure 3–2 shows an example of an anchor **(a)** element with an **href** attribute that links to a home page.

starting anchor tag

text marked as link

```
<a href="index.html">Home</a>
```

href attribute

file name of content to link to

closing anchor tag

Figure 3–2

Relative Links

Hyperlinks that link to other webpages within the same website are known as **relative links**. To create a relative link, use an anchor tag with an **href** attribute that designates the file name of the webpage or the path and the file name of the webpage. Figure 3–2 shows an example of a relative link to the home page named index.html.

Depending on the location of the page or file to be displayed, a relative link may include a file path. Recall that your root fitness folder contains four subfolders: css, images, media, and template. To reference a file in one of the subfolders, you must include the path to the subfolder along with the file name. For example, you would use the following code to create a link to the fitness template:

```
<a href="template/fitness.html">Fitness Template</a>
```

This code means the browser should create a link to the fitness.html file in the template folder using Fitness Template as the link text. To link to the template in this example, you must include the file path because the template file is not stored in the fitness root folder.

Absolute Links

Hyperlinks that link to other webpages outside of your website are known as **absolute links**. To create an absolute link, use an **anchor** element with an **href** attribute that designates a website URL. When assigning the attribute for the absolute link, begin with the http:// text, which references the HTTP protocol and indicates the webpage or other resource is located somewhere on the Internet. Next, include the website domain name such as www.cengage.com to link to that domain's home page. Figure 3–3 shows an example of an absolute link to the home page on the Cengage Learning website. This code means the browser should create a link to www.cengage .com using Cengage as the link text.

BTW

Link Text

When determining the text to use in a link, insert or use text that concisely indicates what appears when visitors tap or click the link. For example, text such as "tap or click here" invites the appropriate action but does not identify what the link is connected to.

Figure 3–3

Image Links

In addition to text, images can also link to another page within the site, another website, an email address, or a telephone number. To configure an image with a link, place the starting anchor tag before the image element and place the ending anchor tag after the image element. Figure 3–4 shows an example of an image with a relative link to the website's home page. This code means the browser should create a link to the index.html file for the website using the image file named image.png as the link object.

BTW

Nesting Elements

To follow proper syntax with nested elements, close each tag in the reverse order as you opened them.

Figure 3–4

Email Links

Hyperlinks that link to an email address are called **email links**. Use `anchor` elements to link to an email address by including the `href` attribute followed by "mailto:" and then the email address. When a user taps or clicks an email link, their default email program runs and opens a new message with the designated email address in the To text box. Figure 3–5 shows an example of an email link. This code means the browser should create an email message addressed to forwardfitness@club.net when someone taps or clicks the "forwardfitness@club.net" link text. Figure 3–6 shows the result of a user tapping or clicking the email link shown in Figure 3–5.

Figure 3–5

Figure 3–6

Telephone Links

Hyperlinks that link to a telephone number are called **telephone links** and work primarily on smartphones. Use an `anchor` element to link to a telephone number by including the `href` attribute, followed by "tel:+1*number*" where +1 is the international dialing prefix (in this case, for the United States) and *number* is the phone number, including the area code. Including the international dialing prefix makes the link accurate in any location. When a user taps or clicks a telephone link from a mobile device, a dialog box is displayed, asking whether the user wants to call the phone number. Figure 3–7 shows an example of a telephone link. This code means the browser should dial the phone number 1-800-555-2356 when someone taps or clicks the "Call us today at 800-555-2356" link text.

BTW

Other Links
You also can create links to other locations on the Internet (that is, non-http) such as FTP sites and newsgroups. To link to an FTP site, type ftp:// URL rather than http:// URL. For a newsgroup, type news:newsgroup name, and for any particular article within the newsgroup, type news:article name as the entry.

starting anchor tag   tel protocol   text marked as telephone link

`<a href="tel:+18005552356">Call us today at 800-555-2356</a>`

href attribute   phone number with country code and area code   ending anchor tag

Figure 3–7

To Add Relative Links in a Website Template

1 ADD HYPERLINKS | 2 ADD IMAGES | 3 ADD DIV ELEMENTS | 4 ADD HEADINGS & LISTS
5 VIEW WEBSITE IN BROWSER & TEST LINKS | 6 VALIDATE PAGES

The **nav** section of the Forward Fitness Club website template and the home page currently contain text, but do not yet contain links to the pages in the website. Start by adding relative links to the navigation area of the website template to link to the home, About Us, Classes, Nutrition, and Contact Us pages. *Why? If you edit the template to include relative links, future pages created from the template will already have these links established.* The following steps add page links to a website template.

1

- Open your text editor to run the program.

- Tap or click File on the menu bar and then tap or click Open to display the Open dialog box.

- Navigate to your fitness folder and then double-tap or double-click the template folder to open it and display the fitness.html template file (Figure 3–8).

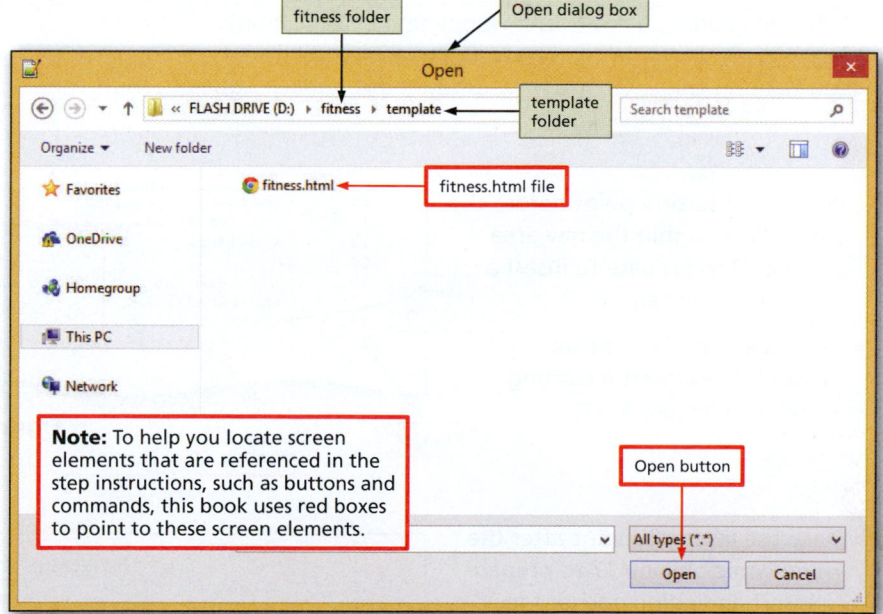

fitness folder   Open dialog box

template folder

fitness.html file

Open button

Note: To help you locate screen elements that are referenced in the step instructions, such as buttons and commands, this book uses red boxes to point to these screen elements.

Figure 3–8

2

- Tap or click the fitness.html file and then tap or click the Open button to open the file in the text editor.

- Place the insertion point before the word *Forward* on Line 12 to prepare to insert a starting anchor tag.

- Type `<a href="index .html">` to insert a starting anchor tag (Figure 3–9).

Figure 3–9

3

- Place the insertion point after the word *Club* on Line 12 to prepare to insert an ending anchor tag.

- Type `</a>` to insert an ending anchor tag (Figure 3–10).

Q&A

Why is the ending tag </a> instead of </a href="index.html">?
An href attribute is defined only within the starting anchor tag. After you define an anchor with an attribute, you close the element with an </a> tag.

Why am I adding a link in the webpage header section?
You will soon replace the text in the header with a company logo, which should link to the home page. On many websites, the company logo links to the home page.

Figure 3–10

4

- Place the insertion point before the word *Home* within the nav area on Line 17 to prepare to insert a starting anchor tag.

- Type `<a href="index .html">` to insert a starting anchor tag (Figure 3–11).

Figure 3–11

5

- Place the insertion point after the word *Home* on Line 17 to prepare to insert an ending anchor tag.

- Type `</a>` to insert an ending anchor tag (Figure 3–12).

Figure 3–12

6

- Place the insertion point before the word *About* on Line 18 to prepare to insert a starting anchor tag.

- Type `<a href="about .html">` to insert a starting anchor tag.

- Place the insertion point after the word *Us* on Line 18 to prepare to insert an ending anchor tag.

- Type `</a>` to insert an ending anchor tag (Figure 3–13).

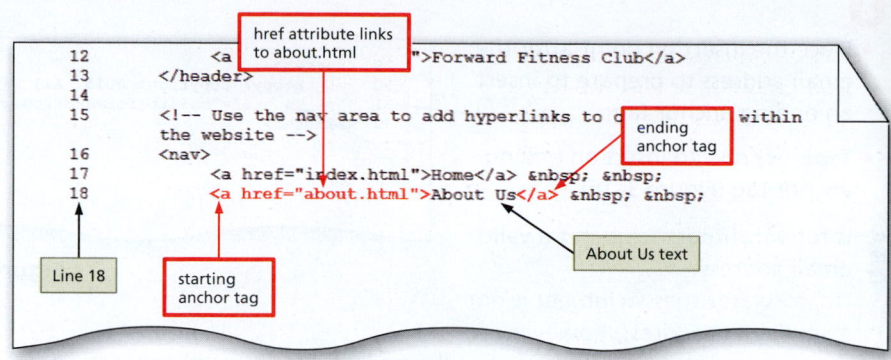

Figure 3–13

Q&A

Why do I need to create a link to about.html when I have not yet created the about.html webpage?

You will use this template to create all future pages for this website. Creating the links now saves time coding for pages you create later.

7

- Using the same method as in Steps 2–5, insert anchor elements as shown in Table 3–1 to add hyperlinks to the remaining pages within the navigation area (Figure 3–14).

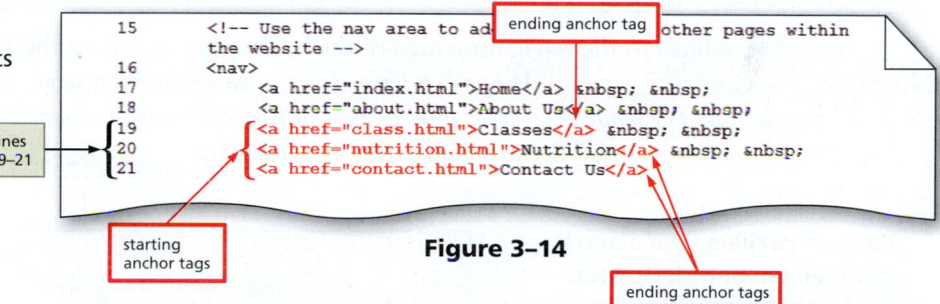

Figure 3–14

Table 3-1 Navigation Anchor Tags

Webpage Link	Anchor Tags
Classes	`<a href="class.html">Classes</a>`
Nutrition	`<a href="nutrition.html">Nutrition</a>`
Contact Us	`<a href="contact.html">Contact Us</a>`

To Add an Email Link in a Website Template

1 ADD HYPERLINKS | 2 ADD IMAGES | 3 ADD DIV ELEMENTS | 4 ADD HEADINGS & LISTS
5 VIEW WEBSITE IN BROWSER & TEST LINKS | 6 VALIDATE PAGES

Next, add an email link to the email address in the footer area of the template. *Why? Visitors can tap or click the link in the footer to quickly send an email message to the Forward Fitness Club.* The following steps insert an email link in a website template.

- Place your insertion point before forwardfitness@club.net on Line 31, located within the footer area, to prepare to insert an email anchor element.

- Type `<a href="mailto: forwardfitness@club.net">` to insert a starting anchor tag (Figure 3–15).

Figure 3–15

- Place the insertion point after the email address to prepare to insert an ending anchor tag.

- Type `</a>` to insert an ending anchor tag (Figure 3–16).

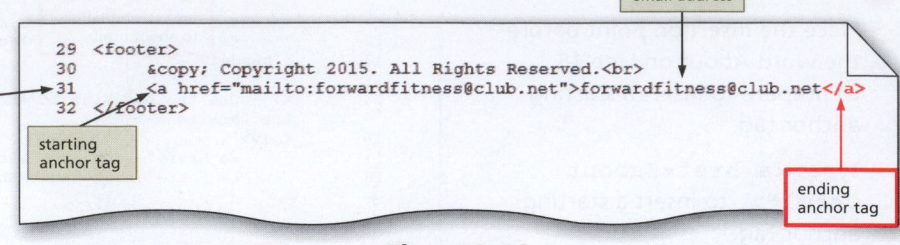

Figure 3–16

Q&A

Is forwardfitness@club.net a valid email address?

No, forwardfitness@club.net is not a valid email address; however, tapping or clicking the email link still runs the default email application on your computer and creates a message addressed to forwardfitness@club.net. If you send a message to this email address, you will receive a delivery failure notice to advise you that the email submission failed.

- Save your changes.

To Add Relative Links in the Home Page

1 ADD HYPERLINKS | 2 ADD IMAGES | 3 ADD DIV ELEMENTS | 4 ADD HEADINGS & LISTS
5 VIEW WEBSITE IN BROWSER & TEST LINKS | 6 VALIDATE PAGES

Add relative links to the navigation area of the home page to link to the home, About Us, Classes, Nutrition, and Contact Us pages. *Why? You have already created the home page, so it cannot benefit from the links you added to the template. The home page needs hyperlinks so visitors can navigate from the home page to other pages within the website.* The following steps add relative links to the home page.

- Tap or click File on the menu bar and then tap or click Open to display the Open dialog box.

- Navigate to your fitness folder to display the index.html file (Figure 3–17).

Figure 3–17

- Tap or click the index.html file and then tap or click the Open button to open the file in the text editor.

- Place the insertion point before the word *Forward* on Line 12 to prepare to insert a starting anchor tag.

- Type `<a href="index .html">` to insert a starting anchor tag (Figure 3–18).

Figure 3–18

3

- Place the insertion point after the word *Club* on Line 12 to prepare to insert an ending anchor tag.
- Type **</a>** to insert an ending anchor tag (Figure 3–19).

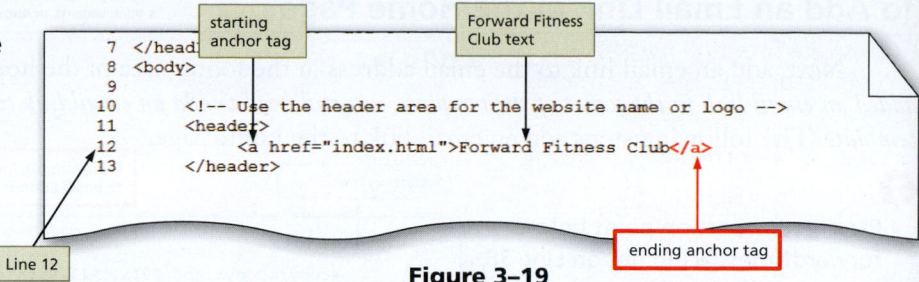

```
 7    </head
 8    <body>
 9
10        <!-- Use the header area for the website name or logo -->
11        <header>
12            <a href="index.html">Forward Fitness Club</a>
13        </header>
```

starting anchor tag

Forward Fitness Club text

ending anchor tag

Line 12

Figure 3–19

4

- Place the insertion point before the word *Home* within the nav area on Line 17 to prepare to insert a starting anchor tag.
- Type **<a href="index .html">** to insert a starting anchor tag (Figure 3–20).

```
           </header>                                .htm    Fitness Club</a>
14
15        <!-- Use the nav area to add hyperlinks to other pages within
              the website -->
16        <nav>
17            <a href="index.html">Home    
```

starting anchor tag

href attribute links to index.html

Home text

Line 17

starting anchor tag

Figure 3–20

5

- Place the insertion point after the word *Home* on Line 17 to prepare to insert an ending anchor tag.
- Type **</a>** to insert an ending anchor tag (Figure 3–21).

```
12            ="index.html">Forward Fitness Club</a>
13        </
14
15        <!-- Use the nav area to add hyperlinks to other pages within
              the website -->
16        <nav>
17            <a href="index.html">Home</a>    
```

starting anchor tag

Home text

Line 17

ending anchor tag

Figure 3–21

6

- Using the same method as in Steps 2–5, insert anchor elements as shown in Table 3–2 to add hyperlinks to the navigation area (Figure 3–22).

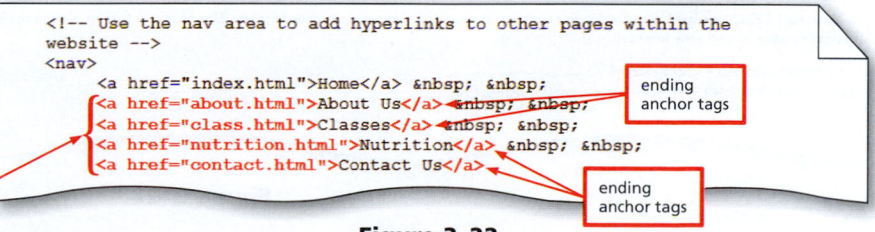

```
<!-- Use the nav area to add hyperlinks to other pages within the
website -->
<nav>
    <a href="index.html">Home</a>    
    <a href="about.html">About Us</a>    
    <a href="class.html">Classes</a>    
    <a href="nutrition.html">Nutrition</a>    
    <a href="contact.html">Contact Us</a>
```

starting anchor tags

ending anchor tags

ending anchor tags

Figure 3–22

Table 3-2 Navigation Anchor Tags

Webpage Link	Anchor Tags
About Us	<a href="about.html">About Us</a>
Classes	<a href="class.html">Classes</a>
Nutrition	<a href="nutrition.html">Nutrition</a>
Contact Us	<a href="contact.html">Contact Us</a>

To Add an Email Link in the Home Page

Next, add an email link to the email address in the footer area of the home page. *Why? Although you added an email link in the footer of the template, you still need to add an email link to the home page to match the website template.* The following steps add an email link to the home page.

1

- Place your insertion point before forwardfitness@club.net on Line 38, located within the footer area, to prepare to insert an email anchor tag.

- Type **<a href="mailto: forwardfitness@club.net">** to insert a starting anchor tag that links to an email address.

Figure 3–23

- Place the insertion point after the email address on Line 38 to prepare to insert an ending anchor tag.

- Type **</a>** to insert an ending anchor tag (Figure 3–23).

2

- Tap or click the Save button on the toolbar to save your changes.

- Open File Explorer (Windows) or Finder (Mac), navigate to the index.html file in the fitness folder, and then double-tap or double-click the file to open it in your default browser (Figure 3–24).

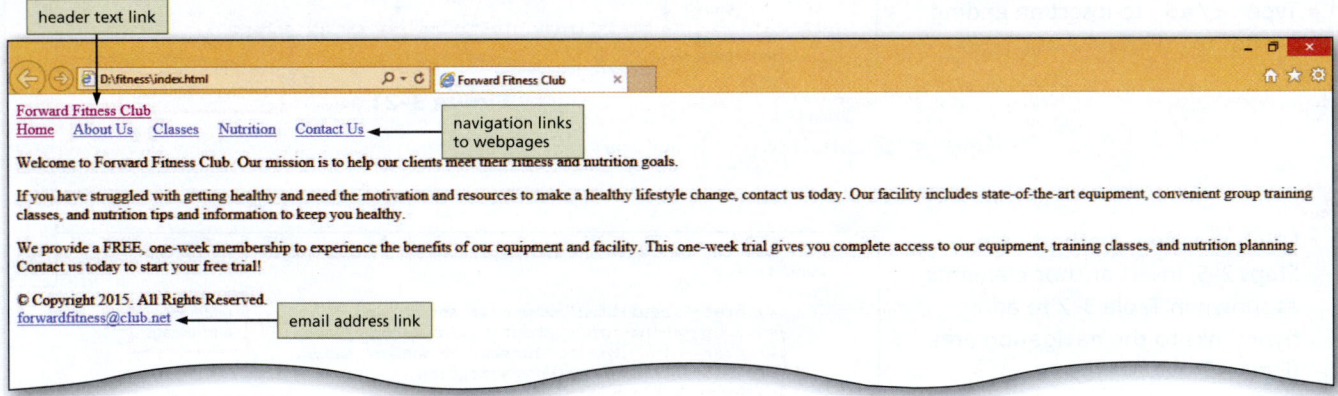

Figure 3–24

Experiment

- Tap or click the Home link and the email link, and then close the window for the new email message and close the browser.

Adding Images to a Website

Images include photos, drawings, diagrams, charts, and other graphics that convey visual information. On a webpage, they help break up text and contribute to the design and aesthetics of a website. However, rather than merely decorate a webpage, images should support the purpose of the page or illustrate content. Images can also provide visual representations of a company's products and services. When determining what images to use within your website, choose those that relate directly to the content. Images that do not support the content can be distracting or confusing. For example, using images on a business website that do not pertain to the business may be perceived as unprofessional or may leave the user wondering what the business is actually selling. Figure 3–25 shows the website for Let's Move, an educational website created by the U.S. government to promote healthy eating. Note the use of the site's logo and photo to demonstrate a healthy lifestyle.

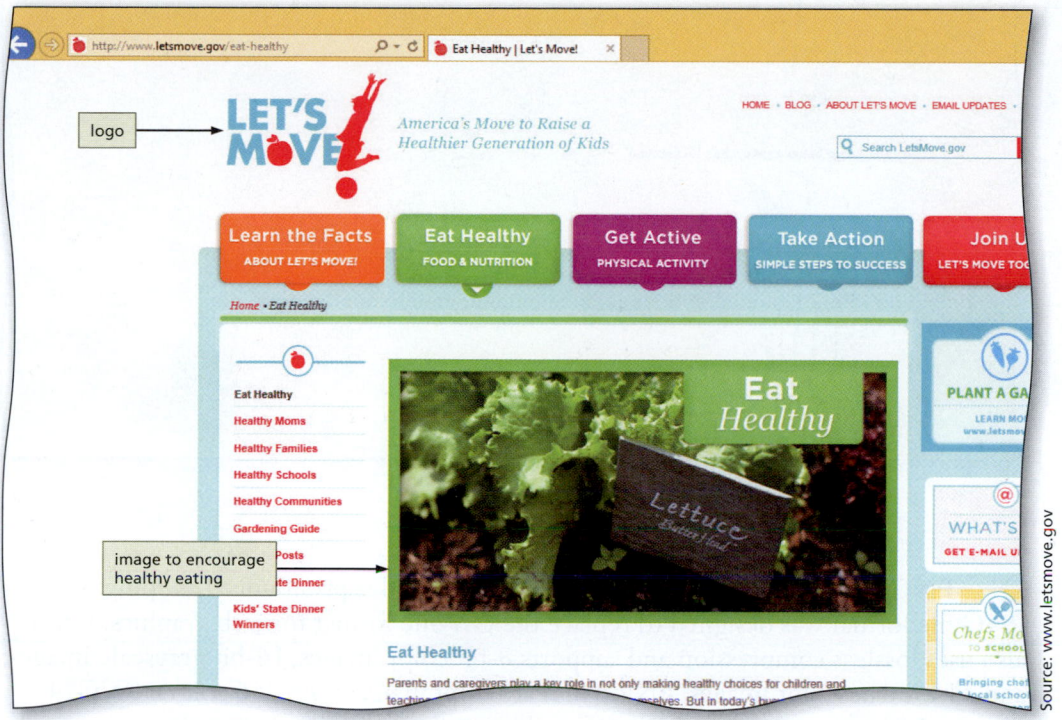

Figure 3–25

Image File Formats

When incorporating images into a website, web designers need to consider the file format, image dimensions, and file size. These factors affect the appearance of an image on a webpage and how long it takes the browser to display the image.

Image files are created in several formats; however, when adding images to a webpage, you must use image files in the GIF, PNG, JPG, or SVG format.

GIF stands for Graphics Interchange Format and is pronounced "jiff." GIF is the oldest web file format and supports transparency and frame animation. To create images that do not display a background color but have a transparent, or clear, background instead, you use a file format that supports transparency, such as GIF. Figure 3–26 shows an example of an image with and without transparency. GIF files can also be images that use frame animation, which is a series of drawings quickly displayed in a sequence to give the illusion of movement. To compress an image, or reduce its file size, the GIF format uses a technique called **lossless compression** that maintains the file's color information. GIF files are 8-bit images that can display up to 256 colors, making the file sizes relatively small. Because of the small color palette in GIF files, they are suitable for icons and line drawings, but not high-quality pictures or photos.

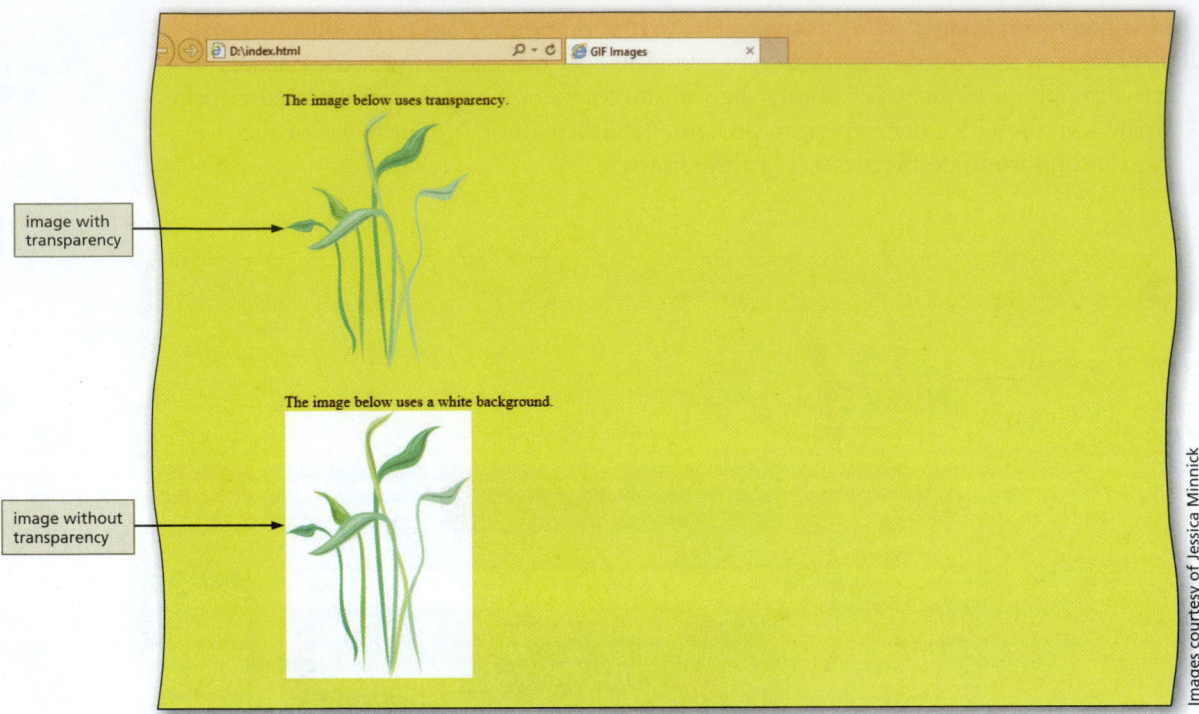

Figure 3–26

Images courtesy of Jessica Minnick

BTW

Animated GIF

To see an example of an animated GIF file, visit en.wikipedia.org/wiki/GIF.

PNG stands for Portable Network Graphics and is pronounced as "ping." The PNG file format was designed to replace the GIF file format for web graphics. PNG also uses lossless compression and supports 8-bit color images, 16-bit grayscale images, and 24-bit true-color images. PNG8 files are 8-bit images with 256 colors. PNG24 files are 24-bit images that can contain millions of colors. This is one advantage to using PNG compared to GIF: PNG24 can support over 16 million colors, whereas GIF supports only 256 colors. PNG also supports transparency, but not animation. In addition, PNG is not ideal for photographic images, as its lossless compression is not as efficient as that of the JPG format. Figure 3–27 shows an example of a website (usa.gov) that contains both GIF and PNG files.

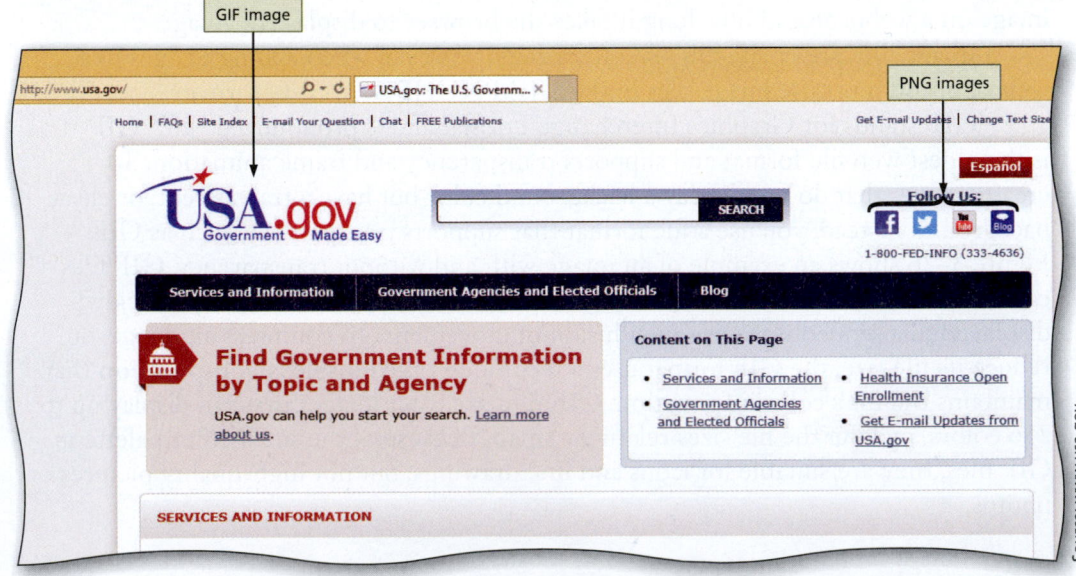

Source: www.usa.gov

Figure 3–27

JPG or **JPEG** stands for Joint Photographic Experts Group and is pronounced "jay-peg." This is the standard file format for a digital photo, such as one taken with a digital camera. The JPG format is a 24-bit image that supports 16.7 million colors, which is why it is used for digital photos and other pictures with a high level of detail or color complexity, such as shadows. JPG uses a **lossy compression** made exclusively for digital photos. To reduce file size, a lossy compression discards some of the color information in the image, which reduces its original quality. If you include a digital photo in your website, use a JPG or JPEG file format. Figure 3–28 shows a page from the National Park Service website that contains several JPG image files.

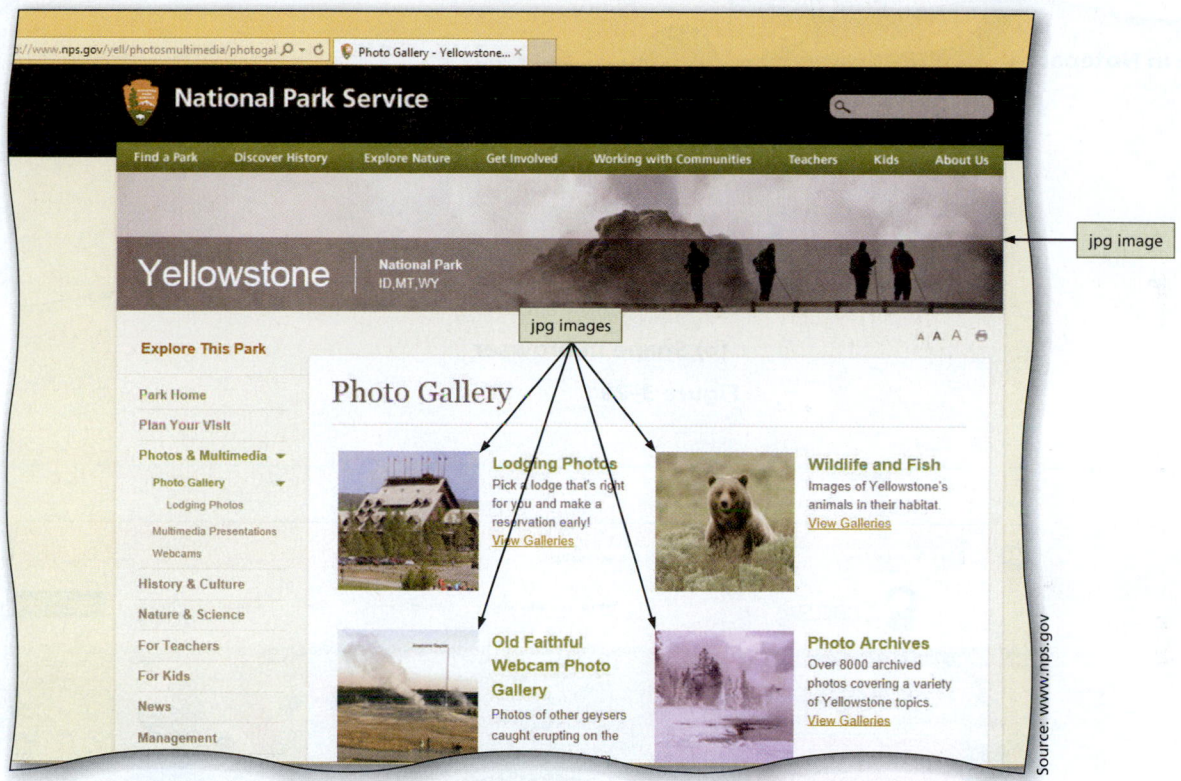

Figure 3–28

Source: www.nps.gov

SVG stands for Scalable Vector Graphics, a format that uses markup language to create two-dimensional graphics, images, and animations. It is a royalty-free graphic format developed by the SVG working group at the W3C. The latest edition of SVG recommended by the W3C is version 1.1, second edition. Use SVG to create shapes such as circles, squares, rectangles, and lines. Only modern browsers can display SVG graphics, though no browser supports all SVG elements, so you must test for browser compatibility, which you can do at caniuse.com/svg. Currently, SVG is not a common image format on the web. Figure 3–29a shows an example of the SVG code required to create the circle shown on the webpage displayed in Figure 3–29b. An example of an SVG animation game is shown in Figure 3–30.

SVG code to create a circle

(a) SVG code in Notepad++

SVG circle

(b) Shape in browser

Figure 3–29

Source: Courtesy of Notepad++

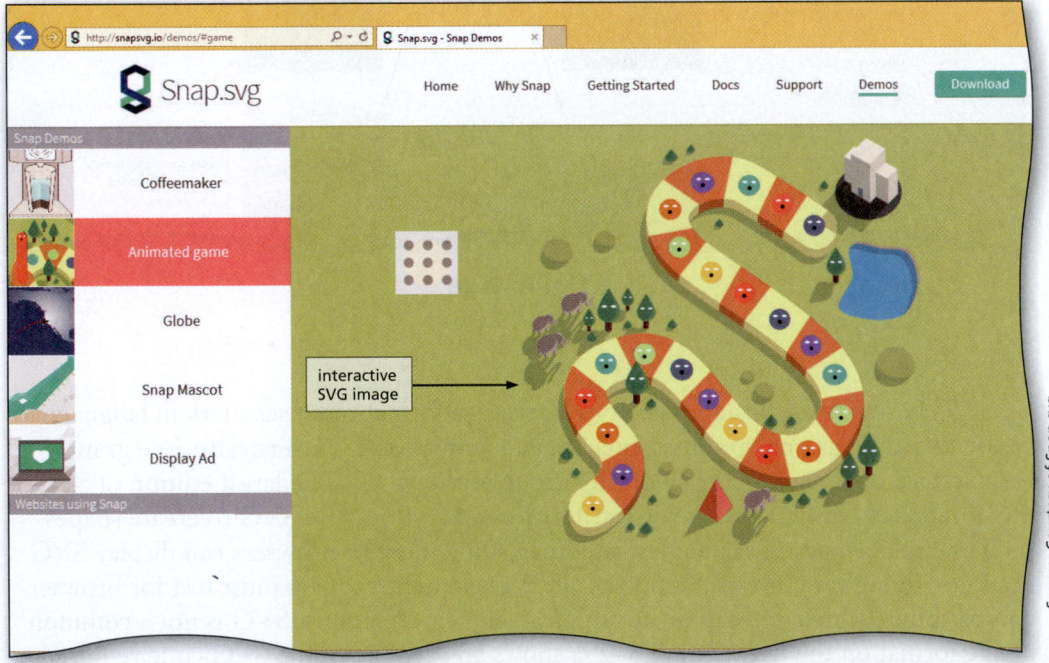

interactive SVG image

Figure 3–30

Source: Courtesy of Snap.svg

Table 3–3 summarizes the pros and cons of each image file format for the web.

Table 3-3 Choosing an Image File Format

Format	Pros	Cons	Use for
GIF	Small file size; supports transparency and animation	Limited to 256 colors	Line drawings; replaced by PNG file format
PNG	Small file size; supports transparency and more than a million colors	Does not support animation	Images that are not digital photos
JPG	Supports more than a million colors	Larger file size	Digital photos
SVG	Flexible; scalable; no files needed because graphics are created with code	Not supported by older browsers and not all modern browsers support it 100 percent	Shapes, lines, text, and gradients

Image Dimensions and File Size

To display content, monitors and other screen devices use pixels. A **pixel**, a term coined from "picture element," is the smallest element of light or color on a device displaying images. Pixels are arranged in rows and columns to compose an image, but are usually so small that you cannot see them, making the image appear smooth and fluid. Webpage images can be measured in pixels. For example, an image may be 200 × 200 pixels, which means it has a height of 200 pixels and a width of 200 pixels.

Monitors and other screen devices have a default resolution, which determines the clarity of the content displayed on the screen. The higher the screen resolution, the sharper text and images appear. A common resolution for today's laptops is 1366 × 768 pixels. The resolution of a device's screen dictates the number of pixels that can appear in an image. The higher the resolution, the greater the number of pixels in the image, resulting in a sharp, clear image.

File size is the number of bytes a file contains, though the size of an image file is usually expressed as kilobytes (KB), thousands of bytes; megabytes (MB), millions of bytes; or gigabytes (GB), billions of bytes. The disadvantage of an image with a high resolution is that it also has a large file size. If a webpage contains an image, the file size of the image can determine how long it takes for the webpage to load in a browser. If a webpage contains several large image files, the page might be slow to load, especially on a mobile device. Today's users expect pages to load as soon as they tap or click a link. The key to reducing page load time is keeping the webpage file small. Though a webpage itself may load quickly, large images on the webpage can take longer to appear.

When you choose a file format for an image, file size is a major factor. For example, JPG files can be large files; a detailed digital photo contains much more data than a simple line drawing in a GIF format. If you are using images with large file sizes, use a photo or graphics editor, such as Adobe Photoshop, to **optimize** the graphic for web use. Optimizing an image reduces its file size and load time. To optimize an image file for web use, you can crop the image, modify its dimensions to make it smaller, adjust the quality, or convert the image file format. When preparing an image file for web use, keep in mind that reducing the file size can also decrease the quality of the image. To retain the original high-quality image, make a copy of the original file and optimize the copy. Figure 3–31 shows the same image at various levels of compression that reduced file size. As the figure shows, too much compression can degrade the quality of the image.

original image

reduced image quality

further reduced image quality

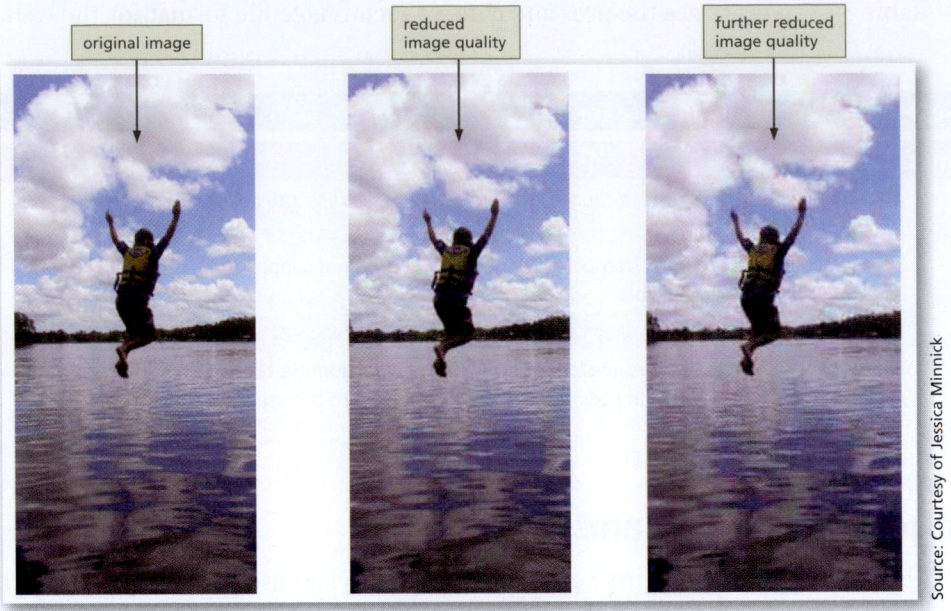

Source: Courtesy of Jessica Minnick

Figure 3–31

In Adobe Photoshop, you use the Save for Web dialog box to adjust the file format, file quality, and size of an image file to optimize the image for web use. The dialog box displays the same image at different quality settings along with the corresponding file size and load time. For example, Figure 3–32 shows the same image as in Figure 3–31, with the file size of 549 K for the original image. Changing the Quality setting to 100 reduces the file size to 142 K and estimates a load time of 7 seconds without a noticeable change in quality. Changing the Quality setting to 10 further reduces the file size to 13.26 K and the load time to 1 second, but also degrades the image quality.

Save for Web dialog box in Adobe Photoshop

file format setting

Quality setting

file size of original file

file size and load time on webpage for image with 100 quality

file size and load time on webpage for image with 10 quality

Adobe product screenshot(s) reprinted with permission from Adobe Systems Incorporated; photo courtesy of Jessica Minnick

Figure 3–32

TO OPTIMIZE AN IMAGE FOR WEB USE WITH ADOBE PHOTOSHOP

Before you use a digital photo on a webpage, you should optimize the photo for web use to reduce its file size. If you want to optimize an image using Photoshop, you would complete the following steps.

1. Open the digital photo in Adobe Photoshop.
2. Tap or click File on the application bar to display the File menu.
3. Tap or click Save for Web to display the Save for Web dialog box.
4. Tap or click the 4-up tab to display the different load times and file sizes of the image.
5. Select the JPEG file format setting, and then adjust the photo quality and the image size.
6. Tap or click the image you want to save, and then tap or click the Save button to save the image file.

Image Tag and Its Attributes

The **image tag**, <img>, is an empty HTML tag used to add an image to a webpage. As an empty tag, the image tag does not have an ending tag. It includes many attributes, such as the required file source attribute, **src**, which identifies the image file being inserted. An example of an image element with a source attribute is <img src="logo .png">. This code tells the browser to display the image file named logo.png. Table 3–4 shows a list of common attributes used with the image element.

Table 3-4 Image Element Attributes	
Attribute	**Function**
src	Identifies the file name of the image to display
alt	Specifies alternate text to display when an image is being loaded
	Especially useful for screen readers, which translate information on a computer screen into audio output
	Should briefly describe the purpose of the image in 50 characters or less
height	Defines the height of the image in pixels, which improves loading time
width	Defines the width of the image in pixels, which improves loading time

You should always use the **alt** attribute in an image tag to specify alternate text in case the image cannot be displayed in a browser. The alternate text briefly describes the image. Screen readers recite alternate text to address accessibility. An example of an image tag with `src` and `alt` attributes is <img src= "logo. png"alt ="Company logo">. This code means the browser should retrieve and display the image file named logo.png and provide "Company logo" as the alternate text. Figure 3–33 shows an example of alternative text displayed in a browser that is unable to display an image.

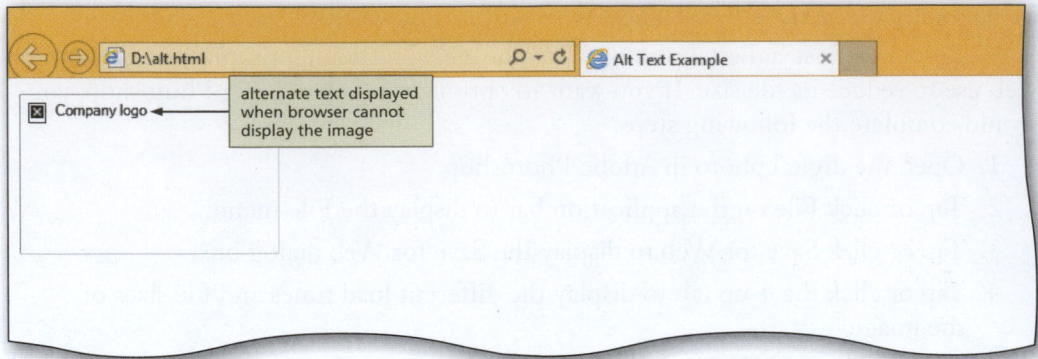

Figure 3–33

When you add an image to a webpage, you can also define the image's height and width. A browser uses these attributes to reserve the amount of space needed for the image. An example of an image tag with attributes is shown in Figure 3–34.

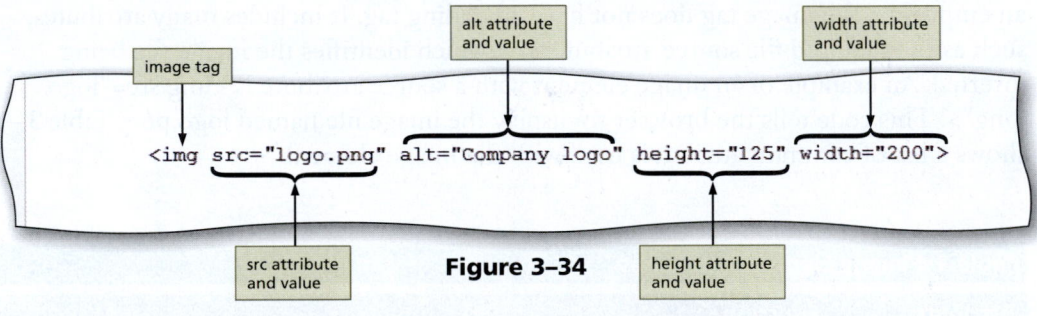

Figure 3–34

A browser interprets the code in Figure 3–34 as follows:

1. First, the browser reads the starting image tag, which indicates the browser should display an image on the webpage.

2. The src="logo.png" attribute and value identify the name of the image to display.

3. The alt="Company logo" attribute and value identify the alternate text to display if the browser cannot display the image.

4. The height="125" attribute and value reserve the height needed to display the image in a browser.

5. The width="200" attribute and value reserve the width needed to display the image in a browser, and the right angle bracket (>) closes the image element.

When specifying values for the **height** and **width** attributes of an image, use the actual dimensions of the image. For example, the code shown in Figure 3–34 is appropriate for an image with a height of 125 pixels and a width of 200 pixels. (You can find the dimensions of an image file by opening it in a graphics editor such as Photoshop or Paint or by displaying the file's properties using File Explorer or Finder.) If you make the dimensions larger than the actual image, you reduce the quality, which can result in a blurry or distorted image. Making the dimensions smaller than the actual image does not improve the browser's page load time because the image file size remains the same. If you need to use a smaller image, adjust its dimensions in a graphics editor first. Many graphics editors, including Photoshop, let you change the width and height of an image. Be sure to use an option such as "Constrain proportions" or "Maintain aspect ratio" to change each dimension in proportion to the other, which is called maintaining the aspect ratio. Otherwise, you are likely to distort the image. Figure 3–35 shows an example of an image displayed in a browser with its original dimensions and with larger dimensions. The bottom image uses dimensions larger than the file size and does not maintain the aspect ratio, which distorts the image.

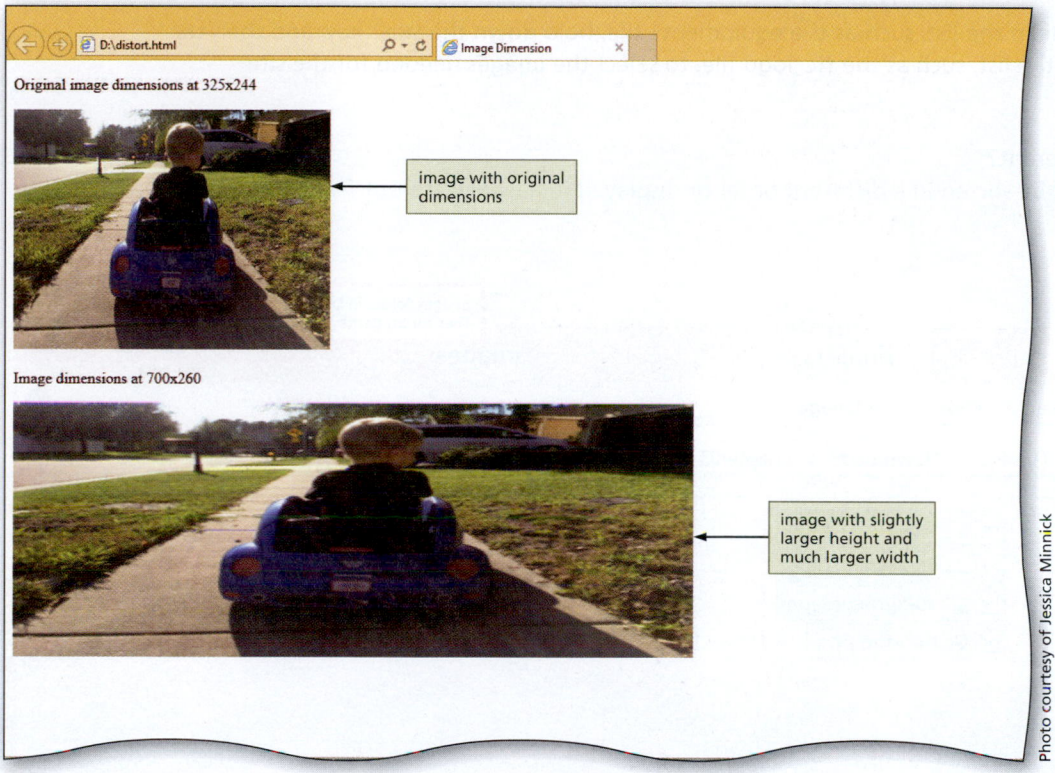

Photo courtesy of Jessica Minnick

Figure 3–35

Using the **height** and **width** attributes in an image element establishes a fixed size for the image, which can affect the webpage layout. A webpage can have a fixed layout or a fluid layout (also called a flexible or a responsive layout). A webpage with a fixed layout does not change when the browser window is resized or the page is displayed at varying resolutions. In a fixed layout, every element has a predefined height and width. However, as you progress further into this book and begin to design responsively for mobile, tablet, and desktop devices, you will learn how to create fluid layouts and images with CSS. Fluid images adjust their size for optimal display on a desktop, tablet, and mobile device.

To Copy Files into the Images Folder

Before you can add an image to a site, you need to acquire the images and store them in the folder designated for images on your website. *Why? You need to have image files and know where they are stored before you can add them to a webpage. In the following steps, you copy image files to your images folder.* The following steps copy four images files from the Data Files for Students to the images folder for the fitness site.

1

- If necessary, insert the drive containing the Data Files for Students into an available port.
- Use File Explorer (Windows) or Finder (Mac) to navigate to the storage location of the Data Files for Students.
- Double-tap or double-click the chapter03 folder, double-tap or double-click the fitness folder, and then double-tap or double-click the images folder to open the images folder and display the image files.
- Tap or click the first file in the list, such as the equipment1 file, hold down the SHIFT key, and then tap or click the last file in the list, such as the ffc_logo file, to select the images needed for the site (Figure 3–36).

◄ Q&A | Why is my file list different?
Your list of files might be sorted in a different order or displayed in a view different from the one shown in Figure 3–36.

Figure 3–36

- Press and hold or right-click the selected files, tap or click Copy on the shortcut menu, and then navigate to the images folder in your fitness folder to prepare to copy the files to your images folder.

- Press and hold or right-click a blank area in the open window, and then tap or click Paste on the shortcut menu to copy the files into the images folder.

- Verify that the folder now contains four images (Figure 3–37).

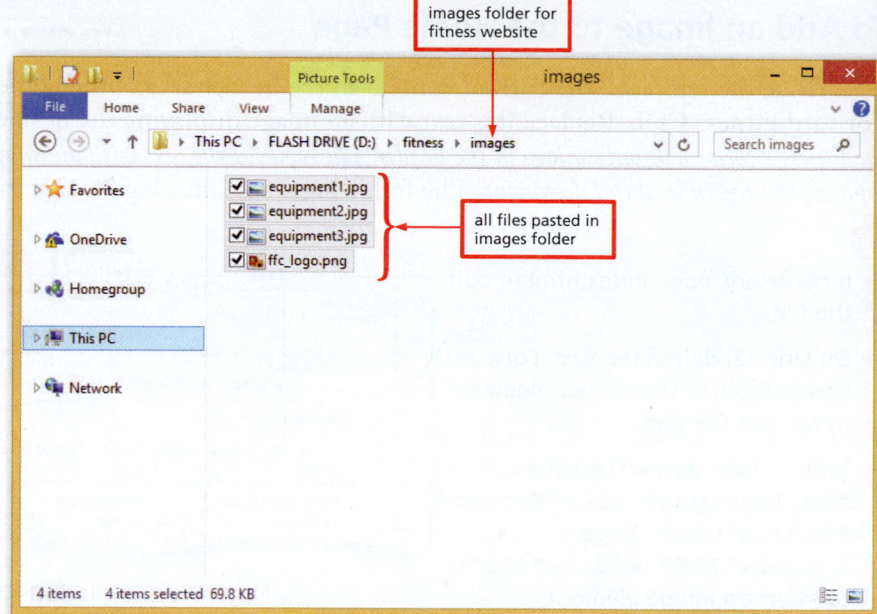

Figure 3–37

Other Ways

1   Select files, tap or click Copy button (Home tab | Clipboard group), navigate to destination folder, tap or click Paste button (Home tab | Clipboard group)

2   Select files, press CTRL+C, navigate to destination folder, press CTRL+V (Mac users: press COMMAND+C and COMMAND+V)

To Add an Image to a Website Template

1 ADD HYPERLINKS | **2 ADD IMAGES** | 3 ADD DIV ELEMENTS | 4 ADD HEADINGS & LISTS
5 VIEW WEBSITE IN BROWSER & TEST LINKS | 6 VALIDATE PAGES

In the template, the current content in the header area is the name of the business, Forward Fitness Club. Replace this text with an image displaying the business logo. *Why? Most businesses use a logo on their webpages to promote their business and brand.* The following steps add a logo image to a website template.

Figure 3–38

- If necessary, open fitness.html to open the template file.

- On Line 12, delete the text, Forward Fitness Club, in the anchor element to remove the text.

- Type `<img src="images/ffc_logo.png" alt="Forward Fitness Club logo" height="275" width="845">` to insert an image element (Figure 3–38).

Q&A | Why do I need to type images/ before the name of the logo file?
All images, including the logo, are stored in the images folder, so you must include the folder name in the path to the logo file.

- Save your changes.

Q&A | After I saved my changes, I viewed the template in my browser and the alternate text appears instead of the logo. Why?
You save the template file in the template folder, so the browser is looking for the ffc_logo.png file in an images subfolder of the template folder, which does not exist. When you create pages based on the template, you will store them in the fitness folder, which does contain the image folder, so this path will be correct for each webpage.

To Add an Image to the Home Page

Like the template, the current content in the header area of the home page is the name of the business, Forward Fitness Club. Replace this text with an image displaying the business logo. *Why? All of the pages in the fitness website will have a logo in the header. You replaced the text with an image in the template file, but still need to replace it in the index.html document.* The following steps add a logo image to the home page.

- If necessary, open index.html to edit the file.

- On Line 12, delete the text, Forward Fitness Club, in the anchor element to remove the text.

- Type `<img src="images/ffc_logo.png" alt="Forward Fitness Club logo" height="275" width="845">` to insert an image element (Figure 3–39).

Figure 3–39

- Save your changes.

- Open File Explorer (Windows) or Finder (Mac), navigate to the index.html file, and then double-tap or double-click the file to open it in your default browser (Figure 3–40).

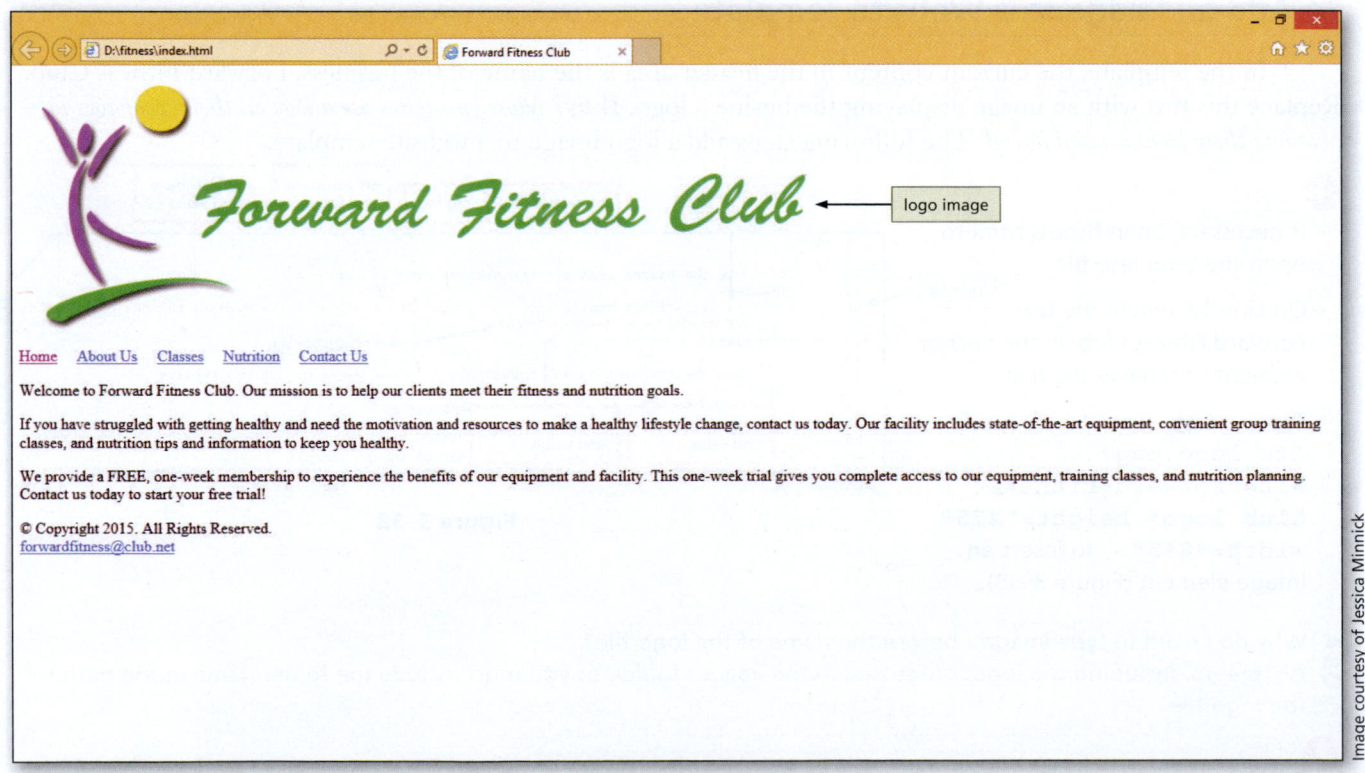

Figure 3–40

Break Point: If you want to take a break, this is a good place to do so. You can exit the text editor now. To resume at a later time, run your text editor, open the file called fitness.html, and continue following the steps from this location forward.

Exploring Div Elements

As you have learned, every webpage consists of several essential lines of HTML code used to display and support content in a browser. In addition, you use HTML5 tags to identify specific areas on a webpage, such as the header, navigation area, main content area, and the footer. These are just a few of the basic HTML tags used to display a webpage. You can use other types of HTML tags to organize and display content on a webpage.

Div Element

Use a **div element** to define an area or a division in a webpage. You insert `div` elements with the <div> and </div> tags. Prior to HTML5, `div` elements defined specific areas on a webpage, such as the header, navigation area, main content area, and footer. The HTML5 semantic elements replace the `div` elements for these areas because the new, more meaningful HTML5 elements better reflect their purpose. However, web designers still use the `div` element on their websites; it is not an obsolete element. One reason is that many well-established websites still have webpages that were created using `div` elements where more semantic HTML5 elements would now apply. Some people and organizations use older browsers that can read `div` elements but not HTML5 elements. More commonly, web designers use `div` elements to structure parts of a webpage to which an HTML5 element does not apply. For example, recall that the `main` element identifies the primary content for the page and that you can have only one `main` element on a webpage. You can also use `div` elements within the `main` element to further divide the primary content area into separate sections, such as the introduction, a long quotation, a list of "See Also" links, and a conclusion. Figure 3–41 shows a wireframe with four `div` elements inside the `main` element.

Figure 3–41

Div Attributes

Like other elements, `div` elements have attributes that provide more meaningful information about the element. One div attribute is **id**, which identifies a unique area on a webpage and distinguishes it from other page divisions. For example, <div id="menu"> is a starting div tag with an `id` attribute that has a value of `menu`. You might use this element to identify a menu of options on the webpage. The `id` attribute value must be unique — no other `div` element on the webpage can have an `id` attribute value of `menu`. Figure 3–42 shows an example of `div` elements used in lieu of HTML5 semantic elements. Because each `div` element has a different `id` attribute value, browsers interpret the content in those elements as belonging to different areas of the webpage.

Figure 3–42

To gain flexibility in formatting the webpages on the Forward Fitness Club website, you can add a `div` element to the wireframe and template of the website. The purpose of the new `div` element is to contain all of the other webpage elements, including **header, nav, main,** and **footer.** Containing these HTML5 elements within a single `div` element prepares the template and future pages for CSS styles, such as one that centers the webpage in a browser window. Figure 3–43 shows the revised wireframe with the `div` element and `id` attribute value defined as `container`.

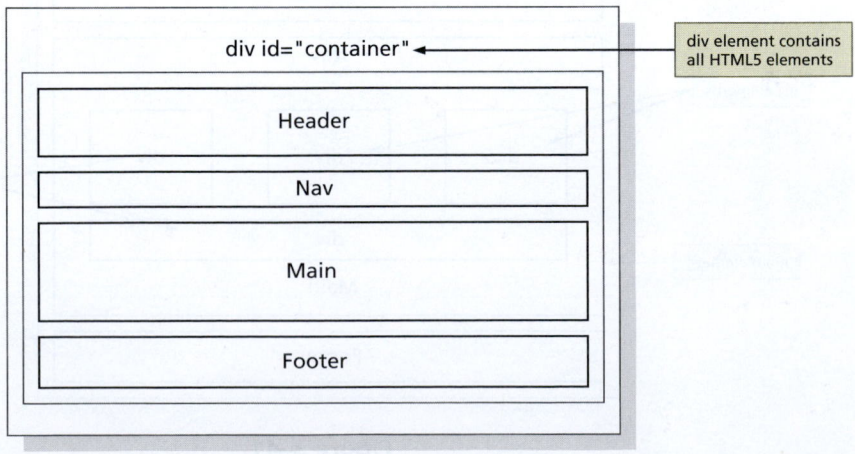

Figure 3–43

Why is "container" the value of the id attribute?

Because this div element will contain all of the webpage elements, it is commonly referred to as the container or the wrapper because it contains or wraps around all of the webpage elements, similar to how a fence wraps around a physical piece of property to contain things on the property.

To Add a Div Element to a Website Template

1 ADD HYPERLINKS | 2 ADD IMAGES | 3 ADD DIV ELEMENTS | 4 ADD HEADINGS & LISTS
5 VIEW WEBSITE IN BROWSER & TEST LINKS | 6 VALIDATE PAGES

Apply the changes from the Forward Fitness website wireframe to the template. Add a **div** element with an **id** attribute and an attribute value of **container** to contain all of the HTML5 webpage elements in the fitness template, including **header, nav, main,** and **footer.** *Why? Because the template will be used to create future pages for the website, edit the template so that all pages use the same layout.* The following steps add a **div** element with an **id** attribute value of **container** to the website template.

- If necessary, open the fitness.html template file to prepare to insert a div element.

- Place the insertion point after the starting <body> tag and then press the ENTER key two times to create a new Line 10.

- Press the TAB key to indent the line.

- Type **<div id="container">** to insert a div element with an id attribute and value (Figure 3–44).

```
            starting                    div element with id
            body tag                    attribute and value

 8  <body>
 9
10      <div id="container">
11
12      <!-- Use the header area for the website name or logo -->
13      <header>
14          <a href="index.html"><img src="images/ffc_logo.png" alt="Forward Fitness Club logo"
                height="275" width="845"></a>
15      </header>
```

Line 10

Figure 3–44

- Place the insertion point after the ending </footer> tag and press the ENTER key two times to create a new Line 36.

- If necessary, press the TAB key to increase the indent.

- Type **</div>** to close the div element (Figure 3–45).

```
                        ending
                        footer tag

31          <footer>
32          &copy; Copyright 2015. All Rights Reserved.<br>
33          <a href="mailto:forwardfitness@club.net">forwardfitness@club.net</a>
34          </footer>
35
36      </div>                          ending
37                                       div tag
38  </body>
39  </html>
```

Line 36

Figure 3–45

Q&A | Why is the ending div tag </div> instead of </div id="container">?
A div attribute is defined only within the starting div tag. After a div is defined with an attribute, you close it with a </div> tag.

3

- Save your changes.

To Add a Div Element to the Home Page

You must also edit the home page of the website by adding a **div** element with an **id** attribute and value of **container** to make it consistent with the website template. *Why? All of the pages within the website should use the same general template layout.* The following steps add a **div** element with an **id** attribute and value to the home page.

- If necessary, open the index.html file to prepare to insert a div element.

- Place the insertion point after the starting <body> tag and then press the ENTER key two times to create a new Line 10.

- Press the TAB key to increase the indent.

- Type **<div id="container">** to insert a div element with an id attribute and value (Figure 3–46).

Figure 3–46

- Place the insertion point after the ending </footer> tag and then press the ENTER key two times to create a new Line 43.

- If necessary, press the TAB key to increase the indent.

- Type **</div>** to close the div element (Figure 3–47).

Figure 3–47

- Save your changes and close index.html.

Class Attributes

The **class** attribute is also commonly used in HTML. Unlike the **id** attribute, a **class** attribute name can be applied to more than one **div** or other HTML element on a webpage. Classes provide another level of control over the styling or formatting of specific elements on a webpage. For example, rather than having all paragraphs of text appear with the same formatting, you might want to format the first paragraph after a heading to be different from other paragraphs of text. You can define the first paragraph after a heading with a class attribute and name, such as <p class="first">. This makes it easier to format every paragraph after a heading the same way. In another example, <img class="product"> is an image tag with a **class** attribute that has a value of `product`. You might use this element to collect all product photos in a single category and then format those images to have a border or to position them in a specific area on a webpage. Figure 3–48 shows an example of a `class` attribute used within an image tag.

Figure 3–48

To mark an element as belonging to a class, add the class attribute and name to the element. In Figure 3–48, `equip` is the name of the class. Any word can be used as a class name, as long as it does not contain spaces. In general, however, you should use descriptive names that illustrate the purpose of a class (for example, `beginning, legallanguage,` or `copyrighttext`), rather than names that describe the appearance of the class (for example, `bluetext, largeritalic,` or `boldsmallarial`). Using names that describe the purpose of the class makes the code more flexible and easier to read. In Chapter 4, you will apply styles to classes to format more than one element at a time.

Adding Headings and Lists

Some HTML elements are designed to group information on a webpage. For example, the `p` element groups text into a paragraph and the `div` element groups elements into an area or section. Two other grouping elements are heading elements and lists. Headings indicate that a new topic is starting and typically identify or summarize the topic. Lists group related items together in a sequence or collection.

Heading Elements

You use **heading elements** to provide a title or heading before a paragraph of text or section of a page. On a webpage, headings appear in a larger font size than normal text, making it easy for users to quickly scan the page and identify its sections. Heading levels run from 1 (the most important) to 6 (the least important). Heading level 1 is designed to mark major headings, while heading levels 2–6 are for subheadings. The start tag for heading level 1 is <h1> and the end tag is </h1>. The start tag for heading level 2 is <h2> and the end tag is </h2>, and so on. Figure 3–49 displays the default formatting for heading levels 1 through 6. In the upcoming steps, you insert headings in the About Us and Contact Us pages for the fitness website.

Figure 3–49

What is the difference between a head element, a header element, and a heading element, and how do I know when to use them?

Recall from Chapter 1 that the *head element* is a required element for an HTML webpage and belongs near the top of the page. A head element is defined by <head> and </head> tags and contains information about the webpage, such as the webpage title and the defined character set, not website content. A *header element* is a set of HTML5 tags (<header> and </header>) that define the header area of a webpage and generally come after the starting <body> tag. Header elements contain webpage content, such as a business name or logo. A *heading element*, h1, h2, h3, h4, h5, or h6, defines a heading in a webpage and is generally placed above other webpage content. Heading elements also contain webpage content. A heading element can appear in a header element, a main element, or other HTML elements. A heading level 1 element is defined by <h1> and </h1> tags.

Lists

Lists structure text into an itemized format. An **unordered list**, also called a bulleted list, displays a small graphic called a bullet before each item of information. In an unordered list, the bulleted items can appear in any sequence. To mark an unordered list, insert the <ul> tag at the start of the list and the </ul> tag at the end of the list. Mark each item in an unordered list with a set of list item tags (<li> and </li>). The following code creates a bulleted list of two items:

```
<ul>
  <li>First item</li>
  <li>Second item</li>
</ul>
```

An **ordered list**, also called a numbered list, displays information in a series using numbers or letters. An ordered list works well to organize items where sequence matters, such as in a series of steps. To mark an ordered list, insert the <ol> and </ol> tags at the start and end of the list. As with unordered lists, you mark each item in an ordered list with a set of <li> and </li> tags. The following code creates a numbered list of two items:

```
<ol>
  <li>First item</li>
  <li>Second item</li>
</ol>
```

Figure 3–50 shows a webpage with an unordered and an ordered list.

Figure 3–50

Unordered and ordered lists have optional bullet and number types. An unordered list can use one of three bullet options: disc, square, or circle. If no type is identified, the browser displays the default type, a disc. You can also specify an image to use as a bullet. An ordered list can use numbers, letters, or Roman numerals. The default option is to use Arabic numbers, such as 1, 2, and 3. Table 3–5 shows the different values and examples of unordered and ordered list options. Although you can use the `style` attribute to specify the style of bullets and numbers, the recommended method for changing bullet list and number styles is with CSS, which is covered in Chapter 4.

Table 3-5 List Type Attributes

Unordered Lists

Value	Example
disc (default)	•
square	■
circle	o

Ordered Lists

Value	Example
1	1. 2. 3.
A	A. B. C.
a	a. b. c.
I	I. II. III.
i	i. ii. iii.

A **description list** contains terms and descriptions. Use a description list to create a glossary or to list questions and answers, for example. A description list includes terms and descriptions or definitions. Define a description list between a pair of <dl> and </dl> tags. Mark each term within a pair of <dt> and </dt> tags. Mark each description or definition between a pair of <dd> and </dd> tags. For each item, the `dt` element must come before the `dd` element. More than one `dd` element can follow a `dt` element. The following code creates a description list of two terms and definitions:

```
<dl>
  <dt>First term</dt>
  <dd>First definition</dd>

  <dt>Second term</dt>
  <dd>Second definition - part 1</dd>
  <dd>Second definition - part 2</dd>
</dl>
```

Figure 3–51 shows an example of a description list.

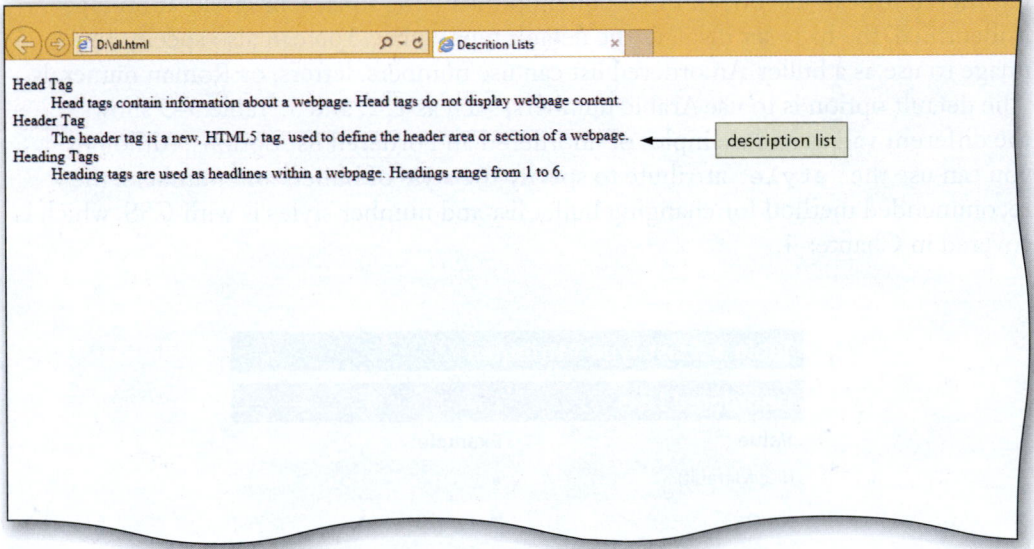

Figure 3–51

To Create the About Us Webpage and Add a Heading and Image

1 ADD HYPERLINKS | 2 ADD IMAGES | 3 ADD DIV ELEMENTS | 4 ADD HEADING ELEMENTS & LISTS
5 VIEW WEBSITE IN BROWSER & TEST LINKS | 6 VALIDATE PAGES

The About Us page provides additional information about the Forward Fitness Club, including pictures of its facility. It also includes headings to identify the topics on the page. Use the website template to create the About Us page. *Why? The website template already contains the basic HTML code for the website. Using the template saves time coding.* The following steps create the About Us page for the fitness website using the website template.

- If necessary, reopen the fitness .html template file to create a new webpage using the template file.

- Tap or click File on the menu bar and then tap or click Save As to display the Save As dialog box.

- If necessary, navigate up one level to access the fitness folder.

- Type **about** in the File name text box to name the file (Figure 3–52).

Figure 3–52

- Tap or click the Save button to save the file in the fitness folder.

- Place your insertion point after the starting <main> tag on Line 27 and then press the ENTER key twice to insert new Lines 28 and 29.

- On Line 29, press the TAB key and then type **<h1>Weights</h1>** to add heading 1 tags and content to the page (Figure 3–53).

Figure 3–53

- Press the ENTER key to insert a new Line 30.

- Type **<img class="equip" src="images/equipment1 .jpg" alt="Weight Equipment" height="195" width="260">** to add an image element to the page (Figure 3–54).

Figure 3–54

What is the purpose of class="equip"?
Including the class attribute identifies this image as belonging to the equip class. In Chapter 4, you will format all the images in the equip class in the same way.

Why am I setting 195 as the height and 260 as the width?
These are the actual dimensions of the equipment1.jpg image file. In Windows, you can verify the dimensions by pressing and holding or right-clicking the image file, and then selecting Properties on the shortcut menu to display the Properties dialog box for the file. Tap or click the Details tab. The dimensions are listed in the Image section of the Details tabbed page.

4

- Press the ENTER key to insert a new Line 31.

- Type `<p>Our facility includes a weight training area with several weight options. Build lean muscle with weights and improve your core with weight training.</p>` to add a paragraph element to the page (Figure 3–55).

Figure 3–55

To Add Unordered Lists to the About Us Webpage

1 ADD HYPERLINKS | 2 ADD IMAGES | 3 ADD DIV ELEMENTS | **4 ADD HEADING ELEMENTS & LISTS**
5 VIEW WEBSITE IN BROWSER & TEST LINKS | 6 VALIDATE PAGES

The About Us page should list the types of equipment the Forward Fitness Club provides to its members. You can include these items using unordered lists. *Why? The types of equipment can appear in any order in the lists, so the items are appropriate for unordered lists.* The following steps add headings and unordered lists to the About Us page.

1

- With the insertion point at the end of Line 31, press the ENTER key to insert a new Line 32.

- Type `<ul>` to insert a starting unordered list tag.

- Press the ENTER key, increase the indent, and then type `<li>Dumbbells</li>` to add the first list item.

- Press the ENTER key and then type `<li>Kettle bells</li>` to add the second list item.

- Press the ENTER key and then type `<li>Barbells</li>` to add the third list item.

- Press the ENTER key, press the SHIFT+TAB keys to decrease the indent, and then type `</ul><br>` to add the ending unordered list tag and a line break (Figure 3–56).

Figure 3–56

②

- Press the ENTER key two times to insert new Lines 37 and 38.

- Type the code shown in Table 3–6 to insert additional elements for headings, images, and unordered lists (Figure 3–57).

Figure 3–57

Table 3-6 About Us Code for Lines 38–54	
Line Number	**Code to Insert**
38	`<h1>Cardio</h1>`
39	`<img class="equip" src="images/equipment2.jpg" alt="Cardio Equipment" height="195" width="260">`
40	`<p>Burn fat through cardio workouts. If you need to lose 20 lbs or more, include at least 30 minutes of cardio each day. We have several equipment choices for your workout.</p>`
41	`<ul>`
42	`<li>Treadmills</li>`
43	`<li>Elliptical Machines</li>`
44	`<li>Exercise Bikes</li>`
45	`</ul> `
46	
47	`<h1>Personal Training</h1>`
48	`<img class="equip" src="images/equipment3.jpg" alt="Personal Training" height="195" width="260">`
49	`<p>Our certified personal trainers work with you one on one to help you obtain your fitness goals. Our personal trainers keep you motivated and push you farther than you would push yourself. When you feel like you cannot do one more rep, they tell you that you can. Personal training has many benefits.</p>`
50	`<ul>`
51	`<li>Accountability</li>`
52	`<li>Personalized Program</li>`
53	`<li>Consistent Support and Motivation</li>`
54	`</ul> `

To Add a Description List and Absolute Link to the About Us Webpage

The About Us page should also describe the types of exercises the Forward Fitness Club recommends for its members. You can include these descriptions using a description list. Below the description list, include an absolute link to fitness.gov with more information about being active. *Why? The webpage can list the exercises by name followed by a description, which is appropriate for a description list.* The following step adds a description list to the About Us page.

1

- With the insertion point at the end of Line 54, press the ENTER key two times to insert new Lines 55 and 56.

- Type the code shown in Table 3–7 to insert a heading 1 element, a paragraph, and a description list (Figure 3–58).

Figure 3–58

Table 3-7 About Us Code for Lines 56–73

Line Number	Code to Insert
56	<h1>Common Exercises</h1>
57	<p>The following are common exercises that we encourage our clients to do as part of their daily exercise routine.</p>
58	<dl>
59	<dt>Burpee</dt>
60	<dd>Burpees are a great, full body exercise to increase your strength and endurance. Begin in a standing position, drop into a squat and extend your hands forward, kick your feet back and then forward again quickly, and then jump up from a squatted position.
61	 </dd>
62	
63	<dt>Plank</dt>
64	<dd>Planks build your core strength. To perform a plank, get in a push up position and rest your forearms on the floor. Hold the position as long as you can.
65	 </dd>
66	
67	<dt>Mountain Climber</dt>
68	<dd>Mountain climbers are a good cardio exercise. Place your hands on the floor in a push up position, then bring one knee up to your chest and then switch as quickly as you can (as though you are climbing a mountain).
69	 </dd>
70	</dl>
71	
72	<p>For more information about how to stay active, visit <a href="http://www.fitness.gov/be-active/ways-to-be -active/">fitness.gov</a>.</p>
73	

To Save the About Us Webpage and View It in a Browser

The About Us page is finished for now. The following steps save the webpage and view it in your default browser.

1 Check the spelling in your document to find misspelled words and correct them as necessary.

2 Save and close the about.html file.

3 Using File Explorer (Windows) or Finder (Mac), navigate to the about.html file, and then open the file to display it in your default browser (Figure 3–59).

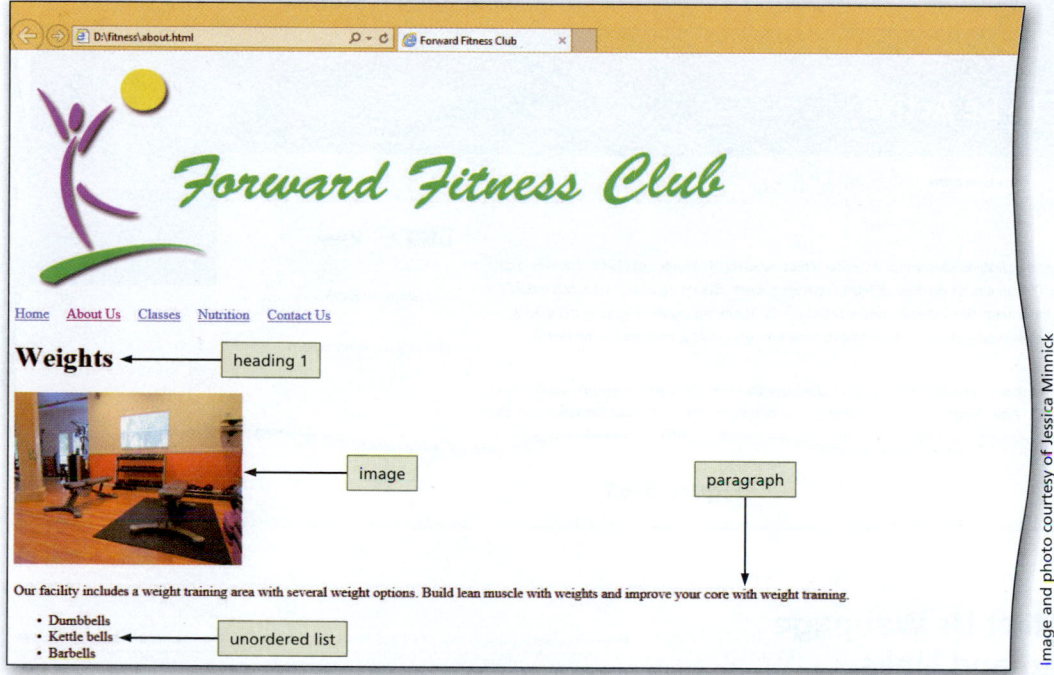

Image and photo courtesy of Jessica Minnick

Figure 3–59

4 Scroll down the page and display the description list (Figure 3–60).

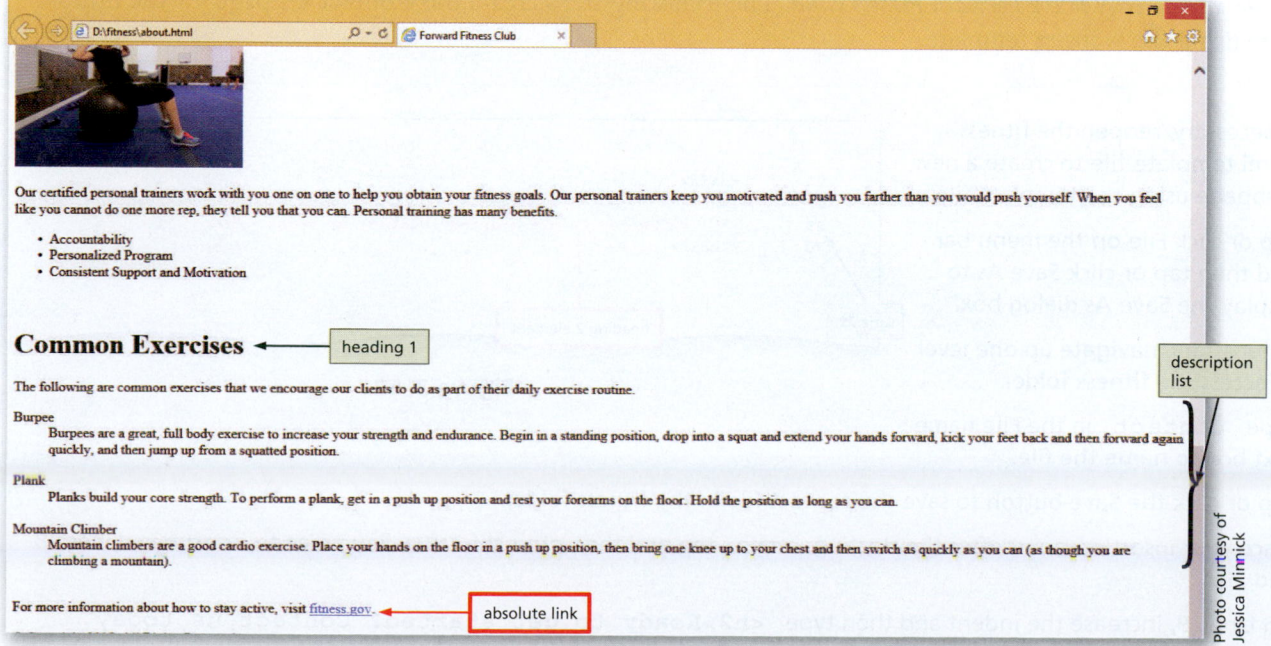

Photo courtesy of Jessica Minnick

Figure 3–60

5 Tap or click the fitness.gov link to open the fitness.gov website (Figure 3–61).

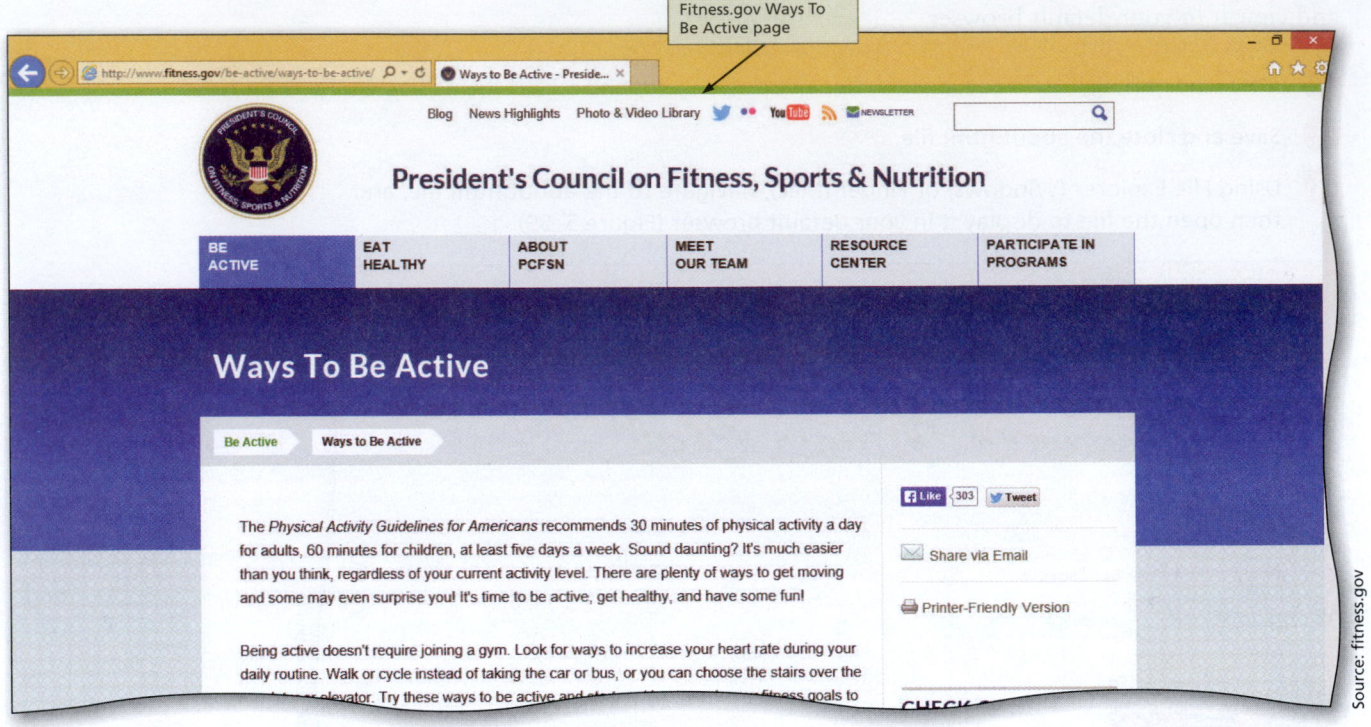

Figure 3–61

To Create the Contact Us Webpage and Add a Heading and Links

1 ADD HYPERLINKS | 2 ADD IMAGES | 3 ADD DIV ELEMENTS | **4 ADD HEADING ELEMENTS & LISTS**
5 VIEW WEBSITE IN BROWSER & TEST LINKS | 6 VALIDATE PAGES

The Contact Us page provides an address, a phone number, and an email address for the Forward Fitness Club. Insert a heading to identify the new information, and then add the phone number and email address to the webpage as link text. *Why? If you mark the text as links, visitors can select the links to make a phone call or send an email message directly to the Forward Fitness Club.* The following steps create the Contact Us page for the fitness website using the website template.

- If necessary, reopen the fitness .html template file to create a new webpage using the template file.

- Tap or click File on the menu bar and then tap or click Save As to display the Save As dialog box.

- If necessary, navigate up one level to access the fitness folder.

- Type **contact** in the File name text box to name the file.

- Tap or click the Save button to save the contact file in the fitness folder.

- Place your insertion point after the starting <main> tag and then press the ENTER key twice to insert new Lines 28 and 29.

- On Line 29, increase the indent and then type **<h2>Ready to get started? Contact us today. </h2>** to add a heading 2 element to the page (Figure 3–62).

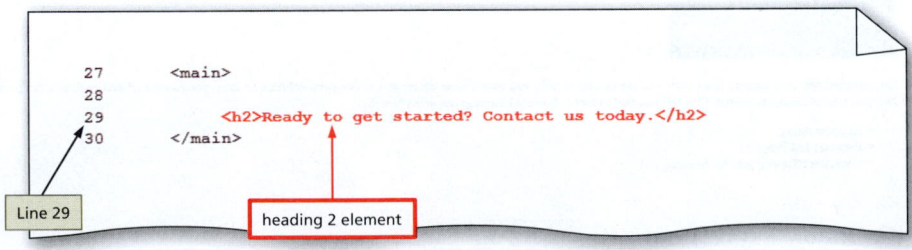

```
27        <main>
28
29            <h2>Ready to get started? Contact us today.</h2>
30        </main>
```

Line 29

heading 2 element

Figure 3–62

Source: fitness.gov

2

- Press the ENTER key to insert a new Line 30.

- Type the code shown in Table 3–8 to add paragraphs and link text, indenting each line beginning on Line 30 and continuing through Line 40 (Figure 3–63).

```
29    <h2>Ready to get started? Contact us today.</h2>
30    <p>We are located at:<br>
31    25743 Bloom Court<br>
32    Locket, GA 85524</p>
33
34    <p>Phone Number<br>
35    <a class="mobile" href="tel:8145559608">(814) 555-9608</a>(814) 555-9608</p>
36
37    <p>Email Address<br>
38    <a href="mailto:forwardfitness@club.net">forwardfitness@club.net</a></p>
39    <br><br>
40
41    </main>
```

paragraph elements · telephone link · link to email address · ending <main> tag

Figure 3–63

Q&A Why is the phone number shown twice?

The first phone number is for mobile display and will allow a mobile device user to tap and call the business. The other phone number is for a desktop and tablet display. You will hide the mobile display for desktop and tablet in a later chapter so that only one number is displayed.

Table 3-8 Contact Us Code for Lines 30–40	
Line Number	**Code to Add**
30	<p>We are located at:
31	25743 Bloom Court
32	Locket, GA 85524</p>
33	
34	<p>Phone Number
35	<a class="mobile" href="tel:8145559608">(814) 555-9608</a>(814) 555-9608</p>
36	
37	<p>Email Address
38	<a href="mailto:forwardfitness@club.net">forwardfitness@club.net</a></p>
39	
40	

To Save the Contact Us Webpage and View It in a Browser

The Contact Us page is finished for now. The following steps save the webpage and view it in your default browser.

1 Check the spelling in your document to find misspelled words and correct them as necessary.

2 Save and close the contact.html file.

3 In File Explorer (Windows) or Finder (Mac), navigate to the contact.html file, and then open the file in your default browser (Figure 3–64).

Q&A Why does the telephone number appear twice on the page?

One telephone number contains a link and the other does not. The telephone number with the link will be used for mobile display. You will format this link in a later chapter so it is not displayed on a desktop view, leaving the telephone number without the link.

Forward Fitness Club

Home   About Us   Classes   Nutrition   Contact Us

Ready to get started? Contact us today. ← heading 2

We are located at:
25743 Bloom Court
Locket, GA 85524

Phone Number
(814) 555-9608(814) 555-9608 ← telephone link

Email Address
forwardfitness@club.net ← email link

Figure 3–64

Image courtesy of Jessica Minnick

To Preview a Website in a Browser and Test Page Links

Now that you have created three webpages, it is time to test the hyperlinks in a browser. ***Why?*** *You need to test your hyperlinks to confirm that your page links work correctly.* The following step displays a webpage in a browser and test hyperlinks.

1

- If necessary, reopen contact.html in your browser to display the page.

- Tap or click the Home link to display the home page.

- Tap or click the About Us link to display the About Us page (Figure 3–65).

Q&A

Why do I receive an error message when I tap or click the classes and nutrition links?
You have not yet created these pages, but specified their file names in the href attribute. The browser looks for the file specified in the href attribute and displays an error message when it cannot find the file.

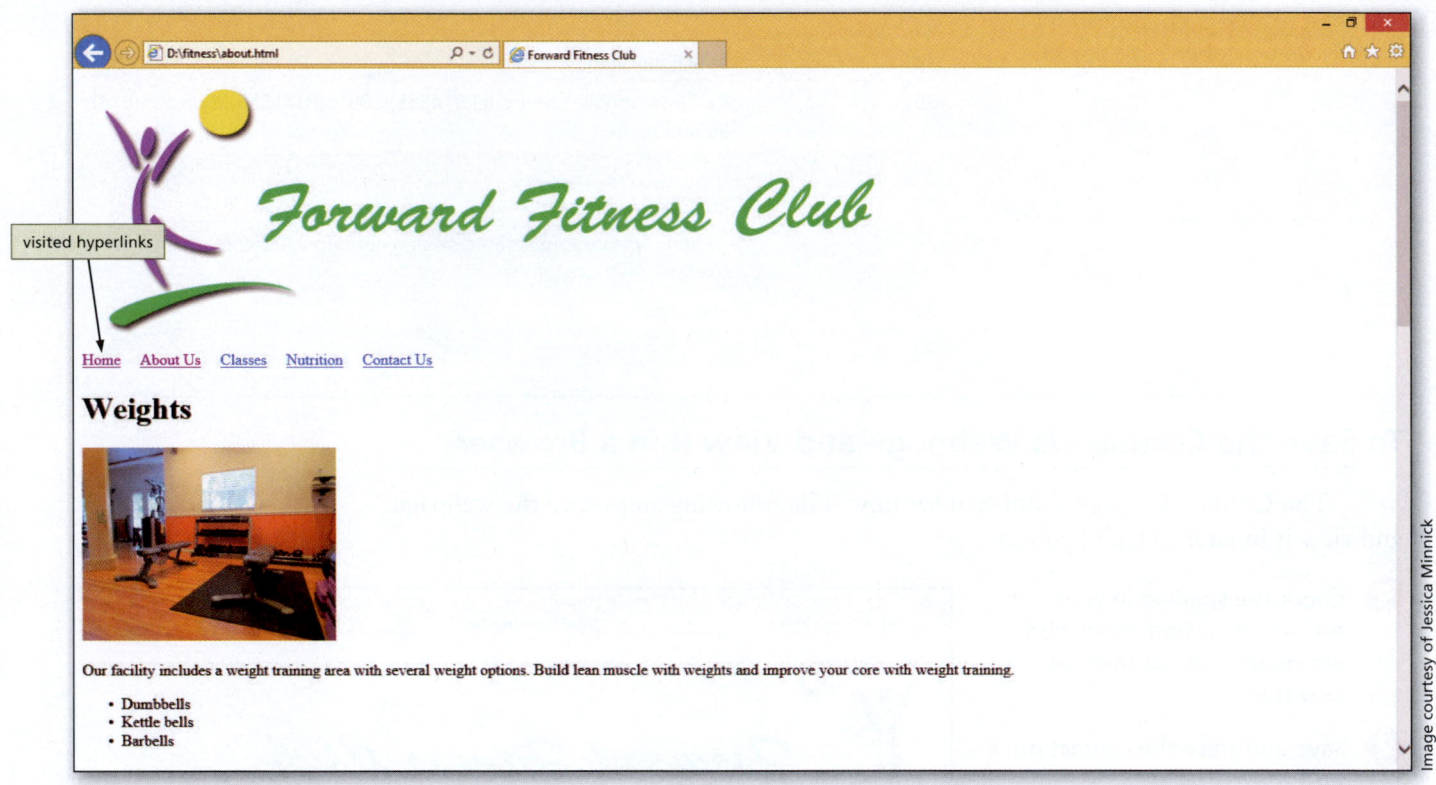

visited hyperlinks

Figure 3–65

Image courtesy of Jessica Minnick

To Validate the About Us and Contact Us Pages

Every time you create a new webpage, run it through the W3C validator to check the document for errors and correct them. The following steps validate an HTML document.

1 Open your browser and type `http://validator .w3.org/` in the address bar to display the W3C validator page.

2 Tap or click the Validate by File Upload tab to display the Validate by File Upload tab information, and then upload the about.html file to the W3C validator.

3 Tap or click the Check button to send the document through the validator and display the validation results page (Figure 3–66).

4 If necessary, correct any errors, save your changes, and run through the validator again to revalidate the page.

5 Perform Steps 1–4 to validate the contact.html page and correct any errors.

6 Close the browser, and then close the HTML text editor.

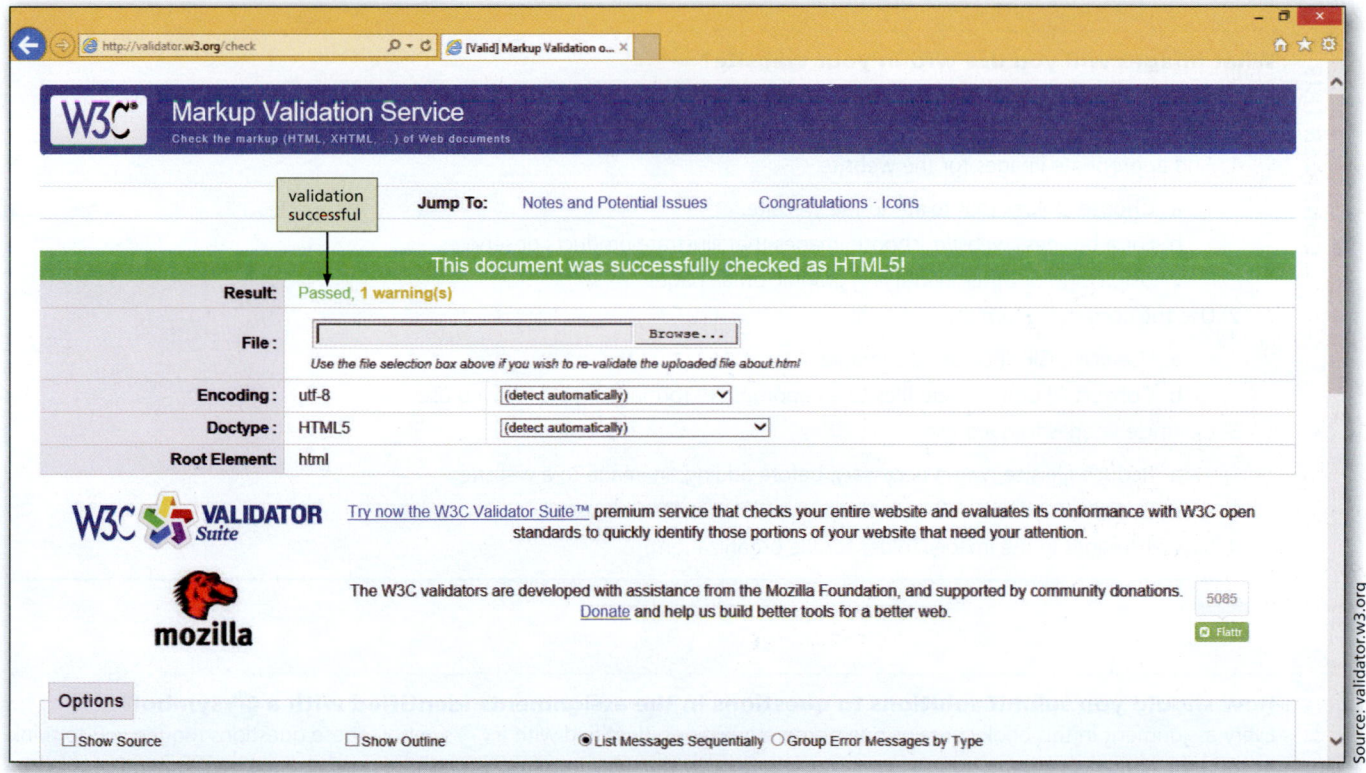

Figure 3–66

Chapter Summary

In this chapter, you have learned how to create many types of hyperlinks. You also inserted new HTML elements, including div elements, image elements, headings, and lists. The items listed below include all the new concepts and skills you have learned in this chapter, with the tasks grouped by activity.

Adding Links to a Webpage
Add Relative Links to a Webpage (HTML 114)
Add an Email Link to a Webpage
  (HTML 89, HTML 92)
Add Absolute Links to a Webpage (HTML 87)
Add Image Links to a Webpage (HTML 88)
Add Telephone Links to a Webpage (HTML 88)

Adding Images to a Website
Copy Files into the Images Folder (HTML 104)
Add an Image to a Webpage (HTML 105,
  HTML 106)

Exploring Div Elements
Add a Div Element to a Webpage (HTML 109)

Adding Headings and Lists
Create the About Us Webpage and Add a Heading
  (HTML 114)
Add Unordered Lists to the About Us Webpage
  (HTML 116)
Add a Description List to the About Us Webpage
  (HTML 118)
Test Page Links (HTML 122)

CONSIDER THIS

What images will you use within your website?
Use these guidelines as you complete the assignments in this chapter and as you create your own webpages outside of this class.

1. Find appropriate images for the website.

    a. Choose images that relate to the website.

    b. For a business website, choose images that illustrate products or services.

    c. Use a logo or other identifying graphic on all pages.

2. Use the correct file format.

    a. Use PNG, GIF, JPG, or SVG images.

    b. Convert all other image files to an appropriate format suitable for web use.

3. Optimize images for web use.

    a. Reduce file size, when necessary, before adding an image to a website.

    b. Use photo-editing software to optimize images for web use.

4. Save all images in the images folder for file organization.

CONSIDER THIS

How should you submit solutions to questions in the assignments identified with a symbol?
Every assignment in this book contains one or more questions identified with a symbol. These questions require you to think beyond the assigned presentation. Present your solutions to the questions in the format required by your instructor. Possible formats may include one or more of these options: create a document that contains the answer; present your answer to the class; discuss your answer in a group; record the answer as audio or video using a webcam, smartphone, or portable media player; or post answers on a blog, wiki, or website.

Apply Your Knowledge

Reinforce the skills and apply the concepts you learned in this chapter.

Creating a Page with Links, Images, Lists, and Headings

Instructions: In this exercise, you will use your HTML editor to enter the needed tags and content to create a template for the pages for a new website as well as the home page for the Durango Jewelry and Gem Shop. The completed home page is shown in Figure 3–67. It contains the content as well as the HTML5 tags required to insert an image, headings, links, lists, and paragraphs of information for this page. You will also use professional web development best practices to indent, space, validate, and check the spelling of your work.

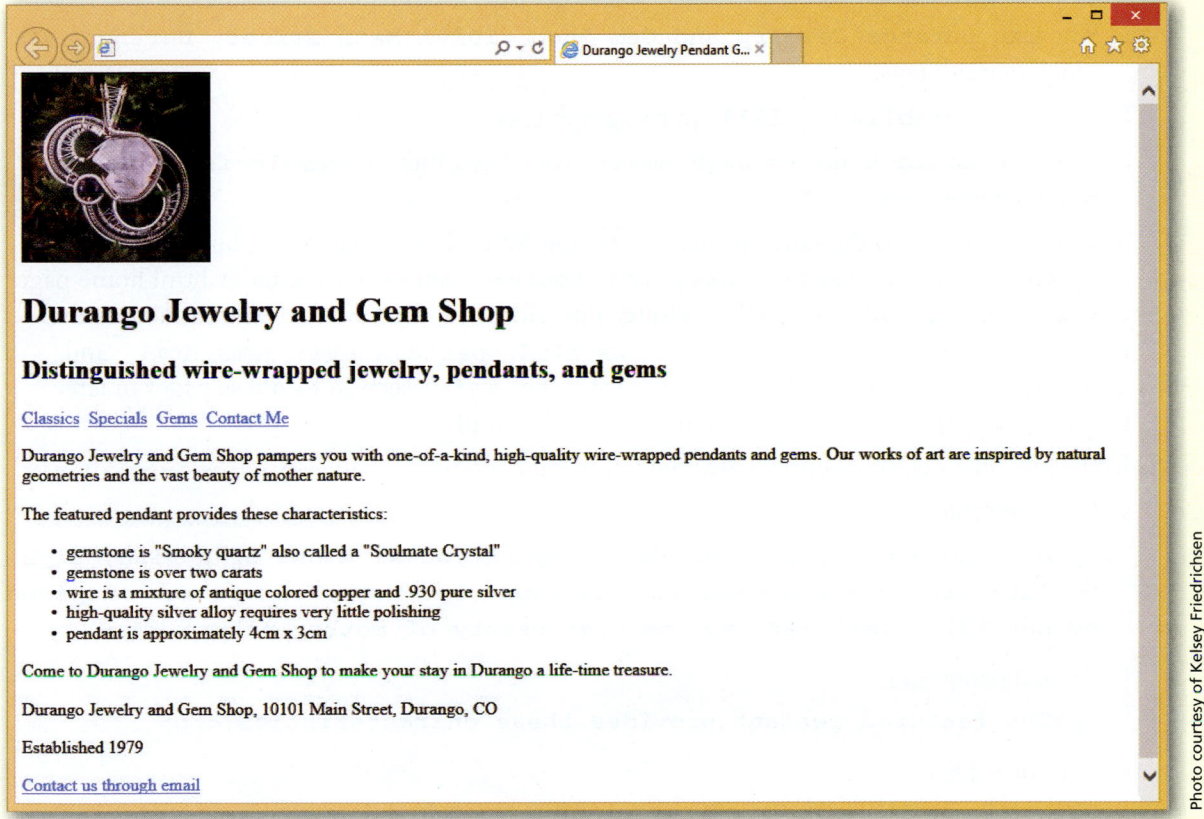

Photo courtesy of Kelsey Friedrichsen

Figure 3–67

Perform the following tasks:

1. Open your HTML editor and then open the apply03.html file from the Data Files for Students. Use the File Save As feature to save the webpage in the chapter03\apply folder with the name `index.html` to create the home page.

2. Modify the comment at the top of the page to include your name and today's date.

3. Enter `Durango Jewelry Pendant Gem` in the <title> tags. Recall that content in the title tags appears in the tab at the top of the browser and is also used by search engines.

4. In the `header` section, enter the following content, each on its own line in the HTML editor.

   a. An image element coded as follows:

   ```
   <img src="wirewrap01.jpg" alt="smoky quartz pendant" width="171"
   height="171">
   ```

Continued >

Apply Your Knowledge *continued*

   b. The text `Durango Jewelry and Gem Shop` in <h1> tags to insert the name of the store.

   c. The text `Distinguished wire-wrapped jewelry, pendants, and gems` in <h2> tags to serve as the tagline.

5. In the `nav` section, enter the following links, each on its own line in the HTML editor.

```
<a href="classics.html">Classics</a> 
<a href="specials.html">Specials</a> 
<a href="gems.html">Gems</a> 
<a href="contact.html">Contact Me</a> 
```

6. In the `footer` section, enter the following content, each on its own line in the HTML editor.

   a. The text `Durango Jewelry and Gem Shop, 10101 Main Street, Durango, CO` in paragraph tags.

   b. The text `Established 1979` in paragraph tags.

   c. The text `Contact us through email` coded as a link to `gemologist@durangogem.com`

7. The content added to the <div id="main"> section for each page will differ, but the content you just added to the `header, nav,` and `footer` sections for the index.html home page will be the same for all pages in the website. Therefore, use the Save As feature to create the four other pages for this website: `classics.html`, `specials.html`, `gems.html`, and `contact.html`. You will fill in the content for the `main` section for these pages in later tutorials, so close these pages and then reopen index.html.

8. In the <div id="main"> section, enter the following content.

   a. First paragraph:

```
<p>Durango Jewelry and Gem Shop pampers you with one-of-a-kind, high-
quality wire wrapped pendants and gems. Our works of art are inspired
by natural geometries and the vast beauty of mother nature.</p>
```

   b. Second paragraph:

```
<p>The featured pendant provides these characteristics:</p>
```

   c. Unordered list:

```
<ul>
  <li>gemstone is "Smoky quartz" also called a "Soulmate Crystal"</li>
  <li>gemstone is over two carats</li>
  <li>wire is a mixture of antique colored copper and .930 pure
silver</li>
  <li>high-quality silver alloy requires very little polishing</li>
  <li>pendant is approximately 4cm x 3cm</li>
</ul>
```

   d. Final paragraph:

```
<p>Come to Durango Jewelry and Gem Shop to make your stay in Durango
a life-time treasure.</p>
```

9. Review and check the spelling of your textual content.

10. Validate your webpage using the W3C validator found at validator.w3.org and fix any errors that are identified. Validation is complete when the validator returns the message *"This document was successfully checked as HTML5!"* in a green bar near the top of the webpage.

11. Submit the `index.html` file in a format specified by your instructor.

12. ✳ In this exercise, you were instructed to use the <div id="main"> tag instead of the HTML5 <main> tag to mark up the main content in the body of the webpage. Because browsers are constantly changing and improving, it's important to make sure that the audience you are trying to reach supports the HTML5 elements and attributes you are using on your website. Find two websites that address the issue of HTML5 browser compatibility. Paste those links and a screenshot of the webpage into a document. (*Hint:* To take a screenshot of the webpage, press the PrtSc or Print Screen key on your keyboard, tap or click your document, and then tap or click the Paste button.)

    Use your research to answer these questions:

    a. When is the div element used within a webpage written with HTML5 tags?

    b. What are the HTML5 semantic tags?

    c. What is the primary advantage and the primary disadvantage of using the <main> tag versus <div id="main">?

Extend Your Knowledge

Extend the skills you learned in this chapter and experiment with new skills. You may need to use additional resources to complete the assignment.

Inserting Links

Instructions: In this exercise, you will use your HTML editor to enter the needed tags and content to create several different types of links. The completed page is shown in Figure 3–68. The starting file contains comments to note the location of links you will add to the page. You will also use professional web development best practices to indent, space, validate, and check the spelling of your work.

Perform the following tasks:

1. Open the `ski03.html` file from the Data Files for Students and then modify the comment at the top of the page to include your name and today's date.

2. After the <!--Insert an image with a link--> comment, insert an <img> tag as follows:

   `<img src="ski.jpg" alt="happy skiers" height="343" width="514">`

3. Make the image a link to `http://www.breckenridge.com`

4. Make each word in the <nav> section a link to another page on the website. Put each link on its own line for readability as follows:

   ```
   <a href="events.html">Events</a> |
   <a href="lessons.html">Lessons</a> |
   <a href="snowreports.html">Snow Reports</a> |
   <a href="employment.html">Employment</a>
   ```

5. In the <div id="content"> section, make the phone number, 1-800-555-4SKI, a telephone link to that number. (*Hint:* The letters SKI translate to the numbers 754 on a phone keypad.)

6. Make the text "Write to Kent" an email link to `kent@ilovesnow.com`

7. In the `footer,` make the text "snow.com" a link to `http://www.snow.com`

8. To make it easier for users to navigate the home page, add two links in the footer section that will quickly take the user back to the top and main areas of the webpage.

Continued >

Extend Your Knowledge continued

Snow Fever Ski and Board School

Let it snow, let it snow, let it snow

Events | Lessons | Snow Reports | Employment

Children's Lessons

Children's full-day lessons meet from 10 am through 3:30 pm and include lift access, rentals (ski or snowboard), and lunch. All children (ages 4-12) are welcome regardless of ability or prior experience. Our expert ski and snowboard instructors provide special care and attention to teach children the correct way to ski and ride, from the basics of carving turns to safety instruction to advanced lessons and multi-week programs. We focus on having fun in a safe and responsible way!

Terrain Park Lessons

Our terrain park lessons meet from 12:30 pm to 4 pm at the base of the Powder Keg Terrain Park and include lift access, rentals (ski or snowboard), and an afternoon snack. We start with the basics and progress through all skill levels. Learn how to ride the rails, half pipe, and jumps. Must be 13 years old. Our proven techniques will teach you how to maneuver through any terrain park in a fun and safe way!

Adult Lessons

Adult full-day lessons from 9 am through 3 pm include lift access, rentals (ski or snowboard), and lunch. Adults are divided by ability and experience. We have expert instructors for all levels!

Cost

All of our lessons are $100/day. If you prepay for three full days, you will receive a free season pass to keep practicing your skiing or snowboarding skills for the rest of the season!

Registration

Call or email our Ski School Manager: Kent Hoiberg
1001 West Main Street
Breckenridge, Colorado 80425

Phone: 1-800-555-4SKI
E-mail: Write to Kent

Our Sponsor: snow.com

Lessons   Top   Rental Agreement

Figure 3–68

In the **footer** section, make Lessons link to the id="content" location on same page. When a link goes to a location on the same page, the **href** attribute value starts with a # (pound sign or hash tag) followed by the **id** value of the target location as follows: `<a href="#content">Lessons</a>`

9. In the **footer**, make Top link to the top of the page. Because the location for this link is not yet identified, you need to insert an appropriate attribute value pair to the opening <header> tag as follows to mark this location: `<header id="top">`

   With the location identified, go back to the **footer** and mark up the Top text with a link as follows: `<a href="#top">Top</a>`

Navigational links at the bottom of the webpage are especially useful to those who are viewing the page on a small device because they help minimize excessive scrolling.

10. In the `footer` section, make Rental Agreement link to a document named legal.pdf as follows: `<a href="legal.pdf">Rental Agreement</a>`

11. Save and view your work in a browser. Tap or click each of the 11 links you inserted starting with the image link to make sure they work as desired. Note that the links in the `nav` section currently point to pages you have not created yet. Also, depending on the device you are using to check your work, the telephone and email links may not work.

12. Check the spelling of the content on the page.

13. Validate your webpage using the W3C validator found at validator.w3.org and fix any errors that are identified. Validation is complete when the validator returns the message *"This document was successfully checked as HTML5!"* in a green bar near the top of the webpage.

14. Submit the `ski03.html` file in a format specified by your instructor.

15. ✹ The html validator at http://validator.w3.org allows you to validate a webpage by entering a URL, uploading a file, or directly inputting the code into the validation window. Which method(s) does the link checker at http://validator.w3.org/checklink use? (*Hint:* A URL is created by software on the web server when you publish a webpage. See your instructor to determine if a web server is available for student use at your school.)

Analyze, Correct, Improve

Analyze a webpage, correct all errors, and improve it.

Correcting Image, Link, Heading, and List Errors

Instructions: Open your HTML editor and then open the resources03.html file from the Data Files for Students. Eight HTML5 resource URLs are listed in the body section of this webpage, but the addresses are not configured as links. Refer to Figure 3–69 to create an unordered list of HTML5 resources using these URLs. You will also use professional web development best practices to indent, space, validate, and check the spelling of your work.

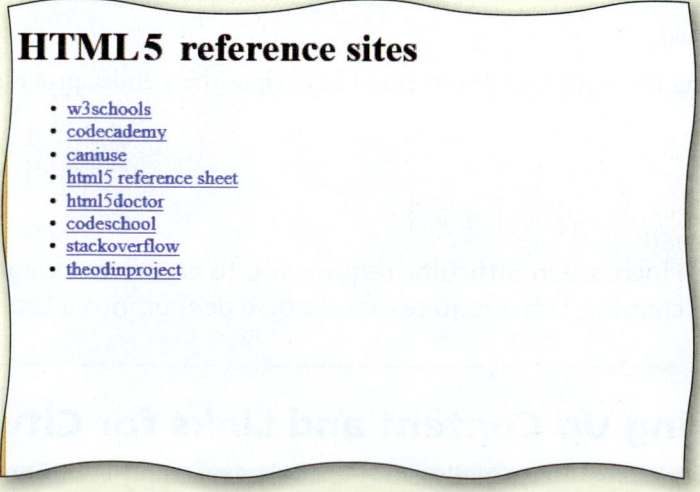

HTML5 reference sites

- w3schools
- codecademy
- caniuse
- html5 reference sheet
- html5doctor
- codeschool
- stackoverflow
- theodinproject

Figure 3–69

Continued >

Analyze, Correct, Improve *continued*

1. Correct

a. With the resources03.html file open in your HTML editor, modify the comment at the top of the page to include your name and today's date.

b. Enter **HTML5 resources** in the <title> tags.

c. Several URLs are listed in the <div id="main"> section of this webpage. Each is a reference to an HTML5 resource. Convert each URL to a link by using the URL as the value for the **href** attribute value and adding text for the link as shown in Figure 3–69.

d. Save the page, and then view it in a browser. Notice that all of the links are positioned on the same line.

e. Tap or click each of the eight links to test them.

2. Improve

a. The **anchor** element is an *inline* element, meaning that the content within the opening and closing <a> tags are displayed in the same line rather than on a new line. Most other paired elements such as all of the heading tags, **h1** through **h6, p, div, ul, ol, dl,** and **li** are *block* elements, meaning that the content within the opening and closing tags creates its own block by starting on a new line. Because this list of links would look better if each item were on its own line, mark up the links as an unordered list. Insert the opening **<ul>** tag on a new line after the <h1> content and before the first link. Add the closing **</ul>** tag after the last link and just before the closing </div> tag.

b. Indent and surround each link with an opening and closing list item tag **<li>** and **</li>** For example, the opening <ul> tag and first link would be coded as:

```
<ul>
  <li><a href="http://www.w3schools.com/">w3schools</a></li>
```

(*Hint:* Note that tags must be *nested properly*. For example, content marked by <li><a> tags must be closed as </a></li>. Improperly nested tags will cause validation errors.)

c. Save the page and view it in a browser. Because the <li> tags are block elements, each link creates its own block by starting on a new line.

d. Check the spelling of the content on the page.

e. Validate your webpage using the W3C validator found at validator.w3.org and fix any errors that are identified.

4. ✸ After reviewing the webpages documented by each of these links, provide a brief description of each website.

In the Lab

Labs 1 and 2, which increase in difficulty, require you to create webpages based on what you learned in the chapter; Lab 3 requires you to dive deeper into a topic covered in the chapter.

Lab 1: Marking Up Content and Links for City Farmer

Problem: You work for a local but rapidly growing gardening supply company called City Farmer that specializes in products that support food self-sufficiency. The company has hired you to add content in the form of images, headings, paragraphs, and lists to the home page. You will also identify several links. Create the webpage shown in Figure 3–70 that contains the textual content that City Farmer wants on their home page.

Figure 3–70

Instructions: Perform the following tasks:

1. Open the `cityfarmer03.html` file in your HTML editor and then modify the comment at the top of the page to include your name and today's date. Make sure the <title>…</title> tags contain the text `City Farmer Home Page`.

2. Delete the first comment in the header section and add an `img` element to insert the cityfarmer.jpg file as follows:

```
<img src="cityfarmer.jpg" alt="City Farmer logo" width="303"
height="252">
```

3. Change the <p>…</p> tags that mark up "City Farmer" in the `header` section to <h1>…</h1> tags.

4. Change the <p>…</p> tags that mark up "…today's urban cowboy" in the `header` section to <h2>…</h2> tags.

5. Modify the content in the `nav` section to create an unordered list of links to each of the future pages of the website as follows:

```
<ul>
    <li><a href="products.html">Products</a> </li>
    <li><a href="order.html">Order</a> </li>
    <li><a href="news.html">News</a> </li>
    <li><a href="events.html">Events</a> </li>
</ul>
```

(*Hint:* Note that the ending anchor tag, </a>, is positioned immediately after the word that becomes the link such as Products or Order. The ending anchor tag, </a>, does not include the nonbreaking space, ` `. This results in a clean link such as <u>Products</u> or <u>Order</u> instead of a link that adds a space on the end such as <u>Products </u>or <u>Order </u>.

Continued >

In the Lab *continued*

Also note that the closing list item tag, </li>, includes the nonbreaking space . The HTML validator will not allow any text, even a nonbreaking space, inside an unordered list <ul> that is not surrounded by list item <li>….</li> tags.)

6. In the `footer` section, modify the email address to be a hyperlink as follows:

   `<a href="mailto:feedback@cityfarmer.com">Send us an email</a>`

7. Validate your code and fix any errors.

8. Check the spelling of the text.

9. Save and open the page within a browser as shown in Figure 3–70.

10. Submit your assignment in the format specified by your instructor.

11. ✸ Current best practices are to code the links in the <nav> section as list items using <li>…</li> tags within an unordered list created with <ul>…</ul> tags. Why are these best practices recommended instead of coding the links as paragraph content using <p>…</p> tags or as heading content using <h1>…</h1> through <h6>…</h6> tags?

Lab 2: Creating a Home Page for Cycle Out Cancer

Problem: You are part of a philanthropic group of motorcyclists, Cycle Out Cancer, who participate in community events and parades to distribute cancer awareness information. Create the webpage shown in Figure 3–71 that marks up the content on the organization's home page.

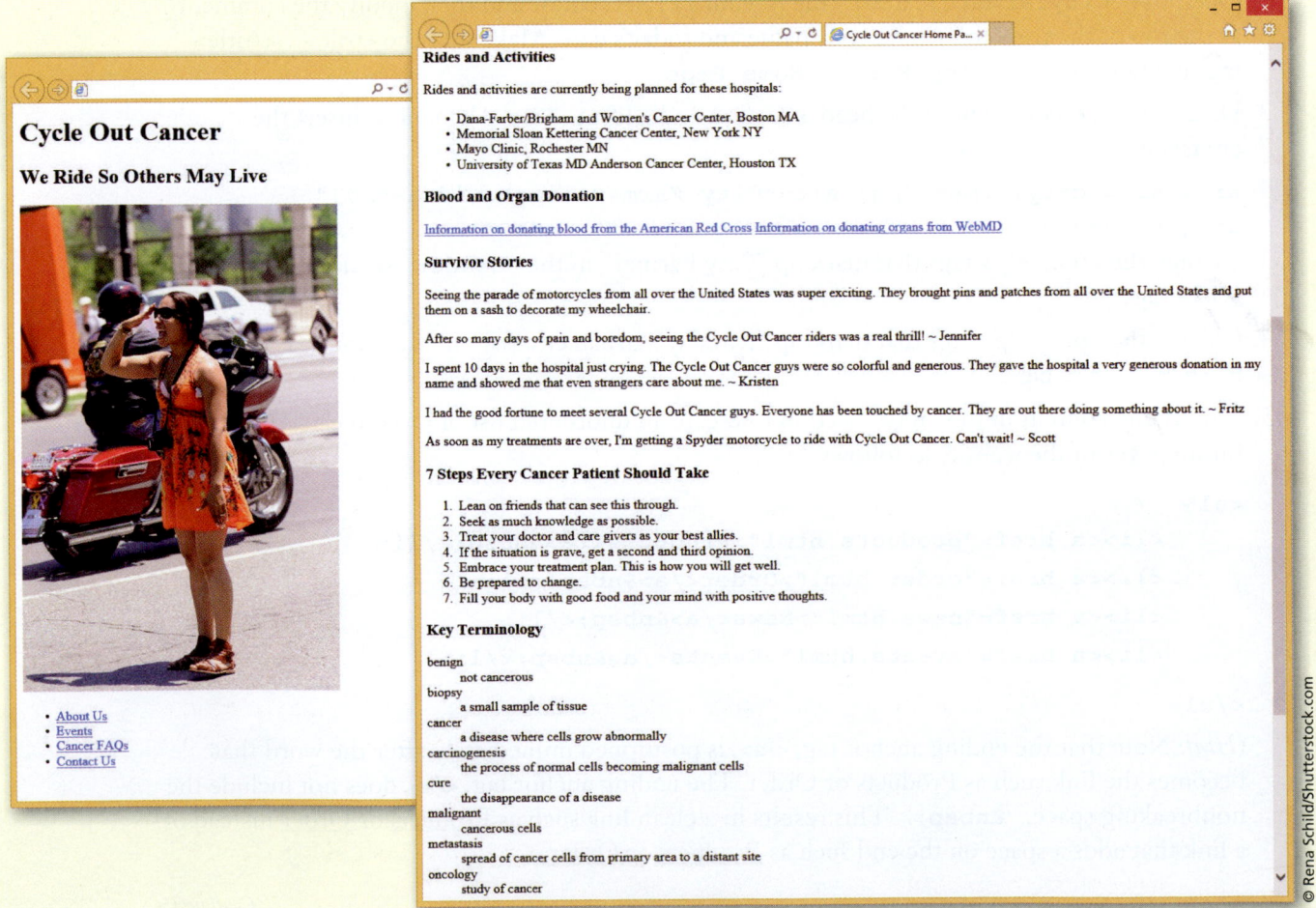

Figure 3–71

Instructions: Perform the following tasks:

1. Open the `cycle03.html` in your HTML editor and then modify the comment at the top of the page to include your name and today's date. Make sure the <title>…</title> tags contain the text `Cycle Out Cancer Home Page`.

2. Change the <p>…</p> tags that mark up "Cycle Out Cancer" in the `header` section to <h1>…</h1> tags.

3. Change the <p>…</p> tags that mark up "We Ride So Others May Live" in the `header` section to <h2>…</h2> tags.

4. Delete the <!-- add photo--> comment in the `header` section and add an `img` tag with the following attributes and values:

   ```
   src="cycle.jpg"
   alt="Woman saluting riders"
   width="385"
   height="578"
   ```

5. Modify the content in the nav section to create links to each of the future pages of the website with the href attribute values as follows:

   ```
   <a href="about.html">About Us</a>
   <a href="events.html">Events</a>
   <a href="faq.html">Cancer FAQs</a>
   <a href="contact.html">Contact Us</a>
   ```

6. Modify the list of links in the `nav` section to be indented list items using <li>…</li> tags within an unordered list created with <ul>…</ul> tags. The two nonbreaking space codes ` ` should be positioned after the closing </a> tag but before the closing </li> tag for each item.

7. In the <div id="main"> section, mark up the following headings with <h3>…</h3> tags:

   Rides and Activities
   Blood and Organ Donation
   Survivor Stories
   7 Steps Every Cancer Patient Should Take
   Key Terminology

8. Below the "Rides and Activities" heading in the <div id="main"> section, mark up the first line ("Rides and activities are…") with <p>…</p> tags. Mark up the list of four hospitals as an unordered list.

9. Below the "Blood and Organ Donation" heading in the <div id="main"> section, use the first URL as the `href` attribute value to create a link with the text `Information on donating blood from the American Red Cross`.

   Use the second URL as the `href` attribute value to create a link with the text `Information on donating organs from WebMD`.

10. Below the "Survivor Stories" heading in the <div id="main"> section, mark up the four testimonials using <p>…</p> tags. (*Hint:* Each paragraph ends with the name of a person.)

11. Below the "7 Steps Every Cancer Patient Should Take" heading in the <div id="main"> section, delete numbers 1 through 7, and then mark up and indent the seven steps as list items using <li>…</li> tags within an ordered list created with <ol>…</ol> tags.

12. Below the "Key Terminology" heading in the <div id="main"> section, mark up the entire section as a description list using <dl>…</dl> tags. Mark up each term as a definition term with <dt>…</dt> tags and each definition with <dd>…</dd> tags.

Continued >

In the Lab *continued*

13. Validate your code and fix any errors.

14. Check the spelling of the text.

15. Save and open the page within a browser as shown in Figure 3–71.

16. Submit your assignment in the format specified by your instructor.

17. ✳ It's easy to confuse head, header, and heading HTML elements. Describe the purpose for each.

Lab 3: Expand Your World
HTML Terminology and Syntax

Problem: Every programming language has its own body of terminology needed to describe the components and capabilities of the language. In addition, every programming language has unique syntax, or rules, by which the code must be authored. In this exercise, you will create a large HTML description list to mark up some of the key terms and definitions for html. The final webpage is shown in Figure 3–72.

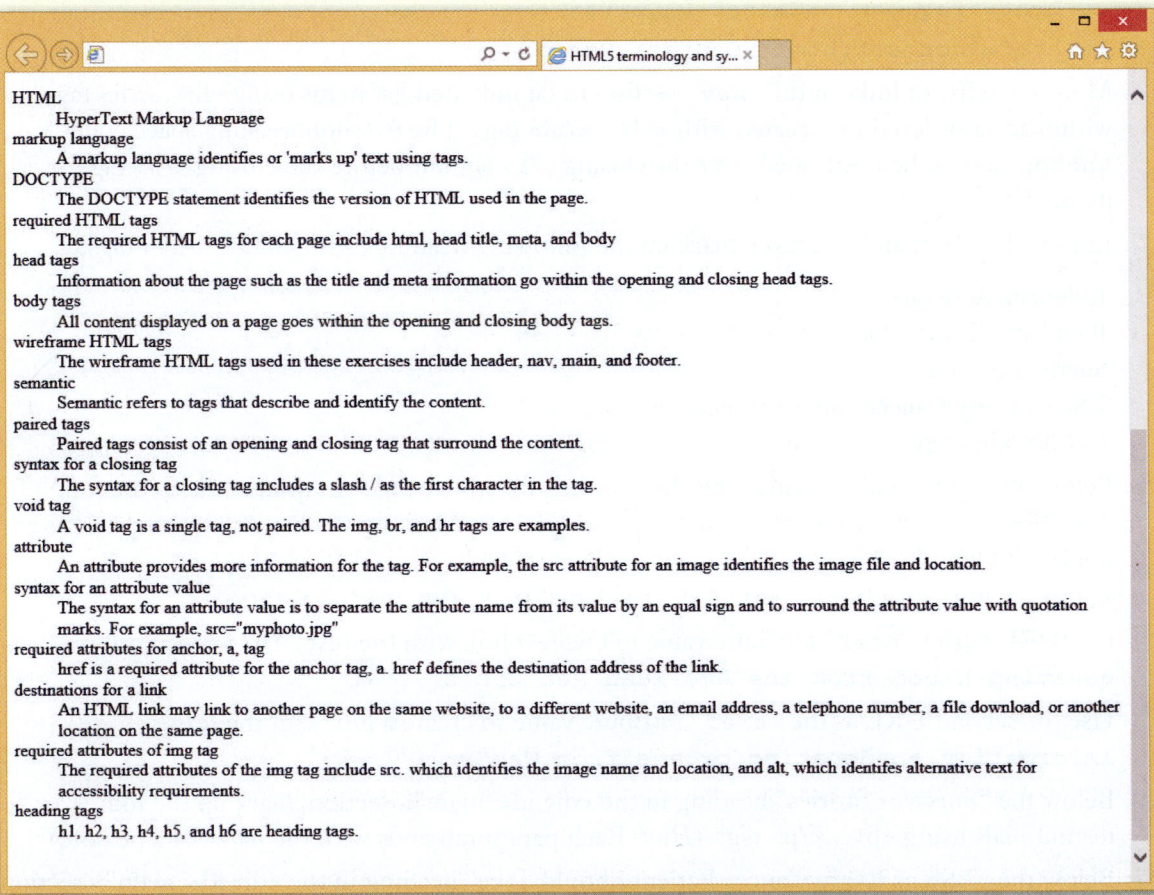

Figure 3–72

Instructions:

1. Open `terminology03.html` in your HTML editor and then modify the comment at the top of the page to include your name and today's date. Enter `HTML5 terminology and syntax` within the <title> tags.

2. Using the information in this chapter as well as the web, mark up the entire content in the <div id="terminology"> section as a description list using <dl>…</dl> tags. Mark up each term as a term using <dt>…</dt> tags.

3. After each term, research and enter a definition for that term using <dd>…</dd> tags. Indent the definition under the term it defines as shown in Figure 3–72.

4. Validate your code and fix any errors.

5. Check the spelling of the text.

6. Save and open the page within a browser as shown in Figure 3–72.

7. Submit your assignment in the format specified by your instructor.

8. ✸ Identify three problems that might occur for a web developer if the terminology and syntax discussed in this exercise are not understood.

Consider This: Your Turn

Apply your creative thinking and problem-solving skills to design and implement a solution.

1. Create the Home Page for Your Personal Portfolio Website

Personal

Part 1: In Chapter 2, you completed a wireframe and site map for your personal portfolio website in the `portfolio.html` webpage. In this exercise, you will update that page with content and HTML tags. Include the following updates:

1. Add an `img` tag as the first line in the `header` section with a professional picture of yourself. Be sure to include appropriate values for the `alt, width,` and `height` attributes. (*Hint:* To determine the actual width and height measurements of any image, open it in an image-editing program such as Paint or Photoshop. Information about the file's width and height measurements is usually presented in the status bar of the program. If your image is larger than 500 × 500 pixels, use the image-editing program to resize the image to make it as small and efficient for the web as possible. As you resize the image, be careful to maintain the current width/height ratio so that you do not skew or distort the image.)

2. In the `nav` section, create an unordered list of links to future pages that link to `education.html, experience.html, samples.html,` and `contact.html`.

3. To make sure the webpage will render successfully in all browsers, identify the main section using the <div id="main"> and </div> tags versus <main> and </main>, and include three <h2> headings in that section that mark up the headings of `Strengths, Technologies,` and `Other`.

4. Include paragraph content listing *your* strengths, technologies, and other applicable business skills below each <h2> heading.

5. Add an email hyperlink and a telephone hyperlink to the email and telephone content in the `header` section.

6. Validate and correct your webpage, spell check the content, and submit your assignment in the format specified by your instructor.

Part 2: ✸ Use your favorite search engine to find articles on search engine optimization (SEO). Identify three tips that you can add to your webpage to improve its SEO performance.

Continued >

Consider This: Your Turn *continued*

2. Create the Home Page for a Web Development and Consulting Business

Professional

Part 1: In Chapter 2, you completed a wireframe and site map for the web development firm website in the `webdev.html` webpage. In this exercise, you will update that page with content and HTML tags. Submit your assignment in the format specified by your instructor.

Validate and correct your webpage, spell check the content, and submit your assignment in the format specified by your instructor.

1. Save the webdev.html page as `index.html` because it will serve as your home page for this site.

2. Add an `img` tag as the first line in the `header` section using the company logo stored in the Data Files for Students as webdevpros.jpg with the following attribute values:

   ```
   alt="WebDevPros logo"
   height="260"
   width="389"
   ```

3. In the `nav` section, create an unordered list of links to future pages that link to `index.html`, `services.html`, `testimonials.html`, `aboutus.html`, and `contactus.html`.

4. To make sure the webpage will render successfully in all browsers, identify the main section using the <div id="main"> and </div> tags versus <main> and </main>.

5. Save the page and then save it with the name `services.html`.

6. In the services.html page, create content in the <div id="main"> section using this text within <p>...</p> tags:

   ```
   WebDevPros offers a full stack of web development services
   from front-end webpage design and development through back-end
   e-commerce solutions. Our development principles consider these web
   development strategies:
   ```

7. In the services.html page, below the paragraph in the <div id="main"> section, create a description list of five principles of web development that start with these three terms. Code the phrases as data terms using <dt>...</dt> tags and their definitions using <dd>...</dd> tags.

   Term: `Separation of presentation, content, and behavior where prudent`
   Definition: `Striving to use html to describe the structure of content, external css style sheets to style and position the content, and external JavaScript files to create interactions between the webpage and the user.`

   Term: `Responsive Web Design`
   Definition: `Building websites to provide an optimal viewing experience across a wide range of devices.`

   Term: `Progressive Enhancement`
   Definition: `Designing websites using a layered approach that provides basic content and functionality to all users while providing enhanced functionality to those using advanced technology.`

   (Add two more terms and definitions that relate to web development.)

Part 2: ✺ In Chapter 2, you contacted a web development consulting firm to interview them about a successful project to showcase as content on your home page. Open the index.html page and save it as `testimonials.html`. Delete the existing content in the <div id="main"> section. Using information from your interview, create a three- or four-sentence testimonial from a satisfied customer and enter it within paragraph tags within the <div id="main"> section. The testimonial will be fictitious, but strive to make it professional and realistic.

Validate and correct your webpages, spell check the content, and check the links between the index.html, testimonial.html, and services.html pages. Submit your assignment in the format specified by your instructor.

3. Create the Home Page for the Dog Hall of Fame

Research and Collaboration

Part 1: In Chapter 2, you completed a wireframe and site map for the Dog Hall of Fame website in the `dogfame.html` webpage. In this exercise, you'll update that page with content and HTML tags. Submit your assignment in the format specified by your instructor.

1. Save the dogfame.html page as `index.html` because it will serve as your home page for this site.

2. Add the banner.jpg image as the first line of content in the <header> section with the following attribute values:

   ```
   alt="banner logo for Dog Hall of Fame"
   height="300"
   width="720"
   ```

3. Create an unordered list of links to future pages that link to `index.html`, `winners.html`, and `nominations.html` in the `nav` section.

4. In Chapter 2, your team collected content, images, and stories to add to the Dog Hall of Fame website in these three areas: Hero dog, Working dog, and Companion dog. Add that content to the <div id="main"> section of the index.html page using heading, paragraph, and list tags as appropriate. Four dog images are provided in the Data Files for Students if needed for this project.

5. Validate and correct your webpage, spell check the content, and check the links between the index.html page and the services.html page. Submit your assignment in the format specified by your instructor.

Part 2: ✺ Anytime you gather information or images from the web, copyright laws and academic fair use policies and ethics come into play. Work with your instructor to identify and apply the fair use and copyright policies that apply to the content you gather on the Internet as applied to the exercises for this class.

4 | Applying CSS Styles to Webpages

Objectives

You will have mastered the material in this chapter when you can:

- Explain the importance of separating design from content

- Describe Cascading Style Sheets (CSS)

- Define inline, embedded, and external styles and their order of precedence

- Describe a CSS rule and its syntax

- Explain the difference between a selector, property, and value

- Create styles that use text and color properties

- Explain the difference between inline and block content

- Describe the CSS box model and how to apply margins, padding, and borders

- Create an external style sheet and link it to an HTML page

- Create styles that use padding, border, and margin properties

- Float an image

- Create styles that use list properties

- Add comments to an external style sheet

- Validate a CSS file

4 | Applying CSS Styles to Webpages

Introduction

Creating a well-designed website that captures your audience's attention is vital in attracting and obtaining new customers. To do so, a web developer can use formatting such as font styles, font colors, white space, and background colors or images to increase the visual appeal of the webpages. Websites developed with HTML5 alone can be functional, but they lack this important element of visual appeal. To improve the appearance of a website by including color, formatting text, and adding margins, borders, and shadows, for example, you need to apply styles created with **Cascading Style Sheets (CSS)**, a language you use to describe the formatting of a document written in a markup language such as HTML5. While HTML provides the structural foundation of a webpage, you use CSS styles to determine the formatting for a webpage. By defining CSS styles in a style sheet separate from the HTML code, you can format a webpage in an unlimited number of ways, such as changing the background color of the webpage, increasing the size of text or bolding it, applying margins to a section, and adding borders to elements.

Project — Format Webpages with CSS

In previous chapters, you created a website template and three webpages for the Forward Fitness Club website. You also added content and links to the home page, the About Us page, and the Contact Us page. However, these pages lack formatting to enhance their appearance.

In Chapter 2, you created a website plan to guide the design and development of the Forward Fitness Club website. The plan provides information about the desired typography and colors to enhance the business brand and logo. The plan includes a wireframe, which specifies passive white space between HTML elements. To add these design elements according to your plan, you create and apply CSS styles in an external style sheet, a separate file that contains the styles for the website.

The project in this chapter enhances a website with CSS. You apply styles to the HTML5 elements on each page to give the site a certain look and feel. After creating a style sheet, you link it to all of the pages in the website, including the template. As you add styles to the style sheet, they immediately format the attached webpages when you open or refresh the pages in a browser. Figure 4–1 shows the home page after it has been enhanced by CSS.

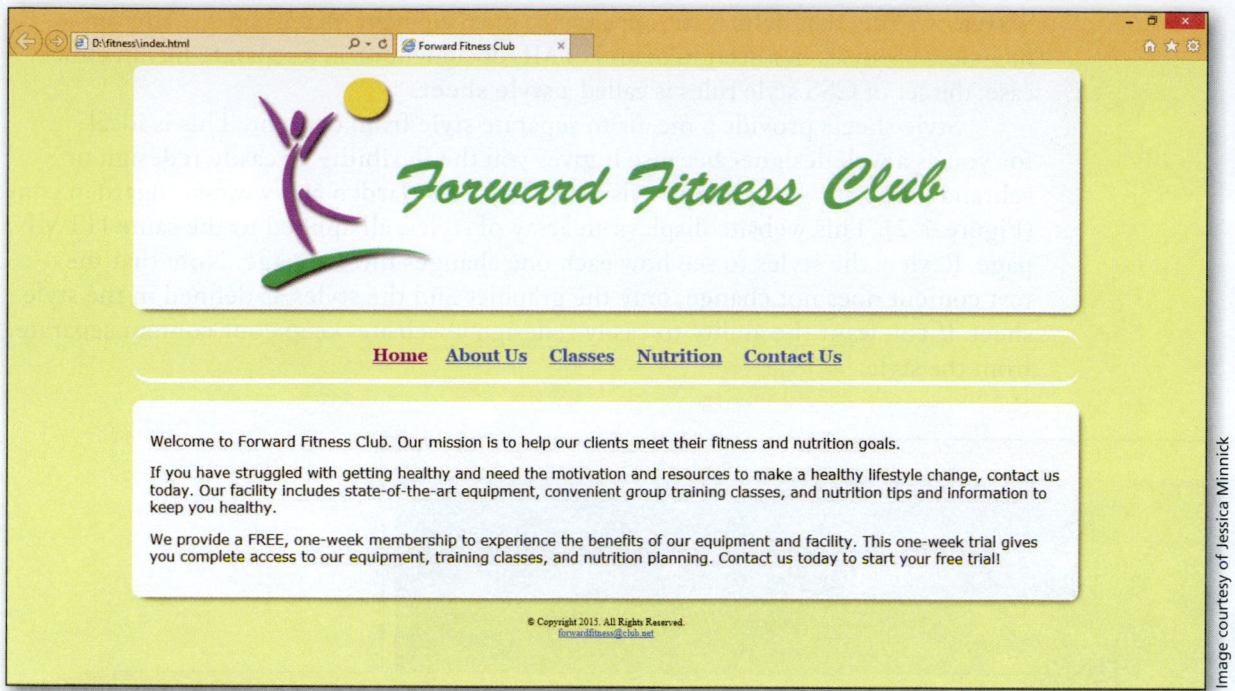

Figure 4–1

Roadmap

In this chapter, you will learn how to create the webpage shown in Figure 4–1. The following roadmap identifies general activities you will perform as you progress through this chapter:

1. CREATE a CSS FILE.
2. LINK HTML PAGES TO a CSS FILE.
3. CREATE STYLE RULES.
4. ADD COMMENTS to the CSS file.
5. VALIDATE the CSS FILE.

At the beginning of step instructions throughout the chapter, you will see an abbreviated form of this roadmap. The abbreviated roadmap uses colors to indicate chapter progress: gray means the chapter is beyond that activity; blue means the task being shown is covered in that activity; and black means that activity is yet to be covered. For example, the following abbreviated roadmap indicates the chapter would be showing a task in the 4 ADD COMMENTS activity.

1 CREATE CSS FILE | 2 LINK PAGES TO CSS FILE | 3 CREATE STYLE RULES
4 ADD COMMENTS | 5 VALIDATE CSS FILE

Use the abbreviated roadmap as a progress guide while you read or step through the instructions in this chapter.

Using Cascading Style Sheets

Although HTML allows web developers to make changes to the structure and content of a webpage, HTML is limited in its ability to define the appearance of one or more webpages. Instead, you use CSS styles to position and format elements on a webpage.

A **style** is a rule that defines the appearance of an element on a webpage. You can include CSS styles in a section of an HTML document or in a separate file. In either case, the set of CSS style rules is called a **style sheet**.

Style sheets provide a means to separate style from content. This is ideal for you as a web designer because it gives you the flexibility to easily redesign or rebrand a website. For example, visit the CSS Zen Garden at www.csszengarden.com (Figure 4–2). This website displays an array of styles, all applied to the same HTML page. Review the styles to see how each one changes the webpage. Note that the text content does not change, only the graphics and the styles as defined in the style sheet. If you want the ability to easily redesign a website, keep your content separate from the style.

Figure 4–2

Separating content from style is even more important when you are maintaining a large website. You can define styles in a single CSS style sheet file, and then attach the single file to several webpages to apply the styles to all the attached pages. If you decide to use a different background color on all the webpages in the site, for example, you can make one change to the CSS style sheet to automatically update every page. Not only does this save a lot of time, it also means less maintenance for you or another web developer. If the site contained styles in the HTML code, locating those styles and removing them could be a time-consuming process.

CSS was developed by the W3C and is still evolving. The first version of CSS, CSS 1, was released in 1996. This version of CSS included styles for text, color, alignment, borders, padding, and margins. The second version of CSS, CSS 2, was released two years later in 1998 and included new styles to control the positioning of elements. The latest version of CSS is CSS3, which adds many new style features, including shadows, rounded borders, and enhanced text effects. CSS3 is currently still in working draft status at the W3C, which means W3C members, the public, and other technical organizations are reviewing it and might change its details. For a full list of CSS3 styles, visit w3.org. To work with an excellent tutorial for HTML5 elements and CSS3 properties, visit w3schools.com.

Modern browsers support CSS 1 and 2 and many of the new CSS3 features. However, browsers may vary in how they apply CSS styles, so be sure to test and view your site in all the major browsers. Visit www.quirksmode.org to learn which browsers support each CSS style.

The W3C developed CSS as the primary way to format webpages, so you should not use HTML tags to style page content. Tags, such as the <font> tag, have been deemed as obsolete by W3C and should not be used.

Inline Styles

CSS supports inline, embedded (or internal), and external styles. With an **inline style**, you add a style to the start tag for an element, such as a heading or paragraph, using the **style attribute**. The style changes the content marked up by a specific pair of tags, but does not affect other content in the document. Because inline styles take precedence over other types of styles and affect the style for individual pieces of content, they are helpful when you need to format only one section of a webpage in a unique way. However, inline styles defeat the purpose and advantages of separating style from content, so they should be used sparingly. An example of an inline style is shown in Figure 4–3. The style rule applies only to the content in this `h1` element, the "Special Note" text. In the starting <h1> tag, you begin writing an inline style using the `style` attribute. The inline style shown in Figure 4–3 defines the font color of the "Special Note" text as navy blue.

BTW

Deprecated and Unsupported Elements

A **deprecated** element or attribute is one that is outdated. Deprecated elements may become obsolete in the future, though most browsers continue to support deprecated elements for backward compatibility. In addition, many tags and attributes are not supported by HTML5, as noted in Appendix A. You can also visit w3c.org to find a list of deprecated HTML tags.

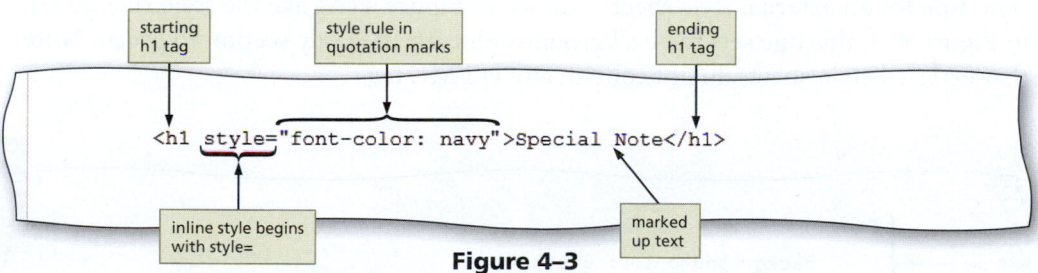

Figure 4–3

Embedded Style Sheets

An **embedded style sheet**, also called an **internal style sheet**, includes the style sheet within the opening <head> and closing </head> tags of the HTML document. Use an embedded style sheet when you want to create styles for a single webpage that are different from the rest of the website. An embedded style sheet takes precedence over an external style sheet. An example of an embedded style sheet is shown in Figure 4–4. In embedded style sheets, you place the style rules between the opening <style> and closing </style> tags. The style rule shown in Figure 4–4 sets the background color for the body section to green for the current webpage only.

Figure 4–4

External Style Sheets

An **external style sheet**, also called a **linked style sheet**, is a CSS file that contains all of the styles you want to apply to more than one page in the website. An external style sheet is a text file with the **.css** file extension. To apply an external style sheet, you link it (or attach it) to a webpage using a link tag in the head section of the webpage. External style sheets give you the most flexibility to quickly change webpage formats because the styles in an external style sheet are applied to every page linked to that style sheet. Changing the look of an entire website is sometimes called **reskinning** the website. You will create an external style sheet for the Forward Fitness Club's website to enhance the styles of the **body,** the **div id="container",** **header, nav, main,** and **footer** sections, lists, and classes. An example of a style rule for an external style sheet is shown in Figure 4–5. Like the style rule shown in Figure 4–4, this one sets the background color for the body section to green. Note that external style sheets do not contain any HTML tags.

Figure 4–5

Style Sheet Precedence

Style sheets are said to "cascade" because each type of style has a specified level of precedence (or priority) in relationship to the others. For example, suppose you create an inline style to change the text color of an **h1** heading to red. In the **head** section of a webpage, you also create a style in an embedded style sheet to change **h1** headings to blue, and in an external style sheet, you create a style to change **h1** headings to green. What color would **h1** headings be in the webpage with the inline style? They would be red because the style closest to the content takes precedence. In other words, inline styles beat embedded styles, and embedded styles beat external styles.

CSS properties can be inherited from a parent element. This principle is called **inheritance**. For example, paragraphs and headings inherit the font and color rules for the body selector. If a selector has more than one CSS rule, **specificity** determines which CSS rule to apply. The more specific selector is applied. For example, if the value of the background-color property for the body selector is green but the one for p is blue, the p elements will have a blue background because the p selector is more specific than the body selector.

The best practice is to apply inline styles when you want to control the style of content within one pair of HTML tags, an embedded style sheet when you want to change the style of one page, and external or linked style sheets for the styles that apply to many or all pages in the website.

Web designers use external style sheets for most of their styles for many reasons. First, they can create or modify all of the styles in one style sheet file and then link the file to all of the HTML documents. This provides consistency throughout the website and lessens the need for coding beyond the single style sheet. Second, when an HTML document is linked to a CSS file, the page can load in a browser quickly. Third, if web designers need to change the appearance of a particular HTML element, they can do so in one file. The browser applies the change to all of the linked pages, reducing errors and redundancies.

CSS Basics

To write an inline CSS style, you use a style attribute within the HTML element, as shown in Figure 4–3. To write a CSS style, or rule, for an embedded or external style sheet, you write a statement that follows the CSS syntax. Each CSS rule consists of a selector and a declaration. See Figure 4–6.

Figure 4–6

The **selector** is the part of the statement that identifies what to style. Any HTML5 element such as body, header, nav, main, or footer may be a selector. For example, if you want to format the content in the `body` section of a webpage, use `body` as the selector in the style statement. A selector may also be the value of an id or class attribute. For example, if you want to format the content in the `div id="container"` section, use `#container` as the selector. (You will learn about including a # sign with selectors shortly.)

The **declaration** defines the exact formatting of the style. A declaration consists of a property and a value, separated by a colon and followed by a semicolon (;). The **property** identifies the style quality or characteristic to apply, such as color (text color), background-color, text-indent, border-width, or font-style. A declaration includes at least one property to apply to the selected element.

For each property, the declaration includes a related **value** that identifies the particular property value to apply, such as green for color or 150% for font-size. You can use only certain values with each property based on the styles that property can define. The font-color property, for example, can accept navy as a value, but cannot

BTW

Style Rule Syntax
The correct syntax for styles is to use all lowercase letters for the property name without any spaces. The same is true for values: use all lowercase characters and no spaces.

accept 150% because that is not a valid value for the color property. See Appendix B for a list of properties and valid values.

Figure 4–7 shows the correct syntax for the style rule shown in Figure 4–4 and Figure 4–5. To create a style for an embedded or external style sheet, you first identify the selector, followed by a space and an opening brace. Next, you specify the property, followed by a colon, and then provide a value for the property, followed by a semicolon. Close the rule with a closing brace.

Figure 4–7

CONSIDER THIS

What is the difference between HTML attributes and CSS properties?
You use attributes in HTML elements to define more information for an element. Enter an attribute in an element's start tag as a name="value" pair. For example, in an `img` element, you include an attribute such as `src="logo.png"` to specify the source of the image. In this example, "src" is the attribute name and "logo.png" is the value. In a similar way, a CSS style defines the formatting for one or more elements. A style rule includes a selector and a declaration that consists of a property: value; pair. For example, `h1 {color: blue;}` formats `h1` elements using blue text. Enter a declaration for a selector in a style sheet.

CSS Text Properties

You can use CSS styles to format webpage text in a variety of ways. For example, use the font-family property to define a specific font. Use the font-size property to define a specific font size.

Table 4–1 lists common text properties and values.

Table 4–1 Common Text Properties and Values		
Property	**Description**	**Common Values**
font-family	Specific and general font names	font-family: Cambria, "Times New Roman", serif; font-family: Verdana, Arial, sans-serif; font-family: Georgia, "Times New Roman", serif;
font-size	Absolute or relative size of a font	font-size: 1.5em; font-size: 50%; font-size: x-large; font-size: 14pt;
font-weight	Weight of a font	font-weight: bold; font-weight: bolder; font-weight: lighter;
font-style	Style of a font	font-style: normal; font-style: italic; font-style: oblique;
text-align	Alignment of text	text-align: center; text-align: right; text-align: justify;
color	Color of text	color: red; color: blue; color: green;

Notice that the font-family property may include multiple values. In fact, you should provide more than one value for this property in case the browser does not support the primary font. The additional values are called **fallback values**. If the browser does not support the primary font, it displays the second font family indicated and if the browser does not support the second font family value, the browser uses the next font family. Commas separate each value. The desired value is listed first and the value of serif or sans-serif is listed last. For example, the declaration `font-family: Cambria, "Times New Roman", serif;` means that the browser should use the Cambria font; if the browser cannot use Cambria, it should use Times New Roman, which is listed in quotation marks because the font family name contains more than one word. Finally, if the browser does not support Cambria or Times New Roman, it should use its default serif font.

BTW
Font Names
The W3C recommends quoting font family names that contain spaces, digits, or punctuation characters other than hyphens.

Why would a browser not support certain fonts?

Fonts are installed on a computer, so a computer must have the font installed before a browser can display it. For a list of common web fonts, visit www.w3schools.com/cssref/css_websafe_fonts.asp.

CONSIDER THIS

CSS measures font size using many measurement units, including pixels, points, and ems, and by keyword or percentage. Table 4–2 lists units for measuring font size.

Table 4–2 Font Size Measurement Units			
Unit	**Definition**	**Example**	**Comments**
em	Relative to the default font size of the element	font-size: 1.25em;	Recommended by W3C; sizes are relative to the browser's default font size
%	Relative to the default font size of the element	font-size: 50%;	Recommended by W3C; sizes are relative to the browser's default font size
px	Number of pixels	font-size: 25px;	Depends on screen resolution
pt	Number of points	font-size: 12pt;	Use for printing webpages
keyword	Relative to a limited range of sizes	font-size: xx-small;	Sizes are relative to the browser's default font size, but size options are limited

The em is a relative measurement unit that the W3C recommends for values of the font-size property. The size of an em is relative to the current font size of the element. For example, 1.25em means 1.25 times the size of the current font. If a browser displays paragraphs using 16-point text by default, a font-size property value of 1em is 16 points and 1.25em is 20 points.

Percentage measurements work in a similar way. A font-size property value of 2em and of 200% appear the same when displayed in a browser. Note that no spaces appear in the font-size property value, so 1.25em and 50% are correct, but 1.25 em is not correct.

CSS Colors

One way to help capture a webpage visitor's attention is to use color as a webpage background or for text, borders, or links. HTML uses color names or codes to designate color values. When using a color name, you specify a word such as aqua or black as a value. Following are 16 basic color names. For more color names, visit www.w3schools.com/htmL/html_colornames.asp.

aqua	navy
black	olive
blue	purple
fuchsia	red
gray	silver
green	teal
lime	white
maroon	yellow

Color codes are more commonly used in web design. You can use two types of color codes with CSS: hexadecimal and RGB.

Hexadecimal values consist of a six-digit number code that corresponds to **RGB (Red, Green, Blue)** color values. When noting color values in CSS, include a number sign (#) before the code. Hexadecimal is a combination of the base-16 numbering system, which includes letters A through F. An example of a hexadecimal color value is 0000FF, which is blue. The first two digits (00) indicate the red value, which is none in this case. The next two digits (00) indicate the green value, which is also none in this case. The last two digits (FF) indicate the blue value. Because FF is the highest two-digit hexadecimal number, 0000FF specifies a pure blue.

RGB notation is used to display colors on a screen, though not in print. RGB blends red, green, and blue color channels to create a color. (A **channel** contains the number of red, green, or blue pixels necessary to create a specified color.) Each color channel is expressed as a number, 0 through 255. For example, the color blue is expressed as rgb(0,0,255). The first number represents the red color channel. The zero represents no pixels from a color channel; in the example, color channels red and green contribute no pixels to the color. The last channel represents the blue color channel; the number 255 represents the truest form of the color channel, in this case, blue. Hexadecimal 0000FF and rgb(0,0,255) are two ways of expressing the same color, pure blue.

Table 4–3 shows a common list of colors, with the corresponding hexadecimal and RGB color codes.

BTW

Colors

For more information about webpage colors, see Appendix C, which includes a list of websites that can help you determine the name, hexadecimal number, and RGB value for colors.

BTW

Quick Color Picker

W3 Schools provides a quick color picker reference at www.w3schools.com/tags/ref_colorpicker.asp. Here, you can select a color, view various shades of the color, and find the hexadecimal color value.

Table 4–3 Color Values		
Color	**Hexadecimal**	**RGB**
Black	#000000	rgb(0,0,0)
White	#FFFFFF	rgb(255,255,255)
Red	#FF0000	rgb(255,0,0)
Green	#008000	rgb(0,128,0)
Blue	#0000FF	rgb(0,0,255)
Yellow	#FFFF00	rgb(255,255,0)
Orange	#FFA500	rgb(255,165,0)
Gray	#808080	rgb(128,128,128)

To use a color in a style rule declaration, use the color value as the property value. For example, to style a background color as gray, you use the background-color property with a value of #808080, as shown in the following example:

```
background-color: #808080;
```

Understanding Inline Elements and Block Elements

When you format webpages with CSS, you set rules that describe how the HTML elements should appear in a browser. As you create rules for the elements, review the structure of the HTML document because it plays a part in how a browser displays the element on a webpage.

HTML elements are positioned on the webpage as a block or as inline content. A **block element** appears as a block because it starts and ends with a new line, such as the main element or a paragraph element. Block elements can contain content, other block elements, and inline elements. **Inline elements** are displayed without line breaks so they flow within the same line. Inline content always appears within block elements. Examples of inline elements are the span tag (<span>) and the anchor tag (<a>). You use the span element to group inline elements. To format one or more words in a paragraph, for example, include an inline style in the opening span tag that groups the words, as in the following example, which formats only "Warning" in red text.

```
<span style="color: red;">"Warning"</span>
```

An **img** element is also an inline element because it flows in the same line, although it has natural height and width properties unlike other inline elements. Figure 4–8 shows an example of an inline element in a block element.

Figure 4–8

Header, nav, main, and footer are all examples of block elements. When you apply CSS styles to these block elements in the website you created for the Forward Fitness Club, you must consider their hierarchical structure to produce the visual effect you intend. Styles applied to elements below or above another element can affect their placement on a webpage. For example, as a block element, the **header** element normally starts on a new line and spans the width of the webpage. A new line also appears after the **header** element. If you want the **nav** element to appear to the right of the header, apply styles to both the **header** element and the **nav** element to accomplish this effect.

CSS Box Model

Each block element such as a header, nav, main, and footer element has a top, right, bottom, and left side. In other words, the element is displayed in a browser as a box with content. The **CSS box model** describes these boxes of content on a webpage. Each content box can have margins, borders, and padding, as shown in Figure 4–9. You refer to the sides of a box in clockwise order: top, right, bottom, and left.

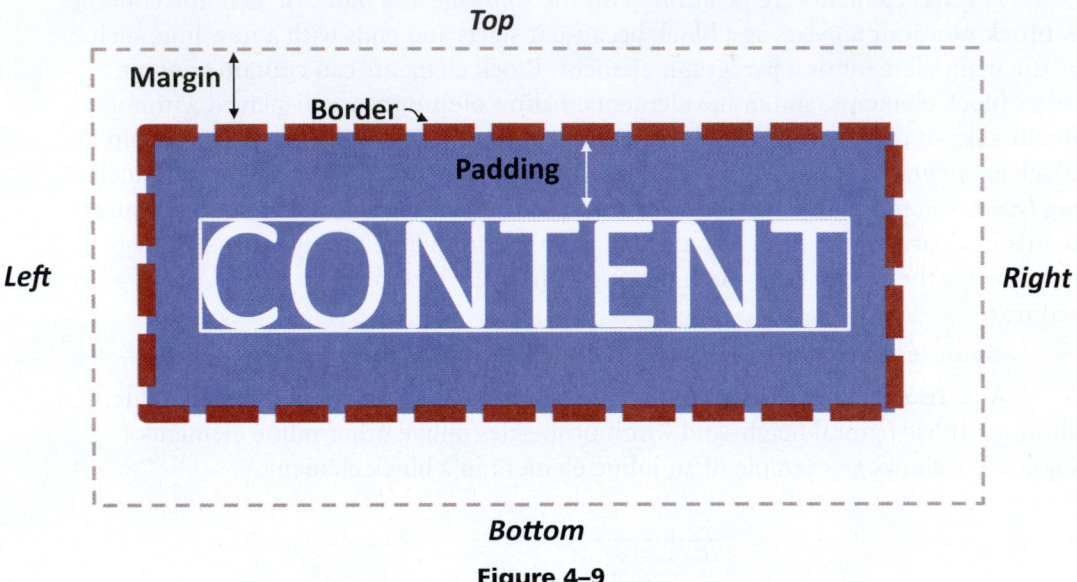

Figure 4–9

The **margin** provides passive white space between block elements or between the top or bottom of a webpage. You can define margins at the top, right, bottom, and left of a block element. Margins are transparent and are measured in pixels (px), ems (em), or percentages (%).

The **border** separates the padding and the margin of the block element. A border can vary in thickness and color and can be defined at the top, right, bottom, and left sides of a block element. A border can also have a style such as solid, dashed, or dotted.

Padding is the passive white space between the content and the border of a block element. Padding is typically measured in pixels (px), ems (em), or percentages (%). By default, padding is set to 0px, so paragraph text, for example, appears at the edges of the block element. You can increase the padding to improve legibility. The box model shown in Figure 4–9 includes more than the default amount of padding. The background color for the padding and content is always the same.

Using CSS, you can set the margin, border, or padding properties for all four sides of a block element using a single declaration. For example, the following declaration sets the top, right, bottom, and left margins of a block element to 2em:

```
margin: 2em;
```

You can use a similar shorthand notation to set the style, width, and color for all four sides of a block element's border. The property values can appear in any order. The following declaration sets the top, right, bottom, and left borders of a block element to a solid line using a width of 1 pixel and a color of black:

```
border: solid 1px #000000;
```

Writing the declaration using shorthand notation is helpful when all four sides of the block element use the same property values. If you want to use different property values on one or more sides of the block element, include a declaration for each side of the block element. For example, you can use the following declarations to set the padding for each side of a block element:

```
padding-top: 5px;

padding-right: 15px;

padding-bottom: 12px;

padding-left: 10px;
```

You can set even more specific property options for the border, such as border-top-width and border-right-color. For example, the following declaration sets only the left border of the block element to a width of 2 pixels:

```
border-left-width: 2px;
```

Table 4–4 lists common CSS box model properties used to style block elements.

Table 4–4 Common CSS Box Model Properties

Property	Description	Examples
margin	Sets the amount of space around the block element (top, right, bottom, left)	margin: 20px; margin-top: 2em; margin-bottom: 150%;
padding	Sets the amount of space between content and the border of its block element	padding: 10px; padding-left: 1.5em; padding-right: 125%;
border	Sets the format of the block element's border	border: solid 1px #000000;
border-style	Designates the style of a border	border-top-style: solid; border-top-style: dotted;
border-width	Designates the width of a border	border-top-width: 1px; border-bottom-width: thick;
border-color	Designates the border color	border-top-color: #000000; border-bottom-color: gray;
border-radius	Rounds the corners of a block element's border	border-radius: 10px;
box-shadow	Adds a shadow to a block element's border	box-shadow: 8px 8px 8px #000000;

To have a border appear around the content in a block element, you must specify a border style in a CSS statement. You can include the style value with the border property or use the border-style property with an assigned value.

The border-radius and box-shadow properties are new to CSS3. As with the other border properties, you can list more than one value to set the top, right, bottom, and left radius values for the border. For the box-shadow property, you must specify the horizontal and vertical offset measurements. In addition, you can set the distance of the shadow's blur, the size of the shadow, and its color. The default color is black.

BTW

CSS Box Properties
Appendix B contains a comprehensive list of the CSS box properties and their acceptable values.

Creating an External Style Sheet

To create styles that apply to more than one webpage in a website, use an external style sheet. Recall that an external style sheet is a text file that contains the style rules (selectors and declarations) you want to apply to more than one page in the website.

Using an external style sheet involves two steps. First, use a text editor to create and save a document with a .css extension. In the CSS document, create style rules for elements such as body, header, nav, main, and footer to improve the visual appeal of the website. Use styles to add color and borders, apply text properties, align items, and increase white space for padding and margins. Next, link the CSS file to the webpages that should be formatted using the styles defined in the external style sheet.

Selectors

Recall that a style rule begins with a selector, which specifies the element to style. A selector can be an HTML element name, an id attribute value, or a class attribute value. If the selector is an HTML element, you use the element name for the selector. Figure 4–10 shows how a selector in a CSS file selects the content to be styled for an HTML element, an id attribute, and a class attribute for HTML elements in an HTML file.

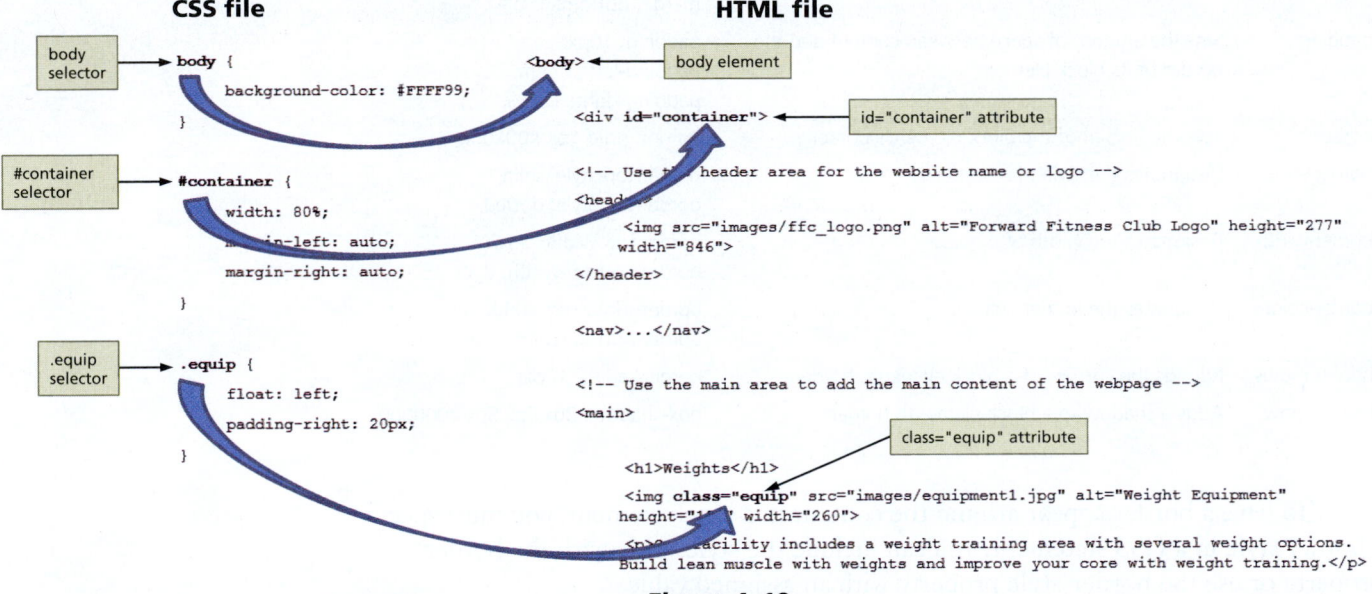

Figure 4–10

For example, to style the header element, use **header** as the name of the selector. To define the style of all p elements so they display white text on a black background, use the following style rule:

```
p {
  color: white;
  background-color: black;
}
```

If you want to apply styles to some p elements but not others, for example, you can create an id or a class selector. An **id selector** uses the id attribute value of an HTML element to select a single element. To create an id selector, you begin the style rule with a number sign (#) followed by the id attribute value. For example, to style the `div id="container"` element, use `#container` as the selector. The following style rule applies a solid 2-pixel border to only the `div id="container"` element:

```
#container {
  border: solid 2px;
}
```

Use a **class selector** to select elements that include a certain class attribute. To create a class selector, you begin the style rule with a period (.) followed by the class attribute value. For example, to style class="mobile", use `.mobile` as the selector. The following style rule sets the font size to 10 points for all elements that use mobile as their class attribute value:

```
.mobile {
  font-size: 10pt;
}
```

If you want to create a style that applies to more than one element, you can list more than one selector in the style rule. For example, the following style rule sets the same font family property and values for the `header, nav,` and `footer` elements:

```
header, nav, footer {
  font-family: Calibri, Arial, sans-serif;
}
```

If you want to create a style that applies to an element contained within another element, you list the elements in the order they appear to create the selector in the style rule. This type of selector is called a **descendant selector**. For example, the following style rule sets the list-style property to none for list items in an unordered list included in the navigation area:

```
nav ul li {
  list-style: none;
}
```

To Create a CSS File and a Style Rule for the Body Element

1 CREATE CSS FILE | 2 LINK PAGES TO CSS FILE | 3 CREATE STYLE RULES
4 ADD COMMENTS | 5 VALIDATE CSS FILE

To apply styles to the Forward Fitness Club website, you can create them in an external style sheet. *Why? The styles defined in the external style sheet will apply to all the webpages in the website.* To create a CSS file, you use your preferred text editor to create a file and save it as a CSS document. Next, include one or more style rules that apply to all the webpages linked to the CSS document. The first style rule you add sets the background color of the webpages. This rule uses "body" as the selector and the background-color property in the declaration. Because the `body` element contains all of the content displayed on a webpage, using "body" as the selector sets the background color of the entire webpage. The following steps create a CSS file and a style rule.

1

- Open your text editor, tap or click File on the menu bar, and then tap or click New if you need to open a new blank document.

- Tap or click File on the menu bar and then tap or click Save As to display the Save As dialog box.

- Navigate to your fitness folder and then double-tap or double-click the css folder to open it.

- In the File name box, type **styles** to name the file.

Figure 4–11

Q&A Is "styles" the required file name for the CSS file?
No. You can give a CSS file any meaningful name, but a common name for an external style sheet is styles.css. An external style sheet must end with a .css extension.

- Tap or click the Save as type button, and then tap or click Cascading Style Sheets or CSS to select the file format.

- Tap or click the Save button to save the file in the css folder.

- On Line 1 of the text editor, type **body {** to begin a new style rule for the body element (Figure 4–11).

Q&A Why should I use "body" as the selector?
Using "body" as the selector means the style rule applies to all of the body elements in the webpages linked to the style sheet. In this case, you are creating a style rule that sets the background color for the entire webpage because the body element contains all of the content displayed on a webpage.

2

- Press the ENTER key to add Line 2, press the TAB key to indent the new line, and then type **background-color: #FFFF99;** to add a declaration that sets the background color.

- Press the ENTER key to add Line 3, press the SHIFT+TAB keys to decrease the indent, and then type **}** to add a closing brace (Figure 4–12).

Figure 4–12

Q&A What color does FFFF99 represent?
The color specified by FFFF99 is a light yellow.

3

- Save your changes.

Linking an HTML Document to a CSS File

After creating a CSS file, link it to all the webpages that will use its styles. Otherwise, the browser will not find and apply the styles in the external style sheet. Insert a `link` element on the HTML page within the <head> and </head> tags, which is the section of an HTML document that provides information to browsers and search engines but is not displayed on the webpage itself.

The `link` element uses two attributes, `rel` and `href`. The `rel` attribute uses the `stylesheet` value to indicate that the document is linked to a style sheet. The `href` attribute value specifies the file path or file name of the CSS file. Following is an example of a link to a style sheet named styles.css and stored in the css folder:

```
<link rel="stylesheet" href="css/styles.css">
```

The `type="text/css"` attribute and value is also commonly used within a `link` element to reference a CSS file. However, with HTML5, the `type` attribute is not necessary. The W3C says that the use of the `type` attribute within the `link` element is "purely advisory."

To Link HTML Pages to the CSS File

1 CREATE CSS FILE | **2 LINK PAGES TO CSS FILE** | 3 CREATE STYLE RULES
| 4 ADD COMMENTS | 5 VALIDATE CSS FILE

To link the styles.css file to an HTML page, you include a link to the style sheet within the `head` section of the document. Next, view the changes to the webpage in a browser. ***Why?*** *To apply the CSS style rules to a webpage, you must link the webpage to the CSS file. To view the applied styles, open the home page in a browser.* If you link the website template to the style sheet file, any new pages created from the template will already be linked to the style sheet. The following steps link the home, about, contact, and template HTML documents to the external style sheet file and then view one page in a browser.

1

- Open index.html in your text editor to prepare to link the page to the CSS file.

- Place the insertion point after the beginning <head> tag on Line 4 and press the ENTER key to create a new Line 5.

- Press the TAB key to indent the line and then type `<link rel="stylesheet" href="css/styles.css">` to create a link to the style sheet file (Figure 4–13).

```
1  <!DOCTYPE html>
2  <!-- This website template was created by: Student's First
      Name Student's Last Name -->
3  <html lang="en">
4  <head>
5      <link rel="stylesheet" href="css/styles.css">
6      <title>Forward Fitness Club</title>
```

Line 5 → 5

link to styles.css

Figure 4–13

◁ | Why do I need to include css/ before the name of the file?
Q&A | The styles.css file is located within the css folder. Because the file is not stored in the same folder as the index.html document, you must include the folder name as well as the file name in the `href` attribute value.

- Save the index.html page to preserve your changes.
- Open about.html in your text editor to prepare to link the page to the CSS file.
- Place the insertion point after the beginning <head> tag on Line 4 and press the ENTER key to create a new Line 5.
- Press the TAB key to indent the line and then type `<link rel="stylesheet" href="css/styles.css">` to create a link to the style sheet file.
- Save your changes and close the file.
- Open contact.html in your text editor, place the insertion point after the beginning <head> tag on Line 4, and then press the ENTER key to create a new Line 5.
- Press the TAB key and then type `<link rel="stylesheet" href="css/styles.css">` to create a link to the style sheet file.
- Save your changes and close the file.
- Open fitness.html, located in the template folder, place the insertion point after the beginning <head> tag on Line 4, and then press the ENTER key to create a new Line 5.
- Press the TAB key and then type `<link rel="stylesheet" href="css/styles.css">` to create a link to the style sheet file.
- Save your changes and close the file.
- View the home page in your default browser to view the page with the linked style sheet (Figure 4–14).

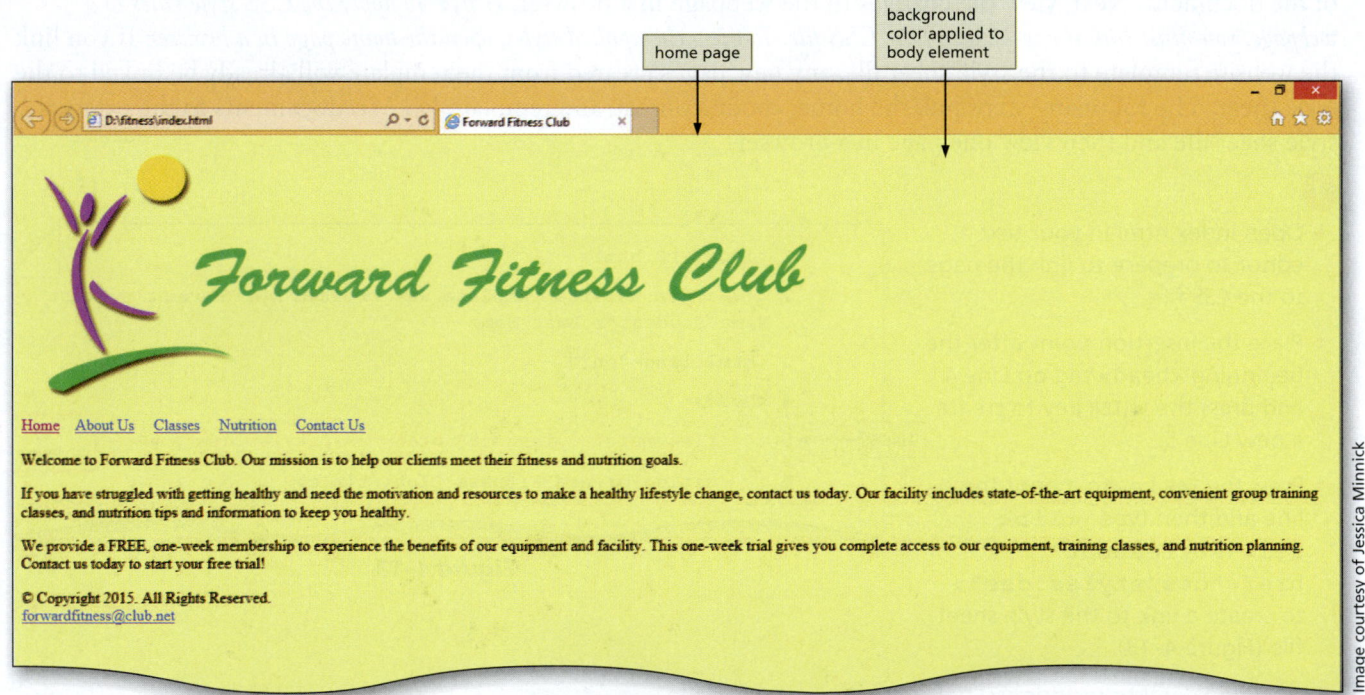

Figure 4–14

Image courtesy of Jessica Minnick

Aligning Webpage Content

One way to align webpage content is to use the text-align property, which applies to block elements. Use the text-align property to set the horizontal alignment for the lines of text in an element. The text-align property can use one of four values: left (the default), center, right, or justify. Use the justify value to align text on the left and right margins by adding white space to the lines of text. Use the center value to center content within an element. For example, the following rule centers an **h1** element:

```
h1 {
  text-align: center;
}
```

Another way to center webpage content is to use the margin property. To center all of the elements so that the page appears centered within a browser window, you create styles to set the left and right margins to auto. You also set the width property to a percentage to specify how much of the page to use for content. For example, if you set the width to 80%, you leave 20 percent of the page for margins. Using "auto" as the property value means that the left and right margins split the available 20 percent equally, leaving 10 percent of the page for the left margin and 10 percent of the page for the right margin. The following declaration specifies the width of the **div id="container"** section as 80 percent of the page and sets the left and right margins to "auto," centering all of the content in that section:

```
container {
  width: 80%;
  margin-left: auto;
  margin-right: auto;
}
```

To Center Content

1 CREATE CSS FILE | 2 LINK PAGES TO CSS FILE | **3 CREATE STYLE RULES**
4 ADD COMMENTS | 5 VALIDATE CSS FILE

Now that you have created a style for the **body** element, return to your CSS file to create style rules for the **div id="container"** section. Recall that this section contains all of the other structural areas of the webpage, including the **header, nav, main,** and **footer** elements. Currently, these elements are not centered on the page when displayed in a browser. To center all of these elements using a single style rule, you set the left and right margins to **auto** for the **div id="container"** element. In addition, set the width to 80% so that the elements do not span 100 percent of the browser window. Because "container" is an id value, use **#container** as the selector. The following steps center the contents of an element using margin and width properties.

1

- In the text editor, return to the styles.css file.

- Place the insertion point after the closing brace on Line 3 and press the ENTER key twice to insert new Lines 4 and 5.

- On Line 5, type **#container { to add the container selector and an opening brace (Figure 4–15).

```
1  body {
2      background-color: #FFFF99;
3  }
4
5  #container {          ← opening brace
```

Line 5 → #container selector

Figure 4–15

Q&A | Why is Line 4 blank?
Reading and reviewing several lines of code can be hard on the eyes. For improved readability, insert blank lines between each style rule.

2

- Press the ENTER key to add Line 6, press the TAB key to indent the line, and then type **width: 80%;** to add a declaration that sets the width of the element.

- Press the ENTER key to add Line 7 and then type **margin-left: auto;** to add a declaration that sets the left margin.

- Press the ENTER key to add Line 8 and then type **margin-right: auto;** to add a declaration that sets the right margin.

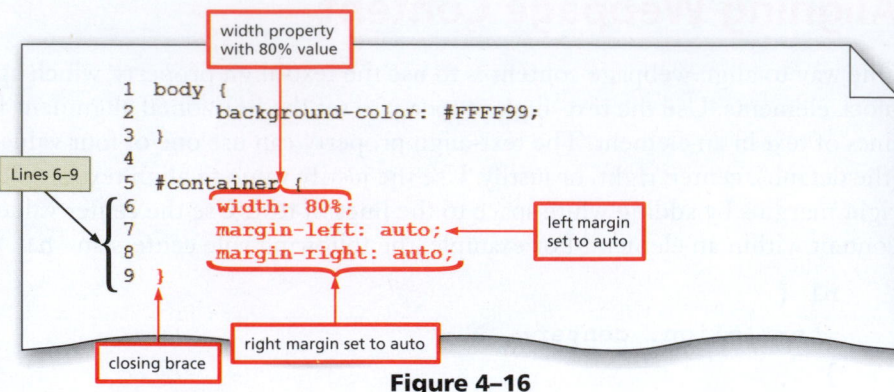

Figure 4–16

- Press the ENTER key to add Line 9, press the SHIFT+TAB keys to decrease the indent, and then type } to close the declarations for the #container selector (Figure 4–16).

Q&A

Why do I need to set the width to 80%?
Currently, the elements on the webpage will span the entire width of the browser window. Setting the width to 80% restricts the width of all the elements in the container to 80 percent of the width of the browser window.

Why am I using the value "auto" for the left and right margins?
Setting the left and right margins of a div element that contains all of the elements of a webpage, such as the container div, centers all of the elements on the page.

Do I have to enter each property and value on a separate line?
No. However, listing each property and value on separate lines enhances the readability of the style sheet. A style rule with many declarations is difficult to read unless the declarations are listed on separate lines. Readability helps to find and correct syntax errors.

3

- Save your changes.

- View the home page in a browser to see the applied styles (Figure 4–17).

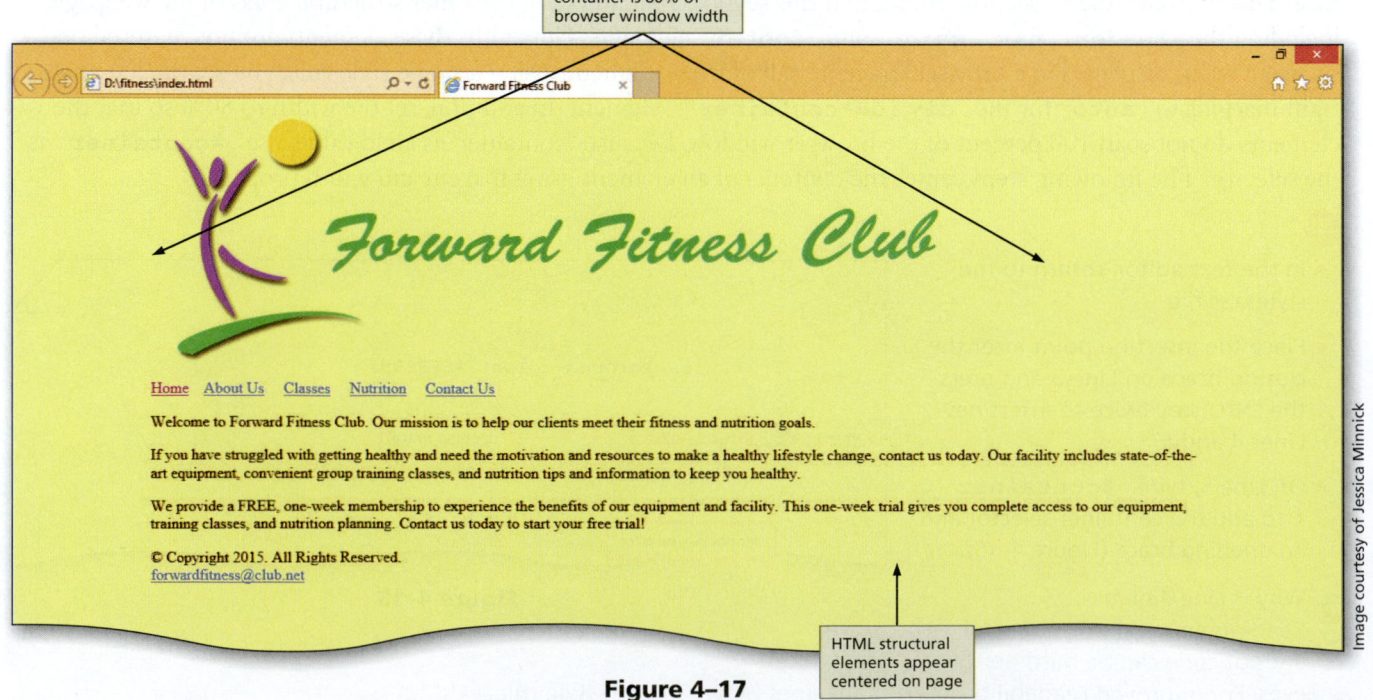

Figure 4–17

Creating Style Rules for Structural Elements

The next formatting task is to create style rules for the HTML5 structural elements used in the Forward Fitness Center website. Because the header section appears at the top of the webpage, it needs formatting that makes the header contents stand out and attract visitors to the page. To achieve this effect, you can use CSS text properties and box model properties to adjust the margins, add a border and background color, and center the contents of the header section.

The nav section should also be prominent and easy to find on the webpage, so you should format it differently from the other structural elements. Because the nav section contains only text, use CSS text properties to determine the text's appearance. Use CSS box model properties to specify the padding, margins, and borders of the **nav** element.

Unlike the other structural sections, the main section should be formatted using the display property. Internet Explorer versions 9 through 11 treat the **main** element as an inline element rather than a block element. To apply text and box model properties to the main section and have them appear as you intend in Internet Explorer, use the **display property**, which determines how the browser displays an element. Including the display property with a value of "block" in the declaration list of the main selector means that all browsers will display the main section as a block element.

Finally, create a style rule that formats the footer section by defining the font size, text alignment, and top margin of the **footer** element.

To Create a Style Rule for the Header Element

1 CREATE CSS FILE | 2 LINK PAGES TO CSS FILE | **3 CREATE STYLE RULES**
4 ADD COMMENTS | 5 VALIDATE CSS FILE

Next, you will create a style rule for the header, which is located at the top of the HTML page and currently contains the Forward Fitness Center logo. The rule will use "header" as the selector and list a few declarations to format the **header** element. To separate the header from the rest of the webpage, add declarations to apply top and bottom margins and a background color. To create a more distinctive design for the header element, apply a rounded border and a shadow. Finally, to improve the appearance of the logo within the header, use the text-align property to center the **header** element's contents. The following steps create a style rule for the **header** element.

- Place the insertion point after the closing brace on Line 9 and press the ENTER key twice to insert new Lines 10 and 11.

- On Line 11, type **header {** to add the header selector and an opening brace (Figure 4–18).

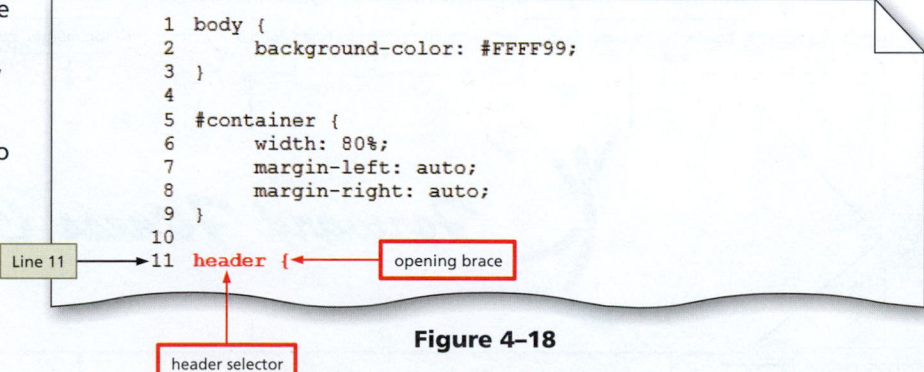

```
1  body {
2      background-color: #FFFF99;
3  }
4
5  #container {
6      width: 80%;
7      margin-left: auto;
8      margin-right: auto;
9  }
10
Line 11 → 11  header {          opening brace
```

header selector

Figure 4–18

2

- Press the ENTER key to add Line 12, press the TAB key to indent the line, and then type **margin- top: 10px;** to add a declaration that sets the top margin.

- Press the ENTER key to add Line 13 and then type **margin-bottom: 20px;** to add a declaration that sets the bottom margin.

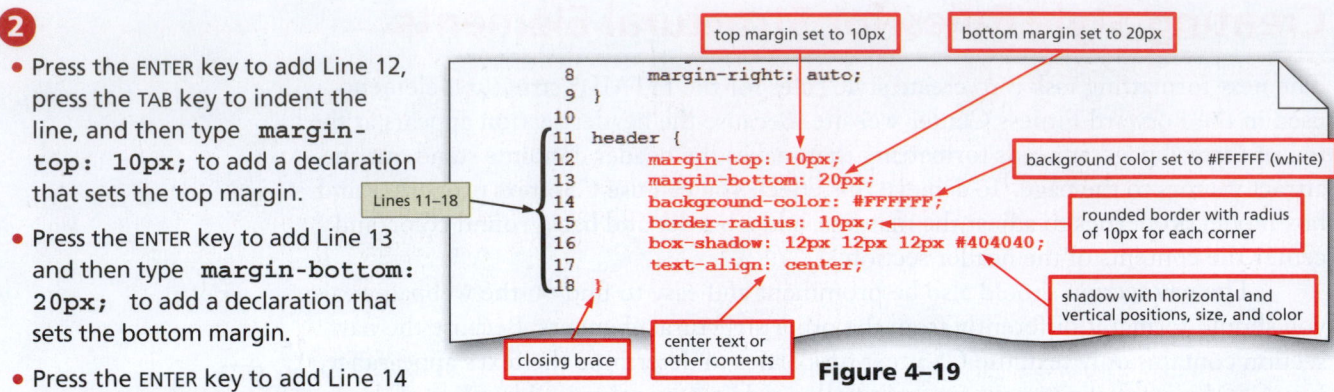

- Press the ENTER key to add Line 14 and then type **background-color: #FFFFFF;** to add a declaration that sets the background color to white.

- Press the ENTER key to add Line 15 and then type **border-radius: 10px;** to add a declaration that defines a rounded border around the element.

- Press the ENTER key to add Line 16 and then type **box-shadow: 12px 12px 12px #404040;** to add a declaration that defines a shadow.

- Press the ENTER key to add Line 17 and then type **text-align: center;** to add a declaration for text alignment.

- Press the ENTER key to add Line 18, press the SHIFT+TAB keys to decrease the indent, and then type **}** to close the declarations for the header selector (Figure 4–19).

Q&A
What do the four values for the box-shadow property mean?
The first value (12px) sets the horizontal position of the shadow in relation to the element. The second value (12px) sets the vertical position of the shadow. The third value (12px) sets the distance of the blur in the shadow, and the fourth value (#404040) sets the color to a dark gray.

The header element does not contain any text. Why do I need to add a text-align property with a value of center for the header?
The text-align property is applied to the header's contents, including image tags such as the one used to display the Forward Fitness Center logo.

3

- Save your changes.
- View the home page in a browser to see the applied styles (Figure 4–20).

Q&A
When I display the home page, the shadow looks different from the one in the figure. Why is that?
Browsers vary in how they interpret the box-shadow property and display shadows. If your CSS code matches the code shown in Figure 4–19, you are entering the style rule correctly.

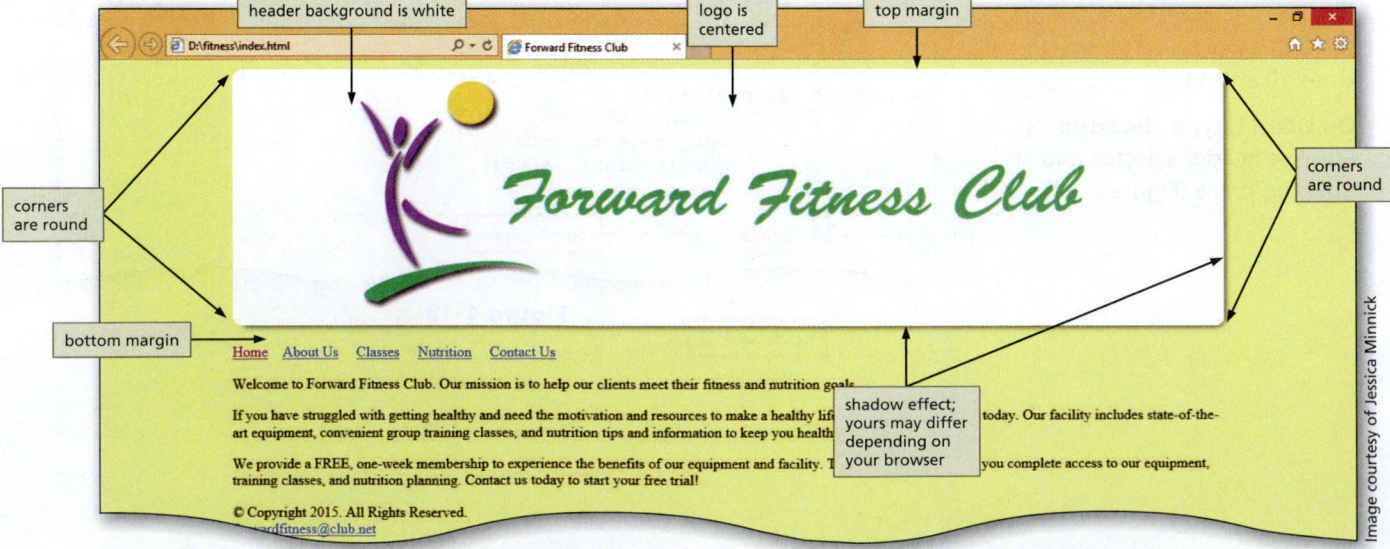

Figure 4–20

To Create a Style Rule for the Nav Element

Next, you will create a style rule for the nav element. The **nav** area is located below the header on the webpage and currently contains links to all pages in the website. As with the header style rule, the one for the **nav** element will include "nav" as the selector and many declarations to format the element's contents. First, you add declarations to format the text, including font-family, font-size, font-weight, and text-align properties and values. You also add declarations to specify the padding, margins, and rounded borders for the nav element. *Why? Applying these properties and values sets the nav element apart from other elements on the webpage.* The following steps create a style rule for the nav element.

①

- Place the insertion point after the closing brace on Line 18 and press the ENTER key twice to insert new Lines 19 and 20.

- On Line 20, type **nav {** to add the nav selector and an opening brace.

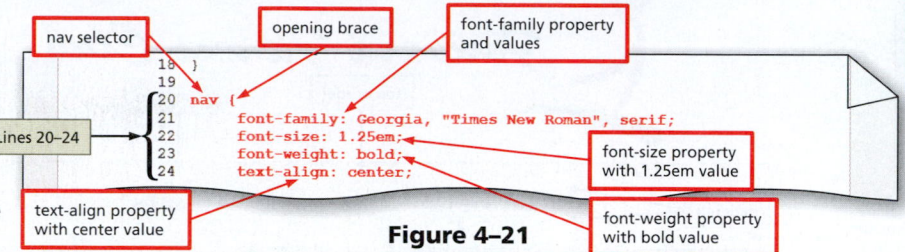

Figure 4–21

- Press the ENTER key to add Line 21, press the TAB key to indent the line, and then type **font-family: Georgia, "Times New Roman", serif;** to add a declaration that specifies a font family with a range of alternative values.

- Press the ENTER key to add Line 22 and then type **font-size: 1.25em;** to add a declaration that sets the font size.

- Press the ENTER key to add Line 23 and then type **font-weight: bold;** to add a declaration that sets the font weight.

- Press the ENTER key to add Line 24 and then type **text-align: center;** to add a declaration for text alignment (Figure 4–21).

Q&A Why do I need to include three values for the font-family property?
If the browser cannot display the first font, it will use the next specified font. If the browser cannot display the second font, it will use a serif font installed on the user's computer.

What does the 1.25em value mean for the font-size property?
Setting the font-size property to 1.25em means the font size of the nav section is 1.25 times larger than the default font size of the browser. If the default size is 16 points, for example, the font size in the nav section is 20 points.

②

- Press the ENTER key to add Line 25 and then type **padding: 15px;** to add a declaration for padding.

- Press the ENTER key to add Line 26 and then type **margin-top: 10px;** to add a declaration that sets the top margin.

- Press the ENTER key to add Line 27 and then type **margin-bottom: 10px;** to add a declaration that sets the bottom margin.

```
        {
22      font-family: Georgia, "Times New
        font-size: 1.25em;
23      font-weight: bold;
24      text-align: center;
25      padding: 15px;
26      margin-top: 10px;
27      margin-bottom: 10px;
28      border-radius: 20px;
29      border-top: 5px solid #FFFFFF;
30      border-bottom: 5px solid #FFFFFF;
31    }
```

Figure 4–22

- Press the ENTER key to add Line 28 and then type **border-radius: 20px;** to add a declaration that defines a rounded border around the element.

- Press the ENTER key to add Line 29 and then type **border-top: 5px solid #FFFFFF;** to add a declaration that formats the top border of the element.

- Press the ENTER key to add Line 30 and then type **border-bottom: 5px solid #FFFFFF;** to add a declaration that formats the bottom border of the element.

- Press the ENTER key to add Line 31, press the SHIFT+TAB keys to decrease the indent, and then type **}** to close the declarations for the nav selector (Figure 4–22).

Q&A Should I apply padding to the top, right, bottom, and left sides of the nav element?
When you use the padding property, the padding value is applied to all sides. If you need to apply padding only to the bottom, for example, use the padding-bottom property.

3

- Save your changes.
- View the home page in a browser to see the applied styles (Figure 4–23).

Figure 4–23

To Create a Style Rule for the Main Element

1 CREATE CSS FILE | 2 LINK PAGES TO CSS FILE | **3 CREATE STYLE RULES**
4 ADD COMMENTS | 5 VALIDATE CSS FILE

The main area is located below the **nav** element and contains the primary content of the webpage. The first declaration to add to the style rule for the **main** element sets the display property to "block." **Why?** *At the time of this writing, Internet Explorer versions 9 through 11 treat the semantic HTML5* **main** *element as an inline element, not a block element. Using the display property with a value of "block" ensures the main element will be displayed consistently as a block.* Next, add text and box model properties to specify the font family, font size, padding, margins, and rounded borders. The following steps create a style rule for the **main** element.

- Place the insertion point after the closing brace on Line 31 and then press the ENTER key twice to insert new Lines 32 and 33.

- On Line 33, type **main {** to add the main selector and an opening brace.

- Press the ENTER key to add Line 34, press the TAB key to indent the line, and then type **display: block;** to add a declaration for the display property.

```
28        border-radius: 20px;
29        border-top: 5px solid #FFFFFF;
30        border-bottom: 5px solid #FFFFFF;
31   }
32
33   main {
34        display: block;
35        font-family: Verdana, Arial, sans-serif;
36        font-size: 1em;
37        margin-top: 20px;
38        margin-bottom: 10px;
```

Figure 4–24

- Press the ENTER key to add Line 35 and then type **font-family: Verdana, Arial, sans-serif;** to add a declaration that specifies a font family with a range of alternate values.

- Press the ENTER key to add Line 36 and then type **font-size: 1em;** to add a declaration that sets the font size.

- Press the ENTER key to add Line 37 and then type **margin-top: 20px;** to add a declaration that sets the top margin.

- Press the ENTER key to add Line 38 and then type **margin-bottom: 10px;** to add a declaration that sets the bottom margin (Figure 4–24).

Q&A
Why do I need to include the display property with a value of "block"?
The main element is an HTML5 block element, but is not fully supported by Internet Explorer 9 through 11. You must add this declaration so that Internet Explorer will correctly display the main element as a block element in the webpage.

Why do I need to set the font-size property to 1em?
When you set the font size to 1em, the browser uses its default font size.

2

- Press the ENTER key to add Line 39 and then type **padding: 20px;** to add a declaration that sets the padding.

- Press the ENTER key to add Line 40 and then type **border-radius: 10px;** to add a declaration that defines a rounded border around the element.

- Press the ENTER key to add Line 41 and then type **background-color: #FFFFFF;** to add a declaration that sets the background color of the element.

- Press the ENTER key to add Line 42 and then type **box-shadow: 12px 12px 12px #404040;** to add a declaration that defines a shadow.

- Press the ENTER key to add Line 43, press the SHIFT+TAB keys to decrease the indent, and then type **}** to close the declarations for the main selector (Figure 4–25).

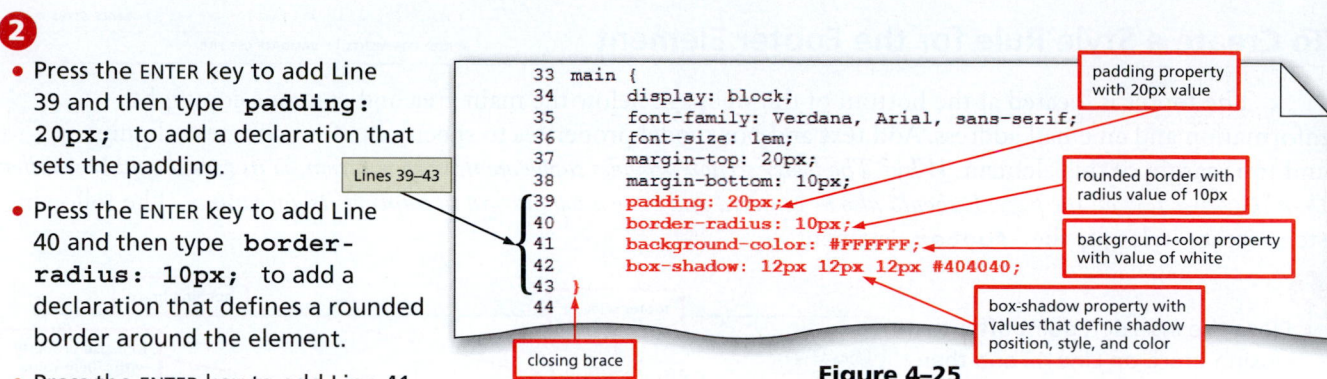

Lines 39–43

```
33  main {
34      display: block;
35      font-family: Verdana, Arial, sans-serif;
36      font-size: 1em;
37      margin-top: 20px;
38      margin-bottom: 10px;
39      padding: 20px;
40      border-radius: 10px;
41      background-color: #FFFFFF;
42      box-shadow: 12px 12px 12px #404040;
43  }
44
```

padding property with 20px value

rounded border with radius value of 10px

background-color property with value of white

box-shadow property with values that define shadow position, style, and color

closing brace

Figure 4–25

3

- Save your changes.

- View the home page in a browser to see the applied styles (Figure 4–26).

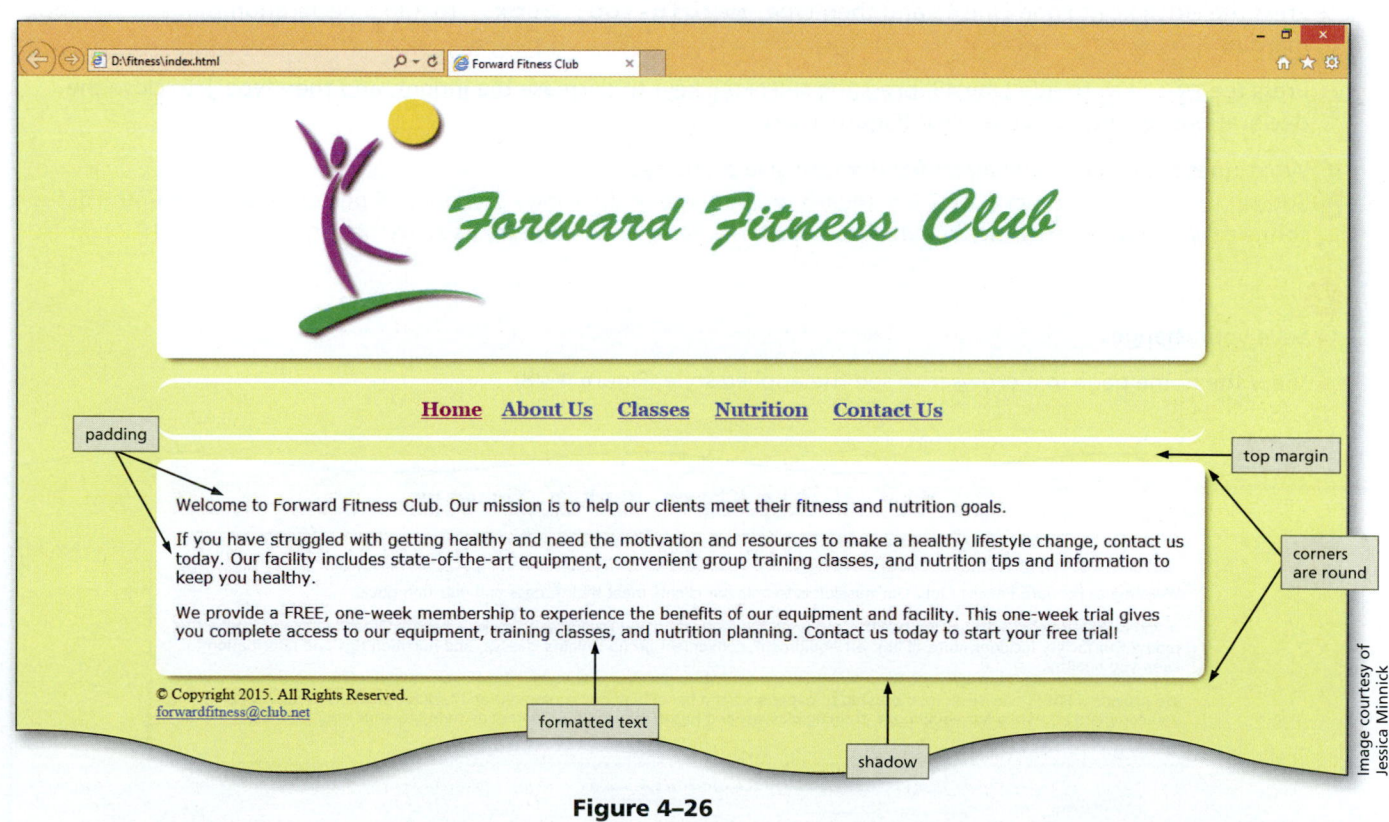

Figure 4–26

To Create a Style Rule for the Footer Element

The footer is located at the bottom of the webpage below the main area and contains copyright information and an email address. Add text and box model properties to specify the font size, text alignment, and top margin of this element. *Why? The footer section provides supplemental information, so its text should be smaller than the other text on the page. It should also be centered and have a top margin to improve its appearance.* The following steps create styles for the `footer` element.

- Place the insertion point after the closing brace on Line 43 and then press the ENTER key twice to insert new Lines 44 and 45.

- On Line 45, type `footer {` to add the footer selector and an opening brace.

- Press the ENTER key to add Line 46, press the TAB key to indent the line, and then type `font-size: .70em;` to add a declaration that sets the font size.

Figure 4–27

- Press the ENTER key to add Line 47 and then type `text-align: center;` to add a declaration for text alignment.

- Press the ENTER key to add Line 48 and then type `margin-top: 20px;` to add a declaration that sets the top margin.

- Press the ENTER key to add Line 49, press the SHIFT+TAB keys to decrease the indent, and then type `}` to close the declarations for the footer selector (Figure 4–27).

Q&A What does the .70em value mean for the font-size property?

Setting the font-size property to .70em means the font size of the footer section is 70 percent smaller than the default font size of the browser. If the default size is 16 points, for example, the font size in the footer section is 11.2 points.

- Save your changes.

- View the home page in a browser to see the applied style (Figure 4–28).

Figure 4–28

Creating Style Rules for Classes

In Chapter 3, you added a class attribute to the `img` elements specifying the images displayed on the About Us page. For example, you added the following `img` element after the Weights heading on the About Us page:

```
<img class="equip" src="images/equipment1.jpg" alt="Weight
Equipment" height="195" width="260">
```

This element displays the equipment1.jpg image. The first attribute and value, `class="equip"`, assigns this element to the equip class. The `img` elements that display the equipment2.jpg and equipment3.jpg images also include the `class="equip"` attribute and value to assign them to the equip class. Including the `class="equip"` attribute and value in each `img` element means you can format all the elements assigned to the equip class with a single style rule. For example, the following style rule adds 20 pixels of padding to the right side of elements in the `equip` class:

```
.equip {
  padding-right: 20px;
}
```

To indicate you are using a class name as a selector, include a period (.) before the class name, similar to the way you include a number sign (#) with an id selector. The effect of this style rule is to add 20 pixels of padding to the right of the three images on the About Us page. However, the three images do not actually need the additional padding as they are currently positioned (Figure 4–29).

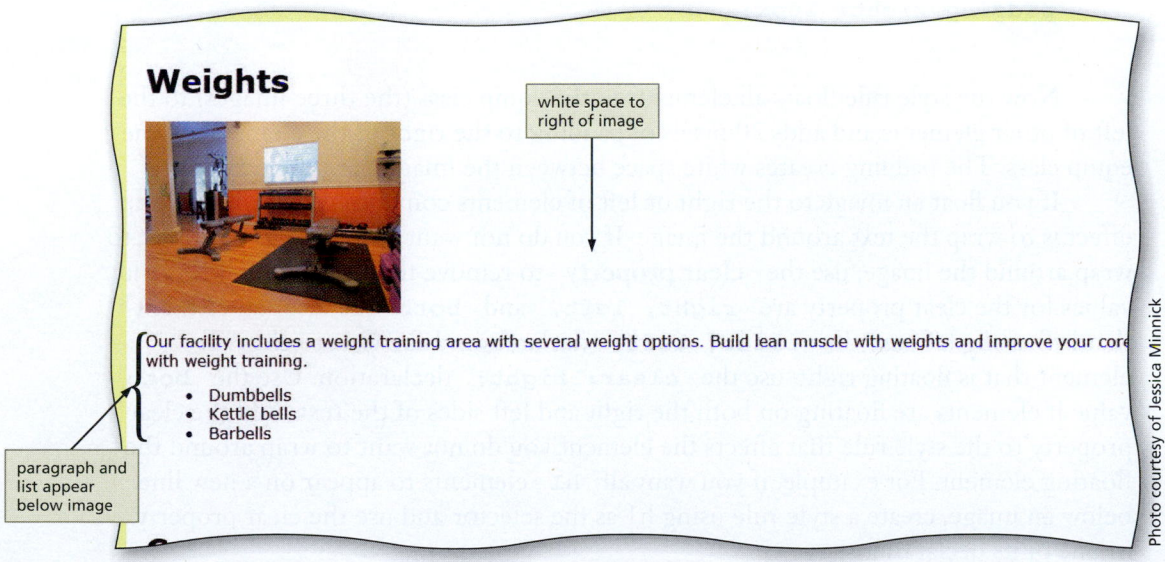

Figure 4–29

The About Us page would look more professional if the paragraph and list currently displayed below each image were displayed to the right of each image instead. To achieve this effect, you use the **float property**, which lets you position an element to the right or left of other elements. The valid values for the float property are `right` and `left,` indicating where to display (or float) the element. Figure 4–30 shows the image floating to the left of the text on the About Us page.

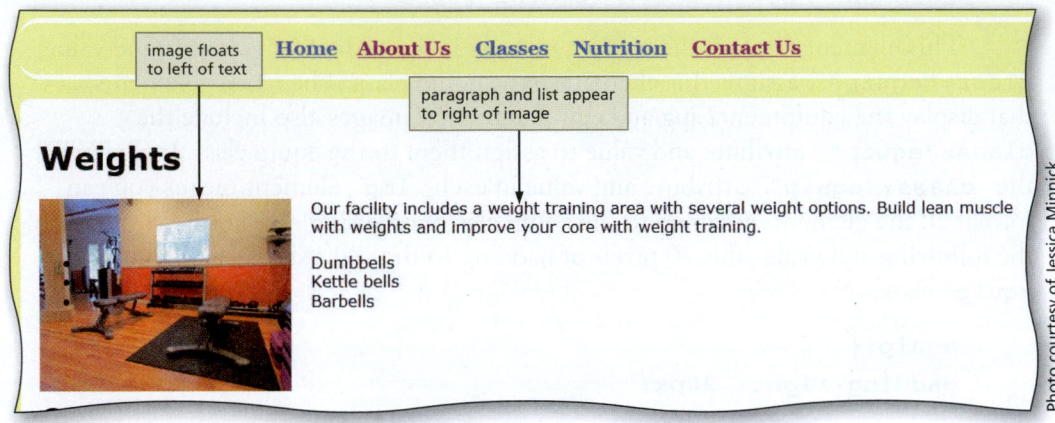

Figure 4–30

To have all three images on the About Us page float to the left of the text, add a `float: left;` declaration to the style rule for the equip class as follows:

```
.equip {
 float: left;
 padding-right: 20px;
}
```

Now the style rule floats all elements in the equip class (the three images) to the left of other elements and adds 20 pixels of padding to the right of the elements in the equip class. The padding creates white space between the images and the text.

If you float an image to the right or left of elements containing text content, the effect is to wrap the text around the image. If you do not want text, such as headings, to wrap around the image, use the **clear property** to remove the float effect. The valid values for the clear property are `right, left,` and `both`. To clear an element that is floating left, use the `clear: left;` declaration. Likewise, to clear an element that is floating right, use the `clear: right;` declaration. Use the `both` value if elements are floating on both the right and left sides of the text. Add the clear property to the style rule that affects the element you do not want to wrap around the floating element. For example, if you want all `h1` elements to appear on a new line below an image, create a style rule using h1 as the selector and use the clear property in one of its declarations.

To Create a Style Rule for the equip Class

1 CREATE CSS FILE | 2 LINK PAGES TO CSS FILE | **3 CREATE STYLE RULES**
4 ADD COMMENTS | 5 VALIDATE CSS FILE

The images on the About Us page should appear on the left and the text should appear on the right side of each image. To accomplish this task, you use the float property to float the images left and then apply padding to the right side of the images to provide white space between each image and the text on the page. Add declarations including the float and padding properties to a style rule that uses the .equip class selector. *Why? Using the .equip class selector will apply the style rule to all elements in the equip class.* The following steps create a style rule for the equip class.

- Place the insertion point after the closing brace on Line 48 and then press the ENTER key twice to insert new Lines 50 and 51.

- On Line 51, type `.equip {` to add the .equip selector and an opening brace.

- Press the ENTER key to add Line 52, press the TAB key to indent the line, and then type `float: left;` to add a declaration that floats elements in the specified class.

Figure 4–31

- Press the ENTER key to add Line 53 and then type `padding-right: 20px;` to add a declaration for padding.

- Press the ENTER key to add Line 54, press the SHIFT+TAB keys to decrease the indent, and then type `}` to close the declarations for the .equip selector (Figure 4–31).

Q&A Why does the .equip selector start with a period?
To style a class, you insert a period before the class name to specify the selector in the CSS file.

How will the `float: left;` declaration change the About Us webpage?
This declaration places images on the left side of the webpage, allowing the text after each image to wrap around the image on the right.

How do you stop content from floating so that it starts on its own line?
To stop floating an element, use the clear property. For example, apply the following declaration to the content that you want to start on its own line, or clear the float: `clear: left;` (clear left float), `clear: right;` (clear right float), or `clear: both;` (clear left and right float).

Using CSS List Properties

To control the appearance of numbered and bulleted lists, you use the CSS **list-style properties**. By default, lists marked with the <ul> and </ul> tags display a solid bullet before each list item. Lists marked with the <ol> and </ol> tags display Arabic numerals (1, 2, 3, and so on) before the list items. You use the list-style-type property to specify a different type of bullet or a different numbering style to use in a list. For example, the following style rule defines a filled square bullet for an unordered list:

```
ul {
  list-style-type: square;
}
```

The following style rule defines lowercase Roman numerals for an ordered list:

```
ol {
  list-style-type: lower-roman;
}
```

If you want to display an image instead of a bullet, use the list-style-image property. To indicate the file name of the image file, begin the value with "url" followed by the file name or path in parentheses. For example, the following style rule defines the image in the arrow.png file as the bullet for unordered lists:

```
ul {
  list-style-image: url(arrow.png);
}
```

To specify the position of the bullet or number in a list, use the list-style-position property. The default value for this property is outside, which displays the list item with a bullet or number `outside` of the list's content block as in the following text:

1. Lorem ipsum dolor sit amet,
   consectetur adipiscing elit.

2. Morbi odio nisl, facilisis non
   egestas a, tristique vitae neque.

Using `inside` as the value displays the bullet or number inside the list's content block, as in the following text:

1. Lorem ipsum dolor sit amet,
consectetur adipiscing elit.

2. Morbi odio nisl, facilisis non
egestas a, tristique vitae neque.

For example, in the bulleted lists on the About Us page, the bullets appear outside the content block for each list by default. After floating the images on the About Us page, the images overlap the bullets in the lists, as shown in Figure 4–30 on page 166. To fix this problem, create a style rule for the lists and use inside as the value for the list-style-position property to display the bullets.

BTW

Lorem Ipsum
Web and print designers often use Latin text that begins with "Lorem ipsum" as filler text when they want to focus on design or formatting rather than content.

BTW

List Properties
Appendix B provides a full description of the list properties and their valid values.

To Create Styles for List Elements

1 CREATE CSS FILE | 2 LINK PAGES TO CSS FILE | **3 CREATE STYLE RULES** | 4 ADD COMMENTS | 5 VALIDATE CSS FILE

Next, you style the bulleted lists and the description list that appear on the About Us page. The HTML elements in this case are the unordered list (`ul` element) and the description list (`dt` and `dd` elements). First, apply a large bottom margin to the unordered list to separate subsequent text from the list. Next, set the position of the bullets so they appear inside the list's content block. *Why? The current position of the bullets is outside, the default, where they are hidden by the floating images. Setting the position to inside makes the bullets visible.* To format the definition list at the bottom of the About Us page, create a style rule that bolds the terms (the `dt` element) and another rule that adds padding below each definition (the `dd` element). The following steps create styles for the `ul, dt,` and `dd` elements.

- Place the insertion point after the closing brace on Line 54 and then press the ENTER key twice to insert new Lines 55 and 56.

- On Line 56, type `ul {` to add the ul selector and an opening brace.

- Press the ENTER key to add Line 57, press the TAB key to indent the line, and then type **margin-bottom: 50px;** to add a declaration that sets the bottom margin.

Figure 4–32

- Press the ENTER key to add Line 58 and then type **list-style-position: inside;** to add a declaration to define the position of list items.

- Press the ENTER key to add Line 59, press the SHIFT+TAB keys to decrease the indent, and then type } to close the declarations for the ul selector (Figure 4–32).

Q&A What is the purpose of the `list-style-position: inside;` declaration?
Including this declaration in the style for the unordered list displays the bullets for the list items. Otherwise, the bullets are not displayed because they are hidden by the images.

2

- Place the insertion point after the closing brace on Line 59 and then press the ENTER key twice to insert new Lines 60 and 61.

- On Line 61, type **dt {** to add the dt selector and an opening brace.

- Press the ENTER key to add Line 62, press the TAB key to indent the line, and then type **font-weight: bold;** to add a declaration that sets the font weight.

- Press the ENTER key to add Line 63, press the SHIFT+TAB keys to decrease the indent, and then type } to close the declaration for the dt selector (Figure 4–33).

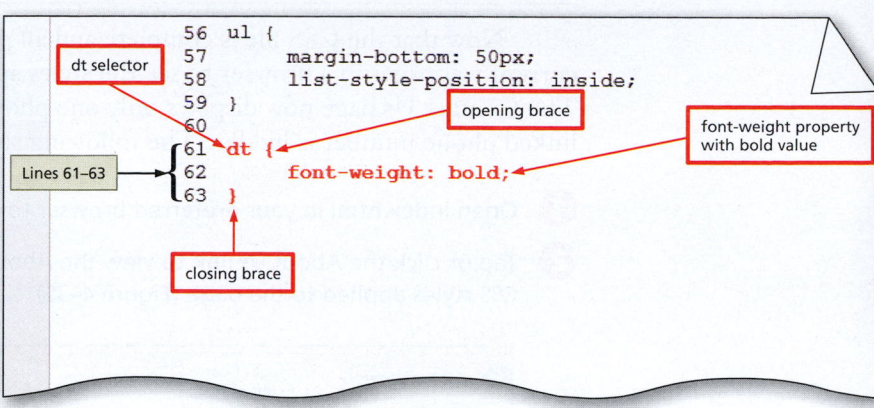

```
56  ul {
57      margin-bottom: 50px;
58      list-style-position: inside;
59  }
60
61  dt {
62      font-weight: bold;
63  }
```

dt selector — opening brace — font-weight property with bold value — Lines 61–63 — closing brace

Figure 4–33

3

- Place the insertion point after the closing brace on Line 63 and then press the ENTER key twice to insert new Lines 64 and 65.

- On Line 65, type **dd {** to add the dd selector and an opening brace.

- Press the ENTER key to add Line 66, press the TAB key to indent the line, and then type **padding-bottom: 20px;** to add a declaration that sets the bottom padding.

- Press the ENTER key to add Line 67, press the SHIFT+TAB keys to decrease the indent, and then type } to close the declaration for the dd selector (Figure 4–34).

```
61  dt {
62      font-weight: bold;
63  }
64
65  dd {
66      padding-bottom: 20px;
67  }
```

dd selector — opening brace — padding-bottom property with 20px value — Lines 65–67 — closing brace

Figure 4–34

To View the Website in a Browser

Now that the CSS file is complete and all pages are linked to the file, view the current webpages in a browser to see the styles applied across all of the HTML pages. The Contact Us page now displays only one phone number, not two, because the linked phone number is hidden. The following steps view a website in a browser.

1 Open index.html in your preferred browser to display the page.

2 Tap or click the About Us link to view the About Us page and scroll down to see the CSS styles applied to the page (Figure 4–35).

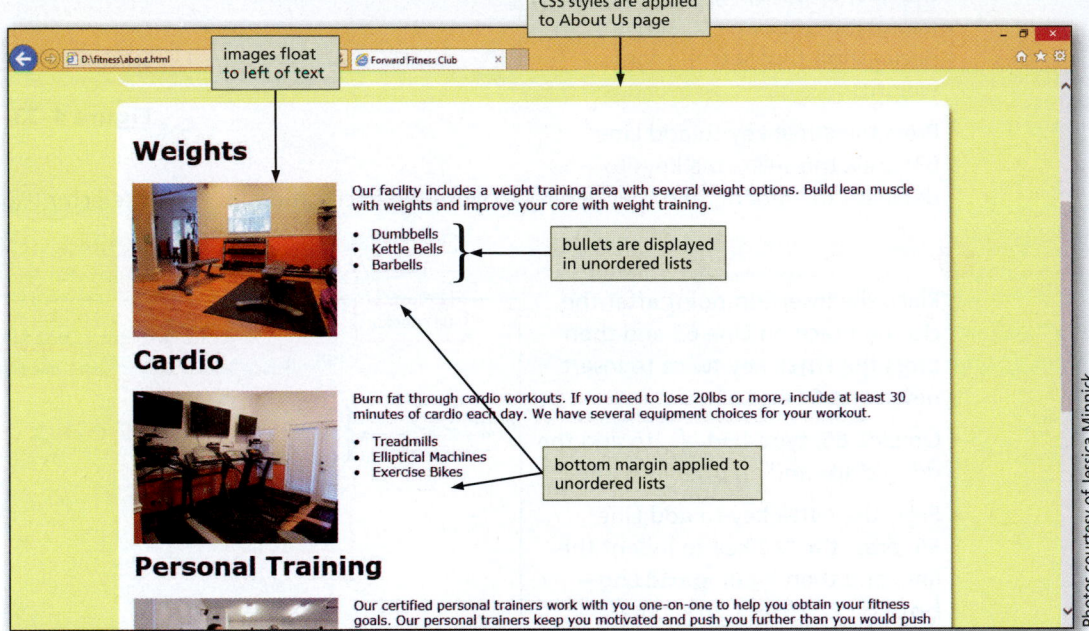

Figure 4–35

Photos courtesy of Jessica Minnick

3 Tap or click the Contact Us link to view the Contact Us page and see the CSS styles applied to the page (Figure 4–36).

Figure 4–36

Image courtesy of Jessica Minnick

4 Close your browser.

Adding Comments to CSS Files

As you create a CSS file, include comments about each rule to identify its purpose. Comments can provide additional information about the area where the styles are applied or other helpful explanations, such as what the styles do. Add a comment above a selector using the following syntax:

```
/* Place your comment here */
```

CSS comment syntax specifies a forward slash at the beginning and at the end of the comment. After the first forward slash, insert an asterisk (*) followed by the comment text. For example, the comment text might identify the group of styles or the author of the style sheet. Close the comment by adding another asterisk, followed by a forward slash.

BTW

CSS Comments in Notepad++

When you correctly add comments to a CSS file using Notepad++, the comments appear in green.

To Add Comments to a CSS File

1 CREATE CSS FILE | 2 LINK PAGES TO CSS FILE | 3 CREATE STYLE RULES

4 ADD COMMENTS | 5 VALIDATE CSS FILE

When you create a CSS file, including comments provides additional information about each style rule. You can also use a comment to identify that you are the author of the webpage. *Why? When you or another web designer are editing a CSS file, comments provide insight on the purpose of the style or its declarations.* The following steps add comments to a CSS file.

1
- Place the insertion point before the body selector on Line 1, and then press the ENTER key twice to place the body selector on Line 3.
- On Line 1 type `/* Style sheet created by: Student's First Name Student's Last Name, Today's Date */` to add a comment at the beginning of the document that identifies the author (Figure 4–37).

Figure 4–37

Q&A Are comments required in a CSS file?

No. Comments are optional, but using comments in a CSS file is a best practice to document the author and date of the last update. Comments also help to organize categories of styles in the style sheet.

2
- Place the insertion point before the body selector on Line 3, and then press the ENTER key to place the body selector on Line 4.
- On Line 3 type `/* Style for body specifies a background color */` to add a comment providing information about the style applied to the body element (Figure 4–38).

Figure 4–38

3

- Place the insertion point before the #container selector on Line 8, and then press the ENTER key to place the #container selector on Line 9.

- On Line 8 type `/* Style for container centers the page and sets the element width */` to add a comment about the style applied to the <div id="container"> element.

- Place the insertion point before the header selector on Line 15, and then press the ENTER key to place the header selector on Line 16.

- On Line 15 type `/* Style for header specifies top and bottom margins, background color, rounded border, shadow, and alignment */` to add a comment about the style applied to the header element.

- Place the insertion point before the nav selector on Line 25, and then press the ENTER key to place the nav selector on Line 26.

- On Line 25 type `/* Style for nav specifies text properties, padding, margins, and borders */` to add a comment about the style applied to the nav element (Figure 4–39).

Figure 4–39

Q&A

I am using Notepad++ and the word *centers* is underlined in red. Is something wrong?

No. Press and hold or right-click the word *centers*, and then tap or click Add "centers" to Dictionary to add the correctly spelled word to the program's dictionary.

4

- Place the insertion point before the main selector on Line 39, and then press the ENTER key to place the main selector on Line 40.

- On Line 39 type `/* Style for main specifies a block display, text properties, margins, padding, rounded border, and shadow */` to add a comment about the style applied to the main element.

- Place the insertion point before the footer selector on Line 52, and then press the ENTER key to place the footer selector on Line 53.

- On Line 52 type `/* Style for footer specifies font size, text alignment, and top margin */` to add a comment about the style applied to the footer element (Figure 4–40).

Figure 4–40

5

- Save your changes.

Validating CSS Files

Once you have created a CSS file, you validate it to verify the validity of the CSS code, similar to how you validate an HTML document to make sure it uses proper HTML syntax. When you validate a CSS document, you confirm that all of the code is correct and follows the established rules for CSS. You can use many online validation services to assure that your CSS code follows standards. Validation should always be a part of your web development testing. The validation service used in this book is the W3C Markup Validation Service (jigsaw.w3.org/css-validator/). You start by uploading your CSS file to the validator, which means you copy the file from your computer to the website. The validator reviews each line of code and locates any errors.

If validation detects an error in your CSS code, a warning such as "Sorry! We found the following error(s)!" appears in the header bar. The results also indicate the number of errors and detailed comments regarding each error.

To Validate the CSS File

1 CREATE CSS FILE | 2 LINK PAGES TO CSS FILE | 3 CREATE STYLE RULES
4 ADD COMMENTS | 5 VALIDATE CSS FILE

After making changes to a CSS file, run the file through W3C's validator to check the document for errors. **Why?** *If the document has any errors, validating gives you a chance to identify and correct them.* The following steps validate a CSS file.

- Open your browser and type `http://jigsaw.w3.org/css-validator/` in the address bar to display the W3C CSS Validation Service page.

- Tap or click the By file upload tab to display the Validate by file upload information.

- Tap or click the Browse button to display the Choose File to Upload dialog box.

- Navigate to your css folder to find the styles.css file (Figure 4–41).

Figure 4–41

- Tap or click the styles.css document to select it.
- Tap or click the Open button to upload the selected file to the W3C CSS validator.
- Tap or click the Check button to send the document through the validator and display the validation results page (Figure 4–42).

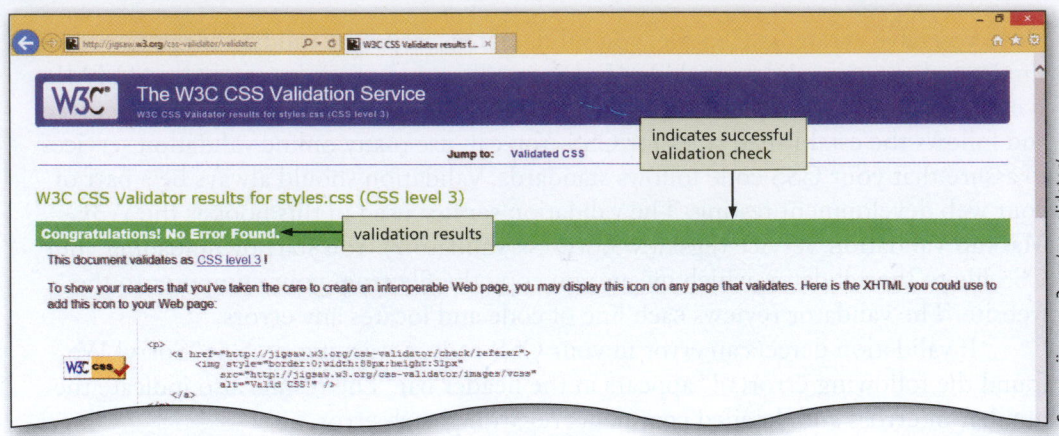

Figure 4–42

Q&A

My results show errors. How do I correct them?

Scroll down the page to display the Notes and Potential Issues section. Review the errors listed below the validation output. Any line number that contains an error is shown in this section.

To Validate a CSS File with Errors

1 CREATE CSS FILE | 2 LINK PAGES TO CSS FILE | 3 CREATE STYLE RULES
4 ADD COMMENTS | 5 VALIDATE CSS FILE

If you created the CSS file correctly, you should not receive any errors, but you can look at what the validator provides when you upload a style sheet file with errors. *Why? When errors are detected in a CSS file, the validator provides information about the location of each error so you can identify and correct them.* The following steps insert an error in the styles CSS file and then validate the document with the W3C CSS validator.

- Return to the styles .css document in your text editor and delete the colon and semicolon on Line 5 to remove the characters from the background-color property and value.
- Save your changes, and then return to the W3C CSS Validation Service page in your browser to display the W3C CSS validator.

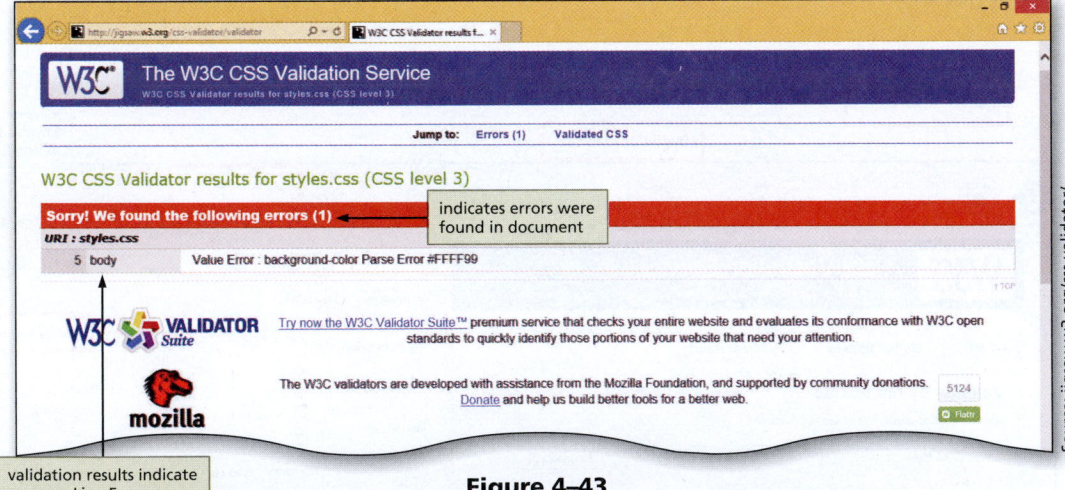

Figure 4–43

- If necessary, tap or click the By file upload tab to display the Validate by File Upload information.
- Tap or click the Browse button to display the Choose File to Upload dialog box.
- Navigate to the css folder in the fitness folder, select the styles.css file, and then tap or click the Open button to upload the file.
- Tap or click the Check button to send the revised document through the validator and display the validation results.
- Review the errors and note their line numbers so you can locate them (Figure 4–43).

- Return to your text editor and type **:** after the background-color property and type **;** after the #FFFF99 value on Line 5 to correct the errors.
- Save your changes and validate the document again to confirm it does not contain any errors.

Chapter Summary

In this chapter, you learned how to create a CSS file with rules to style HTML elements on a webpage. You linked the CSS file to all of the webpages for the fitness website. The items listed below include all the new concepts and skills you have learned in this chapter, with the tasks grouped by activity.

Using Cascading Style Sheets
Inline, Embedded, and External Style Sheets (HTML 143)
CSS Basics (HTML 145)
CSS Text Properties (HTML 146)
CSS Colors (HTML 147)

Understanding Inline Elements and Block Elements
CSS Box Model (HTML 150)

Creating an External Style Sheet
Create a CSS File (HTML 153)
Create a Style Rule for the Body Element (HTML 153)

Linking an HTML Document to a CSS File
Link HTML Pages to the CSS File (HTML 155)

Aligning Webpage Content
Center Content (HTML 157)

Creating Style Rules for Structural Elements
Create Style Rules for the Header, Nav, Main, and Footer Elements (HTML 159–HTML 164)

Creating Style Rules for Classes
Create a Style Rule for the equip Class (HTML 166)

Using CSS List Properties
Create a Style Rule for List Elements (HTML 168)

Adding Comments to CSS Files
Add Comments to a CSS File (HTML 171)

Validating CSS Files
Validate the CSS File (HTML 173)

What decisions will you need to make when creating your next CSS file?

Use these guidelines as you complete the assignments in this chapter and create your own websites outside of this class.

1. Determine properties for your HTML elements (such as header, nav, main, and footer).

   a. Set webpage width and centering characteristics.

   b. Decide on any necessary text properties to use for font face, size, and style.

   c. Set text and background colors.

   d. Decide if you need borders, and then set the style, size, and color of the border.

   e. Float any content that needs to appear on the same line.

   f. Determine the amount of margins and padding to use.

2. Link the CSS file to your HTML pages and website template.

   a. Add comments to your CSS file, noting the declarations for each selector.

   b. Validate your CSS file to confirm that it does not contain any errors.

   c. View your website in a browser to see the applied styles throughout the development process.

   d. Determine any changes that need to be made and revalidate.

3. Depending on the structure of your website, determine if you should create additional CSS files to accommodate multiple wireframes or different media such as mobile or print. Styling for multiple devices will be covered in later chapters.

How should you submit solutions to questions in the assignments identified with a symbol? Every assignment in this book contains one or more questions identified with a symbol. These questions require you to think beyond the assigned presentation. Present your solutions to the questions in the format required by your instructor. Possible formats may include one or more of these options: create a document that contains the answer; present your answer to the class; discuss your answer in a group; record the answer as audio or video using a webcam, smartphone, or portable media player; or post answers on a blog, wiki, or website.

CONSIDER THIS

CONSIDER THIS

Apply Your Knowledge

Reinforce the skills and apply the concepts you learned in this chapter.

Styling a Webpage

Instructions: In this exercise, you will use your text editor to create external, embedded, and inline styles for the Durango Jewelry and Gem Shop home page. You will style the sections of the semantic wireframe (`header, nav, main,` and `footer`) and a `div` element that surrounds all of the content to center the content on the page. You will also float an image to the left so that some of the content can fill the empty space to the right of the image. Finally, you will clear the float and add margins and borders to give your page a professional touch. The completed home page is shown in Figure 4–44. You will also use professional web development practices to indent, space, comment, and validate your code.

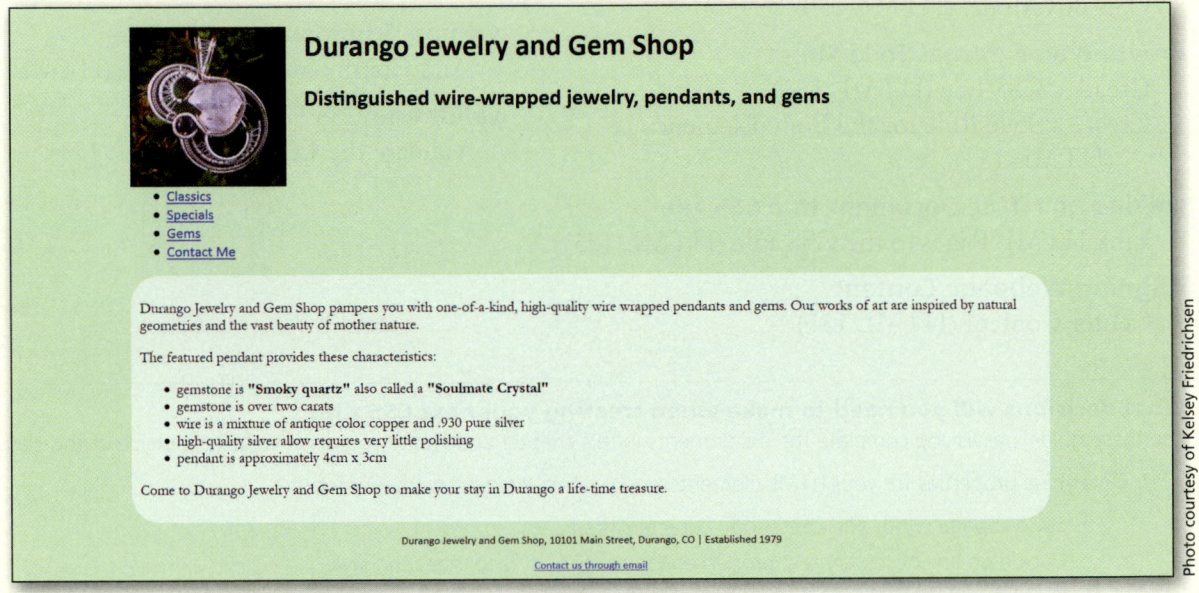

Figure 4–44

Perform the following tasks:

1. Open your text editor, and then open the apply04.html file from the Data Files for Students. Use the File Save As feature to save the webpage in the chapter04\apply folder with the name `index04.html` to create the home page.

2. Modify the comment at the top of the index.html page to include your name and today's date.

3. Start a new file in your text editor, and save it in the chapter04\apply folder with the name `styles04.css` to create a style sheet.

4. Enter a CSS comment as the first line of the external style sheet with *your* name and today's date. Recall that CSS comments are entered within `/*` and `*/` characters.

5. Style the `body` element with a uniform black text color and light-green background color:

```
body { color: #000000;
   background-color: #D9F1C1;
   }
```

6. In the **head** section of the index04.html file, enter an element to connect the page to the external style sheet:

```
<link rel="stylesheet" href="styles04.css">
```

Save your changes. Open or refresh index04.html in a browser to make sure that the style sheet is correctly connected to the HTML file.

7. Your next task is to center the content on the webpage. To do this, add <div> tags to surround the content in the wireframe, and then apply a style to center the content within the <div> tags as follows:

   a. In index04.html, insert the **<div id="outerwrapper">** opening tag just after the opening <body> tag.

   b. In index04.html, insert the **</div> <!--close the outerwrapper-->** closing tag and comment just before the closing </body> tag.

   c. In styles04.css, insert the following declarations to constrain the outerwrapper to 80% of the width of the screen and to center the content within the outerwrapper:

```
#outerwrapper { width: 80%;
  margin: 0 auto 0 auto;
  }
```

   d. Save your changes to both files, and then open or refresh index04.html in a browser to make sure that the content is centered within 80% of the browser window.

8. Apply common sans-serif fonts to the **header, nav,** and **footer** sections, and common serif fonts to the **div id="main"** section by adding the following style to the external stylesheet:

```
header, nav, footer { font-family: Calibri, Arial, sans-serif;
  }

#main { font-family: Garamond, "Times New Roman", serif;
  }
```

(*Hint*: After each step, save index04.html and styles04.css and then refresh index04.html in the browser to make sure that each style is applied successfully.)

9. Style the text in the **footer** section to be 0.75em and centered by adding the following styles to the external stylesheet:

```
footer { font-size: 0.75em;
  text-align: center;
  }
```

10. Style the content within the **div id="main"** section to have a lighter background and 10px of padding on all four sides by adding the following declarations to the existing #main selector:

```
background-color: #F0F9E6;
padding: 10px;
```

11. Float the image to the left with the following style so that the existing **h1** and **h2** content moves to the right of the image:

```
img { float: left;
  }
```

12. Clear the float for the nav section with the following style:

```
nav { clear: both;
    }
```

13. Add a margin to the left of the `h1` and `h2` content in the `nav` section to insert white space between the headings and the image. Given you want to apply the same rule to two specific headings (but not other `h1` and `h2` content on the website), you will first give the tags the same class attribute value and then apply the style to that class as follows:

   a. In index04.html, insert `class="addrightmargin"` to the opening <img> tag in the `header` section.

   b. In styles04.css, insert the following style to increase the size of the right margin for content tagged with class="addrightmargin"

   ```
   .addrightmargin { margin-right: 2%;
       }
   ```

14. In index04.html, insert an embedded style sheet just below the link tag in the `head` section to apply a rounded border to the `div id="main"` section:

```
<style>
    #main { border-radius: 2em; }
</style>
```

15. In index04.html, insert <span> and </span> tags around "Smoky quartz" and "Soulmate Crystal" in the first list item in the unordered list in the `div id="main"` section. Use the `style` attribute to give each opening <span> tag an inline style that bolds the font of the content within the <span> tags as follows:

```
<span style="font-weight:bold;">"Smoky quartz"</span>
<span style="font-weight:bold;">"Soulmate Crystal"</span>
```

16. Validate your HTML document using the W3C validator at validator.w3.org and fix any errors that are identified. Validation is complete when the validator returns the message "*This document was successfully checked as HTML5!*" in a green bar near the top of the webpage.

17. Add indents, spaces, and extra lines to your external style sheet to make it as professional and easy to read as possible. Employ these conventions:

   • Put the selector and opening brace on the first line. Alternatively, put the selector, opening brace, and first declaration on the first line.

   • Add second and subsequent declarations on their own lines.

   • Make sure that each property is separated from its value with a colon (:)

   • Make sure that there are no spaces in values such as 10px or 20%.

   • Make sure that each declaration ends with a semicolon (;)

   • For each set of styles, position the closing brace on its own line

   • Add a blank line before each new selector line.

18. Validate your CSS file using the W3C validator at http://jigsaw.w3.org/css-validator/ and fix any errors that are identified. Validation is complete with the validator returns the message "*Congratulations! No Error Found.*"

19. Submit the index04.html and styles04.css files in a format specified by your instructor. Your instructor may also ask you to submit the wirewrap01.jpg file used with index04.html.

20. ✳ In this exercise you applied linked, embedded, and inline styles to style a home page. Use your experiences and research the web to answer these questions:

a. In step 7, you entered a comment <!--close the outerwrapper--> after the closing </div> tag. Why is a comment especially useful after a closing </div> tag?

b. What is the primary advantage of using an external versus embedded style sheet for the majority of your website styles?

c. In step 15, two <span> tags were given the same inline style. Why would you use inline styles versus embedded or external styles?

Extend Your Knowledge

Extend the skills you learned in this chapter and experiment with new skills. You may need to use additional resources to complete the assignment.

Styling Paragraphs, Headings, Lists, and Images

Instructions: In this exercise, you will use your text editor to create an external style sheet to extend your knowledge of CSS as applied to the home page for Snow Fever Ski and Board School. You will apply new styles to headings, lists, and links. You will use CSS to format an unordered list within the <nav> tags as a horizontal navigation bar. You will also add comments to an existing style sheet. The completed webpage is shown in Figure 4–45. You will also use professional web development practices to indent, space, and validate your code.

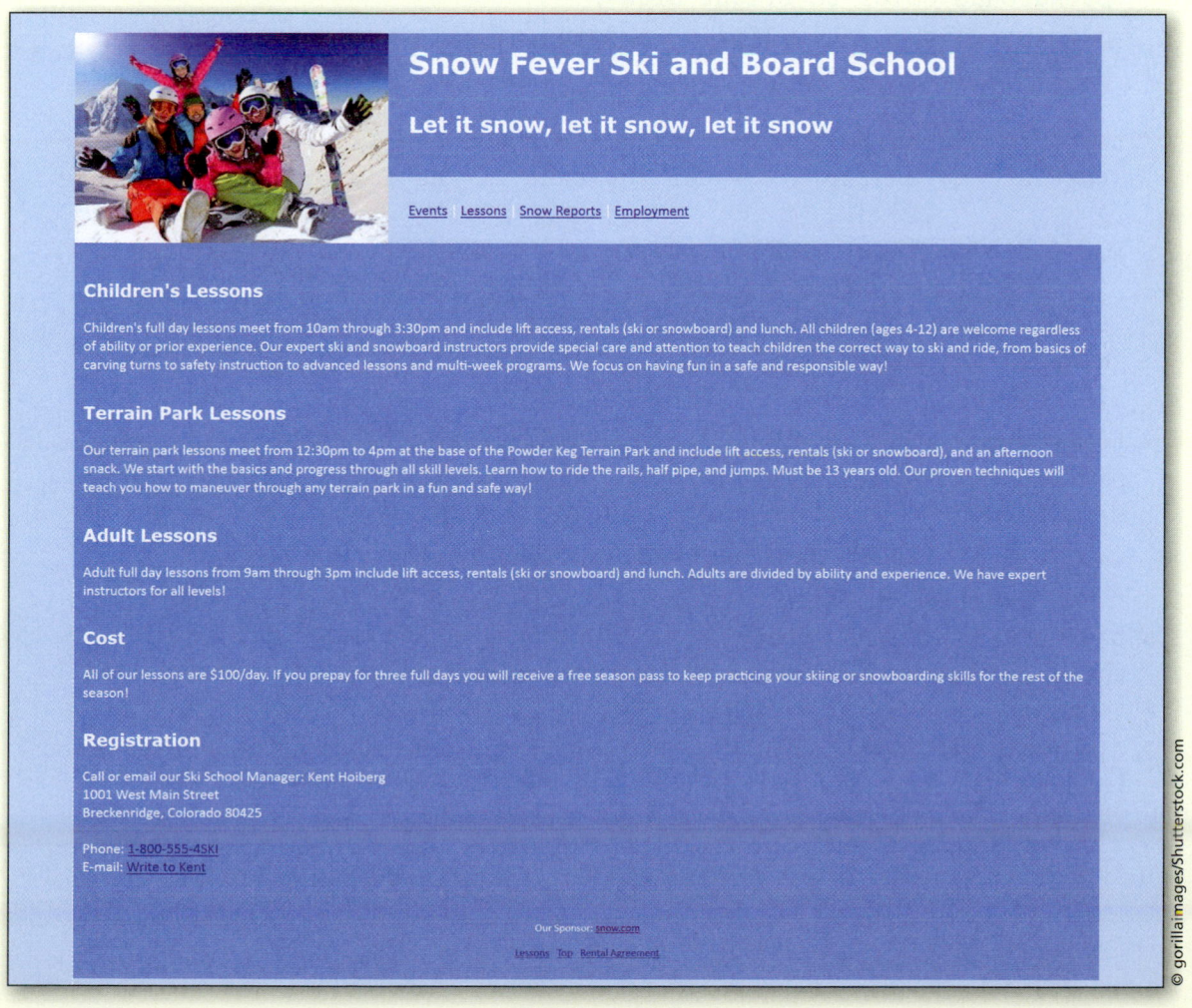

© gorillaimages/Shutterstock.com

Figure 4–45

Perform the following tasks:

1. Open the `ski04.html` file from the Data Files for Students in your text editor and then modify the comment at the top of the page to include your name and today's date.

2. In the `head` section of the ski04.html file, enter a link tag to connect the page to the external style sheet:

   ```
   <link rel="stylesheet" href="skistyles04.css">
   ```

   Save ski04.html and then preview it in a browser to make sure that the style sheet is correctly connected to the HTML file.

3. Open the `skistyles04.css` file from the Data Files for Students in your text editor and then modify the comment in the first line to include your name and today's date.

4. Document the existing style sheet before enhancing it. In the skistyles04.css file, add comments to the end of each declaration to document the existing styles as follows:

   ```
   body { color: #FFFFFF; /*set text color to white*/
    background-color: #C9E4FF; /*set background color to light blue*/
    font-family: Calibri, sans-serif; /*set font to Calibri, or the
    generic sans-serif font*/
    }
   #outer-wrapper { width: 90%; /*set width of id="outer-wrapper" to 90%*/
    margin: 0 auto 0 auto; /*center content within id="outer-wrapper"*/
    }
   header, nav, #content, footer { background-color: #4CA6FF; /*set
    background color to bright blue*/
    padding: 10px; /*add 10px of padding on all four sides of the
    wireframe containers*/
   }
   footer { font-size: 0.75em; /*reduce the font size in the footer*/
    text-align: center; /*center the text in the footer*/
    }
   img { float: left; /*float the image to the left*/
    }
   .rightmargin { margin-right: 2%; /*add 2% right margin to
    class="rightmargin"*/
    }
   ```

5. Format the headings with <h1>, <h2>, or <h3> tags with a Verdana font face and a little padding between the content and top border of the block by adding the following styles to the end of the external style sheet:

   ```
   h1, h2, h3 { font-family: Verdana, sans-serif;
     padding-top: 1%;}
   ```

6. Save the style sheet, and then refresh the ski04.html file in the browser to observe the changes. Refresh the webpage in a browser after each new style you apply to double check your work.

7. Modify the `li` content within the `nav` section so that the unordered list appears without bullets by adding the following style to the end of the external style sheet:

   ```
   li { list-style-type: none; }
   ```

8. Modify the `li` content within the `nav` section so that the items appear on the same line instead of as new blocks of content by inserting the following declaration for the `li` selector. (*Hint*: Make sure you insert the declaration before the } closing brace.)

   `display: inline;`

9. Save the stylesheet and refresh the ski04.html file in the browser to observe the changes.

10. Modify the `nav` section to have a light-blue background by inserting the following style at the end of the external style sheet:

    `nav { background-color: #C9E4FF; }`

11. Make sure that the heading that starts with "Children's Lessons" does not float to the right of the image by clearing the float at that element. In the ski04.html file, add the following attribute/value pair to the opening <h3> tag that marks the Children's Lessons heading:

    `class="clearfloat"`

12. In the skistyles04.css external style sheet, add a style to the end of the style sheet to clear the float for content marked class="clearfloat" as follows:

    `.clearfloat { clear: both; }`

13. Add padding to the `header` section that contains the image, headings, and nav by styling the `header` section separately from the rest of the wireframe elements as follows:

    a. Delete `header` in the `header, nav, #content, footer` selector.

    b. Immediately below the `nav, #content, footer` selector, create a style for the `header` section to apply the desired background color and to change the padding on the `header` section to 0 top, 2% right, 2% bottom, and 0 left.

    ```
    header { background-color: #4CA6FF;
     padding: 0 2% 2% 0; }
    ```

14. Add tabs, spaces, and extra lines to your external style sheet to make it easy to read.

15. Add comments at the end of the new styles to document their application.

16. Validate your CSS file using the W3C validator at http://jigsaw.w3.org/css-validator/ and fix any errors that are identified. Validation is complete when the validator returns the message *"Congratulations! No Error Found."*

17. Validate your HTML webpage using the W3C validator at validator.w3.org and fix any errors that are identified. Validation is complete when the validator returns the message *"This document was successfully checked as HTML5!"* in a green bar near the top of the webpage.

18. Submit the `ski04.html` and `skistyles04.css` files in a format specified by your instructor. Your instructor may also ask you to submit the ski.jpg and legal.pdf files that are referenced by the webpage.

19. ✳ In step 10 you modified the rules for the header as follows:

    ```
    nav, #content, footer { background-color: #4CA6FF;
     padding: 10px;
     }
    header { background-color: #4CA6FF;
     padding: 0 2% 2% 0; }
    ```

    Given that the same background-color rule is found in two areas, rewrite these rules so that the background-color property is referenced only once. (*Hint*: You will need to create three selectors to do this.) What is the benefit of listing the same declaration only once?

Analyze, Correct, Improve

Analyze an external style sheet, correct all errors, and improve it.

Correcting CSS Errors

Instructions: Open your text editor and then open the cssbest04.html and cssbeststyles04.css files from the Data Files for Students. Several CSS "best practices" are listed on this webpage, but there are errors in both the HTML and CSS files that you will need to find and correct. Use Figure 4–46 as a guide to correct these files. You will also use professional web development best practices to comment, indent, space, and validate your work.

20 CSS Best Practices

1. Create HTML first using a semantic wireframe and meaningful names for id and class attributes.
2. Learn the language of css: selector, declaration, and property.
3. Learn css syntax: the characters required to write accurate, readable styles.
4. Put global styles in an external style sheet. Use embedded and inline styles only when appropriate.
5. Write styles in a sensible order starting with reset code.
6. Group styles that apply to similar content such as headings, lists, or forms together.
7. Put each declaration on its own line to make the code easy to read.
8. Save your work and refresh your webpage often to observe incremental updates.
9. Use comments to separate the sections of your style sheet.
10. Use comments to document the author, latest update, or anything else that is important.
11. Use combination selectors such as h1, h2, h3 to code each declaration only once.
12. Use combination properties such as margin when appropriate to cut down on the number of declarations.
13. Study and truly understand the more difficult concepts of css such as float and block versus inline elements.
14. Use an outer wrapper and the margin: 0 auto; declaration to center content within the outer wrapper.
15. Measure widths in % to make the containers responsive.
16. Measure text in ems or % to make the text responsive.
17. Use Firebug or a similar web development tool to analyze and debug errors.
18. When debugging, use comments to "comment out" a rule that you are modifying (instead of deleting it).
19. Validate all html and css.
20. Never stop learning.
    ○ Cascading Style Sheet home page from w3.org - keeper of the official css standards
    ○ CSS Tricks home page - dedicated to providing current information, tutorials, and code samples for css developers
    ○ CSS home page w3schools.com - online css tutorial site
    ○ 25 best CSS practices from a web development company
    ○ Sample CSS reset code
    ○ Provides HTML5 browser compatibility information
    ○ Provides browser compatibility information for individual HTML elements, HTML attributes and CSS properties

Figure 4–46

1. Correct

a. Open the `cssbest04.html` file in your editor and then modify the comment at the top of the document to include your name and today's date.

b. Open the `cssbeststyles04.css` file in your editor and then modify and correct the comment at the top of the style sheet to include your name and today's date. Correct the problem with the h1 style.

c. Enter a tag in the <head> section of the cssbest04.html file just below the <meta> tag to connect the webpage to the external style sheet.

```
<link rel="stylesheet" href="cssbeststyles04.css">
```

Open the webpage in a browser to make sure it is properly connected to the style sheet.

d. The current colors of the webpage are not a pleasing combination. Furthermore, the content goes "wall-to-wall" in your browser, meaning it spans the width of the browser window with no left or right margin. To fix this, add a `div` element to surround the content, and then resize and center it with CSS by completing the following:

• In the cssbest04.html document, after the opening <body> tag, add a `<div id="main">` tag.

• Just before the closing </body> tag, add a `</div><!--close main-->` tag and comment.

- In the cssbeststyles04.css file, add the following style between the body and h1 selectors to constrain the content within the <div id="main"> and </div> tags to 70% of the width of the screen and to center it.

```
#main { width: 70%;
 margin: 0 auto 0 auto;
 }
```

e. Save both files, then preview the webpage in a browser to observe the changes. Next, you will work on the colors. Go to **www.coolors.co** or any color scheme generation site and pick three complimentary colors for the body text, body background, and h1 text. Apply the colors in your style sheet. The color declarations used in Figure 4–46 are:

```
color: #895D88; (for the body selector)
background-color: #F8F991; (for the body selector)
color: #3D315B; (for the h1 selector)
```

f. To improve the spacing between the list items, add the following rule to the end of your style sheet to add a half a line of space between list items:

```
li { line-height: 150%; }
```

2. Improve

a. Use http://validator.w3.org to validate your cssbest04.html page. The page flags an error at Line 34. In your cssbest04.html page, notice that the "Never stop learning" list item contains an unordered list starting on Line 34. Often, the validator flags the line after the actual error occurs. In this case, the closing </li> tag on Line 33 is in the wrong position. Move the </li> tag to below the closing </ul> tag on Line 42. In other words, the "Never stop learning" list item includes not only those three words, but the entire unordered list of links as well.

b. Save and revalidate the cssbest04.html page. Fix any errors and revalidate until you get the message "*This document was successfully checked as HTML5!*" A first step in creating clean CSS code is to validate your HTML code.

c. Use http://jigsaw.w3.org/css-validator/ to validate your CSS code. Unless you've already fixed it, you should see an error on Line 12 because the final brace } was not included for the h1 selector. Add that character and revalidate your CSS code. Fix any errors and revalidate until you get the message "*Congratulations! No Error Found.*"

3. ✳ After reviewing the 20 "best practices," comment on which of these practices you would like to understand better and why.

After reviewing the links in the "Never stop learning" list item, comment on which of these sites you would like to explore further and why.

In the Labs

Labs 1 and 2, which increase in difficulty, require you to create webpages based on what you learned in the chapter; Lab 3 requires you to dive deeper into a topic covered in the chapter.

Lab 1: Creating an External Style Sheet for City Farmer

Problem: You work for a local but rapidly growing gardening supply company called City Farmer that specializes in products that support food self-sufficiency. The company has hired you to help create the home page. The content for the home page is in place, but it needs to be styled. Style the webpage shown in Figure 4–47 with an external style sheet.

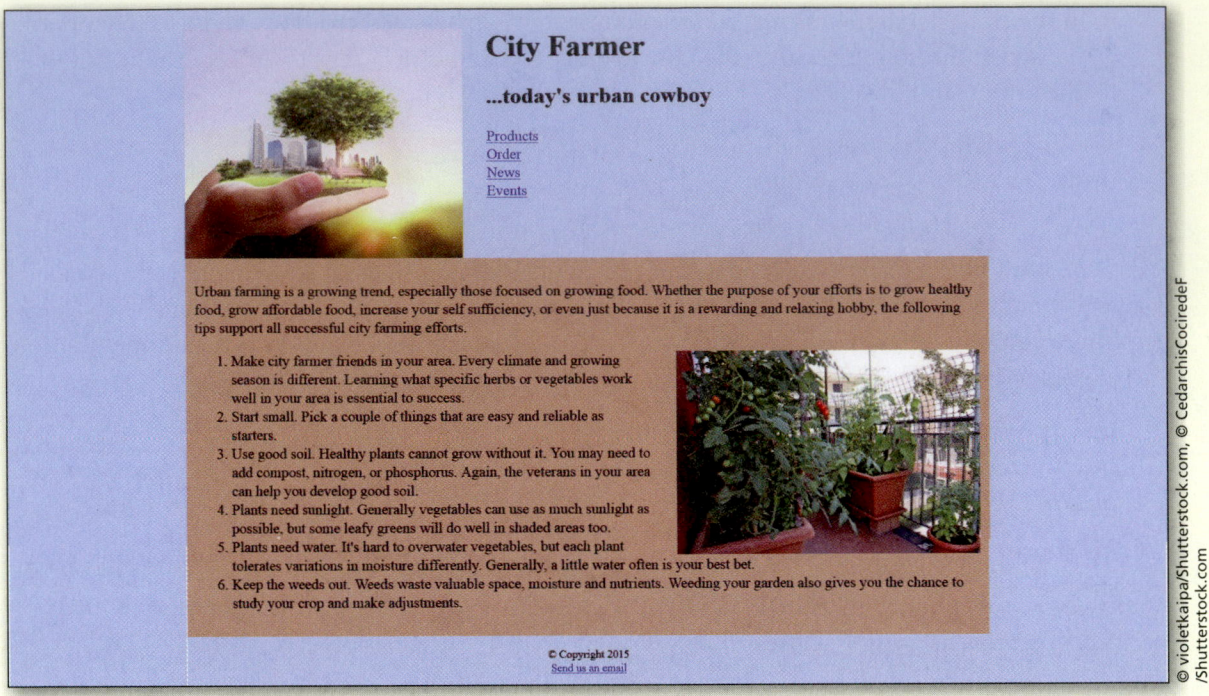

Figure 4–47

Instructions: Perform the following tasks:

1. Open `cityfarmer04.html` in your HTML editor from the Data Files for Students and then modify the comment at the top of the page to include your name and today's date. Make sure the <title>…</title> tags contain the text `City Farmer Home Page`.

2. Start a new file in your text editor, and save it in the lab1\styles folder with the name `farmerstyles04.css`

3. Enter a CSS comment as the first line of the external style sheet with *your* name and today's date. Recall that CSS comments are entered within `/*` and `*/` characters.

4. Enter a style to apply a uniform black text color, a uniform serif font, and light-blue background color to the body:

```
body { color: #000000;
  background-color: #B8D1EB;
  font-family: "Times New Roman", serif;
  }
```

5. In the `head` section of the cityfarmer04.html file, enter an element to connect the page to the external style sheet:

```
<link rel="stylesheet" href="styles/farmerstyles04.css">
```

Save your changes, and then open or refresh cityfarmer04.html in a browser to make sure that the style sheet is correctly connected to the HTML file. Note that in this exercise, the style sheet is saved in the styles folder, so that path needs to be included in the `href` value.

6. Center the content by adding <div> and </div> tags to surround the content in the wireframe, and then applying styles to center the content within the <div> and </div> tags as follows:

   a. In cityfarmer04.html, insert the `<div id="outerwrapper">` opening tag just after the opening <body> tag.

   b. In cityfarmer04.html, insert the `</div> <!-- close the outerwrapper-->` closing tag and comment just before the closing </body> tag. Save your changes to cityfarmer04.html.

c. In farmerstyles04.css, insert the following style to constrain the outerwrapper to 70% of the width of the screen and to center the content within the outerwrapper:

```
#outerwrapper { width: 70%;
 margin: 0 auto 0 auto;
 }
```

Save your changes to farmerstyles04.css, and then open or refresh cityfarmer04.html in a browser to make sure that the content is centered within 70% of the browser window.

7. Style the text in the footer section to have a font size of 0.75em and appear centered by adding the following styles to the external stylesheet:

```
footer { font-size: 0.75em;
 text-align: center;
 }
```

(*Hint*: Save and refresh the cityfarmer04.html file in your browser after every step to observe and study the impact of each style.)

8. Style the content within the `div id="main"` section to have a light-brown background and 10px of padding on the top by adding the following style:

```
#main { background-color: #C5A98B;
 padding: 10px;
 }
```

9. Float the image in the header to the left with the following style so that the <h1>, <h2>, and <nav> content moves to the right of the image:

```
img { float: left;
 }
```

10. Remove the bullets from the list items in the `nav` section by adding the following style:

```
ul { list-style-type: none;
 }
```

11. Push the content away from the image by adding a right margin to the img selector with the following declaration:

```
margin-right: 3%;
```

12. Clear the float so that the content for the `div id="main"` section starts on its own line by adding a second style rule with a #main selector:

```
#main { clear: both;
 }
```

13. You decide to float the second image right instead of left. Right now, your float rule is written using the img selector so all img content is affected. To change the float value for the second image, complete the following:

a. Add a `class="floatleft"` attribute value pair to the first <img> tag (the logo) in the cityfarmer04.html file. (*Hint*: The order of attribute value pairs in the opening html tag do not affect how the code works in the browser, but typically the most important attributes are listed first so the class="floatleft" attribute would often be listed second or third.)

b. Add a `class="floatright"` attribute value pair to the second <img> tag (tomatoes in pots) in the cityfarmer04.html file.

c. In the farmerstyles04.css file, change the img selector to `.floatleft`

d. Just below the .floatleft style in the CSS file, add the following style to float the second image to the right:

```
.floatright { float: right;
  margin-left: 3%;
  }
```

Save both files and then refresh cityfarmer04.html in your browser.

14. To make sure the footer also starts on its own line, modify the selector for the rule that clears all float to include both the #main and footer areas as follows:

```
#main, footer { clear: both;
  }
```

15. Validate your HTML code and fix any errors.

16. Validate your CSS code and fix any errors.

17. Save and open the cityfarmer04.html page within a browser as shown in Figure 4–47.

18. Submit your assignment in the format specified by your instructor.

19. ✳ In step 13, you inserted class="floatleft" and class="floatright" attributes in your HTML page instead of id="floatleft" and id="floatright". Why?

Lab 2: Creating an External Style Sheet for Cycle Out Cancer

Problem: You are part of a philanthropic group of motorcyclists, Cycle Out Cancer, who participate in community events and parades to distribute cancer awareness information. You have created content for the first four webpages of their website and updated the links in the **nav** section for each page. In this exercise you will create an external style sheet and link it to the four pages as shown in Figures 4–48 through 4–51.

Figure 4–48

Cycle Out Cancer

We Ride So Others May Live

Home
About Us
Events
Cancer FAQs

About Us

Cycle Out Cancer is a volunteer organization that promotes cancer awareness. Cycle Out Cancer was founded by a group of three motorcycle enthusiasts from Kansas City who each found their lives interrupted by something else they unfortunately shared in common: cancer. Each made a vow to the other to fight their different forms of cancer to the best of their ability and some day, "ride again."

After a three years and countless medical procedures, their dream came true in May of 2000 when the threesome made their way from Kansas City to Branson, Missouri. At every stop in the short journey the three friends shared their amazing stories of how they fought their cancers. Over time, more and more people have joined their rides. Now Cycle Out Cancer is one of the largest all-volunteer motorcycle clubs in the midwest.

Anyone who is a motorcycle enthusiast is welcome to join. Many say that the best part of the ride are the inspiring stories shared by the members at the finish line.

Contact Cycle Out Cancer

© Jim Pruitt/Shutterstock.com

Figure 4–49

Cycle Out Cancer

We Ride So Others May Live

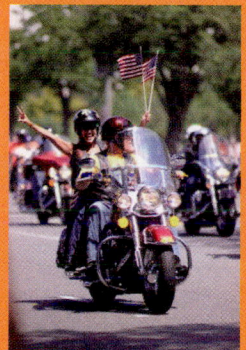

Home
About Us
Events
Cancer FAQs

Monthly Rides

First Friday of the Month - May - June - July - Aug - September

The first Friday of these months we honor past members who have had cancer but are no longer with us. Our route may include a lunch at their favorite watering hole, a visit to their surviving spouse, or a visit to the cemetary to decorate their grave. Contact Cycle Out Cancer for more information on commemorative rides in your area.

Rider Safety

All riders must adhere to basic safety rules while on our rides:

1. Gear up: Wear an approved helmet and protective clothing appropriate for the weather.
2. Maintain the big stuff: Check your tires, breaks, fluids, electronics, and frame before each ride.
3. Check the little stuff: Make sure your lights, blinkers, mirrors, and stands all work correctly.
4. Obey all traffic laws, lights, and signs.
5. Drive defensively and respectfully even when others do not.

Rides and Activities

Rides and activities are currently being planned for these hospitals in the coming year:

Contact Cycle Out Cancer for up-to-date schedules.

- Dana-Farber/Brigham and Women's Cancer Center, Boston MA
- Memorial Sloan Kettering Cancer Center, New York NY
- Mayo Clinic, Rochester MN
- University of Texas MD Anderson Cancer Center, Houston TX

Contact Cycle Out Cancer

© Rena Schild/Shutterstock.com

Figure 4–50

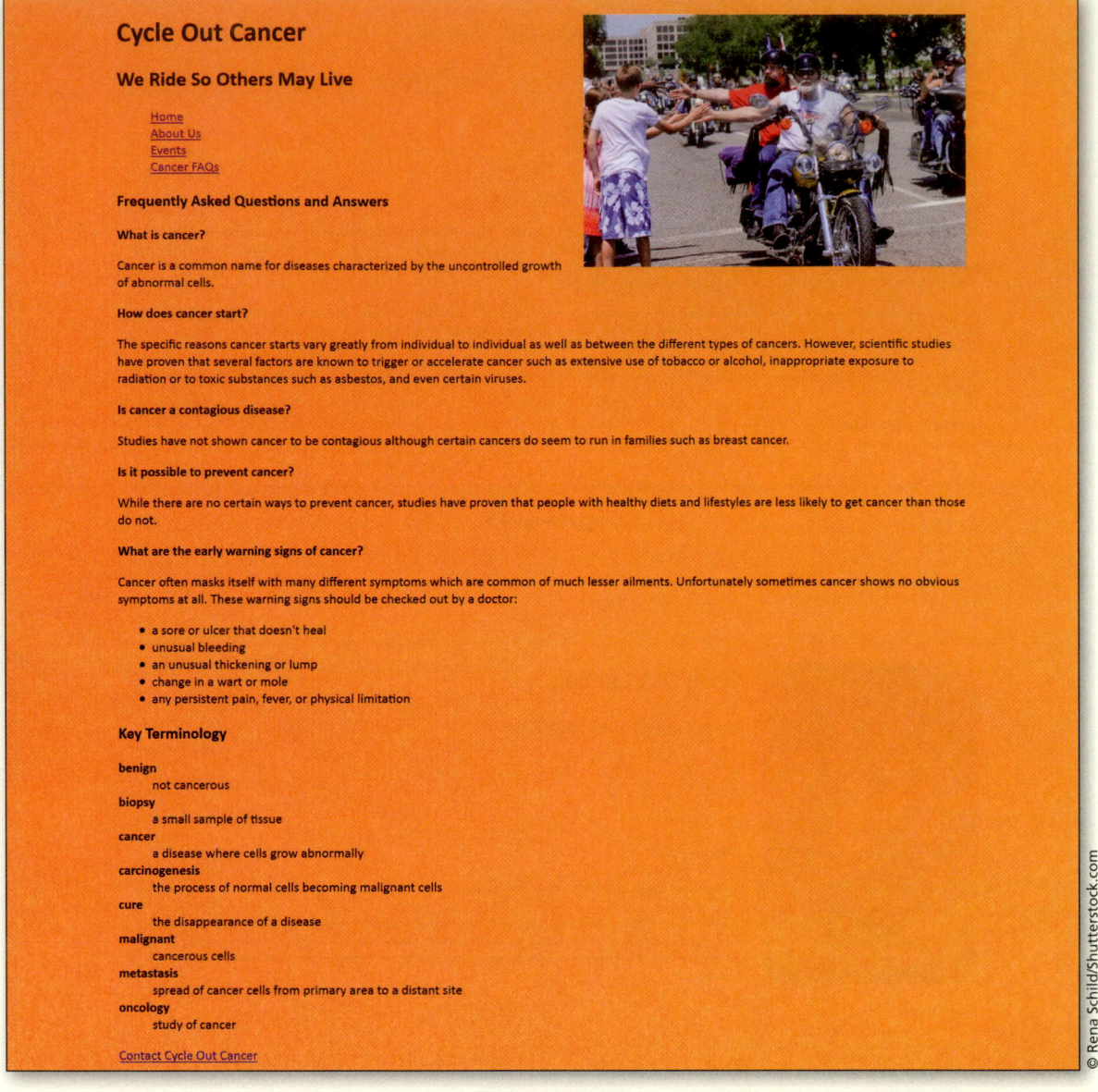

Figure 4–51

Instructions: Perform the following tasks:

1. Open the **cyclehome04.html**, **cycleabout04.html**, **cycleevents04.html**, and **cyclefaq04.html** files in your HTML editor from the Data Files for Students and then modify the comment at the top of each page to include your name and today's date.

2. Start a new file in your text editor, and save it in the lab2\styles folder with the name **cyclestyles04.css**

3. Enter a CSS comment as the first line of the external style sheet with *your* name and today's date.

4. Enter the styles to apply a uniform black text color, Calibri and sans-serif font, and an orange (#FF9900) background color to the body.

5. In the **head** section of each of the four cycle HTML documents, enter an element to connect the page to the external style sheet.

   Save and then open or refresh each page in a browser to make sure that the stylesheet is correctly connected to the HTML files. Note that in this exercise, the style sheet is saved in the styles folder, so that path needs to be included in the **href** value.

6. Center the content by adding <div> and </div> tags to surround the content in the wireframe, and then apply styles to center the content within the <div> and </div> tags as follows:

a. In each HTML page, insert the `<div id="wrapper">` opening tag just after the opening <body> tag.

b. In each HTML page, insert the `</div> <!--close the wrapper-->` closing tag and comment just before the closing </body> tag.

c. In cyclestyles04.css, add the styles to constrain the wrapper to 80% of the width of the window and to center the content within the wrapper.

Save all files and then open or refresh the pages in a browser to make sure that the content is centered within 80% of the browser window. (*Hint*: Note that a `nav` section to link to each of the four pages follows the image on each page.)

9. On the cyclehome04.html and cyclefaq04.html pages, you want to float the image in the header to the right. On the cycleevents04.html and cycleabout04.html pages, you want to float the image in the header to the left. Complete these tasks as follows:

a. Create styles in your style sheet with a selector that addresses the class names of floatleft and floatright. (*Hint*: A `class="floatleft"` attribute and value in the HTML document is referenced by a `.floatleft` selector in the CSS file.)

b. Add two declarations to both the selectors. The first will float the content either left or right. The second will add a 2% margin to the inside edge of the content. For example, the declarations for the .floatleft selector would be:

```
.floatleft { float: left;
margin-right: 2%;
}
```

Complete the declarations for the .floatright selector to make the image float right and add a 2% margin to the left side.

c. Add `class="floatleft"` to the opening `img` tag in the cycleevents04.html and cycleabout04.html pages.

d. Add `class="floatright"` to the opening `img` tag in the cyclehome04.html and cyclefaq04.html pages.

e. Save all files and refresh them in your browser.

11. Remove the bullets from the list items only in the nav section by adding the following style:

```
nav ul { list-style-type: none;
}
```

(*Hint*: In this example, you are using a descendant selector. Only the `ul` content within the `nav` content will be affected.) Save and refresh files and review them in your browser to make sure that only the bullets for the `ul` content within the `nav` section were removed.)

12. Create one more class named `boldtext` for the questions on the cyclefaq04.html page as follows so that you can style the questions in bold:

a. Add `class="boldtext"` to the opening <p> tag for the five questions immediately below the <h3>Frequently Asked Questions and Answers </h3> heading in the cyclefaq04.html file.

b. Add a style in the cyclestyles04.css file to apply bold to the content that is identified by the boldtext class as follows:

```
.boldtext { font-weight: bold; }
```

13. You also decide to bold the `dt` (definition term) content on the cyclefaq04.html page. Given you already have a declaration to apply bold, change the selector to include both the content identified by the boldtext class as well as the content marked up by the `dt` tag as follows:

```
.boldtext, dt { font-weight: bold; }
```

14. Validate your four HTML pages and fix any errors.

15. Validate your CSS code and fix any errors.

16. Save and open the pages within a browser as shown in Figures 4–48, 4–49, 4–50, and 4–51.

17. Submit your assignment in the format specified by your instructor.

18. ✳ Compare the selector of `nav ul` (step 11) to the selector of `.boldtext, dt` (step 13). One contains a comma and one does not. What is the significance of the comma? (*Hint:* Search for information on CSS grouping selectors and descendant selectors.)

Lab 3: Expand Your World
Styling Inline versus Block Content

Problem: CSS has its own terminology, syntax, and concepts such as the box model, float, and inline versus block content, all of which is critical to your ability to successfully apply styles and position content on your webpages. In this exercise you will create an external style sheet to experiment with styles as they relate to inline and block content. The webpages that you are styling summarize CSS terminology, syntax, and tips. The final, styled webpages are shown in Figures 4–52, 4–53, 4–54, and 4–55.

Figure 4–52

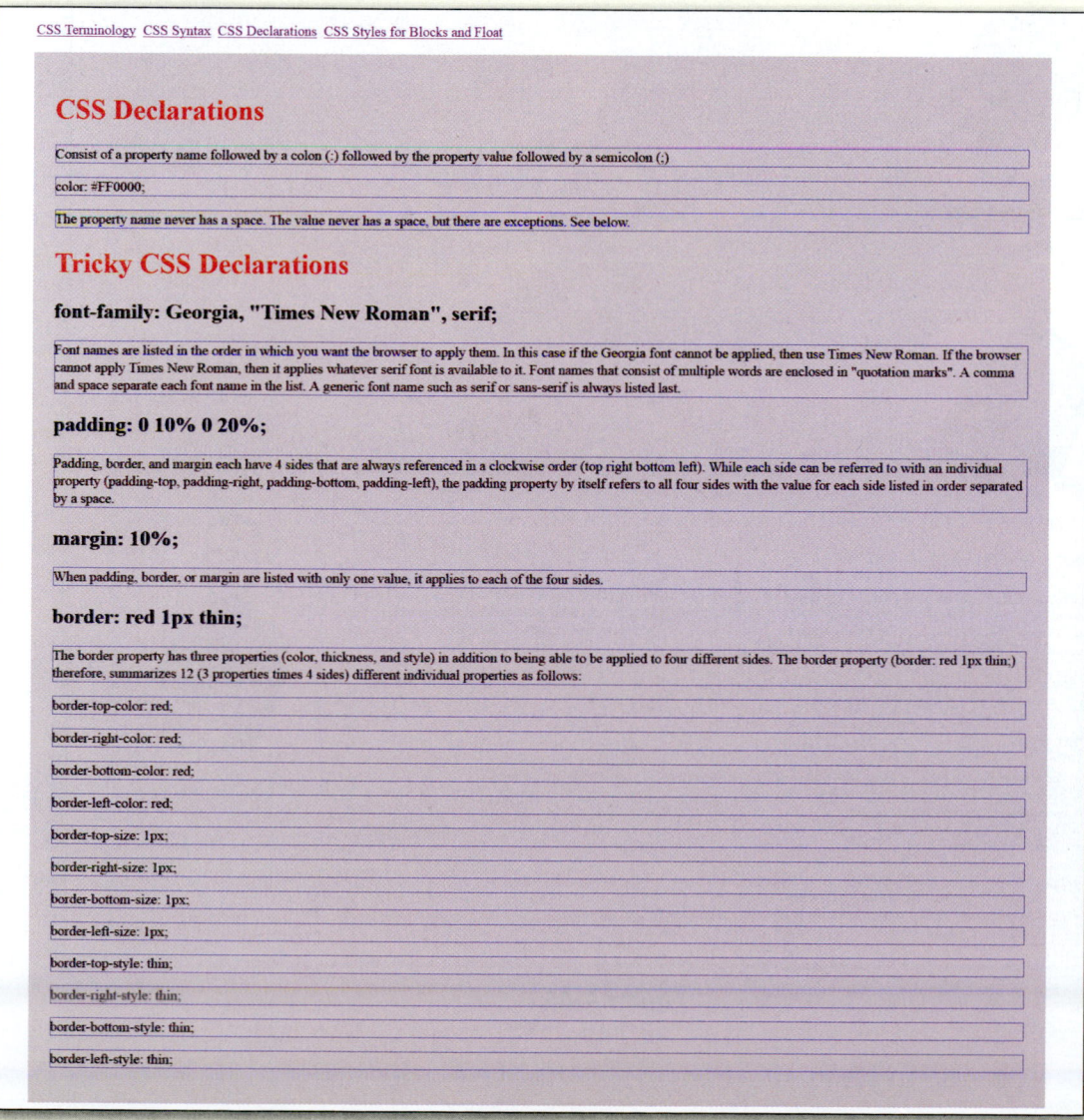

CSS Syntax

The selector is followed by an opening brace {

The declaration may not consist of any spaces with the exception of an optional space after the colon. (See exceptions below.)

If a property value consists of a unit and unit of measure such as 80% or 2em, do not put a space between the unit and unit of measure.

All of the declarations for a particular selector end with a closing brace }

CSS Professionalism

Put all global rules in an external style sheet. Use embedded styles only when the styles apply to one page only. Use inline styles only when the style applies to one element only.

Use comments to document the author, date, and sections of your style sheet. CSS comments are entered within /* these characters */

For maximum readability...

- Position the selector and opening brace { on its own line.
- Position each declaration on its own line. This also helps you see that each declaration is closed with a semicolon ;
- Position the closing brace } on its own line.

Use reset code.

Validate all CSS code.

Figure 4–53

CSS Declarations

Consist of a property name followed by a colon (:) followed by the property value followed by a semicolon (;)

color: #FF0000;

The property name never has a space. The value never has a space, but there are exceptions. See below.

Tricky CSS Declarations

font-family: Georgia, "Times New Roman", serif;

Font names are listed in the order in which you want the browser to apply them. In this case if the Georgia font cannot be applied, then use Times New Roman. If the browser cannot apply Times New Roman, then it applies whatever serif font is available to it. Font names that consist of multiple words are enclosed in "quotation marks". A comma and space separate each font name in the list. A generic font name such as serif or sans-serif is always listed last.

padding: 0 10% 0 20%;

Padding, border, and margin each have 4 sides that are always referenced in a clockwise order (top right bottom left). While each side can be referred to with an individual property (padding-top, padding-right, padding-bottom, padding-left), the padding property by itself refers to all four sides with the value for each side listed in order separated by a space.

margin: 10%;

When padding, border, or margin are listed with only one value, it applies to each of the four sides.

border: red 1px thin;

The border property has three properties (color, thickness, and style) in addition to being able to be applied to four different sides. The border property (border: red 1px thin;) therefore, summarizes 12 (3 properties times 4 sides) different individual properties as follows:

border-top-color: red;

border-right-color: red;

border-bottom-color: red;

border-left-color: red;

border-top-size: 1px;

border-right-size: 1px;

border-bottom-size: 1px;

border-left-size: 1px;

border-top-style: thin;

border-right-style: thin;

border-bottom-style: thin;

border-left-style: thin;

Figure 4–54

CSS Terminology CSS Syntax CSS Declarations CSS Styles for Blocks and Float

Block Versus Inline Content

Most html content renders in a browser as block content.

The most common inline elements are span, a (hyperlink), and img (image).

Images are the trickiest inline elements because they are often followed by block content making them "appear" to be blocks. But consider the following examples.

Example 1: several images positioned together prove that the img is an inline element -- images stay on the same line (inline).

Example 2: one image followed by block content makes the image "appear" that it is also a block element.

Paragraph content is block content which starts on its own line, its own block.

Example 3: one image - float left.

Block content that follows a left float.

Example 4: one image - float right.

Block content that follows a right float.

float: left; and clear: both;

The float property allows content that follows the floated content to occupy the available horizontal space not used by the floated content. Float is commonly applied to images given they have a distinct width which leaves extra horizontal white space beside the image when the next block of content is rendered on the page. Float can also be applied to sections of content to create multiple columns on a page. Content is floated left or right with the float: left; or float: right; declarations.

To "clear" the float use the clear: both; declaration on the content that you want to start on its own line. You may also clear only the left or right float by using clear: left; or clear: right; declarations.

Float tips...

- The content that is floated - whether left or right -- is positioned before other content in the html file.
- Because we read from left to right in the English language, content that is floated right may appear out of order in the html file. Content that is floated right must appear before other content in the html file.
- The "box" (margins, border, and padding) of content that follows a floated element behaves as if the floated element is not there.
- To clear a float which allows a block element to start on its own line, use the clear property. clear: both; is the most common declaration, but you can clear only a left or only a right float using clear: left; or clear: right;
- Textual content that is styled with a float should be given a width value. (Images have an inherent width.)
- It is not possible to float content in the center, only left or right.
- Floating content left or right shifts it to the left or right edge of the containing block.

Figure 4–55

Instructions:

1. Open the **cssterminology04.html, csssyntax04.html, cssdeclarations04.html**, and **cssblock04.html** files in your HTML editor from the Data Files for Students and then modify the comment at the top of each of the four pages to include your name and today's date.

2. Enter **CSS terminology** within the <title> tags of cssterminology04.html, **CSS syntax** within the <title> tags of csssyntax04.html, **CSS declarations** within the <title> tags of the cssdeclarations04.html page, and **CSS block styles** within the <title> tags of the cssblock04.html page.

3. Open the cssterminology04.html page in the browser and read the page. Tap or click the links for the three other pages and read them as well. Note that the content goes "wall-to-wall" in your browser. To center the content within a small left and right margin, add padding between the content and border, and then change the background color to light gray. To do so, create an external style sheet with the following rules for the content marked up between <div id="main"> and </div> tags:

```
#main { width: 90%;
 margin: 0 auto 0 auto;
 padding: 2%;
 background-color: #D7D7D7;
 }
```

4. Save the file as **css04.css** in the same folder as the HTML webpages and then add a comment as the first line of the file with your name and the current date.

5. Link the css04.css stylesheet to each page by entering the following element to the <head> section in each page.

```
<link rel="stylesheet" href="css04.css">
```

6. Save and refresh your webpages after every step and tap or click each link to see the impact of each new set of rules on the four pages. Style <h1> content with a dark red text color by adding the following style to the external style sheet:

```
h1 { color: #CF0000; }
```

7. To study how borders are applied to block paragraph content, add the following rule to apply a blue, 1px, solid border to all sides of every paragraph:

```
p { border: blue 1px solid; }
```

Save your changes and then refresh your webpages and view the borders around the paragraphs.

8. To study how float is applied, you will work with the cssblock04.html page. Read the paragraphs that surround each example. Example 1 proves that when an image is followed by another image, they arrange themselves in a line, as inline content. Example 2 shows how a single image "appears" to be block content, but only because the content that follows the image is a block and thus starts on its own line.

You will modify the image after the Example 3 paragraph to float left. To do this, add **class="floatleft"** to the <img> tag that follows the Example 3 paragraph. (*Hint*: The order of attribute value pairs in an HTML tag is not technically significant, but it is common to put the most important attributes first. Typically class and id attribute values are listed early in the tag.)

Add the following rule to the external style sheet:

```
.floatleft { float: left; }
```

Save css04.css and cssblock04.html and then refresh the cssblock04.html page in the browser to observe how the image after the Example 3 paragraph floats left. Content that follows the floated image fills the space to the right of the floated image.

9. You want the Example 4 paragraph to start on its own line, so you need to clear the float at that point. To study how float is cleared, add **class="clearfloat"** to the opening <p> tag for the Example 4 paragraph. Add the following rule to the external style sheet:

   ```
   .clearfloat { clear: both; }
   ```

   Save the files and refresh the cssblock04.html page in the browser to observe how the Example 4 paragraph is "cleared of the float" and acts as normal block content again, starting on its own line.

10. You want the image after the Example 4 paragraph to float right. To do this, add **class="floatright"** to the <img> tag that follows the Example 4 paragraph. Add the following rule to the embedded style sheet:

    ```
    .floatright { float: right; }
    ```

    Save the files and refresh the cssblock04.html page in the browser to observe how the image following the Example 4 paragraph floats right. Floating content right can be tricky considering that people read English from left to right. Content that floats right is positioned before the content that flows next to it in the HTML file.

11. Change the existing navigation content into a horizontal navigation bar. To do this, first remove the bullets from the list items in the nav area. List item content naturally flows as block content, with each list item on its own line. To create a horizontal navigation system with each of the links on the same line, you also must add a rule to change the list item content from block to inline. To do this, add the following rules to the style sheet:

    ```
    nav li { list-style-type: none;
      display: inline;
      }
    ```

    Save the files and refresh the pages in the browser to observe the new horizontal navigation system.

12. Tap or click the CSS Terminology link to open the cssterminology.html page in the browser. This page lists several key CSS terms. You want to style the terms in bold. To do this, you will mark up the CSS key terms using the <span>…</span> tags. (The **span** element is an inline element that allows you to mark up and style content within a paragraph without creating a new line.) Mark up the following CSS terms using both the <span> tag and a **class="cssterm"** attribute in the opening <span> tag as follows: (*Hint*: Be careful to add only the opening and closing <span> tags and not change or delete any of the existing content or HTML code.)

    <span class="cssterm">External styles**</span>** (first paragraph)

    <span class="cssterm">Embedded styles**</span>** (second paragraph)

    <span class="cssterm">Inline styles**</span>** (third paragraph)

    <span class="cssterm">Rules**</span>** (fourth paragraph)

    <span class="cssterm">selector**</span>** (fifth paragraph)

    <span class="cssterm">declaration**</span>** (sixth paragraph)

    <span class="cssterm">Inheritance**</span>** (seventh paragraph)

    <span class="cssterm">Specificity**</span>** (eighth paragraph)

Add the following rule to the external style sheet to style the terms marked up by the `class="cssterm"` attribute value:

`.cssterm { font-weight: bold;}`

Save the files and refresh the pages in the browser to observe the new bold terms on the cssterminology04.html page.

13. Validate your HTML and CSS pages and fix any errors.

14. Submit your assignment in the format specified by your instructor.

15. ✳ Create a document with these four headings: Terminology, Syntax, Declarations, and Block Versus Inline. Reread cssterminology04.html webpage in your browser. After the Terminology heading in your document, write a sentence or two about something that you want to learn more about or still have questions about in regard to CSS terminology. Repeat this process for the other three pages in this exercise that discuss CSS syntax, CSS declarations, and CSS block versus inline styles. Your answers should prove that you have read the webpages. Save the file with the name **Chapter4Lab3CSS**.

Consider This: Your Turn

Apply your creative thinking and problem-solving skills to design and implement a solution.

1. Style Your Personal Portfolio Website

Personal

Part 1: In Chapter 3, you added content for your personal portfolio website on the `portfolio.html` webpage. In this exercise, you will update the page with an external style sheet that includes the following updates: (*Note:* Your instructor may want you to use the Data Files for Students provided for this exercise instead.)

1. Create an external style sheet with the name `portfoliostyles04.css` and save it in the `styles` folder within the your_turn_1 folder.

2. Add your name and the current date as a comment to the first line of the portfoliostyles04.css file.

3. Open your portfolio.html file in your HTML editor and float the image in the header section to the left by adding the attribute of `class="float-left"` to the <img> tag and a corresponding `.float-left {float: left;}` rule to the external style sheet.

4. Add a tag to the <head> section of the portfolio.html file to link the external style sheet to the portfolio.html page as follows:

`<link rel="stylesheet" href="styles/portfoliostyles04.css">`

Save both the CSS and HTML files, and open the portfolio.html file in your browser to make sure the style sheet is linked and the image is floating properly.

5. Add some space between the image and the content that is floated to the right by adding the following rule to the style sheet:

`img { margin-right: 3%; }`

Also remove the bullets on the list items within the nav section by adding the following rule to the style sheet:

`nav li { list-style-type: none; }`

6. Center the content on the page by containing all of the content within the `body` by surrounding it with `<div id="outerwrapper">...</div>` tags.

Add a comment after the closing </div> tag to identify that section as follows:

```
<!--end outerwrapper-->
```

Style the outerwrapper in the external style sheet to take up 70% of the available space on the screen and to center it within that space as follows:

```
#outerwrapper { width: 70%;
  margin: 0 auto 0 auto;
  }
```

7. To make sure the webpage will render successfully in all browsers, identify the main section using the <div id="main"> and </div> tags versus <main> and </main>, and include three pairs of <h2> tags in that section that mark up the headings of Strengths, Technologies, and Other.

8. Clear the float with the **main** content by adding the following style to the style sheet:

```
#main { clear: both; }
```

9. Push the content below the image by adding the following declaration to the **img** selector in the style sheet:

```
margin-bottom: 2%;
```

10. Style your name at the top of the webpage with a large Futura then Calibri then generic sans-serif font by adding the following class to the opening <p> tag that contains your name. **class="myname"** and by adding the following corresponding styles to the stylesheet:

```
.myname { font-family: Futura, Calibri, sans-serif;
  font-size: 2em;
  }
```

11. Add a light background color to the **#main** selector that goes well with the colors in your image.

12. Add styles for padding and a border with rounded corners to the **#main** selector as follows:

```
padding: 3%;
border: 2px black solid;
border-radius: 25px;
```

13. Link your style sheet to any other pages you have created in your portfolio website.

14. Add any other styles that you think would improve your portfolio webpages.

15. Validate and correct your HTML and CSS files, and then submit your assignment in the format specified by your instructor.

Part 2: ✺ Go to www.csszengarden.com and tap or click the style links to see how the single HTML file appears with different styles. The featured styles change, but at the time of this writing, the featured eight styles were named "Mid Century Modern," "Garments," "Steel," "Apothecary," "Screen Filler," "Fountain Kiss," "A Robot Named Jimmy," and "Verde Moderna." Be careful to tap or click the style names rather than the "by author's name" links to apply the new style to the web-page. Tapping or clicking the author's name links takes you to the home page for that author.

Explore the site to see how the location and appearance of the content changes from style to style. Locate the links to download the HTML file and CSS file. Download both files and open them in your HTML editor. After reviewing the code in each file, comment on what you learned or want to know more about.

2. Style the WebDevPros Webpages

Professional

Part 1: In Chapter 3, you added content within a wireframe and site map for the WebDevPros website. In this exercise, you will update the pages for that website with an external style sheet that includes the following updates: (*Note:* Your instructor may want you to use the Data Files for Students provided for this exercise instead.)

1. Create an external style sheet with the name `webdevstyles04.css` and save it in the `styles` folder within the your_turn_2 folder.

2. Add your name and the current date as a comment to the first line of the webdevstyles04.css file.

3. Open index.html and other files you created for WebDevPros in Chapter 3 in your HTML editor and float the images in the header section to the left or right by adding the attribute of `class="float-right"` or `class="float-left"` to the <img> tag and the corresponding `.float-right { float: right; }` or `.float-left { float: left; }` rules to the external style sheet. Make your decision on whether the image should float left or right based on how it looks best on the page.

4. Add a tag to the <head> section of the index.html file to link the external style sheet to the index.html page as follows:

   ```
   <link rel="stylesheet" href="styles/webdevstyles04.css">
   ```

   Save both the CSS and HTML file, and open the index.html file in your browser to make sure the style sheet is linked and the image is floating properly.

5. Add some space between the image and the content that is floated to the right by adding the following declaration and comment to the `.float-right` selector:

   ```
   margin: 0 0 3% 3%; /* 0 top 0 right 3% bottom 3% left */
   ```

   Add the following declaration and comment to the `.float-left` selector:

   ```
   margin: 0 3% 3% 0; /* 0 top 3% right 3% bottom 0 left */
   ```

6. Center the content on all of the pages by containing all of the content within the `body` by surrounding it with `<div id="outer-wrapper">` ... `</div>` tags.

   Add a comment after the closing </div> tag to identify that section as follows:

   ```
   <!--end outer-wrapper-->
   ```

   Then style the outer-wrapper section in the external style sheet to take up 80% of the available space on the screen and to center within that space as follows:

   ```
   #outer-wrapper { width: 80%;
    margin: 0 auto 0 auto;
    }
   ```

7. Add a style to clear the float as follows:

   ```
   .clear-float { clear: both; }
   ```

8. Add `class="clear-float"` to the first content tag following the <nav> section, which is probably the <div id="main"> tag unless you have modified your site beyond the previous chapter's instructions.

9. Add `class="webdev"` to the "WebDevPros" paragraph content at the top of each page. Style the class with a font face, font size, and font color as follows:

   ```
   .webdev { font-family: "Mission Gothic", "Times New Roman", serif;
    font-size: 3em;
    color: #0033CC;
    }
   ```

10. Add a style to the style sheet to bold and change the font color of the <dt> content using the following style:

```
dt { font-weight: bold;
  color: #0033CC;
  }
```

11. Link your style sheet to any other pages you have created in your WebDevPros website.

12. Add any other styles that you think would improve your WebDevPros webpages.

13. Validate and correct your HTML and CSS files, and submit your assignment in the format specified by your instructor.

Part 2: ✹ You decide to add a horizontal navigation bar to the bottom of each page. Copy the <ul> content from the <nav> section and paste it inside <footer>…</footer> tags just before the closing </div> that closes the outer-wrapper section.

Add a style to your style sheet to remove the bullets from the <li> content in the <footer> section. (*Hint*: Use a `footer li` selector.) Also add a style to your style sheet to set the <li> content in the <footer> section inline.

Save and refresh all of your files. Why is it considered a good practice to add some sort of navigation bar to the bottom of webpages?

3. Styling the Dog Hall of Fame Webpages

Research and Collaboration

Part 1: In Chapter 3, you added content to the Dog Hall of Fame webpages. In this exercise, you will update those pages with an external style sheet that includes the following updates: (*Note:* Your instructor may want you to use the Data Files for Students provided for this exercise instead.)

1. Create an external style sheet with the name `dogstyles04.css` and save it in the `styles` folder within the your_turn_3 folder.

2. Add your name and the current date as a comment to the first line of the dogstyles04.css file.

3. Open the files you created for the Dog Hall of Fame in Chapter 3 in your HTML editor and float the images that do not span the page to the left or right by adding the attribute of `class="float-right"` or `class="float-left"` to the <img> tag and the corresponding `.float-right {float:right;}` or `.float-left {float:left;}` rules to the external style sheet. Make your decision on whether the image should float left or right based on what looks best on the page.

4. Add a 2% left and bottom margin style to the `.float-right` selector using the following declaration:

```
margin: 0 0 2% 2%;
```

Add a 2% right and bottom margin style to the `.float-left` selector using the following declaration:

```
margin: 0 2% 2% 0;
```

5. Add a tag to the <head> section of each page in the website to link the external style sheet to the dogfame04.html page as follows:

```
<link rel="stylesheet" href="styles/dogstyles04.css">
```

Save both the CSS and HTML files, and open the dogfame04.html file in your browser to make sure the style sheet is linked and the image is floating properly.

6. After viewing your pages, determine appropriate places for the float to be cleared. (For example, you probably want to clear the float when the new headings of "Working Dog" and "Companion Dog" are introduced.) Add a `class="clear-float"` to those tags in the HTML document and a corresponding `.clear-float { clear: both; }` rule to the CSS file.

7. Constrain the content to take 70% of the width of the page by inserting `<div id="page-wrapper">` after the opening <body> tag and closing the div with `</div> <!--close page-wrapper-->` before the closing </body> tag on each page.

   Then add a corresponding rule to set the page-wrapper content to 70% and centered in the page as follows:

   ```
   #page-wrapper { width: 70%;
    margin: 0 auto; /* 0 top and bottom, auto left and right */
    }
   ```

8. Save and refresh your files.

9. Have each team member finish the style sheet using their own style decisions. Include styles for these elements:

   - Font color and font face for the body
   - Background color for the main content
   - Any other styles you deem important or appropriate to best display the content on the pages

   Use comments in your CSS file to document these styles.

10. Validate and correct your HTML and CSS files, and submit your assignment in the format specified by your instructor.

Part 2: ✺ As a group, share and compare how each of you styled the webpages. Discuss which features of each style sheet you liked the best. Together, build a final external style sheet that includes the best features from each member of your team. Note the features you chose from each member.

5 Responsive Design Part 1: Designing for Mobile Devices

Objectives

You will have mastered the material in this chapter when you can:

- Explain the principles of responsive design
- Describe the pros and cons of a mobile website
- Explain the design principles of a mobile website
- Describe a mobile-first strategy
- Define a viewport

- Create a fluid layout
- Make images flexible
- Use styles for a mobile viewport
- Insert and style a span element
- Insert a viewport meta tag
- Test a responsive site using a device emulator

5 | Responsive Design Part 1: Designing for Mobile Devices

Introduction

According to searchenginewatch.com, the number of mobile devices browsing the Internet surpassed the number of desktop browsers in 2014. However, have you used a phone to visit a website that does not work well on a small screen? Webpages that require users to zoom and scroll to read and navigate the website drive visitors away.

The good news is that with a web development approach called responsive design, you have the power to create one website that works well with various screen sizes and browsers on devices ranging from phones and tablets through laptops and traditional desktop displays. **Responsive design** is a website development strategy that strives to provide an optimal user experience of a website regardless of the device or browser used. By applying responsive design principles, the webpage and content respond to the screen size of the user's device to minimize unnecessary scrolling and zooming, making reading and interacting with the site as convenient and intuitive as possible.

Project — Redesign a Website for Mobile Devices

In Chapter 4, you created an external CSS file for the Forward Fitness Club and linked it to each page in the fitness website. For this project, you apply responsive web design principles to the fitness website by editing the CSS and HTML files to use a fluid layout, styles appropriate for a mobile device, and flexible images. These enhancements will result in a better experience for users of mobile devices. You will continue to enhance the site with responsive design for tablet and desktop viewports in Chapter 6.

First, you will modify the template, home page, About Us page, and Contact Us page to prepare them for a fluid layout. You will make sure the wireframe and content are styled with proportional measurement units to create a fluid layout that automatically shrinks and grows with the viewport. Next, you will add new styles to format the content when it appears in a mobile device. You will also modify the CSS code to create flexible images. Finally, you will view, validate, and test the website. Figure 5–1 shows the home page, the About Us page, and the Contact Us page of Forward Fitness Club sized for a mobile viewport. Figure 5–1a shows the home page, Figure 5–1b shows the About Us page, and Figure 5–1c shows the Contact Us page.

(a) Home page

(b) About Us page

(c) Contact Us page

Image courtesy of Jessica Minnick

Figure 5–1

Roadmap

In this chapter, you will learn how to create the webpages shown in Figure 5–1. The following roadmap identifies general activities you will perform as you progress through this chapter:

1. CODE the webpage NAVIGATION LINKS as an unordered list.
2. MAKE webpage IMAGES FLEXIBLE.
3. ADD STYLES FOR a MOBILE viewport.
4. INSERT AND STYLE a SPAN ELEMENT.
5. ADD a META TAG to each HTML document.
6. TEST the WEBPAGES in a mobile emulator.

At the beginning of step instructions throughout the chapter, you will see an abbreviated form of this roadmap. The abbreviated roadmap uses colors to indicate chapter progress: gray means the chapter is beyond that activity; blue means the task being shown is covered in that activity, and black means that activity is yet to be covered. For example, the following abbreviated roadmap indicates the chapter would be showing a task in the 5 ADD META TAG activity.

1 CODE NAVIGATION LINKS | 2 MAKE IMAGES FLEXIBLE | 3 ADD STYLES FOR MOBILE
4 INSERT & STYLE SPAN ELEMENT | 5 ADD META TAG | 6 TEST WEBPAGES

Use the abbreviated roadmap as a progress guide while you read or step through the instructions in this chapter.

Exploring Responsive Design

Figure 5–2 shows an example of a website developed using responsive design principles, www.authenticjobs.com. The content appears easy to read and navigate on devices of three sizes: desktop browser, tablet, and phone. If you are working on a desktop computer, you can quickly experience how the webpage responds to different browser sizes by simply resizing your browser window.

(a) Desktop

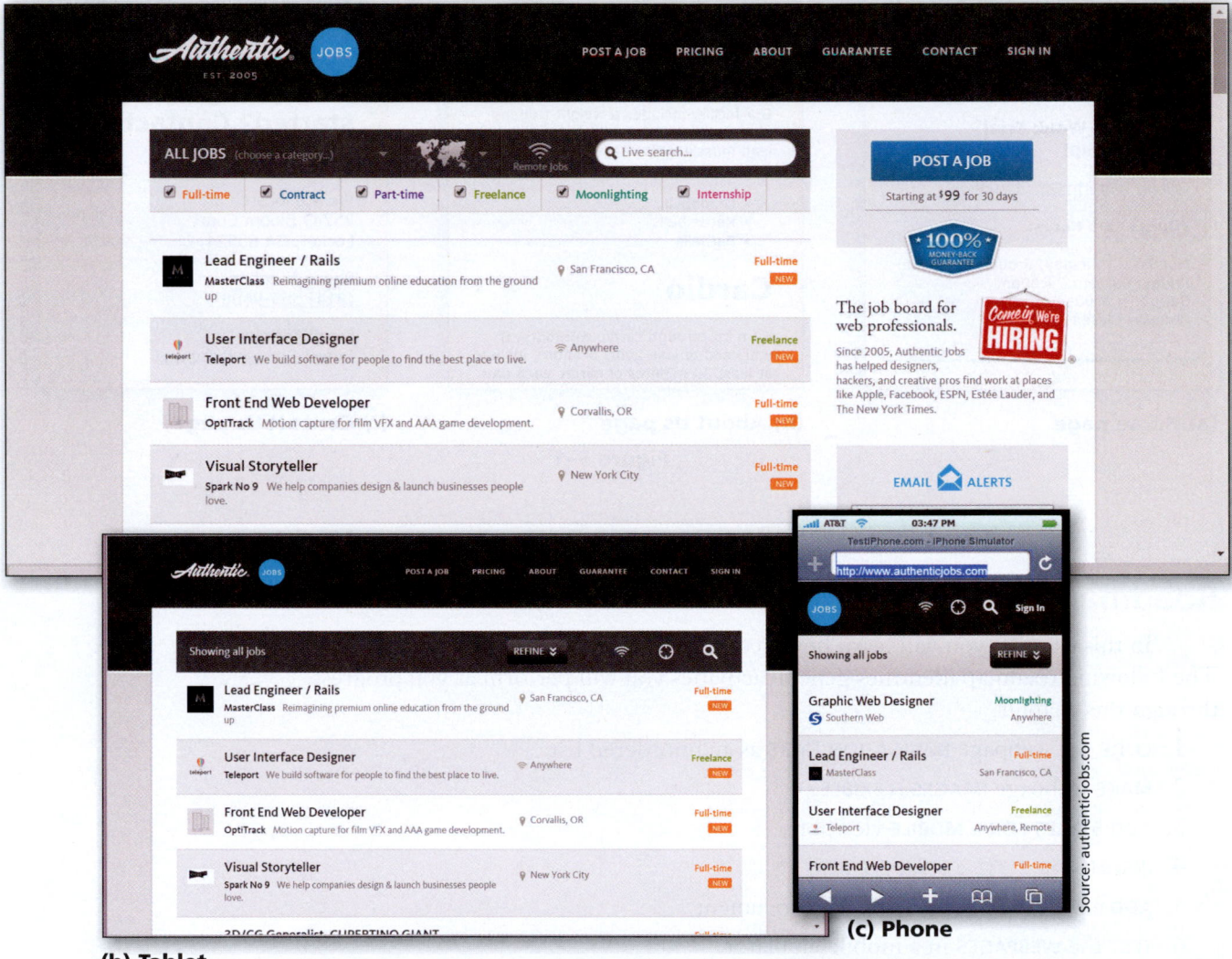

(b) Tablet

(c) Phone

Source: authenticjobs.com

Figure 5–2

Ethan Marcotte is credited with coining the phrase "responsive web design" in a 2010 article he wrote for the web developer community in a magazine called *A List Apart*, alistapart.com. Responsive web design is not a specific set of rules, but is better characterized as a philosophy that is constantly refined as HTML and CSS standards, browsers, and technology evolve and improve. However, most discussions of responsive design highlight the following three concepts:

- Fluid layout: A **fluid layout** applies proportional size measurements to the webpage wireframe and content so that the content stretches, shrinks, and grows as the size of the viewport changes. The **viewport** is the viewing area for the webpage, which is much smaller on a phone than on a traditional desktop. On a traditional Windows desktop computer, the viewport is usually the window itself, but the term "viewport" is preferred over "window" because windows are generally not displayed in the browsers of mobile devices. Furthermore, a window on a traditional desktop display might not be maximized to fill the entire screen. Just keep in mind that the viewport refers to the portion of the webpage that a user sees at any one time, regardless of device, browser, screen size, screen resolution, window size, or orientation.

- Media queries: **Media queries** allow the webpage developer to detect the approximate pixel size of the current viewport. This detection allows the developer to selectively apply CSS rules that work best for that viewport size. CSS3 standards expanded the capabilities of media queries. Media queries will be further discussed in Chapter 6.

- Flexible images: **Flexible images** shrink and grow based on the size of the viewport. Flexible images do not have height and width attributes or values in the HTML document. Rather, flexible images use CSS rules to resize the image relative to the wireframe and viewport.

Designing for Mobile Devices

The explosive growth of mobile browsers including those on phones and tablets quickly created serious problems for webpage developers because smaller viewports often required excessive zooming and scrolling. Different techniques emerged to address this problem, one of which was to build a completely separate, parallel website optimized for mobile users called a **mobile website**. Mobile websites are often identified with an m. or mo. prefix in the URL such as http://m.phsc.edu/, Pasco-Hernando State College's mobile website. Although the word "mobile" applies to any portable device connected to the Internet such as lightweight laptops, tablets, and phones, in this context, mobile websites are generally focused on providing support for browsers on smartphones.

The mobile website approach helps companies that have large existing websites provide a quick solution for mobile users. A large organization's current website may contain a massive number of pages that were developed long ago using unresponsive designs built for traditional desktop browsers. Modifying each of those pages to incorporate responsive techniques is often such a large effort that it is eliminated as a viable solution. The mobile website approach means that developers build a new, parallel website from scratch, specifically designing it for small mobile viewports. This approach can be much faster than converting a large website of existing nonresponsive pages to modern responsive designs.

The major downside of creating a mobile website is that it multiplies the work required to maintain what becomes two separate websites for the same organization. In contrast, responsive design seeks to optimize the viewing experience for a wide range of devices using *one* website. Therefore, a website developed with responsive design principles from the very beginning is less work to maintain down the road.

What is a mobile web application?
A **mobile web application** is an application accessed through a smartphone browser. It is created with a combination of HTML, CSS, and JavaScript programming languages. Unlike a native mobile application, a mobile web application does not reside on the smartphone itself and is only accessible through a browser. In contrast, a native mobile application is downloaded onto a smartphone from an app store, such as Google Play or Apple's App store, and resides on the device itself. A popular tool for creating mobile web applications is **jQuery Mobile**. jQuery Mobile provides a library of JavaScript resources that you can use to create a mobile web application. For more information about jQuery Mobile, visit jquerymobile.com.

A **mobile-first strategy** employs responsive design principles, but with an interesting twist. Following a mobile-first strategy, a web developer designs the flexible wireframe and essential content for the smallest viewport *first*, progressively adding more content as the viewport grows. A web developer then uses media queries to add styles for progressively larger viewports, progressing from tablet to laptop and desktop. See Figure 5–3a. A mobile-first strategy is considered by some to be a more productive and effective way to build a website from scratch because it forces the web developer to focus on the core, essential content first for the smallest viewport. Compare this to Figure 5–3b, the traditional approach, where developers start with a traditional webpage, and then remove or modify nonessential content as the viewport gets smaller. The mobile-first strategy makes the most sense when mobile users are a very high priority for your website and when you have the luxury of building the website from scratch.

Phone   **Tablet**   **Laptop**   **Desktop**

(a) Mobile-first approach

Desktop   **Laptop**   **Tablet**   **Phone**

(b) Traditional approach

Figure 5–3

The website development approach you implement depends on many factors including the current environment, your target audience, available resources, and the time available to tackle the project. Given you are still in the initial stages of developing the Forward Fitness Club website, you will be able to apply a responsive design. Although you already created desktop-sized webpages, you are still in the initial stages of building the Forward Fitness Club website so you can incorporate the mobile-first strategy, which develops an optimum design for a mobile display and focuses on the most essential content.

The following websites provide examples of responsive design. View them using a desktop, tablet, and mobile device to see how they provide an excellent user experience in each environment. You can also create different viewport sizes by opening the website in a desktop browser and then resizing the browser to smaller sizes to simulate the viewports found on tablet and phone devices.

- The Boston Globe: www.bostonglobe.com
- Microsoft: www.microsoft.com
- Engadget: www.engadget.com
- World Wildlife Fund: www.worldwildlife.org
- Awwwards: www.awwwards.com
- Museum of Fine Arts: www.mfa.com
- Silverton Health: www.silvertonhealth.org

Figure 5–4 shows how the Silverton Health (www.silvertonhealth.org) website would look on a desktop, tablet, and phone. Notice how the text, pictures, and content are resized and repositioned to work well in all three environments.

(a) Desktop

(b) Tablet

(c) Phone

Source: silvertonhealth.org

Figure 5–4

CONSIDER THIS

What is the Internet of Things?
The term **Internet of Things (IoT)** refers to the ever-expanding number of devices that connect to the Internet to share information. The IoT includes traditional computers and mobile devices as well as Internet-ready appliances, thermostats, biochips, TVs, and any other device that connects to the Internet to retrieve or send information.

BTW

Web Analytics
Web analytics is the study of how users interact with a website. Web analytics provide statistics on how many people visit a website as well as what browsers, devices, and choices the user made while at a website. This data helps a web developer design a site to meet the needs of their desired audience.

Using Fluid Layouts

A webpage with a liquid layout, also called a **fluid layout**, changes in width based on the size of the viewport. Responsive designs are based on fluid layouts. Before you create a fluid layout for Forward Fitness Club, however, it is helpful to study fixed layouts. **Fixed layouts** do not change in width based on the size of the viewport. Fixed layouts use fixed measurement units such as pixels to define the width of the areas of the wireframe that "fix" the width of the content regardless of the size of the viewport. The noaa.gov website for the National Oceanic and Atmospheric Administration shown in Figure 5–5 is based on a fixed layout. Note how the text does not wrap and how the images do not resize based on the size of the viewport. Fixed layouts can involve a tremendous amount of horizontal scrolling and require much zooming on small viewports.

in fixed layout, content is not resized based on size of viewport

Source: noaa.gov

Figure 5–5

What other types of layouts can I use besides fluid and fixed layouts?

In addition to fluid (also called liquid) and fixed layouts, you can use two other types of layouts. **Elastic layouts** are measured in ems. Elastic layouts also respond to the size of the viewport. **Hybrid layouts** combine aspects of fixed and fluid layouts. For example, you may want to "fix" the size of one column but allow another to be flexible.

Because so many older websites were built for a single, traditional screen resolution such as 1024 by 768 pixels, the Internet is full of webpages with fixed layouts. In fact, it was not uncommon a few years ago to start your wireframe design based on a viewport width of 960 pixels, which generally filled a traditional desktop browser yet allowed for a few pixels of margin on the left and right. Although fixed layouts do not work well for smaller viewports, they are still appropriate for webpages used in controlled environments such as those created for a specific purpose within an internal company intranet. Information-intensive sites such as noaa.gov may also be satisfied with their current fixed layout if their primary audience uses traditional desktop computers to access their site.

You implement fluid layouts by measuring the widths of the wireframe elements and content in relative units such as percentages and ems. Table 5-1 lists the units of measurement you can use in CSS property values as well as the common uses for each. Responsive sites use relative units of measurement.

BTW

Styles and Units of Measurement

Remember that when creating styles that include units of measurement, do not put a space between the value and the unit of measure.

```
font-size: 2em;
/* correct */
font-size: 2 em;
/* incorrect */
```

Table 5–1 Common CSS Units of Measurement

Unit	Description	Relative or Fixed?	Common Uses	CSS Examples

em	An **em** is historically based on the height of the capital letter M of the default font. 1em is typically larger on a desktop browser than on a tablet browser. For example, 1em is usually about 16pt in a desktop browser and about 12pt in a tablet browser.	Relative	Em may be used to scale anything related to textual content such as font size, line sizes, margins, padding. Em sizes are relative to each other. For example, 2em = twice as large as 1em. 0.5em = half as large as 1em.	`p {font-size: 1.0em;` `line-height: 2.0em;` `text-indent: 1.8em;}`
				
				 `h1 {font-size: 3.0em;` `margin: 1.0em;` `padding: 1.5em;}`

%	Percentage. The default font size measurement for most browsers on most devices is 100%.	Relative	Developers use % to measure the widths of the wireframe elements and flexible images. Some use % to measure textual content, too.	`#container {width: 80%;}`
				
				 `img {width: 100%;}`

px	One **pixel** is equal to one dot on the screen. Different screens have different pixel densities.	Pixels on a device are fixed in size, but the number of pixels varies by device	Pixels are commonly used for textual measurements including padding, borders, and margins. Do not use the px measurement for width measurements, as this creates a fixed, unresponsive layout.	`.advertise {border: 1px` `solid red;}`
pt	points (1pt = 1/72 inch)	Fixed	Points are used to measure font and line sizes in **print** media.	
cm mm in	centimeters millimeters inches	Fixed	These measurements are not commonly used for webpage development.	Because these measurements are fixed and do not scale based on the size of the viewport, they should not be used within a responsive design.
pc	picas (1pc = 12pt)	Fixed	The pica measurement harkens back to the "pica typewriter," which produced a **Courier fixed-width font, 12pts tall.**	

Creating a Fluid Layout

To create a fluid layout, use percentages to measure the width of each column in a webpage. At this time, the Forward Fitness Club webpages have only one column, which is identified by <div id="container"> in the HTML document.

Figure 5–6 shows how a fluid layout changes in response to three sizes of the viewport for the w3.org website, which provides technical definitions for the HTML and CSS standards and specifications.

Figure 5–6

In addition to the content stretching or shrinking with the size of the viewport, the smallest viewport in Figure 5–6c hides the first and third columns to give the middle column room to stretch across the entire viewport. The background color of the content in the smallest viewport is also white instead of light blue to make the text easier to read on this smaller device. These formats are automatically applied to the webpage as the viewport changes. The changes are achieved through media queries that detect the size of the viewport and apply the styles that work well for that size.

A media query detects the media type (such as screen or print) and capabilities of the device that the browser is running on (such as the size of the viewport in pixels or its orientation of portrait versus landscape). Based on the information, the media query applies styles that work well for that situation. Several useful examples of how media queries apply styles to resize and reposition content in response to a variety of devices can be found at http://mediaqueri.es/, which is shown in Figure 5–7.

Figure 5–7

Beginning web developers may confuse the capabilities of media queries with the behavior of a liquid layout, but a webpage can have a liquid layout without using media queries. For example, Figure 5–8 shows a webpage with a liquid layout in two widths.

Figure 5–8

No matter how small your browser becomes, the content placeholder boxes on the page shrink and grow in response to the size of the viewport. They resize automatically because the width measurements for the content and placeholders use percentages, which are proportional units of measure, as shown in the CSS code revealed in the lower portion of the webpage.

Navigation Elements in Fluid Layouts

To make the navigation links more appealing and easy to find on the webpage, you can format them so they look more like buttons rather than text links. For the Forward Fitness Club website, you will code the navigation links as an unordered list in the HTML document to better display and position the navigation system as appropriate for your design. For the desktop and tablet viewports, the navigation links can appear as green buttons with white text to match the color scheme of the Forward Fitness Club website. Each button should also have extra space to display the link text clearly and to separate it from adjacent buttons. The navigation system in the phone viewport can use the same color scheme, but each button should be larger so users can find and select each one easily on the small screen of a phone.

To accomplish this design, first code the navigation links as an unordered list. This is a common web design technique that semantically describes the content and lets you format each link using CSS styles. Once the navigation is coded as an unordered list, you can add styles to the style sheet to format the navigation list items without displaying a bullet. You will also apply a background color, text color, and rounded border to make each link look like a button. You will then remove the underlining that appears with links by default.

To Code the Navigation Links as an Unordered List

1 CODE NAVIGATION LINKS | 2 MAKE IMAGES FLEXIBLE | 3 ADD STYLES FOR MOBILE
4 INSERT & STYLE SPAN ELEMENT | 5 ADD META TAG | 6 TEST WEBPAGES

Code the navigation links on the home, About Us, Contact Us, and template pages as list items in an unordered list. *Why? Coding links in a navigation system as an unordered list is a common way to semantically describe the content because a list of links is truly an unordered list. This technique also provides the structure, or "box," around each link, which is required to style the links for different viewport sizes later.* The following steps add the HTML code to mark up the links in the **nav** section as list items in an unordered list.

1

- Open your text editor and then open the index.html file.

- Place the insertion point after the closing bracket on Line 19 and press the ENTER key to insert a new Line 20.

- Starting on Line 20, add the ul and li tags as shown in Figure 5–9 to code the navigation links as list items in an unordered list.

Q&A Do I need to indent the lines of code as I insert the tags?
Yes. Be sure to indent as shown in Figure 5–9 to maintain maximum readability.

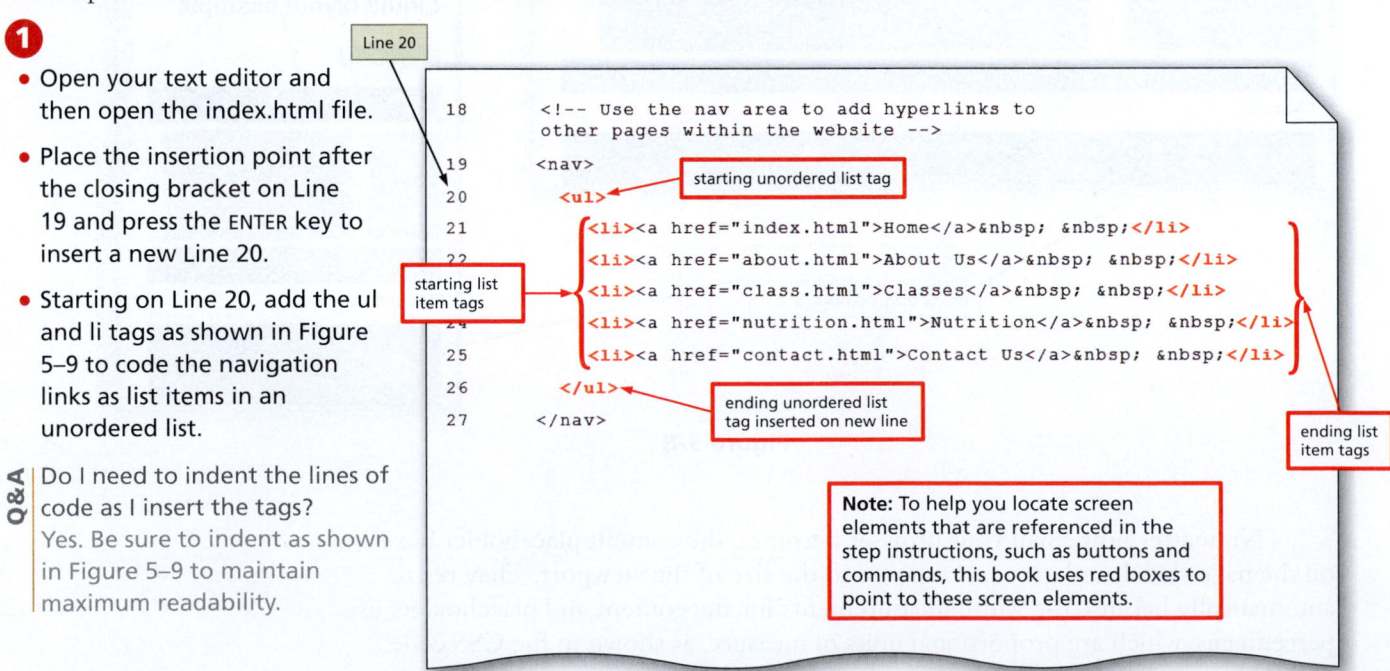

Line 20

```
18      <!-- Use the nav area to add hyperlinks to
        other pages within the website -->

19      <nav>
20          <ul>                    starting unordered list tag
21              <li><a href="index.html">Home</a>    </li>
22              <li><a href="about.html">About Us</a>    </li>
23              <li><a href="class.html">Classes</a>    </li>
24              <li><a href="nutrition.html">Nutrition</a>    </li>
25              <li><a href="contact.html">Contact Us</a>    </li>
26          </ul>               ending unordered list
                                tag inserted on new line
27      </nav>
```

starting list item tags

ending list item tags

Note: To help you locate screen elements that are referenced in the step instructions, such as buttons and commands, this book uses red boxes to point to these screen elements.

Figure 5–9

2

- Delete the two nonbreaking space characters, ** ** after each closing **</a>** tag (Figure 5–10).

Q&A Why am I deleting the nonbreaking space characters? You will use CSS to set the padding and margin between these links so you no longer need the characters to create space between the links.

index.html

nonbreaking spaces deleted

```
18      <!-- Use the nav area to add hyperlinks to
        other pages within the website -->
19      <nav>
20        <ul>
21          <li><a href="index.html">Home</a></li>
22          <li><a href="about.html">About Us</a></li>
23          <li><a href="class.html">Classes</a></li>
24          <li><a href="nutrition.html">Nutrition</a></li>
25          <li><a href="contact.html">Contact Us</a></li>
26        </ul>
27      </nav>
```

Figure 5–10

3

- Copy the unordered list code in the <nav> section starting with the opening <ul> tag on Line 20 through the ending </ul> tag on Line 26.

- Open the about.html file in your text editor.

- Select anchor tags within the <nav>…</nav> tags on Lines 20–24, and then paste the text from index.html containing the links coded as an unordered list (Figure 5-11).

about.html

code pasted from index.html

Figure 5–11

4

- Open the contact.html file in your text editor.

- Select the anchor tags within the <nav>…</nav> tags on Lines 20–24, and then paste the text from index.html containing the links coded as an unordered list (Figure 5-12).

contact.html

code pasted from index.html

Figure 5–12

- Open the template, fitness.html, file in your text editor.
- Select the anchor tags within the <nav>...</nav> tags on Lines 20–24, and then paste the text from index.html containing the links coded as an unordered list (Figure 5–13).

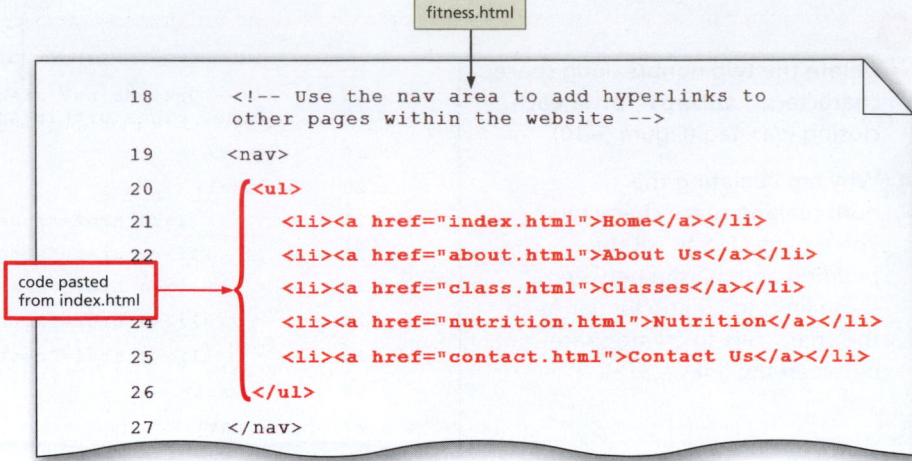

fitness.html

```
18    <!-- Use the nav area to add hyperlinks to
      other pages within the website -->
19    <nav>
20      <ul>
21        <li><a href="index.html">Home</a></li>
22        <li><a href="about.html">About Us</a></li>
                <li><a href="class.html">Classes</a></li>
24        <li><a href="nutrition.html">Nutrition</a></li>
25        <li><a href="contact.html">Contact Us</a></li>
26      </ul>
27    </nav>
```

code pasted from index.html

Figure 5–13

- Save and view all four HTML files in a browser to verify the list items appear as a bulleted list (Figure 5–14).

Q&A Why does each link appear on its own line in the nav area?
Each link appears on its own line because the <li> list item element is a block element.

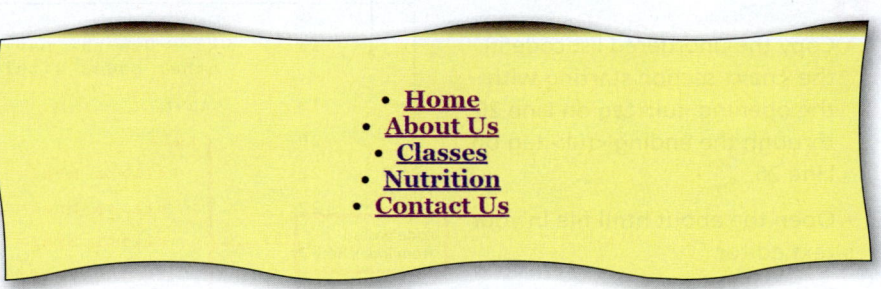

- Home
- About Us
- Classes
- Nutrition
- Contact Us

Figure 5–14

Making Images Flexible

If you reduce the width of the browser window, the Forward Fitness Club logo is cut off because it is not resizing with respect to the viewport. You can tackle that problem next by adding flexible images to your design, another major component of a responsive design strategy. A **flexible image** resizes itself to accommodate the size of the viewport. Flexible images are fairly easy to implement. To create flexible images:

1. Delete the **height** and **width** attribute values for the **img** tags in the HTML files.
2. Add styles for the images in the CSS file to provide the desired flexibility such as the following style: **max-width: 100%;**

By setting the width of the image to 100%, the image automatically stretches to fill 100% of the width of the container element. The height automatically grows in proportion to the width. Use the **max-width** property instead of the **width** property to constrain the image to 100% of its *actual* size in case the viewport grows even larger. For example, you probably do not want the image to stretch beyond its actual size because that degrades the quality of the image even if the webpage is viewed on a very large widescreen TV.

Most of the responsive websites that you have been visiting in the examples in this chapter have employed flexible images. A good example of flexible images along with a deeper discussion of how they support responsive design can be found at http:// demosthenes.info/blog/586/CSS-Fluid-Image-Techniques-for-Responsive-Site-Design shown in Figure 5–15.

Source: demosthenes.info

Figure 5–15

To Add Flexible Images

1 CODE NAVIGATION LINKS | **2 MAKE IMAGES FLEXIBLE** | 3 ADD STYLES FOR MOBILE
4 INSERT & STYLE SPAN ELEMENT | 5 ADD META TAG | 6 TEST WEBPAGES

Add flexible images to the home, About Us, Contact Us, and template pages. *Why? Flexible images shrink and grow in proportion to the viewport, providing a better viewing experience across multiple devices.* The following steps delete the height and width attributes from the `img` tags in the HTML files and add a style using the max-width property to the style sheet file.

1

- Make sure the index .html, about.html, contact.html, and fitness.html files are open in your text editor.

- In the index.html file, select and delete the height and width attributes and values from the logo <img> tag on Line 15 (Figure 5-16).

index.html

```
9    <body>
10
11       <div id="container">
12
13          <!-- Use the header area for the website name or
          logo -->
14          <header>
15          <img src="images/ffc_logo.png" alt="Forward Fitness Club Logo">
16          </header>
17
```

Line 15

height and width attributes and values have been deleted

Figure 5–16

2

- Switch to the about. html file, and then delete the height and width attributes and values from the logo <img> tag on Line 15.

- Delete the height and width attributes and values and from the other images on the page on Lines 33, 42, and 51 (Figure 5-17).

Q&A Should I delete the closing angle bracket for the img tag?

No. Be careful to delete only the height and width attribute values and not the closing angle bracket > for the img tag.

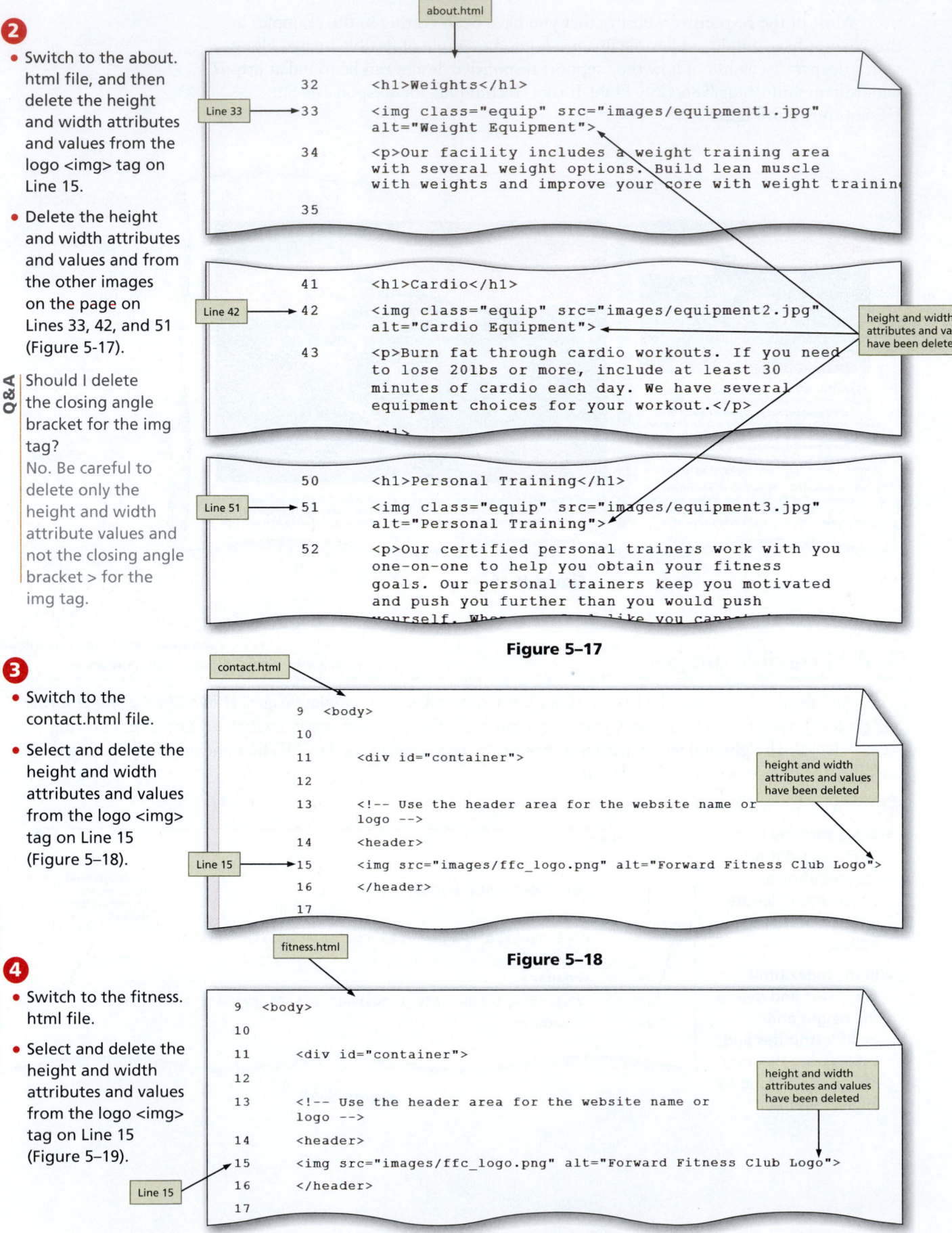

about.html

```
32        <h1>Weights</h1>

33        <img class="equip" src="images/equipment1.jpg"
          alt="Weight Equipment">

34        <p>Our facility includes a weight training area
          with several weight options. Build lean muscle
          with weights and improve your core with weight training

35
```
Line 33

```
41        <h1>Cardio</h1>

42        <img class="equip" src="images/equipment2.jpg"
          alt="Cardio Equipment">

43        <p>Burn fat through cardio workouts. If you need
          to lose 20lbs or more, include at least 30
          minutes of cardio each day. We have several
          equipment choices for your workout.</p>
```
Line 42

height and width attributes and values have been deleted

```
50        <h1>Personal Training</h1>

51        <img class="equip" src="images/equipment3.jpg"
          alt="Personal Training">

52        <p>Our certified personal trainers work with you
          one-on-one to help you obtain your fitness
          goals. Our personal trainers keep you motivated
          and push you further than you would push
          yourself. When
```
Line 51

Figure 5–17

3

- Switch to the contact.html file.

- Select and delete the height and width attributes and values from the logo <img> tag on Line 15 (Figure 5–18).

contact.html

```
9     <body>

10

11        <div id="container">

12

13        <!-- Use the header area for the website name or
          logo -->

14        <header>

15        <img src="images/ffc_logo.png" alt="Forward Fitness Club Logo">

16        </header>

17
```
Line 15

height and width attributes and values have been deleted

Figure 5–18

4

- Switch to the fitness. html file.

- Select and delete the height and width attributes and values from the logo <img> tag on Line 15 (Figure 5–19).

fitness.html

```
9     <body>

10

11        <div id="container">

12

13        <!-- Use the header area for the website name or
          logo -->

14        <header>

15        <img src="images/ffc_logo.png" alt="Forward Fitness Club Logo">

16        </header>

17
```
Line 15

height and width attributes and values have been deleted

Figure 5–19

5

- Open the styles. css file in your text editor.

- Place your insertion point after the closing brace on Line 6 and press the ENTER key twice to insert new Lines 7 and 8.

Figure 5–20

- On Line 8 type `/* Style to create a fluid image */` to insert a comment.

- Press the ENTER key to insert a new Line 9 and then type `img {` to add an img selector and opening brace.

- Press the ENTER key to insert a new Line 10, increase the indent and then type `max-width: 100%;` to add a max-width property with a value of 100%.

- Press the ENTER key, decrease the indent, and then type `}` to insert a closing brace (Figure 5–20).

6

- Save all files in your editor and open the about.html page in your browser.

- Resize the window to a very small viewport and scroll down the page to the see the images (Figure 5–21).

Q&A How does the new style change the images on the webpage?
The logo image automatically resizes with the viewport and the images on the about.html page also resize as the viewport becomes smaller than their natural size.

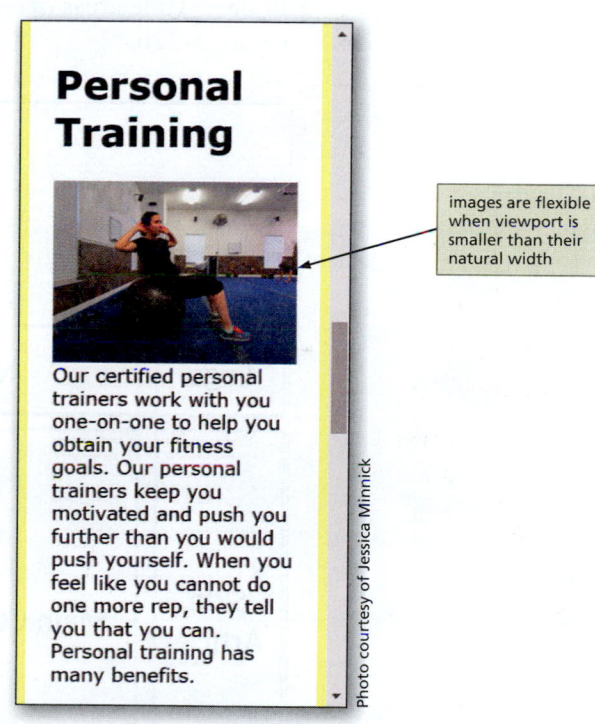

Figure 5–21

Break Point: If you want to take a break, this is a good place to do so. To resume at a later time, continue reading the text from this location forward.

Following a Mobile-First Strategy

The responsive web design approach styles content differently depending on the type of device used to view the site. The mobile-first approach focuses on styling content as appropriate for smaller mobile devices. One goal in designing for mobile devices is to prominently display the content accessed most by users. It is also a best practice to use a single-column layout for a mobile display, as this prevents scrolling horizontally. Displaying what mobile device users need and want on a single screen with minimal scrolling creates a more enjoyable experience.

Styles for Content on Mobile Devices

Styling content for mobile devices is different from styling content for a desktop display. Because the screen size is smaller, you must analyze each page to determine the most important content on the page, and then style that content to attract users of mobile devices. If you do not have an existing website, begin by first determining the most essential content for your site.

If you already have page content, you may need to remove some content for a mobile viewport. Think of this approach as similar to moving from a large home to a small condominium. Before the move can take place, you must determine the essential items you want to take with you to the new home and then downsize.

Figure 5–22a depicts a wireframe example for a traditional desktop viewport. Note the multiple column layout and different areas of content. If you were to use all these same areas of content for a mobile design, the wireframe would look like Figure 5-22b.

(a) Desktop wireframe

(b) Mobile wireframe

Figure 5–22

The mobile layout shown in Figure 5–22b is too long and would require a lot of extra scrolling for a mobile user. An ideal webpage in a mobile viewport requires little or no scrolling. In this example, you need to analyze the page and determine the areas with the most essential content. You then hide the nonessential content areas for a mobile viewport. Figure 5–23 shows how to hide some webpage areas to create a revised mobile wireframe.

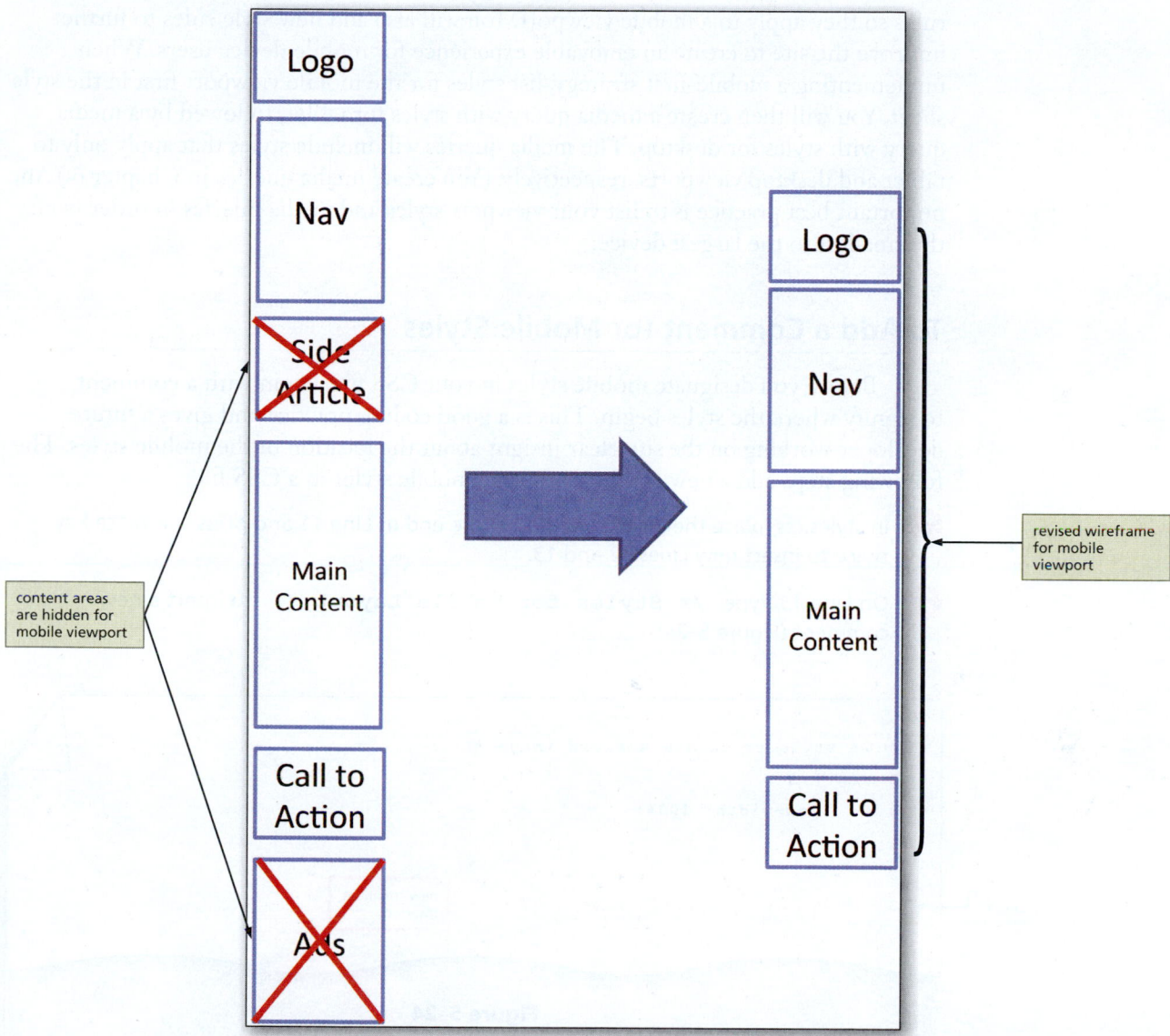

Figure 5–23

Optimize the interface to maximize the mobile user experience. The following are some key best practices when designing for mobile viewports.

1. Make use of 100% of the screen space.
2. Design the navigation to be easy and intuitive.
3. Keep load times minimal. Enhance load times by removing bandwidth-intensive content and streamlining your HTML code.
4. Display essential page content and hide nonessential page content.
5. Make the content easy to access and read.
6. Design a simple layout.

Steps in a Mobile-First Strategy

When you want to implement a mobile-first strategy with an existing website, you must first analyze each page to determine the most essential content and whether to hide some of the content on a mobile device.

The fitness website already has page content, so you need to analyze each page to select the most essential content and then design the content for a mobile viewport.

To apply a mobile-first strategy, open your CSS file and modify the existing style rules so they apply to a mobile viewport. You will also add new style rules to further improve the site to create an enjoyable experience for mobile device users. When implementing a mobile-first strategy, list styles for the mobile viewport first in the style sheet. You will then create a media query with styles for tablet, followed by a media query with styles for desktop. The media queries will include styles that apply only to tablet and desktop viewports, respectively. (You create media queries in Chapter 6.) An important best practice is to list your viewport styles and media queries in order from the smallest to the largest device.

To Add a Comment for Mobile Styles

Before you designate mobile styles in your CSS file, begin with a comment to signify where the styles begin. This is a good coding practice and gives a future developer working on the site clear insight about the location of the mobile styles. The following steps add a new comment to note mobile styles in a CSS file.

1 In styles.css, place the insertion point at the end of Line 11 and press the ENTER key twice to insert new Lines 12 and 13.

2 On Line 13, type `/* Styles for Mobile Layout */` to insert a new comment (Figure 5–24).

```
 8  /* Style to create a fluid image */
 9  img {
10      max-width: 100%;
11  }
12
13  /* Styles for Mobile Layout */
```

Line 13 → Line 13

new comment inserted

Figure 5–24

To Edit the #container Style for Mobile Viewports

When a user views a website from a mobile viewport, the webpage should take up all available screen space because the screen is smaller. The style for the #container selector currently has a width of 80%, which is best for a desktop view. Change the width value to 100% so the page uses all of the screen width in a mobile viewport. The following steps change the width for the #container selector in a CSS file.

1 On Line 17, change the width value from 80% to `100%` (Figure 5–25).

2 Save your changes.

Q&A Why does this style apply to mobile viewports only?
The styles listed at the beginning of the style sheet currently apply to all viewports. When you add media queries and styles for tablet and desktop viewports, the styles at the beginning of the style sheet will apply only to mobile viewports.

```
15    /* Style for the container centers the page and specifies the width */

16    #container {

17        width: 100%;        value changed    ← Line 17

18        margin-left: auto;

19        margin-right: auto;

20    }
```

Figure 5–25

To Edit the header Style for Mobile Viewports

Update the header style for a mobile viewport by using an em unit of measurement for the margin-top and border-radius properties so the margin and border radius are relative to the page. Remove the box-shadow property to create more room for content in the mobile viewport. The following steps edit the styles for the header selector in a CSS file.

1 On Line 22, change the comment text to `Style for the header specifies top margin, background color, rounded corners, and center-aligns content` to edit the comment.

2 On Line 24, change the margin-top value to `0.2em` to edit the value.

Q&A Why am I changing the top margin value to 0.2em?
To use relative measurements for responsive design, change pixel values to em or percent values.

3 On Line 25, delete the margin-bottom property and value to remove it, and then delete the blank line.

4 On Line 26, change the border-radius value to `0.5em` to edit the value.

5 On Line 27, delete the box-shadow property and values to remove them, and then delete the blank line.

6 Remove any blank lines between each property to list each property one after the other (Figure 5–26).

7 Save your changes.

Q&A Why did I remove the box-shadow property?
You removed the shadow effect to allow more room for content on a mobile viewport.

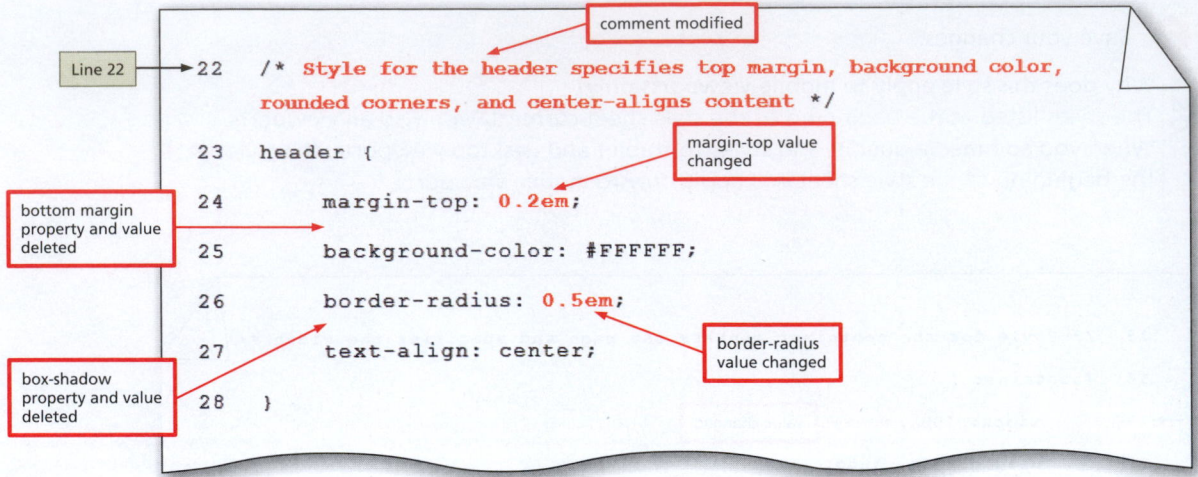

comment modified

Line 22

```
22   /* Style for the header specifies top margin, background color,
        rounded corners, and center-aligns content */

23   header {

24       margin-top: 0.2em;

25       background-color: #FFFFFF;

26       border-radius: 0.5em;

27       text-align: center;

28   }
```

margin-top value changed

bottom margin property and value deleted

border-radius value changed

box-shadow property and value deleted

Figure 5–26

To Edit the nav Style for Mobile Viewports

Next, modify the style rule for the **nav** element to only include text properties. You will create a new style rule to style the unordered list in future steps, however, you must first modify the style rule for the nav selector to use only properties related to text, which are appropriate for list items. The following steps edit the styles for the nav selector in a CSS file.

1 Modify the comment text on Line 30 to **Style for the nav specifies text properties** to edit the comment.

2 Delete Lines 36–41 to delete the properties and values for padding, top and bottom margin, border radius, and top and bottom border (Figure 5–27).

Q&A Why am I removing these properties?
These styles apply to the nav element as a whole. Now that you have created an unordered list, they are no longer necessary. Instead, you will create new style rules for the unordered list, list items, and links in future steps.

3 Save your changes.

comment modified

Line 30

```
30   /* Style for the nav specifies text properties */

31   nav {

32       font-family: Georgia, "Times New Roman", serif;

33       font-size: 1.25em;

34       font-weight: bold;

35       text-align: center;

36   }
```

padding, margin, and border properties and values are removed

Figure 5–27

To Add a nav ul Style for Mobile Viewports

Recall that you inserted an unordered list within the navigation area. Add a nav ul selector to style the unordered list. The style should include a padding property with a value of 0 to allow the links in the list to expand the full width of the mobile viewport. To include some margin before and after the unordered list, add top-margin and bottom-margin properties to the style. The following steps add a nav ul selector and declarations in a CSS file.

1 Place your insertion point at the end of Line 36 and press the ENTER key twice to insert new two new lines, Lines 37 and 38.

2 On Line 38, type `/* Style specifies padding and margins for unordered list */` to insert a comment.

3 Press the ENTER key to insert a new Line 39.

4 On Line 39, type `nav ul {` to add a nav ul selector and opening brace.

5 Press the ENTER key to insert a new Line 40.

6 On Line 40, increase the indent, and then type `padding: 0;` to add a padding property and value.

7 Press the ENTER key to insert a new Line 41 and type `margin-top: 0.5em;` to add a top margin property and value.

8 Press the ENTER key to insert a new Line 42 and type `margin-bottom: 0.5em;` to add a bottom margin property and value.

9 Press the ENTER key, decrease the indent, and then type `}` to insert a closing brace (Figure 5–28).

10 Save your changes.

Q&A Why am I using zero without a unit of measurement for the padding property?
When the value is zero, the unit of measurement does not matter because values such as 0% or 0em are all the same, so you do not need to specify a unit of measurement.

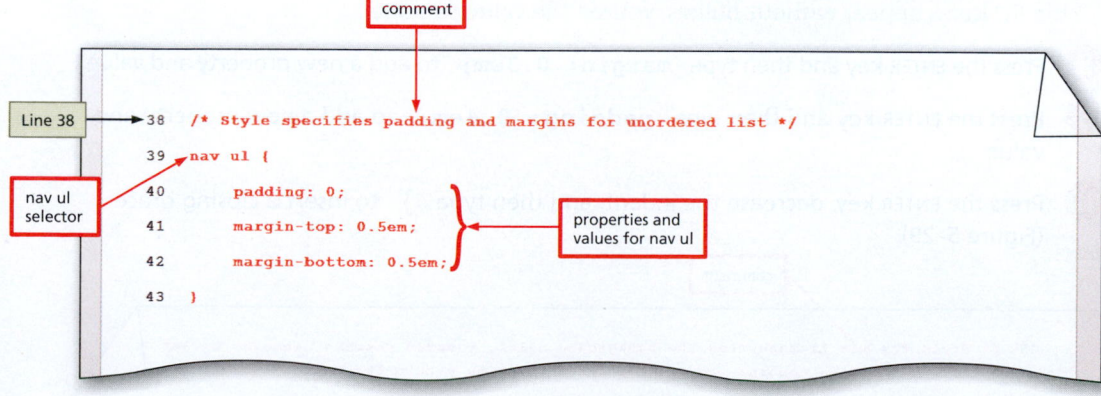

```
        comment

Line 38    ►38   /* Style specifies padding and margins for unordered list */

           39   nav ul {

nav ul     40       padding: 0;
selector
           41       margin-top: 0.5em;              properties and
                                                    values for nav ul
           42       margin-bottom: 0.5em;

           43   }
```

Figure 5–28

To Add a nav li Style for Mobile Viewports

The default marker for each <li> item in an unordered list is a bullet. Add a style for the list items in the navigation area to display the items inline. Also remove the bullets to prepare for displaying the links as a vertical column of buttons. Add declarations to apply a background color to the list items, add padding and margin space, and apply a rounded border to make the list items look like buttons. The following steps add a style rule to the style sheet to format the unordered list as buttons for mobile displays.

1 Place your insertion point at the end of Line 43 and press the ENTER key twice to insert new two new lines, Lines 44 and 45.

2 On Line 45, type `/* Style for nav li specifies the background color, rounded corners, removes bullet style, and applies margins and padding for list items within the navigation */` to insert a comment.

3 Press the ENTER key to insert a new Line 46.

4 On Line 46, type `nav li {` to add a nav li selector and opening brace.

5 Press the ENTER key, increase the indent, and then type `background-color: #009933;` to add a new property and value.

Q&A What color is #009933?
This value is a dark green and will appear in the background of the buttons so they stand out on the page.

6 Press the ENTER key and then type `border-radius: 2em;` to add a new property and value.

Q&A Why am I using the border-radius property?
Including the border-radius property adds a rounded border to each list item.

7 Press the ENTER key and then type `list-style-type: none;` to add a new property and value.

Q&A What is the purpose of this property?
The list-style-type property specifies the type of bullet to use in an ordered list. To have the list items appear without bullets, you set the value to none.

8 Press the ENTER key and then type `margin: 0.3em;` to add a new property and value.

9 Press the ENTER key and then type `padding: 0.4em;` to add a new property and value.

10 Press the ENTER key, decrease the indent, and then type `}` to insert a closing brace (Figure 5–29).

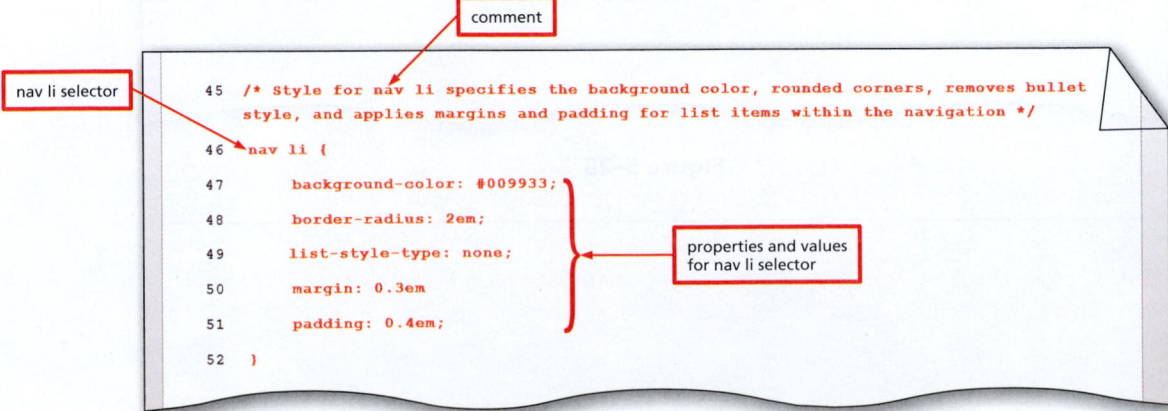

```
45    /* Style for nav li specifies the background color, rounded corners, removes bullet
      style, and applies margins and padding for list items within the navigation */

46    nav li {

47        background-color: #009933;

48        border-radius: 2em;

49        list-style-type: none;

50        margin: 0.3em;

51        padding: 0.4em;

52    }
```

comment

nav li selector

properties and values for nav li selector

Figure 5–29

11 Save your changes, open index.html in your browser, and then adjust the window to the size of a mobile viewport (Figure 5–30).

bullet style removed

rounded corners

margins applied to list items

padding applied to list items

Image courtesy of Jessica Minnick

Figure 5–30

To Add a nav li a Style for Mobile Viewports

Create a new selector in your CSS file, nav li a. This selector applies to the list item anchors, or the page links, in the navigation area. Include the color property to define the color of the link as white (#FFFFFF) so the link text is clear against the dark green background. Set the text-decoration property to none to remove the underlining that appears by default for links. The following steps add a style using the nav li a selector in a CSS file.

1 Place your insertion point at the end of Line 52 and press the ENTER key twice to insert new two new lines, Lines 53 and 54.

2 On Line 54, type `/* Style changes navigation link text color to white and removes the underline */` to insert a comment.

3 Press the ENTER key to insert a new Line 55.

4 On Line 55, type `nav li a {` to add a nav li a selector and opening brace.

5 Press the ENTER key to insert a new Line 56.

6 On Line 56, increase the indent, and then type `color: #FFFFFF;` to add a color property and value.

7 Press the ENTER key to insert a new Line 57 and then type `text-decoration: none;` to add a text-decoration property and value.

8 Press the ENTER key, decrease the indent, and then type ` } ` to insert a closing brace (Figure 5–31).

Q&A What is the purpose of the text-decoration property and value?
Setting the text-decoration property to none removes the underlining from the hyperlinked text.

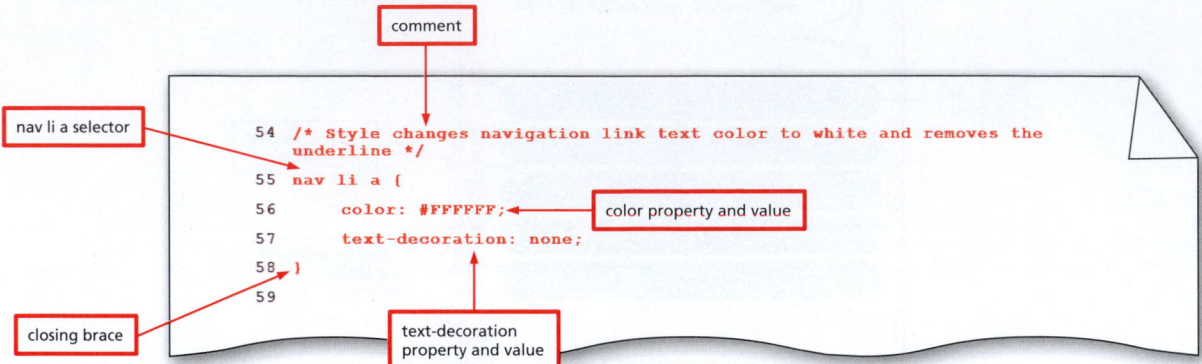

comment

nav li a selector

```
54  /* Style changes navigation link text color to white and removes the
    underline */
55  nav li a {
56      color: #FFFFFF;
57      text-decoration: none;
58  }
59
```

color property and value

closing brace

text-decoration property and value

Figure 5–31

9 Save your changes and refresh the home page in your browser (Figure 5–32).

links are now white and underlining is removed

Image courtesy of Jessica Minnick

Figure 5–32

Analyze the Home Page for Mobile-First Design

The content on the home page is now styled for a productive viewing experience on a mobile device, but the page content is still best suited to a desktop user. Instead of providing an introductory welcome message, use content a mobile device user wants to find quickly, such as the fitness club's hours and phone number with a telephone link.

You can add this essential content to the home page without removing the content for webpage visitors with a desktop device. To accomplish this task, use a **div** element to contain the content for mobile devices and another **div** element to contain the content for desktop displays. You then add a class attribute to each **div** element; add a class="mobile" attribute and value to the **div** element for the mobile content and add a class="desktop" attribute and value for the **div** element for the desktop content. You will then define styles to display the mobile class and hide the desktop class. You create a .tablet class in later steps.

To Modify the Home Page

1 CODE NAVIGATION LINKS | 2 MAKE IMAGES FLEXIBLE | 3 ADD STYLES FOR MOBILE
4 INSERT & STYLE SPAN ELEMENT | 5 ADD META TAG | 6 TEST WEBPAGES

Modify the home page to add essential content for a mobile user. First, create a new **div** element with a class="mobile" attribute and value, and then add the mobile content within this new **div** element. Next, place the desktop paragraph elements within a **div** element and add a class="desktop" attribute and value. *Why? When following a mobile-first strategy, provide the mobile user with the most important, essential page content and remove or hide the desktop content.* The following steps modify the home page content to follow a mobile-first strategy.

1

- Open index.html in your text editor to prepare to modify the page.

- Place your insertion point at the end of Line 32 and press the ENTER key twice to insert new Lines 33 and 34.

- On Line 34, type **<div class= "mobile">** to insert a new div element.

Figure 5–33

- Press the ENTER key twice to insert new Lines 35 and 36.

- On Line 36, increase the indent, and then type **<h3>FREE One-Week Trial Membership!</h3>** to add a heading 3 element.

- Press the ENTER key and type **<p><a href="tel:8145559608">Call Us Today to Get Started</a></p>** on Line 37 to add a paragraph element that contains a telephone link (Figure 5–33).

- Press the ENTER key twice and then type `<h4>Fitness Club Hours:</h4>` on Line 39 to insert a heading 4 element. [Line 39]

- Press the ENTER key and type `<p>Monday - Thursday: 6:00am - 6:00pm<br>` on Line 40 to a new paragraph element and content.

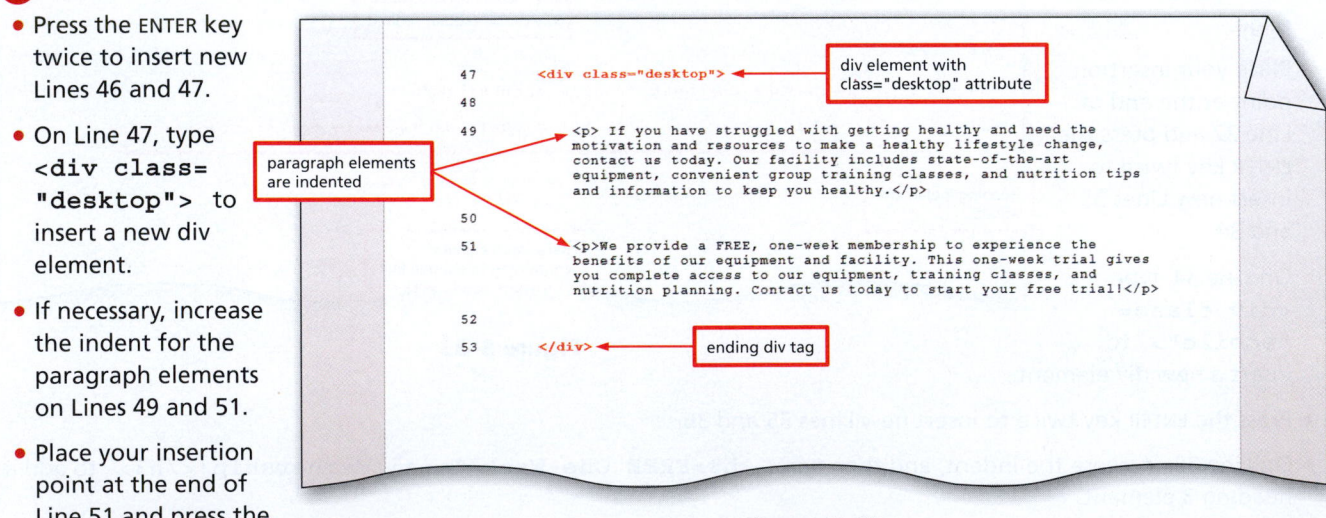

Figure 5–34

- Press the ENTER key and type `Friday: 6:00am - 4:00pm<br>` on Line 41 to add content.

- Press the ENTER key and type `Saturday: 8:00am - 6:00pm<br>` on Line 42 to add content.

- Press the ENTER key and type `Sunday: Closed</p>` on Line 43 to add content and close the paragraph element.

- Press the ENTER key twice, decrease the indent, and then type `</div>` on Line 45 to close the div element (Figure 5–34).

- Press the ENTER key twice to insert new Lines 46 and 47.

- On Line 47, type `<div class="desktop">` to insert a new div element.

- If necessary, increase the indent for the paragraph elements on Lines 49 and 51.

- Place your insertion point at the end of Line 51 and press the ENTER key twice to insert new Lines 52 and 53.

Figure 5–35

- On Line 53, decrease the indent, and then type `</div>` to close the div element (Figure 5–35).

- Save your changes.

To Modify the Style Rule for the mobile Class

Your CSS file contains a style rule for the mobile class, which sets the display to none. When you created this style, it was originally meant to hide the content in the mobile class when the page was displayed in a desktop viewport. You now need to modify the style rule to display the mobile class for the mobile viewport. Modify the style rule for the .mobile selector so it displays content inline. *Why? In the mobile viewport, show the phone number with the link to make it easy for a mobile user to call the business. Use the inline value with the display property to display the phone number as an inline element instead of adding extra space as it would for a block element.* The following steps modify the style rule for the .mobile selector.

- If necessary, reopen styles.css in your text editor to prepare to modify the style rule for the mobile class.

Figure 5–36

- Place your insertion point at the end of Line 58 and press the ENTER key twice to create new Lines 59 and 60.

- On Line 60, type `/* Style displays the mobile class */` to insert a comment.

- Select the style rule for the mobile class on Lines 100 through 102 and press the CTRL+X keys to cut the style rule.

- At the end of Line 60, press the ENTER key and then press the CTRL+V keys to paste the mobile class style rule on Lines 61 through 63.

- Change the display value from none to `inline` to modify the value (Figure 5–36).

2

- Save your changes.

To Add a Style Rule for the desktop Class

Create a style rule to hide content in the desktop class. First, insert a .desktop selector and then set the `display` property to `none`. *Why? You do not want to display desktop content in the mobile viewport.* Later in this chapter, you add a class="desktop" attribute and value to an element that defines desktop-only content. The following steps add the style rule for the .desktop selector.

1

- Place your insertion point at the end of Line 63 and press the ENTER key twice to create new Lines 64 and 65.

Figure 5–37

- On Line 65, type `/* Style hides the desktop class */` to insert a comment.

- Press the ENTER key and type `.desktop {` on Line 66 to add a selector.

- Press the ENTER key, increase the indent, and then type `display: none;` to add a property and value.

- Press the ENTER key, decrease the indent, and then type } to end the new style rule (Figure 5–37).

2

- Save your changes and refresh the index.html file in your browser (Figure 5–38).

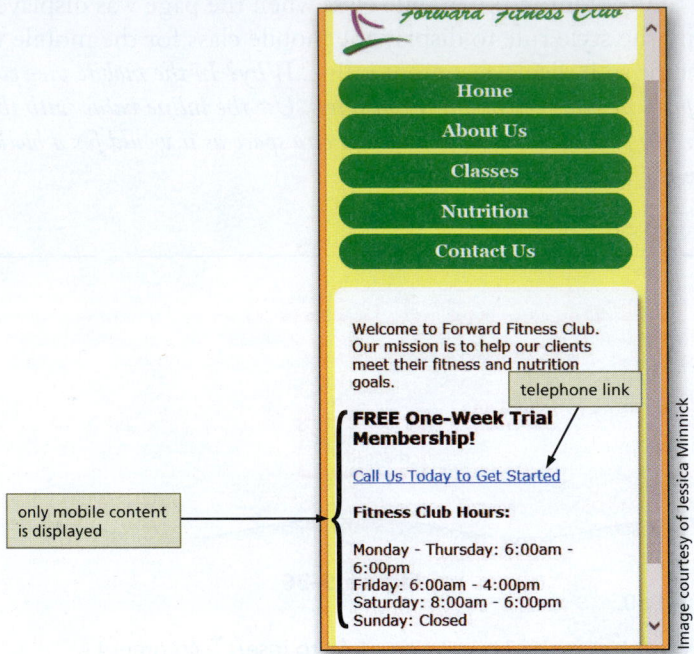

only mobile content is displayed

telephone link

Figure 5–38

To Modify the Style Rule for the main Element

The styles.css file contains a style rule for the main element. Modify the style rule to adjust the padding and margins to display more content in the mobile viewport and change absolute units of measurement to relative units of measurement used for fluid and responsive design layouts. The following steps modify the style rule for main element.

1 On Line 70, change the comment text to `Style for the main element specifies a block display, text properties, margins, padding, rounded corners, and border properties` to edit the comment.

2 On Line 75, change the value for the margin-top property to `0.5em`.

3 Delete the property and value for the bottom margin, and then delete the blank line and extra indent.

4 On Line 76, change the value for padding to `1em`.

5 On Line 77, change the value for border-radius to `1em`.

6 On Line 79, replace the property and value for the box shadow with `border-top: solid 0.2em #009933;` to add a top border.

7 Press the ENTER key and then type `border-bottom: solid 0.2em #009933;` to add a bottom border (Figure 5–39).

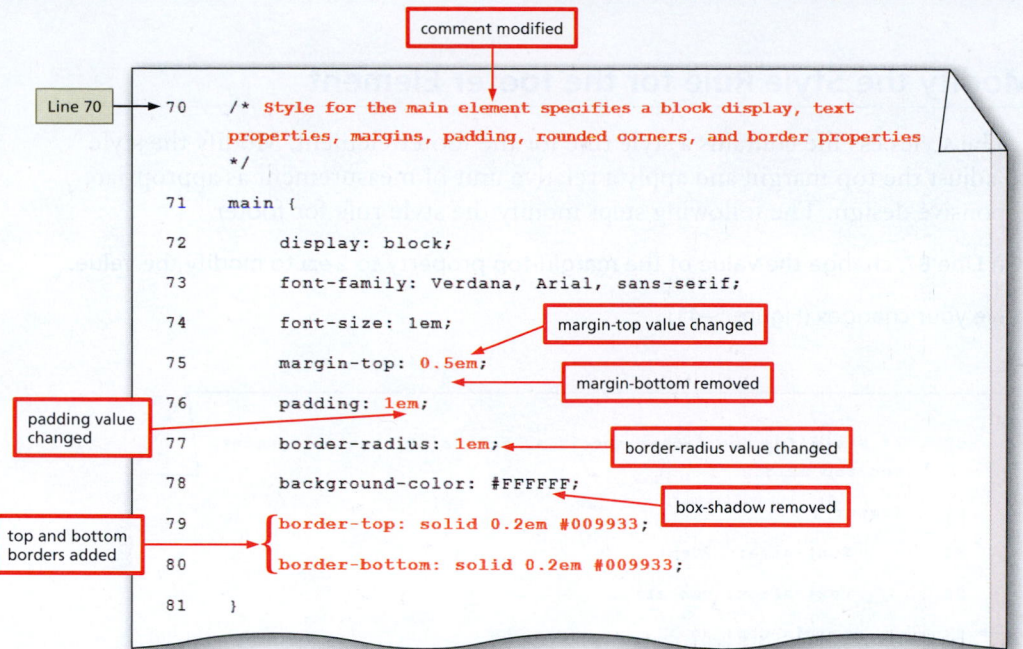

comment modified

Line 70

```
70      /* Style for the main element specifies a block display, text
        properties, margins, padding, rounded corners, and border properties
        */
71      main {
72          display: block;
73          font-family: Verdana, Arial, sans-serif;
74          font-size: 1em;
75          margin-top: 0.5em;
76          padding: 1em;
77          border-radius: 1em;
78          background-color: #FFFFFF;
79          border-top: solid 0.2em #009933;
80          border-bottom: solid 0.2em #009933;
81      }
```

margin-top value changed

margin-bottom removed

padding value changed

border-radius value changed

box-shadow removed

top and bottom borders added

Figure 5–39

8 Save your changes and refresh the index.html page in your browser (Figure 5–40).

top margin

top and bottom borders added

rounded corners

padding applied to main

shadow removed

Image courtesy of Jessica Minnick

Figure 5–40

To Modify the Style Rule for the footer Element

The styles.css file contains a style rule for the footer element. Modify the style rule to adjust the top margin and apply a relative unit of measurement as appropriate for responsive design. The following steps modify the style rule for footer.

1 On Line 87, change the value of the margin-top property to **2em** to modify the value.

2 Save your changes (Figure 5–41).

```
83      /* Style for the footer specifies font size, text alignment,
        and top margin */

84      footer {

85          font-size: .70em;

86          text-align: center;

87          margin-top: 2em;

88      }
```

Line 87 → 87

margin-top value changed

Figure 5–41

Analyze the About Us Page for Mobile-First Design

The content on the home page is now styled for an optimum mobile viewing experience, but take a look at the About Us page. Figure 5–42 shows the areas that can be adjusted to better style the content for a mobile viewport.

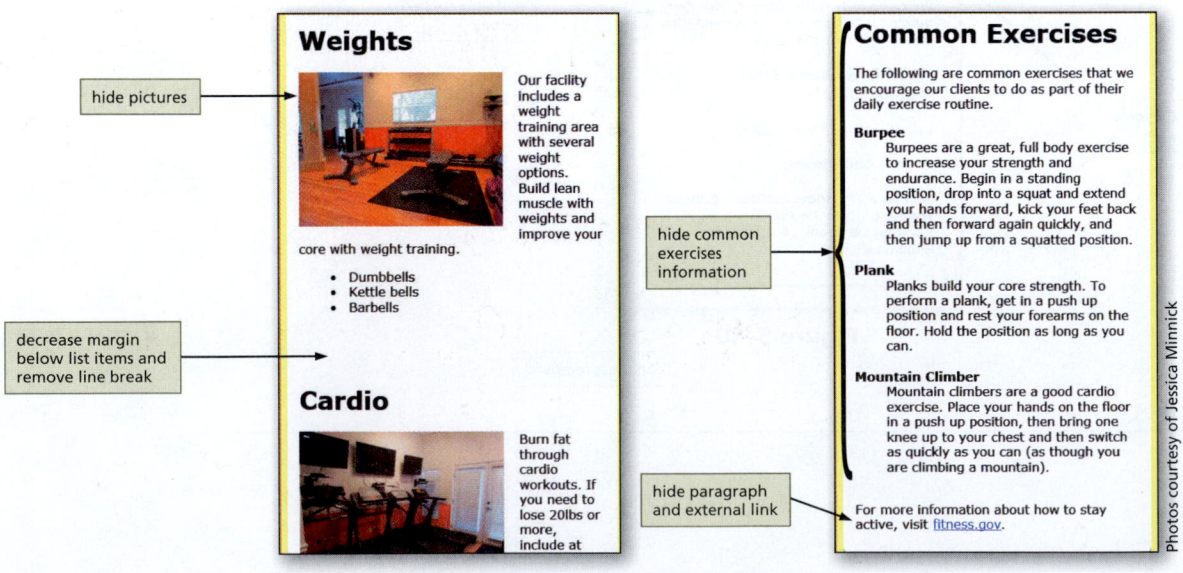

Figure 5–42

The About Us page has more content than the home page. To minimize scrolling, review the page content and determine the most essential information, which describes the equipment and services. In this case, to use as much of the available space as possible, you can hide the pictures, remove the line breaks, and remove the style rules for the ul selector, which set a large bottom margin and position the bullets for the list. (Recall that you set the position of the bullets to inline so they are not covered by the floating pictures. If you hide the pictures, you do not need to set the position of the bullets.) Additionally, you can hide other content in the main element, including the common exercise information and the paragraph with the external link. This content is not essential to mobile users, who want to know the basics about the club's equipment and services.

To take a mobile-first approach with the About Us page, you can open the about .html document and delete all the line breaks, which removes extra space below the lists. Next, add a new `div` element with a class named tablet, which will contain the common exercises content and the paragraph with the external link, as the external website is not optimized for mobile display. Then, open the styles.css file and modify the .equip selector to set the `display` property to `none`. Because the equip class includes the images, setting the `display` property to `none` hides the images in the mobile viewport. Delete the ul style rule to remove the rest of the extra space below the bulleted lists and use the default position for bullets in an unordered list. Because the dt and dl style rules format the common exercise content, and this content is being hidden, you can remove the dt and dl style rules. Finally, create a new style rule that does not display the tablet class.

To Modify the About Us Page

1 CODE NAVIGATION LINKS | 2 MAKE IMAGES FLEXIBLE | 3 ADD STYLES FOR MOBILE
4 INSERT & STYLE SPAN ELEMENT | 5 ADD META TAG | 6 TEST WEBPAGES

Modify the HTML code on the About Us page before you modify the styles.css file so you can see how the changes you make to the styles affect the content on the webpage. In about.html, remove all line breaks and add a `div` element with a class named tablet. *Why? Removing the line breaks removes extra space below the lists.* You will add a .tablet selector to the style sheet in later steps to set the `display` property value to `none` so that this class does not appear in a mobile viewport. The following steps modify the About Us page.

- Open about.html in your text editor to prepare to modify the page.

- Remove the line breaks, <br>, on Lines 39, 48, 57, 64, 68, and 72 (Figure 5–43).

Figure 5–43

- Place the insertion point at the end of Line 57 and press the ENTER key twice to insert new Lines 58 and 59.

- On Line 59, type **<div class= "tablet">** to insert a new div element.

- Place the insertion point at the end of Line 77 and press the ENTER key twice to insert new Lines 78 and 79.

- On Line 79, type **</div>** to close the div element (Figure 5–44).

Figure 5–44

- Save your changes.

To Add a Style Rule for the tablet Class

1 CODE NAVIGATION LINKS | 2 MAKE IMAGES FLEXIBLE | 3 ADD STYLES FOR MOBILE
4 INSERT & STYLE SPAN ELEMENT | 5 ADD META TAG | 6 TEST WEBPAGES

In the previous steps, you added a class named tablet to a **div** element on the About Us page. Now you can insert a style rule with a new selector named .tablet that applies to content in the tablet class. In the style rule, insert a declaration that sets the **display** property to **none** for the mobile viewport. *Why? Hiding nonessential content in the mobile viewport minimizes scrolling.* The following steps create a style rule for the tablet class.

- If necessary, open styles.css to prepare to insert a new style rule.

- Place your insertion point at the end of Line 88 and press the ENTER key twice to insert new Lines 89 and 90.

Figure 5–45

- On Line 90, type **/* Style hides the tablet class */** to insert a comment.

- Press the ENTER key to insert a new Line 91 and type **.tablet {** to begin a new style rule.

- Press the ENTER key to insert a new Line 92, increase the indent, and then type **display: none;** to insert a property and value.

- Press the ENTER key to insert a new Line 93, decrease the indent, and then type } to close the style rule (Figure 5–45).

- Save your changes, open about.html in your browser, and then scroll down to view the changes (Figure 5–46).

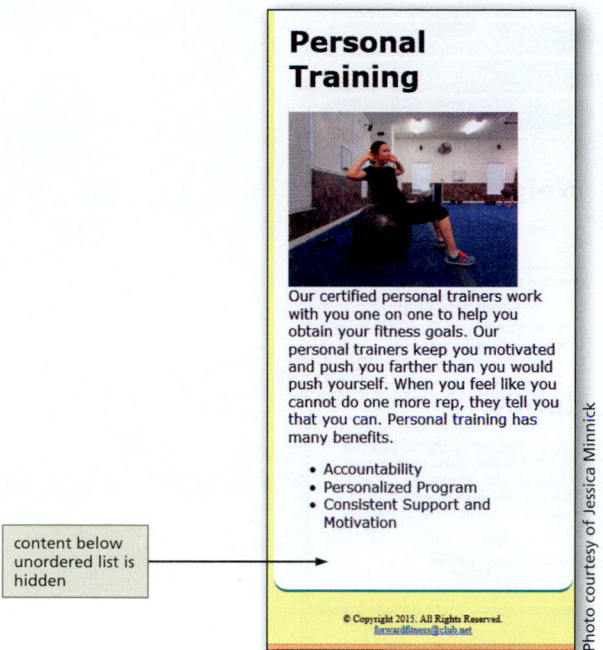

content below unordered list is hidden

Figure 5–46

To Modify the .equip, ul, dt, and dd Style Rules

1 CODE NAVIGATION LINKS | 2 MAKE IMAGES FLEXIBLE | **3 ADD STYLES FOR MOBILE**
4 INSERT & STYLE SPAN ELEMENT | 5 ADD META TAG | 6 TEST WEBPAGES

The styles.css file contains style rules for the equip class and the ul, dt, and dd elements. Modify the .equip style rule by replacing the current properties and values with the **display** property with a value of **none**. Then remove the ul, dt, and dd style rules. ***Why?*** *Setting the display property to none for the equip class hides the pictures on the About Us page to allow more content on the page. The styles for the ul, dt, and dd elements are not needed for the mobile viewport.* The following steps modify the style rule for the equip class and remove the style rules for the ul, dt, and dd elements.

1.
- In styles.css, place your insertion point on Line 94 and press the ENTER key to insert a new Line 95.

comment added

Line 95

```
95    /* Style rule specifies to not display the equip class */

96    .equip {

97        display: none;

98    }

99
```

float and padding properties and values removed

display property and value added

ul, dt, and dd style rules are removed

Figure 5–47

- On Line 95, type **/* Style rule specifies to not display the equip class */** to insert a comment.

- Select Lines 97 and 98 and then type **display: none;** to replace the declarations with a new property and value.

- If necessary, move the closing brace to Line 98.

- Select Lines 100 through 111 and then press the DELETE key to remove the style rules for the ul, dt, and dd elements (Figure 5–47).

2

• Save your changes and refresh your browser to view the changes. If necessary, scroll down to view the changes (Figure 5–48).

Figure 5–48

Analyze the Contact Us Page for Mobile-First Design

Review the Contact Us page to determine how to best style the content for mobile displays. Recall that the Contact Us page includes two telephone numbers; one with a telephone link and one without. The Contact Us page should display the telephone number with the link and hide the telephone number without the link in the mobile viewport. Currently, both telephone numbers are displayed, as shown in Figure 5–49. You will fix this problem using the **span** element.

Figure 5–49

Image courtesy of Jessica Minnick

Using the Span Element

To hide the telephone number that does not include a link, create a **span** element with the class= "desktop" attribute and value. This code adds the **span** element to the desktop class. Because the style sheet sets the **display** property of the desktop class to **none**, the **span** element is not displayed in the mobile viewport.

The **span** element allows you to use CSS to format a span of text separately from its surrounding text. The **span** element begins with a <span> tag and ends with a </span> tag. As an inline element, it can be applied to text within a block. A class can be added to a **span** element to style its text. For example, the following code shows a phone number wrapped in **span** element.

```
<span class="desktop">(814) 555-9608</span>
```

This code defines the telephone number as part of the **span** element and assigns the **span** element to the desktop class. Now the style rule for the desktop class will apply to the phone number. In this case, the phone number will be hidden on a mobile viewport. Later, you create style rules to display the phone number on tablet and desktop viewports.

To Add a Span Element to the Contact Us Page

1 CODE NAVIGATION LINKS | 2 MAKE IMAGES FLEXIBLE | 3 ADD STYLES FOR MOBILE
4 INSERT & STYLE SPAN ELEMENT | 5 ADD META TAG | 6 TEST WEBPAGES

The Contact Us page contains two phone numbers. One of the phone numbers includes a telephone link, which is only helpful to users viewing the page from a mobile device. The telephone number with the link should be displayed only on a mobile device. Likewise, the other telephone number without the link should be displayed only on nonmobile devices. To accommodate this feature, you add a **span** element to the telephone number without a link and include a class named desktop. *Why? A new rule will be added to the CSS file to display the telephone number without the link for nonmobile devices.* The following steps add a **span** element with a class named desktop to the Contact Us page.

- If necessary, open contact.html in your text editor to prepare to insert a span element.

```
37        <p>Phone Number<br>
38            <a class="mobile" href="tel:8145559608">(814) 555-9608</a>
39            <span class="desktop">(814) 555-9608</span></p>
```

Line 39

span element with class attribute

closing span tag

- Place your insertion point before the phone number on Line 39 and then type **<span class="desktop">** to insert a starting span tag with a class named desktop.

Figure 5–50

- Place your insertion point after the phone number on Line 39 and then type **</span>** to insert an ending span tag (Figure 5–50).

2
- Save your changes and open contact.html in your browser to view the changes (Figure 5–51).

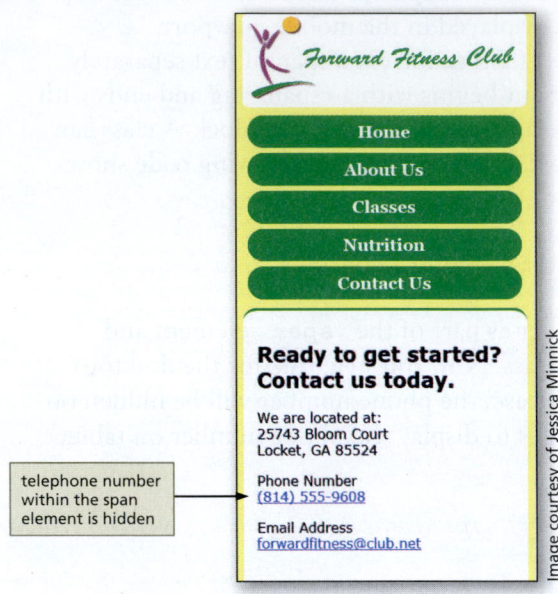

telephone number within the span element is hidden

Figure 5–51

Adding Meta Tags

For responsive sites, add the following **meta** tag to the **head** section of each webpage. This code makes sure that the page *initially loads* in a layout width that matches the viewport of the device. Initially loading the correct layout for each device is particularly helpful for mobile devices because it eliminates extra zooming.

```
<meta name="viewport" content="width=device-width,
initial-scale=1">
```

To Add the Meta Tag for Responsive Design

1 CODE NAVIGATION LINKS | 2 MAKE IMAGES FLEXIBLE | 3 ADD STYLES FOR MOBILE
4 INSERT & STYLE SPAN ELEMENT | 5 ADD META TAG | 6 TEST WEBPAGES

Add the viewport **meta** tag to the **head** section of the home, About Us, Contact Us, and template pages. *Why? The appropriate meta tag helps the webpage initially load in a size that matches the viewport size.* The following steps add the viewport **meta** tag to the home, About Us, Contact, and template pages.

- Return to your text editor and, if necessary, open index.html, about. html, contact.html, and fitness.html.

- In the index.html file, place the insertion point at the end of Line 7 and then press the ENTER key to insert a new Line 8 just above the closing </head> tag.

Figure 5–52

- On Line 8, add the tag `<meta name="viewport" content="width=device-width, initial-scale=1">` to insert a meta tag for responsive design (Figure 5–52).

- Copy the meta element on Line 8, and then in the about.html file, paste the meta element in the same location, on a new Line 8 just above the closing </head> tag.

- In the contact.html file, paste the meta tag in the same location, on a new Line 8 just above the closing </head> tag.

- In the fitness.html file, paste the meta tag in the same location, on a new Line 8 just above the closing </head> tag.

- Save all files.

Testing Webpages in Viewports of Different Sizes

One way to test your webpages for various devices, operating systems, browsers, and viewport sizes is to publish your pages to a web server and access them from all of the configurations you want to test. However, this approach is both expensive and somewhat impractical. Fortunately, many great tools and emulators are available to make the testing process faster and less expensive. A few options are shown in Table 5-2.

Table 5-2 Mobile Device Emulators		
Emulator Name	**Website**	**Description**
Mozilla Firefox Developer	https://www.mozilla.org/en-US/firefox/developer/	Set of authoring and debugging tools built into Firefox
Chrome Developer's Tools	https://developer.chrome.com/devtools	Set of authoring and debugging tools built into Chrome
Viewport Emulator	http://www.viewportemulator.com/	Online tool to test responsive design website in multiple viewports
iPadPeek	http://ipadpeek.com	Online iPad and iPhone simulator
TestiPhone.com	http://www.testiphone.com/	Online iPhone simulator
iOS Simulator	http://developer.apple.com/	Official Apple iOS simulator — downloadable software
Android Emulator	https://developer.android.com/	Official Android simulator — downloadable software
Windows Phone Emulator	http://msdn.microsoft.com/ (then search for Windows Phone Emulator)	Windows Phone Emulator — downloadable software
Opera Mini Emulator	https://dev.opera.com (then search for Opera Mini Emulator)	Opera Mini Emulator — downloadable software

To Preview a Mobile Website in the Google Chrome Emulator

To test your mobile site design, use an emulator to view the site. *Why? Before you publish a website, you should test with as many variable factors as possible. An emulator lets you test across multiple types of devices.* The following steps display the home page in Chrome's emulator.

1

- Open index.html in the Google Chrome browser to display the page.

- Tap or click the Chrome menu button, and then tap or click More tools (Figure 5–53).

Q&A I do not have Google Chrome. What can I do? Google Chrome is a free download at https://www.google.com/chrome/browser/desktop/ Download and install Chrome so you can use it to test your webpages.

Figure 5–53

2

- Tap or click Developer tools to open the Developer tools pane at the bottom of the window.

- If the webpage does not appear in the emulator, tap or click the Toggle device mode button at the top of the Developer tools pane to display the emulator.

- If a message appears at the top of the window advising you to reload the page, press the F5 key to reload the page.

- If necessary, drag the top of the Developer tools pane down to create more room for the emulator.

- Tap or click the Device list arrow, and then tap or click Apple iPhone 6 to select a device.

- Refresh the page to view it as it appears on the selected device (Figure 5–54).

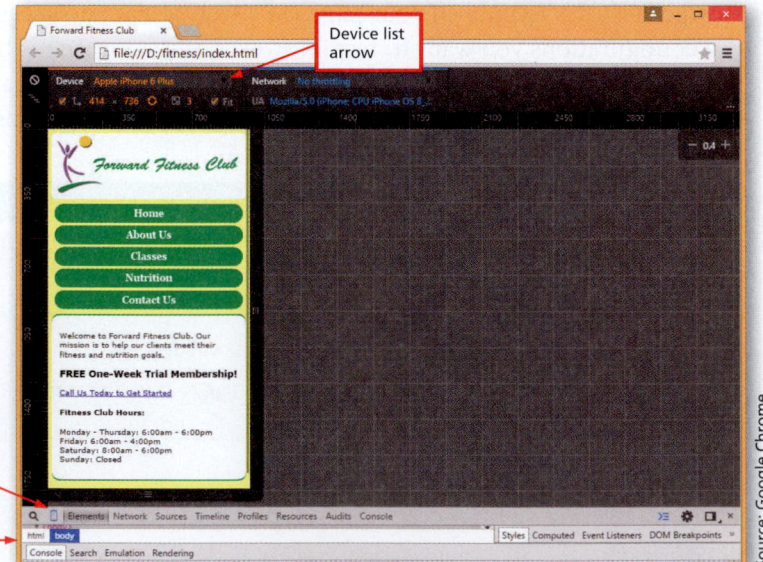

Figure 5–54

Q&A How do I test the page in viewports of different sizes?
Tap or click the Device list arrow and then select a device of a different size.

To Validate the Style Sheet

Always run your files through W3C's validator to check the document for errors. If the document has any errors, validating gives you a chance to identify and correct them. Validation is also an effective troubleshooting tool during the development process and adds a valuable level of professionalism to your work. The following steps validate a CSS document.

1 Open your browser and type `http://jigsaw.w3.org/css-validator/` in the address bar to display the W3C CSS Validation Service page.

2 Tap or click the By file upload tab to display the Validate by File Upload information.

3 Tap or click the Browse button to display the File Upload dialog box.

4 Navigate to your css folder to find the styles.css file.

5 Tap or click the styles.css document to select it.

6 Tap or click the Open button to upload the selected file to the W3C CSS validator.

7 Tap or click the Check button to send the document through the validator and display the validation results page.

To Validate the HTML Files

Every time you create a new webpage, run it through W3C's validator to check the document for errors. If any errors exist, you need to correct them. Validation is also an effective troubleshooting tool during the development process and adds a valuable level of professionalism to your work. The following steps validate an HTML document.

1 Open your browser and type `http://validator.w3.org/` in the address bar to display the W3C validator page.

2 Tap or click the Validate by File Upload tab to display the Validate by File Upload tab information.

3 Tap or click the Browse button to display the File Upload dialog box.

4 Navigate to your website template folder to find the about.html file.

5 Tap or click the about.html document to select it.

6 Tap or click the Open button to upload it to the W3C validator.

7 Tap or click the Check button to send the document through the validator and display the validation results page.

8 If necessary, correct any errors, save your changes, and run through the validator again to revalidate the page.

9 Follow these steps to validate the contact.html, index.html, and fitness.html pages and correct any errors.

Chapter Summary

In this chapter, you learned how to apply responsive design principles to a website. You modified the fitness website to use a fluid layout, coded images to be flexible, and followed a mobile-first strategy to analyze and modify the webpages in the fitness website. Finally, you added meta tags for responsive design. The items listed below include all the new skills you have learned in this chapter, with the tasks grouped by activity.

Creating a Fluid Layout
Code the Navigation Links as an Unordered List (HTML 212)

Making Images Flexible
Add Flexible Images (HTML 215)

Following a Mobile-First Strategy
Modify the Home Page (HTML 227)
Modify the Style Rule for the mobile Class (HTML 229)
Add a Style Rule for the desktop Class (HTML 229)
Modify the About Us Page (HTML 233)

Add a Style Rule for the tablet Class (HTML 234)
Modify the .equip, ul, dt, and dd Style Rules (HTML 235)

Using the Span Element
Add a Span Element to the Contact Us Page (HTML 237)

Adding Meta Tags
Add the Meta Tag for Responsive Design (HTML 238)

Testing Webpages in Viewports of Different Sizes
Preview a Mobile Website in the Google Chrome Emulator (HTML 242)

CONSIDER THIS

How will you apply the principles of responsive web design to your website?
Use these guidelines as you complete the assignments in this chapter and create your own webpages outside of this class.

1. Analyze how the principles of responsive design might be applied to your website.

   a. Determine the importance of mobile traffic.

   b. Consider the pros and cons of responsive design versus a mobile website strategy.

   c. Consider mobile-first principles such as focusing on essential content first.

2. Use a fluid layout.

   a. Width measurements should be in flexible units such as % or ems.

   b. Textual content can be measured in px, but consider ems for maximum flexibility.

3. Apply flexible images.

   a. Remove fixed height and width measurements from the HTML documents.

   b. Size images with CSS percentages.

4. Test and validate your responsive design.

   a. Use emulators to test on multiple devices.

   b. Validate both the HTML and CSS.

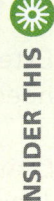

How should you submit solutions to questions in the assignments identified with a ✳ symbol?
Every assignment in this book contains one or more questions identified with a ✳ symbol. These questions require you to think beyond the assigned presentation. Present your solutions to the questions in the format required by your instructor. Possible formats may include one or more of these options: create a document that contains the answer; present your answer to the class; discuss your answer in a group; record the answer as audio or video using a webcam, smartphone, or portable media player; or post answers on a blog, wiki, or website.

Apply Your Knowledge

Reinforce the skills and apply the concepts you learned in this chapter.

Styling for Responsive Design

Instructions: In this exercise, you will use your text editor to apply responsive design principles to an existing webpage. You will make all images flexible, change the layout to a fluid layout, and add a viewport meta tag. The completed webpage is shown in Figure 5–55. You will also use professional web development practices to indent, space, comment, and validate your code.

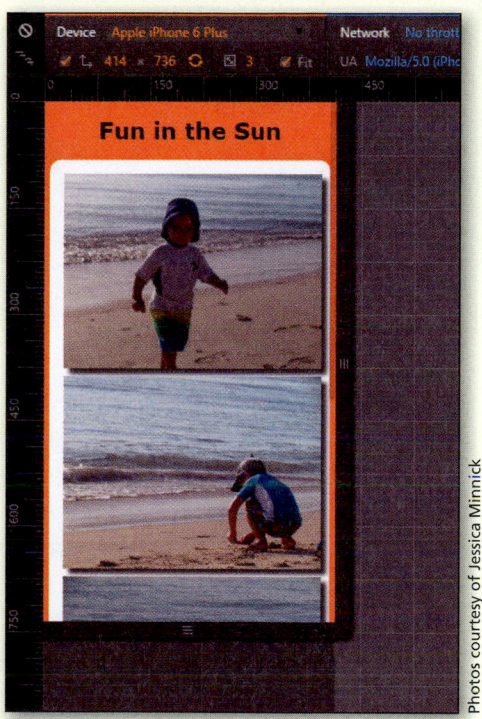

Figure 5–55

Photos courtesy of Jessica Minnick

Perform the following tasks:

1. Open apply05.html in your browser to view the webpage. Adjust the browser window to view the fixed layout.

2. Open apply05.html in your text editor and modify the comment at the top of the page to include your name and today's date.

3. Remove the width and height attributes from the image elements and save your changes.

4. Open the styles05.css file from the apply\css folder. Modify the comment at the top of the styles05.css page to include your name and today's date.

5. In the styles05.css file, add a max-width property with a value of 100% to the img selector.

6. Locate the #container selector and change the width value to use a relative measurement and take up the full width of the page.

7. Save the styles05.css file and refresh the apply05.html file in your browser. Resize the browser to make sure that a fluid layout has been applied and that the images are flexible.

8. In apply05.html, add the following meta tag within the head section of the document:

```
<meta name="viewport" content="width=device-width, initial-scale=1">
```

9. Save your changes to apply05.html and open the file in Google Chrome.

10. Use the developer tools in Google Chrome to view the page in an emulator.

11. Select a device and refresh the page. The page should look similar to Figure 5–55.

12. Validate your HTML document using the W3C validator found at validator.w3.org and fix any errors that are identified.

13. Validate your CSS file using the W3C validator found at http://jigsaw.w3.org/css-validator/ and fix any errors that are identified.

14. Submit the apply05.html and styles05.css files in a format specified by your instructor. Your instructor may also ask you to submit the images folder used with apply05.html.

15. ✳ In step 5, you changed the value to use a percentage (%) measurement. Explain how the percentage unit of measurement makes a fluid layout more flexible as compared to px.

Extend Your Knowledge

Extend the skills you learned in this chapter and experiment with new skills. You may need to use additional resources to complete the assignment.

Learning More About jQuery Mobile

Instructions: In this exercise, you will use your browser to research jQuery Mobile. You will review the information you discover and then answer the following questions. Figure 5–56 shows the flip switch demo page from the jQuery Mobile website.

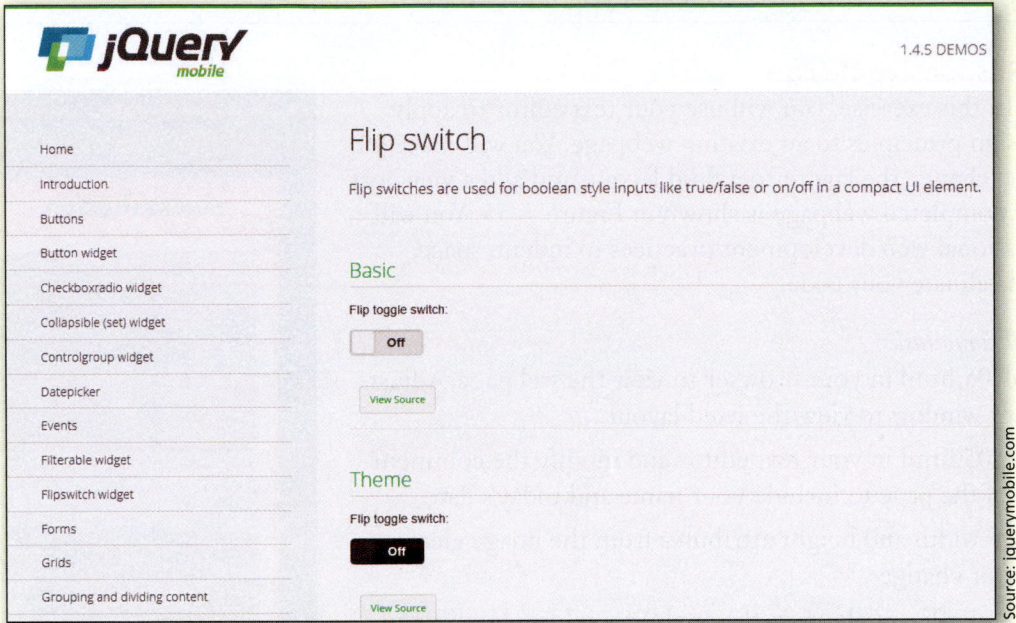

Source: jquerymobile.com

Figure 5–56

Perform the following tasks:

1. Open your browser and go to jquerymobile.com.

2. Review the information on the site.

3. Open your word processor. In your own words, what is jQuery Mobile and how is it used?

4. Tap or click the Demos link and test the demos on the page to view how they work.

5. List and describe three of the demos that you tested. Provide an example of the code required for two of the demos that you tested.

6. Use your browser and visit w3schools.com to research more about jquery mobile.

7. Provide an example of the code needed to create a basic jquery mobile page.

8. Save your file as extend05 and submit it in a format specified by your instructor.

9. ✳ Research mobile web applications and native apps. Identify how they are similar and how they are different.

Analyze, Correct, Improve

Analyze an external style sheet, correct all errors, and improve it.

Changing a Nonresponsive Page into a Responsive Page

Instructions: Work with the responsive05.html file in the analyze folder and the responsivestyles05 .css file in the analyze\css folder from the Data Files for Students. Several responsive web design resources are listed on the responsive05 webpage, but the HTML document and the style sheet are not coded for responsive design as shown in Figure 5–57. Use Figure 5–58 as a guide to correct these files. You will also use professional web development best practices to comment, indent, space, and validate your work.

Figure 5–57

Figure 5–58

1. Correct

a. Open the responsive05.html file in your editor from the Data Files for Students and then modify the comment at the top of the page to include your name and today's date.

b. Open the responsivestyles05.css file in your editor from the Data Files for Students and then modify and correct the comment at the top of the document to include your name and today's date.

c. View responsive05.html in your browser and resize the page to recreate the problems with a nonresponsive webpage as shown in Figure 5–56. The content and images are cut off as the browser width decreases.

d. In the responsive05.html file, add the viewport meta tag right above the closing </head> tag:

```
<meta name="viewport" content="width=device-width, initial-scale=1">
```

Continued >

Analyze, Correct, Improve *continued*

  e. In the responsive05.html file, delete the height and width attributes from the img element.

  f. In the responsivestyles05.css file, make the following property value changes:
     main selector, **width** property, change from **960px** to **100%**

  g. In the responsivestyles05.css file, create a style that has an **img** selector with a **max-width** property and a value of **100%**.

2. Improve

  a. In the responsive05.html file, add indents and spacing for improved readability.

  b. In the responsivestyles05.css file, create a style that has an **ul** selector with a **padding** property and a value of **0**.

  c. In the responsivestyles05.css file, create a style that has an **li** selector with the following properties and values:

     list-style-type property and a value of **none**

     padding property and a value of **1%**

     margin property and a value of **1%**

  d. In the responsivestyles05.css file, create a style that has an **li a** selector with the following properties and values:

     color property and a value of **#FFFFFF**

     text-decoration property and a value of **none**

     list-style-type property and a value of **none**

  e. Save your changes and test your webpage. It should look like Figure 5–58.

  f. Validate your CSS file using the W3C validator found at http://jigsaw.w3.org/css-validator/ and fix any errors that are identified.

  g. Validate your HTML webpage using the W3C validator found at validator.w3.org and fix any errors that are identified.

  h. ✳ Review some of the resources listed on the Responsive Web Design Best Practices page, and then comment on which of these practices you would like to understand better and why.

In the Labs

Labs 1 and 2, which increase in difficulty, require you to create webpages based on what you learned in the chapter; Lab 3 requires you to dive deeper into a topic covered in the chapter.

Lab 1: Creating a Mobile Design for the New Harvest Food Bank

Problem: You volunteer at a local food bank called New Harvest Food Bank that collects community food donations and provides food and other services to those in need. The organization has asked you to create a responsive website. With a growing mobile market, you decide to implement a mobile-first strategy. Style the webpage shown in Figure 5–59 with an external style sheet.

Instructions: Perform the following tasks:

  1. Open your text editor and then open the index.html file in the lab1 folder and the fbstyles.css file in the lab1\css folder from the Data Files for Students.

  2. In the index.html document, modify the comment at the top of the page to include your name and today's date. Make sure the<title>…</title> tags contain the text **New Harvest Food Bank**.

3. In the fbstyles.css file, modify the comment at the top of the page to include your name and today's date.

4. In the index.html file, modify the link to the external style sheet to reference fbstyles.css.

5. Add the following viewport meta tag to the <head> section of the index.html file:

```
<meta name="viewport" content="width=device-
width, initial-scale=1">
```

6. Delete the width and height attributes from all `img` elements.

7. In the `main` element, create a new `div` element with a class= "mobile" attribute and value. Add the following content to the new div element:

```
<p>New Harvest is proud to help and support our
local community</p>

<h3>Volunteer Opportunities Available</h3>

<p>Call Us Today to Inquire, <a
href="tel:5558235555">(555) 823-5555</a></p>
```

8. In the fbstyles.css file, add the following comment and style after the style for the body element to help create flexible images:

```
/* Style to create a fluid image */
img {
    max-width: 100%;
}
```

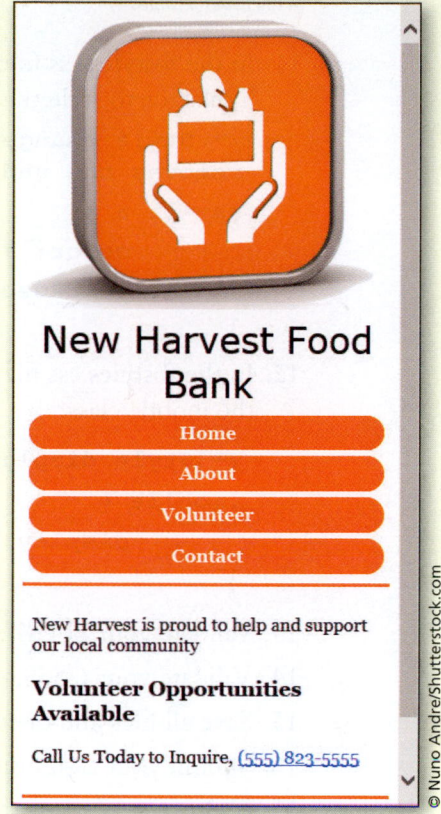

Figure 5–59

© Nuno Andre/Shutterstock.com

9. In the fbstyles.css file, add the following comment and style after the style for the `nav` element to style the unordered list in the nav:

```
/* Style specifies padding and margins for unordered list */
nav ul {
    padding: 0;
    margin-top: 0.5em;
    margin-bottom: 0.5em;
}
```

10. In the fbstyles.css file, add the following comment and style after the one you added for the nav ul selector to style list items within the nav:

```
/* Style for nav li specifies the background color, rounded corners,
removes bullet style, and applies margins and padding for list items
within the navigation */
nav li {
    background-color: #FF6600;
    border-radius: 1em;
    list-style-type: none;
    margin: 0.3em;
    padding: 0.4em;
}
```

Continued >

In the Labs *continued*

11. In the fbstyles.css file, add the following comment and style after the one you added for the nav li selector to style the nav links:

```
/* Style changes navigation link text color to white and
removes the underline */
nav li a {
        color: #FFFFFF;
        text-decoration: none;
}
```

12. In the fbstyles.css file, add the following comment and style to the end of the style sheet to style the mobile class:

```
/* Style displays the mobile class */
.mobile {
        display: inline;
}
```

13. Validate your HTML code and fix any errors.

14. Validate your CSS code and fix any errors.

15. Save all files and open the index.html page within a browser as shown in Figure 5–59.

16. Submit your assignment in the format specified by your instructor.

17. ☀ In step 12, you created a class named mobile. Use your favorite search engine to find an article that discusses popular or appropriate class and id names. Document the website and be prepared to explain or write a short paragraph on what you learned.

Lab 2: Creating a Responsive Website for Steve's Screen Services

Problem: You work for a screening company called Steve's Screen Services that specializes in screening, cleaning, and repairing screened patios, decks, and porches. The company has asked you to create a responsive website. Style the webpage shown in Figure 5–60 with an external style sheet.

Instructions: Perform the following tasks:

1. Open your text editor and then open the index.html file in the lab2 folder and the screenstyles. css file in the lab2\css folder from the Data Files for Students.

2. In the index.html file, modify the comment at the top of the page to include your name and today's date. Make sure the<title>…</title> tags contain the text **Steve's Screen Services.** Add this title to the template file as well.

3. In screenstyles.css, modify the comment at the top of the page to include your name and today's date.

4. In the index.html file, create a link to the external style sheet screenstyles.css. Add this link to the template file as well.

5. Add the following viewport meta tag to the <head> section of the index.html file and the template file:

```
<meta name="viewport" content="width=device-width, initial-scale=1">
```

6. Delete the width and height attributes from all image elements in the index.html file and the template file.

7. In the index.html and template files, code each set of navigation links as an unordered list.

8. In the index.html file, in the `main` element, create a new `div` element with a class="mobile" attribute and value. Add the following content to the new `div` element:

```
<h3>Need your patio screened or just a small
repair?</h3>

<p><a href="tel:5558235555">Call us today</a>
for a FREE estimate and use the reference code
Mobile Offer to receive a 10% discount</p>
```

9. In the screenstyles.css file, add the following style after the style for the body element to help create flexible images:

```
img {
      max-width: 100%;
}
```

10. In the screenstyles.css file, add the following comment and style after the style for the nav element to style the unordered list in the nav:

```
/* Style specifies padding and margins for unor-
dered list */
nav ul {
      padding: 0;
      margin-top: 0.5em;
      margin-bottom: 0.5em;
}
```

Figure 5–60

© Yarek Gora/Shutterstock.com

11. In the screenstyles.css file, add the following comment and style after the one you added for the nav ul selector to style list items within the nav:

```
/* Style for nav li specifies the background color, rounded
corners, removes bullet style, and applies margins and pad-
ding for list items within the navigation */
nav li {
      background-color: #000066;
      list-style-type: none;
      margin: 0.4em;
      padding: 0.5em;
}
```

12. In the screenstyles.css file, add the following comment and style after the style for nav li to style the nav links:

```
/* Style changes navigation link text color to white and
removes the underline */
nav li a {
      color: #FFFFFF;
      text-decoration: none;
}
```

Continued >

In the Labs *continued*

13. In the screenstyles.css file, add the following comment and style to the end of the style sheet to style the mobile class:

```
/* Style displays the mobile class */
.mobile {
        display: inline;
}
```

14. Validate your HTML code and fix any errors.

15. Validate your CSS code and fix any errors.

16. Save all files and open the index.html page within a browser as shown in Figure 5–59.

17. Submit your assignment in the format specified by your instructor.

18. ✳ In steps 7 and 11, you created and styled the navigation element to use an unordered list. Use your browser to research trends in navigation design for responsive web design. Document the website and be prepared to explain or write a short paragraph on what you learned.

Lab 3: Expand Your World
You Be the Judge

Problem: Responsive web design involves a number of technical and artistic elements. In this exercise you will review and document your thoughts on several responsive websites that have been judged by professional web developers to be excellent examples of responsive web design.

Instructions:

1. Go to http://www.awwwards.com/50-examples-of-responsive-web-design.html.

   This link takes you to the awwwards.com site that provides 50 excellent examples of responsive web design. If this site is not available, use your favorite search engine to find a site that highlights excellent examples of responsive web design.

2. Spend some time browsing through the site and reviewing the examples. Responsive web design best practices principles are in constant flux. Review at least three sites and provide your own answers to the following questions in the format specified by your instructor.

   a. Identify three common characteristics you observe for the responsive design winning websites.

   b. Identify three areas that you would like to learn more about.

3. ✳ Images are an important part of the content for any website. Using your favorite search engine, research three articles that provide tips on how to optimize images for the web. Identify the three URLs that you used for your research and provide a list of bullet points (2–5 per article) of tips on how to optimize images for webpages.

✺ Consider This: Your Turn

Apply your creative thinking and problem-solving skills to design and implement a solution.

1. Applying Responsive Design to Your Personal Portfolio Website

Personal

Part 1: In Chapter 4, you styled your personal portfolio website in the `portfolio.html` webpage. In this exercise, you update that page to use responsive design as follows:

1. Open the external style sheet you created in Chapter 4 and save it with the name `portfoliostyles05.css` in the styles folder within the your_turn_1 folder.

2. Add your name and the current date as a comment to the first line of the portfoliostyles05.css file.

3. In your HTML editor, open the files you created for your portfolio website in Chapter 4 and make sure your name and the current date are added as a comment to the first line of all files.

4. Update the HTML files to do the following:

    a. Modify the link to the external style sheet to reference portfoliostyles05.css.

    b. Add the viewport `meta` tag to the head section.

    c. Delete the height and width attributes from all `img` tags.

5. Update the CSS file to do the following:

    a. Measure all width properties in percentages (%).

    b. Add styles to create flexible images.

    c. Determine the most essential content on each page and style the HTML elements for a mobile viewport.

    d. Remove the markers (bullets) from the list items in the `nav` area.

    e. Refine your style sheet as desired to add margins and padding using `em` units of measure.

    f. Add a comment to note where the mobile styles begin.

6. Save and test your files.

7. Validate and correct your HTML and CSS files, and submit your assignment in the format specified by your instructor.

Part 2: ✺

Add the following paragraph and unordered list to an appropriate location on one of your personal portfolio webpages:

```
<p>Have worked with the principles of responsive web design
including:</p>
  <ul>
      <li>fluid layouts</li>
      <li>flexible images</li>
      <li>media queries</li>
  </ul>
```

Why might it be helpful to identify these types of terms on a personal portfolio webpage? Is there any risk in adding this to a personal portfolio?

Continued >

Consider This: Your Turn *continued*

2. Applying Responsive Design to the WebDevPros Webpages

Professional

Part 1: In Chapter 4, you created an external style sheet for WebDevPros website. In this exercise, you will update site to respect the principles of responsive design.

1. Open the external style sheet you created in Chapter 4 and save it with the name **webdevstyles05.css** in the styles folder within the your_turn_2 folder.

2. Add your name and the current date as a comment to the first line of the webdevstyles05.css file.

3. Open the files you created for WebDevPros in Chapter 4 in your HTML editor and make sure your name and the current date are added as a comment to the first line of all files.

4. Update the HTML files to do the following:

    a. Modify the link to the external style sheet to reference webdevstyles05.css.

    b. Add the viewport meta tag.

    c. Delete the height and width attributes from all img tags.

5. You will use a mobile-first strategy that hides images and the top navigation system by default. To do this, add a class="desktop" attribute and value to all images on your pages and to the top navigation system. Review the content on each page and apply the desktop class to nonessential content for a mobile viewport.

6. If you have not already done so, add an unordered list within the <footer> section of each webpage to provide a navigation system at the bottom of each page.

7. Update the CSS file to do the following:

    a. Measure all width properties in %.

    b. Change the measurements of all textual styles to ems or %.

    c. Create flexible images.

    d. Add the following style for the desktop class to remove the images and upper navigation system for mobile users:

    ```
    .desktop { display: none; }
    ```

    e. Set the width of the #outer-wrapper to 100% for mobile users. (*Hint*: You may have a different class name for the <div> that surrounds the entire webpage.)

    f. Determine the essential content for each page to be displayed for a mobile viewport.

    g. Style the navigation links within the footer and remove the default padding from unordered list within the footer.

8. Refine your style sheet as needed to add margins and padding using flexible units of measure.

9. Save and test your files.

10. Validate and correct your HTML and CSS files, and submit your assignment in the format specified by your instructor.

Part 2: In step 6, you added a navigation system to the bottom of each page and in step 7d, you removed images and the upper navigation system for a mobile-first strategy. Why is a navigation system at the bottom of each page a good consideration for a mobile-first strategy?

3. Applying Responsive Design and Mobile-First Strategies to the Dog Hall of Fame Webpages

Research and Collaboration

Part 1: In Chapter 4, you styled the Dog Hall of Fame webpages. In this exercise, you will update those pages to apply the principles of responsive design. Do the following activities as a group:

1. Open the external style sheet you created in Chapter 4 and save it with the name `dogstyles05.css` in the styles folder within the your_turn_3 folder.

2. Add your name and the current date as a comment to the first line of the dogstyles05.css file.

3. Open the files you created for the Dog Hall of Fame in Chapter 4 in your HTML editor and make sure your name and the current date are added as a comment to the first line of all files.

4. Modify the link to the external style sheet to reference dogstyles05.css.

5. Decide what responsive design principles you want to employ. At a minimum, update the HTML and CSS files to do the following:

   a. Add the viewport meta tag.

   b. Create flexible images.

   c. Create a fluid layout.

   d. Determine the essential content for each page to be displayed for a mobile viewport.

   e. Design a navigation system suitable for a mobile viewport.

   f. Refine your style sheet as needed to add margins and padding using em units of measure.

6. Save and test your files.

7. Validate and correct your HTML and CSS files, and submit your assignment in the format specified by your instructor.

Part 2: ✳ Each person in the group should research a current article on responsive web design and bring it to a group discussion. In the discussion, each person should share their article as well as something they learned from it. Secondly, each person should share something that is not completely clear to them or something they want to learn more about. Organize your group's findings as requested by your instructor.

6 Responsive Design Part 2: Designing for Tablet and Desktop Devices

Objectives

You will have mastered the material in this chapter when you can:

- Understand and use media query expressions

- Explain the design principles of a tablet website

- Insert a media query to target tablet viewports

- Create style rules for tablet viewports

- Explain the design principles of a desktop website

- Insert a media query to target desktop viewports

- Create style rules for desktop viewports

- Identify and modify breakpoints

- Explain pseudo-classes

- Apply pseudo-classes to a website

- Explain linear and radial gradients

- Apply a linear gradient to a webpage for a desktop viewport

6 | Responsive Design Part 2: Designing for Tablet and Desktop Devices

Introduction

As you learned in Chapter 5, the responsive web design approach styles content differently depending upon the type of device used to view the site. The mobile-first approach focuses on styling content appropriately for smaller, mobile devices. It also uses a single-column layout to prevent horizontal scrolling and minimize vertical scrolling. This layout creates a more enjoyable experience for users of mobile devices.

The design process for tablet and desktop displays allows more flexibility with the webpage layout. A tablet design can use a two-column layout, while a desktop design can use a multicolumn layout. Designing layouts for tablet and desktop displays is simplified through the use of media queries. Media queries are essential to responsive web design because they let you customize layouts for various viewport sizes. If you take a mobile-first approach, use media queries to create the desired look for tablet and desktop viewports, keeping in mind that desktop viewports include laptop displays.

Project — Use Media Queries to Design for Tablet and Desktop Viewports

In Chapter 5, you began to create a responsive design website by styling the Forward Fitness Club website for a mobile viewport. For the Chapter 6 project, you apply responsive web design principles to the Forward Fitness Club website by editing the site's style sheet to include media queries that will apply styles specific to tablet and desktop viewports. These enhancements will result in a better experience for users of tablet and laptop or desktop devices.

First, you will insert a media query to detect a tablet-sized viewport and then add new styles as appropriate for content displayed in that viewport. Next, you will insert a media query to detect a desktop-sized viewport and then add new styles as appropriate for content displayed in that viewport. To add interactivity and visual appeal to webpages displayed in the desktop viewport, you will add pseudo-classes to the style sheet to further style links within the navigation area. You will also add a linear gradient, which is a CSS3 property style, to the background of webpages displayed in the desktop viewport. Finally, you will validate the website and display all viewports in a browser. Figure 6–1 shows the home page of Forward Fitness Club sized for tablet and desktop viewports. Figure 6–1a shows the home page as it appears on a tablet; Figure 6–1b shows the same page as it appears in a desktop browser.

(a) Home page in tablet viewport

(b) Home page in desktop viewport

Figure 6–1

Images courtesy of Jessica Minnick

Roadmap

In this chapter, you will learn how to create the webpages shown in Figure 6–1. The following roadmap identifies general activities you will perform as you progress through this chapter:

1. ADD TABLET MEDIA QUERY AND STYLES.

2. ADD DESKTOP MEDIA QUERY AND STYLES.

3. MODIFY VIEWPORT BREAKPOINTS.

4. INSERT AND STYLE PSEUDO-CLASSES.

5. ADD a LINEAR GRADIENT.

At the beginning of step instructions throughout the chapter, you will see an abbreviated form of this roadmap. The abbreviated roadmap uses colors to indicate chapter progress: gray means the chapter is beyond that activity; blue means the task being shown is covered in that activity, and black means that activity is yet to be covered. For example, the following abbreviated roadmap indicates the chapter would be showing a task in the 4 INSERT & STYLE PSEUDO-CLASSES activity.

1 ADD TABLET MEDIA QUERY & STYLES | 2 ADD DESKTOP MEDIA QUERY & STYLES | 3 MODIFY VIEWPORT BREAKPOINTS

4 INSERT & STYLE PSEUDO-CLASSES | **5 ADD LINEAR GRADIENT**

Use the abbreviated roadmap as a progress guide while you read or step through the instructions in this chapter.

Using Media Queries

Recall from Chapter 5 that a **media query** detects the media type (such as screen or print) and the capabilities of the device that the browser is running on (such as the size of the viewport in pixels or its orientation of portrait versus landscape). Based on the information, the media query applies styles that work well for that situation.

In Chapter 5, you created a fluid layout and added style rules for a mobile viewport. These styles were not included within a media query so that tablet and desktop viewports will use them by default. To add style rules that target tablet or desktop viewports in particular, create a media query for each viewport.

Media queries take responsiveness to an entirely new level. They allow you to apply *different* CSS styles in response to the environment, such as the media on which the webpage is being viewed (screen or print) or the size of the viewport.

Media queries can apply styles to move, hide, or display content on the page, change text or colors, or add any other styles to make the page easier to read in a particular situation. If you resize a webpage and see the navigation system change or see a multicolumn layout reduce to one column as the viewport narrows to the size of a phone, you know that media queries are working behind the scenes to restyle the webpage in response to the viewport size.

Media queries can be embedded in the `link` tag that connects an external style sheet to an HTML file, or they can be inserted in the external style sheet itself. The following code provides a basic example of a media query inserted into the `link` tag of an HTML page:

```
<link rel="stylesheet" href="css/styles.css"
media="screen">
<link rel="stylesheet" href="css/stylesprint.css"
media="print">
```

The `media` attribute is used to determine which stylesheet should be applied. In this example, the `styles.css` style sheet found in the `css` folder will be applied if the webpage is displayed on the screen. The `stylesprint.css` stylesheet will be applied if the webpage is printed. This is a common technique to allow developers to style with rich colors and colorful images on the screen, but style with black text on a white background when the same webpage is printed.

Breakpoints

Media queries can do more than detect the current media type. They can also determine the size of the viewport, the viewable portion of the webpage.

To understand the code and syntax of how a media query detects viewport size, you set a **breakpoint** (sometimes called threshold), the point at which you want the webpage to change. The breakpoint is where you apply different styles to the webpage to cause it to change in a way that makes it easier to read and navigate for a particular situation, such as a user viewing the webpage on a phone.

For the Forward Fitness Club website, the media queries should detect and apply styles based on the three common viewport sizes listed in Table 6–1.

Table 6–1 Common Viewport Breakpoints		
Device	**Minimum Viewport Width**	**Maximum Viewport Width**
Small smartphones	320px	480px
Tablets and larger smartphones	481px	768px
Tablets in landscape orientation, laptops, and small desktop monitors	769px	1279px
Large desktop monitors	1280px	NA

Figure 6–2 shows how the NASA website uses responsive design with five customized layouts. It uses several breakpoints to determine the layout for various viewports. The designs are similar for the two smartphone viewports, which have maximum widths of 320px and 480px. Viewport widths of 768px and up can use multiple columns.

(a) 320px

(b) 480px

(c) 768px

(d) 1000px

(e) 1280px

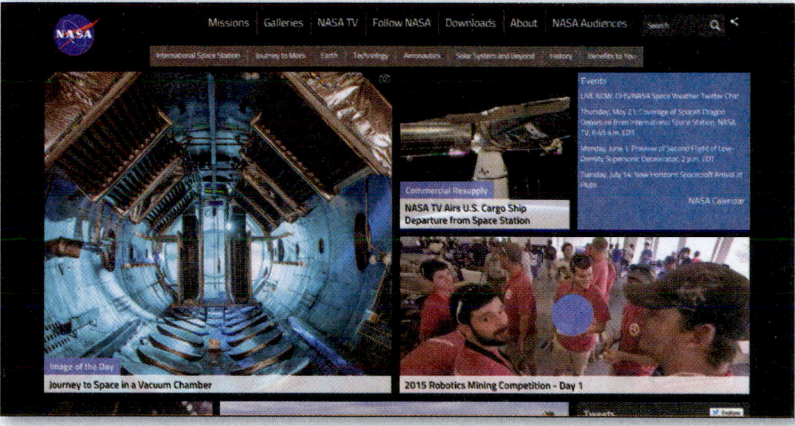

Figure 6–2

Courtesy of nasa.gov

Media Query Expressions

A media query can use a logical expression to test whether a viewport has reached a particular breakpoint. The logical expression includes the name of a **media query feature**, a characteristic of the environment, and a breakpoint value to be tested. If the logical expression evaluates to "true," the media query applies the styles that follow. Following is an example of a media query that includes a media type and a logical expression:

```
<link rel="stylesheet" href="css/styles-mobile.css"
media="screen and (max-width: 480px)">
```

This code directs browsers to use the styles-mobile.css stylesheet in the css folder when screens have a viewport width smaller than or equal to 480px (which is a common maximum viewport size for a phone and thus a common breakpoint for changing styles). In this case, max-width is the feature and 480px is the breakpoint value being tested in the logical condition. A media query can also test for both minimum and maximum breakpoints, as in the following example:

```
<link rel="stylesheet" href="css/styles-tablet.css"
media="screen and (min-width: 481px) and (max-width: 768px)">
```

In this case, the code directs browsers to apply the styles-tablet.css stylesheet in the css folder when screens have a viewport width between 481px and 768px (common breakpoint sizes for tablet devices). When testing for minimum and maximum widths, the word "and" separates each part of the media attribute value. This means that each part must be true to apply the associated styles. The syntax also requires you to surround the logical expression with parentheses and use a colon to separate the media query feature from the value being tested. When writing the CSS code, follow the requirements of the syntax carefully to make sure the media query works correctly.

At this point, you may be wondering how to select the values to use for breakpoint values, especially when so many new mobile devices of all sizes are constantly being introduced. Table 6–1 shows some common viewport breakpoint values as a starting point. After you understand the overall concept of media queries and how to code them, you can always define new breakpoints and add new media queries to refine your webpage design to look better when new devices hit the market.

A second way to implement media queries is to code them directly into a single CSS file using the `@media` rule. An example of a media query added to an external CSS file might be:

```
@media screen {
  body { width: 80%; }
}
```

In this case, `@media screen` identifies the media to which the styles will be applied. Although the example shows only one style, a `width` measurement applied to the `body,` you could list many styles within the outer set of curly braces that surround the styles for that media query. Another application of a media query in a CSS file to apply styles to a printed webpage might look like this:

```
@media print {
  body {
        width: 100%;
        color: #000000;
        background-color: #FFFFFF;
        }
}
```

In this case, three styles are applied to `body` content when the webpage is printed to allow the content to fill 100% of the printable width of the page, change the text color to black `(#000000),` and change the background color of the page to white `(#FFFFFF).`

Add logical expressions to media queries in an external CSS file as follows:

```
@media screen and (min-width: 481px) {
  .mobile { display: none; }
}
```

In this case, `min-width` is the feature of the screen that is tested. If the width is at least `481px,` the style will be applied. The `.mobile` selector means that the following styles will be applied to content identified with `class="mobile"` in the HTML document. The style declaration `display: none;` removes the content from the display. This example would hide content meant only for mobile display.

An example with two logical expressions might be:

```
@media all and (min-width: 481px) and (max-width: 768px) {
  body { color: #000000; }
}
```

This media query applies to `all` types of media when both features are true. The viewport width must be at least `481px` but cannot exceed `768px`. The three most common types of media are `screen, print,` and `all.` Table 6–2 lists common media query features that can be used in a logical expression. For a full explanation of media query syntax, media types, and features, see the w3.org website.

Table 6–2 Common Media Query Features	
Feature	**Description**
max-device-height min-device-height	Height of the screen in pixels
max-device-width min-device-width	Width of the screen in pixels
max-height min-height	Height of the viewport in pixels
max-width min-width	Width of the viewport in pixels
orientation	Orientation of the device (landscape or portrait)

Adding Media Queries to an External Style Sheet

The style sheet for the Forward Fitness Club website, styles.css, contains several style rules for a mobile display. In a mobile-first strategy, you list the mobile styles first, because these are the default styles. Next, you use media queries to add styles for larger viewports, progressing from tablet to desktop (which includes laptops). Styles created for the smaller viewports apply to larger viewports by default. To modify the appearance of an element for a larger viewport, create a media query for the larger viewport, and then create a new style.

For example, the mobile navigation links in the Forward Fitness Club website appear as a column of vertical buttons. To change this appearance for a tablet viewport, create a new style rule for the navigation list items and use the `display` property with a value of `inline` to display the links in a single line, as shown in the following example:

```
@media only screen and (min-width: 481px) {
  nav li { display: inline; }
}
```

This new style rule applies only to viewports with a minimum screen width of 481 pixels. As you continue the responsive design process and create media queries for progressively larger viewports, review the existing style rules for small viewports to know the default settings.

BTW

Using the Keyword "only"
When you write a media query that specifies `@media only screen,` the `only` keyword indicates that older browsers should ignore the media query's style rules.

Designing for Tablet Viewports

The growth of the tablet market continues to rise. Tablet devices vary by operating system, manufacturer, and screen size. With so many tablet sizes, it can seem difficult to design a "one size fits all" layout for a tablet device. Luckily, when you use responsive web design and media queries, you do not need to design multiple tablet layouts to accommodate the growing tablet market. Instead, create one layout to target tablet viewports. If a particular tablet device has a viewport smaller than the minimum size specified in the media query, the layout will default to the mobile viewport layout.

To Create a Media Query for a Tablet Viewport

You have already completed the mobile styles and now need to create a media query to target tablet devices. **Why?** *The media query will change the style of the content to better display content when viewed on tablet device.* The following steps add a media query to target tablet devices.

①
- Open your text editor to run the program.

- Open styles.css file from the css folder to prepare to insert a media query.

- Tap or click at the end of Line 98 and then press the ENTER key twice to insert two new Lines 99 and 100.

- On Line 100, type `/* Media query for tablet viewport targets screen size with a minimum width of 481px. */` to insert a CSS comment that identifies the tablet media query.

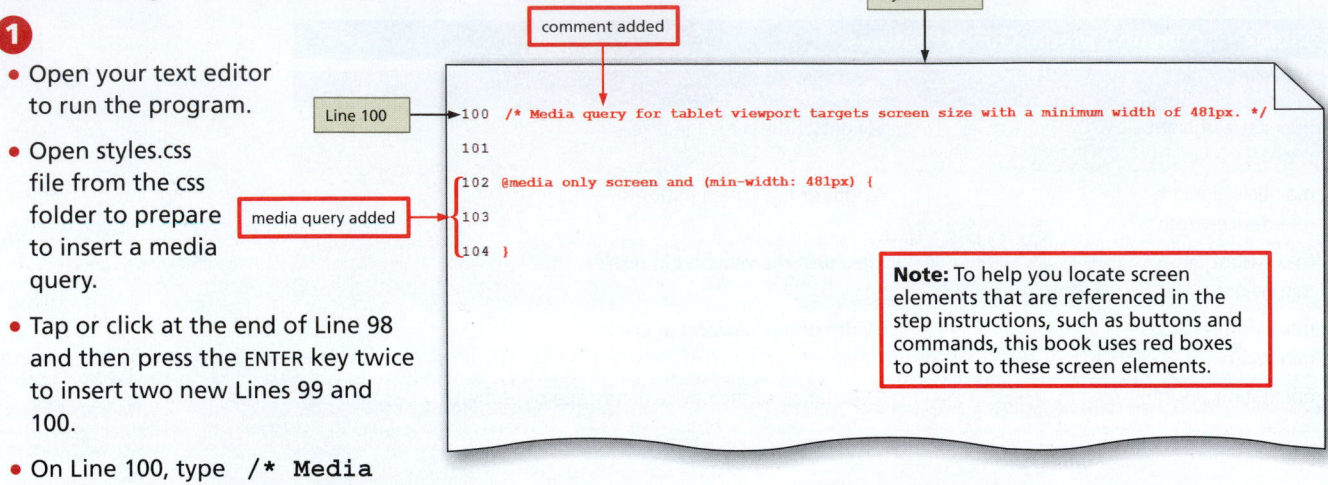

Figure 6–3

- Press the ENTER key twice to insert two new Lines 101 and 102.

- On Line 102, type `@media only screen and (min-width: 481px) {` to insert a media query.

- Press the ENTER key twice to insert two new Lines 103 and 104.

- On Line 104, type `}` to close the media query (Figure 6–3).

Q&A | Why does the media query use `only screen and min-width 481px`?
Because a common breakpoint for mobile devices is 480px, the media query applies the tablet styles starting at a viewport size of 481px.

Page Design for a Tablet Viewport

A tablet viewport is larger than a mobile viewport but smaller than a desktop viewport. The larger screen provides an opportunity for websites to display more content and use a multicolumn layout. Although tablet users expect to see more content than mobile user, they still expect the website to be touch-friendly, which means links and other touch spots that are easy to tap and text that is large enough to read without zooming.

When designing for a tablet viewport, maintain the same color scheme, typography, and general look of the website. The appearance of the website should look the same from viewport to viewport. The only thing that should change is layout and placement of content.

To determine the ideal layout for a website's tablet viewport, first review the mobile site to determine where content should be added and whether any content should be hidden. Figure 6–4 shows tablet viewport design suggestions for the home page of the Forward Fitness Center website.

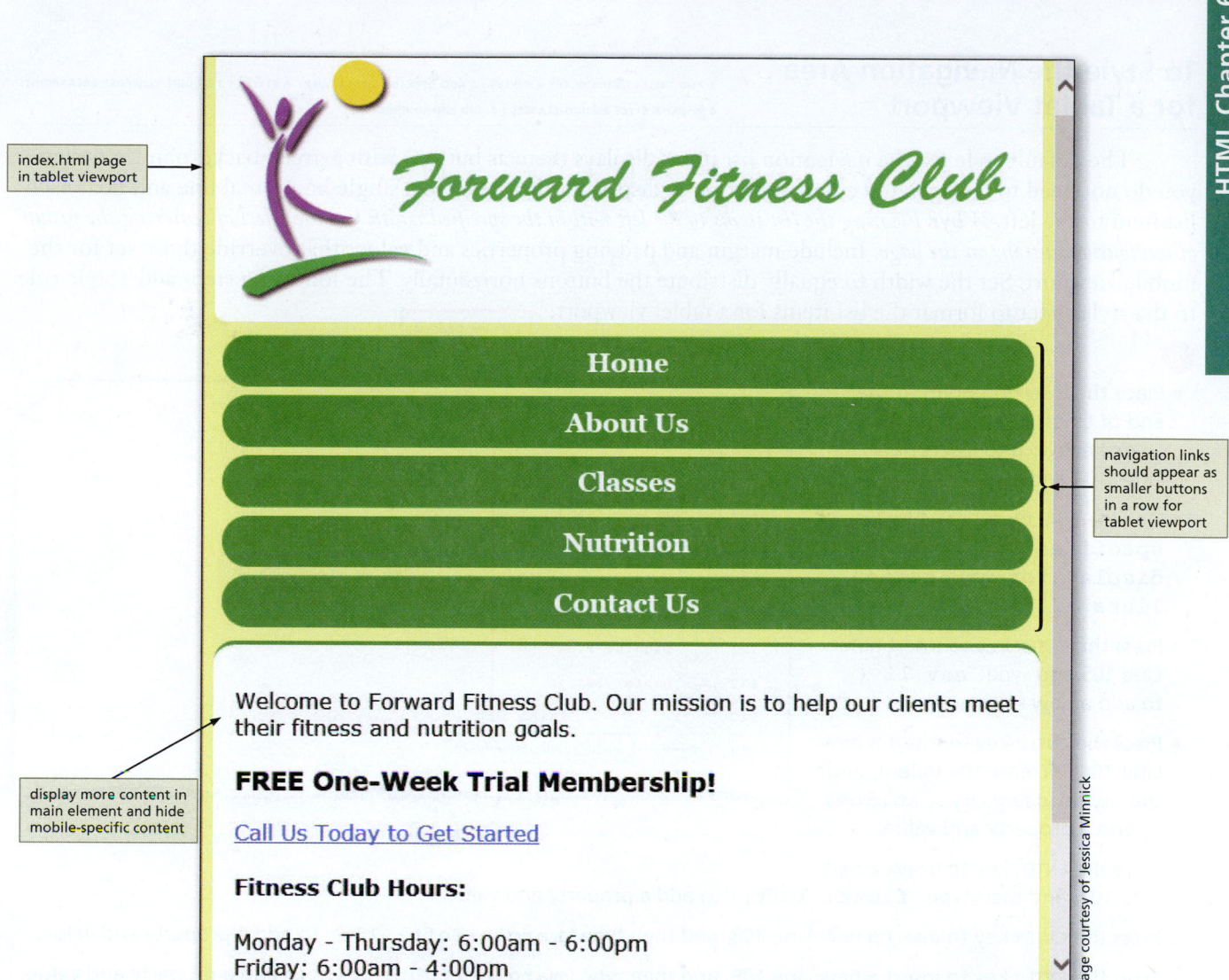

Figure 6–4

Image courtesy of Jessica Minnick

Navigation Design for a Tablet Viewport

Recall that clear, simple, and easy website navigation is vital in attracting new visitors and keeping current customers. If users have a hard time navigating through a website in any viewport, they are likely to become frustrated and leave the site.

The navigation links in the Forward Fitness website currently appear as a vertical list or column of buttons. This design is tailored to the navigation needs of a smartphone user. Because a tablet screen is generally larger than a smartphone screen, maintaining a vertical list of navigation buttons is not necessary. Instead, take advantage of the screen width and align the navigation buttons in one horizontal line. This frees space for the main content below the navigation area, improving its visibility by displaying it in the middle of the screen.

To accomplish this design, create a style rule to display the navigation list items as a single horizontal line when displayed in a tablet viewport. Add other properties and values that override the defaults already set for the mobile viewport.

BTW

Tablet Navigation Tips

As with pages designed for mobile devices, tablet users want to navigate the site easily. Format the navigation area so it is prominent and attractive, design each link so its meaning is clear, and make it easy to return to the home page. To increase accuracy for touchscreen navigation, create large buttons with extra space between each button.

To Style the Navigation Area for a Tablet Viewport

The default style for the navigation list items displays them as buttons with a green background, a design you do not need to change. Add a new style rule to display the list items in a single horizontal line and float each list item to the left. **Why?** *Floating the list items to the left within the specified width has the effect of centering the group of navigation buttons on the page.* Include margin and padding properties and values that override those set for the mobile viewport. Set the width to equally distribute the buttons horizontally. The following steps add a style rule to the style sheet to format the list items for a tablet viewport.

1

- Place the insertion point at the end of Line 102 and press the ENTER key twice to insert new Lines 103 and 104.

- On Line 104, type `/* Style specifies a horizontal display for navigation links */` to insert a comment.

- Press the ENTER key to insert a new Line 105 and type `nav li {` to add a new selector.

- Press the ENTER key to insert a new Line 106, increase the indent, and then type `display: inline;` to add a property and value.

comment added

```
104   /* Style specifies a horizontal display for navigation links */
105   nav li {
106       display: inline;
107       float: left;
108       margin-left: 1%;
109       margin-right: 1%;
110       padding-left: 0;
111       padding-right: 0;
112       width: 18%;
113   }
114   }
```

Line 104

style rule for navigation list items in tablet viewport

media query closing brace

Figure 6–5

- Press the ENTER key to insert a new Line 107, and then type `float: left;` to add a property and value.

- Press the ENTER key to insert a new Line 108, and then type `margin-left: 1%;` to add a property and value.

- Press the ENTER key to insert a new Line 109, and then type `margin-right: 1%;` to add a property and value.

- Press the ENTER key to insert a new Line 110, and then type `padding-left: 0;` to add a property and value.

- Press the ENTER key to insert a new Line 111, and then type `padding-right: 0;` to add a property and value.

- Press the ENTER key to insert a new Line 112, and then type `width: 18%;` to add a property and value.

- Press the ENTER key to insert a new Line 113, decrease the indent, and then type `}` to insert a closing brace (Figure 6–5).

Q&A

How does the inline value change the display of the navigation list items?
The inline value will display the navigation list items horizontally rather than vertically.

What is the purpose of the float property with a value of left?
This property and value improve the appearance of navigation links by placing each list item immediately after the previous list item. With the other properties, `float: left;` improves the horizontal centering of the navigation buttons.

What is the purpose of adding margin properties?
The default left and right margins for nav li are 0.3em. Setting the margin-left and margin-right properties here to 1% increases the margins in the tablet viewport, taking advantage of the increased space and making the navigation buttons look less cluttered.

What is the purpose of the padding properties?
The default left and right padding settings are 0.4em. Remove the padding on the left and right by setting the padding-left and padding-right properties to 0. After setting the width property, the list items no longer need the additional padding.

Why use 18% for the width?
You want the navigation links to be equally distributed across the navigation area. Because the navigation area is set to 100% and there are five navigation links, divide 100 by 5 to calculate a width of 20%. Subtract the left and right margins of 1% each to determine a width for each list item of 18%.

2

- Save your changes, open index.html in your browser, and then adjust the window to the size of a tablet viewport (Figure 6–6).

Q&A Why do the navigation links appear within the main area? The float property with a value of left makes the navigation links appear in the main area. When you clear the float for the main element in upcoming steps, the navigation links will appear above the main element.

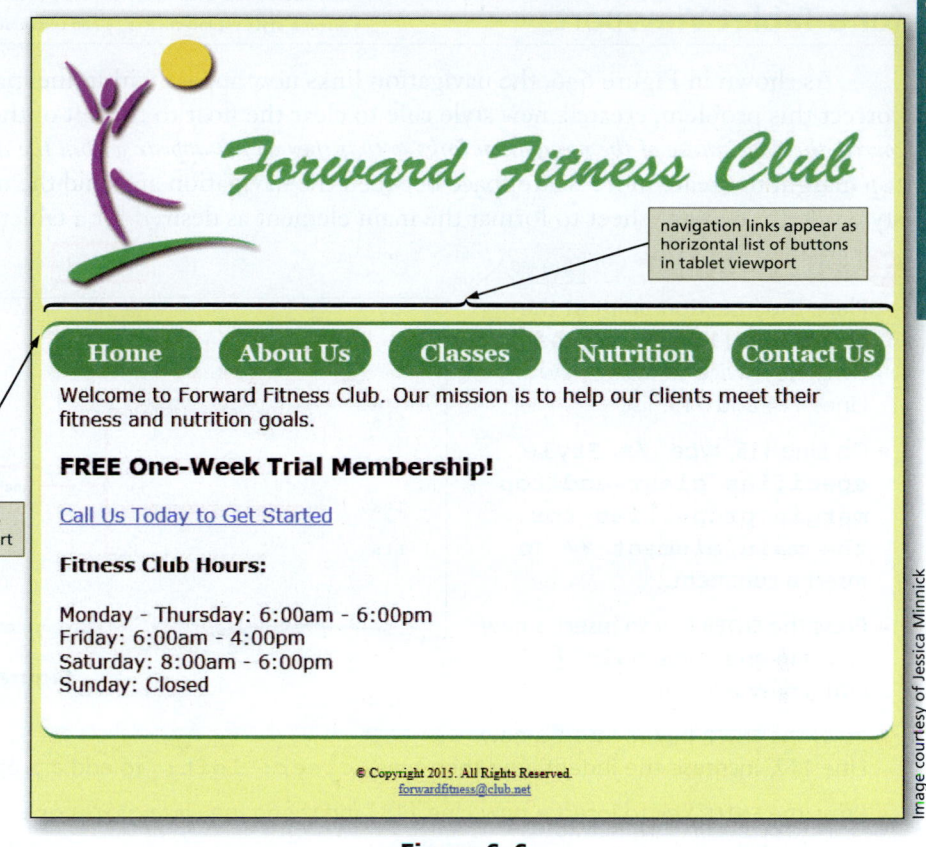

navigation links appear as horizontal list of buttons in tablet viewport

index.html page in tablet viewport

Image courtesy of Jessica Minnick

Figure 6–6

3

- Adjust the window to the size of a mobile viewport to view the change in the navigation links (Figure 6–7).

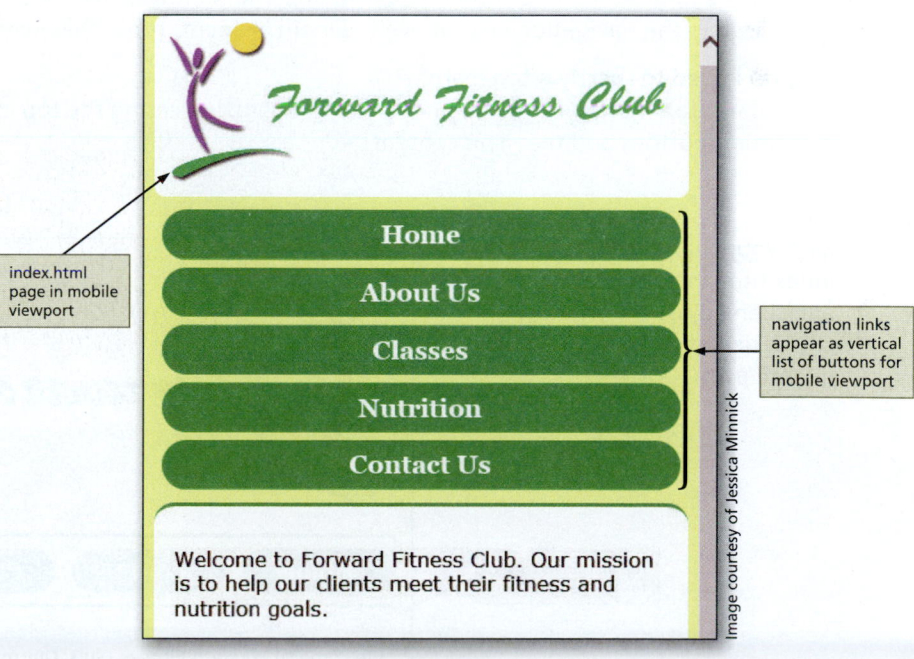

index.html page in mobile viewport

navigation links appear as vertical list of buttons for mobile viewport

Image courtesy of Jessica Minnick

Figure 6–7

To Style the Main Element for a Tablet Viewport

As shown in Figure 6–6, the navigation links now appear within the main area in the tablet viewport. To correct this problem, create a new style rule to clear the float to the left of the main element. *Why? You need to correct the appearance of the navigation links so that they do not appear within the main element.* Additionally, apply a top margin to create more white space between the navigation area and the main area. The following steps add a style rule to the style sheet to format the main element as desired for a tablet viewport.

1

- Place the insertion point at the end of Line 113 and press the ENTER key twice to insert new Lines 114 and 115.

- On Line 115, type **/* Style specifies clear and top margin properties for the main element */** to insert a comment.

- Press the ENTER key to insert a new Line 116 and type **main {** to add a new selector.

```
115  /* Style specifies clear and top margin properties for the
         main element */

116  main {

117      clear: left;

118      margin-top: 4em;

119  }
```

Line 115 — comment — main style rule

Figure 6–8

- Press the ENTER key to insert a new Line 117, increase the indent, and then type **clear: left;** to add a property and value.

- Press the ENTER key to insert a new Line 118, and then type **margin-top: 4em;** to add a property and value.

- Press the ENTER key to insert a new Line 119, decrease the indent, and then type **}** to insert a closing brace (Figure 6-8).

Q&A

What does the **clear: left;** property and value do?

It clears the float to the left of the main element. The float was specified for the navigation list items. Clearing the float displays the navigation links above the main element rather than within it.

Why do I need to specify a top margin?

The default top margin for the main selector is 0.5em. Increasing the top margin to 4em adds space between the navigation buttons and the main content.

2

- Save your changes, refresh index.html in your browser, and then adjust the window to the size of a tablet viewport (Figure 6–9).

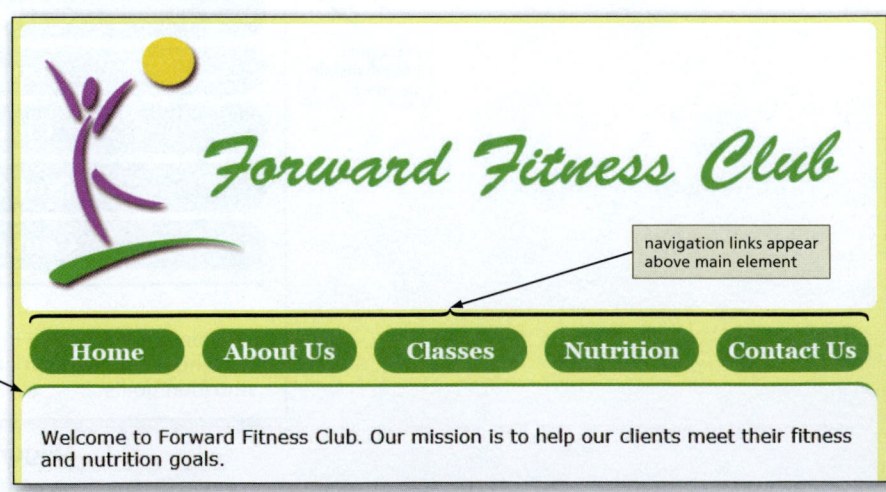

navigation links appear above main element

top margin increased for main element

Welcome to Forward Fitness Club. Our mission is to help our clients meet their fitness and nutrition goals.

Image courtesy of Jessica Minnick

Figure 6–9

To Show and Hide Content for a Tablet Viewport

The content within the main area of the Forward Fitness Club webpages is ideal for a mobile user. In the HTML documents, this content appears in a **div** element with an attribute and value of **class="mobile"**. Create a new style rule to hide the mobile class in the tablet viewport with a **display** property and value of **none**. Because a tablet screen is larger than a mobile screen, it can display more content. The home page already includes additional content that describes the Forward Fitness Club's equipment and services and provides details about the trial membership. This content appears within a **div** element that contains the attribute **class="desktop"**. To display this content in a tablet viewport, create a new style rule to show the desktop class with a **display** property and value of **inline**. *Why? Change the content to better suit the needs of a tablet device user.* The following steps add style rules to hide the mobile class and to display the desktop class for a tablet viewport.

1

- Place the insertion point at the end of Line 119 and press the ENTER key twice to insert new Lines 120 and 121.

- On Line 121, type **/* Style specifies to hide the mobile class */** to insert a comment.

- Press the ENTER key to insert a new Line 122 and type **.mobile {** to add a new selector.

- Press the ENTER key to insert a new Line 123, increase the indent, and then type **display: none;** to add a property and value.

```
          comment

121   /* Style specifies to hide the mobile class */

122   .mobile {

123       display: none;          style rule for mobile class

124   }

125

126   /* Style specifies to display the desktop class */

127   .desktop {

128       display: inline;        style rule for
                                   desktop class
129   }
```

Line 121

Figure 6–10

- Press the ENTER key to insert a new Line 124, decrease the indent, and then type **}** to insert a closing brace.

- Press the ENTER key twice to insert new Lines 125 and 126.

- On Line 126, type **/* Style specifies to display the desktop class */** to insert a comment.

- Press the ENTER key to insert a new Line 127 and type **.desktop {** to add a new selector.

- Press the ENTER key to insert a new Line 128, increase the indent, and then type **display: inline;** to add a property and value.

- Press the ENTER key to insert a new Line 129, decrease the indent, and then type **}** to insert a closing brace (Figure 6–10).

2
- Save your changes, refresh index.html in your browser, and then adjust the window to the size of a tablet viewport (Figure 6–11).

content displayed for tablet viewport

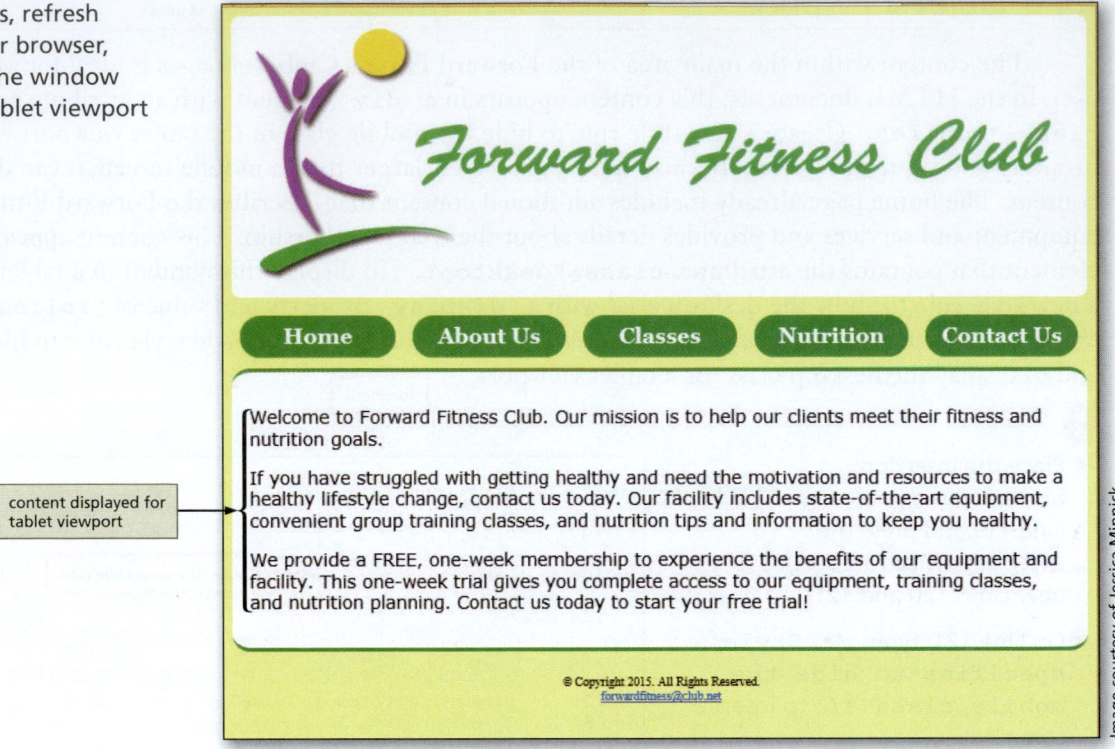

Figure 6–11

About Us Page Design for a Tablet Viewport

The About Us page is currently optimized to display content most pertinent to a mobile user. Figure 6–12 shows the content displayed for both a mobile and tablet device.

about.html page in tablet viewport

current content is for mobile viewport

Figure 6–12

The About Us page contains several images that are not displayed in the mobile viewport. These image elements include a `class="equip"` attribute and value. To display the images on this page, edit the style sheet to add a style rule to display and format the equip class. If you create a new class named items in the unordered list elements, you can create a new style rule to format the items class so the lists appear with bullets next to the images.

The about.html document also contains descriptions of common exercises within a `div` element with a `class="tablet"` attribute and value, but this content is styled so it is not displayed. To display this additional content in the tablet viewport, edit the style sheet to create a new rule to display the tablet class. This content includes a description list, so you should also create new style rules to format the description list terms and definitions.

To Display and Style the equip Class

1 ADD TABLET MEDIA QUERY & STYLES | 2 ADD DESKTOP MEDIA QUERY & STYLES | 3 MODIFY VIEWPORT BREAKPOINTS
4 INSERT & STYLE PSEUDO-CLASSES | 5 ADD LINEAR GRADIENT

The About Us page contains image elements within the main content area. The image elements include a class named equip. Create a new selector for the equip class and then add a style rule to display the equipment pictures on the left of the page. *Why? Show the images in the additional space of a tablet viewport to enhance the user experience.* The following steps add a new style rule to display and format the equip class for a tablet viewport.

1

- Place the insertion point at the end of Line 129 and press the ENTER key twice to insert new Lines 130 and 131.

- On Line 131, type `/* Style specifies a display, float, and padding for the equip class */` to insert a comment.

- Press the ENTER key to insert a new Line 132 and type `.equip {` to add a new selector.

- Press the ENTER key to insert a new Line 133, increase the indent, and then type `display: inline;` to add a property and value.

- Press the ENTER key to insert a new Line 134, and then type `float: left;` to add a property and value.

- Press the ENTER key to insert a new Line 135, and then type `margin-right: 1.5em;` to add a property and value.

- Press the ENTER key to insert a new Line 136, decrease the indent, and then type `}` to insert a closing brace (Figure 6–13).

```
131  /* Style specifies a display, float, and padding for the
     equip class */

132  .equip {

133      display: inline;

134      float: left;

135      margin-right: 1.5em;

136  }
```

Line 131 · comment · style rule for equip class

Figure 6–13

Q&A Why do I need to apply a float property with a value of left?
This property and value places each image to the left of its associated text.

Why do I need to apply a right margin?
The right margin will provide additional white space between the image and its associated text.

2

• Save your changes, open about.html in your browser, and then adjust the window to the size of a tablet viewport (Figure 6–14).

Q&A

What can I do to prevent the headings from appearing below the unordered list instead of above its associated text?
You will fix this style error by adding a new class for the list items and a new style rule in the next set of steps.

about.html displayed in tablet viewport

images displayed in tablet viewport

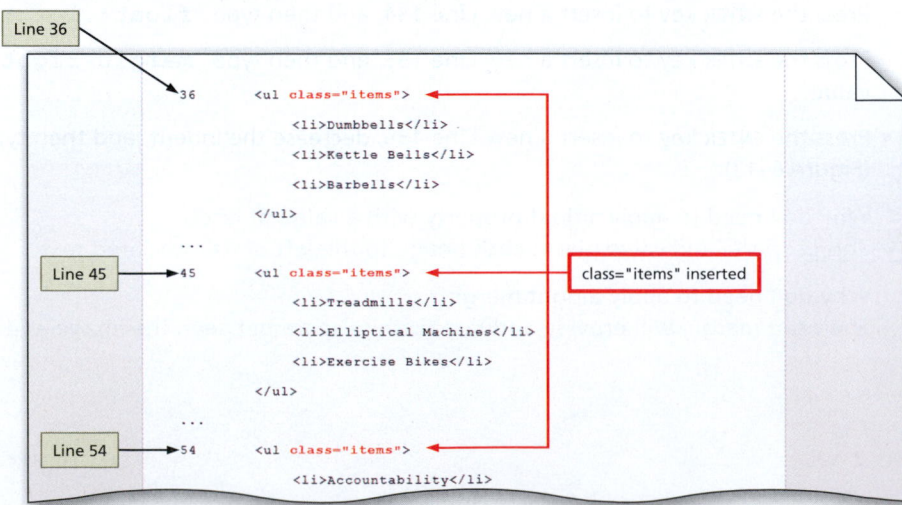

Weights

Our facility includes a weight training area with several weight options. Build lean muscle with weights and improve your core with weight training.

Dumbbells
Kettle bells
Barbells

Cardio

Burn fat through cardio workouts. If you need to lose 20lbs or more, include at least 30 minutes of cardio each day. We have several equipment choices for your workout.

Treadmills
Elliptical Machines
Exercise Bikes

Personal Training

Our certified personal trainers work with you one on one to help you obtain your fitness goals. Our personal trainers keep you motivated and push you farther than you would push yourself. When you feel like you cannot do one more rep, they tell you that you can. Personal training has many benefits.

Accountability
Personalized Program
Consistent Support and Motivation

Photos courtesy of Jessica Minnick

Figure 6–14

To Create and Style the items Class for a Tablet Viewport

1 ADD TABLET MEDIA QUERY & STYLES | 2 ADD DESKTOP MEDIA QUERY & STYLES | 3 MODIFY VIEWPORT BREAKPOINTS
4 INSERT & STYLE PSEUDO-CLASSES | 5 ADD LINEAR GRADIENT

The About Us page now displays images for the tablet viewport; however, depending on your browser, the placement of the Cardio and Personal Training headings are not correct. In addition, again depending on your browser, the bullets for the unordered list are not displayed. To correct this problem, insert a new `class="items"` attribute and value within each unordered list element in the about.html document, and then create a new style rule for the items class within the styles.css file. *Why? Correct how the text is displayed by defining and then styling the items class.* The following steps insert a class and add a new style rule to format list items class in a tablet viewport.

1

• Open about.html and insert `class="items"` within the unordered list elements on Lines 36, 45, and 54.

• Save your changes (Figure 6–15).

Line 36

```
36        <ul class="items">
              <li>Dumbbells</li>
              <li>Kettle Bells</li>
              <li>Barbells</li>
          </ul>
          ...
45        <ul class="items">
              <li>Treadmills</li>
              <li>Elliptical Machines</li>
              <li>Exercise Bikes</li>
          </ul>
          ...
54        <ul class="items">
              <li>Accountability</li>
```

Line 45   class="items" inserted

Line 54

Figure 6–15

2

- Return to styles.css, place the insertion point at the end of Line 136, and then press the ENTER key twice to insert new Lines 137 and 138.

- On Line 138, type **/* Style specifies a display, list-style-position, and bottom margin for the items class */** to insert a comment.

Line 138

comment

```
138   /* Style specifies a display, list style position, and
      bottom margin for the items class */
139   .items  {
140       display: block;
141       list-style-position: inside;          style rule for items class
142       margin-bottom: 5em;
143   }
```

Figure 6–16

- Press the ENTER key to insert a new Line 139, and then type **.items {** to add a new selector.

- Press the ENTER key to insert a new Line 140, increase the indent, and then type **display: block;** to add a property and value.

- Press the ENTER key to insert a new Line 141, and then type **list-style-position: inside;** to add a property and value.

- Press the ENTER key to insert a new Line 142, and then type **margin-bottom: 5em;** to add a property and value.

- Press the ENTER key to insert a new Line 143, decrease the indent, and then type **}** to insert a closing brace (Figure 6–16).

Q&A

Why do I set the `display` value to `block` instead of `inline`?
The `block` value displays the unordered list as a block element.

What is the purpose of the list-style-position property and value?
Using a value of `inside` with this property indents the bullets for the unordered list so that they appear within the block element.

Why do I need to apply a bottom margin?
The bottom margin will provide additional white space after each unordered list.

3

- Save the styles.css file, refresh the about.html page in your browser, and then adjust the window to the size of a tablet viewport.

- Scroll down the page to view the content for Weights and Cardio (Figure 6–17).

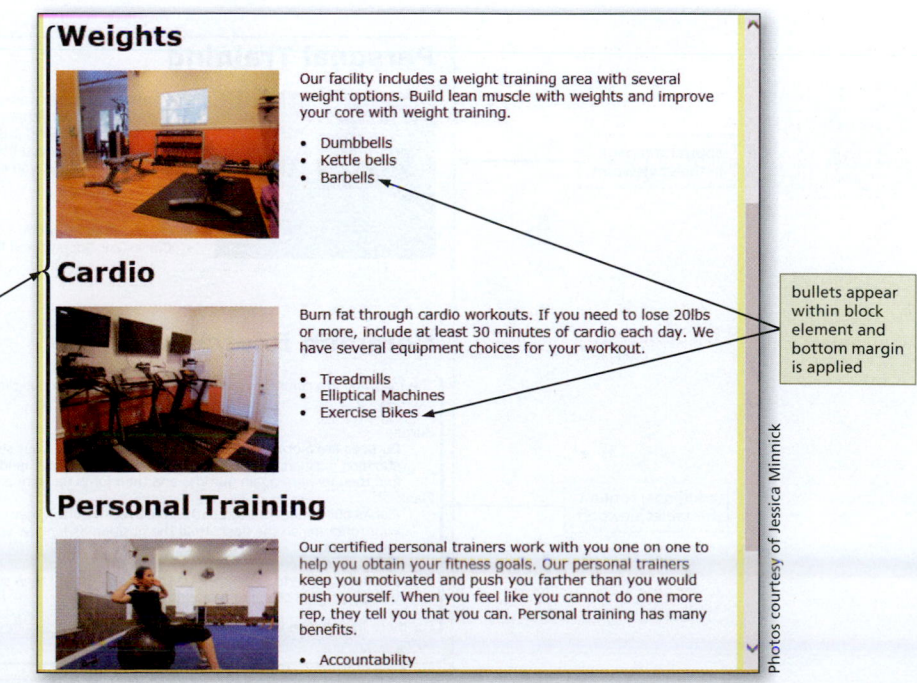

headings appear above each picture

bullets appear within block element and bottom margin is applied

Photos courtesy of Jessica Minnick

Figure 6–17

To Display the tablet Class

A **div** element with a **class="tablet"** attribute and value is located below the last unordered list in the about.html document. This element includes descriptions of common exercises. The mobile styles created in Chapter 5 include a style rule to hide the tablet class. Create a new style rule to display the content in the tablet class as a block. The following steps add a style rule to display the tablet class in the tablet viewport.

1 Place the insertion point at the end of Line 143 and press the ENTER key twice to insert new Lines 144 and 145.

2 On Line 145, type **/* Style specifies to display the tablet class */** to insert a comment.

3 Press the ENTER key to insert a new Line 146 and type **.tablet {** to add a new selector.

4 Press the ENTER key to insert a new Line 147, increase the indent, and then type **display: block;** to add a property and value.

5 Press the ENTER key to insert a new Line 148, decrease the indent, and then type **}** to insert a closing brace (Figure 6–18).

comment

Line 145 ⟶ 145 `/* Style specifies to display the tablet class */`

146 `.tablet {`

147   `display: block;` ⟵ style rule for tablet class

148 `}`

Figure 6–18

6 Save your changes, refresh about.html in your browser, adjust the window to the size of a tablet viewport, and then scroll down to view the additional content (Figure 6–19).

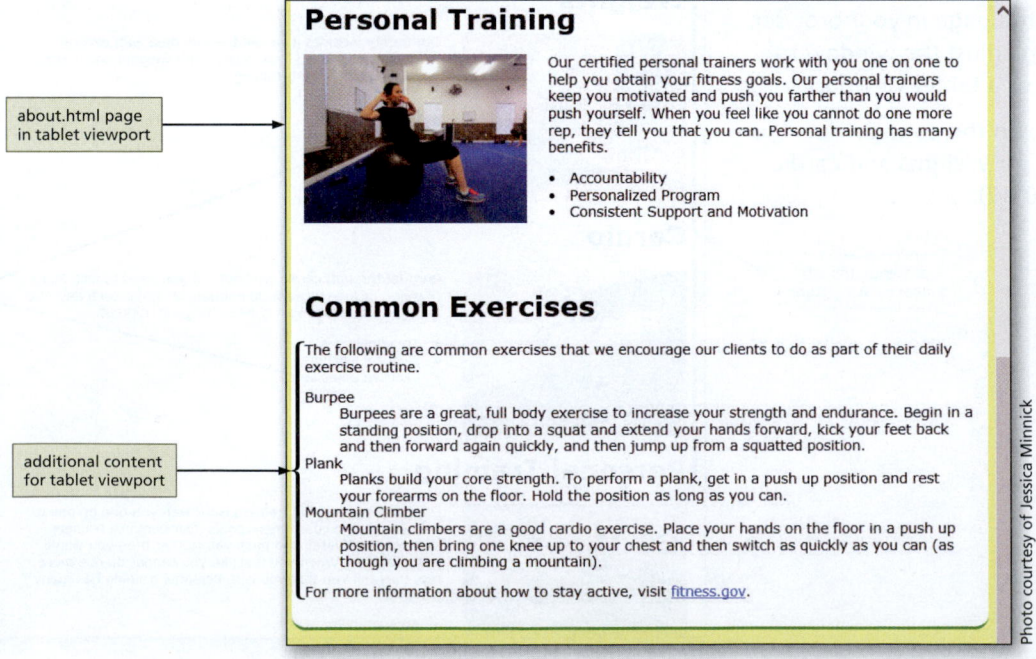

about.html page in tablet viewport

additional content for tablet viewport

Personal Training

Our certified personal trainers work with you one on one to help you obtain your fitness goals. Our personal trainers keep you motivated and push you farther than you would push yourself. When you feel like you cannot do one more rep, they tell you that you can. Personal training has many benefits.

- Accountability
- Personalized Program
- Consistent Support and Motivation

Common Exercises

The following are common exercises that we encourage our clients to do as part of their daily exercise routine.

Burpee
Burpees are a great, full body exercise to increase your strength and endurance. Begin in a standing position, drop into a squat and extend your hands forward, kick your feet back and then forward again quickly, and then jump up from a squatted position.

Plank
Planks build your core strength. To perform a plank, get in a push up position and rest your forearms on the floor. Hold the position as long as you can.

Mountain Climber
Mountain climbers are a good cardio exercise. Place your hands on the floor in a push up position, then bring one knee up to your chest and then switch as quickly as you can (as though you are climbing a mountain).

For more information about how to stay active, visit fitness.gov.

Photo courtesy of Jessica Minnick

Figure 6–19

To Style the Description List Terms

The Common Exercises information is now displayed, but the description list terms below the Common Exercises heading need to be formatted. Bold the terms to emphasize them and add white space between each term and definition to improve readability. The following steps create a new style rule for description list terms within a tablet viewport.

1 Place the insertion point at the end of Line 148 and press the ENTER key twice to insert new Lines 149 and 150.

2 On Line 150, type `/* Style specifies a font weight and top margin for description list terms */` to insert a comment.

3 Press the ENTER key to insert a new Line 151 and type `dt {` to add a new selector.

4 Press the ENTER key to insert a new Line 152, increase the indent, and then type `font-weight: bold;` to add a property and value.

5 Press the ENTER key to insert a new Line 153, and then type `margin-top: 0.7em;` to add a property and value.

6 Press the ENTER key to insert a new Line 154, decrease the indent, type `}` to insert a closing brace, and then press the ENTER key to insert a blank line (Figure 6–20).

```
                              comment
Line 150    150  /* Style specifies a font weight and top margin for
                      description list terms */

            151  dt  {

            152       font-weight: bold;          style rule for
                                                  definition list terms
            153       margin-top: 0.7em;

            154  }

            155

            156  }         media query
                           closing brace
```

Figure 6–20

7 Save your changes, refresh about.html in your browser, adjust the window to the size of a tablet viewport, and then scroll down to view the description list (Figure 6–21).

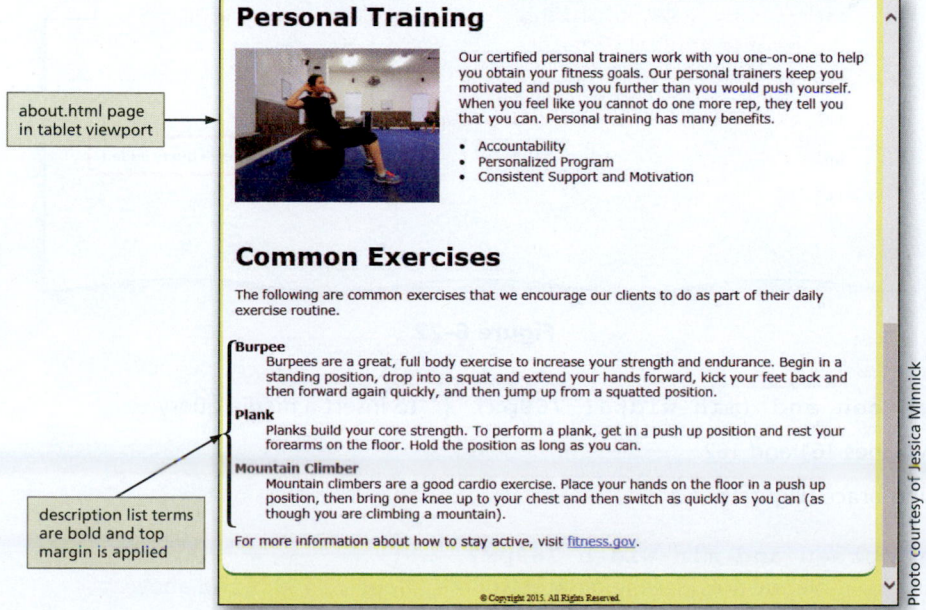

Figure 6–21

Break Point: If you want to take a break, this is a good place to do so. To resume at a later time, continue reading the text from this location forward.

Designing for Desktop Viewports

You used a simple style sheet in Chapter 4 to create a desktop layout. Now you will create a similar layout using responsive design and create a media query for a desktop viewport. The same desktop design principles apply for responsive design; use simple, intuitive navigation, clear images, and typography and apply the same color scheme. Maintain the same look and feel of the site, but change some formatting to best accommodate the desktop viewport. Because desktop screens are often wider than those for other devices, designing for a desktop viewport also provides an opportunity for a multiple-column layout. Multiple-column layouts are covered in Chapter 7.

CONSIDER THIS

How do I begin designing for a desktop viewport?

Before you rearrange elements and add features, such as photos and columns, review the content on each webpage. Consider the design from the user's point of view. What content do most visitors want to find on the home page? Make sure this content is featured prominently. Balance the tradeoffs of providing additional content such as photos and multimedia with potentially reducing performance.

To Create a Media Query for a Desktop Viewport

1 ADD TABLET MEDIA QUERY & STYLES | **2 ADD DESKTOP MEDIA QUERY & STYLES** | 3 MODIFY VIEWPORT BREAKPOINTS
4 INSERT & STYLE PSEUDO-CLASSES | 5 ADD LINEAR GRADIENT

Create a media query for a desktop viewport. *Why? The desktop media query will contain styles to alter the website appearance for desktop users.* The following step adds a media query to target desktop viewports.

1
- In styles.css, tap or click at the end of Line 156 and then press the ENTER key twice to insert two new Lines 157 and 158.

- On Line 158, type `/* Media query for desktop viewport targets screens with a minimum width of 769px. */` to insert a CSS comment.

- Press the ENTER key twice to insert two new Lines 159 and 160.

- On Line 160, type `@media only screen and (min-width: 769px) {` to insert a media query.

- Press the ENTER key twice to insert new Lines 161 and 162.

- On Line 162, type `}` to insert a closing brace (Figure 6–22).

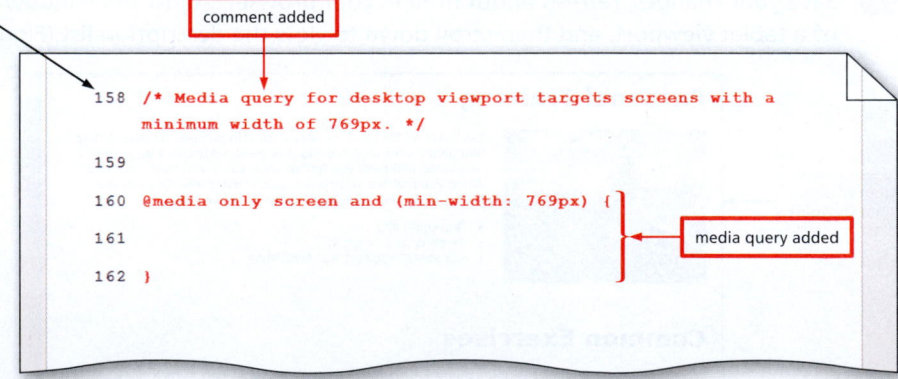

```
        comment added

158  /* Media query for desktop viewport targets screens with a
     minimum width of 769px. */

159

160  @media only screen and (min-width: 769px) {

161                                              media query added

162  }
```

Figure 6–22

Q&A | Why does the media query use `only screen and min-width 769px`?
Because 768px is a common breakpoint for tablet devices, set the desktop styles to apply at 769px and above.

To Create a Style Rule for #container in the Desktop Media Query

There is no need to use 100% of the screen width to display a website for a desktop viewport. Create a new style rule to set the width for the container to 80%. This allows 10% of the screen for the left margin and 10% for the right margin, which is common in a desktop viewport. The following steps create a style rule for #container as desired for a desktop viewport.

1 Place the insertion point at the end of Line 160 and press the ENTER key twice to insert new Lines 161 and 162.

2 On Line 162, type `/* Style specifies a width for container */` to insert a comment.

3 Press the ENTER key to insert a new Line 163 and type `#container {` to add a new selector.

4 Press the ENTER key to insert a new Line 164, increase the indent, and then type `width: 80%;` to add a property and value.

5 Press the ENTER key to insert a new Line 165, decrease the indent, and then type `}` to insert a closing brace (Figure 6–23).

```
                    comment

Line 162  →  162  /* Style specifies a width for container */

             163  #container {

             164      width: 80%;  ←  style rule for container id

             165  }

             166

             167  }  ←  media query closing brace
```

Figure 6–23

6 Save your changes, open index.html in your browser, and then maximize the window to view a desktop viewport (Figure 6–24).

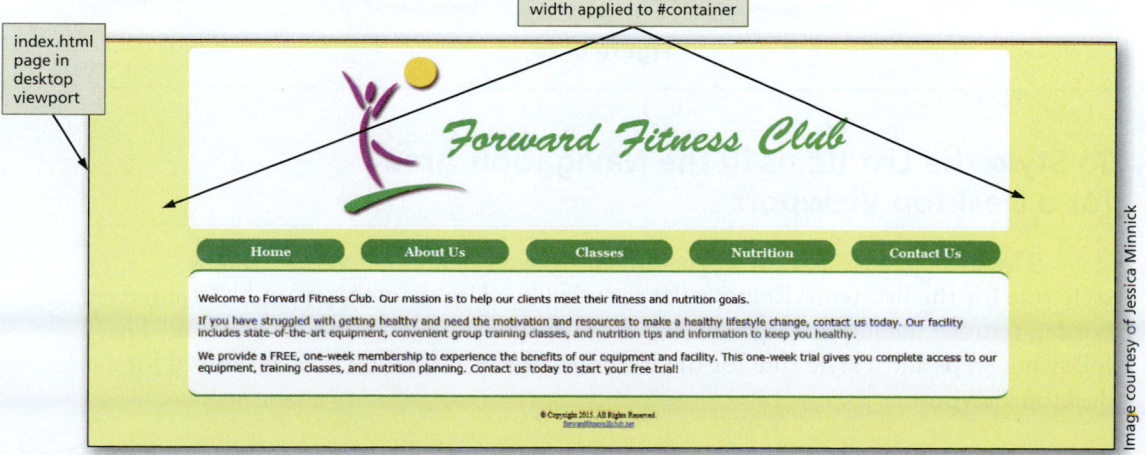

width applied to #container

index.html page in desktop viewport

Forward Fitness Club

| Home | About Us | Classes | Nutrition | Contact Us |

Welcome to Forward Fitness Club. Our mission is to help our clients meet their fitness and nutrition goals.

If you have struggled with getting healthy and need the motivation and resources to make a healthy lifestyle change, contact us today. Our facility includes state-of-the-art equipment, convenient group training classes, and nutrition tips and information to keep you healthy.

We provide a FREE, one-week membership to experience the benefits of our equipment and facility. This one-week trial gives you complete access to our equipment, training classes, and nutrition planning. Contact us today to start your free trial!

© Copyright 2015. All Rights Reserved.
ForwardFitnessClub.net

Image courtesy of Jessica Minnick

Figure 6–24

To Style the Unordered List in the Navigation Area for a Desktop Viewport

Style the navigation area to appear as a single unified element with navigation links evenly distributed within the area. The first step to create this effect is to create a new style rule for the unordered list in the navigation area to remove the existing margin and apply a small amount of left and right padding. The following steps create a style rule for the unordered list within the navigation area as desired for a desktop viewport.

1 Place the insertion point at the end of Line 165 and press the ENTER key twice to insert new Lines 166 and 167.

2 On Line 167, type `/* Style specifies margin and padding for the unordered list within the nav */` to insert a comment.

3 Press the ENTER key to insert a new Line 168 and type `nav ul {` to add a new selector.

4 Press the ENTER key to insert a new Line 169, increase the indent, and then type `margin: 0;` to add a property and value.

5 Press the ENTER key to insert a new Line 170, and then type `padding-left: 0.50%;` to add a property and value.

6 Press the ENTER key to insert a new Line 171, and then type `padding-right: 0.50%;` to add a property and value.

7 Press the ENTER key to insert a new Line 172, decrease the indent, and then type `}` to insert a closing brace (Figure 6–25).

```
comment added

Line 167  →167  /* Style specifies margin and padding for the unordered list
               within the nav */

         168  nav ul {

         169      margin: 0;

         170      padding-left: 0.50%;       ← style rule for unordered
                                               list in nav
         171      padding-right: 0.50%;

         172  }
```

Figure 6–25

To Style the List Items in the Navigation Area for a Desktop Viewport

The next step to create a single unified navigation area is to create a new style rule for the list items. Remove the rounded borders, create a top and bottom border, remove the left and right margins, adjust the width, and remove padding. The following steps add a style rule for the list items in the navigation area as desired for a desktop viewport.

1 Place the insertion point at the end of Line 172 and press the ENTER key twice to insert new Lines 173 and 174.

2   On Line 174, type `/* Style for navigation list items specifies a border radius, border, margin, width, and padding */` to insert a comment.

3   Press the ENTER key to insert a new Line 175 and type `nav li {` to add a new selector.

4   Press the ENTER key to insert a new Line 176, increase the indent, and then type `border-radius: 0;` to add a property and value.

5   Press the ENTER key to insert a new Line 177, and then type `border-top: solid #000000;` to add a property and value.

6   Press the ENTER key to insert a new Line 178, and then type `border-bottom: solid #000000;` to add a property and value.

7   Press the ENTER key to insert a new Line 179, and then type `margin-left: 0;` to add a property and value.

8   Press the ENTER key to insert a new Line 180, and then type `margin-right: 0;` to add a property and value.

9   Press the ENTER key to insert a new Line 181, and then type `padding: 0;` to add a property and value.

10   Press the ENTER key to insert a new Line 182, and then type `width: 20%;` to add a property and value.

11   Press the ENTER key to insert a new Line 183, decrease the indent, and then type `}` to insert a closing brace (Figure 6–26).

Q&A   Why use 20% for the width of each list item?
You want the navigation links to be equally distributed across the navigation area. Because the navigation area is set to 100% with no margins and there are five navigation links, divide 100 by 5 to calculate a width of 20%.

comment added

Line 174

```
174  /* Style for navigation list items specifies a border radius,
         border, margin, width, and padding */

175  nav li {

176      border-radius: 0;

177      border-top: solid #000000;

178      border-bottom: solid #000000;

179      margin-left: 0;

180      margin-right: 0;

181      padding: 0;

182      width: 20%;

183  }
```

style rule for navigation list items

Figure 6–26

12 Save your changes and refresh index.html in your browser to view your changes (Figure 6–27).

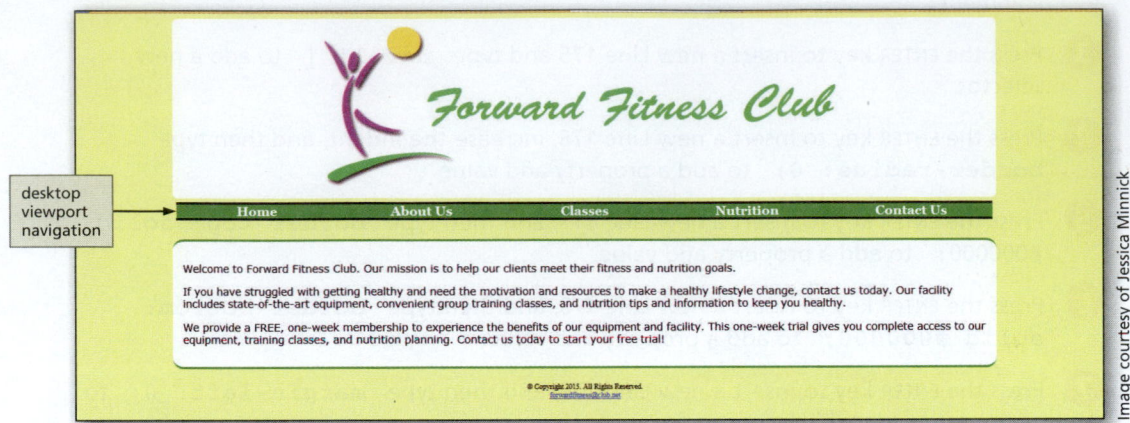

Figure 6–27

Image courtesy of Jessica Minnick

To Style the List Item Links in the Navigation Area for a Desktop Viewport

The navigation area now appears as a single unified line, though the border is too close to the link text. The final step in styling the navigation area is to create a new style rule for the list item links. Display the links as inline block elements so that each list item link appears in the same line, but acts as a block element and expands to the available width. Next, apply a small amount of padding to increase the amount of space between each link and between the links and the borders. The following steps create a new style rule for the list item links within the navigation area as desired for a desktop viewport.

1 Place the insertion point at the end of Line 183 and press the ENTER key twice to insert new Lines 184 and 185.

2 On Line 185, type `/* Style for navigation links specifies display and padding */` to insert a comment.

3 Press the ENTER key to insert new Line 186, and then type `nav li a {` to add a new selector.

4 Press the ENTER key to insert new Line 187, increase the indent, and then type `display: inline-block;` to add a property and value.

5 Press the ENTER key to insert new Line 188, and then type `padding: 0.7em;` to add a property and value.

6 Press the ENTER key to insert new Line 189, decrease the indent, and then type `}` to insert a closing brace (Figure 6–28).

```
185  /* Style for navigation links specifies display and padding */
186  nav li a {
187      display: inline-block;
188      padding: 0.7em;
189  }
190
191  }
```

comment added

Line 185

style rule for links in navigation list

media query closing brace

Figure 6–28

7 Save your changes and refresh index.html in your browser to view your changes (Figure 6–29).

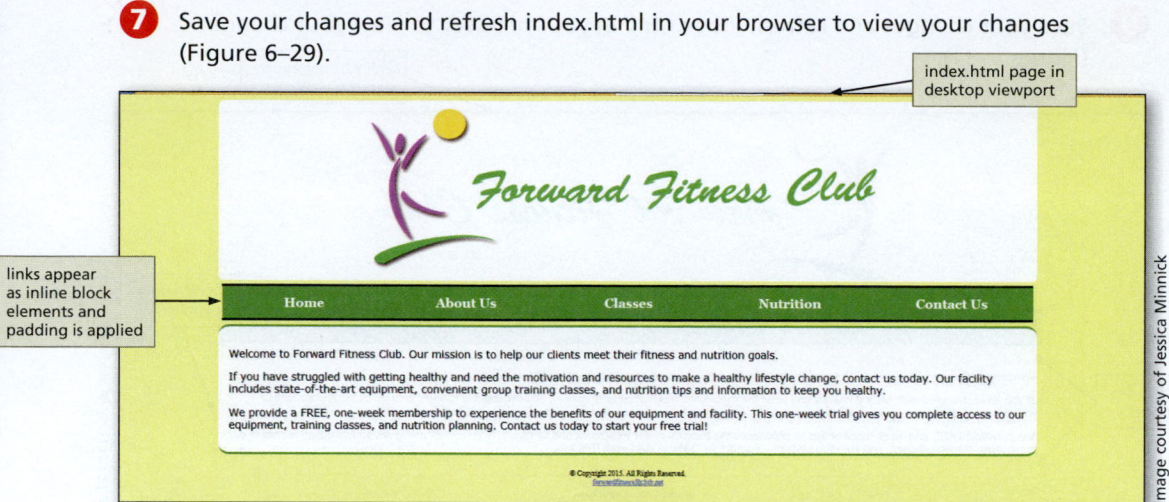

index.html page in desktop viewport

links appear as inline block elements and padding is applied

Image courtesy of Jessica Minnick

Figure 6–29

To Style the Main Element for a Desktop Viewport

The appearance of the main content area is simplified for tablet and mobile viewports. Recall from Chapter 4 that the **main** element previously included a box shadow and no border. Apply those styles for the desktop viewport. Remove the border, add a box shadow effect, and apply a small amount of top and bottom margin. The following steps create a new style rule for the main element as desired for a desktop viewport.

1 Place the insertion point on Line 189 and press the ENTER key twice to insert new Lines 190 and 191.

2 On Line 191, type **/* Style specifies border, shadow, margin, and padding for main element */** to insert a comment.

3 Press the ENTER key to insert a new Line 192, and then type **main {** to add a new selector.

4 Press the ENTER key to insert a new Line 193, increase the indent, and then type **border-style: none;** to add a property and value.

5 Press the ENTER key to insert a new Line 194, and then type **box-shadow: 0.5em 0.5em 0.5em #404040;** to add a property and value.

6 Press the ENTER key to insert a new Line 195, and then type **margin-bottom: 1em;** to add a property and value.

7 Press the ENTER key to insert a new Line 196, and then type **margin-top: 1em;** to add a property and value.

8 Press the ENTER key to insert a new Line 197, decrease the indent, and then type **}** to insert a closing brace (Figure 6–30).

comment added

Line 191

```
191  /* Style specifies border, box shadow, and margins for the main element */
192  main {
193      border-style: none;
194      box-shadow: 0.5em 0.5em 0.5em #404040;
195      margin-bottom: 1em;
196      margin-top: 1em;
197  }
```

style rule for main element

Figure 6–30

9 Save your changes and refresh index.html in your browser to view your changes (Figure 6–31).

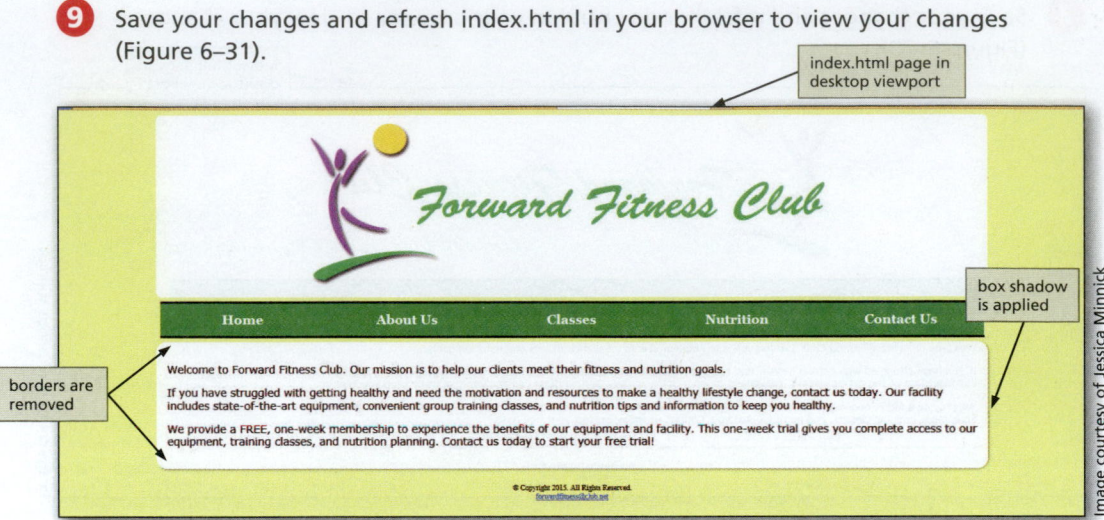

Image courtesy of Jessica Minnick

Figure 6–31

To Style Paragraph Elements Within the Main Element for a Desktop Viewport

Apply left and right padding to the paragraph elements in the main element to add more white space. The following steps create a new style rule for paragraphs within the main element as desired for a desktop viewport.

1 Place the insertion point on Line 197 and press the ENTER key twice to insert new Lines 198 and 199.

2 On Line 199, type `/* Style specifies left and right padding for paragraph elements within the main element */` to insert a comment.

3 Press the ENTER key to insert a new Line 200 and type `main p {` to add a new selector.

4 Press the ENTER key to insert a new Line 201, increase the indent, and then type `padding-left: 0.5em;` to add a property and value.

5 Press the ENTER key to insert a new Line 202, and then type `padding-right: 0.5em;` to add a property and value.

6 Press the ENTER key to insert a new Line 203, decrease the indent, and then type `}` to insert a closing brace (Figure 6–32).

Figure 6–32

7 Save your changes and refresh index.html in your browser to view your changes (Figure 6–33).

index.html page in desktop viewport

right padding applied to paragraph elements

left padding applied to paragraph elements

Image courtesy of Jessica Minnick

Figure 6–33

About Us Page Design for a Desktop Viewport

When the About Us page is displayed in a desktop viewport, the Cardio and Personal Training headings appear below the list items for the previous heading instead of above the associated picture. Figure 6–34 shows the About Us page displayed in a desktop viewport.

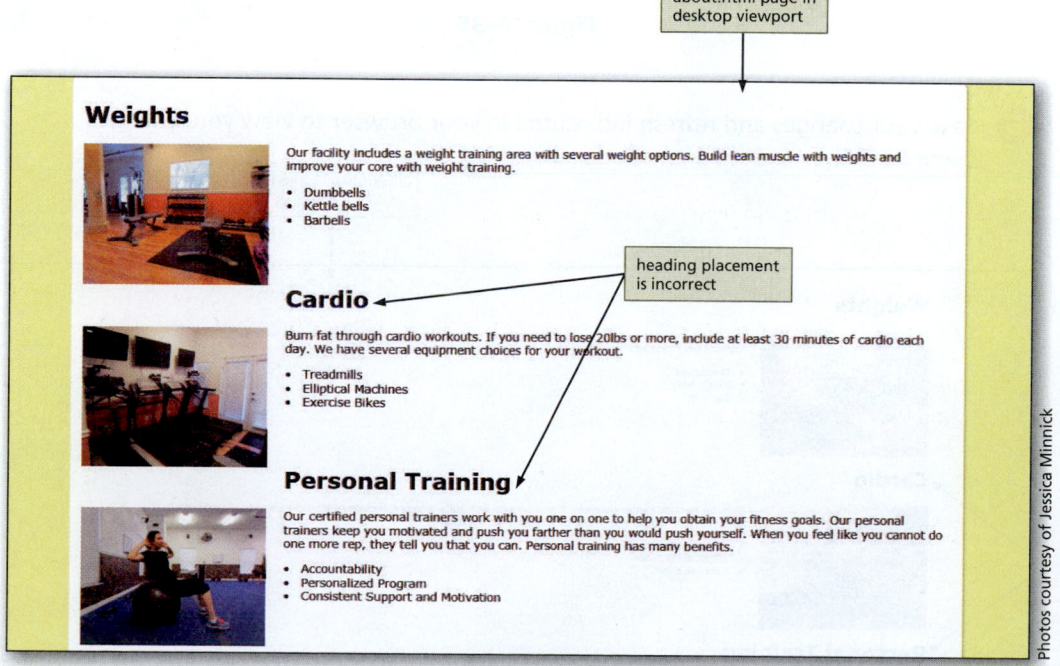

about.html page in desktop viewport

heading placement is incorrect

Photos courtesy of Jessica Minnick

Figure 6–34

Correct the placement of the headings on the About Us page by creating a new style rule to format the items class and add more bottom margin.

To Style the items Class for a Desktop Viewport

Correct the placement of the headings on the About Us page by creating a new style rule to apply more bottom margin to the items class. The following steps create a new style rule for the items class as desired for a desktop viewport.

1 Place the insertion point on Line 203 and press the ENTER key twice to insert new Lines 204 and 205.

2 On Line 205, type `/* Style specifies a bottom margin for the items class */` to insert a comment.

3 Press the ENTER key to insert a new Line 206 and type `.items {` to add a new selector.

4 Press the ENTER key to insert a new Line 207, increase the indent, and then type `margin-bottom: 6em;` to add a property and value.

5 Press the ENTER key to insert a new Line 208, decrease the indent, and then type `}` to insert a closing brace (Figure 6–35).

Figure 6–35

6 Save your changes and refresh index.html in your browser to view your changes (Figure 6–36).

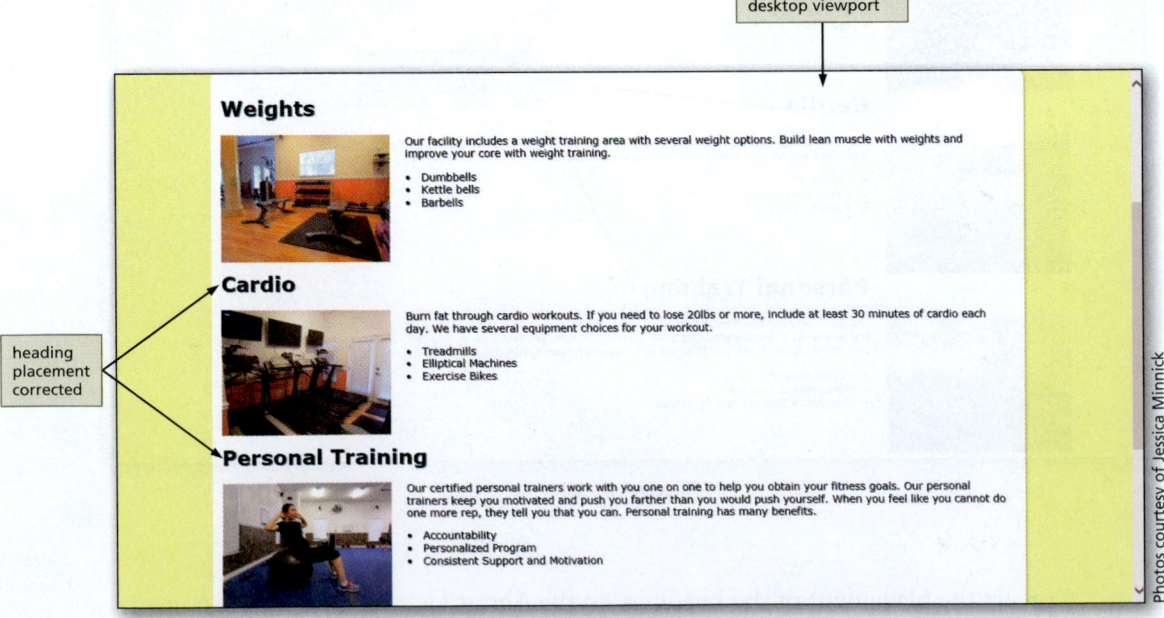

Figure 6–36

Modifying Breakpoints

Recall that a breakpoint is the point at which you want to apply different styles to the webpage, usually depending on the viewport. Set breakpoints as determined by the content on the page. For example, if the navigation area displays link text in buttons for the tablet viewport, as it does for the Forward Fitness Club website, and the link text extends beyond the button's border at a certain page width, modify a breakpoint so the page applies the styles set for the desktop viewport at that point. For the Forward Fitness Club website, the navigation area in the desktop viewport uses a solid bar rather than buttons as the background for the link text, which means the link text will not extend beyond a button's border.

BTW

Browser Developer Tools

Every modern browser provides developer tools that display element dimensions, for example, which are useful when setting breakpoints. You can also use the tools to inspect the HTML, CSS, and other types of code as you view a webpage. For example, you can temporarily remove a CSS declaration to determine its effects on the webpage.

To Determine the Viewport Width for Tablet and Desktop Viewports

1 ADD TABLET MEDIA QUERY & STYLES | 2 ADD DESKTOP MEDIA QUERY & STYLES | **3 MODIFY VIEWPORT BREAKPOINTS**
4 INSERT & STYLE PSEUDO-CLASSES | 5 ADD LINEAR GRADIENT

You have used the standard breakpoints for the tablet and desktop media queries; however, as you resize your browser to view the pages as they appear on a tablet or desktop device, the Contact Us and About Us link text wraps to two lines. To keep the links on one line, modify the style sheet and adjust the `min-width` size for the desktop and tablet media queries. *Why? Currently, the breakpoint value is too small for both desktop and tablet viewports. Using the correct breakpoint value will fix the problem of two-line navigation links.* Increase the breakpoint values for the tablet and desktop media queries so that the style of the `nav` element switches to accommodate the viewport. Use a browser developer tool to help figure out a better value. The following steps modify the style sheet and open the home page in Google Chrome to determine a better breakpoint value for the smallest viewport.

- Place the insertion point at the end of Line 112 and press the ENTER key to insert a new Lines 113.

- On Line 113, type **white-space: nowrap;** to add a property and value.

- Save your changes (Figure 6–37).

Q&A
What is the purpose of the white-space property with a nowrap value?
This property and value will keep the navigation link text together on one line instead of wrapping the second word, such as Us, to the next line.

```
102 @media only screen and (min-width: 481px) {

103

104 /* Style specifies a horizontal display for navigation links
       */

105 nav li {

106     display: inline;

107     float: left;

108     margin-left: 1%;

109     margin-right: 1%;

110     padding-left: 0;

111     padding-right: 0;

112     width: 18%;

113     white-space: nowrap;

114 }
```

property and value added to nav li style rule for tablet media query

Figure 6–37

- Open the index.html file in Google Chrome and maximize the browser window to display the page in the desktop viewport.

- Narrow the browser window until the Contact Us navigation link extends beyond the navigation area (Figure 6–38).

Q&A

Why does the Contact Us navigation link extend beyond the navigation area when I narrow the webpage?

The white-space property with a value of nowrap keeps Contact Us together on one line. As the window is narrowed, the text extends beyond its apparent boundary.

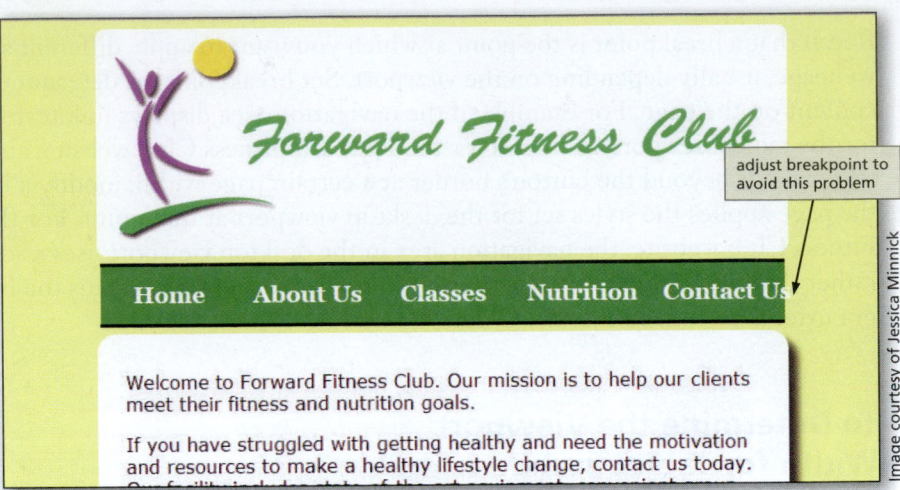

Figure 6–38

3

- Slowly widen the page until the Contact Us link appears within its button area.

- Press and hold or right-click the page, and then tap or click Inspect element on the shortcut menu to open the Inspector pane.

- If the page appears in an emulator, tap or click the Toggle device mode button on the Inspector pane toolbar to display the page without device emulation.

- If necessary, tap or click the Elements tab to display element information.

- In the Inspector pane, tap or click the html tab and hover the pointer over the tab to display the page dimensions (Figure 6–39).

Figure 6–39

Q&A

Why should I widen the page until the Contact Us link appears within the navigation area?

This width represents the smallest viewport size that accommodates the Contact Us link on one line for the desktop viewport.

How can I find the page dimensions if Google Chrome is not installed on my computer?

Most major browsers have built-in development tools that provide information about the HTML and CSS code for the webpage. In Opera, Mozilla Firefox, or Internet Explorer, press and hold or right-click a webpage and choose Inspect element on the shortcut menu. In Safari, open Web Inspector using the key combination COMMAND+OPTION+I.

4

- Narrow the browser window to display a tablet viewport.
- Continue to narrow the browser window until the Contact Us navigation link extends beyond its background (Figure 6–40).

Figure 6–40

adjust breakpoint to avoid this problem

Image courtesy of Jessica Minnick

5

- Slowly widen the page until the Contact Us link appears within its button area.
- In the Inspector pane, tap or click the html tab and hover over the tab to display the page dimensions (Figure 6–41).

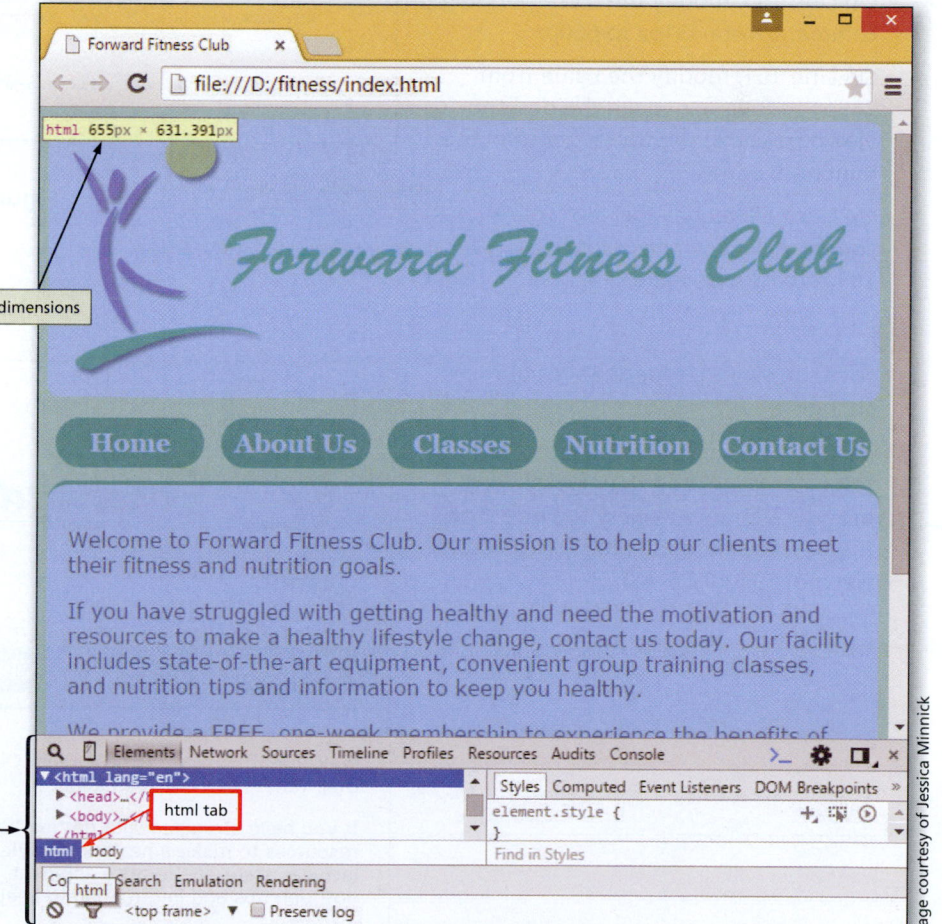

dimensions

Inspector pane

html tab

Figure 6–41

Image courtesy of Jessica Minnick

To Set the New Viewport Widths for the Tablet and Desktop Media Queries

Now that you have determined the minimum widths at which the page displays the link text correctly, you change the viewport widths in the desktop and tablet media queries. *Why? For each viewport, you will make that number the new breakpoint value, which triggers the style that changes the display of the navigation area from inline to block.* Based on your inspection, the width for the desktop viewport is about 825 pixels and the width for the tablet viewport is about 655 pixels. Trigger the change in the appearance of the navigation links to slightly larger than 655px for the tablet viewport and slightly larger than 825px for the desktop viewport. The following steps modify the breakpoint value for the tablet media query from 481px to 660px and modify the breakpoint value for the desktop media query from 769px to 830px.

1

- Return to styles.css to prepare to change the breakpoint value.

- On Line 102, modify the value from 481px to 660px to make the tablet viewport width slightly larger than the minimum width.

- On Line 100, modify the corresponding comment from 481px to 660px.

- On Line 161, modify the value from 769px to 830px to make the desktop viewport width slightly larger than the minimum width.

- On Line 159, modify the corresponding comment from 769px to 830px (Figure 6–42).

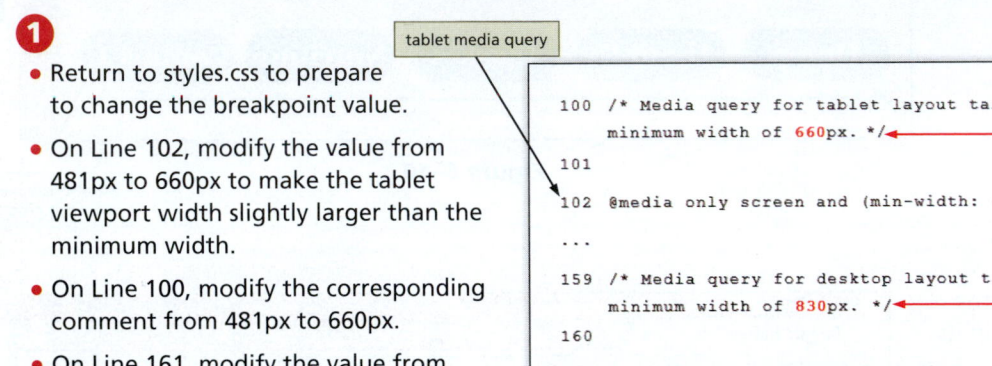

Figure 6–42

2

- Save the styles.css file to save your changes.

- Refresh the index.html page, close the Inspector pane, and then resize your browser window to view the effect of the new breakpoint value for the tablet viewport (Figure 6–43).

Figure 6–43

Image courtesy of Jessica Minnick

3

- Resize your browser window to view the effect of the new breakpoint value for the desktop viewport (Figure 6–44).

navigation area after adjusting breakpoint for desktop viewport

Figure 6–44

Break Point: If you want to take a break, this is a good place to do so. To resume at a later time, continue reading the text from this location forward.

Using Pseudo-Classes

Have you ever visited a website where the links changed colors when you pointed to (hovered over) them or clicked a link? The link color changes due to the use of pseudo-classes in the style sheet. **Pseudo-classes** allow you to change the style of a link based on four link states: link, visited, hover, and active. Table 6–3 describes each link state.

Table 6–3 Pseudo-Classes

Pseudo-class	Used to Style
:link	Unvisited link
:visited	Link that has been clicked
:hover	Link when the mouse is hovering over it
:active	Link at the moment it is clicked

You can define a unique style for normal, visited, hover, and active links by creating four separate style rules with **a:link**, **a:visited**, **a:hover**, and **a:active** as the selectors. A pseudo-class is attached to a selector with a colon to specify a state or relation to the selector to give the web developer more control over that selector. Use the following format to construct a pseudo-class:

```
selector:pseudo-class {
        property: value;
}
```

The colon (:) is part of the pseudo-class and is placed between the selector and the pseudo-class. The following is an example of a navigation :link pseudo-class:

```
nav a:link {
        color: #FFFFFF;
}
```

The selector `nav a:link` identifies the color to apply to a navigation link that has not yet been visited or clicked. In this case, the initial link color is white.

The following is an example of a navigation :visited pseudo-class:

```
nav a:visited {
        color: #000000;
}
```

The selector `nav a:visited` identifies the color to apply to a navigation link that has been visited or clicked. In this case, the link color is black.

The following is an example of a navigation :hover pseudo-class:

```
nav a:hover {
        color: #FFFF00;
}
```

The selector `nav a:hover` identifies the color to apply to a navigation link while the pointer is hovering over the link. In this case, the link color is yellow. The :hover pseudo-class enhances the interactivity between the user and the webpage.

The following is an example of a navigation :active pseudo-class:

```
nav a:active {
        color: #0066CC;
}
```

The selector `nav a:active` identifies the color to apply to a navigation link when the link is being clicked or when it gains focus. In this case, the link color is blue.

Pseudo-classes must be used in the following order: link, visited, hover, active. You do not need to use all of the pseudo-classes; however, if you choose to omit a pseudo-class from your design, be sure to maintain the same order of the pseudo-class styles in the CSS code.

Pseudo-classes are more often used in a desktop viewport because mobile and tablet devices are touch devices and do not have a hover option nor an option to click.

BTW

Other Pseudo-Classes
The most common pseudo-classes are those used to change the style of links. You can also use them to apply style rules to the first letter (:first-letter) or first line (:first-line) of a paragraph to create a drop cap or line of text in small capitals.

To Add Pseudo-Classes to a Style Sheet

1 ADD TABLET MEDIA QUERY & STYLES | 2 ADD DESKTOP MEDIA QUERY & STYLES | 3 MODIFY VIEWPORT BREAKPOINTS
4 INSERT & STYLE PSEUDO-CLASSES | 5 ADD LINEAR GRADIENT

Add new style rules for pseudo-classes to style the links within the navigation area for the desktop viewport. *Why? Pseudo-classes enhance the experience for the desktop user.* First add link, visited, hover, and active pseudo-classes. Save and view your changes, and then remove the visited pseudo-class to maintain the original link color. The following steps add style rules for link, visited, hover, and active pseudo-classes to the desktop media query.

1

- Place the insertion point at the end of Line 190 and press the ENTER key twice to insert new Lines 191 and 192.

- On Line 192, type **/* Style rules for pseudo-classes */** to insert a comment.

- Press the ENTER key to insert a new Line 193 then type **nav li a:link {** to add a new selector.

- Press the ENTER key to insert a new Line 194, increase the indent, and then type **color: #FFFFFF;** to add a property and value.

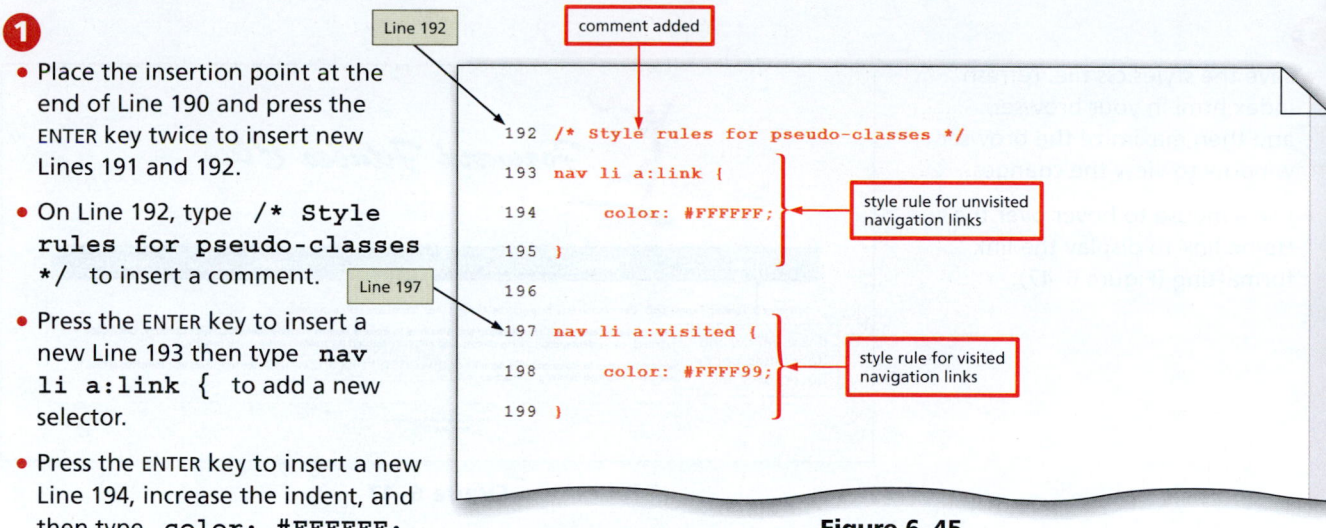

Figure 6–45

- Press the ENTER key to insert a new Line 195, decrease the indent, and then type **}** to insert a closing brace.

- Press the ENTER key twice to insert new Lines 196 and 197.

- On Line 197, type **nav li a:visited {** to add a new selector.

- Press the ENTER key to insert new Line 198, increase the indent, and then type **color: #FFFF99;** to add a property and value.

- Press the ENTER key to insert new Line 199, decrease the indent, and then type } (Figure 6–45).

2

- Press the ENTER key twice to insert new Lines 200 and 201.

- On Line 201, type **nav li a:hover {** to add a new selector.

- Press the ENTER key to insert new Line 202, increase the indent, and then type **color: #FFFF00;** to add a property and value.

- Press the ENTER key to insert new Line 203, and then type **font-style: italic;** to add a property and value.

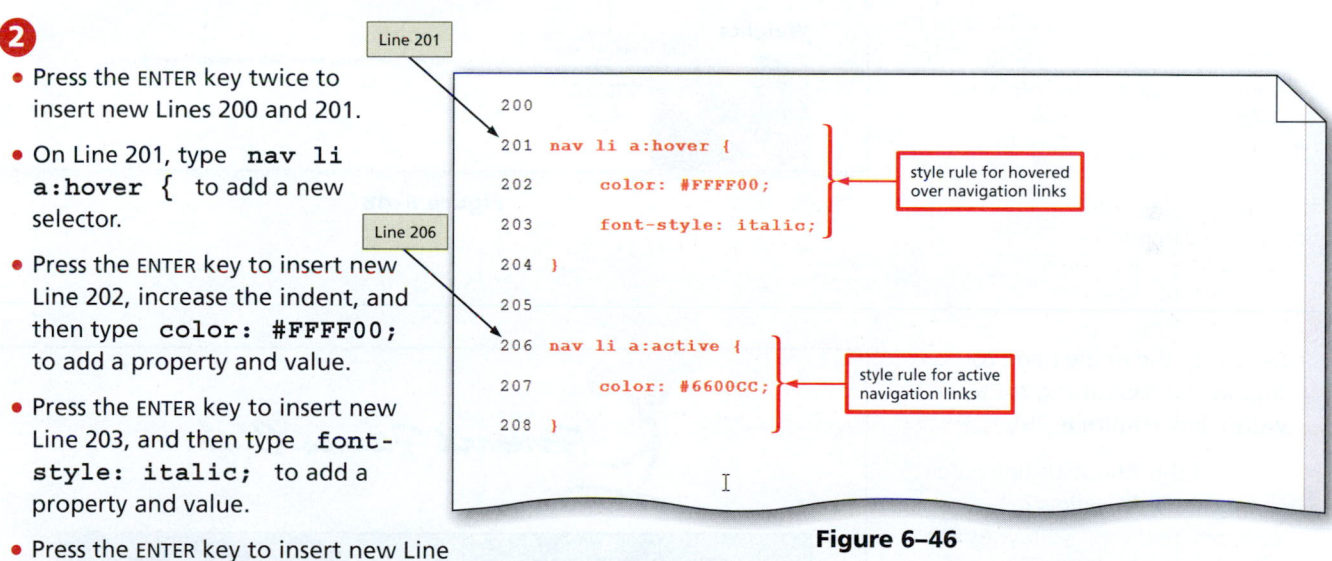

Figure 6–46

- Press the ENTER key to insert new Line 204, decrease the indent, and then type **}** to insert a closing brace.

- Press the ENTER key twice to insert new Lines 205 and 206.

- On Line 206, type **nav li a:active {** to add a new selector.

- Press the ENTER key to insert new Line 207, increase the indent, and then type **color: #6600CC;** to add a property and value.

- Press the ENTER key to insert new Line 208, decrease the indent, and then type **}** to insert a closing brace (Figure 6–46).

3

- Save the styles.css file, refresh index.html in your browser, and then maximize the browser window to view the changes.

- Use a mouse to hover over the Home link to display the link formatting (Figure 6–47).

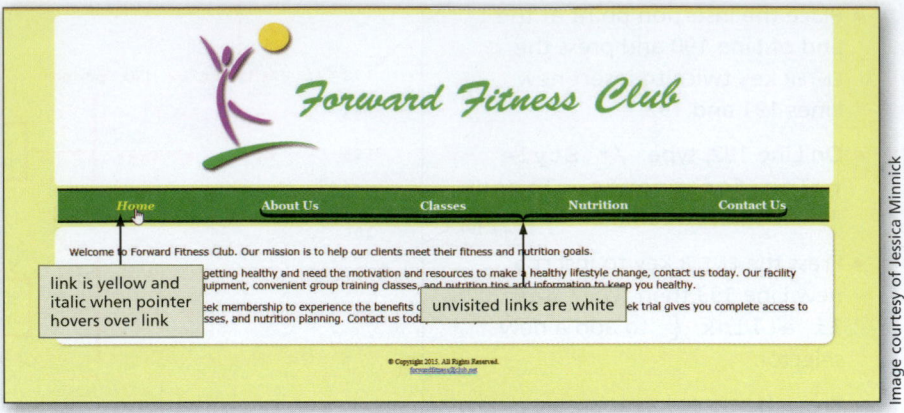

link is yellow and italic when pointer hovers over link

unvisited links are white

Figure 6–47

4

- Click the About Us link to display the formatting for an active link (Figure 6–48).

Q&A Why is the link italicized?
The link is italicized because this font style is specified in the :hover style rule, which precedes :active. To change this, you would need to add the font-style property with a value of normal to the :active style rule.

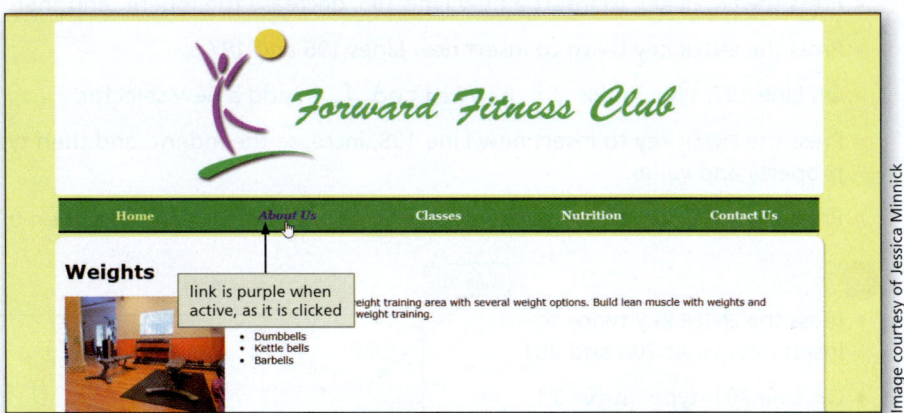

Weights

link is purple when active, as it is clicked

Figure 6–48

5

- Return to the home page to display the formatting for a visited link (Figure 6–49).

Q&A Why did the About Us link color change to light yellow?
You specified light yellow as the color for visited links when you entered the a:visited pseudo-class.

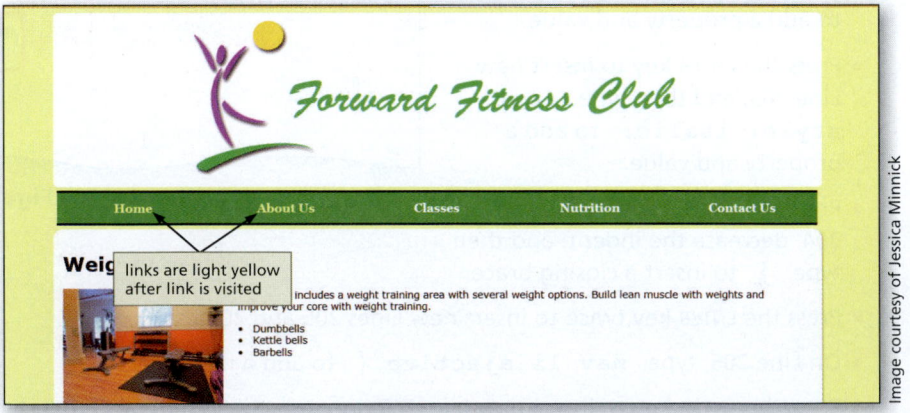

links are light yellow after link is visited

Figure 6–49

Image courtesy of Jessica Minnick

6

- Return to the styles.css file in your text editor to prepare to remove the active pseudo-class.

- Select Lines 206 through 208, and then press the DELETE key to remove the pseudo-class.

- Press the DELETE key one to two more times as necessary to move the comment below the pseudo-classes to Line 206 (Figure 6–50).

```
201  nav li a:hover {

202      color: #FFFF00;

203      font-style: italic;

204  }                          style rule for nav li
                                a:active is removed
205

206  /* Style specifies border, box shadow, and margins for the
     main element */
```

comment below pseudo-classes is moved to Line 206

Figure 6–50

Using Gradients

Recall that the latest version of CSS is CSS3, which introduced several new properties to further enhance a webpage. You have already integrated some CSS3 properties into the Forward Fitness site, such as rounded corners and a box shadow, but CSS3 offers many other formatting options.

One of the new properties introduced with CSS3 is a **gradient**, which is a gradual transition from one color to another. CSS3 has two types of gradients: linear and radial.

Linear gradients can transition from several different angles. The default transition is from the top to the bottom. Linear gradients can also transition up, left, right, or diagonally.

To create a linear gradient, use the `linear-gradient` property. The following is an example of how to apply a linear gradient:

```
body {
        background: linear-gradient(white, blue);
}
```

This example applies a linear gradient that transitions from white at the top to blue at the bottom. To provide support for major browsers, use the following prefixes:

```
-moz- for Mozilla Firefox

-o- for Opera

-webkit- for Google Chrome and Safari
```

The following example of a linear gradient includes all browser support prefixes. When using the prefixes, list the standard syntax last.

```
body {
        background: -moz-linear-gradient(white, blue);
        background: -o-linear-gradient(white, blue);
        background: -webkit-linear-gradient(white, blue);
        background: linear-gradient(white, blue);
}
```

BTW

CSS3 Gradients
Before CSS3, web designers created background gradients by tiling gradient images across a page or element. CSS3 gradients offer two significant advantages over this technique: they use fewer resources, meaning they appear more quickly, and remain sharp and clear when users increase or decrease the webpage zoom setting.

Table 6–4 provides an overview of linear gradients.

Table 6–4 Linear Gradients	
Direction	**Examples**

top to bottom (default)	body {
	background: -moz-linear-gradient: (white, blue);
	background: -o-linear-gradient: (white, blue);
	background: -webkit-linear-gradient: (white, blue);
	background: linear-gradient: (white, blue);
	}

left to right	body {
	background: -moz-linear-gradient: (right, white, blue);
	background: -o-linear-gradient: (right, white, blue);
	background: -webkit-linear-gradient: (left, white, blue);
	background: linear-gradient: (to right, white, blue);
	}

diagonal	body {
	background: -moz-linear-gradient: (bottom right, white, blue);
	background: -o-linear-gradient: (bottom right, white, blue);
	background: -webkit-linear-gradient: (left top, white, blue);
	background: linear-gradient: (to bottom right, white, blue);
	}

specified angle	body {
	background: -moz-linear-gradient: (180deg, white, blue);
	background: -o-linear-gradient: (180deg, white, blue);
	background: -webkit-linear-gradient: (180deg, white, blue);
	background: linear-gradient: (180deg, white, blue);
	}

As shown in these examples, only the standard syntax for left to right and diagonal requires the word "to," as in "to bottom right."

Radial gradients are specified by their center. The color begins in the center and transitions in a radial direction to another color or colors. To create a radial gradient, you must specify at least two colors. The following is an example of a radial gradient:

```
body {
        background: -moz-radial-gradient(red, white, blue);
        background: -o-radial-gradient(red, white, blue);
        background: -webkit-radial-gradient(red, white, blue);
        background: radial-gradient(red, white, blue);
}
```

Gradients create interest on a webpage, especially when used as a background. To complete the project for this chapter, add a linear gradient to the body for the desktop viewport.

Can multiple colors be used within a gradient?
Yes. You can add as many colors as desired to the gradient.

To Add a Linear Gradient

Add a linear gradient to the body element for the desktop viewport. *Why? A gradient background enhances the appearance of the webpage for a desktop display.* The following steps create a new style rule to apply a linear gradient to the body element as desired for a desktop viewport.

1

- Place the insertion point at the end of Line 223 and press the ENTER key twice to insert new Lines 224 and 225.

- On Line 225, type `/* Style specifies a gradient for the body element */` to insert a comment.

- Press the ENTER key to insert a new Line 226, and then type `body {` to add a new selector.

```
225  /* Style specifies a gradient for the body element */
226  body {
227      background: -moz-linear-gradient(#FFFFFF, #FFFF99); /* Firefox */
228      background: -o-linear-gradient(#FFFFFF, #FFFF99); /* Opera */
229      background: -webkit-linear-gradient(#FFFFFF, #FFFF99); /* Chrome, Safari */
230      background: linear-gradient(#FFFFFF, #FFFF99);
231      background-attachment: fixed;
232  }
233
234  }
```
comment added
Line 225
style rule for body element
media query closing brace

Figure 6–51

- Press the ENTER key to insert a new Line 227, increase the indent, and then type `background: -moz-linear-gradient(#FFFFFF, #FFFF99); /* Firefox */` to add a property and value.

- Press the ENTER key to insert a new Line 228, and then type `background: -o-linear-gradient(#FFFFFF, #FFFF99); /* Opera */` to add a property, value, and comment.

- Press the ENTER key to insert a new Line 229, and then type `background: -webkit-linear-gradient(#FFFFFF, #FFFF99); /* Chrome, Safari */` to add a property, value, and comment.

- Press the ENTER key to insert a new Line 230, and then type `background: linear-gradient(#FFFFFF, #FFFF99);` to add a property, value, and comment.

- Press the ENTER key to insert a new Line 231, and then type `background-attachment: fixed` to add a property, value, and comment.

- Press the ENTER key to insert a new Line 232, decrease the indent, and then type `}` to insert a closing brace (Figure 6–51).

Q&A

Why am I using a background-attachment property with a fixed value?

The background-attachment property with a value of fixed will apply the linear gradient to the body element from the top to the bottom of the window.

2

- Save the styles.css file, and then refresh index.html in your browser to view the changes.

 Experiment

- Use Table 6–4 to change the linear gradient to a left to right or to a diagonal gradient, save the styles.css file, and then refresh index.html in your browser.

- Return the background to a linear gradient, save the styles.css file, and then refresh index.html in your browser (Figure 6–52).

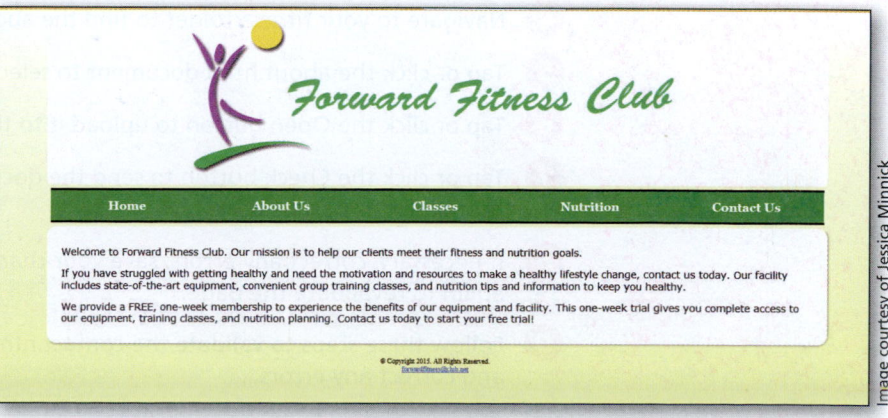

Image courtesy of Jessica Minnick

Figure 6–52

To Validate the Style Sheet

Always run your files through W3C's validator to check the document for errors. If the document has any errors, validating gives you a chance to identify and correct them. Validation is also an effective troubleshooting tool during the development process and adds a valuable level of professionalism to your work. The following steps validate a CSS document.

1 Open your browser and type `http://jigsaw.w3.org/css-validator/` in the address bar to display the W3C CSS Validation Service page.

2 Tap or click the By file upload tab to display the Validate by File Upload information.

3 Tap or click the Choose File button to display the Choose File to Upload dialog box.

4 Navigate to your css folder to find the styles.css file.

5 Tap or click the styles.css document to select it.

6 Tap or click the Open button to upload the selected file to the W3C CSS validator.

7 Tap or click the Check button to send the document through the validator and display the validation results page.

To Validate the HTML Files

Every time you create a new webpage, run it through W3C's validator to check the document for errors. If any errors exist, you need to correct them. Validation is also an effective troubleshooting tool during the development process and adds a valuable level of professionalism to your work. The following steps validate an HTML document.

1 Open your browser and type `http://validator.w3.org/` in the address bar to display the W3C validator page.

2 Tap or click the Validate by File Upload tab to display the Validate by File Upload tab information.

3 Tap or click the Browse button to display the Choose File to Upload dialog box.

4 Navigate to your fitness folder to find the about.html file.

5 Tap or click the about.html document to select it.

6 Tap or click the Open button to upload it to the W3C validator.

7 Tap or click the Check button to send the document through the validator and display the validation results page.

8 If necessary, correct any errors, save your changes, and run through the validator again to revalidate the page.

9 Follow these steps to validate the contact.html, index.html, and fitness.html pages and correct any errors.

Chapter Summary

In this chapter, you learned how to create media queries to target tablet and desktop viewports. You created style rules to format web content displayed on tablet and desktop devices. You modified the media query breakpoints to maintain the integrity of the navigation design. You enhanced the navigation links with pseudo-classes. Finally, you added a linear gradient to the body of the website. The items listed below include all the new skills you have learned in this chapter, with the tasks grouped by activity.

Using Media Queries

Adding Media Queries to an External Style Sheet (HTML 261)

Designing for Tablet Viewports

Create a Media Query for a Tablet Viewport (HTML 262)

Style the Navigation Area for a Tablet Viewport (HTML 264)

Style the Main Element for a Tablet Viewport (HTML 266)

Show and Hide Content for a Tablet Viewport (HTML 267)

Display and Style the equip Class (HTML 269)

Create and Style the items Class for a Tablet Viewport (HTML 270)

Designing for Desktop Viewports

Create a Media Query for a Desktop Viewport (HTML 274)

Style the items Class for a Desktop Viewport (HTML 282)

Modifying Breakpoints

Determine the Viewport Width for Tablet and Desktop Viewports (HTML 283)

Set the New Viewport Widths for the Tablet and Desktop Media Queries (HTML 286)

Using Pseudo-Classes

Add Pseudo-Classes to a Style Sheet (HTML 288)

Using Gradients

Add a Linear Gradient (HTML 293)

How will you design your tablet and desktop layouts?

Use these guidelines as you complete the assignments in this chapter and create your own webpages outside of this class.

1. Determine the layout of the tablet display.

    a. Restrict the design to one or two columns.

    b. Determine the best navigation design for your audience.

    c. Consider a strategy to focus on essential content.

2. Determine the layout of the desktop display.

    a. Determine number of columns for your layout.

    b. Incorporate active white space between content areas.

3. Test media query viewports.

    a. Use browser inspection tools to help determine viewport width.

    b. Modify breakpoints to maintain the tablet design, if necessary.

    c. Modify breakpoints to maintain the desktop design, if necessary.

4. Enhance links with pseudo-classes.

    a. Use a high color contrast between the link color and background color.

    b. Determine which pseudo-classes to use.

5. Evaluate the use of a gradient.

    a. Determine the best location for a gradient.

    b. Determine the type of gradient to use, its direction, and the gradient colors.

CONSIDER THIS

How should you submit solutions to questions in the assignments identified with a ✷ symbol?
Every assignment in this book contains one or more questions identified with a ✷ symbol. These questions require you to think beyond the assigned presentation. Present your solutions to the questions in the format required by your instructor. Possible formats may include one or more of these options: create a document that contains the answer; present your answer to the class; discuss your answer in a group; record the answer as audio or video using a webcam, smartphone, or portable media player; or post answers on a blog, wiki, or website.

Apply Your Knowledge

Reinforce the skills and apply the concepts you learned in this chapter.

Creating Media Queries

Instructions: In this exercise, you will use your text editor to add tablet and desktop media queries to a style sheet. You will create style rules for a tablet viewport and a desktop viewport. You then add a style rule for an image element to style the pictures in two columns for a tablet viewport and three columns for a desktop viewport. The completed webpage is shown in Figure 6–53 for a tablet viewport and Figure 6–54 for a desktop viewport. You will also use professional web development practices to indent, space, comment, and validate your code.

Figure 6–53

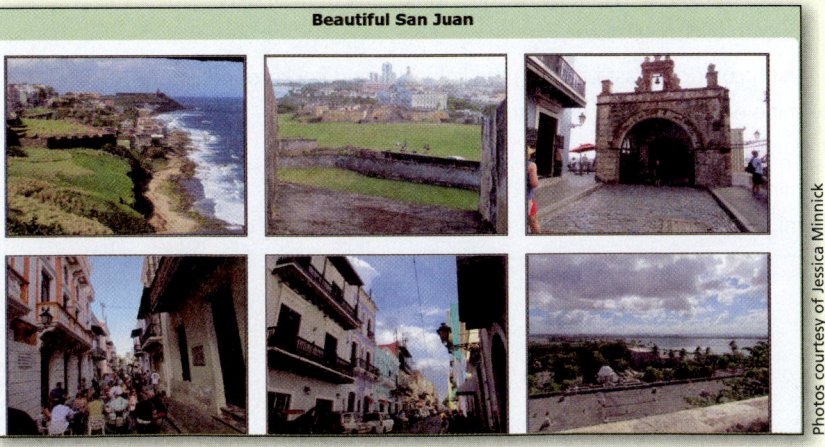

Figure 6–54

Perform the following tasks:

1. Open apply06.html in your browser to view the webpage.

2. Open apply06.html in your text editor, review the page, and modify the comment at the top of the page to include your name and today's date.

3. Open the applystyles06.css file from the apply\css folder. Modify the comment at the top of the style sheet to include your name and today's date.

4. In the applystyles06.css file, add a media query to target a tablet viewport. Use `min-width: 481px` and include the following comment, `Styles for tablet layout.`

5. Create a new style rule for the `img` element to set the `width` to `45%` within the tablet media query.

6. In the applystyles06.css file, add a media query to target a desktop viewport. Use `min-width: 769px` and include the following comment, `Styles for desktop layout.`

7. Create a new style rule for the `img` element to set the `width` to `30%` within the desktop media query.

8. Save all of your changes and open the apply06.html in Google Chrome.

9. Use the developer tools in Google Chrome to view each viewport's dimensions and determine a better viewport size for the desktop viewport.

10. Modify the desktop media query with the new value in the applystyles06.css file.

11. Validate your HTML document using the W3C validator found at validator.w3.org and fix any errors that are identified.

12. Validate your CSS file using the W3C validator found at http://jigsaw.w3.org/css-validator/ and fix any errors that are identified.

13. Submit the files in a format specified by your instructor.

14. ✳ In steps 4 and 6, you created media queries to target tablet and desktop viewports by using `min-width` and a value. Describe how you could use `max-width` and provide the value you would use for each media query.

Extend Your Knowledge

Extend the skills you learned in this chapter and experiment with new skills. You may need to use additional resources to complete the assignment.

Exploring Gradients

Instructions: In this exercise, you will explore how to work with different kinds of gradients. You will discover how to modify linear gradients and how to create angled gradients, diagonal gradients, radial gradients, and gradients with multiple colors. The completed webpage is shown in Figure 6–55.

Figure 6–55

Continued >

Extend Your Knowledge *continued*

Perform the following tasks:

1. Open extend06.html in your browser to view the webpage. Adjust the browser window to a desktop viewport.

2. Open extend06.html in your text editor and modify the comment at the top of the page to include your name and today's date.

3. Open the styles06.css file from the extend\css folder. Modify the comment at the top of the style sheet to include your name and today's date.

4. In the styles.css file, add a linear gradient to the background for the #gradient1 selector. Include comments to note which prefix is needed for each browser:

   ```
   background: -moz-linear-gradient(to right, #000066, #99FF99 25%);

   background: -o-linear-gradient(to right, #000066, #99FF99 25%);

   background: -webkit-linear-gradient(to right, #000066, #99FF99 25%);

   background: linear-gradient(to right, #000066, #99FF99 25%); /* List
   the standard syntax last */
   ```

5. Save your changes and view extend06.html in your browser to view the changes.

6. In the styles.css file, add a linear gradient to the #gradient2 selector, but style it to the left, using the same colors, and 10% as the color stop. Add the same linear gradient with a prefix for all major browsers and include comments to note the prefix needed for each browser.

7. Save your changes and view extend06.html in your browser to view the changes.

8. In the styles.css file, add the following radial gradient to the background for the #gradient3 selector. Include comments to note which prefix is needed for each browser:

   ```
   background: -webkit-radial-gradient(#006699, #00CC00, #FF0000);
   background: -o-radial-gradient(#006699, #00CC00, #FF0000);
   background: -moz-radial-gradient(#006699, #00CC00, #FF0000);
   background: radial-gradient(#006699, #00CC00, #FF0000); /* List the
   standard syntax last */
   ```

9. Save your changes and view extend06.html in your browser to view the changes.

10. In the styles.css file, add the following repeating radial gradient to the background for the #gradient4 selector. Add the same repeating radial gradient with a prefix for all major browsers above the standard syntax and include comments to note the prefix needed for each browser:

    ```
    background: repeating-radial-gradient(#006699, #00CC00 10%, #FF0000)
    15%; /* List the standard syntax last */
    ```

11. Save your changes and view extend06.html in your browser to view the changes.

12. In the styles.css file, add the following linear gradient to the background for the #gradient5 selector. Add the same linear gradient with a prefix for all major browsers above the standard syntax and include comments to note the prefix needed for each browser:

    ```
    background: linear-gradient(to top left, #FFFF00, #FF6600, #006699,
    #3333FF); /* List the standard syntax last */
    ```

13. Save your changes and view extend06.html in your browser to view the changes.

14. In the extend06.html file, add a heading three element with title above each `div` gradient element.

15. Save your files and submit them in a format specified by your instructor.

16. ✳ In this exercise, you explored more about gradients and used percentages to set color stops. Use your browser to research how to set gradient color stops using percentages. Include a description of your findings.

Analyze, Correct, Improve

Analyze a responsive design website, correct all errors, and improve it.

Modifying Media Queries

Instructions: Work with the analyze06.html file in the analyze folder and the analyzestyles06.css file in the analyze\css folder from the Data Files for Students. The analyze06.html webpage is a draft template, but must be corrected and improved for responsive design before presenting it to the client. Use Figure 6–56 and Figure 6–57 as a guide to correct these files.

Figure 6–56

Figure 6–57

Continued >

Analyze, Correct, Improve *continued*

1. Correct

a. Open the analyze06.html file in your editor from the Data Files for Students and then modify the comment at the top of the page to include your name and today's date.

b. Open the analyzestyles06.css file in your editor from the Data Files for Students and then modify and correct the comment at the top of the document to include your name and today's date.

c. View analyze06.html in your browser and resize the page to display mobile, tablet, and desktop viewports. The navigation links for the tablet viewport extend beyond their boundary at the current breakpoint.

d. Open analyze06.html in Google Chrome and use the developer tools to determine the dimensions for a tablet viewport.

e. In the analyzestyles06.css file, modify the tablet media query with a suitable breakpoint value.

f. In the analyzestyles06.css file, modify the #container width within the desktop media query with a suitable value for a desktop viewport.

2. Improve

a. In the analyzestyles06.css file, pseudo-class properties are included within the desktop media query, but they all use the same value. Use `#FFCCFF` for the hover color value and `#9900FF` for the active color value.

b. In the analyzestyles06.css file, add a `font-size` property with value of `1.05em` for the :hover pseudo-class.

c. In the analyzestyles06.css file, create new style rule for the body selector within the desktop media query that uses a background property with a value of `linear-gradient(#FFFFFF, #336699);` and then add the properties and values needed to accommodate the major browsers. Place the standard syntax at the bottom.

d. In the analyzestyles06.css file, add the property `background-attachment` with a value of `fixed` to the style rule for the body selector.

e. Save your changes and test your webpage. It should look like Figure 6–56 for the tablet viewport and Figure 6–57 for the desktop viewport.

f. Validate your CSS file using the W3C validator found at http://jigsaw.w3.org/css-validator/ and fix any errors that are identified.

g. Validate your HTML webpage using the W3C validator found at validator.w3.org and fix any errors that are identified.

h. ✳ Identify other ways to style a pseudo-class and provide an example.

In the Labs

Labs 1 and 2, which increase in difficulty, require you to create webpages based on what you learned in the chapter; Lab 3 requires you to dive deeper into a topic covered in the chapter.

Lab 1: Designing for Tablet and Desktop Viewports for the New Harvest Food Bank

Problem: You volunteer at a local food bank called New Harvest Food Bank that collects community food donations and provides food and other services to those in need. The company has asked you to create a responsive website. Start with the fbstyles.css and index.html files you completed in Chapter 5. You have already created the mobile layout, but now need to design a tablet and desktop layout. Style the webpage shown in Figure 6–58 for the tablet viewport and shown in Figure 6–59 for the desktop viewport.

Figure 6–58

Figure 6–59

Instructions: Perform the following tasks:

1. Open your text editor and then open the index.html file in the lab1 folder and the fbstyles.css file in the lab1\css folder.

2. In the index.html document, modify the comment at the top of the page to include today's date.

3. In the index.html document, insert a `div` element, `div class="desktop"` below the div class="mobile" element.

4. In the index.html document, insert the following paragraph elements in the new div `class="desktop"` element.

```
<p>Too many people in our local community go to bed hungry, many of
whom are children. We can reduce that number, but we need your help.
</p>
```

Continued >

In the Labs *continued*

```
<p>New Harvest Food Bank is proud to help and support our local commu-
nity. Through your donations, we are able to help feed those in need.
Please partner with us and help those in your local community with
food donations, clothing donations, or by volunteering your time.</p>
```

5. In the fbstyles.css file, modify the comment at the top of the page to include today's date.

6. In the fbstyles.css file, create a media query for a tablet viewport and use `min-width: 481px`.

7. Add the following style rules to the tablet media query and include comments for each.

```
img {
        width: 25%;
        float: left;
}

header p {
        margin-bottom: 4em;
        padding-top: 1.5em;
}

nav li {
        display: inline;
        float: left;
        margin-left: 1%;
        margin-right: 1%;
        padding-left: 0;
        padding-right: 0;
        width: 23%;
}

main {
        clear: left;
        margin-top: 12em;
}

.mobile {
        display: none;
}

.desktop {
        display: inline;
}
```

8. In the fbstyles.css file, create a media query for a desktop viewport and use `min-width: 769px`.

9. Add the following styles to the desktop media query and include comments for each.

```
#container {
        width: 80%;
}
```

```
nav {
        margin-top: -5em;
}

nav ul {
        margin: 0;
        padding-left: 0.50%;
        padding-right: 0.50%;
}

nav li {
        background-color: #FFFFFF;
        border-radius: 0;
        margin-left: 0;
        margin-right: 0;
        padding: 0;
        width: 18%;
}

nav li a {
        color: #FF6600;
        display: inline-block;
        padding: 0.7em;
        font-size: 1.25em;
}

nav li a:link {
        color: #FF6600;
}

nav li a:hover {
        color: #4C1F00;
        font-style: italic;
}

main {
        border: none;
        border-radius: 1em;
        box-shadow: 1em 1em 1em #331400;
        margin-top: 1em;
}
```

10. In the fbstyles.css file, add a style rule to hide the desktop class for the mobile layout and include a comment.

11. Validate your HTML code and fix any errors.

12. Validate your CSS code and fix any errors.

13. Save all files and open the index.html page within a browser as shown in Figure 6–58 for a tablet viewport and Figure 6–59 for a desktop viewport.

Continued >

In the Labs *continued*

14. Submit your assignment in the format specified by your instructor.

15. ✳ In step 9, you created a style rule for the nav element and used a negative number for the top margin value. Discuss the effect of this property and value on the `nav` element.

Lab 2: Designing for Tablet and Desktop Viewports for Steve's Screen Services

Problem: You work for a screening company called Steve's Screen Services that specializes in screening, cleaning, and repairing screened patios. The company has asked you to create a responsive website. Start with the screenstyles.css and index.html files you completed in Chapter 5. You have already created the mobile layout, but now need to design a tablet and desktop layout. Style the webpage shown in Figure 6–60 for a tablet viewport and Figure 6–61 for a desktop viewport.

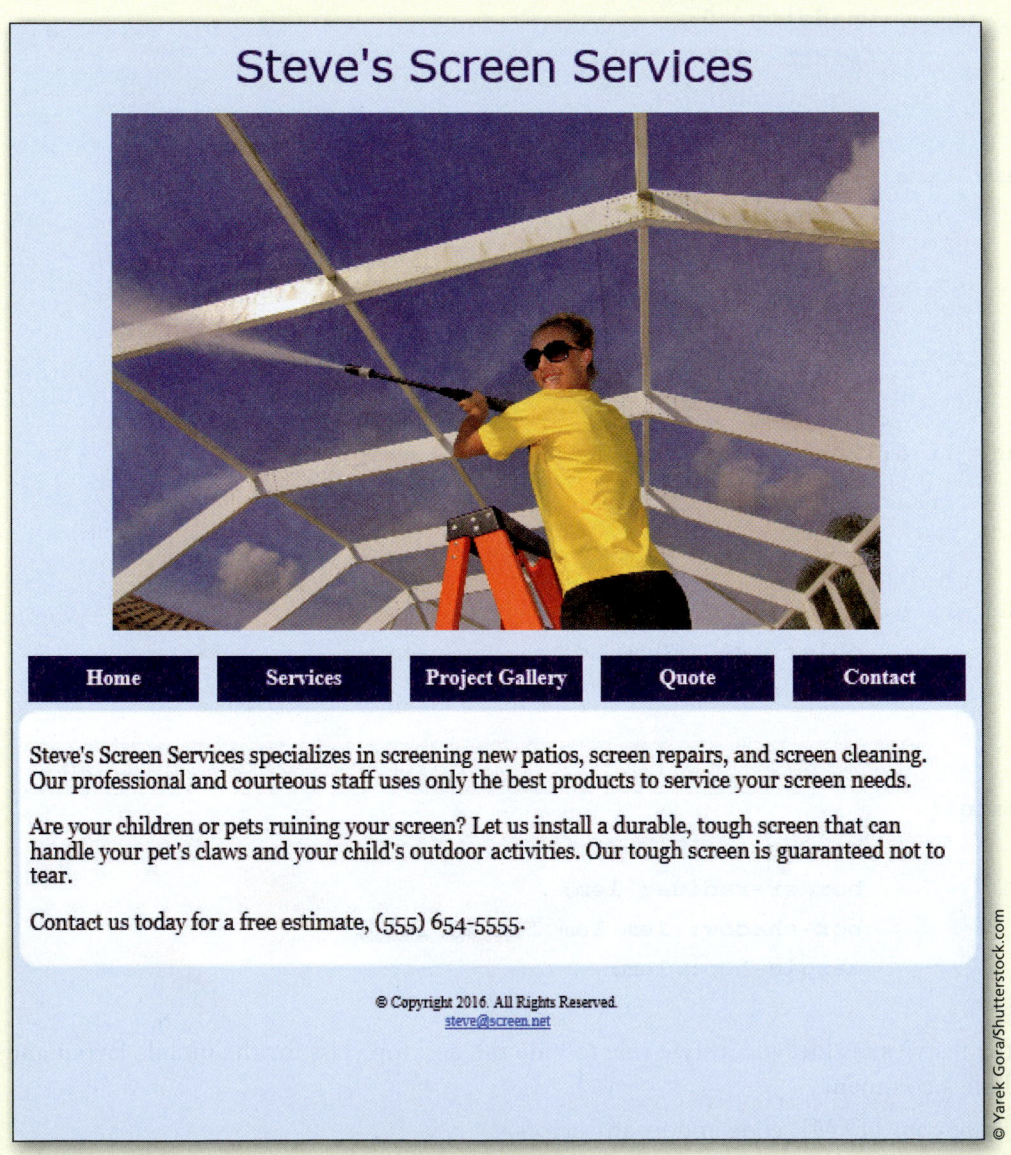

© Yarek Gora/Shutterstock.com

Figure 6–60

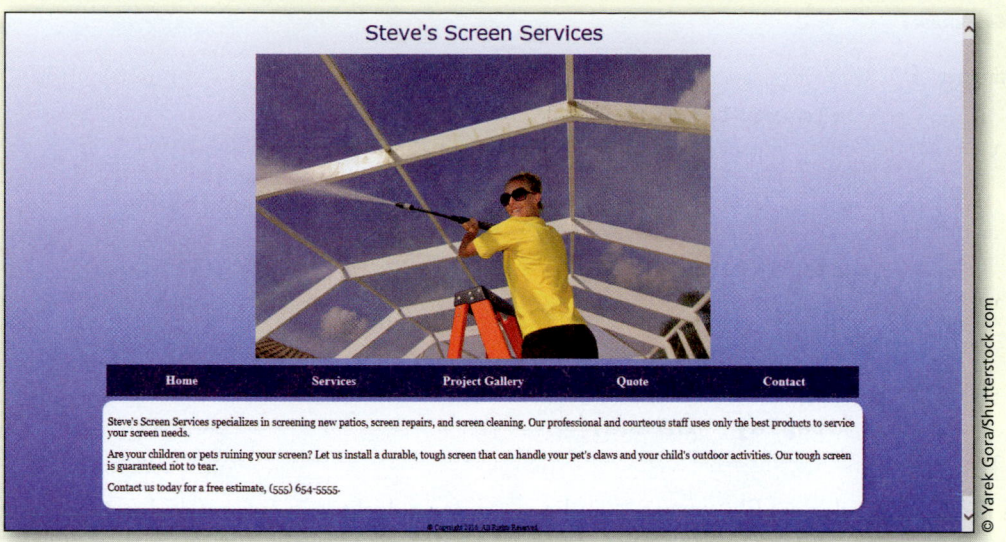

© Yarek Gora/Shutterstock.com

Figure 6–61

Instructions: Perform the following tasks:

1. Open your text editor and then open the index.html file in the lab2 folder and the screenstyles.css file in the lab2\css folder.

2. In the index.html document, modify the comment at the top of the page to include today's date.

3. In the index.html document, insert a div element, `div class="desktop"` below the div `class="mobile"` element.

4. In the index.html document, insert the following paragraph elements in the new div `class="desktop"` element.

   `<p>Steve's Screen Services specializes in screening new patios, screen repairs, and screen cleaning. Our professional and courteous staff uses only the best products to service your screen needs.</p>`

   `<p>Are your children or pets ruining your screen? Let us install a durable, tough screen that can handle your pet's claws and your child's outdoor activities. Our tough screen is guaranteed not to tear.</p>`

   `<p>Contact us today for a free estimate, (555) 654-5555.</p>`

5. In the screenstyles.css file, modify the comment at the top of the page to include today's date.

6. In the screenstyles.css file, create a media query for a tablet viewport and use `min-width: 481px`.

7. Add the following style rules to the tablet media query and include comments for each.

```
img {
        width: 80%;
}


nav li {
        display: inline;
        float: left;
        margin-left: 1%;
        margin-right: 1%;
        padding-left: 0;
        padding-right: 0;
        width: 18%;
}
```

Continued >

In the Labs *continued*

```
main {
        clear: left;
}

.mobile {
        display: none;
}

.desktop {
        display: inline;
}
```

8. In the screenstyles.css file, create a media query for a desktop viewport and use `min-width: 769px`.

9. Add the following styles to the desktop media query and include comments for each.

```
#container {
        width: 80%;
}

img {
        width: 60%;
}

nav ul {
        margin: 0;
        padding-left: 0.50%;
        padding-right: 0.50%;
}

nav li {
        border-radius: 0;
        margin-left: 0;
        margin-right: 0;
        padding: 0;
        width: 20%;
        white-space: nowrap;
}

nav li a {
        display: inline-block;
        padding: 0.7em;
        font-size: 1.25em;
}
```

```
main {
        border: none;
        border-radius: 1em;
        box-shadow: 1em 1em 1em #331400;
        margin-top: 1em;
}
```

10. In the screenstyles.css file, add the following pseudo-classes:

```
nav li a:link {
        color: #FFFFFF;
}
```

```
nav li a:hover {
        color: #CCFFCC;
        font-size: 1.5em;
}
```

11. In the screenstyles.css file, add a style rule to the desktop viewport to apply the following linear gradient to the background. Insert additional properties and values required to accommodate all major browsers. Include comments for all.

```
background: linear-gradient(#FFFFFF, #3366CC);
```

12. In the screenstyles.css file, add a style rule to hide the desktop class for the mobile layout and include a comment.

13. Open index.html in Google Chrome and use the developer tools to determine a suitable breakpoint value for the desktop media query and modify the desktop media query.

14. Validate your HTML code and fix any errors.

15. Validate your CSS code and fix any errors.

16. Save all files and open the index.html page within a browser as shown in Figure 6–60 and Figure 6–61.

17. Submit your assignment in the format specified by your instructor.

18. ✳ In step 11, you created a style rule for a gradient. Discuss at least three different ways this gradient could be applied.

Lab 3: Expand Your World
Discovering More About CSS3 Properties

Problem: In this chapter, you applied a gradient to a webpage; a gradient is a CSS3 property. In this exercise, you will explore other CSS3 properties that you have not yet used in this book.

Instructions:

1. Use your browser to research CSS3 properties and read the information you find.

2. Spend some time browsing through examples. Locate at least three CSS3 properties that you have not yet used and answer the following questions for each property.

   a. Describe the purpose of the property.

   b. Provide an example of the code and include a list of possible property values and what each means.

   c. Identify where you might apply this property within a webpage.

   d. Include a link to your resource.

Continued >

In the Labs *continued*

3. Submit your answers in the format specified by your instructor.

4. ✸ CSS is an integral part of the web design process. Use your browser to research the latest CSS trends and tips for today's websites. Identify at least three trends or tips and include the URL for each.

✸ Consider This: Your Turn

Apply your creative thinking and problem-solving skills to design and implement a solution.

1. Applying Additional Responsive Design Techniques to Your Personal Portfolio Website

Personal

Part 1: In Chapter 5, you styled your personal portfolio website for a mobile layout. In this exercise, you update that page to use responsive design as follows:

1. Open the external style sheet you created in Chapter 5 and save it with the name **portfoliostyles06.css** in the styles folder within the your_turn_1 folder.

2. Add your name and the current date as a comment to the first line of the portfoliostyles06.css file.

3. In your HTML editor, open the files you created for your portfolio website in Chapter 5 and make sure your name and the current date are added as a comment to the first line of all files.

   a. Update the HTML files to modify the link to the external style sheet to reference portfoliostyles06.css.

   b. Apply a class named mobile to elements that should only be displayed on a mobile viewport, such as the telephone link.

   c. Apply a class named desktop to elements that should only be displayed on a tablet or desktop viewport.

4. Update the CSS file to:

   a. Create a media query for tablet and desktop viewports.

   b. Create style rules for tablet and desktop viewports.

   c. Hide the desktop class for the mobile layout.

   d. Hide the mobile class for the desktop layout.

   e. Refine your style sheet as desired.

   f. Adjust viewport widths if necessary.

   g. Add comments to note all changes and updates.

5. Save and test your files.

6. Validate and correct your HTML and CSS files, and submit your assignment in the format specified by your instructor.

Part 2: ✸

Use your browser to research responsive storytelling and discuss how this web design process could be helpful to your portfolio site.

2. Applying Additional Responsive Design Techniques to the WebDevPros Webpages

Professional

Part 1: In Chapter 5, you created a mobile layout for WebDevPros. In this exercise, you will update the site to include media queries for tablet and desktop viewports.

1. Open the external style sheet you created in Chapter 5 and save it with the name **webdevstyles06.css** in the styles folder within the your_turn_2 folder.

2. Add your name and the current date as a comment to the first line of the webdevstyles06.css file.

3. Open the files you created for WebDevPros in Chapter 5 in your HTML editor and make sure your name and the current date are added as a comment to the first line of all files.

4. Update the HTML files to:

   a. Apply a class named mobile to elements that should only be displayed on a mobile viewport, such as the telephone link.

   b. Apply a class named desktop to elements that should only be displayed on a tablet or desktop viewport.

5. Update the CSS file to:

   a. Create a media query for tablet and desktop viewports.

   b. Create style rules for tablet and desktop viewports.

   c. Create style rules for pseudo-classes within the desktop media query.

   d. Hide the mobile class for the tablet and desktop viewports.

   e. Display the desktop class for tablet and desktop viewports.

   f. Refine your style sheet as desired.

   g. Adjust viewport widths if necessary.

   h. Add comments to note all changes and updates.

6. Save and test your files.

7. Validate and correct your HTML and CSS files, and submit your assignment in the format specified by your instructor.

Part 2: ✺ In step 5c, you added style rules for pseudo-classes. Use your browser to research pseudo-classes. Identify two other types of pseudo-classes not covered in this chapter and provide an example of each.

3. Applying Additional Responsive Design Strategies to the Dog Hall of Fame Webpages

Research and Collaboration

Part 1: In Chapter 5, you styled the Dog Hall of Fame webpages for a mobile viewport. In this exercise, you will update those pages to apply media queries for tablet and desktop viewports. Do the following activities as a group:

1. Open the external style sheet you created in Chapter 5 and save it with the name **dogstyles06.css** in the styles folder within the your_turn_3 folder.

2. Add your name and the current date as a comment to the first line of the dogstyles06.css file.

3. Open the files you created for the Dog Hall of Fame in Chapter 5 in your HTML editor and make sure your name and the current date are added as a comment to the first line of all files.

4. Modify the link to the external style sheet to reference dogstyles06.css.

5. Decide how you will design the tablet and desktop viewports. At a minimum, update the HTML and CSS files to do the following:

   a. Create a media query for tablet and desktop viewports.

   b. Create style rules for tablet and desktop viewports.

   c. Create style rules for pseudo-classes within the desktop viewport.

   d. Apply a gradient to the webpages in the tablet and desktop viewports.

Continued >

Consider This: Your Turn *continued*

   e. Hide the mobile class for the tablet and desktop viewports.

   f. Display the desktop class for the tablet and desktop viewports.

   g. Refine your style sheet as desired.

   h. Adjust viewport widths where necessary.

   i. Add comments to note all changes and updates.

6. Save and test your files.

7. Validate and correct your HTML and CSS files, and submit your assignment in the format specified by your instructor.

Part 2: ✳ Each person in the group should research web design trends for tablet and desktop viewports and bring it to a group discussion. In the discussion, each person should share at least three trends for each viewport. Secondly, each person should share an example of a website using the current trends. Organize your group's findings as requested by your instructor.

7 Improving Web Design with New Page Layouts

Objectives

You will have mastered the material in this chapter when you can:

- Explain when to use article, aside, and section elements
- Define figure and figcaption elements
- Redesign wireframes for tablet and desktop viewports
- Explain and use the opacity property
- Describe and use the text-shadow property

- Add a banner image to a website
- Insert and style a figure element
- Insert and style a section element
- Insert and style an article element
- Insert and style an aside element
- Create a three-column layout
- Describe and use the overflow property

7 | Improving Web Design with New Page Layouts

Introduction

Web design involves a daily pursuit of perfection in layout, function, and efficiency. Every site you create expresses your personal creativity while balancing your customers' demands with content and design that captures and holds the attention of your dynamic audience. To meet these requirements, you must constantly reevaluate your content and design and apply new technologies and innovations to keep your audience engaged and your customers elated.

As you have learned, HTML5 provides new tools for improving webpage design, including semantic elements for specific types of content. You have already integrated four semantic elements in a website: header, nav, main, and footer. In this chapter, you will discover other HTML5 semantic elements and learn how to integrate them into webpages. You will also learn how to improve your current design for mobile, tablet, and desktop viewports.

Project — Use HTML5 Structural Elements to Redesign a Website

In Chapters 5 and 6, you discovered how to create a responsive-design website. In Chapter 7, you continue to improve the website design by modifying page layout and learning how to use additional HTML5 semantic elements.

The owners of the Forward Fitness Club are rebranding their image and plan to launch a strategic marketing campaign to gain new clients. As part of the rebranding process, they updated their logo and created a new look. They ask you to apply the new look to the website. Because the website is not yet complete, this is a good time to improve and redesign the site to fit the updated brand.

The project in this chapter enhances a website with HTML5 semantic elements to structure added content. To complete this task, you create a new wireframe for the home and About Us pages. Next, you integrate additional HTML5 semantic elements within the home, About Us, and Contact Us pages. You also update and create style rules for the new and existing elements. Next, you create a wireframe for the Nutrition page, a new webpage in the site. After creating the Nutrition page using HTML5 semantic elements, add style rules for these elements to the style sheet. You apply styles to the HTML5 elements on each page to give the site an enhanced look and feel. As you add styles to the style sheet, they immediately format the attached webpages when you open or refresh the pages in a browser. Figure 7–1 shows the home page, Figure 7–2 shows the About Us page, and Figure 7–3 shows the Nutrition page, each for the mobile, tablet, and desktop viewports after the improvements are applied.

(a) Home page in mobile viewport

(b) Home page in tablet viewport

(c) Home page in desktop viewport

Figure 7–1

(a) About Us page in mobile viewport

(b) About Us page in tablet viewport

(c) About Us page in desktop viewport

Figure 7–2

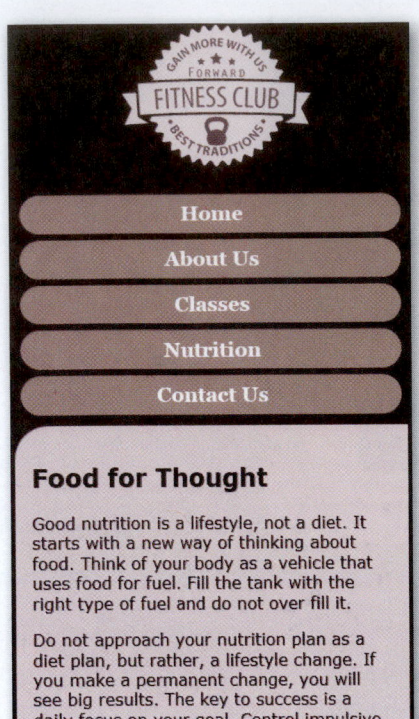

(a) Nutrition page in mobile viewport

(b) Nutrition page in tablet viewport

(c) Nutrition page in desktop viewport

Figure 7–3

Roadmap

In this chapter, you will learn how to create the webpage shown in Figure 7–1. The following roadmap identifies general activities you will perform as you progress through this chapter:

1. MODIFY the HOME PAGE.

2. STYLE the HOME PAGE elements.

3. MODIFY the ABOUT US PAGE.

4. STYLE the ABOUT US PAGE elements.

5. MODIFY AND STYLE the CONTACT US PAGE elements.

6. CREATE AND STYLE the NURTITION PAGE elements.

At the beginning of step instructions throughout the chapter, you will see an abbreviated form of this roadmap. The abbreviated roadmap uses colors to indicate chapter progress: gray means the chapter is beyond that activity; blue means the task being shown is covered in that activity, and black means that activity is yet to be covered. For example, the following abbreviated roadmap indicates the chapter would be showing a task in the 5 MODIFY & STYLE CONTACT US PAGE activity.

1 MODIFY HOME PAGE | 2 STYLE HOME PAGE | 3 MODIFY ABOUT US PAGE | 4 STYLE ABOUT US PAGE

5 MODIFY & STYLE CONTACT US PAGE | 6 CREATE & STYLE NUTRITION PAGE

Use the abbreviated roadmap as a progress guide while you read or step through the instructions in this chapter.

Using HTML5 Semantic Elements

Recall from Chapter 2 that HTML5 semantic elements are sets of starting and ending HTML tags that provide meaning about the content of the tags. For example, the navigation system is contained within the <nav> and </nav> tags; likewise, footer content is contained within the <footer> and </footer> tags.

Use HTML5 semantic elements for specific types of content within a webpage. The name of the tag reflects its purpose. Using semantic HTML5 elements provides a standard naming convention for webpage content, making webpages more universal, accessible, and meaningful to search engines.

The Forward Fitness Club website contains the header, nav, main, and footer semantic elements. HTML5 includes several other semantic elements, some of which you will learn about and use to complete this project. Table 7–1 lists other HTML5 semantic elements.

Table 7–1 HTML5 Semantic Elements	
Element	**Description**
<article> … </article>	Indicates the start and end of an article area of a webpage. Contains content such as forum or blog posts.
<aside> … </aside>	Indicates the start and end of an aside area of a webpage. Contains information about nearby content and is typically displayed as a sidebar.
<details> … </details>	Indicates the start and end of a details area of a webpage. Contains additional information that the user can display or hide. Note that this element is not supported by all major browsers at the time of this publication.
<figure> … </figure>	Indicates the start and end of a figure area of a webpage. Contains pictures and images.
<figcaption> … </figcaption>	Indicates the start and end of a figure caption area of a webpage. Defines a caption for a figure element.
<section> … </section>	Indicates the start and end of a section area of a webpage. Contains a specific grouping of content on a webpage.
<summary> … </summary>	Indicates the start and end of a summary area of a webpage. Contains a visible heading for the details element on a webpage. Note that this element is not supported by all major browsers at the time of this publication.
<time> … </time>	Indicates the start and end of a time area of a webpage. Contains a date/time on a webpage.

Article Element

The **article element**, as described by the W3C, is "a complete, self-contained composition in a document, page, application, or site and that is, in principle, independently distributable or reusable, e.g. in syndication. This could be a forum post, a magazine or newspaper article, a blog entry, a user-submitted comment, an interactive widget or gadget, or any other independent item of content." The article element starts with an <article> tag and ends with an </article> tag. Content placed between these tags will appear on a webpage as part of the `article` element. Articles may be nested within other HTML elements, such as the `main` element, the `section` element, or other `article` elements. Articles are commonly used to contain news articles, blog and forum posts, or comments. The `article` element is supported by the major modern browsers. The following is an example of three `article` elements nested within a `main` element.

```
<main>

    <article>
      <h1>Article 1 Title</h1>
      <p>Information about article 1</p>
    </article>

    <article>
      <h1>Article 2 Title</h1>
      <p>Information about article 2</p>
    </article>

    <article>
      <h1>Article 3 Title</h1>
      <p>Information about article 3</p>
    </article>

</main>
```

An example wireframe that uses the `article` element is shown in Figure 7–4. An example of a webpage that uses an `article` element is shown in Figure 7–5.

Figure 7–4

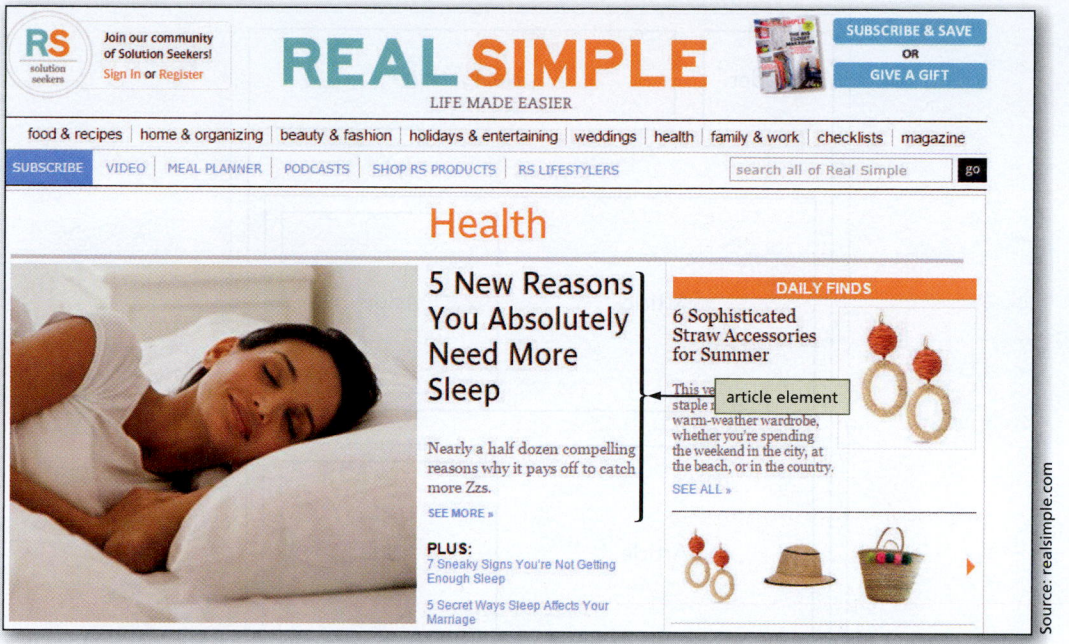

Figure 7–5

Aside Element

The **aside element**, as described by the W3C, is an element that "represents a section of a page that consists of content that is tangentially related to the content around the aside element, and which could be considered separate from that content." The `aside` element is used as a sidebar and contains additional information about a particular item mentioned within another element, such as an `article` or `section` element. For example, if an article on a webpage contains a recipe and a list of ingredients, you could include an `aside` element with more information about one of the key ingredients, such as its origin or where to purchase it. Aside elements can be nested within `article` elements or within `main` or `section` elements. Aside elements are commonly used for pull-out quotes, glossary terms, or related links. The following is an example of an `aside` element nested within an `article` element.

```
<article>
    <h1>Recipe</h1>
      <p>Recipe ingredients and instructions</p>
    <aside>
      <p>More information about a specific ingredient</p>
    </aside>
</article>
```

An example wireframe that uses the `aside` element is shown in Figure 7–6. An example of a webpage that uses an `aside` element is shown in Figure 7–7.

Figure 7–6

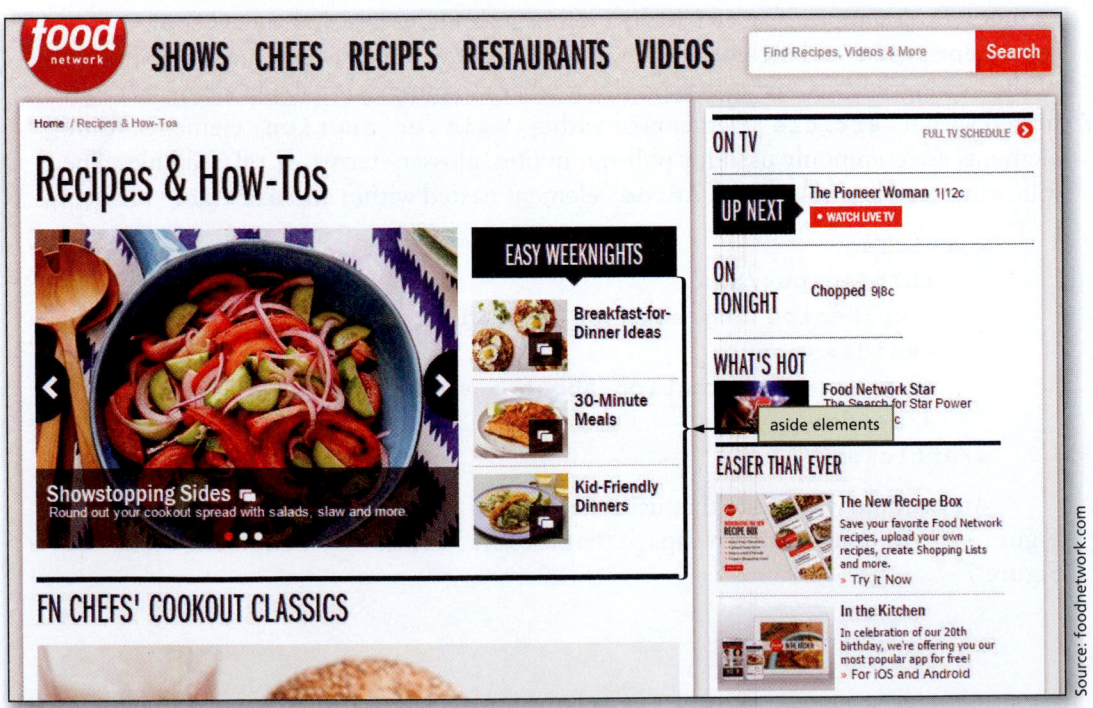

Figure 7–7

Section Element

The **section element**, as described by the W3C, is an element that "represents a generic section of a document or application. A section, in this context, is a thematic grouping of content. The theme of each section should be identified, typically by including a heading (h1-h6 element) as a child of the section element." The `section` element defines different parts of a webpage document, such as chapters. For example, in a webpage that contains a list of tutorials, Tutorials 1-3, each tutorial can be placed within a section and include a heading element with an appropriate title, Tutorial 1, Tutorial 2, Tutorial 3, followed by the tutorial content. Be sure to include a heading element within a `section` element or the page will receive a warning from the W3C HTML validator. Use a `section` element for content that naturally contains a heading. The W3C encourages designers to use `article` elements for other types of subdivided content. The W3C also states that the `section` element "is not a generic container element. When an element is needed only for styling purposes or as a convenience for scripting, authors are encouraged to use the div element instead. A general rule is that the section element is appropriate only if the element's contents would be listed explicitly in the document's outline." The following is an example of a several `section` elements nested within an article element.

```
<article>

    <h1>Tutorials: Cooking Basics</h1>
      <p>Watch our tutorials to learn the basics of
         good cooking.</p>

    <section>
      <h1>Tutorial 1</h1>
      <p>Assembling basic kitchen tools.</p>
    </section>

    <section>
      <h1>Tutorial 2</h1>
      <p>Cooking with essential spices.</p>
    </section>

    <section>
      <h1>Tutorial 3</h1>
      <p>Following food prep basics.</p>
    </section>

</article>
```

An example wireframe that uses the `section` element is shown in Figure 7–8. An example of a webpage that uses a `section` element is shown in Figure 7–9.

Figure 7–8

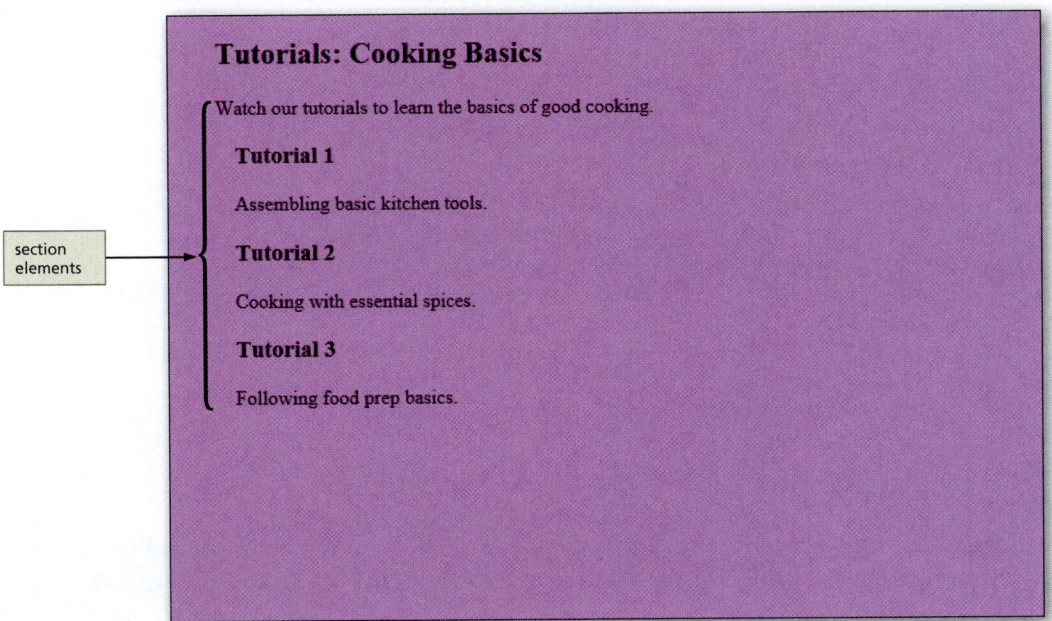

Figure 7–9

Figure and Figure Caption Elements

The **figure element** is used to group content, such as illustrations, diagrams, and photos. According to the W3C, the figure element "represents some flow content, optionally with a caption, that is self-contained (like a complete sentence) and is typically referenced as a single unit from the main flow of the document." Though the `figure` element is commonly used to contain images, it can also display a chart, graph, or table. Do not confuse the `figure` element with the `img` element.

The `figure` element is a semantic element with self-contained content. A `figure` element can contain one or more `img` elements.

The `figure` element may contain an optional **figure caption** element, which is used to provide a caption for the figure element. The `figure caption` element uses a <figcaption> tag as the starting tag and a </figcaption> tag as the ending tag. The following is an example of the `figure` element and the `figure caption` element.

```
<figure>
    <figcaption>New York City Highlights</figcaption>
    <img src="ny1.jpg" alt="Statue of Liberty">
    <img src="ny2.jpg" alt="Central Park">
    <img src="ny3.jpg" alt="New York at Night">
</figure>
```

An example wireframe that uses the `figure` and `figure caption` elements is shown in Figure 7–10. An example of a webpage that uses the elements is shown in Figure 7–11.

Figure 7–10

Figure 7–11

Can I use figure and figure caption elements to wrap image elements separately?
Yes. You can wrap each image element within separate figure and figure caption elements.

Website Layout

Many of today's modern websites use one or more images that consume most of the browser window for desktop viewports. Many of these websites display little text on the home page and use key words or phrases, or call-to-action items, to entice the user to further explore the website. Figures 7–12 and 7–13 show two websites that have been recognized by the web design community for their modern designs.

Figure 7–12

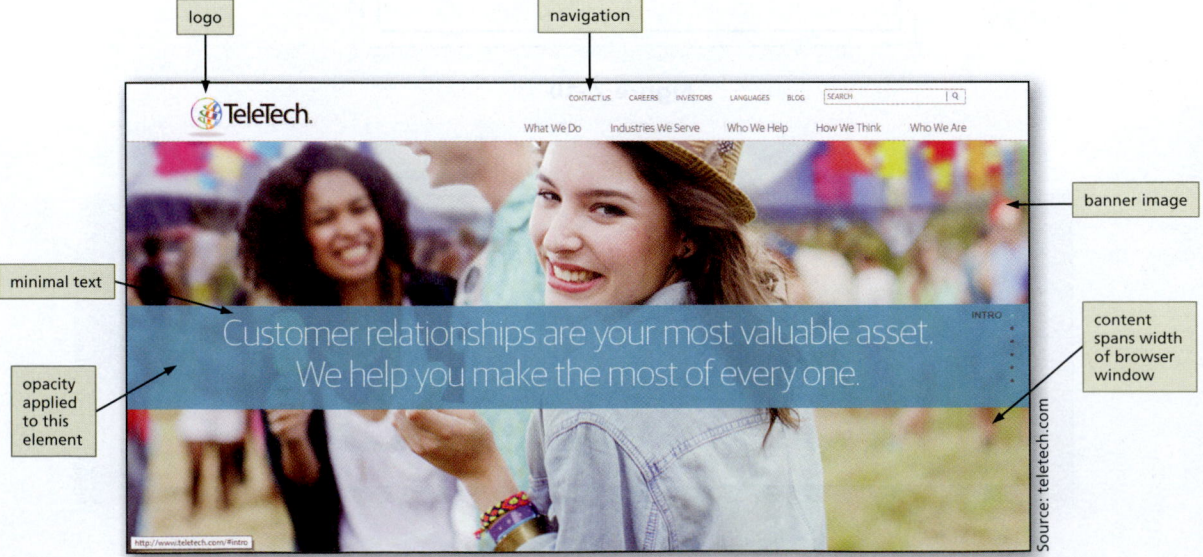

Figure 7–13

In both examples, the logos appear in the upper-left corner and the navigation appears to the right of the logo. The large banner image is shown below the navigation area and takes up a majority of the screen. (A **banner** is a graphic that spans the width of a webpage and usually brands a website, often by displaying its name or an identifying image.) Textual content is kept to a minimum. Each website also takes up the entire screen. Both sites use HTML, CSS, and other web technologies to accomplish their modern look and interaction.

What is the difference between a logo and a banner?
A logo is a graphical representation of a business, used to promote the business brand and market presence. A banner image is used as a focal point on a webpage to capture the user's attention.

Figure 7–13 also demonstrates the use of the CSS3 **opacity** property, which specifies the transparency of an element. The default value of the opacity property is 1, which does not make the element transparent. An opacity property value of 0.50 makes an element 50 percent transparent and a value of 0 makes an element completely transparent. Major modern browsers support this CSS3 property.

The **text-shadow** property is another CSS3 property that applies a shadow to text. This property requires a minimum of two values: the h-shadow value, which designates the horizontal position of the shadow, and the v-shadow value, which designates the vertical position of the shadow. Optional values include a blur radius and a color. Below is an example of a style rule that applies a text shadow to an element.

```
h1 {
    text-shadow: 0.2em 0.1em #292933;
}
```

In this example, a text shadow with a horizontal position of 0.2em, a vertical position of 0.1em, and a dark gray color is applied to an h1 element.

Redesigning the Home Page

Owners of the Forward Fitness Club have provided you with their new logo and other marketing materials to show you how they have rebranded the business. The marketing materials use dark gray to emphasize a refined and contemporary look. The new logo is light gray. You can incorporate these colors and updated design features in the Forward Fitness Club website.

Start by reviewing the existing wireframe for each viewport to determine how to improve it. You can keep the same wireframe for the home page mobile viewport because it is basic, adaptable, and works well in limited space. However, you can modify the wireframes for tablet and desktop viewports because the additional space allows you to include extra content, such as images in a figure element. New wireframes for the tablet and desktop viewports, which integrate a div for a banner image and a figure element, are shown in Figures 7–14 and 7–15.

Home page wireframe for tablet viewport

Figure 7–14

Home page wireframe for desktop viewport

Figure 7–15

To Add a New div Element to the Home Page

Modify the home page by adding a new **div** element to contain the banner image. To begin, download the new images and save them in your images folder. Next, open the index.html file in your text editor and insert a **div** element for the banner image and add the banner image. The following steps add a **div id="banner"** element to the home page.

1 Copy the files from the chapter07 folder provided with the Data Files for Students to the fitness\images folder. When prompted to replace the existing ffc_logo.png file, select the option to replace the file.

2 Open index.html in your text editor, tap or click at the end of Line 28, and then press the ENTER key twice to insert new Lines 29 and 30.

3 On Line 30, type `<!-- Home Page Banner -->` to insert a comment.

4 Press the ENTER key to insert new Line 31, and then type `<div id="banner" class="desktop">` to insert a div tag.

5 Press the ENTER key to insert new Line 32, increase the indent, and then type `<img src="images/homeBanner.jpg" alt="home banner image">` to insert an image.

6 Press the ENTER key to insert new Line 33, decrease the indent, and then type `</div>` to insert a closing div tag (Figure 7–16).

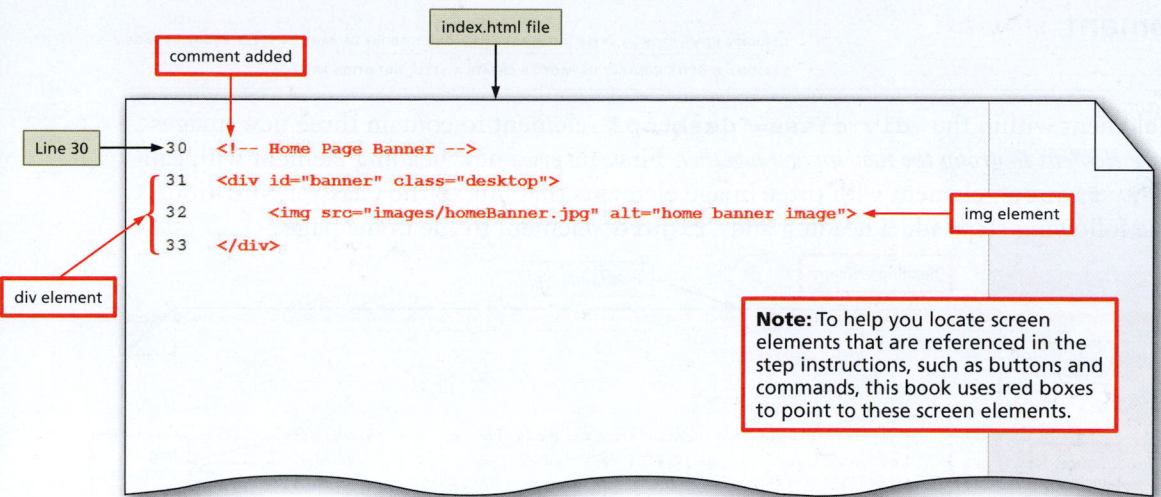

comment added

index.html file

Line 30

```
30    <!-- Home Page Banner -->
31    <div id="banner" class="desktop">
32        <img src="images/homeBanner.jpg" alt="home banner image">
33    </div>
```

img element

div element

Note: To help you locate screen elements that are referenced in the step instructions, such as buttons and commands, this book uses red boxes to point to these screen elements.

Figure 7–16

7 Save your changes, open index.html in your browser, and then adjust the window to the size of a desktop viewport (Figure 7–17).

Q&A Why is the Forward Fitness Center logo different?
The new logo reflects the updated design for the business and is a new image with the same name as the previous logo file. You saved the new file in the images folder from the Data Files for Students.

new logo

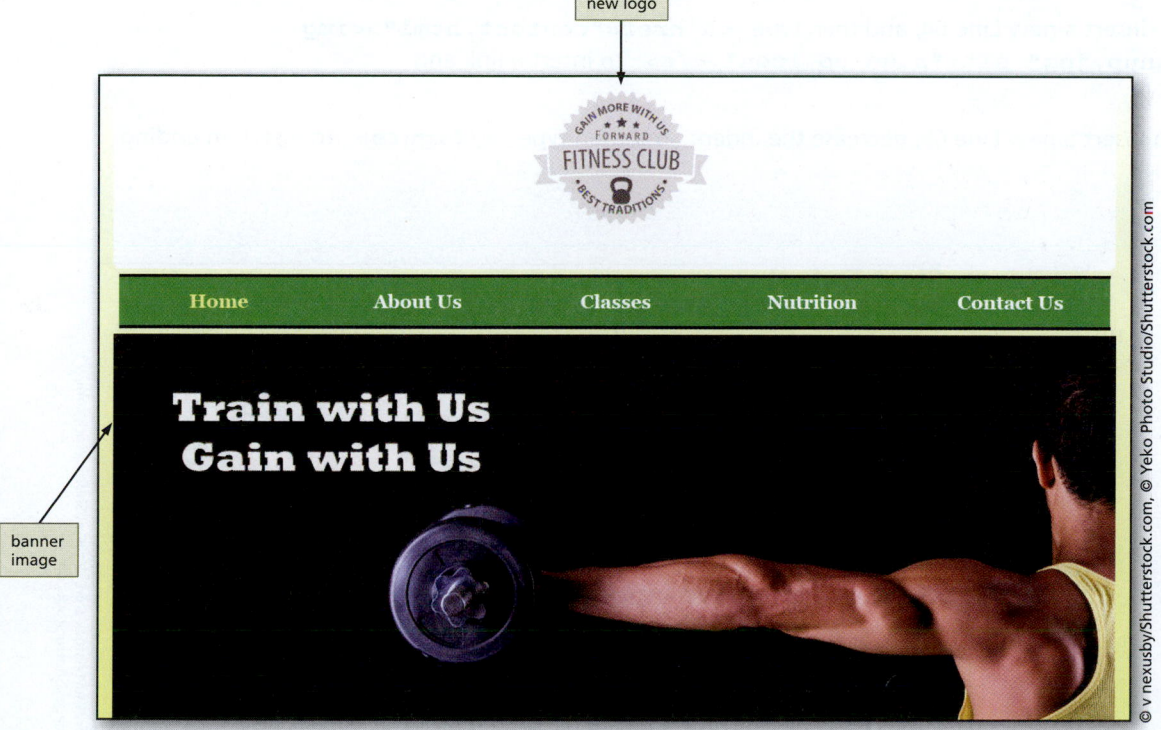

banner image

© v nexusby/Shutterstock.com, © Yeko Photo Studio/Shutterstock.com

Figure 7–17

To Add a figure Element to the Home Page

Insert a `figure` element within the `div class="desktop"` element to contain three new images and links. *Why? Use a figure element to group the new images together.* First, insert a new heading element with call-to-action text. Next, insert a `figure` element with three image elements that link to the Classes, Nutrition, and Contact Us pages. The following steps add a heading and `figure` element to the home page.

1

- Tap or click at the end of Line 57, and then press the ENTER key twice to insert new Lines 58 and 59.

- On Line 59, type `<h1>Start Today!</h1>` to insert a heading element.

- Press the ENTER key twice to insert new Lines 60 and 61, and then type `<figure>` to insert a starting figure tag.

Figure 7–18

- Press the ENTER key to insert a new Line 62, increase the indent, and then type `<a href="classes.html"><img src="images/group.jpg" alt="group fitness"></a>` to insert a link and an image.

- Press the ENTER key to insert a new Line 63, and then type `<a href="nutrition.html"><img src="images/nutrition.jpg" alt="good nutrition"></a>` to insert a link and an image.

- Press the ENTER key to insert a new Line 64, and then type `<a href="contact.html"><img src="images/signup.jpg" alt="sign up icon"></a>` to insert a link and an image.

- Press the ENTER key to insert a new Line 65, decrease the indent, and then type `</figure>` to insert an ending figure tag (Figure 7–18).

2

- Save your changes and refresh index.html in your browser (Figure 7–19).

Figure 7–19

© Rob Marmion/Shutterstock.com, © Faysal/Shutterstock.com,
© Milleflore Images/Shutterstock.com

To Update the Style Sheet for the New Design in a Mobile Viewport

1 MODIFY HOME PAGE | 2 STYLE HOME PAGE | 3 MODIFY ABOUT US PAGE | 4 STYLE ABOUT US PAGE
5 MODIFY & STYLE CONTACT US PAGE | 6 CREATE & STYLE NUTRITION PAGE

Update the style sheet for the mobile viewport. *Why? The new and modified styles update the body background color and styles for the structural elements in the mobile viewport to reflect the rebranding of the Forward Fitness Club.* The following steps modify the style rules for the mobile viewport.

1

- Open the styles.css file in your text editor to prepare to edit it.

- On Line 5, replace the background-color value with **1D1D1C** to modify it (Figure 7–20).

Q&A

What color is represented by this color value?
This color value is dark gray.

Figure 7–20

2

- Remove Lines 24 through 26 to delete these properties and values.

- If necessary, press the DELETE key to move the text-align property and value to Line 24 (Figure 7–21).

Figure 7–21

3

- Tap or click at the end of Line 32, and then press the ENTER key to insert a new Line 33.

- On Line 33, type **margin-top: -1.5em;** to insert a new property and value (Figure 7–22).

Q&A

Why is the value a negative number?
The negative value places the top margin of the nav element within the area of header element. This helps achieve part of the desired look for the new design.

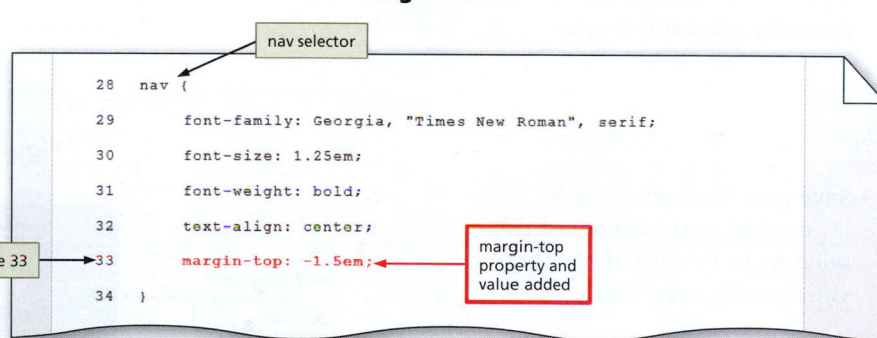

Figure 7–22

4

- On Line 45, replace the background-color value with **9D9D93** to modify it (Figure 7–23).

Q&A

What color is represented by this color value?
This color value is light gray.

Figure 7–23

5
- On Line 75, replace the border-radius value with **2em 0 2em 0** to modify it.

- Remove Lines 77 through 78 to delete these properties and values.

- On Line 77, type **opacity: 0.85;** to add a new property and value (Figure 7–24).

Q&A

How does the new value for the border-radius affect the main element?
This new value curves the top-left and bottom-right corners, and squares the top-right and bottom-left corners.

How does the opacity property with a value of 0.85 affect the main element?
This value makes the background of the main element 85 percent transparent.

```
main selector

69    main {
70        display: block;
71        font-family: Verdana, Arial, sans-serif;
72        font-size: 1em;
73        margin-top: 0.5em;
74        padding: 1em;
Line 75   75    border-radius: 2em 0 2em 0;     border-radius value
76        background-color: #FFFFFF;
Line 77   77    opacity: 0.85;                  opacity property and value
78    }
```

Figure 7–24

6
- Tap or click at the end of Line 84, and then press the ENTER key to insert a new Line 85.

- On Line 85, type **color: #FFFFFF;** to insert a new property and value (Figure 7–25).

```
footer selector

81    footer {
82        font-size: .70em;
83        text-align: center;
84        margin-top: 2em;
Line 85   85    color: #FFFFFF;        color property and
86    }                            value (white)
```

Figure 7–25

7
- Save your changes, refresh index.html, and then adjust the window to the size of a mobile viewport (Figure 7–26).

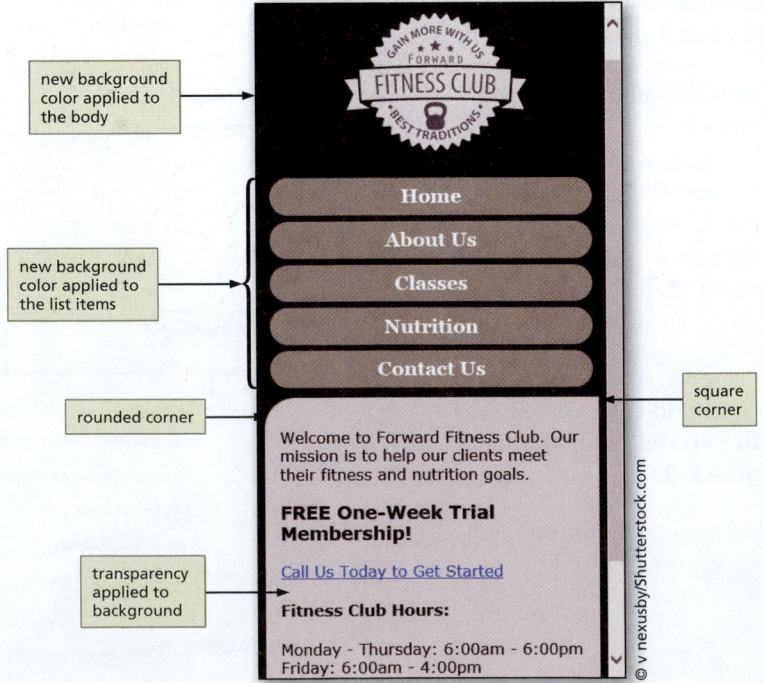

new background color applied to the body

new background color applied to the list items

rounded corner

square corner

transparency applied to background

Figure 7–26

© v nexusby/Shutterstock.com

To Add New Style Rules for Anchor Elements in a Mobile Viewport

Create two new style rules for the fitness website when displayed in a mobile viewport. The first rule styles anchor elements within the **main** element and the second rule styles anchor elements within the footer. *Why? Update the style of the anchor elements to be consistent with the new look of the website.* The following steps create style rules for the mobile viewport.

1

- In styles.css, tap or click at the end of Line 78, and then press the ENTER key twice to insert new Lines 79 and 80.

- On Line 80, type **/* Style for anchor elements within the main element*/** to insert a new comment.

- Press the ENTER key to insert a new Line 81, and then type **main a {** to insert a new selector.

- Press the ENTER key to insert a new Line 82, increase the indent, and then type **background-color: #9D9D93;** to insert a new property and value.

```
        comment
              ↓
Line 80 →  80   /* Style for anchor elements within the main element*/
           81   main a {
           82       background-color: #9D9D93;
           83       border-radius: 1em;
           84       color: #FFFFFF;                  ←  style rule for
           85       font-weight: bold;                  main a
           86       padding: 0.5em;
           87       text-decoration: none;
           88   }
```

Figure 7–27

- Press the ENTER key to insert a new Line 83, and then type **border-radius: 1em;** to insert a new property and value.

- Press the ENTER key to insert a new Line 84, and then type **color: #FFFFFF;** to insert a new property and value.

- Press the ENTER key to insert a new Line 85, and then type **font-weight: bold;** to insert a new property and value.

- Press the ENTER key to insert a new Line 86, and then type **padding: 0.5em;** to insert a new property and value.

- Press the ENTER key to insert a new Line 87, and then type **text-decoration: none;** to insert a new property and value.

- Press the ENTER key to insert a new Line 88, decrease the indent, and then type **}** to insert a closing brace (Figure 7–27).

Q&A How does the new style affect the anchor elements in the main element?
The new style displays links as bold white text in a gray rectangle with rounded corners with a small amount of padding and no text decoration (such as underlining).

2

- Tap or click at the end of Line 96, and then press the ENTER key twice to insert new Lines 97 and 98.

- On Line 98, type `/* Style for anchor elements within the footer element */` to insert a new comment.

- Press the ENTER key to insert a new Line 99, and then type `footer a {` to insert a new selector.

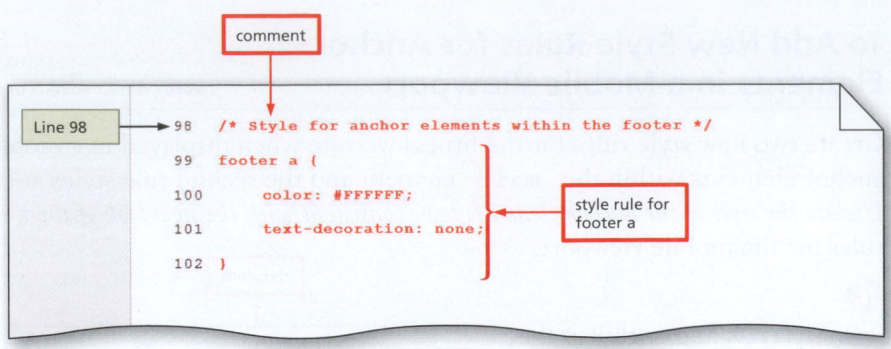

Figure 7–28

- Press the ENTER key to insert a new Line 100, increase the indent, and then type `color: #FFFFFF;` to insert a new property and value.

- Press the ENTER key to insert a new Line 101, and then type `text-decoration: none;` to insert a new property and value.

- Press the ENTER key to insert a new Line 102, decrease the indent, and then type `}` to insert a closing brace (Figure 7–28).

3

- Save your changes and refresh index.html in your browser (Figure 7–29).

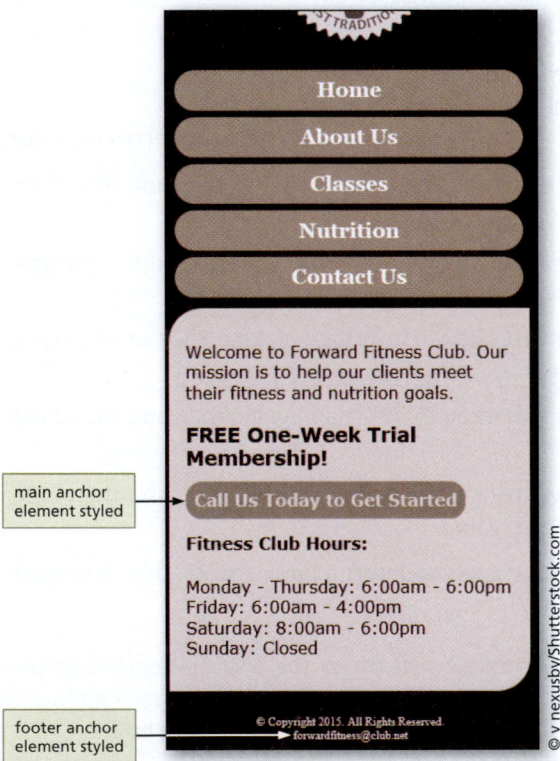

Figure 7–29

To Update the Style Sheet for the New Design in a Tablet Viewport

1 MODIFY HOME PAGE | **2 STYLE HOME PAGE** | 3 MODIFY ABOUT US PAGE | 4 STYLE ABOUT US PAGE

5 MODIFY & STYLE CONTACT US PAGE | 6 CREATE & STYLE NUTRITION PAGE

Update the style sheet for the tablet viewport. *Why? The new and modified styles update the list items in the navigation element and refine the styles for the main element in the tablet viewport to reflect the rebranding of the Forward Fitness Club.* First, add new properties to the navigation list item style rule to remove the background color and rounded corners. Then, modify the styles for the main element to apply a top margin and to remove the margin and rounded corners. The following steps modify the style rules for the tablet viewport.

1

- In styles.css, tap or click at the end of Line 127, and then press the ENTER key to insert a new Line 128.

- On Line 128, type **border-radius: 0;** to insert a new property and value.

- Press the ENTER key to insert a new Line 129, and then type **background-color: transparent;** to insert a new property and value (Figure 7–30).

nav li selector in tablet media query

```
119  nav li {
120       display: inline;
121       float: left;
122       margin-right: 1%;
123       margin-left: 1%;
124       padding-left: 0;
125       padding-right: 0;
126       width: 18%;
127       white-space: nowrap;
128       border-radius: 0;
129       background-color: transparent;
130  }
```

Line 128

background-color property and value

border-radius property and value

Figure 7–30

2

- On Line 135, replace the margin-top value with **-0.3em** to modify it.

- Press the ENTER key to insert a new Line 136, and then type **border-radius: 0;** to insert a new property and value (Figure 7–31).

main selector

```
133  main {
134       clear: left;
135       margin-top: -0.3em;
136       border-radius: 0;
137  }
```

Line 135

margin-top value changed

border-radius property and value

Figure 7–31

3

- Save your changes, refresh index.html, and then adjust the window to the size of a tablet viewport (Figure 7–32).

rounded corners and background color are removed from navigation list items

rounded corners are removed and top margin is modified for main element

Home   About Us   Classes   Nutrition   Contact Us

Train with Us Gain with Us

Welcome to Forward Fitness Club. Our mission is to help our clients meet their fitness and nutrition goals.

If you have struggled with getting healthy and need the motivation and resources to make

© v nexusby/Shutterstock.com, © Yeko Photo Studio/Shutterstock.com

Figure 7–32

To Add New Style Rules to the Tablet Viewport

1 MODIFY HOME PAGE | **2 STYLE HOME PAGE** | 3 MODIFY ABOUT US PAGE | 4 STYLE ABOUT US PAGE
5 MODIFY & STYLE CONTACT US PAGE | 6 CREATE & STYLE NUTRITION PAGE

You added heading and figure elements to the home page and now need to create style rules to format the elements. Create three new style rules: one for the heading element and two for the figure element. *Why? Create the style rules for the new elements to format them to suit the updated design.* First, create a new style rule for the heading one element to center-align its content. Next, create a new style rule for the images within the figure element to specify a background color, display setting, height, width, margin, and padding. Finally, create a new style rule to style the anchor elements in the figure element. The following steps create new style rules for the tablet viewport.

1

- In styles.css, tap or click at the end of Line 172, and then press the ENTER key twice to insert new Lines 173 and 174.

- On Line 174, type **/* Style for h1 element */** to insert a new comment.

- Press the ENTER key to insert a new Line 175, and then type **h1 {** to insert a new selector.

Figure 7–33

- Press the ENTER key to insert a new Line 176, increase the indent, and then type **text-align: center;** to insert a new property and value.

- Press the ENTER key to insert a new Line 177, decrease the indent, and then type **}** to insert a closing brace (Figure 7–33).

2

- Press the ENTER key twice to insert new Lines 178 and 179.

- On Line 179, type **/* Style for images within the figure element */** to insert a new comment.

- Press the ENTER key to insert a new Line 180, and then type **figure img {** to insert a new selector.

- Press the ENTER key to insert a new Line 181, increase the indent, and then type **background-color: #1D1D1C;** to insert a new property and value.

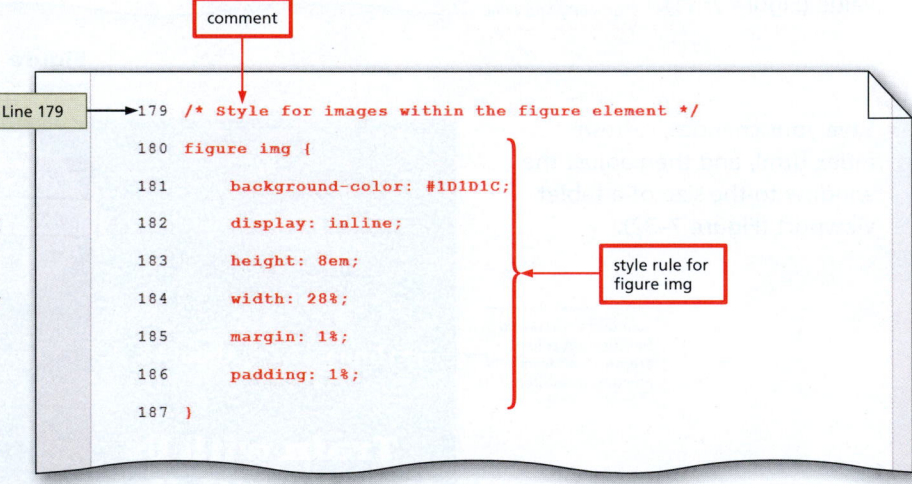

Figure 7–34

- Press the ENTER key to insert a new Line 182, and then type **display: inline;** to insert a new property and value.

- Press the ENTER key to insert a new Line 183, and then type **height: 8em;** to insert a new property and value.

- Press the ENTER key to insert a new Line 184, and then type **width: 28%;** to insert a new property and value.

- Press the ENTER key to insert a new Line 185, and then type **margin: 1%;** to insert a new property and value.

- Press the ENTER key to insert a new Line 186, and then type **padding: 1%;** to insert a new property and value.

- Press the ENTER key to insert a new Line 187, decrease the indent, and then type **}** to insert a closing brace (Figure 7–34).

3

- Press the ENTER key twice to insert new Lines 188 and 189.

- On Line 189, type **/* Style for anchor elements within the figure element */** to insert a new comment.

- Press the ENTER key to insert a new Line 190, and then type **figure a {** to insert a new selector.

- Press the ENTER key to insert a new Line 191, increase the indent, and then type **background-color: transparent;** to insert a new property and value.

- Press the ENTER key to insert a new Line 192, and then type **padding: 0;** to insert a new property and value.

- Press the ENTER key to insert a new Line 193, and then type **text-decoration: none;** to insert a new property and value.

- Press the ENTER key to insert a new Line 194, decrease the indent, and then type **}** to insert a closing brace (Figure 7–35).

comment

Line 189

```
189  /* Style for anchor elements within the figure element */
190  figure a {
191      background-color: transparent;
192      padding: 0;
193      text-decoration: none;
194  }
195
196  }
```

style rule for figure a

media query closing brace

Figure 7–35

4

- Save your changes, refresh index.html in your browser, and scroll down if necessary to view your changes (Figure 7–36).

h1 element aligned center

images and links formatted in figure element

Welcome to Forward Fitness Club. Our mission is to help our clients meet their fitness and nutrition goals.

If you have struggled with getting healthy and need the motivation and resources to make a healthy lifestyle change, contact us today. Our facility includes state-of-the-art equipment, convenient group training classes, and nutrition tips and information to keep you healthy.

We provide a FREE, one-week membership to experience the benefits of our equipment and facility. This one-week trial gives you complete access to our equipment, training classes, and nutrition planning. Contact us today to start your free trial!

Start Today!

Group Fitness   Meal Plans   SIGN UP Get Started

Figure 7–36

To Update the Style Sheet for the New Design in a Desktop Viewport

1 MODIFY HOME PAGE | **2 STYLE HOME PAGE** | 3 MODIFY ABOUT US PAGE | 4 STYLE ABOUT US PAGE
5 MODIFY & STYLE CONTACT US PAGE | 6 CREATE & STYLE NUTRITION PAGE

Update the style sheet for the desktop viewport to apply the new theme colors and desired layout for the Forward Fitness Club. **Why?** *The new and modified styles reflect the rebranding of the Forward Fitness Club.* First, modify the style rule for the **#container** element to remove the width and to apply a background color. Next, modify the style rule for the navigation list item elements to remove the borders. Then, modify the style rule for the navigation anchor elements to apply a text shadow. Modify the style rules for the active and hover pseudo-classes by changing their color values, and then modify the style rule for the main element by removing the currently properties and values and adding a background property and value. Also modify the style rule for paragraph elements within the main element by removing the current properties and values and adding a color, width, and margins. Finally, modify the style rule for the **body** element by removing the gradient background and applying a solid background color. The following steps modify the style rules for the desktop viewport.

- On Line 204 of styles.css, remove the width property and value, and then type **background-color: #1D1D1C;** to insert a new property and value (Figure 7–37).

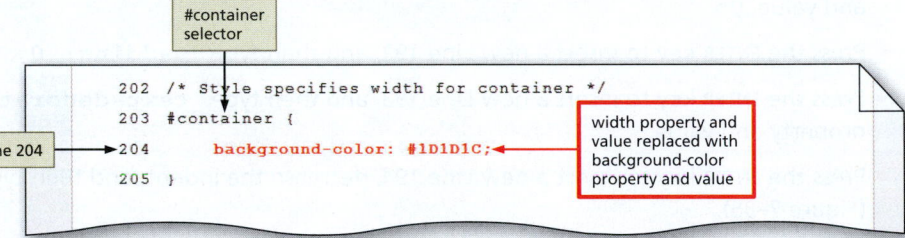

Figure 7–37

2

- Delete Lines 216 through 218 to remove these properties and values.

- If necessary, move the margin-left property and value up to Line 216 (Figure 7–38).

Figure 7–38

3

- Tap or click at the end of Line 225 then press the ENTER key to insert a new Line 226.

- On Line 226, type **text-shadow: 0.2em 0.1em #3D3D35;** to insert a new property and value (Figure 7–39).

Figure 7–39

Q&A
What does this value mean?
The first value is the position of the horizontal shadow. The second value is the position of the vertical shadow. The third value is the color of the shadow, which, in this case instance, is dark gray.

4

- On Line 235, replace the current color value with **#CCCCFF;** to modify the value.

- On Line 239, replace the current color value with **#9D9D93;** to modify the value (Figure 7–40).

Q&A What colors do #CCCCFF and #9D9D93 represent?
The color value #CCCCFF is very light blue and #9D9D93 is light gray.

```
234  nav li a:visited {
235       color: #CCCCFF;
236  }
237
238  nav li a:hover {
239       color: #9D9D93;
240       font-style: italic;
241  }
```

visited pseudo-class
Line 235
hover pseudo-class
Line 239
color values replaced

Figure 7–40

5

- Delete Lines 245 through 248 to remove these properties and values.

- On Line 245, type **background-color: #1D1D1C;** to insert a new property and value (Figure 7–41).

```
244  main {
245       background-color: #1D1D1C;
246  }
```

main selector
Line 245
border-style, box-shadow, and margin properties and values are removed
background-color property and value added

Figure 7–41

6

- Delete Lines 250 through 251 to remove these properties and values.

- On Line 250, type **color: #FFFFFF;** to insert a new property and value.

- Press the ENTER key to insert a new Line 251, and then type **margin-left: auto;** to insert a new property and value.

```
249  main p {
250       color: #FFFFFF;
251       margin-left: auto;
252       margin-right: auto;
253       width: 90%;
254  }
```

main p selector
Line 250
left and right padding properties and values are removed
new properties and values added

Figure 7–42

- Press the ENTER key to insert a new Line 252, and then type **margin-right: auto;** to insert a new property and value.

- Press the ENTER key to insert a new Line 253, and then type **width: 90%;** to insert a new property and value (Figure 7–42).

7

- Delete Lines 263 through 267 to remove these properties and values.

- On Line 263, type **background-color: #FFFFFF;** to insert a new property and value (Figure 7–43).

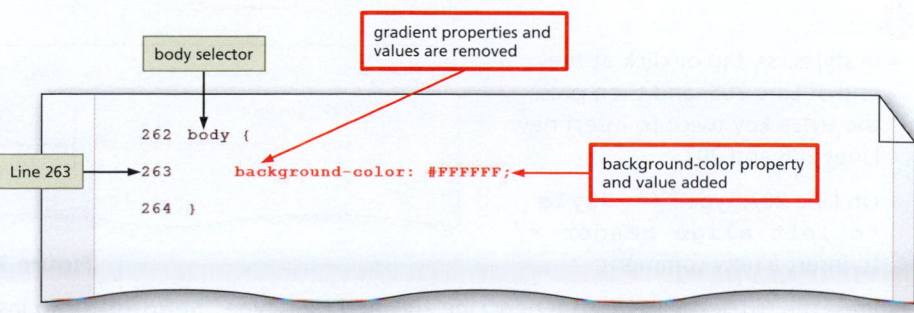

```
262  body {
263       background-color: #FFFFFF;
264  }
```

body selector
Line 263
gradient properties and values are removed
background-color property and value added

Figure 7–43

8

- Save your changes, refresh index.html, and then adjust the window to the size of a desktop viewport (Figure 7–44).

body background color applied

#container background color applied

text-shadow applied to navigation list items

Home   About Us   Classes   Nutrition   Contact Us

Train with Us Gain with Us

© v nexusby/Shutterstock.com, © Yeko Photo Studio/ Shutterstock.com

Figure 7–44

CONSIDER THIS

How big should I make my banner image?
The size of a banner image should be at least 1940 pixels wide to cover a large desktop screen. If you are using a digital photo- graph, select a high-resolution photograph, and then use a photo editor, such as Adobe Photoshop, to optimize the image for web use, as this will reduce the file size and reduce the time it takes to load the image on a page.

To Add New Style Rules to the Desktop Viewport

1 MODIFY HOME PAGE | **2 STYLE HOME PAGE** | 3 MODIFY ABOUT US PAGE | 4 STYLE ABOUT US PAGE
5 MODIFY & STYLE CONTACT US PAGE | 6 CREATE & STYLE NUTRITION PAGE

Create style rules to format the header and navigation elements so that both appear side-by-side, as indicated in the new wireframe. Create other style rules to apply opacity to the figure element to give it a rich, interactive look. In addition, create style rules to format the heading one element and the footer element. *Why? The new style rules format the pages according to the design specified in the wireframe and for optimum desktop display.* First, create a new style rule for the **header** element to align the content to the left. Then, create a new style rule for the **nav** element to specify a float, margins, and width. Next, create two new style rules for the image elements contained within the figure element to apply and remove opacity and to adjust the height of the image elements. Create a style rule for the heading one element to format its color. Finally, style the footer element to apply a background color, margin, and padding. The following steps create new style rules for the desktop viewport.

1

- In styles.css, tap or click at the end of Line 205, and then press the ENTER key twice to insert new Lines 206 and 207.

- On Line 207, type **/* Style to left align header */** to insert a new comment.

comment

Line 207

```
207  /* Style to left align header */
208  header {
209      text-align: left;
210  }
```

header style rule

Figure 7–45

- Press the ENTER key to insert a new Line 208, and then type **header {** to insert a new selector.

- Press the ENTER key to insert a new Line 209, increase the indent, and then type **text-align: left;** to insert a new property and value.

- Press the ENTER key to insert a new Line 210, decrease the indent, and then type **}** to insert a closing brace (Figure 7–45).

2

- Press the ENTER key twice to insert new Lines 211 and 212.

- On Line 212, type `/* Style for nav specifies a float, margin, and width */` to insert a new comment.

- Press the ENTER key to insert a new Line 213, and then type `nav {` to insert a new selector.

- Press the ENTER key to insert a new Line 214, increase the indent, and then type `float: right;` to insert a new property and value.

Figure 7–46

- Press the ENTER key to insert a new Line 215, and then type `margin-top: -7em;` to insert a new property and value.

- Press the ENTER key to insert a new Line 216, and then type `margin-right: 3em;` to insert a new property and value.

- Press the ENTER key to insert a new Line 217, and then type `margin-bottom: 0;` to insert a new property and value.

- Press the ENTER key to insert a new Line 218, and then type `width: 65%;` to insert a new property and value.

- Press the ENTER key to insert a new Line 219, decrease the indent, and then type `}` to insert a closing brace (Figure 7–46).

Q&A | Why is the value for margin-top a negative value?
Use a negative value to push the navigation element up and appear horizontally centered with the logo.

3

- Save your changes and refresh index.html in your browser to view the changes (Figure 7–47).

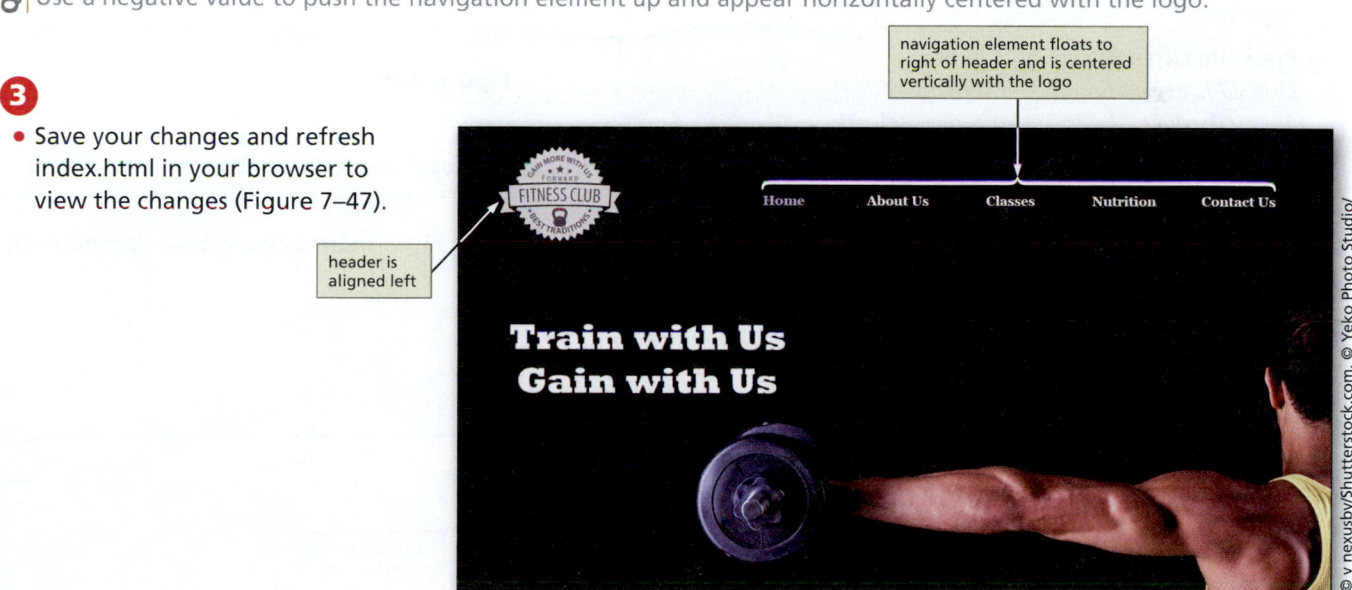

Figure 7–47

4

- Tap or click at the end of Line 268, press the ENTER key twice to insert new Lines 269 and 270.

- On Line 270, type `/* Style applies height and opacity to images within figure element */` to insert a new comment.

Figure 7–48

- Press the ENTER key to insert a new Line 271, and then type `figure img {` to insert a new selector.

- Press the ENTER key to insert a new Line 272, increase the indent, and then type `height: 15em;` to insert a new property and value.

- Press the ENTER key to insert a new Line 273, and then type `opacity: 0.7;` to insert a new property and value.

- Press the ENTER key to insert a new Line 274, decrease the indent, and then type `}` to insert a closing brace (Figure 7–48).

Q&A How will the opacity value affect the images within the figure element?
The opacity value will make the images appear with 70 percent opacity, or 30 percent transparent.

5

- Press the ENTER key twice to insert new Lines 275 and 276.

- On Line 276, type `/* Style removes transparency on hover */` to insert a new comment.

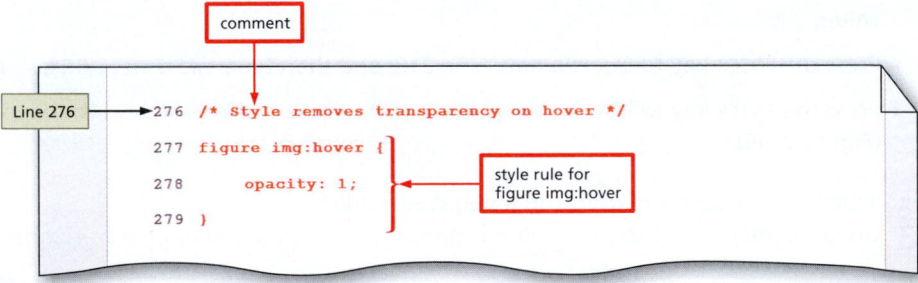

Figure 7–49

- Press the ENTER key to insert a new Line 277, and then type `figure img: hover {` to insert a new selector.

- Press the ENTER key to insert a new Line 278, increase the indent, and then type `opacity: 1;` to insert a new property and value.

- Press the ENTER key to insert a new Line 279, decrease the indent, and then type `}` to insert a closing brace (Figure 7–49).

Q&A How does this style affect the images within the figure element?
When a mouse hovers over an image, the opacity is removed.

- Tap or click at the end of Line 268, and then press the ENTER key twice to insert new Lines 269 and 270.

- On Line 270, type `/* Style applies color to h1 element */` to insert a new comment.

Figure 7–50

- Press the ENTER key to insert a new Line 271, and then type `h1 {` to insert a new selector.

- Press the ENTER key to insert a new Line 272, increase the indent, and then type `color: #FFFFFF;` to insert a new property and value.

- Press the ENTER key to insert a new Line 273, decrease the indent, and then type `}` to insert a closing brace (Figure 7–50).

7

- Tap or click at the end of Line 294, and then press the ENTER key twice to insert new Lines 295 and 296.

- On Line 296, type `/* Style specifies a background color, margin, and padding for footer element */` to insert a new comment.

```
          comment
Line 296    296  /* Style specifies a background color, margin, and padding
                     for footer element */
            297  footer {                                      style rule for
            298      background-color: #2A2A2A;                footer
            299      margin-top: -0.2em;
            300      padding: 2em;
            301  }
```

Figure 7–51

- Press the ENTER key to insert a new Line 297, and then type `footer {` to insert a new selector.

- Press the ENTER key to insert a new Line 298, increase the indent, and then type `background-color: #2A2A2A;` to insert a new property and value.

- Press the ENTER key to insert a new Line 299, and then type `margin-top: -0.2em;` to insert a new property and value.

- Press the ENTER key to insert a new Line 300, and then type `padding: 2em;` to insert a new property and value.

- Press the ENTER key to insert a new Line 301, decrease the indent, and then type `}` to insert a closing brace (Figure 7–51).

Q&A | What color does the value #2A2A2A represent?
The value #2A2A2A represents a slightly lighter gray compared to the #container background color.

8

- Save your changes, refresh index.html in your browser, and scroll down if necessary to view your changes (Figure 7–52).

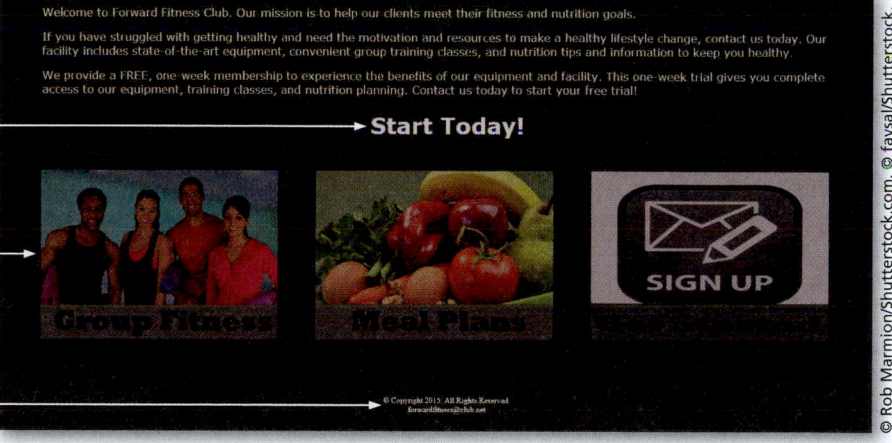

color applied to h1

height and opacity applied to images

background color, margin, and padding applied to footer element

Figure 7–52

9

- Hover over the images in the figure element to view the change in opacity (Figure 7–53).

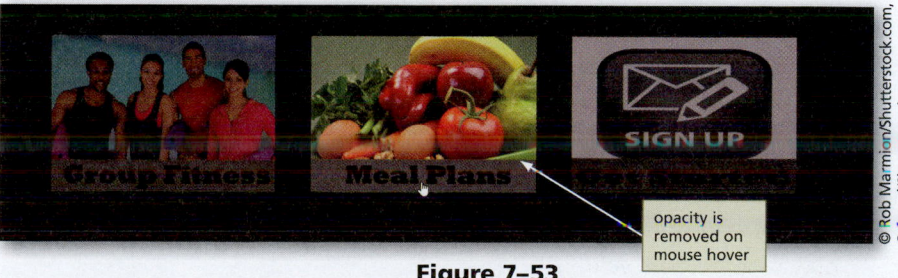

opacity is removed on mouse hover

Figure 7–53

Updating the About Us Page

The home page now displays the new look and design for the Forward Fitness Club. Next, revise the About Us page to integrate additional HTML5 semantic elements and then style the page according to the new design.

The About Us page contains groups of content that are not currently wrapped within a semantic element. These groups of content include the Weights group, the Cardio group, and the Personal Training group. Use a section element to group each of these areas together. The Common Exercises group is contained within a **div** element; however, change this from a **div** to a **section** element to integrate a semantic element. Once you have modified the About Us page, update the style sheet for tablet and desktop viewports.

To Add Section Elements to the About Us Page

1 MODIFY HOME PAGE | 2 STYLE HOME PAGE | 3 MODIFY ABOUT US PAGE | 4 STYLE ABOUT US PAGE
5 MODIFY & STYLE CONTACT US PAGE | 6 CREATE & STYLE NUTRITION PAGE

Add **section** elements to the About Us page to group content. *Why? Group content to improve semantic design and search engine results.* Wrap each group of content on the page within a **section** element. These include the Weights group, the Cardio group, the Personal Training group, and the Common Exercises group. The following steps add **section** elements to the About Us page.

1

- Open about.html in your text editor to prepare to modify it.

- Tap or click the blank Line 32, and then press the ENTER key to insert a new Line 33.

- On Line 33, increase the indent, and then type **<section>** to insert a starting section tag.

- Tap or click at the end of Line 41, and then press the ENTER key to insert a new Line 42.

- On Line 42, type **</section>** to insert an ending section tag (Figure 7–54).

Figure 7–54

2

- Tap or click the blank Line 43, and then press the ENTER key to insert a new Line 44.

- On Line 44, increase the indent, and then type **<section>** to insert a starting section tag.

- Tap or click at the end of Line 52, and then press the ENTER key to insert a new Line 53.

- On Line 53, type **</section>** to insert an ending section tag (Figure 7–55).

Line 44 · starting section tag · about.html

```
44        <section>

45        <h1>Cardio</h1>

46        <img class="equip" src="images/equipment2.jpg"
          alt="Cardio Equipment">

47        <p>Burn fat through cardio workouts. If you need to lose
          20lbs or more, include at least 30 minutes of cardio each
          day. We have several equipment choices for your
          workout.</p>

48        <ul class="items">

49            <li>Treadmills</li>

50            <li>Elliptical Machines</li>

51            <li>Exercise Bikes</li>

52        </ul>

53        </section>
```

Line 53 · ending section tag

Figure 7–55

3

- Tap or click the blank Line 54, and then press the ENTER key to insert a new Line 55.

- On Line 55, increase the indent, and then type **<section>** to insert a starting section tag.

- Tap or click at the end of Line 63, and then press the ENTER key to insert a new Line 64.

- On Line 64, type **</section>** to insert an ending section tag (Figure 7–56).

Line 55

```
55        <section>          starting section tag

56        <h1>Personal Training</h1>

57        <img class="equip" src="images/equipment3.jpg"
          alt="Personal Training">

58        <p>Our certified personal trainers work with you one on
          one to help you obtain your fitness goals. Our personal
          trainers keep you motivated and push you farther than you
          would push yourself. When you feel like you cannot do one
          more rep, they tell you that you can. Personal training
          has many benefits.</p>

59        <ul class="items">

60            <li>Accountability</li>

61            <li>Personalized Program</li>

62            <li>Consistent Support and Motivation</li>

63        </ul>

64        </section>
```

Line 64 · ending section tag

Figure 7–56

4

- On Line 66 replace the word "div" with **section** to modify the tag.

- On Line 86 replace the word "div" with **section** to modify the tag.

- Save your changes (Figure 7–57).

Line 66 · div replaced with section

```
66        <section class="tablet">

67

68        <h1>Common Exercises</h1>

...

86        </section>
```

Line 86 · div replaced with section

Figure 7–57

To Style the About Us Page for a Tablet Viewport

Update the style sheet for the tablet viewport to format the `section` elements and to revise style rules for the classes on the About Us page. *Why? Update the styles for the tablet viewport in the new design.* First, update the style rule for the items and tablet classes. Next, add a new style rule for a `section` element to apply margin and padding. Then, create a new style rule to format heading one elements within a section. Finally, create a style rule to format section anchor elements. The following steps update the style rules for the tablet viewport.

- If necessary, reopen styles.css file in your text editor to prepare to edit it.

- On Line 160, delete the margin-bottom property and value to remove it. If necessary, move the closing brace to Line 160.

- Tap or click at the end of Line 164, and then press the ENTER key to insert a new Line 165.

- On Line 165, type `margin-top: -3em;` to insert a new property and value.

- Press the ENTER key to insert a new Line 166, and then type `margin-bottom: -1em;` to insert a new property and value (Figure 7–58).

```
156 /* Style specifies a display, list style position, and bottom
    margin for the items class */
157 .items   {
158     display: block;
159     list-style-position: inside;
160 }                              ← margin-bottom property and
161                                  value are removed
162 /* Style specifies to display the tablet class */
163 .tablet {
164     display: block;
165     margin-top: -3em;          ← margin-top property and value
166     margin-bottom: -1em;       ← margin-bottom property and value
167 }
```

Figure 7–58

Q&A
Why do I need to remove the bottom margin from the items class and add top and bottom margin to the tablet class?
The style rules you add for the section elements in subsequent steps need the additional space that these modifications create.

- Tap or click at the end of Line 195, and then press the ENTER key twice to insert new Lines 196 and 197.

- On Line 197, type `/* Style specifies bottom padding for the section element */` to insert a comment.

- Press the ENTER key to insert a new Line 198, and then type `section {` to insert a new selector.

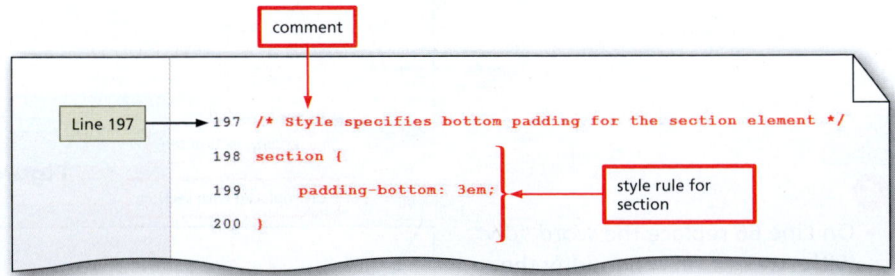

Figure 7–59

- Press the ENTER key to insert a new Line 199, increase the indent, and then type `padding-bottom: 3em;` to insert a new property and value.

- Press the ENTER key to insert a new Line 200, decrease the indent, and then type `}` to insert a closing brace (Figure 7–59).

- Press the ENTER key twice to insert new Lines 201 and 202.

- On Line 202, type **/* Style for h1 element within the section element */** to insert a new comment.

- Press the ENTER key to insert a new Line 203, and then type **section h1 {** to insert a new selector.

- Press the ENTER key to insert a new Line 204, increase the indent, and then type **text-align: left;** to insert a new property and value.

- Press the ENTER key to insert a new Line 205, decrease the indent, and then type **}** to insert a closing brace.

```
comment

Line 202  →  202  /* Style for h1 element within the section element */

             203  section h1 {
                                                    style rule for
             204      text-align: left;             section h1

             205  }

             206

             207  /* Style for anchor element within the section element */  ←  comment

             208  section a {

             209      background-color: transparent;

             210      color: #1D1D1C;

             211      font-weight: normal;          style rule for
                                                    section a
             212      padding: 0;

             213      text-decoration: underline;

             214  }

             215

             216  }  ←  tablet media query closing brace
```

Figure 7–60

- Press the ENTER key twice to insert new Lines 206 and 207.

- On Line 207, type **/* Style for anchor element within the section element */** to insert a new comment.

- Press the ENTER key to insert a new Line 208, and then type **section a {** to insert a new selector.

- Press the ENTER key to insert a new Line 209, increase the indent, and then type **background-color: transparent;** to insert a new property and value.

- Press the ENTER key to insert a new Line 210, and then type **color: #1D1D1C;** to insert a new property and value.

- Press the ENTER key to insert a new Line 211, and then type **font-weight: normal;** to insert a new property and value.

- Press the ENTER key to insert a new Line 212, and then type **padding: 0;** to insert a new property and value.

- Press the ENTER key to insert a new Line 213, and then type **text-decoration: underline;** to insert a new property and value.

- Press the ENTER key to insert a new Line 214, decrease the indent, and then type **}** to insert a closing brace (Figure 7–60).

4

- Save your changes, refresh about.html, and then adjust the window to the size of a tablet viewport.

- Scroll down the page to view your changes (Figure 7–61).

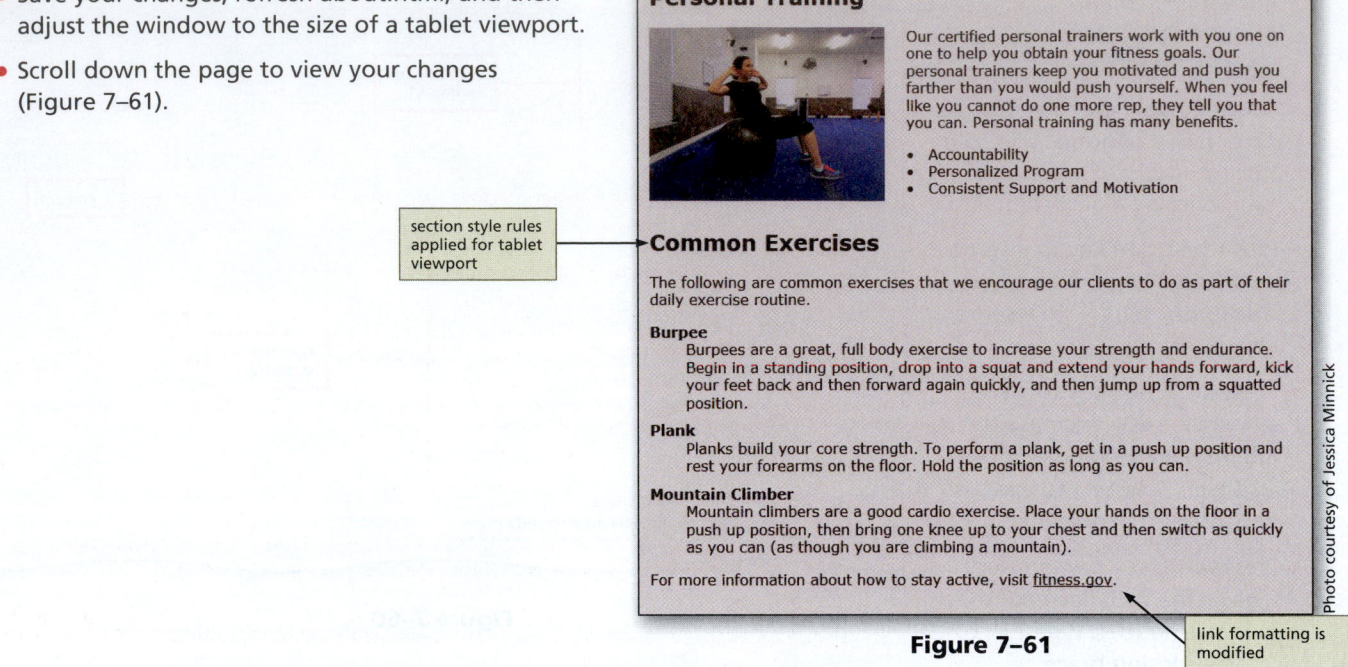

section style rules applied for tablet viewport

link formatting is modified

Photo courtesy of Jessica Minnick

Figure 7–61

To Style the About Us Page for a Desktop Viewport

1 MODIFY HOME PAGE | 2 STYLE HOME PAGE | 3 MODIFY ABOUT US PAGE | **4 STYLE ABOUT US PAGE**
5 MODIFY & STYLE CONTACT US PAGE | 6 CREATE & STYLE NUTRITION PAGE

Update the style sheet for the desktop viewport to format the **section** elements and to revise style rules for the classes on the About Us page. *Why? Update the styles for the desktop viewport in the new design.* First, remove the style rule for the items class. Next, add a new style rule for a **section** element to apply color and margin properties. Then, create a new style rule to specify the color of anchor elements within a section. The following steps update the style rules for the desktop viewport.

 1

- Delete Lines 306 through 309 to remove the style rule. If necessary, move the body comment up to Line 306.

- Tap or click at the end of Line 316, and then press the ENTER key twice to insert new Lines 317 and 318.

- On Line 318, type **/* Style specifies color and left margin for the section element */** to insert a comment.

- Press the ENTER key to insert a new Line 319, and then type **section {** to insert a new selector.

.items style rule removed

Line 306

```
306  /* Style specifies a gradient for the body element */
307  body {
308      background-color: #FFFFFF;
309  }
...
318  /* Style specifies color and left margin for the section
         element */
319  section {
320      color: #FFFFFF;
321      margin-left: 1em;
322      padding-bottom: 5em;
323  }
```

comment

style rule for section

Figure 7–62

- Press the ENTER key to insert a new Line 320, increase the indent, and then type **color: #FFFFFF;** to insert a new property and value.

- Press the ENTER key to insert a new Line 321, and then type **margin-left: 1em;** to insert a new property and value.

- Press the ENTER key to insert a new Line 322, and then type **padding-bottom: 5em;** to insert a new property and value.

- Press the ENTER key to insert a new Line 323, decrease the indent, and then type **}** to insert a closing brace (Figure 7–62).

2

- Press the ENTER key twice to insert new Lines 324 and 325.

- On Line 325, type `/* Style for anchor element within the section element */` to insert a new comment.

- Press the ENTER key to insert a new Line 326, and then type `section a {` to insert a new selector.

- Press the ENTER key to insert a new Line 327, increase the indent, and then type `color: #FFFFFF;` to insert a new property and value.

```
                                                                    comment

  Line 325          325  /* Style for anchor element within the section element */
                    326  section a {
                    327      color: #FFFFFF;              style rule for
                    328  }                                section a
                    329
                    330  /* Style for paragraph within the section element */     comment
                    331  section p {
                    332      margin-left: 0;              style rule for
                    333  }                                section p
                    334
                    335  }                          desktop media query closing brace
```

Figure 7–63

- Press the ENTER key to insert a new Line 328, decrease the indent, and then type `}` to insert a closing brace.

- Press the ENTER key twice to insert new Lines 329 and 330.

- On Line 330, type `/* Style for paragraph element within the section element */` to insert a new comment.

- Press the ENTER to insert a new Line 331, and then type `section p {` to insert a new selector.

- Press the ENTER key to insert a new Line 332, increase the indent, and then type `margin-left: 0;` to insert a new property and value.

- Press the ENTER key to insert a new Line 333, decrease the indent, and then type `}` to insert a closing brace (Figure 7–63).

3

- Save your changes, refresh about.html, and then adjust the window to the size of a desktop viewport.

- Scroll down the page to view your changes (Figure 7–64).

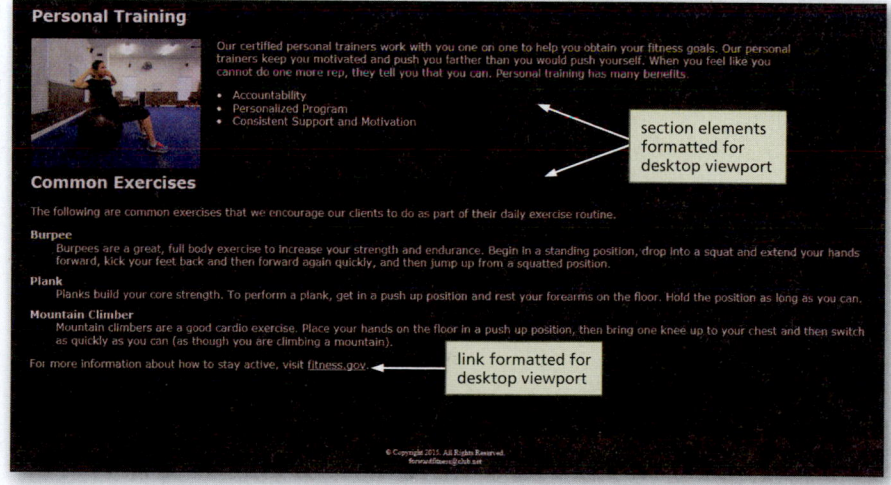

Figure 7–64

Photo courtesy of Jessica Minnick

Updating the Contact Us Page

The home page and About Us pages now display the new look and design for the Forward Fitness Club. Next, revise the Contact Us page elements and style the page according to the new design.

The Contact Us page contains a telephone link and an email link; however, these links cover surrounding content. Wrap the telephone link and email link within paragraph elements, and then create a new style rule for tablet and desktop viewports to remove the button look of these elements.

To Modify the Contact Us Page

Wrap the telephone link and email link within separate paragraph elements on the Contact Us page. **Why?** *Wrapping these elements within a paragraph element places each element within its own paragraph and subsequently unblocks its surrounding content.* The following steps add paragraphs elements, add a class attribute and value, and delete line breaks in the Contact Us page.

- Open contact.html in your text editor to prepare to modify it.

- Tap or click at the end of Line 38, and then replace the line break tag with a `</p>` tag to insert an ending paragraph tag.

- Tap or click at the beginning of Line 39, and then insert a `<p>` tag to insert a starting paragraph tag.

Figure 7–65

- Tap or click at the end of Line 42, and then replace the line break tag with a `</p>` tag to insert an ending paragraph tag.

- Tap or click at the beginning of Line 43, and then insert a `<p>` tag to insert a starting paragraph tag.

- On Line 43, insert `class="contact"` within the email anchor element to insert a new class.

- Delete the line breaks on Line 44 to remove them (Figure 7–65).

Q&A What is the purpose of the contact class?

In future steps, you will create a style rule for the contact class to format the email link for tablet and desktop viewports.

- Save your changes.

To Style the Contact Us Page

Update the style sheet for the tablet viewport to format heading two elements and the email link on the Contact Us page. **Why?** *Change the text color of the heading two element and remove the button appearance of the email link, as this style is for the mobile viewport.* Create a new style rule within the tablet media query to style the heading two element within the `main` element. Then create a new style rule within the tablet media query to style the contact class. Specify a background color, color, and text decoration. The following steps update the style rules for the tablet desktop viewports.

1

- If necessary, reopen styles.css to prepare to modify it.

- Tap or click at the end of Line 214, and then press the ENTER key twice to insert new Lines 215 and 216.

- On Line 216, type /* Style for contact class */ to insert a comment.

- Press the ENTER key to insert a new Line 217, and then type .contact { to insert a new selector.

Figure 7–66

- Press the ENTER key to insert a new Line 218, increase the indent, and then type background-color: transparent; to insert a new property and value.

- Press the ENTER key to insert a new Line 219, and then type color: #1D1D1C; to insert a new property and value.

- Press the ENTER key to insert a new Line 220, and then type padding: 0; to insert a new property and value.

- Press the ENTER key to insert a new Line 221, and then type text-decoration: underline; to insert a new property and value.

- Press the ENTER key to insert a new Line 222, decrease the indent, and then type } to insert a closing brace (Figure 7–66).

2

- Save your changes, open contact.html in a browser, and then adjust the window to the size of a tablet viewport (Figure 7–67).

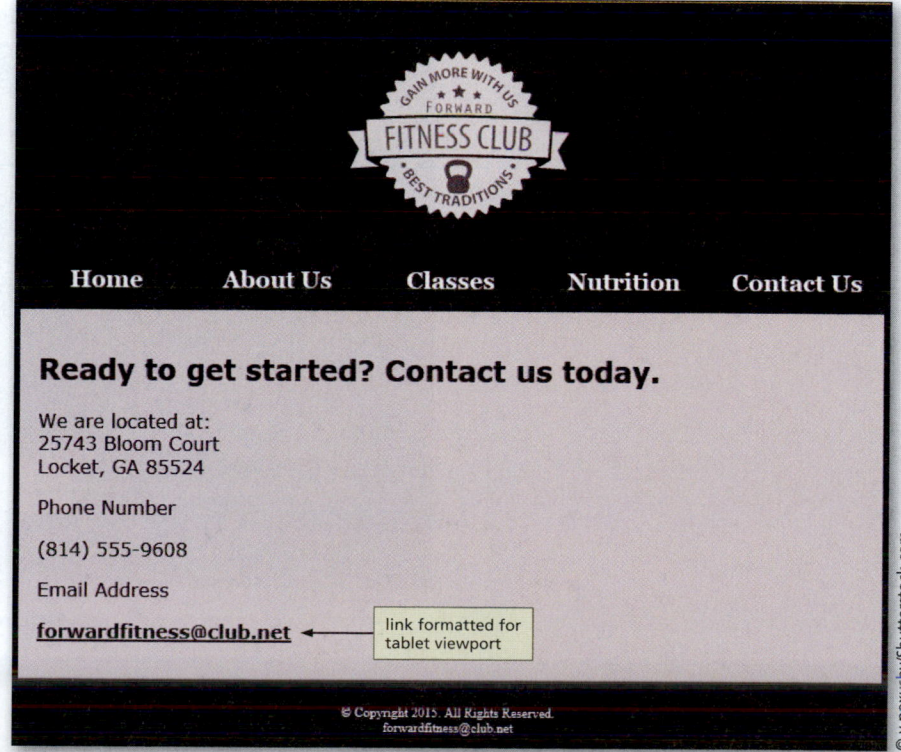

Figure 7–67

3

- Tap or click at the end of Line 341, and then press the ENTER key twice to insert new Lines 342 and 343.

- On Line 343, type `/* Style for main h2 element */` to insert a new comment.

- Press the ENTER key to insert a new Line 344, and then type `main h2 {` to insert a new selector.

- Press the ENTER key to insert a new Line 345, increase the indent, and then type `color: #FFFFFF;` to insert a new property and value.

Figure 7–68

- Press the ENTER key to insert a new Line 346, decrease the indent, and then type `}` to insert a closing brace.

- Press the ENTER key twice to insert new Lines 347 and 348.

- On Line 348, type `/* Style for contact class */` to insert a new comment.

- Press the ENTER key to insert a new Line 349, and then type `.contact {` to insert a new selector.

- Press the ENTER key to insert a new Line 350, increase the indent, and then type `color: #FFFFFF;` to insert a new property and value.

- Press the ENTER key to insert a new Line 351, decrease the indent, and then type `}` to insert a closing brace (Figure 7–68).

4

- Save your changes, refresh contact.html, and then adjust the window to the size of a desktop viewport (Figure 7–69).

Figure 7–69

Break Point: If you want to take a break, this is a good place to do so. You can exit the text editor now. To resume at a later time, run your text editor, open the file called styles.css, and continue following the steps from this location forward.

Creating the Nutrition Page

The home, About Us, and Contact Us pages now display the new look and design for the Forward Fitness Club. Next, you create the Nutrition page, which provides tips for good nutrition, guidelines for a healthy diet, and a featured recipe of the week. To have the new page follow the same design as the other pages in the site, use the fitness template to create the page and then add HTML5 semantic elements. Style the page to be consistent with the other pages.

You drafted a wireframe for the Nutrition page in tablet and desktop viewports, which uses article and aside elements, as shown in Figures 7–70 and 7–71. This page uses a three-column layout for tablet and desktop viewports. The mobile layout will remain the same as the other pages, a one-column layout. Create the nutrition page and then update the style sheet.

Nutrition page wireframe for tablet viewport

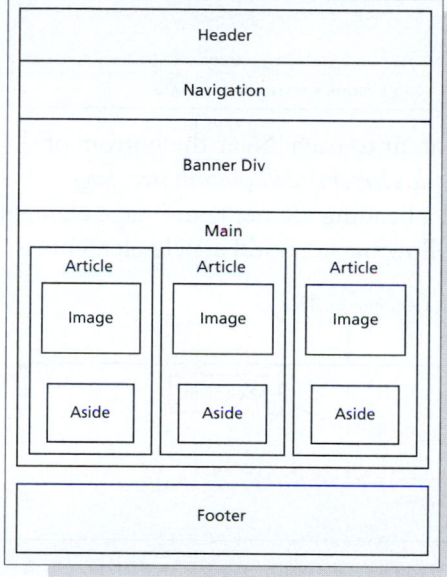

Figure 7–70

Nutrition page wireframe for desktop viewport

Figure 7–71

To create the three-column layout, modify existing style rules and create new style rules for tablet and desktop viewports. Use the **overflow property** to specify how to manage content when it "spills over" into another element. Similar to the clear property, the overflow property can help resolve display issues related to a nearby floating element.

To Create the Nutrition Page

Use the template, fitness.html, to create the Nutrition page. After creating the page, insert a banner image. The following step creates the Nutrition page.

1 Open fitness.html in your text editor, and then save the page as nutrition.html in your fitness folder.

2 Update the comment with your name and today's date, tap or click at the end of Line 28, and then press the ENTER key twice to insert new Lines 29 and 30.

3 On Line 30, type `<!-- Nutrition Page Banner -->` to insert a comment.

4 Press the ENTER key to insert new Line 31, and then type `<div id="banner" class="desktop">` to insert a div tag.

BTW

Multiple Columns Using CSS3
You can create columns using the CSS3 property called column-count. The value used for this property indicates the desired number of columns. Several other properties can be used with the column-count property, such as column-gap, column-width, and column-rule.

5 Press the ENTER key to insert new Line 32, increase the indent, and then type `<img src="images/nutritionBanner.jpg" alt="nutrition banner image">` to insert an image.

6 Press the ENTER key to insert new Line 33, decrease the indent, and then type `</div>` to insert a closing div tag (Figure 7–72).

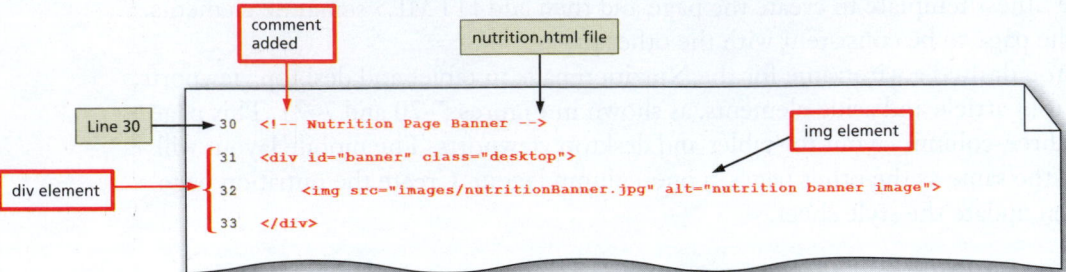

Figure 7–72

To Add article and aside Elements to the Nutrition Page

1 MODIFY HOME PAGE | 2 STYLE HOME PAGE | 3 MODIFY ABOUT US PAGE | 4 STYLE ABOUT US PAGE

5 MODIFY & STYLE CONTACT US PAGE | **6 CREATE & STYLE NUTRITION PAGE**

Insert three article elements within the **main** element and add content to each. Near the bottom of each article, insert an aside element with additional content. **Why?** *The article elements will contain new page content, including tips, guidelines, and recipes.* Inside each article element, add a heading element, an image element, paragraph elements, unordered list elements, and an aside element. The following steps add article elements to the Nutrition page.

1

- In nutrition.html, tap or click at the end of Line 36, and then press the ENTER key twice to insert new Lines 37 and 38.

- On Line 38, type `<article>` to insert an article tag.

- Press the ENTER key to insert a new Line 39, increase the indent, and then type `<h2>Food for Thought</h2>` to insert a heading two element.

- Press the ENTER key to insert a new Line 40, and then type `<img src="images/nutrition1. jpg" alt="food for thought image" class="desktop">` to insert an image element.

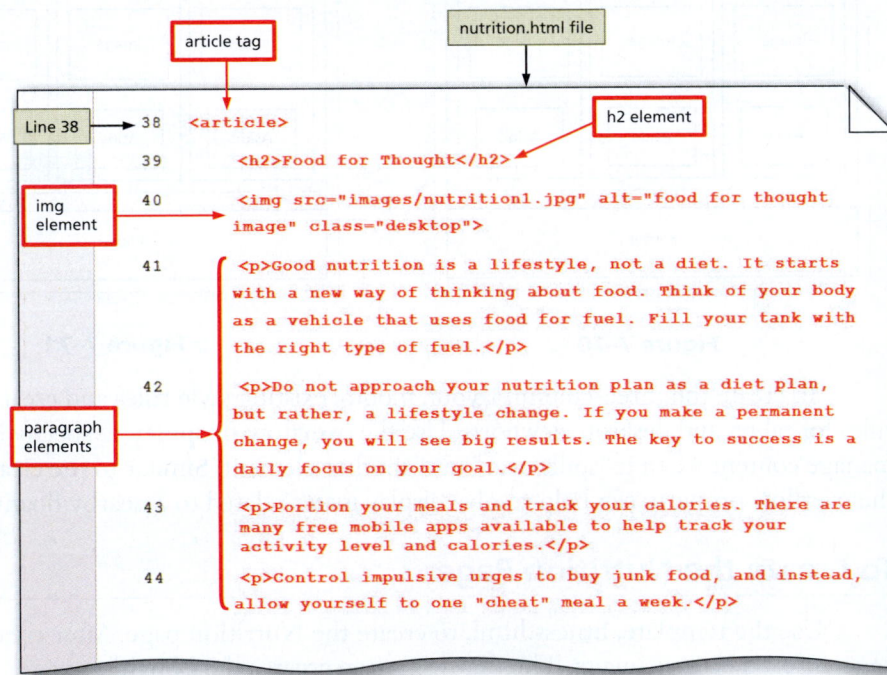

Figure 7–73

- Open the nutritionText.txt file located in the fitness folder provided with the Data Files for Students, select Lines 2 through 5, and then press CTRL+C to copy the text.

- In the nutrition.html file, press the ENTER key to insert a new Line 41, and then press CTRL+V to paste the new content.

- Indent Lines 42 through 44 to align with the img element on Line 40 (Figure 7–73).

2

- Tap or click at the end of Line 44, press the ENTER key to insert a new Line 45, and then type `<aside>Did you know the average American consumes 3 lbs of sugar each week?</aside>` to insert an aside element.

- Press the ENTER key to insert a new Line 46, decrease the indent, and then type `</article>` to insert an ending article tag (Figure 7–74).

aside element

```
45      <aside>Did you know the average American consumes 3 lbs
            of sugar each week?</aside>

46      </article>
```

Line 45

ending article tag

Figure 7–74

3

- Press the ENTER key twice to insert new Lines 47 and 48.

- On Line 48 type `<article>` to insert an article tag.

- Press the ENTER key to insert a new Line 49, increase the indent, and then type `<h2>What to Eat</h2>` to insert a heading two element.

- Press the ENTER key to insert a new Line 50, and then type `<img src="images/nutrition2. jpg" alt="food image" class="desktop">` to insert an image element.

- In the nutritionText.txt file, select Lines 8 through 17, and then press CTRL+C to copy the text.

- In the nutrition.html file, press the ENTER key to insert a new Line 51, and then press CTRL+V to paste the new content.

- Indent Lines 52 through 60 to line up with the img element on Line 50 (Figure 7–75).

article tag

```
48      <article>

49          <h2>What to Eat</h2>

50          <img src="images/nutrition2.jpg" alt="food image"
                class="desktop">

51          <p>Use the following as a guideline:</p>

52          <ul>

53              <li>Protein, such as eggs, chicken, and lean red
                    meat</li>

54              <li>Vegetables, but avoid corn and peas</li>

55              <li>Fruit</li>

56              <li>Fat, such as olive oil, nuts, and seeds</li>

57          </ul>

58          <p>Limit the consumption of bread, pasta, white potatoes,
                and processed food. These foods are high in
                carbohydrates.</p>

59          <p>When you shop for groceries, shop the outside isles
                and buy organic when possible. Stock up on fresh
                vegetables, almond flour, and flax seed.</p>

60          <p>Check out our Meal of the Week for new meal ideas.</p>
```

Line 48

h2 element

img element

paragraph element

unordered list

paragraph element

Figure 7–75

4

- Tap or click at the end of Line 60, press the ENTER key to insert a new Line 61, and then type `<aside>Did you know that avocados are a good source of Vitamin B?</aside>` to insert an aside element.

- Press the ENTER key to insert a new Line 62, decrease the indent, and then type `</article>` to insert an ending article tag (Figure 7–76).

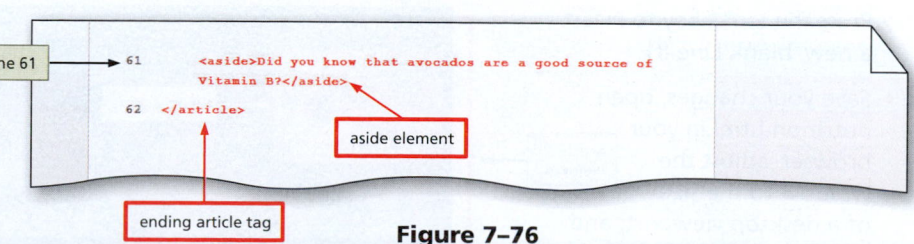

```
61      <aside>Did you know that avocados are a good source of
            Vitamin B?</aside>

62      </article>
```

Line 61

aside element

ending article tag

Figure 7–76

5

- Press the ENTER key twice to insert new Lines 63 and 64.

- On Line 64, type `<article>` to insert an article tag.

- Press the ENTER key to insert a new Line 65, increase the indent, and then type `<h2>Meal of the Week</h2>` to insert a heading two element.

- Press the ENTER key to insert a new Line 66, and then type `<img src="images/nutrition3. jpg" alt=" herb roasted chicken image" class="desktop">` to insert an image element.

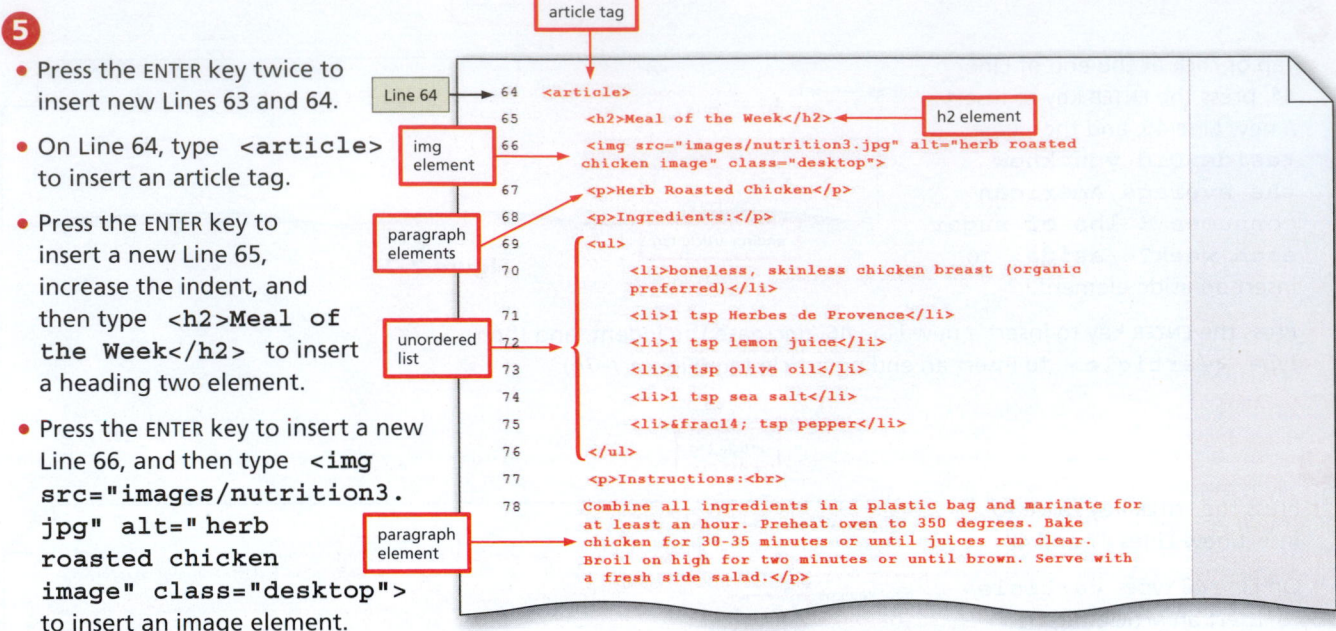

Figure 7–77

- In the nutritionText.txt file, select Lines 20 through 31, and then press CTRL+C to copy Lines 20 through 31.

- In the nutrition.html file, press the ENTER key to insert a new Line 67, and then press CTRL+V to paste the new content.

- Indent Lines 68 through 78 to line up with the img element on Line 66 (Figure 7–77).

Q&A | What does ¼ represent?
This is an HTML entity used to display ¼ on a webpage.

6

- Tap or click at the end of Line 78, press the ENTER key to insert a new Line 79, and then type `<aside>Did you know the average active adult should consume 2,000 calories a day?</aside>` to insert an aside element.

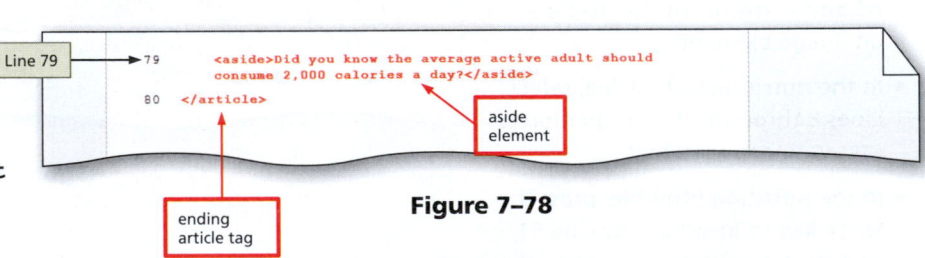

Figure 7–78

- Press the ENTER key to insert a new Line 80, decrease the indent, and then type `</article>` to insert an ending article tag (Figure 7–78).

7

- Press the ENTER key to insert a new, blank Line 81.

- Save your changes, open nutrition.html in your browser, adjust the window to the size of a desktop viewport, and then scroll down the page to view the main content (Figure 7–79).

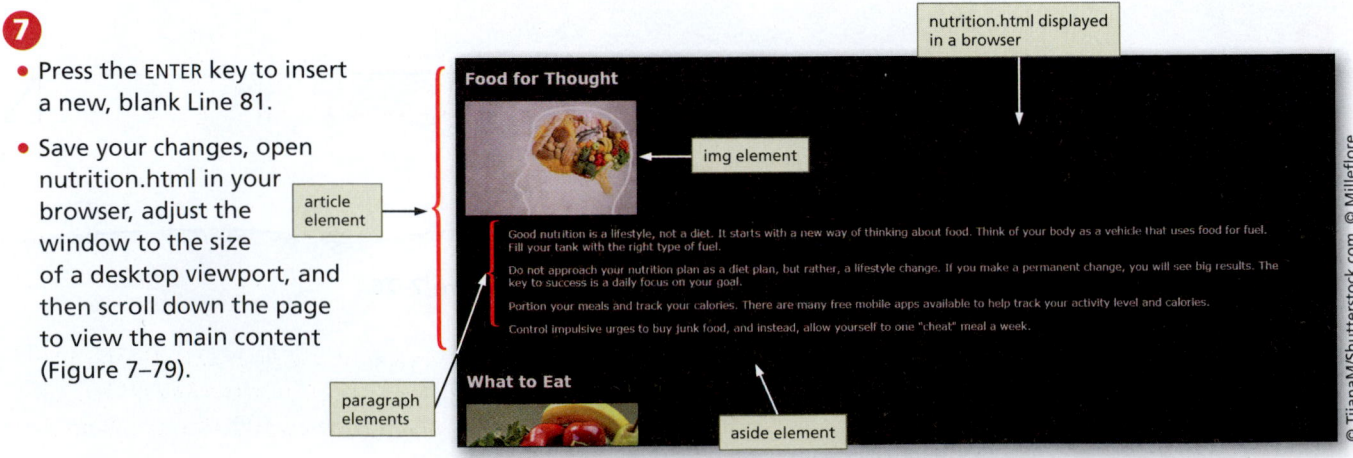

Figure 7–79

To Style the Nutrition Page for a Mobile Viewport

Create a new style rule to format the aside elements with an italic font style. ***Why?*** *Format the aside element differently from the rest of the article so it stands out.* The following steps create a style rule for the aside element.

- If necessary, reopen styles.css to prepare to modify it.

- Tap or click at the end of Line 112, and then press the ENTER key twice to insert new Lines 113 and 114.

- On Line 114, type **/* Style for aside element */** to insert a comment.

- Press the ENTER key to insert a new Line 115, and then type **aside {** to insert a new selector.

- Press the ENTER key to insert a new Line 116, increase the indent, and then type **font-style: italic;** to insert a new property and value.

- Press the ENTER key to insert a new Line 117, decrease the indent, and then type **}** to insert a closing brace (Figure 7–80).

Figure 7–80

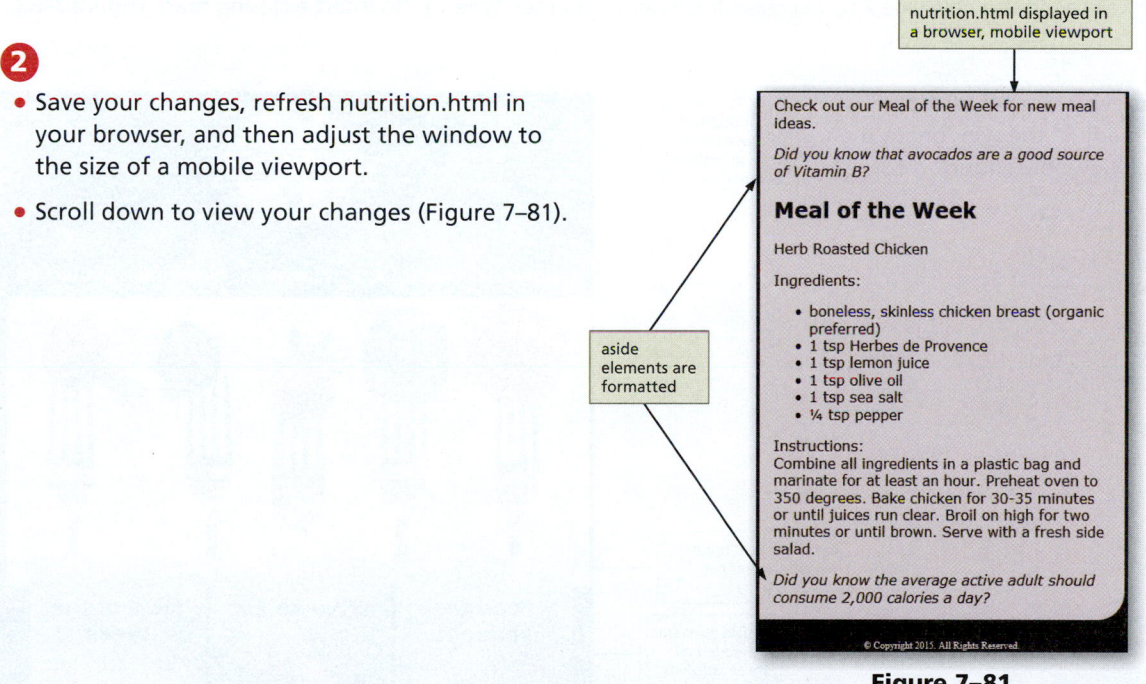

- Save your changes, refresh nutrition.html in your browser, and then adjust the window to the size of a mobile viewport.

- Scroll down to view your changes (Figure 7–81).

Figure 7–81

To Create a Three-Column Layout for the Nutrition Page in a Tablet Viewport

The wireframe for the Nutrition page uses a three-column layout. Create a new style rule to float each article element to the left. ***Why?*** *This style rule formats each article element so it appears in its own column.* Update the style sheet for the tablet viewport to format other aspects of the new article elements added to the Nutrition page. The following steps add a style rule for the tablet viewport.

1

- In styles.css, tap or click at the end of Line 227, and then press the ENTER key twice to insert new Lines 228 and 229.

- On Line 229, type `/* Style for article element */` to insert a comment.

- Press the ENTER key to insert a new Line 230, and then type `article {` to insert a new selector.

- Press the ENTER key to insert a new Line 231, increase the indent, and then type `background-color: #C1D9CA;` to insert a new property and value.

- Press the ENTER key to insert a new Line 232, and then type `float: left;` to insert a new property and value.

- Press the ENTER key to insert a new Line 233, and then type `margin: 0.5%;` to insert a new property and value.

- Press the ENTER key to insert a new Line 234, and then type `padding: 0.5%;` to insert a new property and value.

- Press the ENTER key to insert a new Line 235, and then type `text-align: center;` to insert a new property and value.

- Press the ENTER key to insert a new Line 236, and then type `width: 31%;` to insert a new property and value.

- Press the ENTER key to insert a new Line 237, decrease the indent, and then type `}` to insert a closing brace (Figure 7–82).

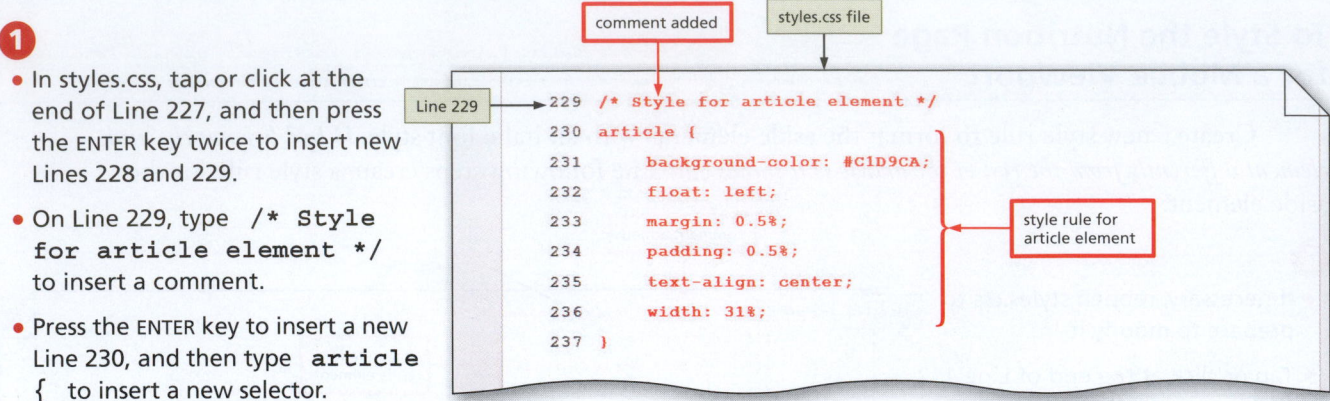

comment added · styles.css file · Line 229 · style rule for article element

```
229    /* Style for article element */
230    article {
231        background-color: #C1D9CA;
232        float: left;
233        margin: 0.5%;
234        padding: 0.5%;
235        text-align: center;
236        width: 31%;
237    }
```

Figure 7–82

2

- Save your changes, refresh nutrition.html, and then adjust the window to the size of a tablet viewport (Figure 7–83).

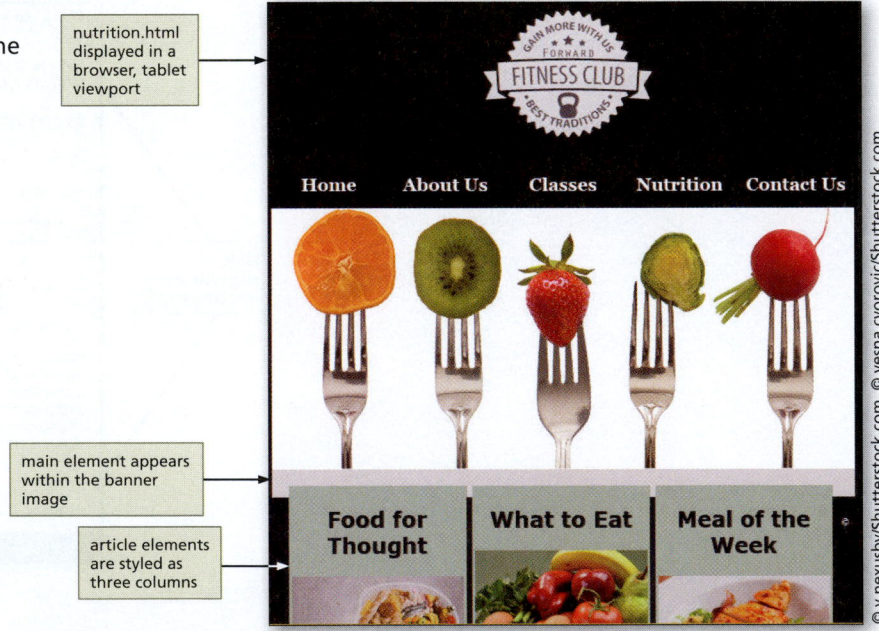

nutrition.html displayed in a browser, tablet viewport

main element appears within the banner image

article elements are styled as three columns

© v nexusby/Shutterstock.com, © vesna cvorovic/Shutterstock.com, © TijanaM/Shutterstock.com, © Milleflore Images/Shutterstock.com, © verchik/Shutterstock.com

Figure 7–83

To Apply the Overflow Property to the main Element Style Rule

1 MODIFY HOME PAGE | 2 STYLE HOME PAGE | 3 MODIFY ABOUT US PAGE | 4 STYLE ABOUT US PAGE
5 MODIFY & STYLE CONTACT US PAGE | 6 CREATE & STYLE NUTRITION PAGE

As shown in Figure 7–83, the **main** element is not in the correct area. The **float** property used within the article style rule displaces the **main** element to the banner image area. To correct this issue, apply an **overflow** property with a value of **auto** to the **main** style rule contained within the tablet media query. **Why?** *Apply the overflow property to the main element so it is displayed below the banner image.* The following step updates the main style rule for the tablet viewport.

1

- Tap or click at the end of Line 141, and then press the ENTER key to insert a new Line 142.

- On Line 142, type **overflow: auto;** to add a property and value.

- Save your changes, refresh nutrition.html, and scroll down if necessary to view the changes (Figure 7–84).

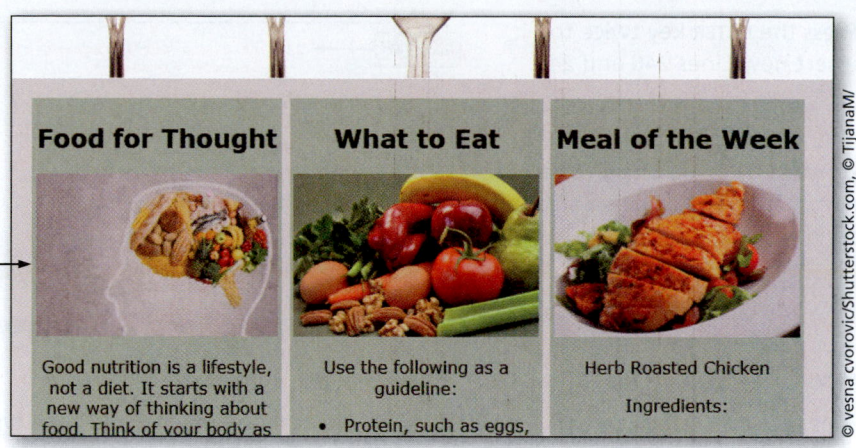

main element appears below banner image

Food for Thought

Good nutrition is a lifestyle, not a diet. It starts with a new way of thinking about food. Think of your body as

What to Eat

Use the following as a guideline:

- Protein, such as eggs,

Meal of the Week

Herb Roasted Chicken

Ingredients:

© vesna cvorovic/Shutterstock.com, © TijianaM/ Shutterstock.com, © Milleflore Images/Shutterstock. com, © verchik/Shutterstock.com

Figure 7–84

To Style the article Element for the Nutrition Page

1 MODIFY HOME PAGE | 2 STYLE HOME PAGE | 3 MODIFY ABOUT US PAGE | 4 STYLE ABOUT US PAGE
5 MODIFY & STYLE CONTACT US PAGE | 6 CREATE & STYLE NUTRITION PAGE

The Nutrition page now uses a three-column layout; however, the content within each article needs to be formatted. Center-align the image elements and apply a border around image. Left-align the paragraph and unordered list elements and change the font color. *Why? Applying these changes improves readability.* First, create a new style rule for the main article **img** element. Next, create a new style rule for the main article paragraph element. Next, create a new style rule for the main article unordered list element. The following steps update the style rules for the tablet viewport.

1

- Tap or click at the end of Line 238, and then press the ENTER key twice to insert new Lines 239 and 240.

- On Line 240, type **/* Style for image element contained within the main article element */** to insert a comment.

- Press the ENTER key to insert a new Line 241, and then type **main article img {** to insert a new selector.

- Press the ENTER key to insert a new Line 242, increase the indent, and then type **border: solid 0.1em #1D1D1C;** to insert a new property and value.

- Press the ENTER key to insert a new Line 243, and then type **margin-left: auto;** to insert a new property and value.

- Press the ENTER key to insert a new Line 244, and then type **margin-right: auto;** to insert a new property and value.

- Press the ENTER key to insert a new Line 245, decrease the indent, and then type **}** to insert a closing brace (Figure 7–85).

comment added

Line 240

```
240  /* Style for image element contained within the main article
     element */
241  main article img {
242      border: solid 0.1em #1D1D1C;
243      margin-left: auto;
244      margin-right: auto;
245  }
```

style rule for main article img element

Figure 7–85

2

- Press the ENTER key twice to insert new Lines 246 and 247.

- On Line 247, type **/* Style for paragraph element contained within the main article element */** to insert a comment.

- Press the ENTER key to insert a new Line 248, and then type **main article p {** to insert a new selector.

Figure 7–86

- Press the ENTER key to insert a new Line 249, increase the indent, and then type **color: #000000;** to insert a new property and value.

- Press the ENTER key to insert a new Line 250, and then type **margin-top: 2%;** to insert a new property and value.

- Press the ENTER key to insert a new Line 251, and then type **padding: 1%;** to insert a new property and value.

- Press the ENTER key to insert a new Line 252, and then type **text-align: left;** to insert a new property and value.

- Press the ENTER key to insert a new Line 253, decrease the indent, and then type **}** to insert a closing brace (Figure 7–86).

3

- Press the ENTER key twice to insert new Lines 254 and 255.

- On Line 255, type **/* Style for unordered list element contained within the main article element */** to insert a comment.

Figure 7–87

- Press the ENTER key to insert a new Line 256, and then type **main article ul {** to insert a new selector.

- Press the ENTER key to insert a new Line 257, increase the indent, and then type **text-align: left;** to insert a new property and value.

- Press the ENTER key to insert a new Line 258, decrease the indent, and then type **}** to insert a closing brace (Figure 7–87).

4

- Save your changes, refresh nutrition.html, and then scroll down the page to view your changes (Figure 7–88).

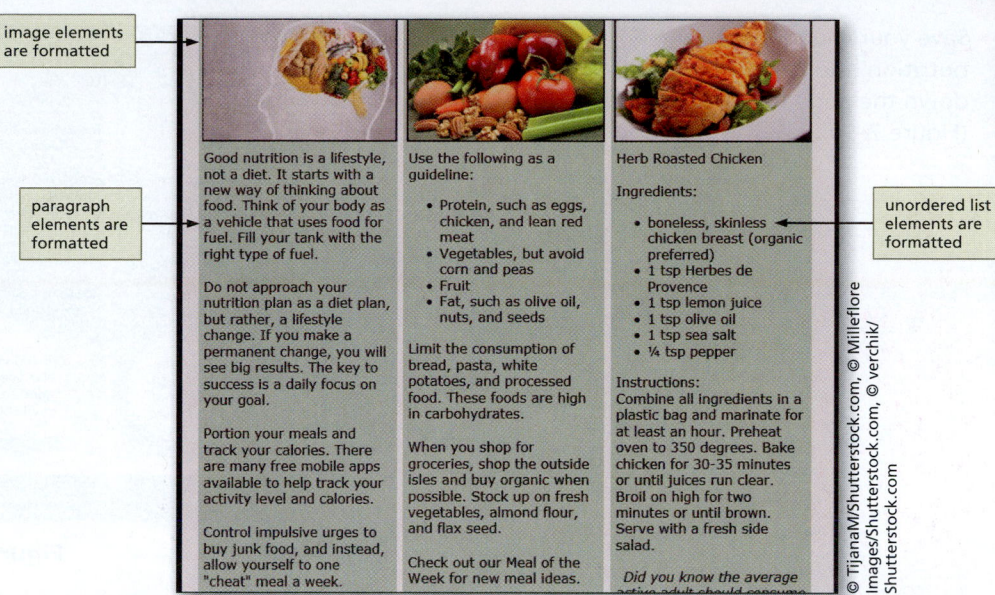

image elements are formatted

paragraph elements are formatted

unordered list elements are formatted

© TijanaM/Shutterstock.com, © Milleflore Images/Shutterstock.com, © verchik/ Shutterstock.com

Figure 7–88

To Style the aside Element for the Nutrition Page

1 MODIFY HOME PAGE | 2 STYLE HOME PAGE | 3 MODIFY ABOUT US PAGE | 4 STYLE ABOUT US PAGE
5 MODIFY & STYLE CONTACT US PAGE | 6 CREATE & STYLE NUTRITION PAGE

An **aside** element is contained at the bottom of each **article** element. The content provided in the **aside** element gives more information pertaining to that particular article. Format this element to stand out and improve its visibility. *Why? The format of an aside element should distinguish it from other elements on the webpage.* Create a style rule for the **aside** element and apply a rounded border, a background color, box-shadow effect, padding, and margin. The following steps create a new style rule for the tablet viewport.

- Tap or click at the end of Line 258, and then press the ENTER key twice to insert new Lines 259 and 260.

- On Line 260, type **/* Style for aside element */** to insert a comment.

- Press the ENTER key to insert a new Line 261, and then type **aside {** to insert a new selector.

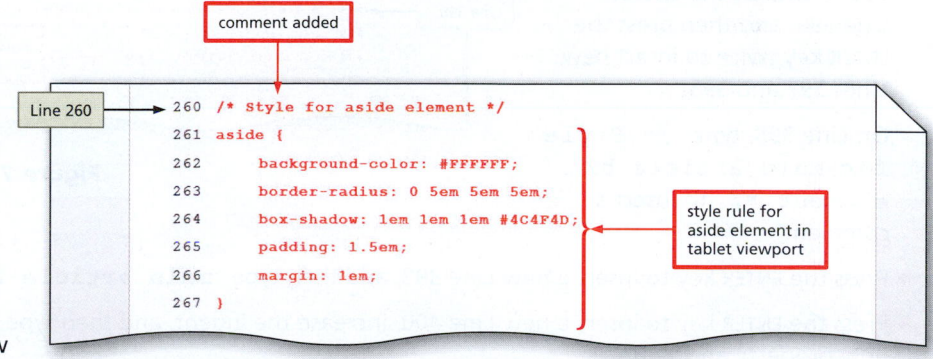

comment added

Line 260

```
260   /* Style for aside element */
261   aside {
262       background-color: #FFFFFF;
263       border-radius: 0 5em 5em 5em;
264       box-shadow: 1em 1em 1em #4C4F4D;
265       padding: 1.5em;
266       margin: 1em;
267   }
```

style rule for aside element in tablet viewport

Figure 7–89

- Press the ENTER key to insert a new Line 262, increase the indent, and then type **background-color: #FFFFFF;** to insert a new property and value.

- Press the ENTER key to insert a new Line 263, and then type **border-radius: 0 5em 5em 5em;** to insert a new property and value.

- Press the ENTER key to insert a new Line 264, and then type **box-shadow: 1em 1em 1em #4C4F4D;** to insert a new property and value.

- Press the ENTER key to insert a new Line 265, and then type **padding: 1.5em;** to insert a new property and value.

- Press the ENTER key to insert a new Line 266, and then type **margin: 1em;** to insert a new property and value.

- Press the ENTER key to insert a new Line 267, decrease the indent, and then type **}** to insert a closing brace (Figure 7–89).

2

- Save your changes, refresh nutrition.html, and then scroll down the page to view your changes (Figure 7–90).

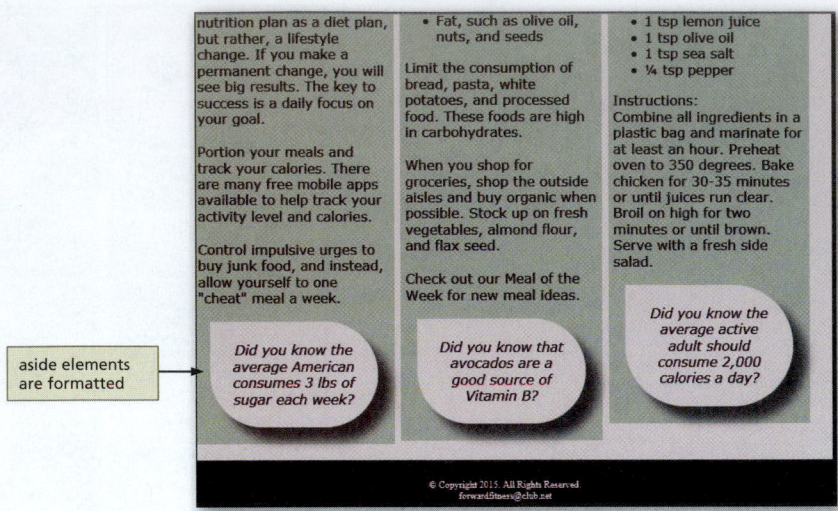

Figure 7–90

To Style the article h2 Element for the Nutrition Page in a Desktop Viewport

1 MODIFY HOME PAGE | 2 STYLE HOME PAGE | 3 MODIFY ABOUT US PAGE | 4 STYLE ABOUT US PAGE

5 MODIFY & STYLE CONTACT US PAGE | **6 CREATE & STYLE NUTRITION PAGE**

The **h2** element in a desktop viewport is the last element that needs to be formatted. Create a style rule to apply a different font color. *Why? The font color is too light to read the text easily in a desktop viewport.* Create a new style rule for the main article **h2** element to apply a font color. The following steps update the style rules for the desktop viewport.

1

- Tap or click at the end of Line 396, and then press the ENTER key twice to insert new Lines 397 and 398.

- On Line 398, type **/* Style for main article h2 element */** to insert a comment.

Figure 7–91

- Press the ENTER key to insert a new Line 399, and then type **main article h2 {** to insert a new selector.

- Press the ENTER key to insert a new Line 400, increase the indent, and then type **color: #000000;** to insert a new property and value.

- Press the ENTER key to insert a new Line 401, decrease the indent, and then type **}** to insert a closing brace (Figure 7–91).

2

- Save your changes, refresh nutrition.html, adjust the browser window to the size of a desktop viewport, and then scroll down the page to view your changes (Figure 7–92).

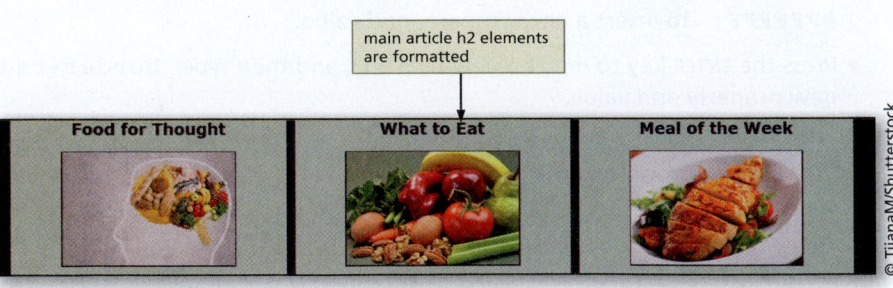

Figure 7–92

To Validate the Style Sheet

Always run your files through W3C's validator to check the document for errors. If the document has any errors, validating gives you a chance to identify and correct them. Validation is also an effective troubleshooting tool during the development process and adds a valuable level of professionalism to your work. The following steps validate a CSS document.

1 Open your browser and type `http://jigsaw.w3.org/css-validator/` in the address bar to display the W3C CSS Validation Service page.

2 Tap or click the By file upload tab to display the Validate by File Upload information.

3 Tap or click the Choose file button to display the File Upload dialog box.

4 Navigate to your css folder to find the styles.css file.

5 Tap or click the styles.css document to select it.

6 Tap or click the Open button to upload the selected file to the W3C CSS validator.

7 Tap or click the Check button to send the document through the validator and display the validation results page.

To Validate the HTML Files

Every time you create a new webpage, run it through W3C's validator to check the document for errors. If any errors exist, you need to correct them. Validation is also an effective troubleshooting tool during the development process and adds a valuable level of professionalism to your work. The following steps validate an HTML document.

1 Open your browser and type `http://validator.w3.org/` in the address bar to display the W3C validator page.

2 Tap or click the Validate by File Upload tab to display the Validate by File Upload tab information.

3 Tap or click the Browse button to display the Choose File to Upload dialog box.

4 Navigate to your website template folder to find the nutrition.html file.

5 Tap or click the nutrition.html document to select it.

6 Tap or click the Open button to upload it to the W3C validator.

7 Tap or click the Check button to send the document through the validator and display the validation results page.

8 If necessary, correct any errors, save your changes, and run through the validator again to revalidate the page.

9 Follow these steps to validate the about.html, contact.html, index.html, and fitness.html pages and correct any errors.

Chapter Summary

In this chapter, you learned how to use the HTML5 figure, section, article, and aside semantic elements. You added these elements to the webpages in the website and then created and modified style rules in the style sheet to format the new elements and adapt to a new design. Finally, you added a new page to the website and formatted some of its contents in three columns.

Redesigning the Home Page

Add a figure Element to the Home Page (HTML 326)

Update the Style Sheet for the New Design in a Mobile Viewport (HTML 327)

Add New Style Rules for Anchor Elements in a Mobile Viewport (HTML 329)

Update the Style Sheet for the New Design in a Tablet Viewport (HTML 330)

Add New Style Rules to the Tablet Viewport (HTML 332)

Update the Style Sheet for the New Design in a Desktop Viewport (HTML 334)

Add New Style Rules to the Desktop Viewport (HTML 336)

Updating the About Us Page

Add Section Elements to the About Us Page (HTML 340)

Style the About Us Page for a Tablet Viewport (HTML 342)

Style the About Us Page for a Desktop Viewport (HTML 344)

Updating the Contact Us Page

Modify the Contact Us Page (HTML 346)

Style the Contact Us Page (HTML 346)

Creating the Nutrition Page

Create the Nutrition Page (HTML 349)

Add article and aside Elements to the Nutrition Page (HTML 350)

Style the Nutrition Page for a Mobile Viewport (HTML 353)

Create a Three-Column Layout for the Nutrition Page in a Tablet Viewport (HTML 353)

Apply the Overflow Property to the main Element Style Rule (HTML 354)

Style the article Element for the Nutrition Page (HTML 355)

Style the aside Element for the Nutrition Page (HTML 357)

Style the article h2 Element for the Nutrition Page in a Desktop Viewport (HTML 358)

CONSIDER THIS

How will you improve the design of your website?

Use these guidelines as you complete the assignments in this chapter and create your own webpages outside of this class.

1. Determine a new look and layout for each viewport.

   a. Review color meanings and the best colors to capture your audience's attention.

   b. Design a wireframe for mobile, tablet, and desktop viewports.

   c. Determine what images you will use and whether to display them on a mobile viewport.

2. Determine the layout for tablet and desktop viewports.

   a. Determine the semantic elements needed for your design.

   b. Determine how to style each element.

3. Determine the use of a banner image.

   a. Find banner images appropriate to your site.

   b. Modify the size of the images to use a minimum width of 1,940 pixels.

   c. Optimize the images for web use.

4. Enhance site design with CSS3 properties.

   a. Determine the best use of the opacity property.

   b. Determine the best use of the text-shadow property.

5. Revise media query style rules.

   a. Determine which style rules need to be modified.

   b. Add new style rules as needed to suit your design.

How should you submit solutions to questions in the assignments identified with a ✳ symbol?
Every assignment in this book contains one or more questions identified with a ✳ symbol. These questions require you to think beyond the assigned presentation. Present your solutions to the questions in the format required by your instructor. Possible formats may include one or more of these options: create a document that contains the answer; present your answer to the class; discuss your answer in a group; record the answer as audio or video using a webcam, smartphone, or portable media player; or post answers on a blog, wiki, or website.

Apply Your Knowledge

Reinforce the skills and apply the concepts you learned in this chapter.

Using HTML5 Semantic Elements

Instructions: In this exercise, you will use your text editor to add and style HTML5 semantic elements. You insert section, article, and aside elements in an HTML document. You then add a style rule to format each element. Work with the apply07.html file in the apply folder and the applystyles07.css file in the apply\css folder from the Data Files for Students. The completed webpage is shown in Figure 7–93. You will also use professional web development practices to indent, space, comment, and validate your code.

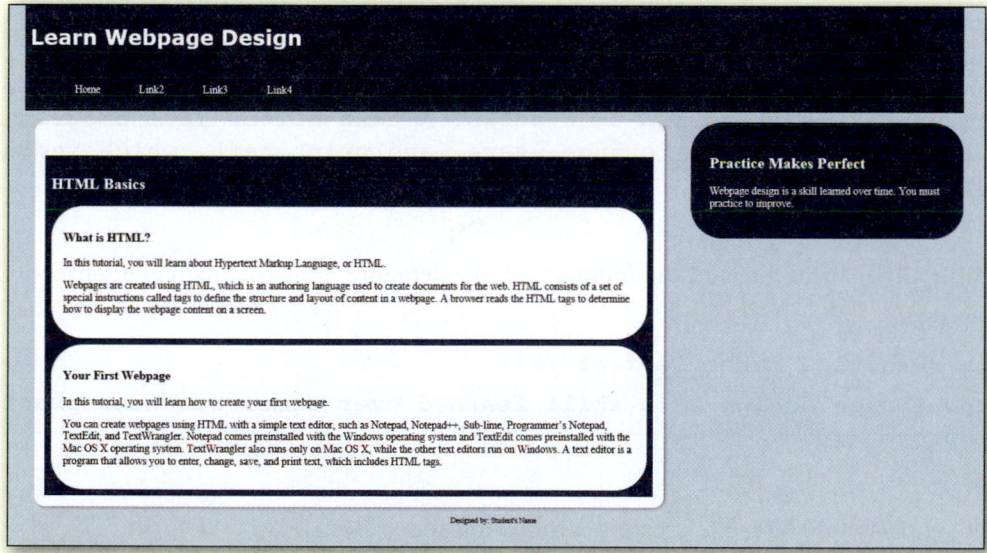

Figure 7–93

Perform the following tasks:

1. Open apply07.html in your browser to view the webpage.

2. Open apply07.html in your text editor, review the page, add a title, modify the comment at the top of the page to include your name and today's date, and replace "Student's Name" with your name in the footer element.

3. Open the applystyles07.css file from the apply\css folder. Modify the comment at the top of the style sheet to include your name and today's date.

4. In the apply07.html file, add a section element within the main element.

5. Add the following heading within the section element:

```
<h2>HTML Basics</h2>
```

Continued >

Apply Your Knowledge *continued*

6. Add the following two article elements within the section element:

```
<article>
   <h3>What is HTML?</h3>
   <p>In this tutorial, you will learn about Hypertext Markup Language,
   or HTML.</p>
   <p>Webpages are created using HTML, which is an authoring language
   used to create documents for the web. HTML consists of a set of spe-
   cial instructions called tags to define the structure and layout of
   content in a webpage. A browser reads the HTML tags to determine how
   to display the webpage content on a screen.</p>
</article>


<article>
   <h3>Your First Webpage</h3>
   <p>In this tutorial, you will learn how to create your first web-
   page.</p>
   <p>You can create webpages using HTML with a simple text editor,
   such as Notepad, Notepad++, Sublime, Programmer's Notepad, TextEdit,
   and TextWrangler. Notepad comes preinstalled with the Windows oper-
   ating system and TextEdit comes preinstalled with the Mac OS X op-
   erating system. TextWrangler also runs only on Mac OS X, while the
   other text editors run on Windows. A text editor is a program that
   allows you to enter, change, save, and print text, which includes
   HTML tags.</p>
</article>
```

7. In the apply07.html file, add the following aside element below the main element:

```
<aside>
   <h2>Practice Makes Perfect</h2>
   <p>Webpage design is a skill learned over time. You must practice to
   improve.</p>
</aside>
```

8. In the applystyles07.css file, create the following style rules:

```
section {
   background-color: #183440;
   color: #FFFFFF;
   margin-top: 4%;
   padding: 1%;
}


article {
   background-color: white;
   border-radius: 3em;
   color: #000000;
   margin-top: 1%;
   padding: 2%;
}
```

```
aside {
    background-color: #183440;
    border-radius: 3em;
    width: 25%;
    float: right;
    padding: 2%;
    margin-top: 1%;
    color: #FFFFFF;
}
```

9. Add appropriate comments above each style rule.

10. Save all of your changes and open the apply07.html in your browser.

11. Validate your HTML document using the W3C validator found at validator.w3.org and fix any errors that are identified.

12. Validate your CSS file using the W3C validator found at http://jigsaw.w3.org/css-validator/ and fix any errors that are identified.

13. Submit the files in a format specified by your instructor.

14. ✸ In step 8, you applied a float property to the aside element. Describe the purpose of the float property and discuss another way to achieve similar results.

Extend Your Knowledge

Extend the skills you learned in this chapter and experiment with new skills. You may need to use additional resources to complete the assignment.

Exploring Column Layouts

Instructions: In this exercise, you research other ways to create a column layout for a webpage.

Perform the following tasks:

1. Use your browser to research different ways to create a multiple-column layout for webpage design.

2. Find at least two different ways to create a column layout and describe the process to create the column layout for each. Include a link to your resources.

3. Provide an example of the code needed to create the column layout.

4. Using what you have learned, create an example HTML webpage and CSS file that uses one of the methods described.

5. Submit your answers in the format specified by your instructor.

6. ✸ In this exercise, you discovered other ways to create a column layout. Use your browser to research grid layouts. Include a description of your findings and a link to your resource(s).

Analyze, Correct, Improve

Analyze a website, correct all errors, and improve it.

Improving an HTML Document with Semantic Markup

Instructions: Work with the analyze07.html file in the analyze folder and the analyzestyles07.css file in the analyze\css folder from the Data Files for Students. The analyze07.html webpage contains generic **div** elements for content and needs to be revised to use HTML5 semantic elements. You then create new style rules to format the semantic elements. Use Figure 9-94 as a guide to correct these files.

Continued >

Analyze, Correct, Improve *continued*

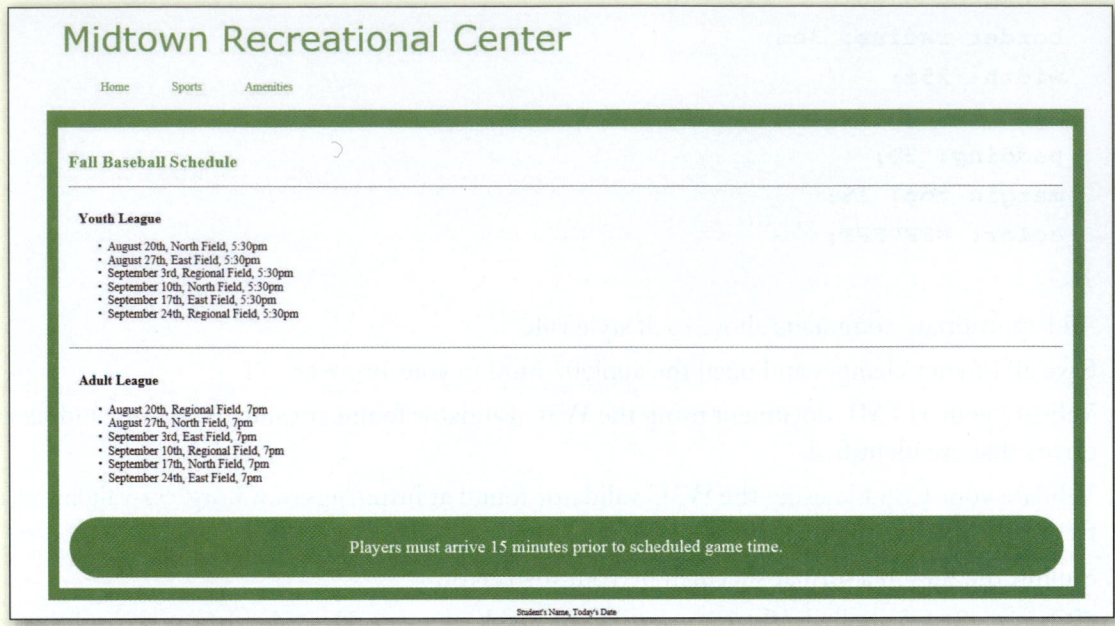

Figure 7–94

1. Correct

    a. Open the analyze07.html file in your editor from the Data Files for Students and then modify the comment at the top of the page to include your name and today's date.

    b. Open the analyzestyles07.css file in your editor from the Data Files for Students and then modify and correct the comment at the top of the document to include your name and today's date.

    c. In analyze07.html, insert a title. Review the current `div` elements used to structure content and replace them with header, nav, main, section, article, aside, and footer HTML5 semantic elements. Do not replace the `div id="container"` tag.

2. Improve

    a. Open the analyzestyles07.css file in your text editor. Create new style rules to format the main, section, article, and aside elements and include comments for each style rule.

    b. Display the `main` element as a `block` with `1em` of padding and a background color of `#4E9657`.

    c. Apply a white background color to the `section` element, use `#4E9657` for the color property, and apply a small amount of padding and top margin.

    d. Use black as the font color for the `article` element, add a thin border on the top of the element, and apply a small amount of padding and top margin.

    e. Apply a border-radius property to the `aside` element, use a background color of `#4E9657`, align the text center, increase the font size, use white as the font color, and apply a small amount of padding and top margin.

    f. Validate your CSS file using the W3C validator found at http://jigsaw.w3.org/css-validator/ and fix any errors that are identified.

    g. Validate your HTML webpage using the W3C validator found at validator.w3.org and fix any errors that are identified.

    h. ✺ Identify another way to modify the HTML structure of the page using the `div` elements instead of the HTML5 semantic elements and provide an example.

In the Labs

Labs 1 and 2, which increase in difficulty, require you to create webpages based on what you learned in the chapter; Lab 3 requires you to dive deeper into a topic covered in the chapter.

Lab 1: Integrating HTML5 Semantic Elements for the New Harvest Food Bank Website

Problem: You volunteer at a local food bank called New Harvest Food Bank that collects community food donations and provides food and other services to those in need. The company has asked you to create a responsive website. You have already created the website but now need to add section, article, and aside elements to the About page and then format them. Create and style the webpage shown in Figure 7–95 for the mobile, tablet, and desktop viewports.

(a) Mobile viewport

(b) Tablet viewport

(c) Desktop viewport

Figure 7–95

Continued >

In the Labs *continued*

Instructions: Perform the following tasks:

1. Copy the foodbank.html template file in the lab1\template folder from the Data Files for Students to your lab1\template folder.

2. Open your text editor and then open the foodbank.html template file in the lab1 folder and use it to create the about.html file.

3. In the about.html document, add a `section` element within the `main` element. Create an `h2` element within the `section` element, `<h2>We Need Your Donations</h2>`.

4. Add an `article` element within the `section` element and then add the following elements within the `article` element:

```
<h4>Items We Need</h4>
        <p>Our pantry is in need of the following items:</p>
          <ul>
            <li>Canned chicken or tuna</li>
            <li>Canned Vegetables</li>
            <li>Oatmeal</li>
            <li>Pasta</li>
            <li>Peanut butter</li>
            <li>Rice</li>
          </ul>
```

5. Add another article element after the first article element, but within the section element, and then add the following elements within the second article element:

```
<h4>Food Drive</h4>
  <p>If you would like to host a food drive, we will provide
  everything you need to get started. Food drives are a great way for
  employees to help their local community. Employees can donate food
  items or make monetary donations.</p>
```

6. Add the following aside element after the section element:

```
<aside>Note that we cannot accept perishable goods, opened food
containers, or home made goods.</aside>
```

7. In the fbstyles.css file, modify the comment at the top of the page to include today's date.

8. In the fbstyles.css file, create a new style rule above the media queries for div p and add `padding-left: 1em;` and `padding-right: 1em;` to the style rule. Include a comment for this new style rule.

9. Add the following style rules to apply to the mobile viewport and include comments for each:

```
section {
    padding: 1%;
    text-align: center;
}

article {
    border-top: solid 0.2em #FF6600;
    padding: 2%;
    margin: 0.5%;
    text-align: left;
}
```

```
aside {
    text-align: center;
    color: #FFFFFF;
    background-color: #FF6600;
    font-size: 1.25em;
    margin: 1em;
    padding: 1em;
}
```

10. Add the following style rules to apply to the tablet viewport and include comments for each:

```
section {
    background-color: #FF6600;
}


article {
    background-color: #FFFFFF;
    border-top: 0;
    border-radius: 0 3em 3em 3em;
    margin-bottom: 1em;
}


aside {
    text-align: center;
    color: #FF6600;
    background-color: #FFFFFF;
    box-shadow: 1em 1em 1em #000000;
    border-radius: 8em;
}
```

11. In the fbstyles.css file, add **overflow: auto;** to the main style rule for the desktop viewport.

12. Add the following style rules to apply to the desktop viewport and include comments for each:

```
section {
    float: left;
    width: 60%;
}


aside {
    float: right;
    width: 25%;
    background-color: #FF6600;
    color: #FFFFFF;
}
```

13. Validate your HTML code and fix any errors.

14. Validate your CSS code and fix any errors.

15. Save all files and open the about.html page within a browser and view the page in all three viewports, as shown in Figure 7–95.

Continued >

In the Labs *continued*

16. Submit your assignment in the format specified by your instructor.

17. ✸ In this assignment, you created several HTML5 semantic elements. Research the `time` semantic element, identify its use, and then discuss its attribute and the different ways in which time can be displayed.

Lab 2: Designing for Tablet and Desktop Viewports for Steve's Screen Services

Problem: You work for a screening company called Steve's Screen Services that specializes in screening, cleaning, and repairing screened patios. The company has asked you to create a responsive website. You have already created the website, but now need to create the Services and Gallery page. You add and style semantic elements for both pages. Style the webpages as shown in Figure 7–96 and Figure 7–97 for mobile, tablet, and desktop viewports.

(a) Mobile viewport

(b) Tablet viewport

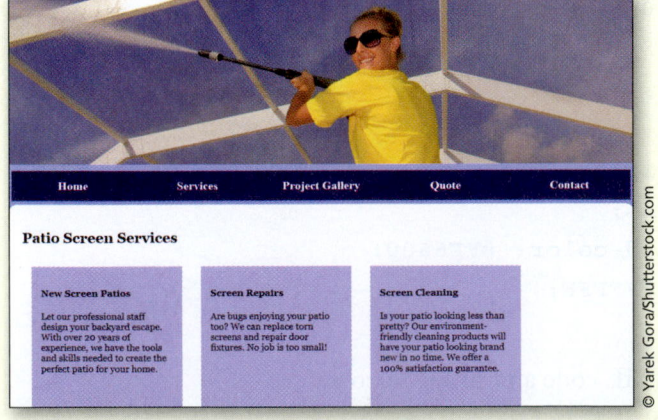

(c) Desktop viewport

© Yarek Gora/Shutterstock.com

Figure 7–96

(a) Mobile viewport

(b) Tablet viewport

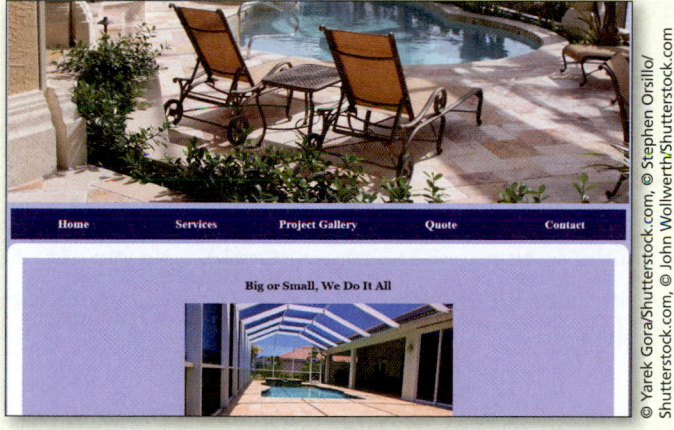

(c) Desktop viewport

© Yarek Gora/Shutterstock.com, © Stephen Orsillo/
Shutterstock.com, © John Wollwerth/Shutterstock.com

Figure 7–97

Instructions: Perform the following tasks:

1. Copy the image files in the lab2\images folder from the Data Files for Students to your lab2\ images folder and replace the old screen1.jpg file with the new screen1.jpg file.

2. Open your text editor and then open the stevescreen.html template file in the template folder and use it to create the services.html file.

3. In the services.html document, add a **section** element within the **main** element. Create an **h2** element within the section, **<h2>Patio Screen Services</h2>**.

4. Add an **article** element within the **section** element and then add the following elements within the **article** element:

```
<article>
<h4>New Screen Patios</h4>
<p>Let our professional staff design your backyard escape. With over
20 years of experience, we have the tools and skills needed to cre-
ate the perfect patio for your home.</p>
</article>
```

Continued >

In the Labs *continued*

5. Add a second `article` element after the first `article` element, but within the `section` element, and then add the following elements within the second `article` element.

```
<article>
<h4>Screen Repairs</h4>
<p>Are bugs enjoying your patio too? We can replace torn screens and
repair door fixtures. No job is too small!</p>
</article>
```

6. Add a third `article` element after the second `article` element, but within the `section` element, and then add the following elements within the third `article` element:

```
<article>
<h4>Screen Cleaning</h4>
<p>Is your patio looking less than pretty? Our environment-friendly
cleaning products will have your patio looking brand new in no time.
We offer a 100% satisfaction guarantee.</p>
</article>
```

7. Open your text editor and then open the stevescreen.html template file in the template folder and use it to create the gallery.html file.

8. In the gallery.html document, replace the image file name on Line 22, screen1.jpg, with `galleryBanner.jpg`.

9. In the gallery.html document, add an article element within the main element. Create an h3 element within the section, `<h3>Big or Small, We Do It All</h3>`.

10. In the gallery.html document, add the following figure element within the article element, below the h3 element:

```
<figure>
    <img src="images/screen2.jpg" alt="Gallery picture 1">
    <img src="images/screen3.jpg" alt="Gallery picture 2">
    <img src="images/screen4.jpg" alt="Gallery picture 3">
<figcaption>Small patios, large patios, pool enclosures</figcaption>
</figure>
```

11. In the screenstyles.css file, modify the comment at the top of the page to include today's date.

12. In the screenstyles.css file, add the following style rules to apply to the mobile viewport and include comments for each:

```
article h3 {
    text-align: center;
}

figure {
    text-align: center;
}

figcaption {
    color: #000066;
}
```

```
section {
    padding: 1em;
}

article {
    margin: 1em;
    padding: 1em;
    background-color: #ACB7E6;
}
```

13. In the screenstyles.css file, remove the img style rule from the tablet and desktop media queries.

14. Add the following style rules to the desktop media query and include a comment for the style rule:

```
section article {
    width: 22%;
    float: left;
    height: 15em;
}
```

15. Save your changes for all files and open the Services page in your browser, and the page in a mobile, tablet, and desktop viewports, as shown in Figure 7–96.

16. Open the Gallery page in your browser in mobile, tablet, and desktop viewports, as shown in Figure 7–97.

17. Validate your HTML code and fix any errors.

18. Validate your CSS code and fix any errors.

19. Submit your assignment in the format specified by your instructor.

20. ✳ In step 12, you created a style rule for a figcaption element. Discuss at least three different properties you would use to improve the appearance of this element.

Lab 3: Expand Your World
Working with Full Image Backgrounds and Opacity

Problem: In this chapter, you worked with banner images and the CSS3 opacity property. Work with the index07.html file in the lab3 folder and the lab3styles07.css file in the lab3\css folder from

Figure 7–98

Continued >

In the Labs *continued*

the Data Files for Students. In this exercise, you will explore ways to apply a background image and to work the opacity property. The complete webpage is shown in Figure 7–98.

Instructions:

1. Open index07.html in your text editor, review the page, add a title, modify the comment at the top of the page to include your name and today's date, and replace "Student's Name" with your name in the footer element.

2. Open the lab3styles07.css file from the lab3\css folder. Modify the comment at the top of the style sheet to include your name and today's date.

3. In the lab3styles07.css file, add the following properties and values to the body style rule to apply a background image to an entire webpage:

```
background: url(beach.jpg) no-repeat center center fixed;
-webkit-background-size: cover;
-moz-background-size: cover;
-o-background-size: cover;
background-size: cover;
```

4. In the lab3styles07.css file, add an opacity property and value to the header, nav, main, and footer elements. Use a different value for each element to view the changes in transparency.

5. Submit your answers in the format specified by your instructor.

6. ✳ In step 3, you applied a background image to the body element so that it would consume the entire webpage. Use your browser to research the background-size property and discuss other areas where this property could be applied.

Consider This: Your Turn

Apply your creative thinking and problem-solving skills to design and implement a solution.

1. Improving Your Personal Portfolio Website Design

Personal

Part 1: In Chapter 6, you completed your personal portfolio website for a responsive design. In this exercise, you update the page as follows:

1. Open the external style sheet you created in Chapter 6 and save it with the name **portfoliostyles07.css** in the styles folder within the your_turn_1 folder.

2. Add your name and the current date as a comment to the first line of the portfoliostyles07.css file.

3. In your HTML editor, open the files you created for your portfolio website in Chapter 6 and make sure your name and the current date are added as a comment to the first line of all files.

   a. Update the HTML files to modify the link to the external style sheet to reference portfoliostyles07.css.

   b. Wrap your picture in a figure element.

   c. Integrate an article element on the portfolio page.

   d. Integrate a section element on the education page.

4. Update the CSS file to:

   a. Style the figure element for mobile, tablet, and desktop viewports.

   b. Style the article element for mobile, tablet, and desktop viewports.

   c. Style the section element for mobile, tablet, and desktop viewports.

   d. Apply a text-shadow property to your name.

    e. Refine your style sheet as desired.

    f. Adjust viewport widths if necessary.

    g. Add comments to note all changes and updates.

5. Save and test your files.

6. Validate and correct your HTML and CSS files, and submit your assignment in the format specified by your instructor.

Part 2: ✳

Use your browser to research the HTML5 details and summary semantic elements. Discuss where you could integrate these elements with your site and why.

2. Improving the Design of the WebDevPros Website

Professional

Part 1: In Chapter 6, you completed a responsive design website for WebDevPros. In this exercise, you update the site as follows:

1. Open the external style sheet you created in Chapter 6 and save it with the name **webdevstyles07.css** in the styles folder within the your_turn_2 folder.

2. Add your name and the current date as a comment to the first line of the webdevstyles07.css file.

3. Open the files you created for WebDevPros in Chapter 6 in your HTML editor and make sure your name and the current date are added as a comment to the first line of all files.

4. Update the HTML files to:

    a. Integrate figure and figcaption elements.

    b. Integrate a section element.

    c. Integrate an article element.

    d. Integrate an aside element.

5. Update the CSS file to:

    a. Style the figure element for mobile, tablet, and desktop viewports.

    b. Style the article element for mobile, tablet, and desktop viewports.

    c. Style the section element for mobile, tablet, and desktop viewports.

    d. Style the aside element for mobile, tablet, and desktop viewports.

    e. Apply an opacity property to an element.

    f. Refine your style sheet as desired.

    g. Adjust viewport widths if necessary.

    h. Add comments to note all changes and updates.

6. Save and test your files.

7. Validate and correct your HTML and CSS files, and submit your assignment in the format specified by your instructor.

Part 2: ✳ In step 5d, you added a style rule for the aside element. Use your browser to research different ideas for styling the aside element. Provide a screen shot of the designs you found and a link to each resource.

Continued >

Consider This: Your Turn *continued*

3. Improving the Design of the Dog Hall of Fame Website

Research and Collaboration

Part 1: In Chapter 6, you completed the responsive design website for the Dog Hall of Fame. In this exercise, you will update those pages to apply new HTML5 semantic elements and then style those element. Do the following activities as a group:

1. Open the external style sheet you created in Chapter 6 and save it with the name **dogstyles07.css** in the styles folder within the your_turn_3 folder.

2. Add your name and the current date as a comment to the first line of the dogstyles07.css file.

3. Open the files you created for the Dog Hall of Fame in Chapter 6 in your HTML editor and make sure your name and the current date are added as a comment to the first line of all files.

4. Modify the link to the external style sheet to reference dogstyles07.css.

5. Decide how you will integrate new HTML5 semantic elements. At a minimum, update the HTML and CSS files to do the following:

   a. Update the winner.html document content and integrate figure and figcaption elements. Three dog images are provided in the Data Files for Students if needed for this project.

   b. Integrate a section element.

   c. Integrate an article element.

   d. Integrate an aside element.

   e. Style the figure element.

   f. Style a section element.

   g. Style an article element.

   h. Style an aside element.

   i. Apply a multiple-column layout.

   j. Use the opacity and text-shadow properties.

   k. Refine your style sheet as desired.

   l. Adjust viewport widths where necessary.

   m. Add comments to note all changes and updates.

6. Save and test your files.

7. Validate and correct your HTML and CSS files, and submit your assignment in the format specified by your instructor.

Part 2: ✳ Each person in the group should research different layout design strategies for the website and present to the group for a discussion. In the discussion, the group should review each strategy and make a decision to apply the most popular layout strategy. Organize your group's findings as requested by your instructor.

8 | Creating Tables and Forms

Objectives

You will have mastered the material in this chapter when you can:

- Define table elements
- Describe the steps used to plan, design, and code a table
- Create a table with rows and data
- Insert a table caption
- Style a table for tablet and desktop viewports
- Describe form controls and their uses

- Use the form and input elements
- Create text input controls, labels, and check boxes
- Create a selection menu with multiple options
- Use the textarea element
- Create a Submit button
- Create a Reset button

8 | Creating Tables and Forms

Introduction

Content you can organize into categories and items is often best presented in a table format. A **table** presents related information in rows and columns, and is especially useful when comparing types of data or listing topics and details. Tables can use column headings or row headings to identify categories or topics. Tables are also helpful when you need to provide a lot of content in a compact form.

Many businesses use **forms** to collect information about their customers. Common information to collect includes a customer's first and last names, address, email address, and phone number. Websites provide forms so visitors can create an account, register for an event, or make a purchase, for example.

In this chapter, you will learn how to use HTML to create a table and a form on separate webpages. After creating the table using several HTML elements, you format the table using CSS styles. To create the form, you will include several controls on a webpage, including check boxes, a drop-down menu, and text boxes. You will also learn to add Submit and Reset buttons that customers can use to submit the completed form or clear the information previously entered into the form. Finally, you will learn to style the form elements using CSS styles.

Project — Create a Table and a Form

In Chapter 8, you create the Classes page, which contains information about the classes offered at the Forward Fitness Club. The classes are offered on various days and times during the week, led by an instructor, and held in a room at the club. You create and style a table to display a class schedule in a compact format for tablet and desktop viewports. You display a brief version of the class schedule as a list for the mobile viewport because the table cannot be adapted to fit on the screens of mobile devices.

In addition, you add a form to the Contact Us page. The goal of the projects completed thus far has been to present content *to* website visitors. In this chapter, you will learn how to get information *from* website visitors by adding a form for user input. The form collects information about potential new clients and provides the information to the Forward Fitness Club owners for follow-up. You then style the form for mobile, tablet, and desktop viewports.

The project in this chapter improves a website by including a table and a form. To perform these tasks, you first create the Classes page and insert a table. Next, you complete the table by adding a table caption, table headings, table rows, and table data. In the style sheet, you add style rules for the table elements for tablet and desktop viewports. For the mobile viewport, you add a short version of the class information to the new Classes page. Next, you create a form on the Contact Us page, and then apply styles to the form for mobile, tablet, and desktop viewports. Figure 8–1 shows the new Classes page for mobile, tablet, and desktop viewports. Figure 8–2 shows the form on the Contact Us page for mobile, tablet, and desktop viewports.

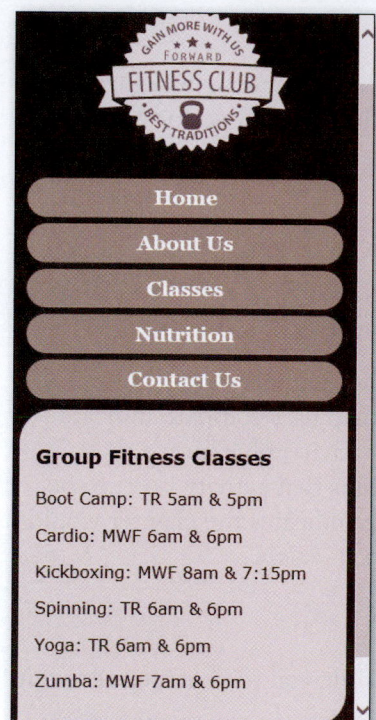

(a) Classes page in mobile viewport

(b) Classes page in tablet viewport

(c) Classes page in desktop viewport

Figure 8–1

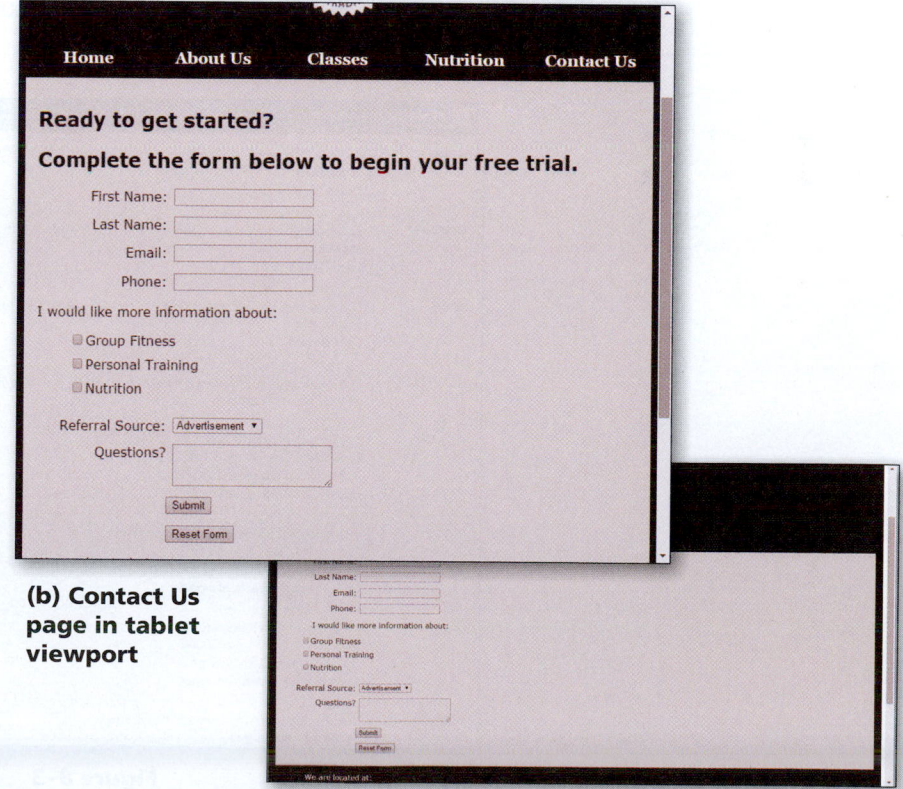

(a) Contact Us page in mobile viewport

(b) Contact Us page in tablet viewport

(c) Contact Us page in desktop viewport

Figure 8–2

Roadmap

In this chapter, you will learn how to create the webpages shown in Figures 8-1 and 8-2. The following roadmap identifies general activities you will perform as you progress through this chapter:

1. CREATE the CLASSES PAGE AND its TABLE.
2. STYLE the TABLE for tablet and desktop viewports.
3. CREATE a FORM on the Contact Us page.
4. STYLE the FORM for mobile, tablet, and desktop viewports.

At the beginning of step instructions throughout the chapter, you will see an abbreviated form of this roadmap. The abbreviated roadmap uses colors to indicate chapter progress: gray means the chapter is beyond that activity; blue means the task being shown is covered in that activity, and black means that activity is yet to be covered. For example, the following abbreviated roadmap indicates the chapter would be showing a task in the 3 CREATE FORM activity.

1 CREATE CLASSES PAGE & TABLE | 2 STYLE TABLE

3 CREATE FORM | **4 STYLE FORM**

Use the abbreviated roadmap as a progress guide while you read or step through the instructions in this chapter.

Discovering Tables

Tables compare data or outline a detailed topic, such as an event in a compact format. For example, Figure 8–3 shows how the White House uses a table on its website to list the president's daily schedule.

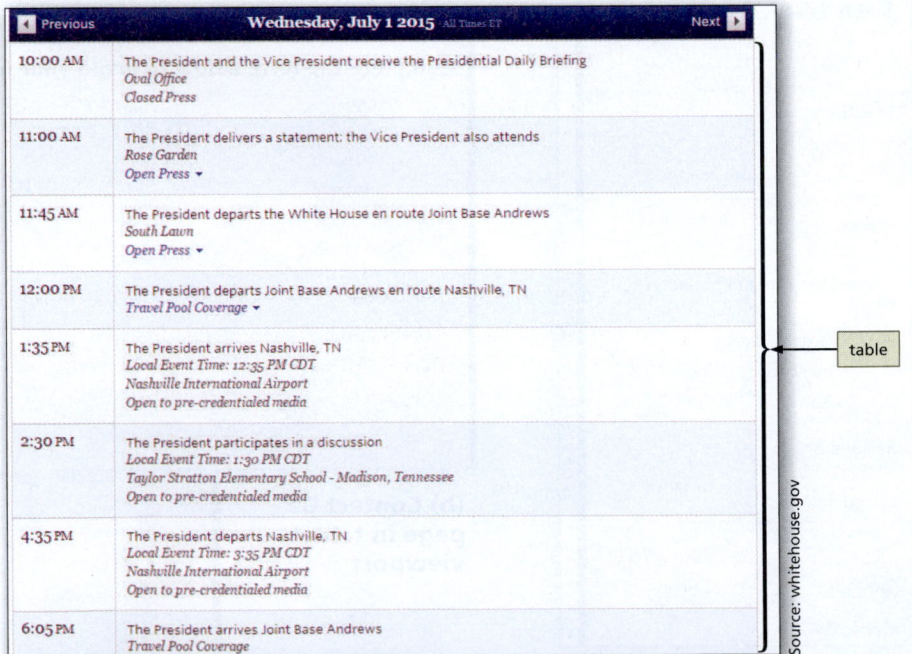

Figure 8–3

A table consists of rows, columns, and cells, much like a spreadsheet. A **row** is a horizontal line of information. A **column** is a vertical line of information. A **cell** is the intersection of a row and a column and usually contains data. Figure 8–4 shows examples of these three elements.

Figure 8–4

A cell can be one of two types: a heading cell or a data cell. A **heading cell** displays text as bold and center-aligned. For example, you use heading cells to display column headings that identify the information in each column. A **data cell** displays normal, left-aligned text and contains information appropriate for the column and row. You should understand the differences among table row, heading cell, and data cell elements so you can use HTML to create a table that matches your design.

Creating a Table with HTML Elements

Table 8–1 lists the HTML elements you use to create a table.

Table 8–1 HTML Table Elements		
Element	**Indicates the start and end of:**	**Contains:**
<table> … </table>	Table within a webpage	All related table elements
<tr> … </tr>	Table row within a table	Table data cells
<th> … </th>	Table header cell	Table header content
<td> … </td>	Table data	Table cell content
<caption> … </caption>	Table caption	Table caption or title
<thead> … </thead >	Table header area	Grouped header content
<tbody> … </tbody >	Table body area	Grouped body content
<tfooter> … </tfooter >	Table footer area	Grouped footer content

To create a table on a webpage, start with the <table> and </table> tags and then add table rows and table data within those tags. The following is an example of code used to create the table shown in Figure 8–5, which consists of four rows and four columns.

```
<table>
  <tr>
        <td>Semester 1</td>
        <td>Semester 2</td>
        <td>Semester 3</td>
        <td>Semester 4</td>
  </tr>
  <tr>
        <td>English I</td>
        <td>English II</td>
        <td>Spanish I</td>
        <td>Spanish II</td>
  </tr>
```

```
    <tr>
            <td>College Algebra</td>
            <td>College Geometry</td>
            <td>Calculus</td>
            <td>Trigonometry</td>
    </tr>
    <tr>
            <td>Physical Science</td>
            <td>Biology</td>
            <td>Humanities</td>
            <td>World History</td>
    </tr>
</table>
```

td elements

Semester 1	Semester 2	Semester 3	Semester 4
English I	English II	Spanish I	Spanish II
College Algebra	College Geometry	Calculus	Trigonometry
Physical Science	Biology	Humanities	World History

tr elements

Figure 8–5

The <table> tag indicates the beginning of the table. Likewise, the </table> tag indicates the end of a table. Each table row is indicated by a starting <tr> tag and an ending </tr> tag. The table shown in Figure 8–5 has four table row elements. Each table row element contains table data elements, indicated by a starting <td> tag and an ending </td> tag. The number of table data elements in each table row element determines the number of columns in the table. In this example, four table data elements are used within each table row element, which means this table consists of four columns.

The table shown in Figure 8–5 does not have any applied style rules, so typical table formatting, such as borders and spacing, is not included by default. You specify properties, such as borders, margins, and padding in a style sheet.

Table Borders, Headers, and Captions

In addition to columns and rows, tables also include features such as borders, headers, and captions. A **table border** is the line that defines the perimeter of the table. You display table borders using a style rule in a style sheet. A **table header** is a heading cell, which is formatted with bold, centered text that indicates the purpose of the row or column. Headers are typically used to identify row or column content. Nonvisual browsers also use headers to identify table content. (See the guidelines in Appendix D for specific information about making your webpages accessible to those with disabilities.) Define a table header with a starting **<th>** tag and an ending **</th>** tag.

A **table caption** is descriptive text that serves as a title or identifies the table's purpose. The table caption text appears above a table, spans its length, and is center-aligned by default. Define a table caption with a starting <caption> tag and an ending </caption> tag. When using a table caption, insert it after the starting <table> tag. A table can have only one caption.

Tables can include headers and captions individually or in combination. The purpose for the table dictates which of these features you use. Figure 8–6 shows a table created with the following code, which includes a table caption and table headers. The figure also shows a table border as defined by an external style sheet.

```
<table>
  <caption>College Course Recommendations by Semester</caption>
  <tr>
        <th>Semester 1</th>
        <th>Semester 2</th>
        <th>Semester 3</th>
        <th>Semester 4</th>
  </tr>
  <tr>
        <td>English I</td>
        <td>English II</td>
        <td>Spanish I</td>
        <td>Spanish II</td>
  </tr>
  <tr>
        <td>College Algebra</td>
        <td>College Geometry</td>
        <td>Calculus</td>
        <td>Trigonometry</td>
  </tr>
  <tr>
        <td>Physical Science</td>
        <td>Biology</td>
        <td>Humanities</td>
        <td>World History</td>
  </tr>
</table>
```

Figure 8–6

CONSIDER THIS

What is the difference between the <th> and the <thead> tags?

The table header element uses the <th> and </th> tags to create table header cells. A header cell contains a header title, such as a column or row title, which describes the column or row content. The table head element uses the <thead> and </thead> tags to group table header content within a table and is used with the table body and table footer elements to identify each part of a table. When you use the table head, table body, and table footer elements, users can scroll the table body content separate from the table head and table footer. For a large table that spans more than one page, users can also print the table head at the top of the page and the table footer at the bottom.

Table Tag Attributes

Prior to HTML5, the table tags had many attributes that could be used to format tables. However, HTML5 does not support the majority of those attributes. Instead of using table tag attributes, use CSS to style tables on a webpage. You will learn more about how to style a table later in this chapter.

Use of Tables

Using tables for web design and page layout was quite popular in the late 1990s; however, this was a misuse of the table elements. Tables are meant to display data in rows and columns and should not be used to design a layout for a webpage.

Before you add a table, you must first determine whether it is necessary on the webpage. As general rule, use a table when it will help organize information so that that it is easier for the user to read. Tables are also useful if the webpage needs to display a structured, organized list of information. Figures 8–7a and 8-7b show examples of information displayed as text in a bulleted list and a table. The bulleted list (Figure 8–7a) provides the schedule information, but the table (Figure 8–7b) presents the same information more clearly.

- Work Schedule
  - o T. Anderson: M 12-5pm, T 2-7pm, W Off, R 8-12pm, F 8-12pm
  - o E. Davis: M 8-12pm, T 8-12pm, W 12-5pm, R Off, F 2-7pm
  - o J. Smith: M 8-12pm, T 12-5pm, W 8-12pm, R 2-7pm, F Off
  - o S. Watson: M 12-7pm, T Off, W 2-7pm, R 12-5pm, F 12-5pm

(a) Schedule as bulleted list

Work Schedule

Employee	Mon	Tue	Wed	Thu	Fri
T. Anderson	12 – 5pm	2 – 7pm	Off	8 – 12pm	8 – 12pm
E. Davis	8 – 12pm	8 – 12pm	12 – 5pm	Off	2 – 7pm
J. Smith	8 – 12pm	12 – 5pm	8 – 12pm	2 – 7pm	Off
S. Watson	12 – 7pm	Off	2 – 7pm	12 – 5pm	12 – 5pm

(b) Schedule as table

Figure 8–7

Planning the Table

To create effective tables, you must plan the information that will appear in columns and rows and then create a design that presents the information clearly. Before writing any HTML code, sketch the table on paper or in an electronic document to see how many rows and columns to create and determine whether the table needs headers or a caption. Conceptualizing the table first saves time when you are determining which HTML table elements to use to create the table. Because you enter the content of a table row by row in an HTML document, you also need a sketch of the finished table to create the table accurately as you are coding.

BTW

HTML Entities in Tables
You often use symbols, such as dollar signs ($) and ampersands (&) in tables to save space. To create these symbols on a webpage, use HTML entities, such as $ for a dollar sign and & for an ampersand.

When planning a table for responsive web design, give careful consideration to the mobile viewport. Because the screen on a mobile viewport is much smaller than a tablet or desktop viewport, tables with several columns are not conducive for mobile viewports. You might need to display only the most important table content in another form, such as a list.

Before adding a table to the Forward Fitness Club website, create the webpage that will contain the table, a schedule for the group classes the club offers.

To Create the Classes Page

Use the template, fitness.html, to create the Classes page, and then insert a banner image to match the other pages on the site. The following steps create the Classes page.

1 Copy the image file from the chapter08\fitness folder provided with the Data Files for Students to the fitness\images folder.

2 Open fitness.html in your text editor, and then save the page as classes.html in your fitness folder.

3 Update the comment with your name and today's date, tap or click at the end of Line 28, and then press the ENTER key twice to insert new Lines 29 and 30.

4 On Line 30, type `<!-- Classes Page Banner -->` to insert a comment.

5 Press the ENTER key to insert a new Line 31, and then type `<div id="banner" class="desktop">` to insert a div tag.

6 Press the ENTER key to insert a new Line 32, increase the indent, and then type `<img src="images/classesBanner.jpg" alt="classes banner image">` to insert an image.

7 Press the ENTER key to insert a new Line 33, decrease the indent, and then type `</div>` to insert a closing div tag (Figure 8–8).

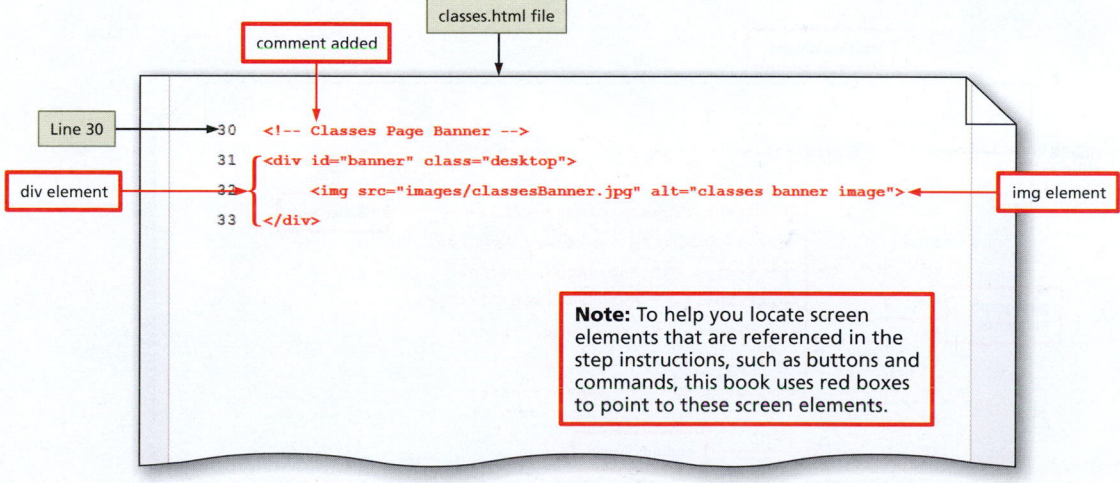

Figure 8–8

To Add a div Element to the Classes Page

Create a `div` element on the Classes page to provide separate content for a mobile user. The following step adds a `div` element to the Classes page.

1 In the classes.html file, tap or click at the end of Line 36 and press the ENTER key twice to insert new Lines 37 and 38.

2 On Line 38, increase the indent, and then type `<div class="mobile">` to insert a div tag.

3 Press the ENTER key twice to insert new Lines 39 and 40.

4 On Line 40, increase the indent, and then type `<h3>Group Fitness Classes </h3>` to insert a heading element.

5 Press the ENTER key to insert a new Line 41 and then type `<p>Boot Camp: TR 5am &amp; 5pm</p>` to insert a paragraph element.

6 Press the ENTER key to insert a new Line 42 and then type `<p>Cardio: MWF 6am &amp; 6pm</p>` to insert a paragraph element.

7 Press the ENTER key to insert a new Line 43 and then type `<p>Kickboxing: MWF 8am &amp; 7:15pm</p>` to insert a paragraph element.

8 Press the ENTER key to insert a new Line 44 and then type `<p>Spinning: TR 6am &amp; 6pm</p>` to insert a paragraph element.

9 Press the ENTER key to insert a new Line 45 and then type `<p>Yoga: TR 6am &amp; 6pm</p>` to insert a paragraph element.

10 Press the ENTER key to insert a new Line 46 and then type `<p>Zumba: MWF 7am &amp; 6pm</p>` to insert a paragraph element.

11 Press the ENTER key twice to insert new Lines 47 and 48, decrease the indent, and then type `</div>` to insert a closing div tag (Figure 8–9).

Q&A What does & represent?

The & code is an HTML entity used to display an ampersand (&) on a webpage.

```
                              starting div tag

Line 38  →  38         <div class="mobile">

            39

            40                <h3>Group Fitness Classes</h3>     ← h3 element

            41                <p>Boot Camp: TR 5am &amp; 5pm</p>

            42                <p>Cardio: MWF 6am &amp; 6pm</p>

paragraph   43                <p>Kickboxing: MWF 8am &amp; 7:15pm</p>
elements
            44                <p>Spinning: TR 6am &amp; 6pm</p>

            45                <p>Yoga: TR 6am &amp; 6pm</p>

            46                <p>Zumba: MWF 7am &amp; 6pm</p>

            47

            48         </div>     ← ending div tag
```

Figure 8–9

12 Save your changes, open classes.html in your browser, adjust the window to the size of a mobile viewport, and then scroll down the page to view the main content (Figure 8–10).

Figure 8–10

To Add a Table Element to the Classes Page

1 CREATE CLASSES PAGE & TABLE | 2 STYLE TABLE
3 CREATE FORM | 4 STYLE FORM

Next, insert a table element within a new `div class="desktop"` element and then insert a table to display information about the classes offered at the Forward Fitness Club. Although the class is named desktop, the table will appear in tablet and desktop viewports. *Why? Only the elements specified as belonging to the mobile class will appear in a mobile viewport.* After inserting a new `div` element to contain the table, insert a starting table tag and a `caption` element. Insert table rows, table headings, and table data elements followed by an ending table tag. The following steps add a `div` and `table` element to the Classes page.

1

- Tap or click at the end of Line 48, and then press the ENTER key twice to insert new Lines 49 and 50.

- On Line 50, type `<div class="desktop">` to insert a div tag.

- Press the ENTER key twice to insert new Lines 51 and 52, increase the indent, and then type `<table><!-- Start Table -->` to insert a starting table tag and a comment.

Figure 8–11

- Press the ENTER key to insert a new Line 53, increase the indent, and then type `<caption>Group Fitness Class Schedule</caption>` to insert a table caption element.

- Press the ENTER key to insert a new Line 54, and then type `<tr><!-- Row 1 -->` to insert a starting table row tag and a comment.

- Press the ENTER key to insert a new Line 55, increase the indent, and then type `<th>Class</th>` to insert a table header element (Figure 8–11).

Q&A Where will the "Class" content appear in the table?

"Class" will appear in the first row of the table, also called the header row, as indicated by the comment on Line 54. Because it is specified as a `th` element, "Class" will be bold and centered.

2

- Press the ENTER key to insert a new Line 56, and then type `<th>Days</th>` to insert a table header element.

- Press the ENTER key to insert a new Line 57, and then type `<th>Times</th>` to insert a table header element.

- Press the ENTER key to insert a new Line 58, and then type `<th>Instructor</th>` to insert a table header element.

- Press the ENTER key to insert a new Line 59, and then type `<th>Room</th>` to insert a table header element.

```
50   <div class="desktop">
51
52          <table><!--Start Table -->
53              <caption>Group Fitness Class Schedule</caption>
54              <tr><!-- Row 1 -->
55                  <th>Class</th>
56                  <th>Days</th>
57                  <th>Times</th>
58                  <th>Instructor</th>
59                  <th>Room</th>
60              </tr>
```

Line 56 — ending table row tag — new th elements

Figure 8–12

- Press the ENTER key to insert a new Line 60, decrease the indent, and then type `</tr>` to insert a closing table row tag (Figure 8–12).

Q&A What does the table consist of so far?
At this point, the table has one row (the header row) and five columns, one each for Class, Days, Times, Instructor, and Room.

3

- Press the ENTER key to insert a new Line 61, and then type `<tr><!-- Row 2 -->` to insert a starting table row tag and a comment.

- Press the ENTER key to insert a new Line 62, increase the indent, and then type `<td>Cardio</td>` to insert a table data element.

- Press the ENTER key to insert a new Line 63, and then type `<td>Mon, Wed, Fri</td>` to insert a table data element.

starting table row tag — comment

```
61              <tr><!-- Row 2 -->
62                  <td>Cardio</td>
63                  <td>Mon, Wed, Fri</td>
64                  <td>6:00am, 6:00pm</td>
65                  <td>Schultz</td>
66                  <td>B</td>
67              </tr>
```

Line 61 — ending table row tag — td elements

Figure 8–13

- Press the ENTER key to insert a new Line 64, and then type `<td>6:00am, 6:00pm</td>` to insert a table data element.

- Press the ENTER key to insert a new Line 65, and then type `<td>Schultz</td>` to insert a table data element.

- Press the ENTER key to insert a new Line 66, and then type `<td>B</td>` to insert a table data element.

- Press the ENTER key to insert a new Line 67, decrease the indent, and then type `</tr>` to insert a closing table row tag (Figure 8–13).

Q&A What did I add to the table in this step?
You added the second row of the table, which contains details about the Cardio class.

4

- Press the ENTER key to insert a new Line 68, and then type `<tr><!-- Row 3 -->` to insert a starting table row tag and a comment.

- Press the ENTER key to insert a new Line 69, increase the indent, and then type `<td>Boot Camp</td>` to insert a table data element.

- Press the ENTER key to insert a new Line 70, and then type `<td>Tue, Thu</td>` to insert a table data element.

starting table row tag

comment

Line 68

```
68          <tr><!-- Row 3 -->
69              <td>Boot Camp</td>
70              <td>Tue, Thu</td>
71              <td>5:00am, 5:00pm</td>
72              <td>Taylor</td>
73              <td>B</td>
74          </tr>
```

td elements

ending table row tag

Figure 8–14

- Press the ENTER key to insert a new Line 71, and then type `<td>5:00am, 5:00pm</td>` to insert a table data element.

- Press the ENTER key to insert a new Line 72, and then type `<td>Taylor</td>` to insert a table data element.

- Press the ENTER key to insert a new Line 73, and then type `<td>B</td>` to insert a table data element.

- Press the ENTER key to insert a new Line 74, decrease the indent, and then type `</tr>` to insert a closing table row tag (Figure 8–14).

Q&A What did I add to the table in this step?
You added the third row of the table, which contains details about the Boot Camp class.

5

- Press the ENTER key to insert a new Line 75, and then type `<tr><!-- Row 4 -->` to insert a starting table row tag and a comment.

- Press the ENTER key to insert a new Line 76, increase the indent, and then type `<td>Spinning</td>` to insert a table data element.

starting table row tag

comment

Line 75

```
75          <tr><!-- Row 4 -->
76              <td>Spinning</td>
77              <td>Tue, Thu</td>
78              <td>6:00am, 6:00pm</td>
79              <td>Roberts</td>
80              <td>A</td>
81          </tr>
```

td elements

ending table row tag

Figure 8–15

- Press the ENTER key to insert a new Line 77, and then type `<td>Tue, Thu</td>` to insert a table data element.

- Press the ENTER key to insert a new Line 78, and then type `<td>6:00am, 6:00pm</td>` to insert a table data element.

- Press the ENTER key to insert a new Line 79, and then type `<td>Roberts</td>` to insert a table data element.

- Press the ENTER key to insert a new Line 80, and then type `<td>A</td>` to insert a table data element.

- Press the ENTER key to insert a new Line 81, decrease the indent, and then type `</tr>` to insert a closing table row tag (Figure 8–15).

Q&A What did I add to the table in this step?
You added the fourth row of the table, which contains details about the Spinning class.

6

- Press the ENTER key to insert a new Line 82, and then type `<tr><!-- Row 5 -->` to insert a starting table row tag and a comment.

- Press the ENTER key to insert a new Line 83, increase the indent, and then type `<td>Kickboxing</td>` to insert a table data element.

- Press the ENTER key to insert a new Line 84, and then type `<td>Mon, Wed, Fri</td>` to insert a table data element.

- Press the ENTER key to insert a new Line 85, and then type `<td>8:00am, 7:15pm</td>` to insert a table data element.

- Press the ENTER key to insert a new Line 86, and then type `<td>Lawrence</td>` to insert a table data element.

- Press the ENTER key to insert a new Line 87, and then type `<td>A</td>` to insert a table data element.

- Press the ENTER key to insert a new Line 88, decrease the indent, and then type `</tr>` to insert a closing table row tag (Figure 8–16).

Figure 8–16

7

- Press the ENTER key to insert a new Line 89, and then type `<tr><!-- Row 6 -->` to insert a starting table row tag and a comment.

- Press the ENTER key to insert a new Line 90, increase the indent, and then type `<td>Yoga</td>` to insert a table data element.

- Press the ENTER key to insert a new Line 91, and then type `<td>Tue, Thu</td>` to insert a table data element.

- Press the ENTER key to insert a new Line 92, and then type `<td>6:00am, 6:00pm</td>` to insert a table data element.

- Press the ENTER key to insert a new Line 93, and then type `<td>Schultz</td>` to insert a table data element.

- Press the ENTER key to insert a new Line 94, and then type `<td>B</td>` to insert a table data element.

- Press the ENTER key to insert a new Line 95, decrease the indent, and then type `</tr>` to insert a closing table row tag (Figure 8–17).

Figure 8–17

8

- Press the ENTER key to insert a new Line 96, and then type `<tr><!-- Row 7 -->` to insert a starting table row tag and a comment.

- Press the ENTER key to insert a new Line 97, increase the indent, and then type `<td>Zumba </td>` to insert a table data element.

- Press the ENTER key to insert a new Line 98, and then type `<td>Mon, Wed, Fri </td>` to insert a table data element.

```
96              <tr><!-- Row 7 -->
97                  <td>Zumba</td>
98                  <td>Mon, Wed, Fri</td>
99                  <td>7:00am, 6:00pm</td>
100                 <td>Roberts</td>
101                 <td>A</td>
102             </tr>
103
104         </table><!-- End Table -->
```

starting table row tag

comment

Line 96

td elements

ending table row tag

ending table tag

comment

Figure 8–18

- Press the ENTER key to insert a new Line 99, and then type `<td>7:00am, 6:00pm</td>` to insert a table data element.

- Press the ENTER key to insert a new Line 100, and then type `<td>Roberts</td>` to insert a table data element.

- Press the ENTER key to insert a new Line 101, and then type `<td>A</td>` to insert a table data element.

- Press the ENTER key to insert a new Line 102, decrease the indent, and then type `</tr>` to insert a closing table row tag.

- Press the ENTER key twice to insert new Lines 103 and 104, decrease the indent, and then type `</table> <!-- End Table-->` to insert a closing table tag and comment (Figure 8–18).

Q&A What did I add to the table in the last three steps?
You added the rows 5, 6, and 7 of the table, which contain details about the Kickboxing, Yoga, and Zumba classes.

9

- Press the ENTER key to insert a new Line 105 and then type `</div>` to insert a closing div tag.

- Save your changes, refresh classes. html in your browser, adjust the window to the size of a tablet viewport, and then scroll down to view the table (Figure 8–19).

Q&A Why do the columns appear to run together?
You have not applied styles to the table. In later steps, you will apply borders, margins, and padding so that each column and data cell appear separately.

Why is the table displayed in the tablet viewport when I added the table to the `div class="desktop"` section?
The tablet media query contains a rule that displays elements in the desktop class.

classes.html displayed in tablet viewport

Home   About Us   Classes   Nutrition   Contact Us

banner image

Classes Designed to Meet Your Busy Schedule

table caption

Group Fitness Class Schedule

Class	Days	Times	Instructor	Room
Cardio	Mon, Wed, Fri	6:00am, 6:00pm	Schultz	B
Boot Camp	Tue, Thu	5:00am, 5:00pm	Taylor	B
Spinning	Tue, Thu	6:00am, 6:00pm	Roberts	A
Kickboxing	Mon, Wed, Fri	8:00am, 7:15pm	Lawrence	A
Yoga	Tue, Thu	6:00am, 6:00pm	Schultz	B
Zumba	Mon, Wed, Fri	7:00am, 6:00pm	Roberts	A

table header elements

table element

table data elements

© Rob Marmion/Shutterstock.com

Figure 8–19

Styling Table Elements

After creating a table, style it by adding new style rules to the style sheet for the website. You can specify style rules for each table element. Table 8–2 lists common CSS properties and examples for styling tables.

Table 8–2 Common CSS Table Properties		
Property	**Example**	**Explanation**

background-color	th {
	    background-color: #F5F5F0;
	}
		Displays the table header with a light gray background

border	table, th, td {
	    border: 0.1em solid #000000;
	}
		Displays the table, table header, and data cells with a thin solid black border

border-collapse	table {
	    border-collapse: collapse;
	}
		Collapses borders in the table so that adjacent cells share borders

color	caption {
	    color: #003300;
	}
		Displays the table caption in dark green text

height	td {
	    height: 2em;
	}
		Sets the height of a table data cell to 2em

margin	table {
	    margin-top: 2em;
	}
		Applies a 2em top margin to the table

padding	caption, th, td {
	    padding: 1em;
	}
		Applies 1em of padding to the table caption, header, and data cells

text-align	td {
	    text-align: center;
	}
		Aligns the table data in the center of the cell

vertical-align	td {
	    vertical-align: center;
	}
		Aligns the table data vertically in the middle of the cell

width	table {
	    width: 80%;
	}
		Sets the width of the table to 80% of the page width

When a border is applied to table elements, by default, each cell has its own border, making the table appear to use double lines between each table data cell. This type of border is called a separated border. Figure 8–20 shows a table with the default border applied.

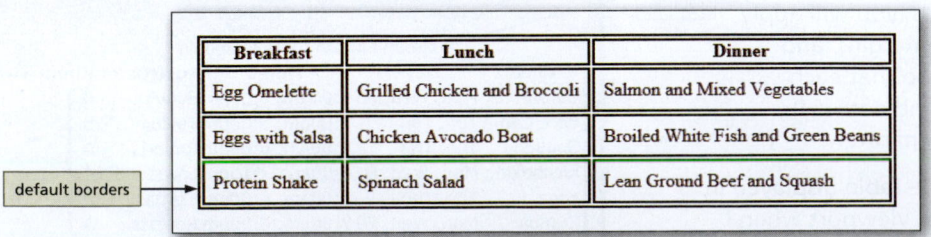

Figure 8–20

If you want to display a table with single, consolidated borders as shown in Figure 8–21, use the `border-collapse` property with a value of `collapse`. This type of border is called a collapsed border.

Breakfast	Lunch	Dinner
Egg Omelette	Grilled Chicken and Broccoli	Salmon and Mixed Vegetables
Eggs with Salsa	Chicken Avocado Boat	Broiled White Fish and Green Beans
Protein Shake	Spinach Salad	Lean Ground Beef and Squash

collapsed borders →

Figure 8–21

Styling Tables for Responsive Web Design

It is often difficult to style a table for a mobile viewport, especially when the table consists of several columns. Many times, viewing a table requires extra horizontal and vertical scrolling by the user. Other times, the table is so small that it is difficult to read. Determine whether you can format the table so it is still easy to read in a mobile viewport. If the table is too large or complex to format, you can display the content in a different format such as a list or a chart in a mobile viewport.

BTW

Converting a Table to a Chart
If your table contains numeric information, such as financial data or compares information among categories, consider converting your table to a chart for the mobile viewport.

1 CREATE CLASSES PAGE & TABLE | **2 STYLE TABLE**
3 CREATE FORM | 4 STYLE FORM

To Style a Table for a Tablet Viewport

Create new style rules to style the table for the tablet viewport. *Why? Format the table to clearly present its information in a tablet viewport.* First, create a style rule for the `table` element to specify borders, including collapsed borders, to center the table on the page, and to set a width. Next, create a style rule for `th` and `td` elements to specify borders and padding for the table header and data cells. Create a separate style rule for the `th` element to format the table header with a dark background color and light font color. Finally, create a style rule to specify the font size, font color, and bottom padding of the table caption.

Add these new style rules to the end of the media query for the tablet layout so the rules will apply to webpages displayed in a tablet viewport. The following steps create style rules for table elements in the tablet viewport.

1

- Open the styles.css file in your text editor to prepare to edit it.

- Tap or click at the end of Line 267, and then press the ENTER key twice to insert new Lines 268 and 269.

- On Line 269, type **/* Style for table element */** to insert a new comment.

- Press the ENTER key to insert a new Line 270, and then type **table {** to insert a new selector.

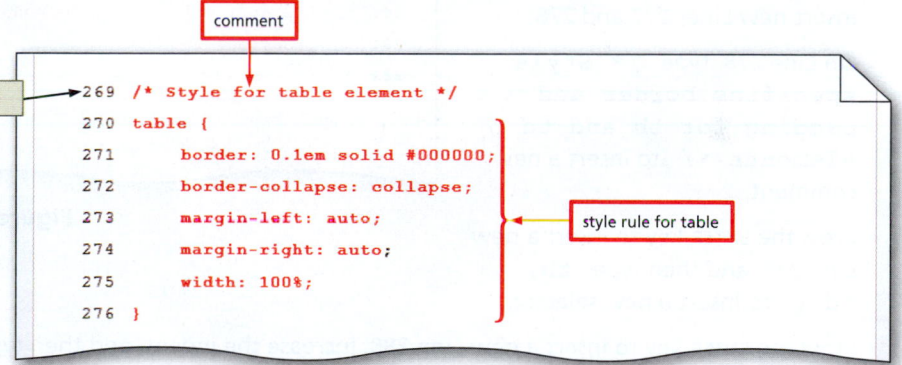

```
269   /* Style for table element */
270   table {
271       border: 0.1em solid #000000;
272       border-collapse: collapse;
273       margin-left: auto;
274       margin-right: auto;
275       width: 100%;
276   }
```

comment
Line 269
style rule for table

Figure 8–22

- Press the ENTER key to insert a new Line 271, increase the indent, and then type **border: 0.1em solid #000000;** to insert a new property and value.

- Press the ENTER key to insert a new Line 272, and then type **border-collapse: collapse;** to insert a new property and value.

- Press the ENTER key to insert a new Line 273, and then type **margin-left: auto;** to insert a new property and value.

- Press the ENTER key to insert a new Line 274, and then type **margin-right: auto;** to insert a new property and value.

- Press the ENTER key to insert a new Line 275, and then type **width: 100%;** to insert a new property and value.

- Press the ENTER key to insert a new Line 276, decrease the indent, and then type **}** to insert a closing brace (Figure 8–22).

◄ | What is the result of setting the left and right margins to a value of auto?
Q&A | Specifying left and right margins of auto centers the table on the page.

2

- Save your changes and refresh classes.html in your browser (Figure 8–23).

Why does the border appear only around the sides of the table? The style rule you created applies to the table only. You will style the `th` and `td` elements in subsequent steps.

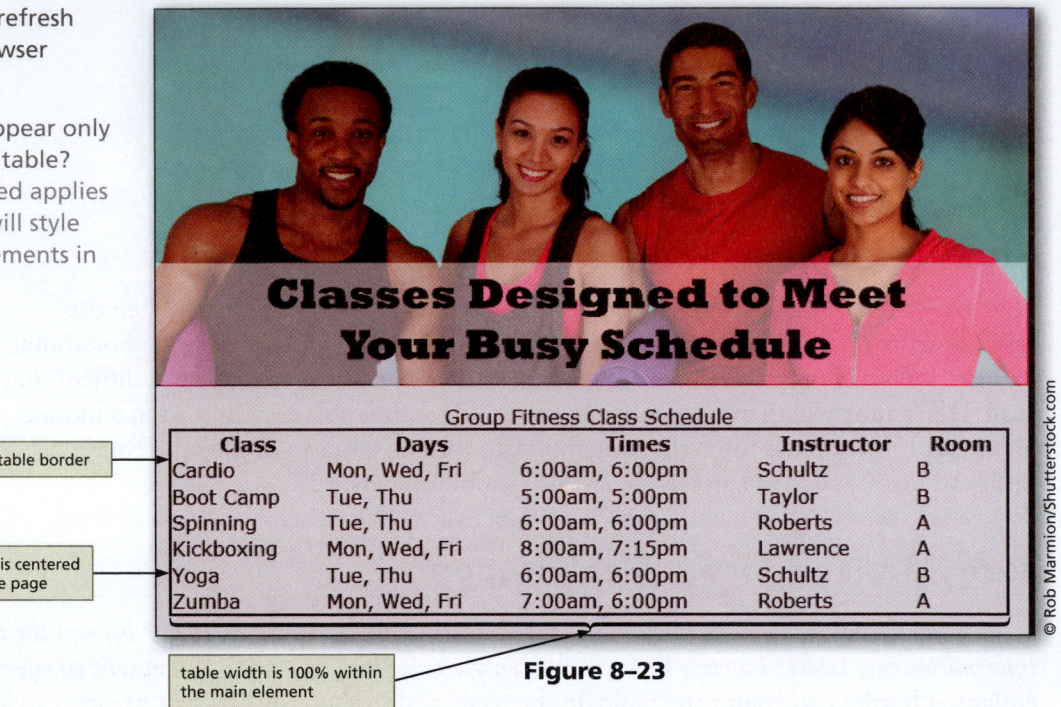

table border

table is centered on the page

table width is 100% within the main element

Figure 8–23

© Rob Marmion/Shutterstock.com

3

- In the styles.css file, tap or click at the end of Line 276, if necessary, and then press the ENTER key twice to insert new Lines 277 and 278.

- On Line 278, type `/* Style specifies border and padding for th and td elements */` to insert a new comment.

comment

Line 278

```
278  /* Style specifies border and padding for th and td elements */
279  th, td {
280      border: 0.1em solid #000000;
281      padding: 1em;
282  }
```

style rule for th and td elements

Figure 8–24

- Press the ENTER key to insert a new Line 279, and then type `th, td {` to insert a new selector.

- Press the ENTER key to insert a new Line 280, increase the indent, and then type `border: 0.1em solid #000000;` to insert a new property and value.

- Press the ENTER key to insert a new Line 281, and then type `padding: 1em;` to insert a new property and value.

- Press the ENTER key to insert a new Line 282, decrease the indent, and then type `}` to insert a closing brace (Figure 8–24).

What is the result of the new style? The style applies a thin (0.1em) solid black (#000000) border and 1em of padding to all sides of the table header and the table data elements.

4

- Save your changes and refresh classes.html in your browser (Figure 8–25).

borders and padding applied to th and td elements

Group Fitness Class Schedule				
Class	**Days**	**Times**	**Instructor**	**Room**
Cardio	Mon, Wed, Fri	6:00am, 6:00pm	Schultz	B
Boot Camp	Tue, Thu	5:00am, 5:00pm	Taylor	B
Spinning	Tue, Thu	6:00am, 6:00pm	Roberts	A
Kickboxing	Mon, Wed, Fri	8:00am, 7:15pm	Lawrence	A
Yoga	Tue, Thu	6:00am, 6:00pm	Schultz	B
Zumba	Mon, Wed, Fri	7:00am, 6:00pm	Roberts	A

Figure 8–25

5

- In the styles.css file, tap or click at the end of Line 282, if necessary, and then press the ENTER key twice to insert new Lines 283 and 284.

- On Line 284, type /* Style for th element */ to insert a new comment.

- Press the ENTER key to insert a new Line 285, and then type th { to insert a new selector.

comment

```
Line 284   284  /* Style for th element */
           285  th {
           286      background-color: #1D1D1C;
           287      color: #FFFFFF;
           288  }
```

style rule for th element

Figure 8–26

- Press the ENTER key to insert a new Line 286, increase the indent, and then type background-color: #1D1D1C; to insert a new property and value.

- Press the ENTER key to insert a new Line 287, and then type color: #FFFFFF; to insert a new property and value.

- Press the ENTER key to insert a new Line 288, decrease the indent, and then type } to insert a closing brace (Figure 8–26).

Q&A Why do I need to create another style rule for the th element?

The previous style rule applied to both the th and the td elements. This style rule applies only to the th element and uniquely formats the table header elements to have a dark gray background and white text.

6

- Save your changes and refresh classes.html in your browser (Figure 8–27).

formatting applied to th element

Group Fitness Class Schedule				
Class	**Days**	**Times**	**Instructor**	**Room**
Cardio	Mon, Wed, Fri	6:00am, 6:00pm	Schultz	B
Boot Camp	Tue, Thu	5:00am, 5:00pm	Taylor	B
Spinning	Tue, Thu	6:00am, 6:00pm	Roberts	A
Kickboxing	Mon, Wed, Fri	8:00am, 7:15pm	Lawrence	A
Yoga	Tue, Thu	6:00am, 6:00pm	Schultz	B
Zumba	Mon, Wed, Fri	7:00am, 6:00pm	Roberts	A

Figure 8–27

7

- In the styles.css file, tap or click at the end of Line 288, if necessary, and then press the ENTER key twice to insert new Lines 289 and 290.

- On Line 290, type `/* Style for caption element */` to insert a new comment.

- Press the ENTER key to insert a new Line 291, and then type `caption {` to insert a new selector.

```
        comment
Line 290  ──▶ 290  /* Style for caption element */
              291  caption {
              292      font-size: 1.5em;
              293      font-weight: bold;        ◀── style rule for
              294      padding-bottom: 0.5em;         caption element
              295  }
              296
              297  }  ◀── tablet media query
                         closing brace
```

Figure 8–28

- Press the ENTER key to insert a new Line 292, increase the indent, and then type `font-size: 1.5em;` to insert a new property and value.

- Press the ENTER key to insert a new Line 293, and then type `font-weight: bold;` to insert a new property and value.

- Press the ENTER key to insert a new Line 294, and then type `padding-bottom: 0.5em;` to insert a new property and value.

- Press the ENTER key to insert a new Line 295, decrease the indent, and then type `}` to insert a closing brace (Figure 8–28).

8

- Save your changes and refresh classes.html in your browser (Figure 8–29).

formatting applied to caption element ──▶

Group Fitness Class Schedule

Class	Days	Times	Instructor	Room
Cardio	Mon, Wed, Fri	6:00am, 6:00pm	Schultz	B
Boot Camp	Tue, Thu	5:00am, 5:00pm	Taylor	B
Spinning	Tue, Thu	6:00am, 6:00pm	Roberts	A
Kickboxing	Mon, Wed, Fri	8:00am, 7:15pm	Lawrence	A
Yoga	Tue, Thu	6:00am, 6:00pm	Schultz	B
Zumba	Mon, Wed, Fri	7:00am, 6:00pm	Roberts	A

Figure 8–29

1 CREATE CLASSES PAGE & TABLE | 2 STYLE TABLE
3 CREATE FORM | 4 STYLE FORM

To Style a Table for a Desktop Viewport

Create new style rules to style the table for the desktop viewport. *Why? Format the table to use a different background color and format the caption to use a different font color so that users can read them easily in a desktop viewport.* First, add a new style rule to the end of the desktop media query to format the table with a white background and a width of 85 percent. Next, create a style rule to format the caption text with a white font color. The following steps create new style rules for the desktop viewport.

1

- In the styles.css file, tap or click at the end of Line 429, and then press the ENTER key twice to insert new Lines 430 and 431.

- On Line 431, type `/* Style for table element */` to insert a new comment.

- Press the ENTER key to insert a new Line 432, and then type `table {` to insert a new selector.

- Press the ENTER key to insert a new Line 433, increase the indent, and then type `background-color: #FFFFFF;` to insert a new property and value.

- Press the ENTER key to insert a new Line 434, and then type `width: 85%;` to insert a new property and value.

- Press the ENTER key to insert a new Line 435, decrease the indent, and then type `}` to insert a closing brace (Figure 8–30).

Figure 8–30

2

- Press the ENTER key twice to insert new Lines 436 and 437.

- On Line 437, type `/* Style for caption element */` to insert a new comment.

- Press the ENTER key to insert a new Line 438, and then type `caption {` to insert a new selector.

- Press the ENTER key to insert a new Line 439, increase the indent, and then type `color: #FFFFFF;` to insert a new property and value.

- Press the ENTER key to insert a new Line 440, decrease the indent, and then type `}` to insert a closing brace (Figure 8–31).

Figure 8–31

3

🔍 **Experiment**

- By default, table captions are positioned above a table. To see what the caption looks like at the bottom of the table, add the caption-side property with a value of bottom to the caption style rule. Save your changes and then refresh classes.html in your browser. After you view the effect, remove the caption-side property from the caption style rule.

- Save your changes, refresh classes.html in your browser, and adjust the window to the size of a desktop viewport (Figure 8–32).

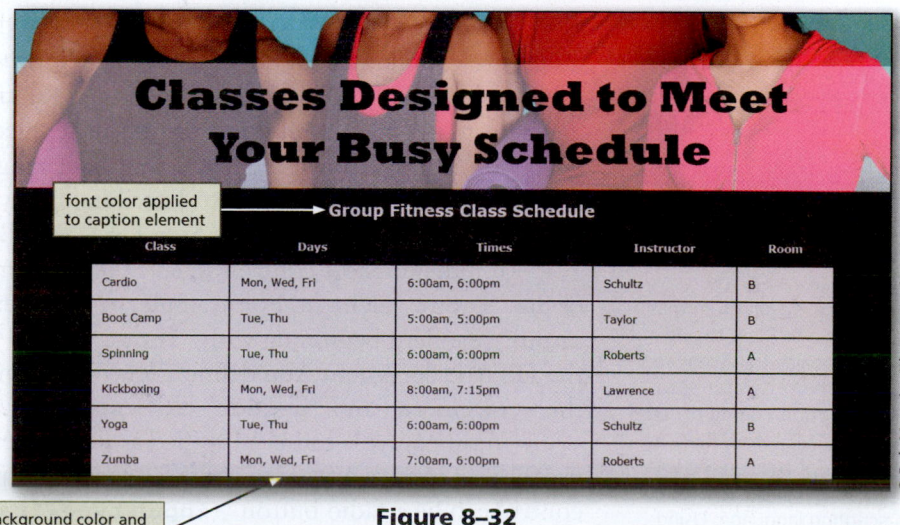

Figure 8–32

© Rob Marmion/Shutterstock.com

Q&A Why do the table's caption and background color look gray instead of white?

Recall that in Chapter 7, you added a style rule for the main element that sets an opacity of 85%. Because the table appears in the main element, the opacity is applied to the table, making the white look gray.

Break Point: If you want to take a break, this is a good place to do so. You can exit the text editor now. To resume at a later time, run your text editor, open the file called styles.css, and continue following the steps from this location forward.

Creating Webpage Forms

Forms provide a structured way to collect information from webpage visitors, such as a visitor's first name, last name, address, email, and telephone number. Visitors often complete webpage forms to register for an account or to make a purchase. Businesses use forms to gather visitor or customer information and store it in a database for future use. Figure 8–33 shows the Sign Up form on Facebook.com. Visitors complete the form to create a new Facebook account.

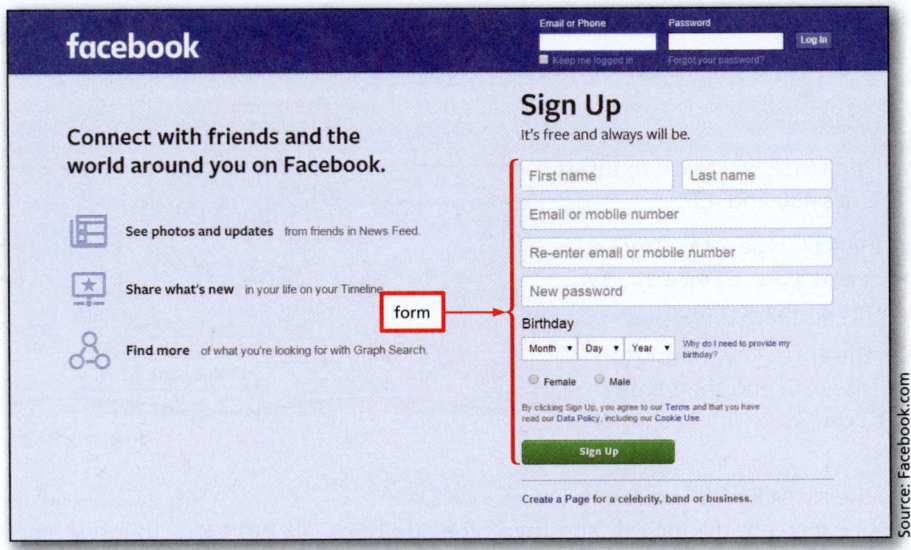

Figure 8–33

Form Controls

A form consists of a starting <form> tag and an ending </form> tag. All form elements are contained with the <form> and </form> tags. Input controls are used within the form element to collect visitor information. An **input control** is an interactive mechanism in which users enter text or make selections on a form. For example, on the Facebook Sign Up form, the text boxes requesting a visitor's first name and last name are input controls. A **label** is text describing the type of information to enter with an input control. On the Facebook Sign Up form, "Birthday" is a label.

You define most controls in an HTML form by using the `type` attribute of the `input` element. For example, to add a text box to a form, you include an `input` element beginning with `input type="text"` in the `form` element in the HTML document. You define a few other controls using separate elements, such as the `textarea` and `select` elements.

Input controls can be classified as data or text input controls. A webpage visitor uses a **data input control** to make a selection or perform a command. A data input control can be a radio button (`input type="radio"`), a check box (`input type="checkbox"`), a Submit button (`input type="submit"`), a Reset button (`input type="reset"`), or a selection menu (`select` element). A **text input control** accepts text, such as names, dates, and passwords, and is often called an input field. Table 8–3 lists input types for an input control.

BTW

HTML Forms and JavaScript
A **script** is a program that runs in a browser to add functionality to a webpage. You can use JavaScript to write scripts commonly used with HTML forms. Because JavaScript runs on the user's computer, it is a client-side scripting language. Using JavaScript, you can create pop-up messages and alerts, validate a form, and perform other beneficial tasks within a webpage.

Input Type	Description	Code Example
button	Creates a button; typically used to run a script when clicked	`<input type="button" onclick="alert('Good Morning!')" value="My Button")`
checkbox	Creates a single item or a list of items	`<input type="checkbox" name="fruit" value="banana">`
date	Creates an input field used to contain a date; the field may appear as a date picker, depending on the browser	`<input type="date" name="birthday">`
datetime	Creates an input field for a date and time with a time zone	`<input type="datetime" name="bdaydatetime">`
datetime-local	Creates an input field for a date and time without a time zone	`<input type="datetime-local" name="bddatetime">`
email	Creates an input field for an email address	`<input type="email" name="email" id="email">`
file	Creates a file-select field and a Browse button	`<input type="file" name="doc">`
hidden	Creates a control that is hidden from the user but contains information to process the form	`<input type="hidden" name="ship">`
image	Creates a graphical button instead of the default button	`<input type="image" name="reset" src="reset.png" alt="Reset">`
month	Creates an input field for a month and year; the field may appear as a date picker, depending on the browser	`<input type="month" name="bdaymth">`
number	Creates an input field for a numeric value	`<input type="number" name="cost">`
password	Creates a single-line field for a relatively small amount of text and masks the entered text as asterisks or bullets	`<input type="password" name="pw" id="pw">`

radio	Creates a list item	`<input type="radio" name="state" value="AL">`
		`<input type="radio" name="state" value="AK">`
		`<input type="radio" name="state" value="AZ">`

range	Creates an input field for a value within a range; the field may appear as a slider control, depending on the browser	`<input type="range" name="survey" min="0" max="10">`
reset	Resets the form	`<input type="reset" value="Reset Form">`
search	Creates an input field used as a search field	`<input type="search" name="search">`
submit	Submits a form for processing	`<input type="submit" value="Submit Form">`
tel	Creates an input field for a telephone number	`<input type="tel" name="phone" id="phone">`
text	Creates a single-line field for text	`<input type="text" name="fName" id="fName">`
time	Creates an input field for a time without a time zone; the field may appear as a time picker, depending on the browser	`<input type="time" name="time">`
url	Creates an input field for a URL	`<input type="url" name="page">`
week	Creates an input field for a week and year; the field may appear as a date picker, depending on the browser	`<input type="week" name="week">`

Table 8–3 Input Types

Regardless of the specific type, each input control has attributes that are used more frequently than the others:

- **name**, which identifies the specific information that is being sent when the form is submitted for processing. All controls have a name.

- **id**, which provides a unique ID for the element. Use the `id` attribute with input controls.

- **value**, which specifies the value of an `input` element and varies depending on input type. For text, password, and hidden controls, the `value` attribute defines the default value. For checkbox, radio, and image controls, it specifies the data submitted with the form when the control is selected. For button, reset, and submit controls, the `value` attribute defines the text on the button. All controls except textarea also have a `value` attribute. For a textarea field, no `value` attribute is possible because of the variability of the input.

Common input controls used with a form include text, password, email, tel, date, textarea, checkbox, radio, select, submit, and reset. Text input controls include the following types:

- **text box** (text control), for small amounts of text
- **password text box** (password control), for entering a password
- **email text box** (email control), for entering an email address
- **telephone text box** (tel control), for entering a telephone number
- **date text box** (date control), for entering a date
- **text area box** (textarea control), for larger amounts of text

Text, password, email, tel, and date controls accept a single line of text, such as a name or password. These text input controls have two frequently used attributes:

- **size**, which determines the width of the control in characters
- **maxlength**, which specifies the maximum number of characters accepted

For example, the first line of the following code creates a 25-character text box for the user's last name and the second line creates an eight-character text box for the user's password:

```
<p>Last Name: <input name="lastname" type="text"
        size="25"></p>
<p>Password: <input name="password" type="password"
        size="8"></p>
```

Because each **input** element uses the **size** attribute, a user can enter a last name longer than 25 characters and a password longer than eight characters. If the **input** elements used the **maxlength** attribute instead of **size**, a user could only enter up to 25 characters for the last name and up to eight characters for the password.

The maximum length of the text box may exceed the size of the text box that appears on the form. For example, consider a size of three characters and a maximum length of nine characters. If a webpage visitor enters more than three characters, the characters scroll to the left, allowing the visitor to enter a maximum of nine characters.

A **password control** is like a text control because it provides a text box for a single line of input—the password a visitor enters. However, as the visitor enters the password, the characters appear as asterisks or bullets, one per character. This feature helps protect the visitor's password from being observed by others as it is entered.

An **email control** is a text box where visitors enter an email address. Some browsers validate that the email address is in the proper format before submitting the form for processing. If the email address is not in the proper format, the browser displays a message asking the user to correct the data. A **tel control** is a text box where visitors enter a telephone number. A **date control** is a text box that accepts a date. Some browsers display a calendar when a visitor taps or clicks a date control.

A **textarea control** creates a text box that allows multiple lines of input. Textarea controls are useful to collect more than a single line of text from a webpage visitor, such as a product review. To create a textarea control, you use the **textarea** element instead of the **input** element. The **textarea** element has two primary attributes, which set the size of the textarea control:

rows, which specifies the number of rows, or lines, in the textarea control

cols, which sets the width of the textarea control as the number of columns, with each column containing one character.

The following is an example of HTML code defining a textarea control:

```
<label>What products would you like to see us offer?</label>
<textarea name="feedback" rows="3" cols="100"></textarea>
```

This textarea control provides three lines of 100 characters each to let visitors describe the products they want the website to offer.

A **checkbox control** allows a webpage visitor to select items from a list of one or more choices. Each choice appears with a graphical box, which can be checked (selected or on) or unchecked (deselected or off). By default, all check boxes are deselected. To set a particular check box to be preselected as the default, use the `checked` attribute and value (`checked="checked"`) within the <input> tag. The following is sample code for two checkbox controls that might appear on a form for a grocery store website where visitors select the kind of fruit they want to buy. The first line creates a check box for the Apple choice, which is selected (or checked) when the webpage opens. The second line shows the Peach choice.

```
<input name="fruit" type="checkbox" value="apple"
      checked="checked">Apple

<input name="fruit" type="checkbox" value="peach">Peach
```

Users can select more than one item in a check box list. For example, a user could select both apple and peach when selecting fruit on the grocery store website form.

A **radio control** limits the webpage visitor to only one choice from a list of choices. Each choice has a **radio button**, or option button, which typically appears as an open circle. When the visitor selects one of the radio buttons, all other radio buttons in the list are automatically deselected. By default, all radio buttons are deselected. To set a particular button as the default, you use the `checked` attribute and value within the <input> tag as you do with the checkbox control. The following is sample code to create two radio controls that might appear in a rental car website form:

```
<input name="car" type="radio" checked="checked"
      value="car">Car

<input name="truck" type="radio" value="truck">Truck
```

A visitor can choose to rent a car or a truck, with the Car radio button already selected when the form opens.

A **select control** creates a selection menu from which the visitor makes one or more choices. This prevents the visitor from having to type information into a text or textarea control. A select control is suitable when a limited number of choices are available. It appears on a form as a text box with a list arrow. The user taps or clicks the list arrow to view all the choices in the menu. The default choice appears first in the menu and is highlighted to indicate that it is selected.

Instead of using the `type` attribute of the `input` element, you define a select control using the `select` and `option` elements. The following is sample code for a select control:

```
<select name="station">
   <option>Pandora</option>
   <option>Internet Radio</option>
   <option>Live365</option>
   <option>Jango</option>
</select>
```

This selection menu contains four options—Pandora, Internet Radio, Live365, and Jango—with "Pandora" appearing as the selected option.

The **submit control** and the **reset control** create the Submit and Reset buttons. The **Submit button** sends the form information to the appropriate location for processing. When a webpage visitor taps or clicks the Submit button on the form, the name of each control and the value of its data are sent to the server to be processed.

BTW

Radio Buttons
Antique car radios were operated by a row of large black plastic buttons. Push one button, and you would get one preset radio station. You could push only one button at a time. Radio buttons on forms work the same way as the antique radio buttons—one button at a time. With check boxes, more than one option can be selected at a time.

The **Reset button** clears any input entered in the form, resetting the input controls to their defaults. A webpage form must include a submit control, and must also include a reset control. You use the `value` attribute to specify the text that appears on the button. The submit and reset controls are created with the following code:

```
<input type="submit" value="Submit">

<input type="reset" value="Reset">
```

Figure 8–34 shows an example of a form with several input controls, including text, email, tel, date, select, and textarea.

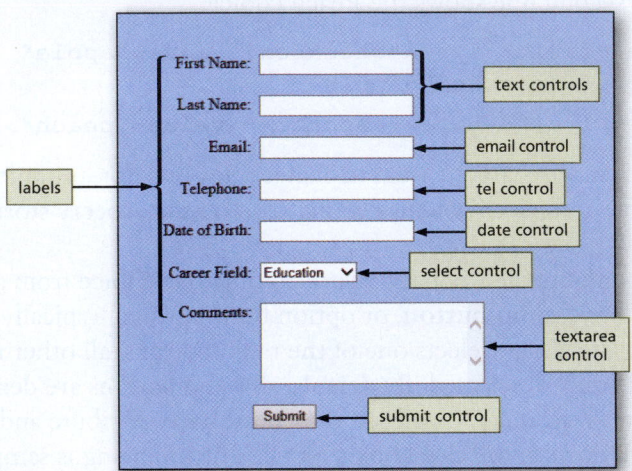

Figure 8–34

BTW

Customer Feedback

One way to use forms is to request and receive feedback from your visitors. Suggestions from visitors can help improve the website and give your visitors the sense that you care about their opinions. Taking visitor feedback into account leads to greater customer satisfaction.

Form Labels

Form labels identify the type of information to enter into or select from an input control. You add a label to a form using the `label` element. To connect a label to its control, include the `for` attribute with the same value as the input control's `id` value. The following code creates a label and a text box for a visitor's first name:

```
<label for="fName">First Name:</label>

<input type="text" name="fName" id="fName">
```

Attributes of HTML Tags Used to Create Forms

Many of the HTML tags used to create forms have several attributes. Table 8–4 lists common form attributes, including several new HTML5 attributes for the input elements. However, many of the new attributes are not yet supported by all major browsers, so be sure to test them first.

Table 8–4 Common Form Attributes

Attribute	Description	Code Example
accept-charset	Specifies the character set used for the form submission	`<form accept-charset="UTF-8">`
action	Specifies where to submit the form data (a URL)	`<form method="POST" action="form.php">`
autocomplete	Specifies whether a form or input field should use autocomplete; when enabled, the browser can complete input fields based on information entered in previous input fields	`<form autocomplete="on">`

Table 8–4 (*continued*)

Attribute	Description	Code Example
autofocus	Specifies that an input field should have focus when the page is displayed, which places the insertion point within a specific input field	`<input type="text" name="fName" id="fName" autofocus>`
disabled	Specifies that the input field is disabled and not available for user input	`<input type="radio" name="terms" value="Accept" disabled>`
enctype	Specifies the encoding of the form for submitting data.	`<form enctype="app/urlencoded">`
form	Specifies which form an input field belongs to when multiple forms are used within a website	`<input type="text" name="fName" id="fName" form="form1">`
formaction	Specifies the URL of a file that will process the input control when the form is submitted, overriding the form action attribute; use the formaction attribute with type="submit" and type="image" input types	`<input type="submit" value="Submit" formaction="process.asp">`
formenctype	Specifies how to encode form data during form submission; use the formenctype attribute with type="submit" and type="image" input types	`<input type="submit" formenctype="multipart/form-data">`
formmethod	Specifies the HTTP method used to transfer the form data, overriding the method attribute	`<input type="submit" value="Submit" formmethod="post">`
formnovalidate	Specifies to not validate an input element	`<input type="submit" value="Submit" formnovalidate>`
formtarget	Specifies a keyword that determines how to display a response when the form is submitted, such as a new, blank window	`<input type="submit" value="Submit" formtaget="_blank">`
height and width	Specifies the height and width for an image input type; always specify a height and width for the image input type	`<input type="image" src="btn1" alt="button 1" height="25" width="30">`

list	Used with the datalist element to specify predefined options for an input element	`<input list="music">`
		`<datalist id="music">`
		`<option value="Country">`
		`<option value="Classical">`
		`<option value="Hip Hop">`
		`<option value="Rock">`
		`</datalist>`

max and min	Specifies the maximum and minimum values for an input element	`<input type="number" name="survey" min="1" max="10">`
maxlength	Specifies the maximum number of characters allowed within the input field	`<input type="text" name="fName" id="fName" maxlength="15">`
method	Specifies the HTTP method used to submit the form data	`<form method="POST">`
multiple	Specifies that user may input more than one value within an input element; used with email and file input types	`<input type="email" name="email" id="email" multiple>`
novalidate	A form attribute that specifies not to validate form data when the submit button is clicked	`<form novalidate>`
pattern	Specifies a regular expression for checking an input element value; used with text, search, url, tel, email, and password input types	`<input type="password" name="pw" id="pw" pattern="[A-Za-z]{8}">`
placeholder	Specifies a hint of the type of information expected within an input field	`<input type="email" name="email" id="email" placeholder="youremail@domain.com">`
readonly	Specifies that the input field is a read-only field and cannot be modified	`<input type="text" name="ssn" id="ssn" value="555123654" readonly>`
required	Specifies that an input field is required	`<input type="text" name="fName" id="fName" required>`
size	Specifies the size (length) of an input field	`<input type="text" name="fName" id="fName" size="20">`
step	Specifies the legal number intervals for an `<input>` element	`<input type="number" name="math" step="5">`
target	Specifies the target address in the action attribute	`<form target="_blank">`
value	Specifies the value for an input field.	`<input type="text" name="fName" id="fName" value="Kate">`

Can I group certain types of form data?

Yes. You can use the fieldset element to group form elements. Use the legend element to provide a caption for the fieldset element.

Form Processing

After creating a form on a webpage, you need to identify how to process the form and when to submit it. Use the `action` attribute of the <form> tag to specify the action the browser takes when submitting the form. Browsers can send information entered in forms to a database on a web server or sent by email to an email address. Many websites use form processing software tools available from the web server. Another common way to transfer form information is through a **Common Gateway Interface (CGI) script**, a program written in a programming language (such as PHP or Perl) that communicates with the web server. The CGI script sends the information on the webpage form to the server for processing.

The `method` attribute of the <form> tag specifies how to send the data entered in the form to the server to be processed. HTML provides two primary ways to send form data: the get method and the post method. The **get method** appends the name-value pairs to the URL indicated in the action attribute. You need to be cautious when using the get method. Some web servers limit the size of a URL, so you run the risk of truncating relevant information when using the get method. The following is an example of a form tag with the get method and specified action:

```
<form method="GET" action="formInfo.php">
```

The **post method** sends a separate data file with the name-value pairs to the URL (or email address) indicated in the action attribute. The post method is the more common method because it can be used to send sensitive form data and does not have a size limitation. The following is an example of a form tag with the post method and specified action:

```
<form method="POST" action="formInfo.php">
```

Because using CGI scripts to process form data involves programming tasks that are beyond the scope of this book, the information entered in the form created in this chapter will not contain a `method` or an `action` attribute, and therefore, no data will be submitted to a web server or email address.

BTW

Security

Security is an important consideration when using web forms, especially when you are collecting credit card information. Search the web for specific information concerning the usage of the SSL-encrypted HTTPS protocol versus the unencrypted HTTP protocol.

How do I send the form data to my email address?

To send form data to an email address, use the action attribute with a value of mailto: followed by your email address within the form tag. Also include the method attribute with a value of post. An example is <form action="mailto:myemail@domain.com" method="POST">

To Add a Form, Labels, and Text Input Controls to the Contact Us Page

1 CREATE CLASSES PAGE & TABLE | 2 STYLE TABLE
3 CREATE FORM | 4 STYLE FORM

Insert a form on the Contact Us page to collect information from prospective clients. *Why? The Forward Fitness Club wants to create a database of prospective clients and use it to market their services. Most of this client data can come from the form on the Contact Us page.* Start by including a heading that alerts visitors to the form. Add the starting <form> tag to the page, and then insert label elements and input text controls. Finally, insert the ending </form> tag to complete the form. The following steps add a form to the Contact Us page.

1

- Open contact.html in your text editor to prepare to modify the document.

- On Line 33, delete the text and period, Contact us today., to remove them.

- Tap or click at the end of Line 33 and press the ENTER key to insert a new Line 34.

Figure 8–35

- On Line 34, type `<h2>Complete the form below to begin your free trial.</h2>` to insert a heading.

- Press the ENTER key twice to insert new Lines 35 and 36, and then type `<form><!-- Start Form -->` to insert a starting form tag and a comment.

- Press the ENTER key to insert a new Line 37, increase the indent, and then type `<label for="fName">First Name:</label>` to insert a label element.

- Press the ENTER key to insert a new Line 38, and then type `<input type="text" name="fName" id="fName">` to insert an text input control (Figure 8–35).

Q&A | What is the effect of the code I entered?

The form contains a First Name: label and a text box. The `fName` value for the `for` attribute in the `label` element matches the `fName` value for the `id` attribute in the `input` element to bind the controls together.

2

- Press the ENTER key twice to insert new Lines 39 and 40, and then type `<label for="lName">Last Name:</label>` to insert a label element.

Figure 8–36

- Press the ENTER key to insert a new Line 41, and then type `<input type="text" name="lName" id="lName">` to insert an text input control.

- Press the ENTER key to insert a new Line 42, decrease the indent, and then type `</form>` to insert an ending form tag (Figure 8–36).

Q&A | What is the difference between the `name` and the `id` attributes?

The `name` attribute identifies the information being sent when the form is submitted for processing. The `id` attribute is a unique identifier used for this specific form element and can be used by scripts.

3

- Save your changes, open contact. html in your browser, and adjust the window to the size of a tablet viewport to display the form on a light background (Figure 8–37).

Q&A | Why do the first name and last name labels and input elements appear on the same line?

You need to set a style rule to display these elements as block elements so they appear on separate lines. You will add style rules in later steps.

Figure 8–37

To Add email and tel Input Controls to a Form

Add email and tel input controls to collect the customer's email address and telephone number. *Why? Using these input controls instead of text controls makes it easier for visitors to enter the appropriate information.* First, add a new label and an **input** element with an **email** type. Then, add a new label and an **input** element with a **tel** type. The following steps add email and tel input controls to the form on the Contact Us page.

- Tap or click at the end of Line 41 and press the ENTER key twice to insert new Lines 42 and 43.

- On Line 43, type **<label for="email">Email:</label>** to insert a label element.

- Press the ENTER key to insert a new Line 44, and then type **<input type="email" name="email" id="email">** to insert an email input control (Figure 8–38).

Figure 8–38

- Press the ENTER key twice to insert new Lines 45 and 46, and then type **<label for="phone">Phone:</label>** to insert a label element.

- Press the ENTER key to insert a new Line 47, and then type **<input type="tel" id="phone" name="phone">** to insert a tel input control (Figure 8–39).

Figure 8–39

3

- Save your changes and refresh contact.html in your browser (Figure 8–40).

Q&A | Why does the email label appear on one line and the email input control appear on the next line? You need to add a style rule to format the controls. The style rule you add later that displays labels and input controls as block elements will solve this problem.

Figure 8–40

To Add Check Boxes to a Form

Add check boxes to collect information from customers about their primary interest in the fitness club. *Why? Using check boxes lets customers select more than one interest.* First, add a new paragraph element to introduce the check boxes. Next, insert checkbox input elements as list items in an unordered list. The following steps add check boxes to the form on the Contact Us page.

1

- Tap or click at the end of Line 47 and press the ENTER key twice to insert new Lines 48 and 49.

- On Line 49, type `<p>I would like more information about:</p>` to insert a paragraph element.

- Press the ENTER key to insert a new Line 50, and then type `<ul>` to insert a starting unordered list tag.

Figure 8–41

- Press the ENTER key to insert a new Line 51, increase the indent, and then type `<li><input type="checkbox" name="grpfit" id="grpfit" value="grpfit" class="chkbx">Group Fitness</li>` to insert a checkbox input element as a list item.

- Press the ENTER key to insert a new Line 52, and then type `<li><input type="checkbox" name="prtrain" id="prtrain" value="prtrain" class="chkbx">Personal Training</li>` to insert a checkbox input element as a list item.

- Press the ENTER key to insert a new Line 53, and then type `<li><input type="checkbox" name="nutr" id="nutr" value="nutr" class="chkbx">Nutrition</li>` to insert an checkbox input element as a list item.

- Press the ENTER key to insert a new Line 54, decrease the indent, and then type `</ul>` to insert a closing unordered list tag (Figure 8–41).

Q&A Why am I entering the check boxes in an unordered list?
Using an unordered list is an easy way to list the check boxes vertically.

What is the purpose of the class="chkbox" attribute and value?
The chkbox class will be used to style the checkbox input elements.

2

- Save your changes and refresh contact.html in your browser (Figure 8–42).

Q&A Why do bullets appear to the left of each checkbox?
You need to add a style rule to the style sheet that removes the bullets from the unordered list in the form.

Figure 8–42

1 CREATE CLASSES PAGE & TABLE | 2 STYLE TABLE
3 CREATE FORM | 4 STYLE FORM

To Add a select Element to a Form

Add a **select** element to learn how customers discovered the Forward Fitness Club. ***Why?*** *A select element lets users select from a list of options, restricting them to a valid option.* First, add a new label element for the referral source. Then, create a **select** element with five **option** elements. The following steps add a **select** element to the form on the Contact Us page.

1

- Tap or click at the end of Line 54 and press the ENTER key twice to insert new Lines 55 and 56.

- On Line 56, type `<label for="reference">Referral Source:</label>` to insert a label element.

- Press the ENTER key to insert a new Line 57, and then type `<select name="reference" id="reference">` to insert a starting select tag.

- Press the ENTER key to insert a new Line 58, increase the indent, and then type `<option value="ad">Advertisement</option>` to insert an option element.

- Press the ENTER key to insert a new Line 59, and then type `<option value="friend">Friend</option>` to insert an option element (Figure 8–43).

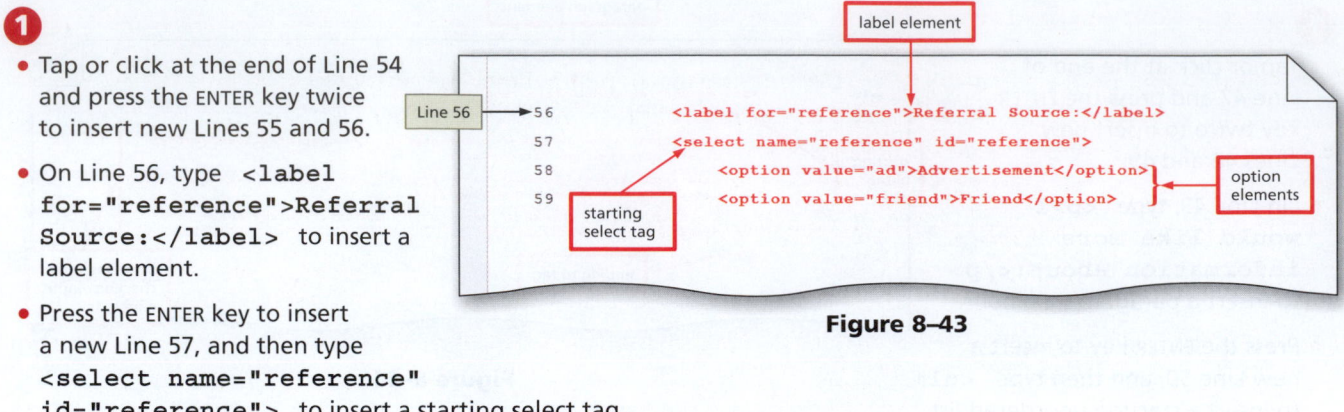

Figure 8–43

Q&A What is the effect of the code I entered?
The selection menu now includes two options: Advertisement and Friend. You add three other options in the next step.

2

- Press the ENTER key to insert a new Line 60, and then type `<option value="google">Google</option>` to insert an option element.

- Press the ENTER key to insert a new Line 61, and then type `<option value="social">Social Media</option>` to insert an option element.

- Press the ENTER key to insert a new Line 62, and then type `<option value="other">Other</option>` to insert an option element.

- Press the ENTER key to insert a new Line 63, decrease the indent, and then type `</select>` to insert a closing select tag (Figure 8–44).

Figure 8–44

3

- Save your changes, refresh contact.html in your browser, and then tap or click the new select control (Figure 8–45).

Q&A Does the order of the options matter?
Yes. The first option in the list appears in the select control before a visitor taps or clicks the control. The first option also appears as selected when a visitor taps or clicks the control.

Figure 8–45

To Add a textarea Element to a Form

Add a `textarea` element to the form to provide an opportunity for customers to ask questions. *Why?* *Customers can enter more than one line of text in a textarea control.* The following steps add a label and a `textarea` element to the form on the Contact Us page.

1

- Tap or click at the end of Line 63 and press the ENTER key twice to insert new Lines 64 and 65.

- On Line 65, type `<label for="questions"> Questions?</label>` to insert a label element.

- Press the ENTER key to insert a new Line 66, and then type `<textarea id="questions" name="questions" rows="3" cols="25"></textarea>` to insert a textarea element (Figure 8–46).

label element

Line 65 → 65   `<label for="questions">Questions?</label>`
66   `<textarea id="questions" name="questions" rows="3" cols="25"></textarea>`

textarea element

Figure 8–46

Q&A | What do the rows and cols attributes mean?
The rows and cols attributes set the size of the textarea control. In this case, the textarea control provides three 25-character lines where visitors can enter questions.

2

- Save your changes and refresh contact.html in your browser (Figure 8–47).

Q&A | Why does the textarea element appear to the right of the select element?
You need to create a style rule to display the textarea element as a block so it is positioned below the select element.

label element

Referral Source: [Advertisement ▾] Questions? [textarea element ⌃⌄]

We are located at:
25743 Bloom Court
Locket, GA 85524

Figure 8–47

To Add Submit and Reset Buttons to a Form

After adding text input controls and other form elements to a form, insert a submit control so that visitors can submit the form with their responses. Also include a button to reset the form in case a customer wants to clear the responses and enter new ones. *Why?* *Every form requires a submit control to send the information to a web server for processing if specified. Provide a reset control as a courtesy to users so they can remove all responses easily.* The following steps add submit and reset controls to the form on the Contact Us page.

1

- Tap or click at the end of Line 66 and press the ENTER key twice to insert new Lines 67 and 68.

- On Line 68, type `<input type="submit" id="submit" value ="Submit" class="btn">` to insert a submit input type.

- Press the ENTER key to insert a new Line 69, and then type `<input type="reset" id="reset" value="Reset Form" class="btn">` to insert a reset input type (Figure 8–48).

Line 68   submit input type element

68   `<input type="submit" id="submit" value="Submit" class="btn">`
69   `<input type="reset" id="reset" value="Reset Form" class="btn">`

reset input type element

Figure 8–48

Q&A | What is the purpose of the btn class?
The btn class will be used to specify a style rule for the submit and reset buttons.

Do I have to use Submit as the value for submit controls?
No. You can use other values, such as Send or OK. The value you specify appears as text on the button.

2

- Save your changes and refresh contact.html in your browser (Figure 8–49).

Q&A How can I make sure the Submit button and Reset Form button appear at the bottom of the form? You can create a style rule that displays the submit control as a block, which positions the submit and reset controls on separate lines at the bottom of the form. You will add this style rule in later steps.

Figure 8–49

Styling Forms

You apply CSS styles to forms for the same reason you style other webpage elements: to improve the appeal and usefulness of the form and its controls. For example, you position labels and form controls so users can quickly and clearly understand what type of information to provide in each control. As with tables, consider forms in the context of responsive design. Start with a simple, basic form for the mobile viewport. This form requests only the most essential information. You can modify the appearance and the content of the form for the tablet and desktop viewports. For example, you can change a form that is long and narrow in a mobile viewport so it is wider and arranges controls in columns in a desktop viewport. You can also include controls to collect optional information, such as product feedback, in tablet and desktop viewports.

To Style a Form for a Mobile Viewport

1 CREATE CLASSES PAGE & TABLE | 2 STYLE TABLE
3 CREATE FORM | **4 STYLE FORM**

Now that the form is complete, you can style the form for a mobile viewport. Start with a style rule that sets the display and bottom margin for the controls. *Why? To avoid horizontal scrolling, display the form elements as blocks so that each element appears on its own line.* Create another style rule to specify a block display for label elements. Create two other style rules: one to remove the bullet from the checkbox input elements, and another to format the chkbx class. The following steps create style rules for form elements in a mobile viewport.

1

- Open styles.css to prepare to modify it.

- Tap or click at the end of Line 117 and press the ENTER key twice to insert new Lines 118 and 119.

- On Line 119, type `/* Style rule for input, select, and textarea form elements */` to add a comment.

Figure 8–50

- Press the ENTER key to insert a new Line 120, and then type `input, select, textarea {` to add a new selector.

- Press the ENTER key to insert a new Line 121, increase the indent, and then type `display: block;` to insert a property and value.

- Press the ENTER key to insert a new Line 122, and then type `margin-bottom: 1em;` to insert a property and value.

- Press the ENTER key to insert a new Line 123, decrease the indent, and then type `}` to insert a closing brace (Figure 8–50).

Q&A Why did I enter the style rule by pressing the ENTER key at the end of Line 117 in the style sheet? Line 117 is the last line of the style sheet before the tablet media query. Any style you add after pressing the ENTER key applies to all viewports unless a later style in the tablet or desktop media query overrides it.

Why does the style rule use input, select, textarea as the selector? The purpose of the style rule is to format the form elements, and input, select, and textarea are the three form elements included in the form.

2

- Press the ENTER key twice to insert new Lines 124 and 125.

- On Line 125, type **/* Style rule for label element */** to insert a comment.

- Press the ENTER key to insert a new 126, and then type **label {** to add a new selector.

Line 125

```
125 /* Style rule for label element */
126 label {
127     display: block;
128 }
```

comment

style rule for label element

Figure 8–51

- Press the ENTER key to insert a new Line 127, increase the indent, and then type **display: block;** to insert a property and value.

- Press the ENTER key to insert a new Line 128, decrease the indent, and then type **}** to insert a closing brace (Figure 8–51).

Q&A Why am I adding this style rule to the style sheet?
By displaying each label on a separate line, this style rule helps to solve the positioning problems that appeared as you created the form.

3

- Press the ENTER key twice to insert new Lines 129 and 130.

- On Line 130, type **/* Style rule for unordered list within a form */** to insert a comment.

Line 130

```
130 /* Style rule for unordered list within a form */
131 form ul {
132     list-style-type: none;
133 }
```

comment

style rule for unordered list in form

Figure 8–52

- Press the ENTER key to insert a new Line 131, type **form ul {** to insert a new selector.

- Press the ENTER key to insert a new Line 132, increase the indent, and then type **list-style-type: none;** to insert a property and value.

- Press the ENTER key to insert a new Line 133, decrease the indent, and then type **}** to insert a closing brace (Figure 8–52).

Q&A What is the effect of the style rule I entered in this step?
This style rule removes the bullets from the unordered list of check boxes in the form by specifying none as the value of the list-style-type property.

4

- Press the ENTER key twice to insert new Lines 134 and 135.

- On Line 135, type **/* Style rule for chkbx class */** to insert a comment.

- Press the ENTER key to insert a new Line 136, and then type **.chkbx {** to insert a new selector.

Line 135

```
135 /* Style rule for chkbx class */
136 .chkbx {
137     display: inline-block;
138 }
```

comment

style rule for chkbx class

Figure 8–53

- Press the ENTER key to insert a new Line 137, increase the indent, and then type **display: inline-block;** to insert a property and value.

- Press the ENTER key to insert a new Line 138, decrease the indent, and then type **}** to insert a closing brace (Figure 8–53).

Q&A Why am I setting a display of inline-block for the chkbx class?
This style rule displays elements in the chkbx class (the check boxes) inline while retaining their block element characteristics. The result is that each check box appears on its own line but allows the list item text to appear to its right.

5

- Save your changes, refresh contact.html in your browser, and adjust the browser window to a mobile viewport (Figure 8–54).

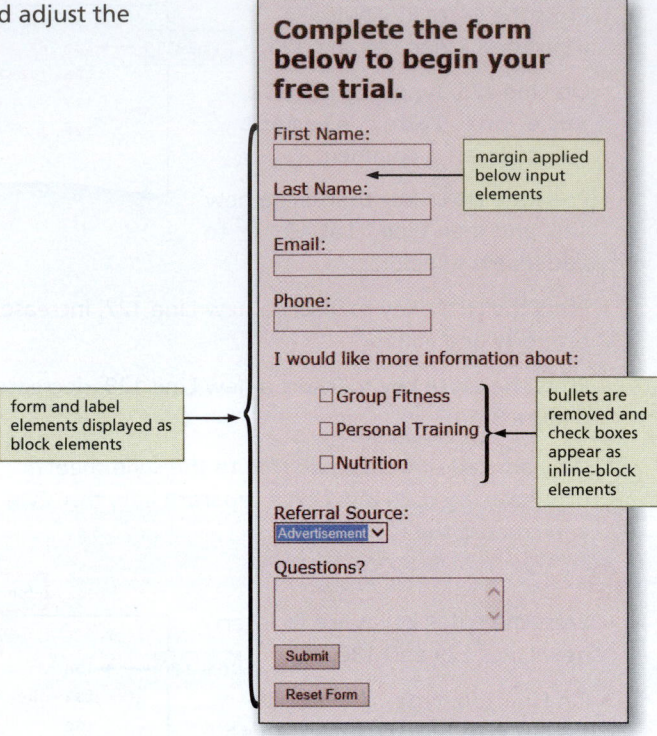

Figure 8–54

To Style a Form for a Tablet Viewport

1 CREATE CLASSES PAGE & TABLE | 2 STYLE TABLE
3 CREATE FORM | 4 STYLE FORM

Now that you have styled the form for a mobile viewport, you can also style the form for a tablet viewport. *Why? The current styles work best for the form in a mobile viewport. Optimize the form for the best viewing experience by a tablet user.* In the tablet media query, change the format of the label elements so they appear to the left of each input element. Also create a style rule to format the btn class, which includes the submit and reset controls. Move the buttons to the right to take advantage of increased screen space by setting a wide left margin. The following steps create new style rules for form elements within the tablet media query of the styles.css file:

1

- Tap or click at the end of Line 316 and press the ENTER key twice to insert new Lines 317 and 318.

- On Line 318, type `/* Style rule label element */` to add a comment.

- Press the ENTER key to insert a new Line 319, and then type `label {` to add a new selector.

- Press the ENTER key to insert a new Line 320, increase the indent, and then type `float: left;` to insert a property and value.

- Press the ENTER key to insert a new Line 321, and then type `padding-right: 0.5em;` to insert a property and value.

- Press the ENTER key to insert a new Line 322, and then type `text-align: right;` to insert a property and value.

- Press the ENTER key to insert a new Line 323, and then type `width: 10em;` to insert a property and value.

- Press the ENTER key to insert a new Line 324, decrease the indent, and then type `}` to insert a closing brace (Figure 8–55).

```
318   /* Style rule for label element */
319   label {
320       float: left;
321       padding-right: 0.5em;
322       text-align: right;
323       width: 10em;
324   }
```

Figure 8–55

Q&A

Q&A

Why did I enter the style rule starting on Line 318 of the style sheet?
Line 318 is part of the tablet media query, so the new label style overrides the one you set earlier when the form is display in a tablet viewport.

What is the effect of the new style rule?
In a tablet viewport, the form labels float to the left of the controls. They also include a small amount of padding to separate each label from its control, and are right-aligned within a 10em-wide area.

- Press the ENTER key twice to insert new Lines 325 and 326.

- On Line 326, type `/* Style rule for btn class */` to insert a comment.

- Press the ENTER key to insert a new Line 327, and then type `.btn {` to add a new selector.

- Press the ENTER key to insert a new Line 328, increase the indent, and then type `margin-left: 12em;` to insert a property and value.

- Press the ENTER key to insert a new Line 329, decrease the indent, and then type `}` to insert a closing brace (Figure 8–56).

Figure 8–56

- Save your changes, refresh contact.html in your browser, and adjust the browser window to a tablet viewport (Figure 8–57).

Figure 8–57

To Style a Form for a Desktop Viewport

Now that you have styled the form for a mobile and tablet viewports, you can also style the form for a desktop viewport. ***Why?*** *The main area of the webpage in a desktop viewport has a dark gray background. Use a light background color for the form to make it readable in a desktop viewport.* The paragraph introducing the form also appears in white text, so you should change its color to a darker one that is easy to read against a light background. In the desktop media query, create a new style rule to apply a background color and padding to the form element. Then, create a new style rule to apply color to the paragraph within the form element. The following steps create style rules for a form element and form paragraph element within the desktop media query of the styles.css file.

1

- Tap or click at the end of Line 474 and press the ENTER key twice to insert new Lines 475 and 476.

- On Line 476, type `/* Style rule for form element */` to add a comment.

- Press the ENTER key to insert a new Line 477, and then type `form {` to add a new selector.

- Press the ENTER key to insert a new Line 478, increase the indent, and then type `background-color: #FFFFFF;` to insert a property and value.

Figure 8–58

- Press the ENTER key to insert a new Line 479, and then type `padding: 1em;` to insert a property and value.

- Press the ENTER key to insert a new Line 480, decrease the indent, and then type `}` to insert a closing brace.

- Press the ENTER key twice to insert new Lines 481 and 482.

- On Line 482, type `/* Style rule for paragraph with form element */` to insert a comment.

- Press the ENTER key to insert a new 483, and then type `form p {` to add a new selector.

- Press the ENTER key to insert a new Line 484, increase the indent, and then type `color: #000000;` to insert a property and value.

- Press the ENTER key to insert a new Line 485, decrease the indent, and then type `}` to insert a closing brace (Figure 8–58).

Q&A

How do these style rules change the appearance of the form?

In a desktop viewport, the form's background changes from dark gray to white, allowing you to read the form contents. The paragraph introducing the check boxes changes from white to black so you can read its text against the white background of the form.

2

- Save your changes, refresh contact.html in your browser, and adjust the browser window to a desktop viewport (Figure 8–59).

Figure 8–59

To Validate the Style Sheet

Always run your files through W3C's validator to check the document for errors. If the document has any errors, validating gives you a chance to identify and correct them. Validation is also an effective troubleshooting tool during the development process and adds a valuable level of professionalism to your work. The following steps validate a CSS document:

1 Open your browser and type `http://jigsaw.w3.org/css-validator/` in the address bar to display the W3C CSS Validation Service page.

2 Tap or click the By file upload tab to display the Validate by file upload information.

3 Tap or click the Browse button to display the Choose File to Upload dialog box.

4 Navigate to your css folder to find the styles.css file.

5 Tap or click the styles.css document to select it.

6 Tap or click the Open button to upload the selected file to the W3C CSS validator.

7 Tap or click the Check button to send the document through the validator and display the validation results page.

8 If necessary, correct any errors, save your changes, and run through the validator again to revalidate the page.

To Validate the HTML Files

Every time you create a new webpage or modify an existing webpage, run it through W3C's validator to check the document for errors. If any errors exist, you need to correct them. Validation is also an effective troubleshooting tool during the development process and adds a valuable level of professionalism to your work. The following steps validate an HTML document.

1 Open your browser and type `http://validator.w3.org/` in the address bar to display the W3C validator page.

2 Tap or click the Validate by File Upload tab to display the Validate by File Upload information.

3 Tap or click the Choose File button to display the Open dialog box.

4 Navigate to your fitness folder to find the classes.html file.

5 Tap or click the classes.html document to select it.

6 Tap or click the Open button to upload it to the W3C validator.

7 Tap or click the Check button to send the document through the validator and display the validation results page.

8 If necessary, correct any errors, save your changes, and run through the validator again to revalidate the page.

9 Follow these steps to validate the contact.html page and correct any errors.

Chapter Summary

In this chapter, you learned how to include tables and forms on webpages. You created a table that displays related information and then formatted it using CSS properties you have used before and one new property specific to tables. You also learned about webpage forms and form controls, including the HTML elements, attributes, and values for creating the controls you need. Finally, you used CSS styles to format a form for mobile, tablet, and desktop viewports. The items listed below include all the new skills you have learned in this chapter, with the tasks grouped by activity.

Discovering Tables
Add a Table Element to the Classes Page
(HTML 385)

Styling Table Elements
Style a Table for a Tablet Viewport (HTML 391)
Style a Table for a Desktop Viewport
(HTML 394)

Creating Webpage Forms
Add a Form, Labels, and Text Input Controls to the
Contact Us Page (HTML 402)

Add email and tel Input Controls to a Form
(HTML 404)
Add Check Boxes to a Form (HTML 404)
Add a select Element to a Form (HTML 405)
Add a textarea Element to a Form (HTML 407)
Add Submit and Reset Buttons to a Form
(HTML 407)

Styling Forms
Style a Form for a Mobile Viewport (HTML 408)
Style a Form for a Tablet Viewport (HTML 410)
Style a Form for a Desktop Viewport (HTML 412)

 How will you improve the design of your website?

Use these guidelines as you complete the assignments in this chapter and create your own webpages outside of this class.

1. Determine if a table is right for your webpage.

   a) Determine if the information is best presented in a tabular format.

   b) Determine the number of rows and columns needed for the table.

   c) Determine whether or not the table can be easily displayed within a mobile viewport of if another format is needed to summarize the content for a mobile viewport.

2. Determine how to style the table elements.

   a) Determine how to style the table caption to make it stand out.

   b) Determine how to style each table element for mobile, tablet, and desktop viewports.

3. Determine the type of information your form should collect.

   a) Identify the different input types needed within your form.

   b) Determine the attributes needed for each input element.

   c) Determine what other form elements to use within your form.

4. Style the form for mobile, tablet, and desktop viewports.

   a) Determine the alignment and look of the form elements for a mobile viewport and then style.

   b) Determine the alignment and look of the form elements for a tablet viewport and then style.

   c) Determine the alignment and look of the form elements for a desktop viewport and then style.

5. Determine the action and method used to submit the form.

   a) Evaluate web server software capabilities to determine the best action and method for the form submission.

   b) Determine security measures needed to encode confidential data.

CONSIDER THIS

How should you submit solutions to questions in the assignments identified with a ✳ symbol?
Every assignment in this book contains one or more questions identified with a ✳ symbol. These questions require you to think beyond the assigned presentation. Present your solutions to the questions in the format required by your instructor. Possible formats may include one or more of these options: create a document that contains the answer; present your answer to the class; discuss your answer in a group; record the answer as audio or video using a webcam, smartphone, or portable media player; or post answers on a blog, wiki, or website.

Apply Your Knowledge

Reinforce the skills and apply the concepts you learned in this chapter.

Using Tables

Instructions: In this exercise, you will use your text editor to create a table and apply table styles. First, you insert a table element. Next, you add a table caption, table rows, table headers, and table data. Then, you create style rules to format the table. Work with the apply08.html file in the apply folder and the applystyles08.css file in the apply\css folder from the Data Files for Students. The completed webpage is shown in Figure 8–60. You will also use professional web development practices to indent, space, comment, and validate your code.

2017 Sales by Quarter

Product	Quarter 1	Quarter 2	Quarter 3	Quarter 4
Tablets	$24,500	$21,525	$20,217	$28,575
Monitors	$12,825	$12,400	$11,900	$14,233
Laptops	$33,000	$32,750	$31,595	$32,465
Desktops	$21,478	$20,895	$18,200	$21,625

Designed by: Student's Name

Figure 8–60

Perform the following tasks:

1. Open apply08.html in your text editor, review the page, add a title, modify the comment at the top of the page to include your name and today's date, and replace "Student's Name" with your name in the footer element.

2. Open the applystyles08.css file from the apply\css folder. Modify the comment at the top of the style sheet to include your name and today's date.

3. In the apply08.html file, add a `table` element within the `main` element.

4. In the apply08.html file, add the following caption to the `table` element:

```
<caption>2017 Sales by Quarter</caption>
```

5. In the apply08.html file, add the following elements within the `table` element:

```
<tr>
<th>Product</th>
<th>Quarter 1</th>
```

Continued >

Apply Your Knowledge *continued*

```
      <th>Quarter 2</th>
      <th>Quarter 3</th>
      <th>Quarter 4</th>
   </tr>

   <tr>
     <th>Tablets</th>
            <td>&#36;24,500</td>
            <td>&#36;21,525</td>
            <td>&#36;20,217</td>
            <td>&#36;28,575</td>
   </tr>

   <tr>
     <th>Monitors</th>
            <td>&#36;12,825</td>
            <td>&#36;12,400</td>
            <td>&#36;11,900</td>
            <td>&#36;14,233</td>
   </tr>

   <tr>
     <th>Laptops</th>
            <td>&#36;33,000</td>
            <td>&#36;32,750</td>
            <td>&#36;31,595</td>
            <td>&#36;32,465</td>
   </tr>

   <tr>
     <th>Desktops</th>
            <td>&#36;21,478</td>
            <td>&#36;20,895</td>
            <td>&#36;18,200</td>
            <td>&#36;21,625</td>
   </tr>
```

6. In the applystyles08.css file, create the following style rules:

```
table {
        width: 80%;
        margin-left: auto;
        margin-right: auto;
}
```

```
table, tr, th, td {
        border-collapse: collapse;
        border: solid 0.1em #000000;
        padding: 1em;
}

td {

        text-align: center;

}

caption {
        font-size: 2em;
        padding: 1em;
        margin-top: 1em;

}
```

7. Add appropriate comments above each style rule.

8. Save all of your changes and open the apply08.html in your browser.

9. Validate your HTML document using the W3C validator found at validator.w3.org and fix any errors that are identified.

10. Validate your CSS file using the W3C validator found at http://jigsaw.w3.org/css-validator/ and fix any errors that are identified.

11. Submit the files in a format specified by your instructor.

12. ✳ In step 5, you coded a table header as the first element within rows two through five. What was the purpose of using the table header elements here? What steps would you take to style these table header elements to left-align the text?

Extend Your Knowledge

Extend the skills you learned in this chapter and experiment with new skills. You may need to use additional resources to complete the assignment.

Discovering HTML5 Input Types and Browser Support

Instructions: In this exercise, you research HTML5 form input types, discover which input types are supported by each browser, and then create a table using HTML that displays your findings. Work with the extend08.html file in the extend folder and the extendstyles08.css file in the extend\css folder from the Data Files for Students. An example of the table is shown in Figure 8–61. You will also use professional web development practices to indent, space, comment, and validate your code.

Perform the following tasks:

1. Use your browser to research HTML5 form input types.

2. Find at least 10 HTML5 input types and note which input types are supported by each major browser.

3. Open extend08.html in your text editor, review the page, add a title, modify the comment at the top of the page to include your name and today's date, link the file to extendstyles08.css, and replace "Student's Name" with your name in the **footer** element.

Continued >

Extend Your Knowledge *continued*

		HTML5 Input Types Browser Support			
Input Type	**IE**	**Chrome**	**Firefox**	**Safari**	**Opera**
input type 1	No	Yes	Yes	No	Yes
input type 2	No	Yes	No	Yes	Yes
input type 3	No	No	No	Yes	Yes
input type 4	Yes	Yes	Yes	No	Yes
input type 5	Yes	Yes	Yes	No	Yes
input type 6	Yes	Yes	Yes	Yes	Yes
input type 7	Yes	Yes	Yes	No	Yes
input type 8	No	Yes	No	Yes	No
input type 9	Yes	Yes	Yes	No	Yes
input type 10	Yes	Yes	Yes	No	Yes

Designed by: Student's Name

Figure 8–61

4. Open the extendstyles08.css file from the extend\css folder. Modify the comment at the top of the style sheet to include your name and today's date.

5. In the extend08.html file, create a `table` element to summarize your findings and use the following as column headers for the first row: `Input Type`, `IE`, `Chrome`, `Firefox`, `Safari`, `Opera`.

6. Include a table caption.

7. Apply table styles and use Figure 8–61 as a reference.

8. Add appropriate comments above each style rule.

9. Save all of your changes and open extend08.html in your browser.

10. Validate your HTML document using the W3C validator found at validator.w3.org and fix any errors that are identified.

11. Validate your CSS file using the W3C validator found at http://jigsaw.w3.org/css-validator/ and fix any errors that are identified.

12. Submit the files in a format specified by your instructor.

13. ✺ In this exercise, you discovered which HTML5 input types were supported by each major browser. Provide an example of code for two of the input types you listed in your table and include at least three attributes for the input element.

Analyze, Correct, Improve

Analyze a website, correct all errors, and improve it.

Improving an HTML Form

Instructions: Work with the analyze08.html file in the analyze folder and the analyzestyles08.css file in the analyze\css folder from the Data Files for Students. The analyze08.html webpage contains a form with various input controls. Analyze the page to determine the type of information

Figure 8–62

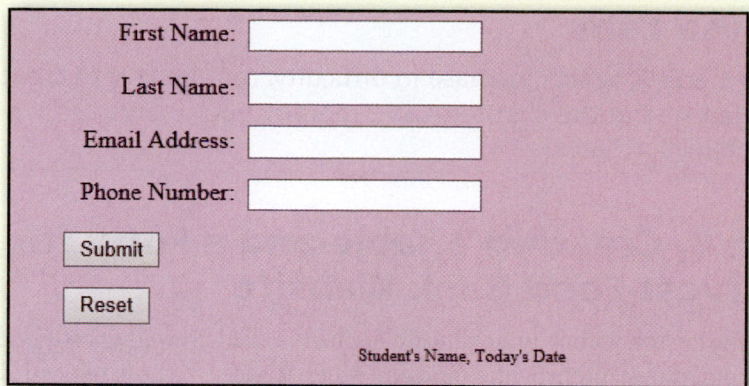

Figure 8–63

being collected by the form and add labels for each input control. Next, create submit and reset buttons, and then style the form for mobile and tablet viewports. Use Figures 8-62 and 8-63 as a guide to correct these files.

1. Correct

 a. Open the analyze08.html file in your text editor from the Data Files for Students. Modify the comment at the top of the page to include your name and today's date and then link the file to analyzestyles08.css.

 b. Open the analyzestyles08.css file in your text editor from the Data Files for Students and then modify and correct the comment at the top of the document to include your name and today's date.

 c. Review the form elements within the analyze08.html file and add labels to all input controls. Be sure to include the `for` attribute.

2. Improve

 a. In the analyze08.html file, add submit and reset buttons.

 b. Create style rules in the analyzestyles08.css file to style the form elements for a mobile viewport. Display input controls and label elements as block elements. Apply `1em` of bottom margin to input controls.

 c. Create style rules in the analyzestyles08.css file to style the form elements for a tablet viewport. Float the label elements left, apply `0.5em` of right padding, align the text `right`, and apply a width of `7em`. Apply `1em` of bottom margin to input controls.

 d. Save all of your changes and open the analyze08.html in your browser.

 e. Validate your CSS file using the W3C validator found at http://jigsaw.w3.org/css-validator/ and fix any errors that are identified.

 f. Validate your HTML webpage using the W3C validator found at validator.w3.org and fix any errors that are identified.

 g. ✸ Identify at least three steps you would take to further improve this form.

Continued >

In the Labs

Labs 1 and 2, which increase in difficulty, require you to create webpages based on what you learned in the chapter; Lab 3 requires you to dive deeper into a topic covered in the chapter.

Lab 1: Creating a Table and a Form for the New Harvest Food Bank Website

Problem: You volunteer at a local food bank called New Harvest Food Bank that collects community food donations and provides food and other services to those in need. The company has asked you to create a responsive website. You have already created the website but now need to create the Volunteer page and insert a table. You also need to create the Contact Us page and insert a form. Create and style the table on the Volunteer page as shown in Figure 8–64 for the mobile, tablet, and desktop viewports. Create and style the form on the Contact Us page as shown in Figure 8–65 for the mobile, tablet, and desktop viewports.

(a) Mobile viewport

(b) Tablet viewport

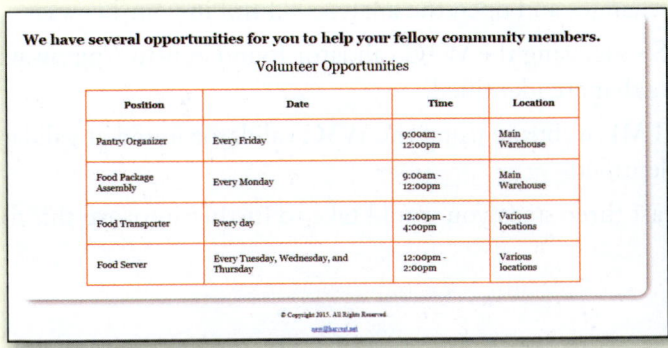

(c) Desktop viewport

Figure 8–64

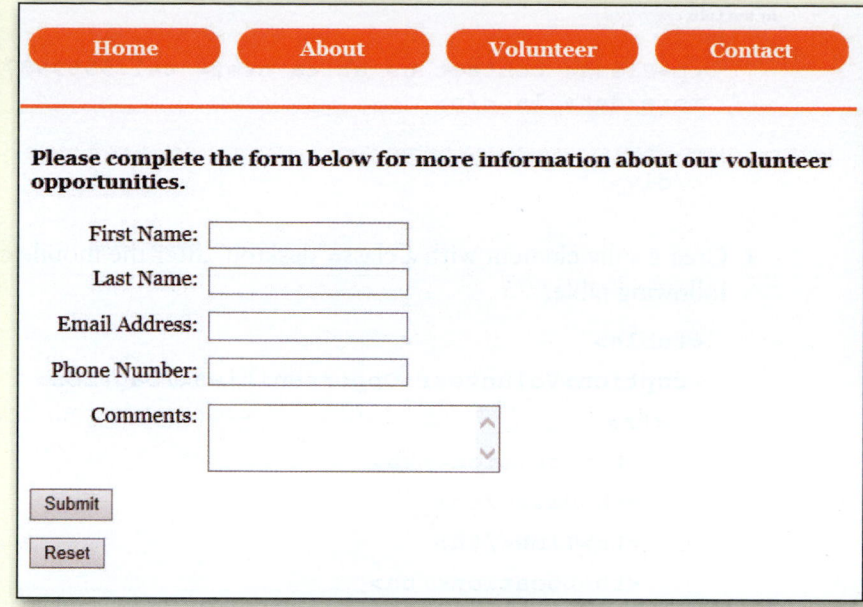

(a) Mobile viewport

(b) Tablet viewport

(c) Desktop viewport

Figure 8–65

Instructions: Perform the following tasks:

1. Open your text editor and then open the foodbank.html template file in the lab1 folder and use it to create the volunteer.html file.

2. In the volunteer.html document, update the comment at the top of the page to include today's date, then create an h2 element within the main element: `<h2>We have several opportunities for you to help your fellow community members.</h2>`.

3. Create the following div element below the h2 element.

```
<div class="mobile">

<p>Our Volunteer Opportunities include:</p>
  <ul>
     <li>Pantry Organizer</li>
     <li>Food Package Assembly</li>
     <li>Food Transporter</li>
     <li>Food Server</li>
  </ul>
```

Continued >

In the Labs *continued*

```
<p>Please contact us at <a href="tel:5559987">(555) 555-9987</a> for
more details.</p>

</div>
```

4. Create a div element with a class="desktop" after the mobile class div and then add the following table:

```
<table>
<caption>Volunteer Opportunities</caption>
  <tr>
    <th>Position</th>
    <th>Date</th>
    <th>Time</th>
    <th>Location</th>
  </tr>

  <tr>
      <td>Pantry Organizer</td>
      <td>Every Friday</td>
      <td>9:00am - 12:00pm</td>
      <td>Main Warehouse</td>
  </tr>

  <tr>
      <td>Food Package Assembly</td>
      <td>Every Monday</td>
      <td>9:00am - 12:00pm</td>
      <td>Main Warehouse</td>
  </tr>

  <tr>
      <td>Food Transporter</td>
      <td>Every day</td>
      <td>12:00pm - 4:00pm</td>
      <td>Various locations</td>
  </tr>

  <tr>
      <td>Food Server</td>
      <td>Every Tuesday, Wednesday, and Thursday</td>
      <td>12:00pm - 2:00pm</td>
      <td>Various locations</td>
  </tr>

</table>
```

5. In the fbstyles.css file, modify the comment at the top of the page to include today's date.

6. In the fbstyles.css file, create the following new style rules within the tablet media query and include comments for each:

```
table, th, td {
    border: solid 0.1em #FF6600;
    border-collapse: collapse;
    padding: 1em;
}


caption {
    font-size: 1.5em;
    padding-bottom: 1em;
}
```

7. In the fbstyles.css file, create the following new style rules within the desktop media query and include a comment:

```
table {
    width: 80%;
    margin-left: auto;
    margin-right: auto;
    margin-bottom: 1em;
}
```

8. Save all files and open the volunteer.html page within a browser and view the page in all three viewports, as shown in Figure 8–64.

9. Open your text editor and then open the foodbank.html template file in the lab1 folder. Use the template to create the contact.html file.

10. In the contact.html document, update the comment at the top of the page to include today's date, and then create an h4 element within the main element: `<h4>Please complete the form below for more information about our volunteer opportunities.</h4>`.

11. Create the following form below the h4 element within the main element:

```
<form>
    <label for="fName">First Name:</label>
    <input type="text" name="fName" id="fName">

    <label for="lName">Last Name:</label>
    <input type="text" name="lName" id="lName">

    <label for="email">Email Address:</label>
    <input type="email" name="email" id="email">

    <label for="phone">Phone Number:</label>
    <input type="tel" name="phone" id="phone">
```

Continued >

In the Labs *continued*

```
<label for="comments">Comments:</label>
<textarea id="comments" name="comments" rows="3" cols="25">
</textarea>


<input type="submit" value="Submit">
<input type="reset" value="Reset">
</form>
```

12. In the fbstyles.css file, create the following new style rules above the media queries and include comments for each:

```
input, textarea {
    display: block;
    margin-bottom: 1em;
}


label {
    display: block;
}
```

13. In the fbstyles.css file, create the following new style rules within the tablet media query and include a comment:

```
label {
    float: left;
    padding-right: 0.5em;
    text-align: right;
    width: 8em;
}
```

14. Save all files, open the contact.html page within a browser, and view the page in all three viewports, as shown in Figure 8–65.

15. Validate your HTML code and fix any errors.

16. Validate your CSS code and fix any errors.

17. Submit your assignment in the format specified by your instructor.

18. ✳ In this assignment, you created a form on the Contact Us page. Research the radio button, describe how you could add it to this form, and provide an example of the HTML code required.

Lab 2: Creating Two Forms for Steve's Screen Services

Problem: You work for a screening company called Steve's Screen Services that specializes in screening, cleaning, and repairing screened patios. The company has asked you to create a responsive website. You have already created the website, but now need to create the Quote and Contact Us pages. You add and style a form for both pages. Style the webpages as shown in Figure 8–66 and Figure 8–67 for mobile, tablet, and desktop viewports.

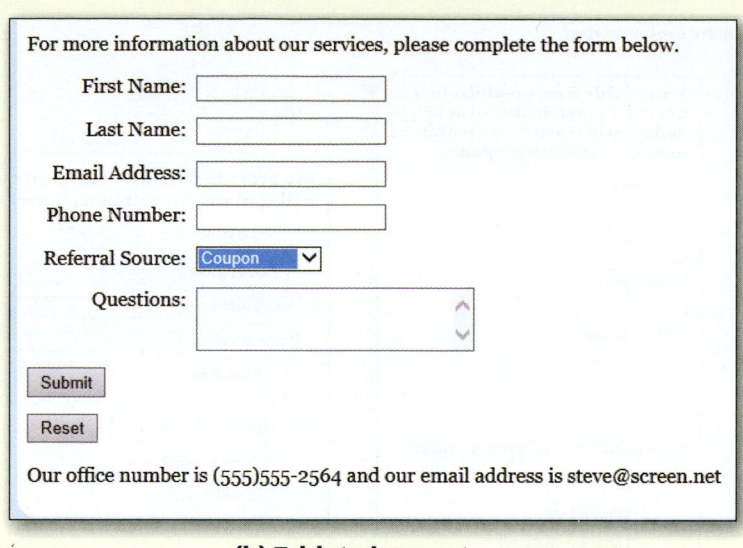

(a) Mobile viewport

(b) Tablet viewport

(c) Desktop viewport

Figure 8–66

Instructions: Perform the following tasks:

1. Open your text editor, open the stevescreen.html template file in the lab2 folder, and then use it to create the contact.html file.

2. In the contact.html document, update the comment at the top of the page to include today's date, and then create an paragraph element within the main element: `<p>For more information about our services, please complete the form below.</p>`.

3. Create the following form below the paragraph element within the main element:

```
<form>
   <label for="fName">First Name:</label>
   <input type="text" name="fName" id="fName">

   <label for="lName">Last Name:</label>
   <input type="text" name="lName" id="lName">
```

Continued >

In the Labs continued

(a) Mobile viewport

(b) Tablet viewport

(c) Desktop viewport

Figure 8–67

```
<label for="email">Email Address:</label>
<input type="email" name="email" id="email">


<label for="phone">Phone Number:</label>
<input type="tel" name="phone" id="phone">


<label for="reference">Referral Source:</label>
<select name="reference" id="reference">
    <option value="ad">Coupon</option>
    <option value="friend">Friend</option>
    <option value="google">Google</option>
    <option value="social">Social Media</option>
    <option value="other">Other</option>
</select>
```

```
<label for="questions">Questions:</label>
<textarea id="questions" name="questions" rows="3" cols="25"></tex-
tarea>

<input type="submit" value="Submit">
<input type="reset" value="Reset">
</form>
```

4. Create a new paragraph element below the form element, `<p>Our office number is (555)555-2564 and our email address is steve@screen.net</p>`.

5. In the screenstyles.css file, modify the comment at the top of the page to include today's date.

6. In the screenstyles.css file, create the following new style rules above the media queries and include comments for each:

```
input, select, textarea {
    display: block;
    margin-bottom: 1em;
}

label {
    display: block;
}
```

7. In the screenstyles.css file, create the following new style rules within the tablet the media query and include a comment:

```
label {
    float: left;
    padding-right: 0.5em;
    text-align: right;
    width: 8em;
}
```

8. Save all files and open the contact.html page within a browser and view the page in all three viewports, as shown in Figure 8–66.

9. Open your text editor, open the stevescreen.html template file in the lab2 folder, and then use it to create the quote.html file.

10. In the quote.html document, update the comment at the top of the page to include today's date, and then create an paragraph element within the main element: `<h3>We provide free, no-obligation quotes. Complete the form below and we will contact you within 24 hours with your free quote.</h3>`.

11. Create the following form below the paragraph element within the main element.

```
<form>
    <label for="fName">First Name:</label>
    <input type="text" name="fName" id="fName">

    <label for="lName">Last Name:</label>
    <input type="text" name="lName" id="lName">
```

In the Labs *continued*

```
<label for="email">Email Address:</label>
<input type="email" name="email" id="email">

<label for="phone">Phone Number:</label>
<input type="tel" name="phone" id="phone">

<label for="area">Patio Size:</label>
<textarea name="area" id="area" rows="2" cols="15"></textarea>

<p>Please indicate the type of service needed:</p>
<ul>
    <li><input type="checkbox" name="ns" id="ns" value="ns"
class="svc">New Screen Patio</li>
    <li><input type="checkbox" name="srepair" id="srepair"
value="srepair" class="svc">Small Repair</li>
    <li><input type="checkbox" name="lrepair" id="lrepair"
value="lrepair" class="svc">Large Screen Repair</li>
    <li><input type="checkbox" name="hw" id="hw" value="hw"
class="svc">Door and Hardware Replacement</li>
    </ul>

<input type="submit" value="Submit">
<input type="reset" value="Reset">
</form>
```

12. In the screenstyles.css file, create the following new style rules above the media queries and include comments for each:

```
form ul {
    list-style-type: none;
}

.svc {
    display: inline-block;
}
```

13. Save all files, open the quote.html page within a browser, and then view the page in all three viewports, as shown in Figure 8–67.

14. Validate your HTML code and fix any errors.

15. Validate your CSS code and fix any errors.

16. Submit your assignment in the format specified by your instructor.

17. ✳ Research the requirements to submit a form to a server for processing and provide a summary of your findings.

Lab 3: Expand Your World
Working with Form Elements

Problem: In this chapter, you worked with many types of input controls. In this exercise, you will explore input controls that were not used in this chapter to gain more insight on how to use and code other types of form elements. Work with the form08.html file in the lab3 folder and the lab3styles08.css file in the lab\css folder from the Data Files for Students. The complete webpage is shown in Figure 8–68.

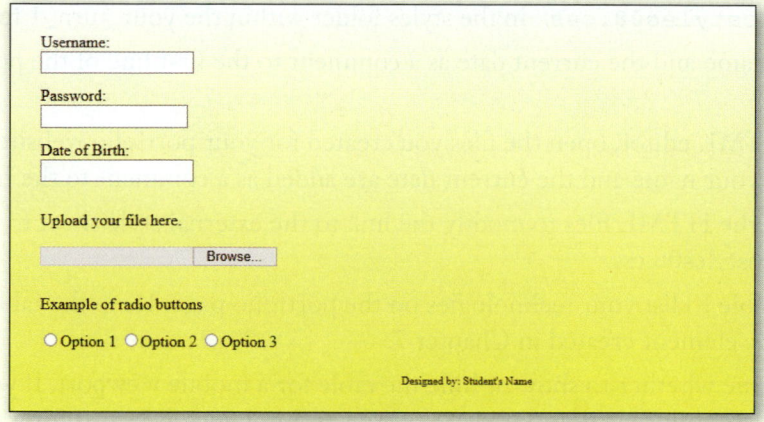

Figure 8–68

Instructions:

1. Open form08.html in your text editor, review the page, add a title, link the file to lab3styles08.css, modify the comment at the top of the page to include your name and today's date, and replace "Student's Name" with your name in the footer element.

2. Open the lab3styles08.css file from the lab3\css folder. Modify the comment at the top of the style sheet to include your name and today's date.

3. In form08.html, create a new form within the main element.

4. Create a new label and text input element for **Username**. Include all appropriate attributes.

5. Create a new label and password type input element for **Password**. Include all appropriate attributes.

6. Create a new label and date type input element for **Date of Birth**. Include all appropriate attributes.

7. Add a file type input control to the form with an attribute of **size="20"**.

8. Create a new paragraph element for a file type input control with the content, **Upload your file here**.

9. Create three radio buttons and include a new paragraph element with the content, **Example of Radio Buttons**.

10. In the lab3styles08.css file, create style rules for these form elements. Use Figure 8–68 as a guide. Include comments for each.

11. Submit your answers in the format specified by your instructor.

12. ✳ In step 7, you inserted a date type input control. Describe the difference in how this field displays in Internet Explorer and Google Chrome.

Consider This: Your Turn

Apply your creative thinking and problem-solving skills to design and implement a solution.

1. Improving Your Personal Portfolio Website Design

Personal

Part 1: In Chapter 7, you integrated additional HTML5 semantic elements. In this exercise, you update the page as follows:

1. Open the external style sheet you created in Chapter 7 and save it with the name `portfoliostyles08.css` in the styles folder within the your_turn_1 folder.

2. Add your name and the current date as a comment to the first line of the portfoliostyles08.css file.

3. In your HTML editor, open the files you created for your portfolio website in Chapter 7 and make sure your name and the current date are added as a comment to the first line of all files.

   a. Update the HTML files to modify the link to the external style sheet to reference portfoliostyles08.css.

   b. Use a table to list your technologies on the portfolio page. Keep the table within the semantic element created in Chapter 7.

   c. Determine whether to show or hide the table for a mobile viewport. If you hide the table from the mobile viewport, keep the current technologies area as is for a mobile viewport.

4. Update the CSS file to:

   a. Style the table element for mobile, tablet, and desktop viewports.

   b. Refine your style sheet as desired.

   c. Adjust viewport widths if necessary.

   d. Add comments to note all changes and updates.

5. Save and test your files.

6. Validate and correct your HTML and CSS files, and submit your assignment in the format specified by your instructor.

Part 2: ✳

List at least three pros and three cons of using a table.

2. Improving the Design of the WebDevPros Website

Professional

Part 1: In Chapter 7, you integrated additional HTML5 semantic elements for WebDevPros. In this exercise, you update the site as follows:

1. Open the external style sheet you created in Chapter 7 and save it with the name `webdevstyles08.css` in the styles folder within the your_turn_2 folder.

2. Add your name and the current date as a comment to the first line of the webdevstyles08.css file.

3. Open the files you created for WebDevPros in Chapter 7 in your HTML editor and make sure your name and the current date are added as a comment to the first line of all files.

4. Update the HTML files to:

   a. Integrate a table element.

   b. Create a form.

   c. Use appropriate labels and input types.

   d. Use the required attribute for at least two input fields.

5. Update the CSS file to:

   a. Style the table elements for mobile, tablet, and desktop viewports.

   b. Style the form elements for mobile, tablet, and desktop viewports.

   c. Refine your style sheet as desired.

   d. Adjust viewport widths if necessary.

   e. Add a comments to note all changes and updates.

6. Save and test your files.

7. Validate and correct your HTML and CSS files, and submit your assignment in the format specified by your instructor.

Part 2: ✳ Research SSL (Secure Socket Layer) and then provide a summary of your findings and a link to your resource.

3. Improving the Design of the Dog Hall of Fame Website

Research and Collaboration

Part 1: In Chapter 7, integrated additional HTML5 semantic elements for the Dog Hall of Fame. In this exercise, you create and style a form to accept dog nominations. Do the following activities as a group:

1. Open the external style sheet you created in Chapter 7 and save it with the name **dogstyles08.css** in the styles folder within the your_turn_3 folder.

2. Add your names and the current date as a comment to the first line of the dogstyles08.css file.

3. Open the files you created for the Dog Hall of Fame in Chapter 7 in your HTML editor and make sure your names and the current date are added as a comment to the first line of all files.

4. Modify the link to the external style sheet to reference dogstyles08.css.

5. Create a form on the nominations page. Decide what input controls you will use and how you will style the form elements for mobile, tablet, and desktop viewports. At a minimum, update the HTML and CSS files to do the following:

   a. Update the nominations.html document to include a form.

   b. Integrate text input controls, include appropriate attributes and determine which fields should be required.

   c. Integrate a select and textarea element.

   d. Integrate a form element not used within the chapter project.

   e. Integrate submit and reset buttons.

   f. Style the form elements for mobile, tablet, and desktop viewports.

6. Save and test your files.

7. Validate and correct your HTML and CSS files, and submit your assignment in the format specified by your instructor.

Part 2: ✳ Research the mailto action and discuss the pros and cons of using the mailto action.

9 | Integrating Audio and Video

Objectives

You will have mastered the material in this chapter when you can:

- Describe the benefits and limitations of multimedia in websites
- Identify audio formats
- Identify video formats
- Describe a plug-in
- Understand codecs
- Understand and create audio elements
- Understand and create video elements
- Identify common audio attributes
- Identify common video attributes
- Understand the source element
- Test audio elements
- Test video elements

9 | Integrating Audio and Video

Introduction

A website provides several creative opportunities to capture the attention of your audience. Many websites use multimedia (digital media such as audio, video, and animation) to enrich the user experience and provide interactivity. For example, websites include videos to share news updates, promote products and services, or demonstrate how to use a product. Videos add visual appeal and can pack a huge amount of information into a few seconds. According to a recent study by Forrester Research, consumers prefer videos to text, find them more memorable, and stay on websites that include videos longer than websites that do not.

Audio on webpages can set a mood or tone and further entice a user to make a purchase. Audio can also provide information more quickly or effectively than text, such as a guided tour that describes the features of a product or testimonials from customers that support a product or service.

In this chapter, you will learn how to use HTML5 to embed audio and video on an HTML webpage. You will learn how to use the `audio` element and its attributes to add audio to a webpage. Similarly, you will learn how to use the `video` element and its attributes to add a video to webpage. You will also learn about the various audio and video file formats and which formats to use for the web. Finally, you will learn how to style the video using CSS.

Project — Add Audio and Video to a Webpage

In Chapter 9, you enhance the Forward Fitness Club website by adding audio to the home page to improve the user experience. Additionally, you insert a video in the About Us page to engage the user and promote the club.

This chapter provides an introduction to using multimedia in web development, focusing on two forms of multimedia: audio and video. The finished webpages contain relevant audio and video clips that provide valuable multimedia content for visitors of the Forward Fitness Club website.

The project in this chapter improves a website by integrating HTML5 `audio` and `video` elements. To perform these tasks, you first copy the media files to your media folder. Next, you add an `audio` element to a webpage. Then, you add a `video` element to a webpage. In the style sheet, you add style rules for the `video` element for tablet and desktop viewports. Figure 9–1 shows the home page with the embedded audio and controls. Figure 9–2 shows the video on the About Us page.

Figure 9–1

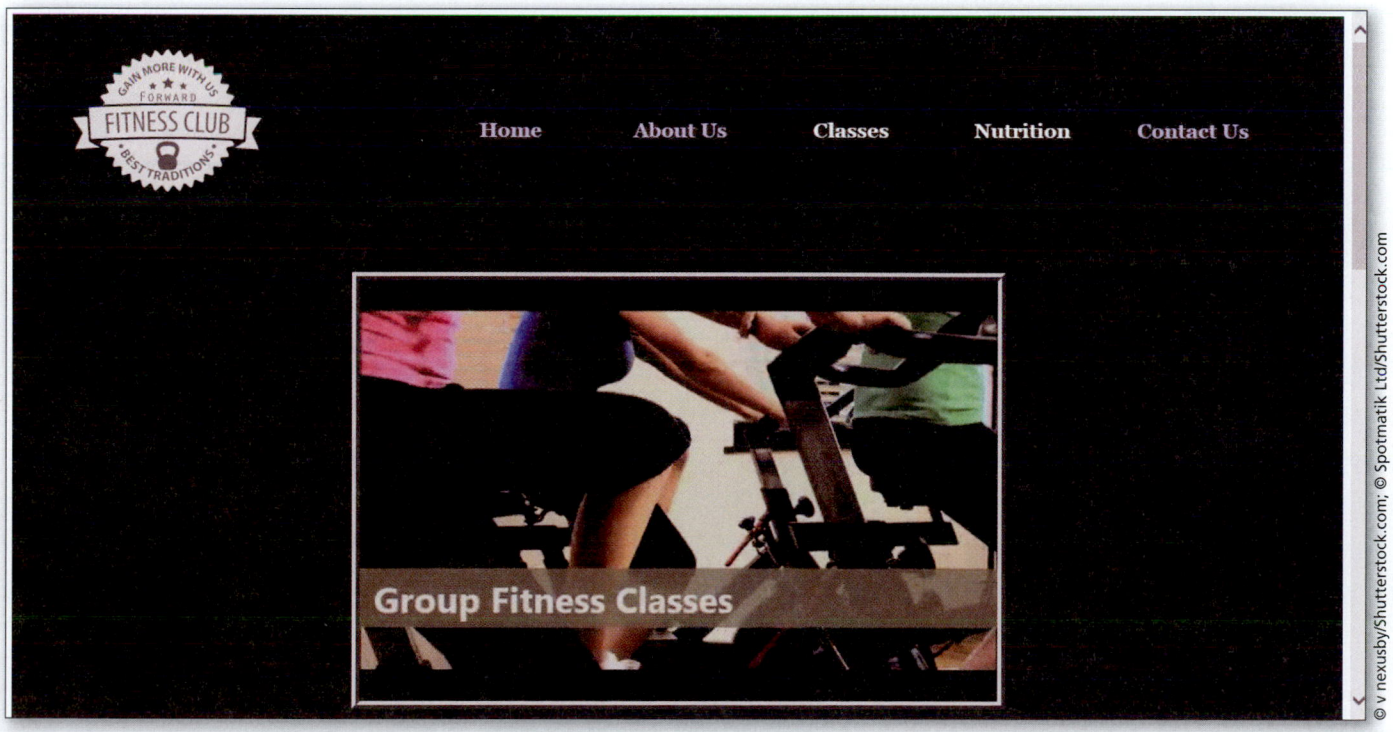

Figure 9–2

Roadmap

In this chapter, you will learn how to create the webpages shown in Figures 9–1 and 9–2. The following roadmap identifies general activities you will perform as you progress through this chapter:

1. **INSERT** the **AUDIO ELEMENT**.
2. **INSERT** the **VIDEO ELEMENT**.
3. **STYLE** the **VIDEO ELEMENT**.

At the beginning of step instructions throughout the chapter, you will see an abbreviated form of this roadmap. The abbreviated roadmap uses colors to indicate chapter progress: gray means the chapter is beyond that activity; blue means the task being shown is covered in that activity; and black means that activity is yet to be covered. For example, the following abbreviated roadmap indicates the chapter would be showing a task in the 2 INSERT VIDEO ELEMENT activity.

| 1 INSERT AUDIO ELEMENT | **2 INSERT VIDEO ELEMENT** |
| **3 STYLE VIDEO ELEMENT** | |

Use the abbreviated roadmap as a progress guide while you read or step through the instructions in this chapter.

Using Multimedia

The popularity of the web is due in part to its ability to display webpages that include graphic images, audio, and video. These additions can boost the visual appeal of a website and make the browsing experience more enjoyable and interactive. Sometimes, however, multimedia can distract from the website message. When deciding whether to include multimedia, remember the purpose of the website. If the multimedia content enhances that purpose, it should be included. If the multimedia content distracts from the purpose of the website, then you should reconsider using it.

Multimedia is the combination of text, images, sound, and video to express an idea or convey a message. Because most people have broadband Internet connections that can transfer data quickly, multimedia webpages that include large graphics, audio, and video are common. Figure 9–3 shows an example of multimedia used on the PBS website.

Figure 9–3

Source: www.pbs.org/nationalparks

Many websites use videos to advertise products, to entertain visitors, or to provide instruction. For example, you may be able to review a medical procedure online before having the procedure done yourself. You can view clips of movies or hear segments of audio recordings from webpages that provide content in those formats. **Podcasts**, a series of audio or video clips that are released in a sequence, are popular in home, academic, and corporate settings. Figure 9–4 shows an example of a website, Podcast Alley, with several podcasts on current technology topics.

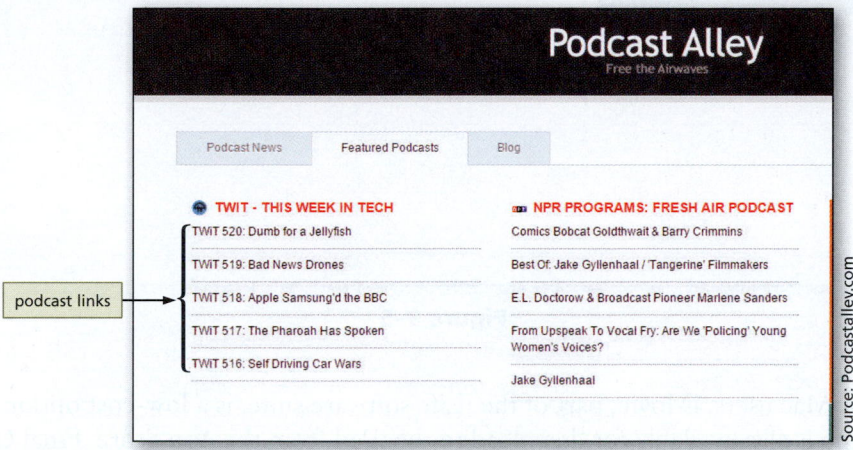

Figure 9–4

Creating Multimedia Files

You can obtain multimedia files by creating them yourself or by finding files that are already available. If you create your own multimedia files, you do not have to be concerned with copyright or licensing agreements. On the other hand, the multimedia files might not have the same quality and effectiveness as professional content. You can create your own audio files using a microphone and software designed to edit digital files, such as Audacity, a free, open-source audio editor, and Adobe Audition, which can be purchased as part of the Adobe Creative Cloud. If you do use any portion of files that have been professionally developed, such as those from an online multimedia provider, be certain that you understand and follow the copyright and licensing requirements.

For video files, you can use a digital camcorder, a digital camera, or even a smartphone to create clips that can be included on a webpage. For the Windows operating system, a popular, free video editing application is Windows Movie Maker (Figure 9–5). This application is available for download from the Microsoft website as part of the Windows Live Essentials software package. MAGIX Movie Edit Pro software and training is available for a fee, with an active online community for additional support. Corel VideoStudio Pro has simple and more advanced menu system options that novice movie editors and professionals alike can use comfortably. CyberLink PowerDirector is another software option that allows you to create professional-quality videos.

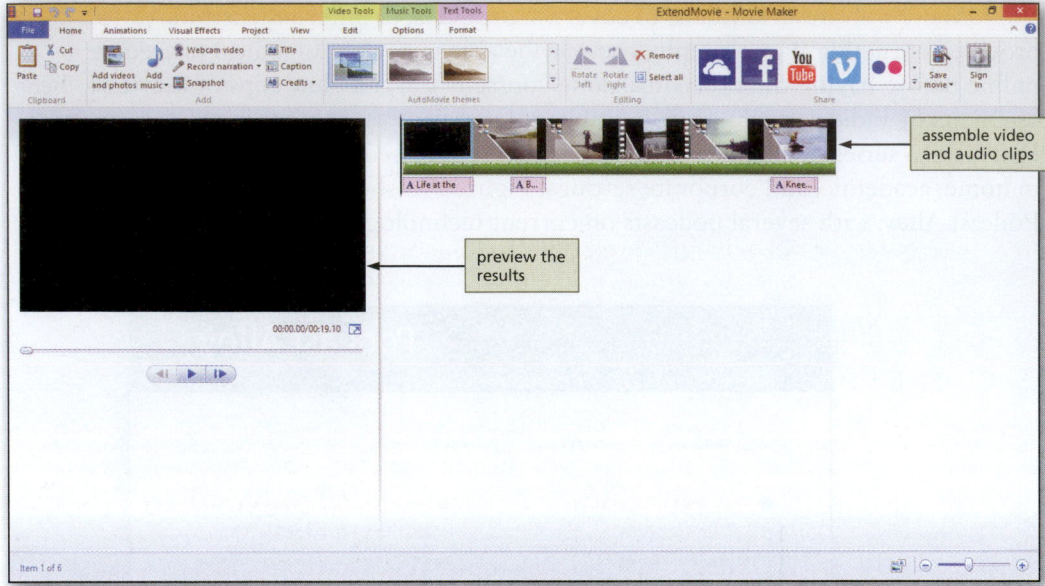

Figure 9–5

For Mac users, iMovie, part of the iLife software suite, is a low-cost option. The iMovie app is also available for download to the iPad from the App Store. Final Cut Pro X is a video editor for the Mac that offers professional-level editing.

Adobe Premiere Pro is another highly rated application for movie editing that can be used on either the Mac or Windows operating systems. As with many multimedia software products, Adobe Premiere Pro lets novice users create professional-quality video. Figure 9–6 shows the Adobe Premiere Pro Creative Cloud application.

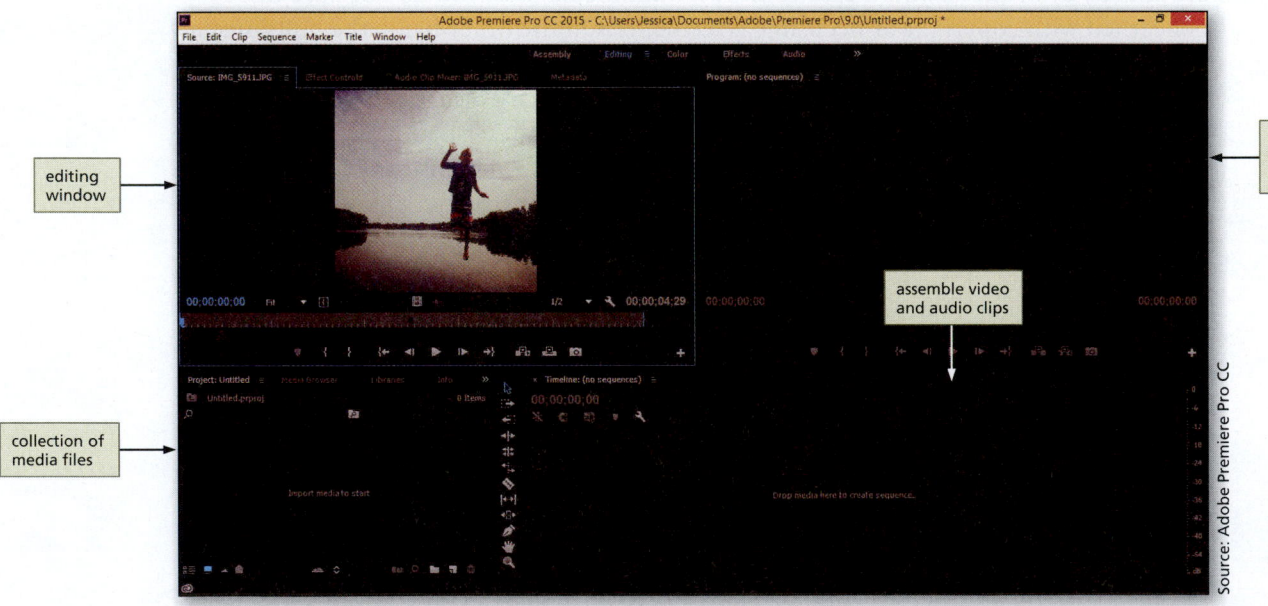

Source: Adobe Premiere Pro CC

Figure 9–6

Many audio- and video-editing applications offer a free trial period. You might try downloading a free trial of the software, if available, and using it to create or edit a movie. You could also try a few different programs to see how they work. Most multimedia software operates in a similar fashion and has a user-friendly help utility that guides you through the process of editing. Most products also provide templates and effects that enhance the creative aspects of presenting multimedia.

To find multimedia resources on the web, search for "public domain audio or video." These resources are available free of copyright restrictions. Websites that provide stock photos often provide music, sound, and video files for a fee. Before using any content, be sure to understand and follow the copyright license agreements that accompany any multimedia content that you find on the web.

Can I use any images, audio, or video I find on the Internet to create a multimedia file?

In general, no, you cannot use any file you find. However, as a student, you are permitted to use some for academic purposes. This is known as Fair Use. For more information about copyright laws, visit copyright.gov.

Embedded vs. External Multimedia

Embedding media is similar to inserting inline images. The embedded media files appear within the webpage along with the audio or video player controls. Visitors use the controls to play or stop the media. Because the media file is embedded directly into the webpage, you can complement the audio or video clip resource with surrounding text or graphical images. Before HTML5, the **object** element was used to insert embedded content, including multimedia. HTML5 introduces two new elements, **audio** and **video**, to use as an alternative to the **object** element. Figure 9–7 shows an example of how the U.S. Department of Defense uses the **video** element on its webpage.

Figure 9–7

To access external media files, website visitors click a link. They can then decide whether to link directly to the external source or download the file. Unlike embedded media, the external media is displayed out of context with the webpage that contains the link. Using external links is a common web development practice. For example, sites that provide many video resources, such as YouTube, use external media files and the **embed** element, which defines a container for an external application or interactive content (also called a plug-in). Figure 9–8 shows an example of a White House video provided on YouTube through an external link.

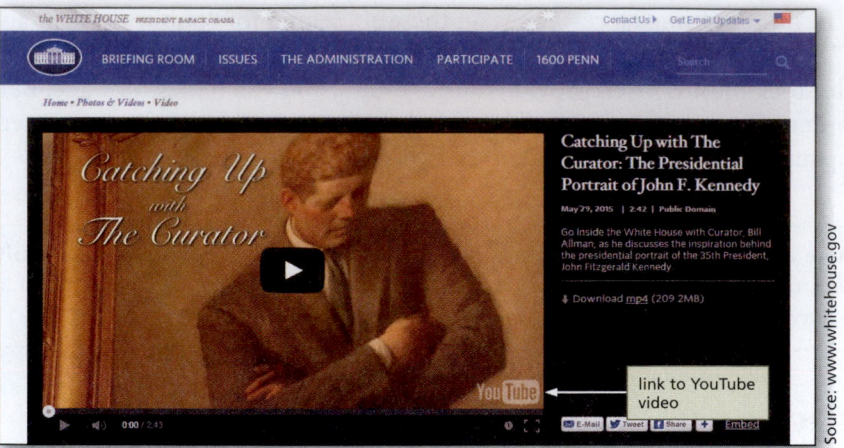

Figure 9–8

Media Players and Plug-Ins

As you know, browsers can display text and the graphics formats discussed in earlier chapters without using external software. To play an audio or video file, however, some browsers need the help of an application called a media player or a plug-in. A **media player** is computer software that plays multimedia files. Most software media players support an array of media formats, including audio and video files. This chapter uses an .mp3 audio file and an .mp4 video file. The Internet Explorer browser can play files in both formats. Windows Media Player, included as part of Windows, also plays both audio and video. The Mac operating system comes with QuickTime Player for playing movies, while iTunes can be downloaded for Windows or Mac OS to play a variety of media formats.

A **plug-in** (also called an add-in or add-on) is extra software added to the browser (or other program) to provide a capability that is not inherent to the browser. In other words, for an embedded media file to work in a browser, the website visitor needs to have the correct plug-in. Most browsers have a variety of plug-ins installed, but website visitors can also download and install necessary plug-ins from the browser manufacturers. Common plug-ins are Windows Media Player, Apple QuickTime Player, Adobe Flash, Microsoft Silverlight, and Adobe Acrobat. Figure 9–9 shows an example of plug-ins installed on the Internet Explorer 11 browser.

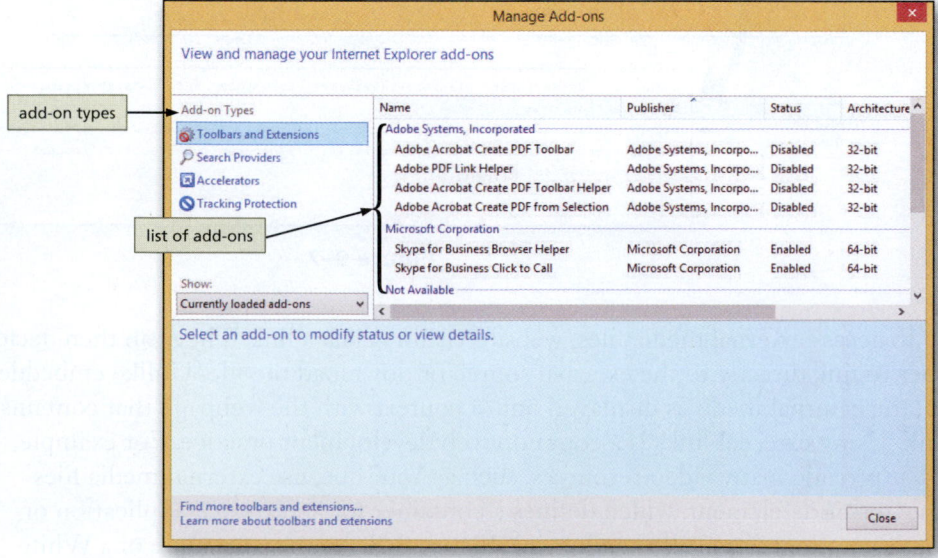

Figure 9–9

Internet Explorer uses proprietary ActiveX controls. When Internet Explorer encounters a multimedia file, it searches for the appropriate ActiveX control to play the file. If Internet Explorer cannot find the control, users are usually asked if they want to install it. Some browsers direct users to the website from which they can download the required plug-in. A suggestion to web developers is to use media files in common formats, such as .wmv, .mp4, .flv, and .mp3, so users can access the plug-ins easily. It is also a good idea to let your users know what format is being used. If the plug-in is not installed, Internet Explorer generally provides the capability to install it. Many websites also provide a link to the appropriate manufacturer for an ActiveX control needed to play the file.

As you will see in the following section, the various audio and video formats can be played on a variety of players. For embedded multimedia, use a format supported by multiple players.

BTW
Plug-ins and Add-ons
Investigate the plug-ins available for the version of browser that you use. (In Internet Explorer, display the Command bar, click Tools on the Command bar, and then select Manage add-ons.) Search the web for information about the listed add-ons and determine if you can download other add-ons that you might need.

HTML5 and Multimedia

HTML5 introduces built-in media support via the `audio` and `video` elements. Using these elements, web developers can easily embed media into HTML documents. This chapter teaches you how to use the new HTML5 `audio` and `video` elements. Additional multimedia types discussed in this chapter include Flash, Java applets, and the HTML `object` element.

CONSIDER THIS

Will the ActiveX controls and security notification appear if I use a browser other than Internet Explorer?
No. ActiveX controls are displayed only in the Internet Explorer web browser.

Flash

Flash, or Adobe Flash, has been used within websites for nearly 20 years. Using Flash, you can create animations or movie files. Flash files have the .swf file extension and require the browser to have a Flash plug-in. Incorporating Flash animation was popular on websites before using smartphones and tablets became widespread. Some websites were developed exclusively with Flash. However, many of today's websites use Flash sparingly, if at all, partly because the iPhone and iPad, which run the iOS operating system, do not support Flash. Instead, many web developers have embraced JavaScript to incorporate additional interactivity within their websites. Figure 9–10 shows an example of an interactive Flash video used on the National Parks Service website.

Java Applets

A **Java applet** is a small program created with Java, a programming language. A Java applet can be embedded within a webpage, though the browser must have Java installed and enabled. Java applets were very popular in the late 1990s; however, their use in today's modern websites is in decline.

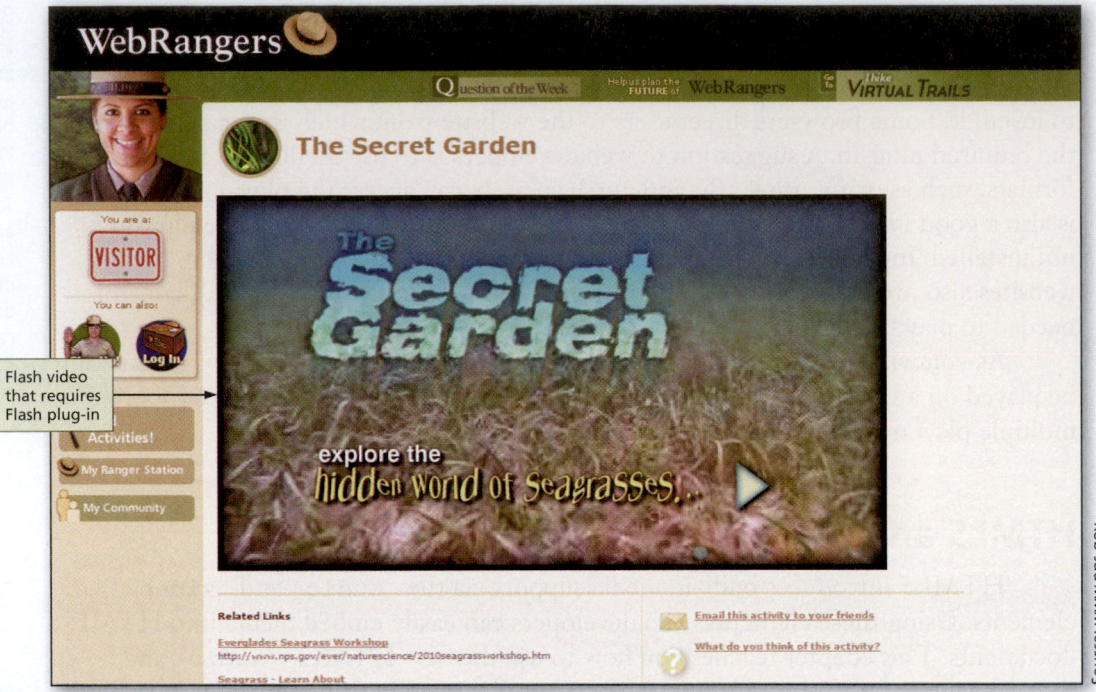

Figure 9–10

Source: www.nps.gov

Object Element

You use the HTML **object** element to embed multimedia objects such as Flash files, Java applets, PDF files, and ActiveX controls. Use the **param** element to define parameters for plug-ins embedded with an **object** element. The following is an example of the **object** element.

```
<object data="audio.wav">
    <param name="autoplay" value="true">
</object>
```

In this example, an audio file named audio.wav is embedded on the webpage. The autoplay parameter is set to true, meaning the audio starts playing when the webpage opens.

BTW

Parameters
Many other object parameters are available that are not discussed in this chapter. Each ActiveX control has particular parameters. Review online other parameters that might be effective for you to use in your web development.

Integrating Audio

Adding audio to a webpage can help set a desired mood or tone. It can also be a distraction to some users, so you must first determine if the audio is appropriate for the webpage and its audience. Audio integrated within a webpage should have a distinct purpose and should provide added value or instruction. You should also consider the time it takes for the browser to load the audio file. If your audience includes users with dial-up connections rather than broadband access, they will likely experience a delay, especially if the audio files are large. Keep in mind that using audio or video on a mobile device requires a data plan if the device is not connected to a wireless network. One popular way that websites use audio is to provide links to music files that visitors can play or download. Figure 9–11 shows list of music files to listen to on the Noisetrade.com website.

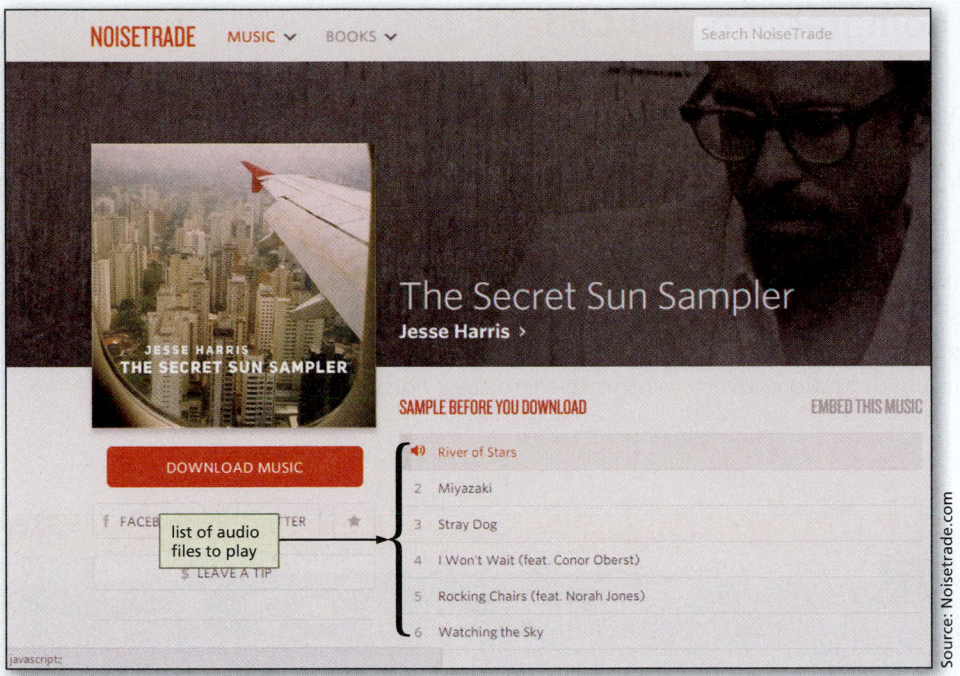

Source: Noisetrade.com

Figure 9–11

Audio File Formats

Table 9–1 lists the most common audio file formats for webpages. The HTML5 `audio` element supports only three audio file formats: .mp3, .ogg, and .wav. These supported formats are indicated with an asterisk in Table 9–1. However, you can use audio converter software to convert files from one audio format to a supported format. Audio files for the web often use file compression techniques to reduce the size of the file, though they can also diminish the sound quality. Uncompressed audio formats listed in Table 9–1 include .aiff, .au, and .wav.

Table 9–1 Common Audio File Formats		
File Format	**File Extension**	**Description**
AIFF	.aiff	Standard audio file format developed by Apple As an uncompressed and lossless format, it uses more disk space than the MP3 format
AU	.au	Standard audio file format used by Sun, Unix, and Java Can be compressed
MIDI	.mid .rmi	Musical Instrument Digital Interface (MIDI) Limited to electronic musical instruments (such as synthesizers) and other electronic equipment Files can be much smaller than in other formats
MP3*	.mp3	One of the most popular formats for music storage Compresses files to approximately one-tenth the size of uncompressed files
MP4	.mp4	Based on the QuickTime format; used for audio and video Creates quicker, faster, high-quality media Not supported by Windows Media Player
Ogg*	.ogg	Maintained by Xiph.Org Foundation Designed to provide for efficient streaming and high-quality digital multimedia Can be used with `audio` element
RealAudio	.ra .ram	Designed for streaming audio over the Internet; declining use Sound quality not as good as other formats
WAV*	.wav	Standard audio format for Windows Commonly used for storing uncompressed CD-quality sound files Compression is available to reduce file size

File Compression and Codecs

When embedding an audio or video file onto a webpage, you should keep the file size small and compress the file when necessary. A **codec** is a compression technology used to compress images, audio, and video files. The word codec is short for code/decode because it consists of an encoder, which compresses the file, and a decoder, which decompresses the file. An audio editor uses a codec to reduce the size of an audio file, while maintaining enough quality to play the audio file on a computer. Although codecs improve the page load time, compressing a media file too much results in a loss of sound quality. On the other hand, if you do not compress a media file enough, the file may take too long to download into a browser. Figure 9–12 shows an example of audio converter software that uses a codec to compress files.

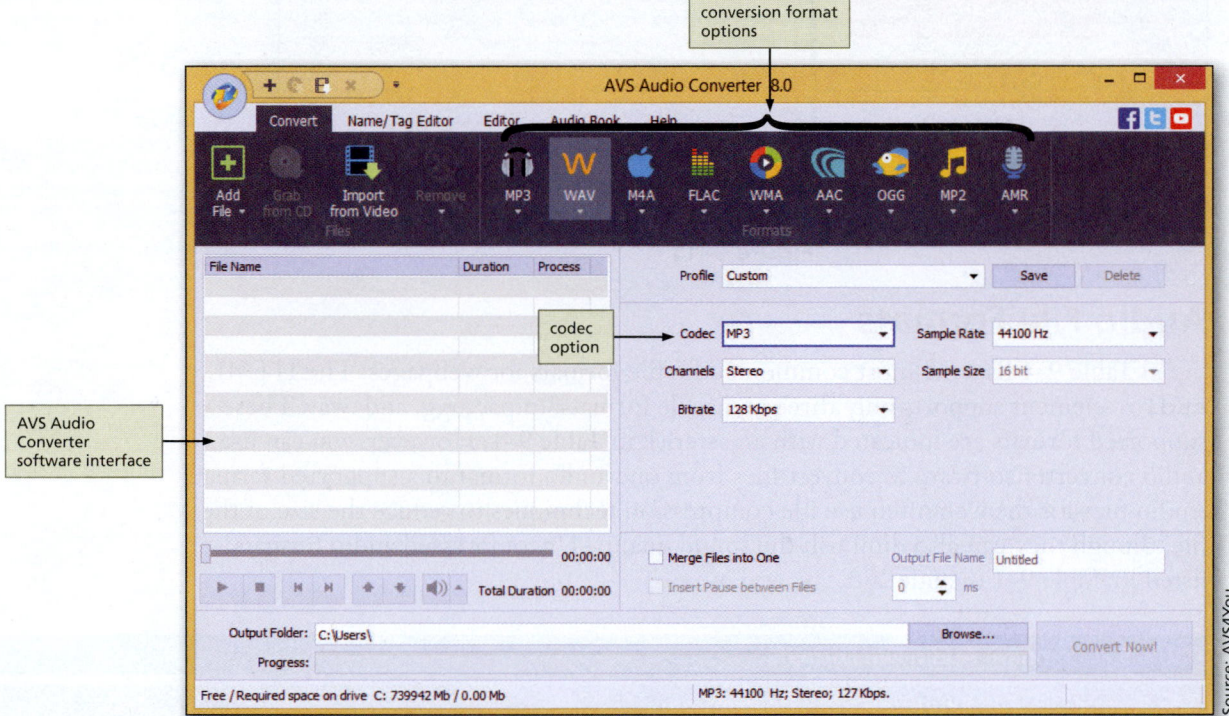

Figure 9–12

HMTL5 audio Element

One of the most long-awaited features in HTML5 is the **audio** element, which you use to define sound, such as music or other audio streams. Table 9–2 shows the attributes and values that can be used with the **audio** element.

The following sample code shows how to use the **audio** element to insert an audio file named music.mp3. Because browsers that do not support the **audio** element ignore the <audio> tag, you should insert text content between the <audio> and </audio> tags to alert users, as the paragraph element does in the following code.

```
<audio controls="controls" autoplay="autoplay">
  <source src="music.mp3" type="audio/mp3">
  <p>Your browser does not support the HTML5 audio element.</p>
</audio>
```

In this example, an audio file named music.mp3 is embedded on the webpage. The first line shows the beginning **audio** tag and includes two attributes: **controls** and **autoplay**. The **controls** attribute specifies to display the audio controls, such

Table 9–2 Audio Element Attributes

Attribute	Value	Description
autoplay	autoplay	Specifies that the audio will automatically start playing
controls	controls	Specifies that audio controls should be displayed (such as a play/pause button)
loop	loop	Specifies that the audio will start playing every time it is finished
muted	muted	Specifies that the audio should be muted
preload	auto metadata none	Specifies whether and how the audio should be loaded when the page loads
src	URL	Specifies the URL of the audio file

as play/pause and volume control. The `autoplay` attribute specifies to start playing the audio file once the page is loaded in the browser. The second line uses the `source` tag with two attributes, `src` and `type`. The `src` attribute specifies the location of the audio file. The `type` attribute specifies the type of audio file, in this instance, MP3. The third line is a `paragraph` element with fallback text to let the user know that their browser does not support the audio element. The sentence, "Your browser does not support the HTML5 audio element" appears in a legacy browser that does not support HTML5. The fourth line includes the ending `audio` tag.

If you use the `object` element instead of the `audio` element, you must include the `data` attribute to specify the source file. Only one `data` attribute can be specified within one `object` element. In addition, you need to include the `param` element in the `object` element to specify additional parameters, such as `autoplay`. However, many of the attributes for the object element and the parameter element are not supported in HTML5.

The `controls` attribute adds audio controls, such as play, pause, and volume. It can be set up in any of the three following ways:

```
<audio controls="controls">
<audio controls>
<audio controls="">
```

Similarly, the autoplay attribute can be set up in any of these ways:

```
<audio autoplay>
<audio autoplay="autoplay">
<audio autoplay="">
```

To enable the `audio` element to work in all browsers, use `source` elements inside the `audio` element. The `source` elements can link to the same or different audio files as appropriate. Including the `source` elements accommodates visitors who use any of the five major browsers. The browser will use the first recognized format. The following is an example of an `audio` element with multiple `source` elements:

```
<audio controls="controls" autoplay="autoplay">
    <source src="music.mp3" type="audio/mp3">
    <source src="music.ogg" type="audio/ogg">
    <source src="music.wav" type="audio/wav">
    <p>Your browser does not support the HTML5 audio
    element.</p>
</audio>
```

In this example, if the browser cannot play MP3 files, it checks to determine whether it can play Ogg files. If it can, it plays the music.ogg file. If it cannot play Ogg files, it checks to determine whether it can play WAV files. If it can, it plays the music.wav file. Otherwise, it does not play any audio. If the browser cannot play the audio, then it does not support HTML5. Table 9–3 lists the three audio file formats supported by the `audio` element and identifies whether each file format is also supported by the five major browsers. While most of these browsers support more than the audio file formats listed in Table 9–3, at this time, the `audio` element only supports three.

Other attributes include the `preload` attribute, which tells the browser to begin downloading the audio file immediately when it encounters the `audio` element. However, if you use the `autoplay` attribute, which also begins downloading immediately, you do not need to also use the `preload` attribute. The `loop` attribute restarts the audio immediately once it has finished playing.

Table 9–3 Audio File Browser Support					
Audio File Format	Internet Explorer	Google Chrome	Mozilla Firefox	Apple Safari	Opera
MP3	•	•	•	•	•
Ogg		•	•		•
Wav		•	•	•	•

To Add Audio to the Home Page

1 INSERT AUDIO ELEMENT | 2 INSERT VIDEO ELEMENT
3 STYLE VIDEO ELEMENT

Insert an `audio` element on the home page of the Forward Fitness Center website to add sound to the page. *Why? Set an energetic tone with a short audio file to further enhance the user's interest.* Include three file sources to accommodate all browsers and include attributes to autoplay the audio file and to display controls on the webpage. The following steps add audio to the home page.

1

• Copy the media files from the chapter09\fitness\media folder provided with the Data Files for Students to the fitness\media folder.

• Open index.html in your text editor and update the comment with today's date.

• Tap or click at the end of Line 67, and then press the ENTER key twice to insert new Lines 68 and 69.

• On Line 69, type `<audio autoplay controls>` to insert a starting audio tag.

• Press the ENTER key to insert a new Line 70, increase the indent, and then type `<source src="media/ffc_aud.mp3" type="audio/mp3">` to insert a source element (Figure 9–13).

index.html file

```
69    <audio autoplay controls>
70        <source src="media/ffc_aud.mp3" type="audio/mp3">
```

Line 69

audio element

source element

Note: To help you locate screen elements that are referenced in the step instructions, such as buttons and commands, this book uses red boxes to point to these screen elements.

Figure 9–13

Q&A What is the purpose of the `autoplay` and `controls` attributes?
The `autoplay` attribute specifies to automatically play the audio file in the browser. The `controls` attribute specifies to display the audio controls within the browser, which allows the user to play or pause the music and adjust the volume.

Why did I begin inserting the code on Line 69?
The code appears at the end of the main element, so the audio controls will appear at the end of the page, before the footer.

2

- Press the ENTER key to insert a new Line 71, and then type `<source src="media/ffc_aud.ogg" type="audio/ogg">` to insert a source element.

```
69      <audio autoplay controls>
70          <source src="media/ffc_aud.mp3" type="audio/mp3">
71          <source src="media/ffc_aud.ogg" type="audio/ogg">
72          <source src="media/ffc_aud.wav" type="audio/wav">
73          <p>Your browser does not support the audio tag.</p>
74      </audio>
```

Line 71 →

paragraph element

source elements

closing audio tag

Figure 9–14

- Press the ENTER key to insert a new Line 72, and then type `<source src=" media/ffc_aud.wav" type="audio/wav">` to insert a source element.

- Press the ENTER key to insert a new Line 73, and then type `<p>Your browser does not support the audio tag.</p>` to insert a paragraph element.

- Press the ENTER key to insert a new Line 74, decrease the indent, and then type `</audio>` to insert a closing audio tag (Figure 9–14).

Q&A Why do I need to include three source elements?
To accommodate all major browsers, you specify three audio source files, MP3, Ogg, and WAV. These are the three file formats supported by the audio element.

Will the webpage display the paragraph element?
The webpage displays the paragraph element only if the browser does not support the `audio` element.

3

- Save your change, open index.html in your browser, adjust the window to the size of a desktop viewport, and then scroll down to view the audio controls (Figure 9–15).

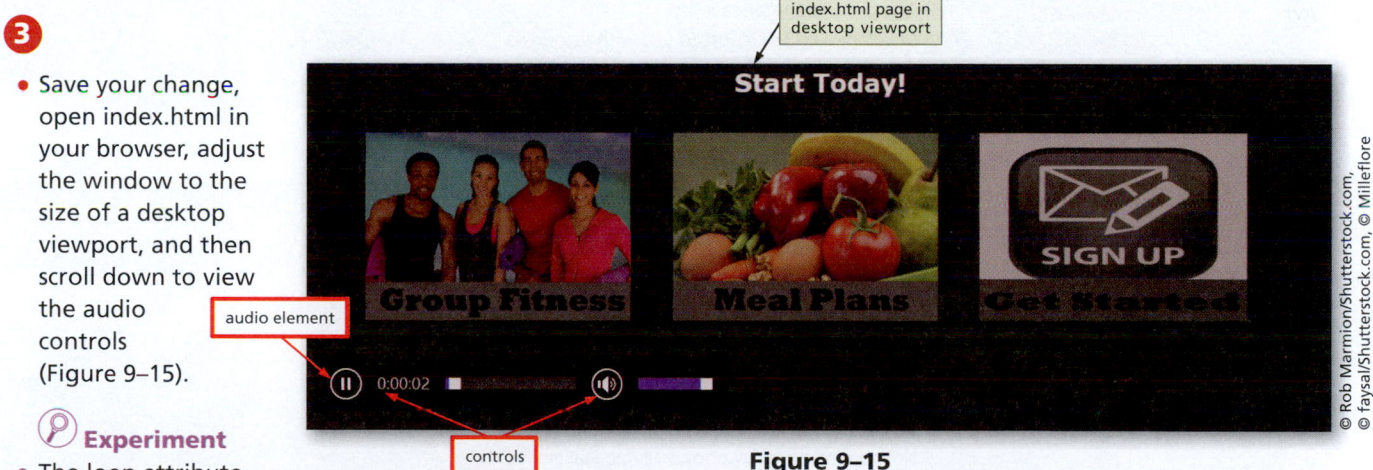

index.html page in desktop viewport

Start Today!

Group Fitness   Meal Plans   Get Started

audio element

controls

© Rob Marmion/Shutterstock.com,
© faysal/Shutterstock.com, © Milleflore
Images/Shutterstock.com

Figure 9–15

Experiment

- The loop attribute automatically replays the audio file after it is finished. To see how this works, add the loop attribute to the audio tag, save your changes, and then refresh index.html in your browser.

- Remove the controls attribute from the audio element to view the page without controls, save your changes, and then refresh index.html in your browser.

- Remove the loop attribute, add the controls attribute to the audio tag, and then save your changes.

Q&A A message appears at the bottom of my window, "Internet Explorer restricted this webpage from running scripts or ActiveX controls." How should I proceed?
Tap or click the Allow blocked content button to play the audio file and display the audio controls.

My controls do not look like the controls in Figure 9–15. Why?
Figure 9–15 shows the controls in Internet Explorer 11. If you are using a different browser, your controls will look different.

Break Point: If you want to take a break, this is a good place to do so. You can exit the text editor now. To resume at a later time, run your text editor, open the file called about.html, and continue following the steps from this location forward.

Integrating Video

Adding video to a webpage can increase traffic to your website if the video is informative and meaningful. As with audio files, consider the time it takes for the browser to load the video file. Non-broadband users will likely experience a delay, especially if the video files are large, and mobile device users might incur costs on a data plan. For these reasons, include only those videos that create a rich experience for the user.

Video File Formats

Table 9–4 lists the most commonly used video file formats for the web. The HTML5 `video` element supports only three of these video file formats: .mp4, .ogg, and .webm. The supported formats are indicated with an asterisk in Table 9–4. If you want to use an unsupported video file format with the `video` element, use video converter software to convert the file to a supported format. The `video` element does not work in legacy browsers, so consider your audience before using the `video` element. Most video file formats for the web use codec compression techniques to reduce the file size.

Table 9–4 Common Video File Formats		
File Format	**File Extension**	**Description**
AVI	.avi	Audio / Video Interleaved Developed by Microsoft to use with Windows Can contain both audio and video data
Flash	.swf	Small Web Format Can contain audio, video, or animations Requires Adobe Flash Player
Flash Video	.flv .f4v	Developed by Adobe Format of choice for embedded video on the web Used by YouTube and Hulu
MPEG	.mpg .mpeg .mp3	Moving Picture Experts Group Can be highly compressed, resulting in small file size Supported by most major browsers
MP4*	.mp4	Based on QuickTime format; used for audio and video Creates quicker, faster, high-quality media Not supported by Windows Media Player
Ogg*	.ogg	Maintained by Xiph.org Foundation Designed for efficient streaming and high-quality digital multimedia Can be used with HTML5 `video` element
QuickTime	.mov	Developed by Apple for both Windows and Mac operating systems File compression can result in smaller file size Requires QuickTime Player or Adobe Flash Player, which are easily downloaded
RealVideo	.rm .rv	Proprietary video format developed by RealNetworks Requires RealPlayer
WebM*	.webm	Developed by Google Royalty-free, open format Can be used with HTML5 <video> tag
Windows Media	.wmv	Developed by Microsoft Originally designed for Internet streaming applications Requires Windows Media Player or RealPlayer

HTML5 video Element

Until the new HTML5 `video` element was introduced, browsers did not have a standard for playing video on a webpage. Most videos were shown through a plug-in (such as Adobe Flash). The problem with plug-ins is that browsers may have different plug-ins or only recognize specific video formats. The HTML5 `video` element solves this problem and provides a standard way to play web videos in today's modern browsers.

You can use three HTML elements to incorporate video: `embed`, `object`, and `video`. You would have to add all three elements and use different video formats to make sure your video can play in all browsers and browser versions (Internet Explorer, Chrome, Firefox, Safari, and Opera) and on all hardware (PC, Mac, Android Tablet, Android Smartphone, iPad, and iPhone).

The purpose of the `embed` element is to embed multimedia elements in HTML pages. However, the `embed` element is unknown to HTML4 and is not validated correctly. In addition, the `embed` element causes other problems: if the browser does not support Flash, the video specified in the `embed` element will not play; iOS devices such as the iPad and iPhone do not display Flash videos; and if you convert the video to another format, it still does not play in all browsers.

You can also use the `object` element to embed multimedia elements in HTML pages. Although the code with an `object` element is validated correctly, the `object` element causes other problems: if the browser does not support Flash, your video will not play; iOS devices such as the iPad and iPhone do not display Flash videos; and if you convert the video to another format, it still does not play in all browsers.

Using the video Element

Use the `video` element to specify a video, such as a movie clip or other video stream, on a webpage. Table 9–5 lists the attributes and values that can be used with the `video` element.

Table 9–5 Video Element Attributes

Attribute	Value	Description
autoplay	autoplay	Specifies that the video will start playing as soon as it is ready
controls	controls	Specifies that video controls should be displayed (such as a play/pause button)
height	*pixels*	Sets the height of the video player
loop	loop	Specifies that the video will start playing every time it is finished
muted	muted	Specifies that the audio output of the video should be muted
poster	*URL*	Specifies an image to be shown while the video is downloading, or until the user clicks the play button
preload	auto metadata none	Specifies whether and how the video should be loaded when the page loads
src	*URL*	Specifies the URL of the video file
width	*pixels*	Sets the width of the video player

The following sample code shows how to use the `video` element to insert a video file named advertisement.mp4 in a webpage. Because browsers that do not support the `video` element ignore the <video> tag, you should insert text content between the <video> and </video> tags to alert users, as the paragraph element does in the following code.

```
<video width="320" height="240" controls="controls">
  <source src="advertisement.mp4" type="video/mp4">
  <p>Your browser does not support the HTML5 video element.</p>
</video>
```

In this example, the code sets the dimensions of the video (320 pixels by 240 pixels) and displays the playback controls. The browser plays the advertisement.mp4 file, which is an MP4 video file. If the browser does not support the `video` element, the user is alerted.

It is a good idea to include width and height attributes when you are not designing a responsive website. If you set the width and height, the space required for the video is reserved when the page is loaded. However, without these attributes, the browser does not know the size of the video and cannot reserve the appropriate space for it. The effect is that the page layout will change when the video loads. If you are designing a responsive website, do not include width and height attributes. Instead, use CSS to set the height to `auto` and the `max-width` attribute to 100%, as this will allow the video to automatically resize to fit the user's viewport.

As with the `audio` element, the `controls` attribute adds video controls including play, pause, and volume. It can be set up in any of the three following ways:

```
<video controls="controls">
<video controls>
<video controls="">
```

You can use the `src` attribute in the `video` element itself, as shown in the sample below:

```
<video controls autoplay src="advertisement.mp4">
  <p>Your browser does not support the HTML5 video element.</p>
</video>
```

Also, as you did with the `audio` element, you should use the `source` elements inside the `video` element. The `video` element allows multiple `source` elements, which can link to different video files. Including the `source` elements accommodates visitors who use any of the five major browsers. The browser will use the first recognized format. The following is an example of a `video` element with multiple `source` elements:

```
<video controls="controls" autoplay="autoplay">
  <source src="advertisement.mp4" type="video/mp4">
  <source src="advertisement.ogg" type="video/ogg">
  <source src="advertisement.webm" type="video/webm">
  <p>Your browser does not support the HTML5 video element.</p>
</video>
```

BTW

Aligning Videos on a Webpage
The video element is merely a container to hold a video. To center a video on a page, wrap the video element within a div element and then style the div element.

In this example, if the browser cannot play MP4 files, it checks to determine whether it can play Ogg files. If it cannot play the advertisement.ogg file, it checks to determine whether it can play WebM files. If it cannot play MP4, Ogg, or WebM files, then the browser does not support the HTML5 `video` element. Table 9–6 lists the three video file formats supported by the `video` element and identifies whether or not each file format is supported by the five major browsers. While most of these browsers support more than the video file formats listed in Table 9–6, at this time, the `video` element only supports three.

BTW
Video Clips
Video clips can have a large file size depending on the length and the quality of the clip. Search for rules-of-thumb for file sizes when video clips are incorporated into a website.

To Add Video to the About Us Page

1 INSERT AUDIO ELEMENT | 2 INSERT VIDEO ELEMENT
3 STYLE VIDEO ELEMENT

Next, insert a video on the About Us page to highlight its services. *Why? You can use a video to promote the benefits of joining the Forward Fitness Club.* Include three file sources to accommodate all browsers. Also include attributes to automatically play the video file and to display controls on the webpage. The following steps add video to the About Us page.

- Open about.html in your text editor and update the comment with today's date.

- Tap or click at the end of Line 31, and then press the ENTER key twice to insert new Lines 32 and 33.

- On Line 33, increase the indent, and then type `<div class="video">` to insert a div tag.

Figure 9–16

- Press the ENTER key to insert a new Line 34, and then type `<video autoplay controls>` to insert a starting video tag.

- Press the ENTER key to insert a new Line 35, increase the indent, and then type `<source src="media/ffc_vid.mp4" type="video/mp4">` to insert a source element (Figure 9–16).

Q&A
Why am I creating a new div element with a class value of video?
In future steps, you will style the video. In order to center the video on the webpage, wrap it within a div element and include a class value of video.

- Press the ENTER key to insert a new Line 36, and then type `<source src="media/ffc_vid.ogg" type="video/ogg">` to insert a source element.

- Press the ENTER key to insert a new Line 37, and then type `<source src="media/ffc_vid.webm" type="video/webm">` to insert a source element.

Figure 9–17

- Press the ENTER key to insert a new Line 38, and then type `<p>Your browser does not support the video tag.</p>` to insert a paragraph element.

- Press the ENTER key to insert a new Line 39, decrease the indent, and then type `</video>` to insert a closing audio tag.

- Press the ENTER key to insert a new Line 40, and then type `</div>` to insert a closing div tag (Figure 9–17).

© v nexusby/Shutterstock.com; © Spotmatik Ltd/Shutterstock.com

Q&A | Why do I need to include three source elements?
To accommodate all major browsers, you specify the video source files in three formats: MP4, Ogg, and WebM. The video element supports these three file formats.

3
- Save your changes, open about.html in your browser, and then adjust the window to the size of a desktop viewport (Figure 9–18).

Q&A | Why does the video appear on the left side of the page? The default alignment is left. You will create a style rule to center the video in future steps.

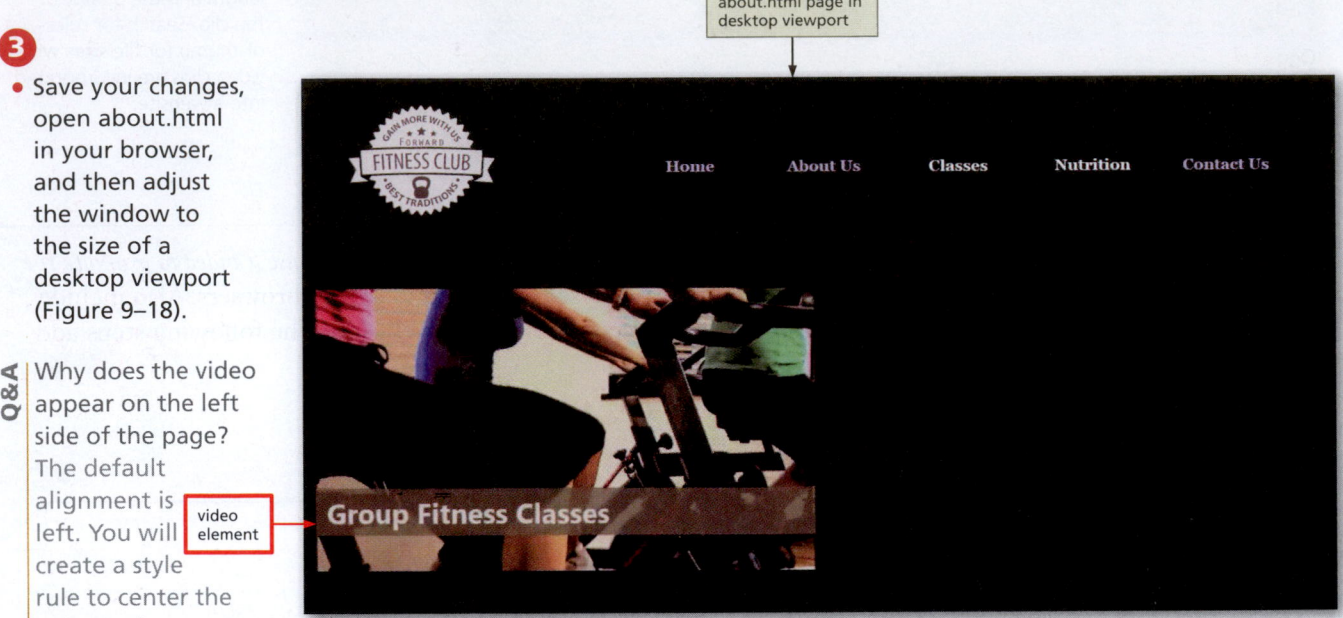

Figure 9–18

To Style the Video

1 INSERT AUDIO ELEMENT | **2 INSERT VIDEO ELEMENT**

3 STYLE VIDEO ELEMENT

You have added a video to the About Us page, but need to format the video so it is appealing on the webpage. Start by centering the video, and then apply borders and padding to further improve the video's appearance on the page. *Why? Formatting videos enhances their visual appeal to the user.* Also create a style rule for the `video` element to accommodate responsive design by specifying height and max-width attribute values. The following steps format the video by adding styles to the styles.css file.

1
- Open styles.css in your text editor and update the comment with today's date.

- Tap or click at the end of Line 138, and then press the ENTER key twice to insert new Lines 139 and 140.

- On Line 140, type `/* Style rule for the video class */` to insert a comment.

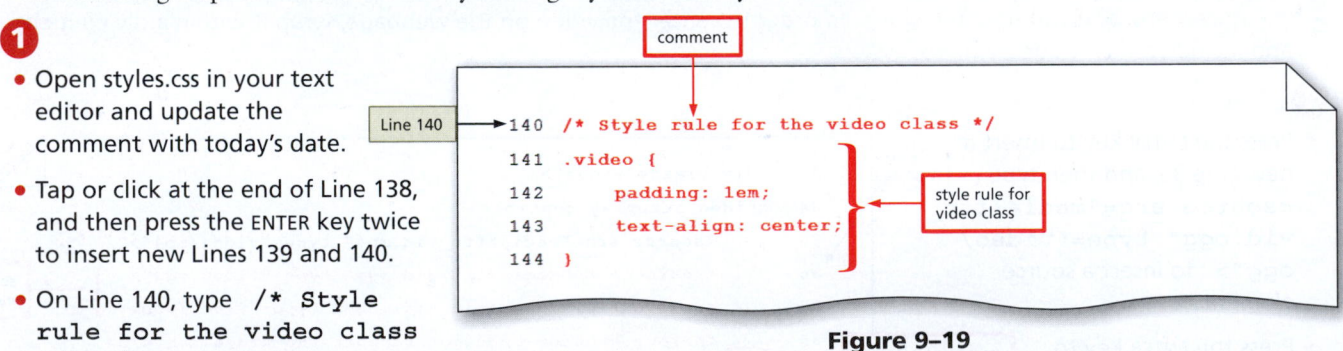

Figure 9–19

- Press the ENTER key to insert a new Line 141, and then type `.video {` to insert a new selector.

- Press the ENTER key to insert a new Line 142, increase the indent, and then type `padding: 1em;` to insert a new property and value.

- Press the ENTER key to insert a new Line 143, and then type `text-align: center;` to insert a new property and value.

- Press the ENTER key to insert a new Line 144, decrease the indent, and then type `}` to insert a closing brace (Figure 9–19).

2

- Save your changes and refresh about.html in your browser (Figure 9–20).

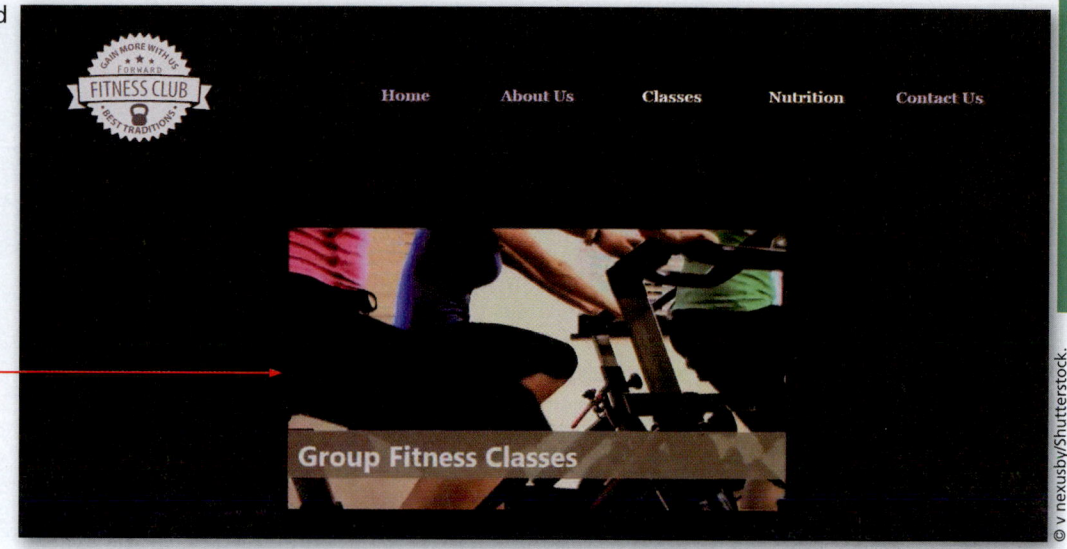

video element is center aligned

Figure 9–20

3

- Return to styles.css and then press the ENTER key twice to insert new Lines 145 and 146.

- On Line 146, type `/* Style rule for video element */` to insert a comment.

- Press the ENTER key to insert a new Line 147, and then type `video {` to insert a new selector.

comment

Line 146

```
146  /* Style rule for video element */
147  video {
148      border: 0.5em ridge #FFFFFF;
149      height: auto;
150      max-width: 100%;
151  }
```

style rule for video element

Figure 9–21

- Press the ENTER key to insert a new Line 148, increase the indent, and then type `border: 0.5em ridge #FFFFFF;` to insert a new property and value.

- Press the ENTER key to insert a new Line 149, and then type `height: auto;` to insert a new property and value.

- Press the ENTER key to insert a new Line 150, and then type `max-width: 100%;` to insert a new property and value.

- Press the ENTER key to insert a new Line 151, decrease the indent, and then type `}` to insert a closing brace (Figure 9–21).

Q&A | What is the result of the ridge value specified with the border property?
The ridge value defines a 3-D ridged border.

4

• Save your changes and refresh about. html in your browser (Figure 9–22).

© v nexusby/Shutterstock.com; © Spotmatik Ltd/ Shutterstock.com

Q&A Why does the border color appear white and gray?
The color combination is the result of specifying a ridge border.

Figure 9–22

5

• Adjust your browser to a tablet viewport (Figure 9–23).

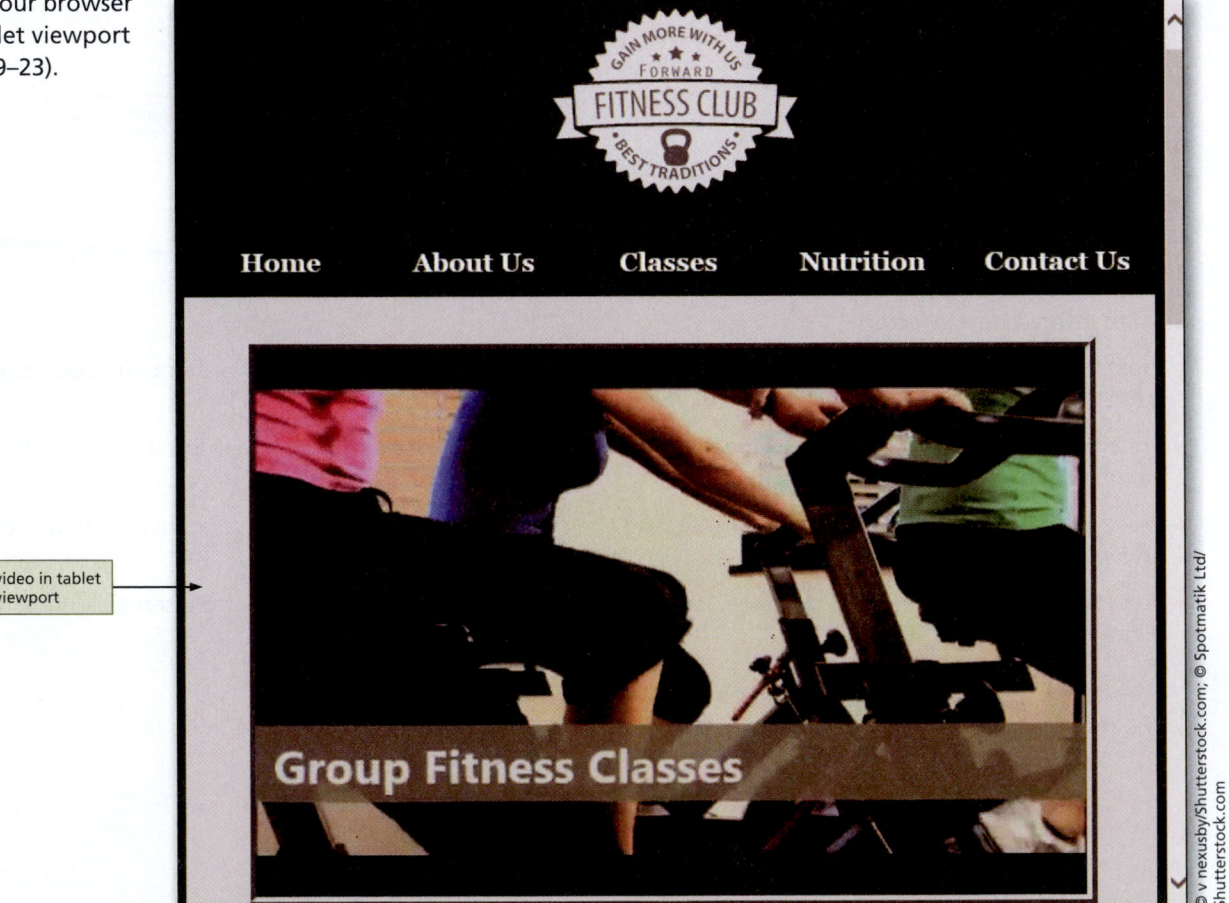

© v nexusby/Shutterstock.com; © Spotmatik Ltd/ Shutterstock.com

Figure 9–23

6

- Adjust your browser to a mobile viewport (Figure 9–24).

video in mobile viewport

Group Fitness Classes

Weights

Our facility includes a weight training area with several weight options. Build lean muscle with weights and improve your core with weight training.

- Dumbbells

© v nexusby/Shutterstock.com; © Spotmatik Ltd/Shutterstock.com

Figure 9–24

To Validate the Style Sheet

Always run your files through W3C's validator to check the document for errors. If the document has any errors, validating gives you a chance to identify and correct them. Validation is also an effective troubleshooting tool during the development process and adds a valuable level of professionalism to your work. The following steps validate a CSS document.

1 Open your browser and type `http://jigsaw.w3.org/css-validator/` in the address bar to display the W3C CSS Validation Service page.

2 Tap or click the By file upload tab to display the Validate by file upload information.

3 Tap or click the Browse button to display the Choose File to Upload dialog box.

4 Navigate to your css folder to find the styles.css file.

5 Tap or click the styles.css document to select it.

6 Tap or click the Open button to upload the selected file to the W3C CSS validator.

7 Tap or click the Check button to send the document through the validator and display the validation results page.

8 If necessary, correct any errors, save your changes, and run through the validator again to revalidate the page.

To Validate the HTML Files

Every time you create a new webpage or modify an existing webpage, run it through W3C's validator to check the document for errors. If any errors exist, you need to correct them. Validation is also an effective troubleshooting tool during the development process and adds a valuable level of professionalism to your work. The following steps validate an HTML document.

1 Open your browser and type `http://validator.w3.org/` in the address bar to display the W3C validator page.

2 Tap or click the Validate by File Upload tab to display the Validate by File Upload information.

3 Tap or click the Browse button to display the Choose File to Upload dialog box.

4 Navigate to your fitness folder to find the index.html file.

5 Tap or click the index.html document to select it.

6 Tap or click the Open button to upload it to the W3C validator.

7 Tap or click the Check button to send the document through the validator and display the validation results page.

8 If necessary, correct any errors, save your changes, and run through the validator again to revalidate the page.

9 Follow these steps to validate the about.html page and correct any errors.

Chapter Summary

In this chapter, you learned how to integrate audio and video elements within a website. You used HTML5 audio element to insert three audio source elements and specified that it automatically play and display controls. You also learned how to use the HTML5 video element and insert a video onto a webpage and coded for cross-browser compatibility. Finally, you used CSS styles to format a video for all viewports. The items listed below include all the new skills you have learned in this chapter, with the tasks grouped by activity.

Integrating Audio
Add Audio to the Home Page
(HTML 456)

Integrating Video
Add Video to the About Us Page (HTML 451)
Style the Video (HTML 452)

How will you use multimedia?

CONSIDER THIS

Use these guidelines as you complete the assignments in this chapter and create your own webpages outside of this class.

1. Determine if audio has a defined purpose for your website.

   a) Determine if the audio should automatically play when the page loads.

   b) Determine whether to show or hide the audio controls.

2. Determine if a video can enhance your website.

   a) Determine the ideal placement of your video to make it stand out.

   b) Determine how to style the video for mobile, tablet, and desktop viewports.

3. Determine how to best obtain multimedia for your website.

   a) Identify tools and software necessary to create your own video.

   b) Identify public domain content available for use.

   c) Learn how to use multimedia and converter software.

4. Determine if other forms of multimedia are appropriate for your website.

   a) Identify the pros and cons of using Adobe Flash.

   b) Determine which HTML elements are best for including your multimedia.

How should you submit solutions to questions in the assignments identified with a ✳ symbol?
Every assignment in this book contains one or more questions identified with a ✳ symbol. These questions require you to think beyond the assigned presentation. Present your solutions to the questions in the format required by your instructor. Possible formats may include one or more of these options: create a document that contains the answer; present your answer to the class; discuss your answer in a group; record the answer as audio or video using a webcam, smartphone, or portable media player; or post answers on a blog, wiki, or website.

Apply Your Knowledge

Reinforce the skills and apply the concepts you learned in this chapter.

Adding Audio to a Webpage

Instructions: In this exercise, you will use your text editor to add audio to a webpage. Insert an audio element and three source elements. Work with the apply09.html file in the apply folder and audio files in the apply\media folder from the Data Files for Students. The completed webpage is shown in Figure 9–25. You will also use professional web development practices to indent, space, comment, and validate your code.

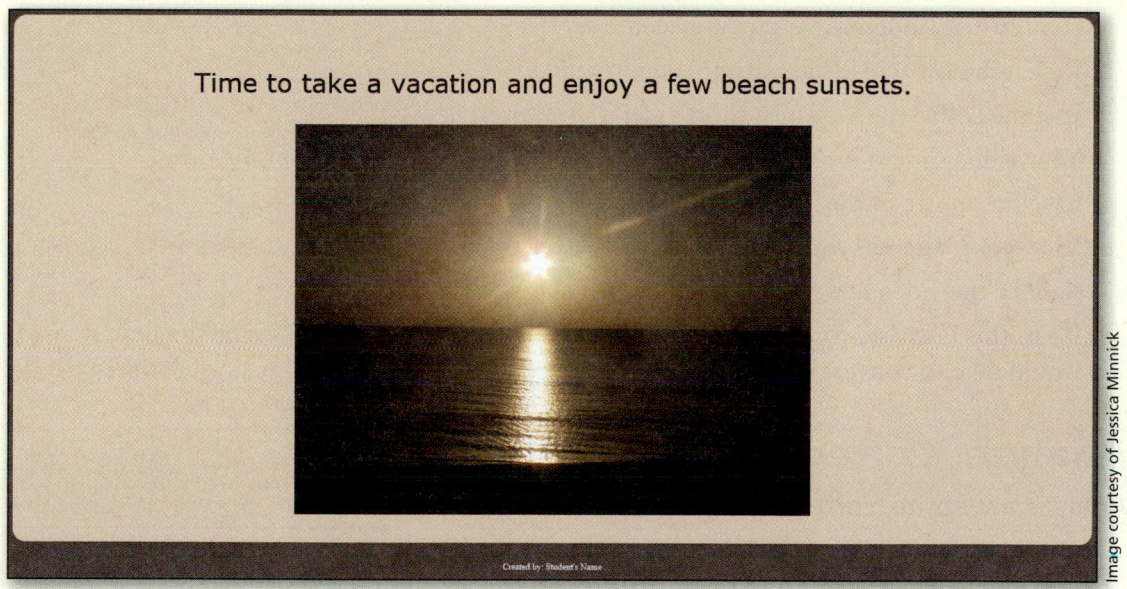

Time to take a vacation and enjoy a few beach sunsets.

Created by: Student's Name

Image courtesy of Jessica Minnick

Figure 9–25

Perform the following tasks:

1. Open apply09.html in your text editor, review the page, add a title, modify the comment at the top of the page to include your name and today's date, and replace "Student's Name" with your name in the footer element.

2. Insert an **audio** element below the **figure** element.

3. Set the **audio** element to play automatically and to repeat continuously.

4. Insert three **source** elements within the **audio** element and use the three audio files contained within the apply\media folder.

5. Include a paragraph element within the **audio** element that advises legacy browser users that their browser does not support the **audio** element.

6. Save all of your changes and open the apply09.html in your browser.

7. Validate your HTML document using the W3C validator found at validator.w3.org and fix any errors that are identified.

Continued >

Apply Your Knowledge *continued*

8. Submit the files in a format specified by your instructor.

9. ✳ In this exercise, you specified three source files, one of which was an Ogg file. Use your browser to research free resources available to convert an audio file to the Ogg format. Summarize your findings and provide a link to at least three different resources.

Extend Your Knowledge

Extend the skills you learned in this chapter and experiment with new skills. You may need to use additional resources to complete the assignment.

Using Multimedia Software

Instructions: In this exercise, you download and use multimedia software. If you use a Windows PC, download Windows Movie Maker. Use multimedia software to create a short video. If you use a Mac and have iMovie on your system, use iMovie to complete this project.

Perform the following tasks:

1. If you use a Windows PC, download and install Windows Movie Maker at windows.microsoft. com/en-us/windows-live/movie-maker.

2. Research how to use the software you installed.

3. Use the software to create a short video (30 seconds or less).

4. Your video should include, at a minimum, images, sound, and captions or titles.

5. Save the movie in the MP4 file format.

6. View your video in your preferred video player.

7. Submit the video in a format specified by your instructor.

8. ✳ In this exercise, you learned how to use multimedia software. Describe the next steps you would take to convert the video file you created to accommodate all major browsers.

Analyze, Correct, Improve

Analyze a website, correct all errors, and improve it.

Improving a Webpage with Video and Audio

Instructions: Work with the analyze09.html file in the analyze folder, the analyzestyles09.css file in the analyze\css folder, and the media files in the analyze\media folder from the Data Files for Students. The analyze09.html webpage needs multimedia to advertise its services. Insert a video element with appropriate source files to accommodate all major browsers. Set the video to play automatically, continuously, display controls, and specify width and height. Next, insert an audio element that continuously plays and does not display controls. Finally, style the video element. Use Figure 9–26 as a guide to correct these files.

1. Correct

a. Open the analyze09.html file in your text editor from the Data Files for Students. Modify the comment at the top of the page to include your name and today's date and then link the file to analyzestyles09.css.

b. Open the analyzestyles09.css file in your text editor from the Data Files for Students and then modify and correct the comment at the top of the document to include your name and today's date.

c. Review the **video** element within the analyze09.html file and add appropriate attributes to specify that the video plays automatically when the page loads, displays controls, and plays continuously. Also specify a width and height for the video. (*Hint*: Review the video's properties.)

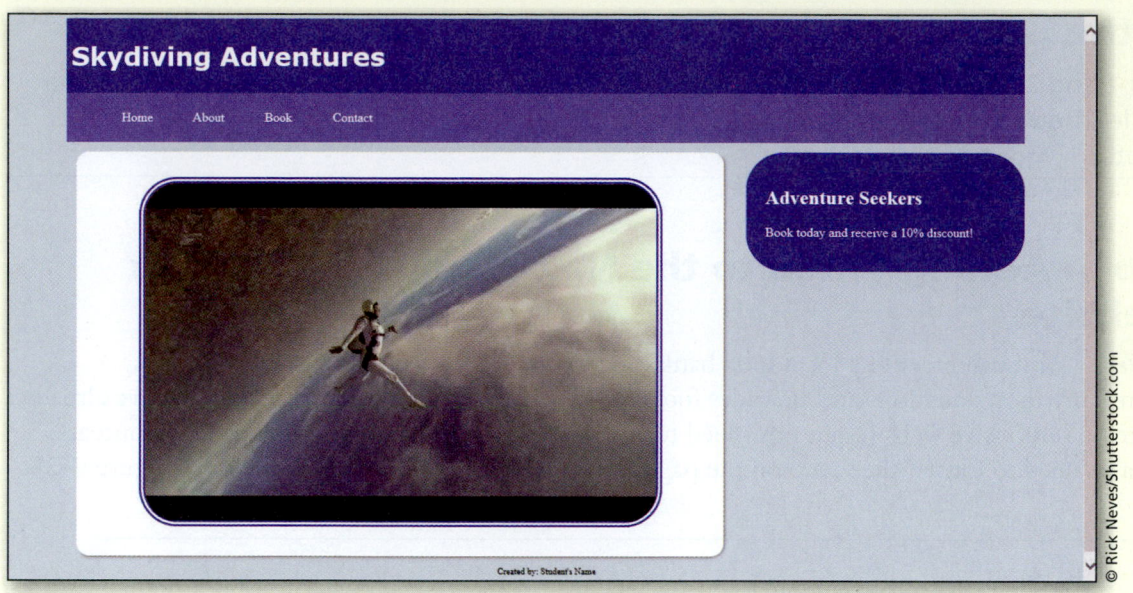

Figure 9–26

d. Modify the `video` element to enable the video to play with all major, modern browsers and provide fallback text for legacy browsers that do not support the `video` element.

e. Wrap the `video` element in a `div` element with a class value of `video`.

2. Improve

a. In the analyze09.html file, add an `audio` element below the `div` element you just created.

b. Specify three audio source files and provide fallback text for legacy browsers that do not support the `audio` element.

c. Set the audio to play automatically and continuously.

d. In the analyzestyles09.css file, create a style rule for the `video` class to center the `div` element and to apply 1em of padding. Include a comment for the style rule.

e. Create a style rule for the `video` element and specify a border with rounded corners. Include a comment for the style rule.

f. Save all of your changes and open the analyze09.html in your browser.

g. Validate your CSS file using the W3C validator found at http://jigsaw.w3.org/css-validator/ and fix any errors that are identified.

h. Validate your HTML webpage using the W3C validator found at validator.w3.org and fix any errors that are identified.

i. ✳ Identify the steps you would take to accommodate legacy browsers when including a Flash video on a webpage.

In the Labs

Labs 1 and 2, which increase in difficulty, require you to create webpages based on what you learned in the chapter; Lab 3 requires you to dive deeper into a topic covered in the chapter.

Lab 1: Adding Video to the New Harvest Food Bank Website

Problem: You volunteer at a local food bank called New Harvest Food Bank that collects community food donations and provides food and other services to those in need. You have already created a responsive website but now need to add a video to the home page to attract volunteers. You also need to format the video on the page. Create and style the video as shown in Figure 9–27.

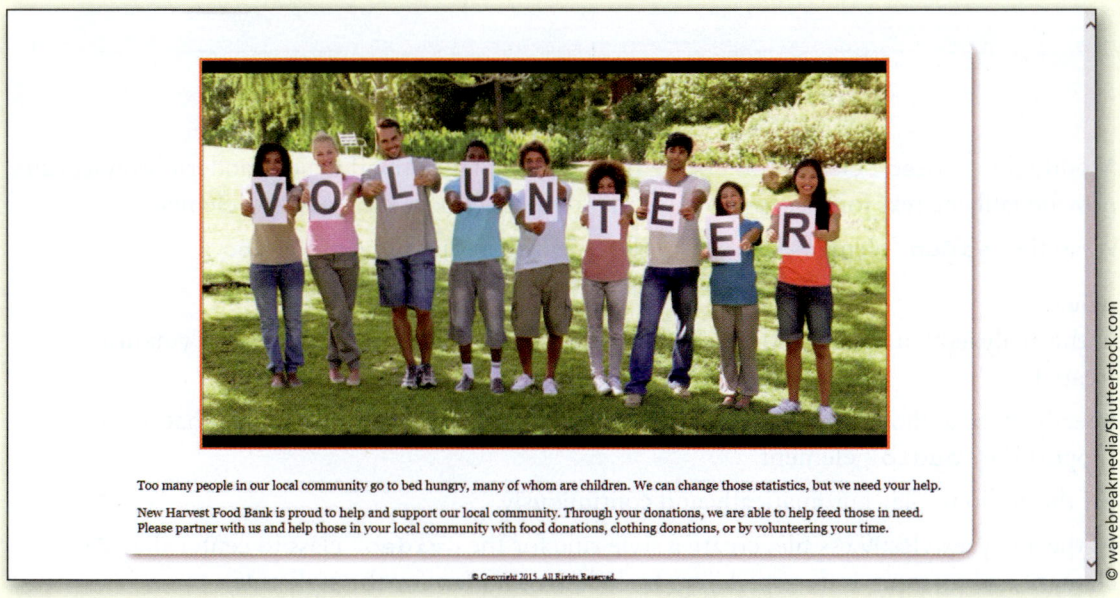

Too many people in our local community go to bed hungry, many of whom are children. We can change those statistics, but we need your help.

New Harvest Food Bank is proud to help and support our local community. Through your donations, we are able to help feed those in need. Please partner with us and help those in your local community with food donations, clothing donations, or by volunteering your time.

© Copyright 2015. All Rights Reserved.

Figure 9–27

Instructions: Perform the following tasks:

1. Save the lab1\media folder from the Data Files for Students to your lab1 folder.

2. Open your text editor and then open the index.html document in the lab1 folder and update the comment at the top of the page to include today's date.

3. In the **main** element of the index.html document, insert a **video** element with **autoplay** and **controls** attributes.

4. Specify the following three source files within the **video** element and insert the appropriate **type** attribute and value for each source.

   ```
   src="media/volunteer.mp4"
   src="media/volunteer.ogg"
   src="media/volunteer.webm"
   ```

5. Create a paragraph element below the source elements with text that states **Your browser does not support the video element.**

6. Wrap the video element in a **div** element and include a **class="video"** attribute and value.

7. In the fbstyles.css file, update the comment with today's date, and then create the following new style rules above the media queries and include comments for each:

```
.video {
text-align: center;
padding: 1em;
}


video {
border: 0.2em solid #FF6600;
height: auto;
max-width: 100%;
}
```

8. Save all files, open the index.html page within a browser, and then view the page, as shown in Figure 9–27.

9. Validate your HTML code and fix any errors.

10. Validate your CSS code and fix any errors.

11. Submit your assignment in the format specified by your instructor.

12. ✹ In this assignment, you wrapped a `video` element within a `div` element. Could the `video` element be wrapped within an HTML5 semantic element, such as an article, aside, or a section? Why or why not?

Lab 2: Adding Audio to the Website for Steve's Screen Services

Problem: You work for a screening company called Steve's Screen Services that specializes in screening, cleaning, and repairing screened patios. You have already created a responsive website, but now need to enhance the Gallery page with audio. You add and style an audio element for the Gallery page. The webpage with the audio element is shown in Figure 9–28.

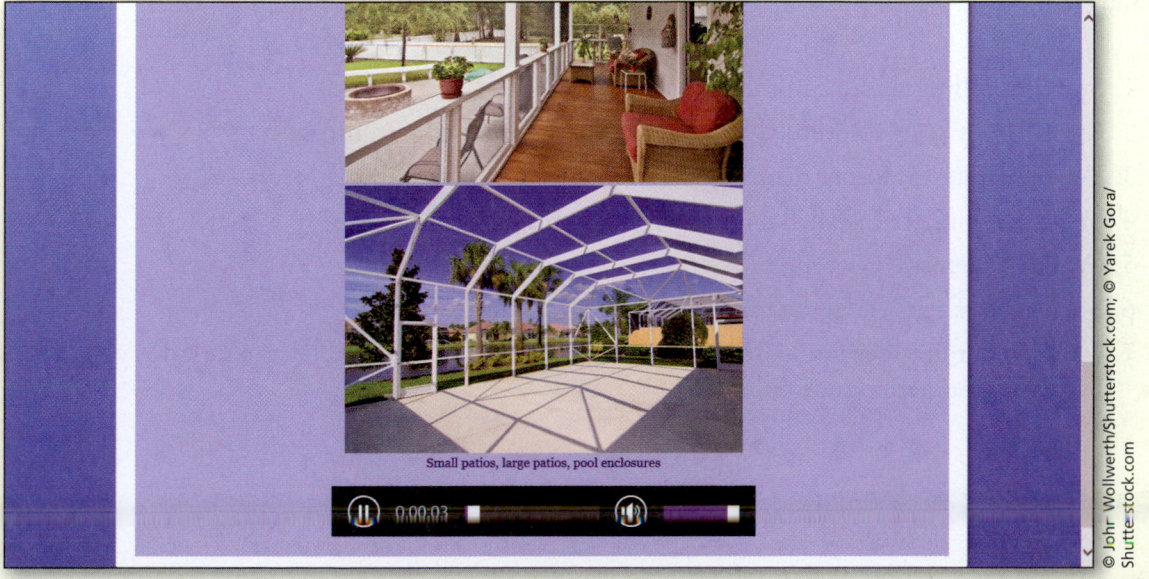

Figure 9–28

Continued >

In the Labs *continued*

Instructions: Perform the following tasks:

1. Save the lab2\media folder from the Data Files for Students to your lab2 folder.

2. Open the gallery.html document and update the comment at the top of the page to include today's date.

3. Insert an **audio** element below the **figure** element (within the **article** element) and set the element to automatically play the sound and to display the controls.

4. Insert three **source** elements and reference each audio file within the media folder. Insert the appropriate **type** attribute and value for each source.

5. Create a paragraph element with a fallback message to legacy browser users, notifying them that their browser does not support the audio element.

6. Wrap the **audio** element within a div element with the attribute and value **class="sound"**.

7. In the screenstyles.css file, modify the comment at the top of the page to include today's date.

8. In the screenstyles.css file, create a new style rule for the **sound** class above the media queries that specifies a center alignment. Include a comment for this new style rule.

9. Save all files and open the gallery.html page within a browser to view the page, as shown in Figure 9–28.

10. Validate your HTML code and fix any errors.

11. Validate your CSS code and fix any errors.

12. Submit your assignment in the format specified by your instructor.

13. ❇ Research the Internet to locate free resources for audio files and provide a summary of your findings. Include at least three resource links.

Lab 3: Expand Your World
Exploring Multimedia File Formats and Plug-ins

Problem: In this chapter you worked with many types of file formats and learned about different kinds of multimedia. In this exercise, you will research to learn more about plug-ins.

Instructions:

1. Search the Internet for information about plug-ins.

2. Identify why plug-ins were created and how they are used by a browser.

3. Why are plug-ins losing their popularity?

4. What plug-ins are installed on your desktop browser?

5. What is Microsoft Silverlight?

6. Submit your answers in the format specified by your instructor.

7. ❇ Use your browser to research how to update the Adobe Flash Player plugin for your browser. Summarize your findings.

Consider This: Your Turn

Apply your creative thinking and problem-solving skills to design and implement a solution.

1. Improving Your Personal Portfolio Website Design

Personal

Part 1: In Chapter 8, you added a table to your portfolio page. In this exercise, you update the page as follows:

1. Open the external style sheet you created in Chapter 8 and save it with the name `portfoliostyles09.css` in the styles folder within the your_turn_1 folder.

2. Add your name and the current date as a comment to the first line of the portfoliostyles09.css file.

3. In your HTML editor, open the files you created for your portfolio website in Chapter 8 and make sure your name and the current date are added as a comment to the first line of all files.

   a. Update the HTML files to modify the link to the external style sheet to reference portfoliostyles09.css.

   b. Insert an `audio` element on the portfolio page.

   c. Determine which attributes to include for the `audio` element.

   d. Include at least two source files. Audio files for this exercise are available in the your_turn_1\media folder in the Data Files for Students.

4. Save and test your files.

5. Validate and correct your HTML and CSS files, and submit your assignment in the format specified by your instructor.

Part 2: ✳

Discuss the reasons you should or should not include audio on your portfolio webpage.

2. Improving the WebDevPros Website

Professional

Part 1: In Chapter 8, you added a table and a form for webDevPros. In this exercise, you update the site as follows:

1. Open the external style sheet you created in Chapter 8 and save it with the name `webdevstyles09.css` in the styles folder within the your_turn_2 folder.

2. Add your name and the current date as a comment to the first line of the webdevstyles09.css file.

3. Open the files you created for webDevPros in Chapter 8 in your HTML editor and make sure your name and the current date are added as a comment to the first line of all files.

4. Update the HTML files to:

   a. Integrate a `video` element on the home page.

   b. Set the video to play automatically and to display controls.

   c. Set a width and height for the `video` element.

   d. Specify two source elements. Video files are provided for this exercise in the your_turn_2\media folder in the Data Files for Students.

   e. Include fallback text in case the user's browser does not support the `video` element.

   f. Wrap the `video` element within a `div` element with a class named ad.

Continued >

Consider This: Your Turn *continued*

5. Update the CSS file to:

a. Style the `div` element to center the video on the page and to apply a small amount of padding.

b. Style the `video` element for responsive design and include a border, and rounded corners.

c. Add comments to note all changes and updates.

6. Save and test your files.

7. Validate and correct your HTML and CSS files, and submit your assignment in the format specified by your instructor.

Part 2: ✷ In this exercise, you integrated two video file formats, MP4 and WebM. Search the Internet for an Ogg converter, create an Ogg file format, and add it as a third source file to the `video` element. Identify the website source that you used to create the Ogg file.

3. Improving the Dog Hall of Fame Website

Research and Collaboration

Part 1: In Chapter 8, you added a form to the Dog Hall of Fame website. In this exercise, you create and style a video for the website. Do the following activities as a group:

1. Open the external style sheet you created in Chapter 8 and save it with the name `dogstyles09.css` in the styles folder within the your_turn_3 folder.

2. Add your names and the current date as a comment to the first line of the dogstyles09.css file.

3. Open the files you created for the Dog Hall of Fame in Chapter 8 in your HTML editor and make sure your names and the current date are added as a comment to the first line of all files.

4. Modify the link to the external style sheet to reference dogstyles09.css.

5. Insert a video element on the nominations page. At a minimum, update the HTML page to do the following:

a. Integrate a `video` element on the page.

b. Set the video to play automatically and to display controls.

c. Set a width and height for the `video` element.

d. Specify three source elements. Video files are provided for this exercise in the your_turn_3\ media folder in the Data Files for Students.

e. Include fallback text in case the user's browser does not support the `video` element.

f. Wrap the `video` element within a `div` element with a class named dog.

6. Update the CSS file to:

a. Style the `div` element to center the video on the page and to apply a small amount of padding.

b. Style the `video` element for responsive design and include a border, rounded corners, and a box shadow effect.

c. Add comments to note all changes and updates.

7. Save and test your files.

8. Validate and correct your HTML and CSS files, and submit your assignment in the format specified by your instructor.

Part 2: ✷ As a group, discuss the benefits of uploading a video file to YouTube and then linking the YouTube video to a website. List the steps you would take to accomplish this task.

10 | Creating Interactivity with Social Media and JavaScript

Objectives

You will have mastered the material in this chapter when you can:

- Understand social media
- Identify and describe forms of social media
- Understand and describe a blog
- Understand JavaScript
- Describe JavaScript code
- Understand and use the script element
- Understand where JavaScript code may be written

- Create an external JavaScript file
- Describe pop-up windows
- Understand and use the alert() method
- Understand and use the open() method
- Understand events
- Use an onclick event handler

10 | Creating Interactivity with Social Media and JavaScript

Introduction

Many individuals, organizations, and companies rely on their websites as a key vehicle to communicate with friends, members, and current and future customers. Webpages often announce upcoming events, provide updated information, or act as a sales tool or product catalog. Regardless of the content, webpage features should spark visitors' interests and entice them to return to the website. As with an advertisement, a webpage has six to seven seconds to attract and retain a visitor's attention.

Word of mouth is one of the best forms of advertisement, and happens when a friend or family member recommends a specific product, service, or business to you. This form of advertisement is powerful because most people trust the word of a friend or family member more than a magazine advertisement or commercial. With the use of social media, word-of-mouth advertising spreads quickly, which is why businesses use social media to interact and engage with customers.

Besides including social media links, many of today's websites use a combination of HTML5, CSS3, and JavaScript. JavaScript is a web programming language used to enhance a website and create interactivity. An effective way to create interesting and useful webpages is to include dynamic content to make the webpage interactive. To engage and interact with customers on a webpage is to use JavaScript code to display messages.

In this chapter, you will learn about the different forms of social media. You will learn how to use Facebook, Twitter, Google+, YouTube, Instagram, and Pinterest and how to link your social media pages to your website. You will also insert social media icons onto a webpage and link them to a social media page. Next, you will explore JavaScript and use the `script` element and its attributes to add JavaScript to a webpage. You will also learn how to create an external JavaScript file and create several functions. Finally, you will learn how to reference the external JavaScript file within an HTML webpage.

Project — Add Social Media and JavaScript to a Webpage

In Chapter 10, you make the Forward Fitness Club website more engaging by adding social media icons and links to every page within the website. You also add interactivity to the home page, the About Us page, and the Contact Us page using JavaScript.

This chapter provides an overview of the popular social media sources available today. The chapter focuses on Facebook, Twitter, Google+, YouTube, Instagram, and Pinterest and details how businesses use these social media outlets to interact and engage with their customers.

This chapter also provides a basic introduction to JavaScript and discusses how to use JavaScript to enhance a webpage through interactivity.

The project in this chapter improves a website by adding social media icons and links to all pages within the website. To perform these tasks, you first copy the image files to your image folder. Next, you add social media images and links within the footer element on each webpage and style the social media icons to improve their appearance. Next, you create your first JavaScript code to create a pop-up message on the home page. After copying the script folder to your fitness folder, you create an external JavaScript file that contains four functions. Finally, you reference the external JavaScript file within the Contact Us and the About Us pages. Figure 10–1 shows the Classes page with the social media icons at the bottom of the page. Figure 10–2 shows the pop-up message on the home page. Figure 10–3 shows the pop-up message on the Contact Us page. Figure 10–4 shows the new window that opens as a result of a JavaScript function.

Group Fitness Class Schedule

Class	Days	Times	Instructor	Room
Cardio	Mon, Wed, Fri	6:00am, 6:00pm	Schultz	B
Boot Camp	Tue, Thu	5:00am, 5:00pm	Taylor	B
Spinning	Tue, Thu	6:00am, 6:00pm	Roberts	A
Kickboxing	Mon, Wed, Fri	8:00am, 7:15pm	Lawrence	A
Yoga	Tue, Thu	6:00am, 6:00pm	Schultz	B
Zumba	Mon, Wed, Fri	7:00am, 6:00pm	Roberts	A

© Copyright 2015. All Rights Reserved.
forwardfitness@club.net

Connect with us:

Figure 10–1

Figure 10–2

Figure 10–3

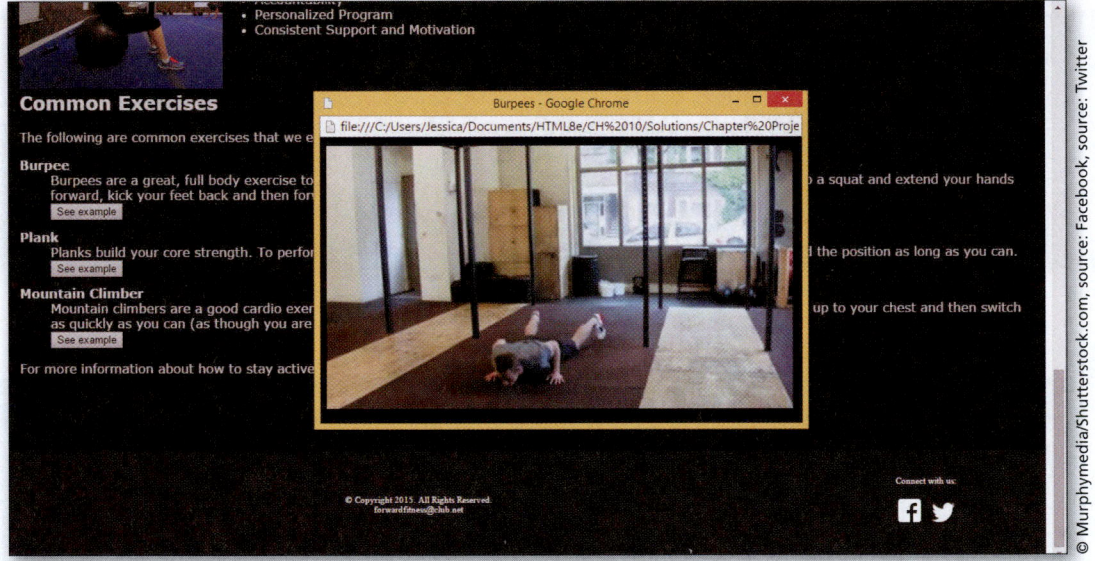

Figure 10–4

Roadmap

In this chapter, you will learn how to create the webpages shown in Figures 10–1, 10–2, 10–3, and 10–4. The following roadmap identifies general activities you will perform as you progress through this chapter:

1. INSERT SOCIAL MEDIA ICONS and LINKS.

2. STYLE SOCIAL MEDIA ICONS.

3. CREATE JAVASCRIPT ALERT MESSAGE.

4. CREATE EXTERNAL JAVASCRIPT FILE.

5. CALL JAVASCRIPT FUNCTIONS.

At the beginning of step instructions throughout the chapter, you will see an abbreviated form of this roadmap. The abbreviated roadmap uses colors to indicate chapter progress: gray means the chapter is beyond that activity, blue means the task being shown is covered in that activity, and black means that activity is yet to be covered. For example, the following abbreviated roadmap indicates the chapter would be showing a task in the 2 STYLE SOCIAL MEDIA ICONS activity.

1 INSERT SOCIAL MEDIA ICONS & LINKS | 2 STYLE SOCIAL MEDIA ICONS | 3 CREATE JAVASCRIPT ALERT MESSAGE
4 CREATE EXTERNAL JAVASCRIPT FILE MESSAGE | 5 CALL JAVASCRIPT FUNCTIONS

Use the abbreviated roadmap as a progress guide while you read or step through the instructions in this chapter.

Using Social Media

A **social network** is an online community where members post and exchange **social media** content, such as pictures, videos, and music. A social networking site allows members to share information and ideas with fellow online community members, who can view and comment on the shared social media. Social networking is a very popular and powerful medium for advertising your brand and product. As shown in Figure 10–5, the web has many social networking sites, such as Facebook, Twitter, Google+, YouTube, Instagram, Vine, and Pinterest.

Social media can be a significant opportunity to market your product to potential customers because it encourages word-of-mouth advertising. Social networking sites allow businesses to immediately connect with their customers and potential customers and instantly engage them with new product information.

© rvlsoft/Shutterstock

Figure 10–5

Facebook

Facebook is a social networking site with more than one billion users, most users of any social networking site. Users include individuals and businesses. Individuals can exchange comments, share personal updates, and post pictures and video. With so many users Facebook provides another medium for advertising. A business can create a Facebook page and use it to advertise its products and services. Individuals can "like" a business by clicking a button to indicate that they use or approve of a produce. Businesses can engage with people who have "liked" their page by posting a picture of their latest work, create community events, or provide new product updates. Individuals who like the business's page see the new posts made by the business within their home page feed. Obtaining "likes" is a goal for most businesses, as this increases its presence and positive perception. As shown in Figure 10–6, you can create several types of Facebook pages, including a local business page, a company page, a brand or product page, a public figure page, an entertainment page, or a community page.

types of pages on Facebook Create a Page →

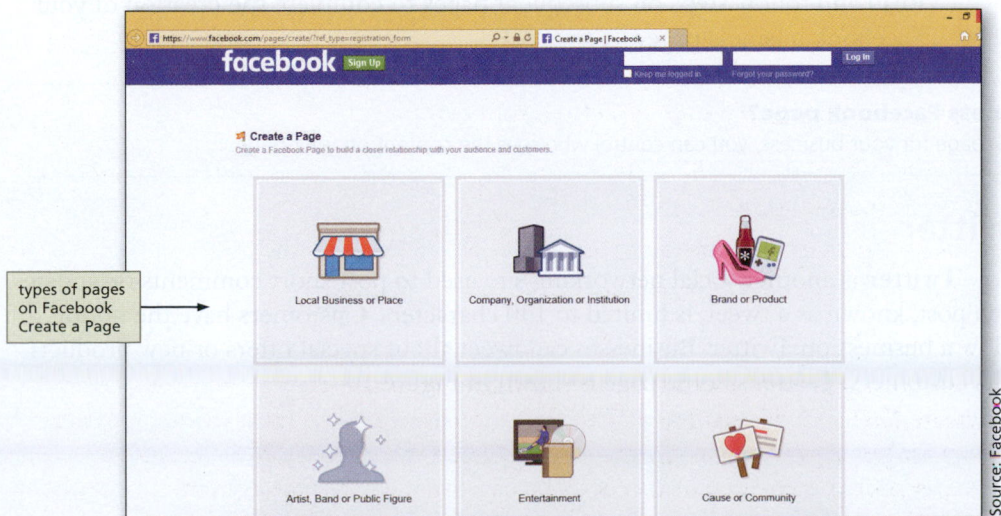

Source: Facebook

Figure 10–6

There is no cost to create a business Facebook page, and the page allows businesses to instantly connect and engage with customers. Businesses leverage Facebook to increase traffic to their website and increase sales. For a fee, businesses can also create an ad on Facebook to further drive potential customers to its website. Facebook matches a target audience with a company's ad and displays the ad on potential customers' news feeds, located on their home pages. Facebook provides several tools to measure the success of your ad and your Facebook page.

The following are several key items to consider when creating a Facebook post.

1. Set a positive tone within the first sentence of the status update, which yields interest and engagement.

2. Announce a special offer with a link for more information to drive traffic to your website.

3. Include an image with your posts, as this helps to further engage potential customers.

4. Keep your images mobile-friendly, as many Facebook users use the Facebook app on their mobile device.

5. Positively respond to customer comments to help build relationships.

6. Create a schedule for posts and post consistently.

To Create a Local Business Facebook Page

As shown in Figure 10–6, you can create several types of pages within Facebook. If you choose to create a Facebook page for your local business, you would use the following steps.

1 Open your browser and type www.facebook.com/business within your address bar.

2 Tap or click the CREATE PAGE link at the top of the page.

3 Tap or click the Local Business or Place icon.

4 You will then be prompted to login to Facebook or to sign up for Facebook.

5 If necessary, tap or click the Sign up for Facebook link and follow the steps to create a new account. Otherwise, enter your email and password and then tap or click the Log In button to login.

6 Tap or click the Local Business or Place icon again, complete the form, and then tap or click the Get Started button.

7 Read and follow steps on subsequent pages to complete the creation of your Facebook business page.

Who can view my business Facebook page?
Once you create a Facebook page for your business, you can control who sees the content on your page.

Twitter

Twitter is another social networking site used to post short comments or updates. Each post, known as a tweet, is limited to 140 characters. Customers have the option to follow a business on Twitter. Businesses can tweet about special offers or new products to its customers. Twitter's home page is shown in Figure 10–7.

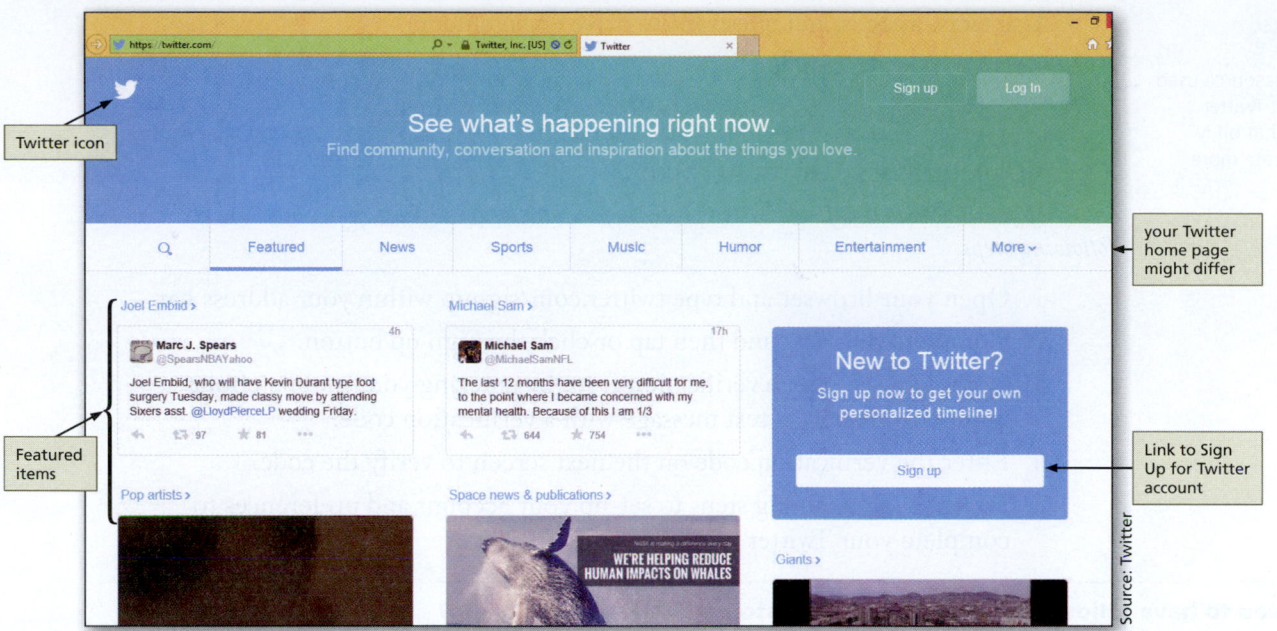

Figure 10–7

Creating a business Twitter account is free and allows businesses to instantly connect and engage with its customers. Businesses can follow their competition and learn about special offers made by their competitors. Businesses can also display ads on Twitter for a fee. Twitter provides many marketing opportunities for business to help with a content strategy, to engage and obtain more customers, and to measure marketing results in real time. Figure 10–8 shows the Twitter business page (business.twitter.com).

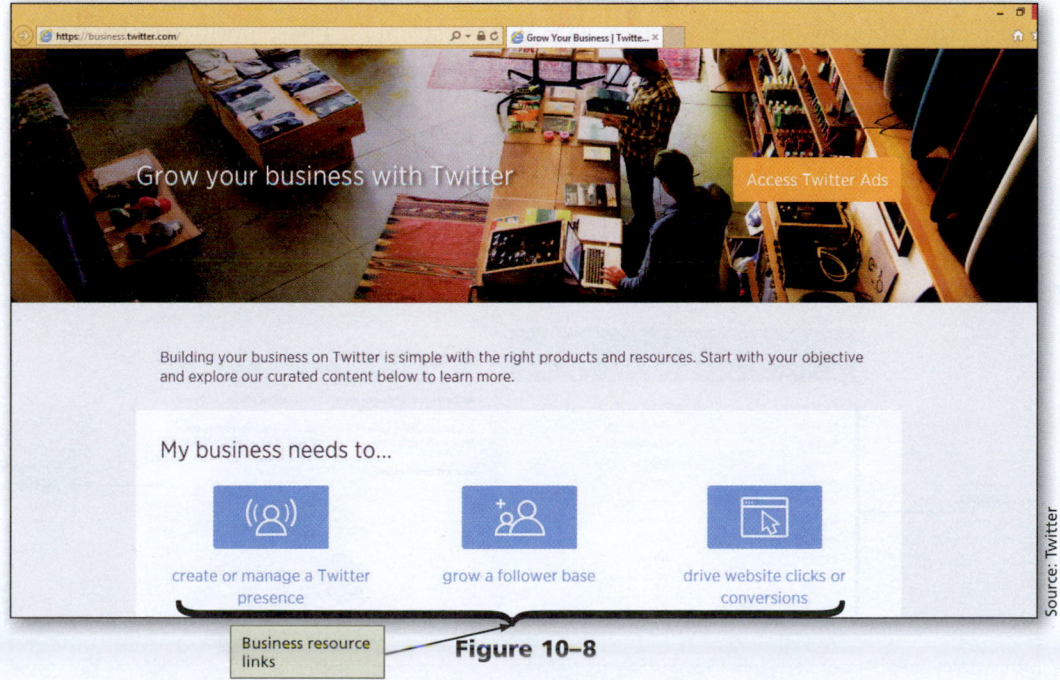

Figure 10–8

The following are several key items to consider when creating a tweet.

1. Include a clear call to action.

2. Avoid using abbreviations and all caps.

3. Use links with short URLs.

4. Use facts, images, and questions to drive engagement.

5. Retweet relative content.

6. Use Twitter's tools to schedule tweets and tweet campaigns.

To Create a Business Twitter Account

If you choose to create a Twitter presence for your local business, you would use the following steps.

1. Open your browser and type twitter.com/signup within your address bar.

2. Complete the form and then tap or click the Sign up button.

3. Complete the phone verification form by entering your mobile phone number to receive a text message with a verification code.

4. Enter the verification code on the next screen to verify the code.

5. Follow the remaining steps to set-up your account and preferences to complete your Twitter account.

CONSIDER THIS

Do I need to have followers before potential customers can see my tweets?
No. If you use Twitter ads, your tweets or ad will be displayed on pages of potential customers. You can set a budget for Twitter ads and view ad results in real-time.

Google+

Google+ joined the social media phenomenon in 2011 but has quickly gained in popularity among individuals and especially businesses. To use Google+, you must have a Google account, which you can create for free at plus.google.com. Once you have established your account, you add people to your circles. Circles are groups or categories, such as friends, family, and acquaintances. You can share content within all your circles or only select circles.

Like Facebook and Twitter, businesses using Google+ can post special offers and pictures of new products to share with their customers. These businesses have an added benefit because Google+ works with Google's search engine, increasing the probability of a potential customer finding the business through Google's search engine. An example of a Google+ page is shown in Figure 10–9.

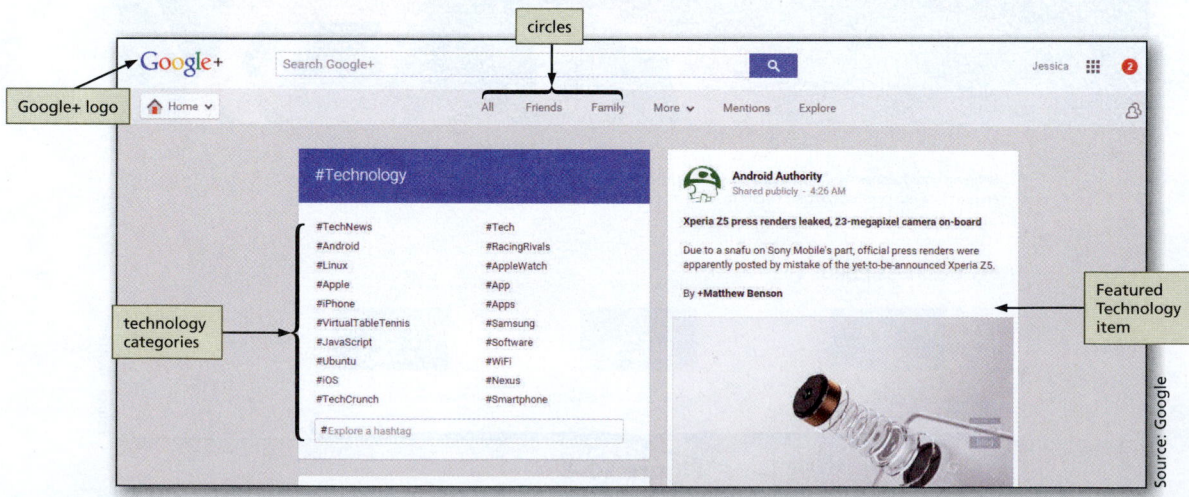

Figure 10–9

YouTube

YouTube is a social media website where members can upload and share original videos. YouTube was founded in 2005 and has grown to over one billion users.

Every day, YouTube's visitors watch several hundred hours of video and generate billions of views. This provides businesses a good opportunity to advertise and market their products. More than a million people advertise on YouTube, and the bulk of the advertisers are small businesses. YouTube also has a Facebook and Twitter presence.

Businesses can purchase ad space on YouTube to attract its target audience. Business ads can be a banner image that is displayed on the lower part of a video or a full-length commercial that plays before the selected video. Figure 10–10 shows an example of banner ad. Figure 10–11 shows an example of commercial ad that plays before a video.

Figure 10–10

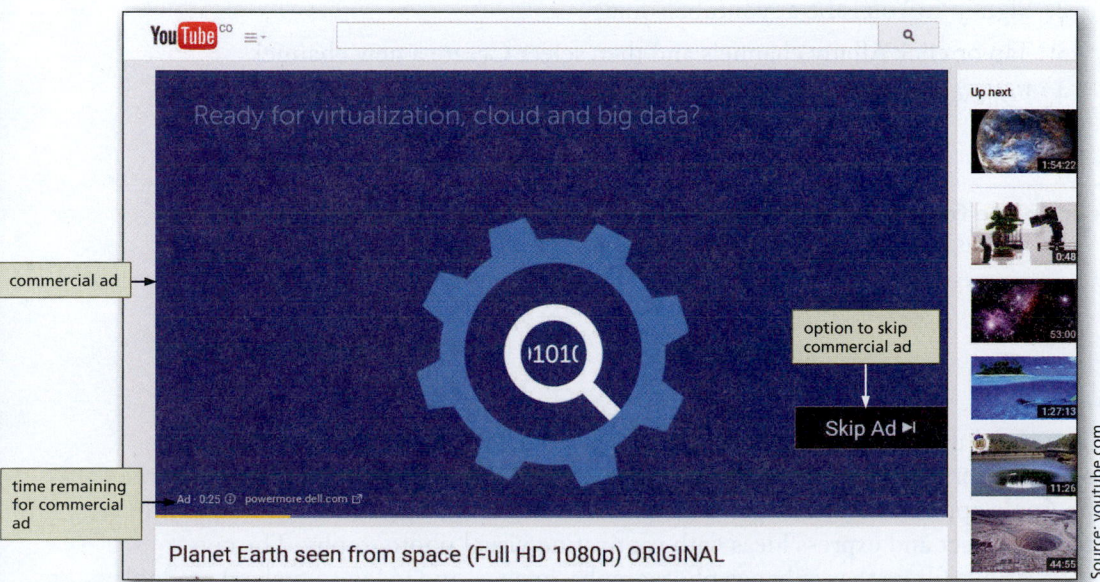

Figure 10–11

Businesses can create their own channel on YouTube and upload videos to their channel. Users can subscribe to a channel and view the business' latest video. The Cengage Learning channel video page is shown in Figure 10–12.

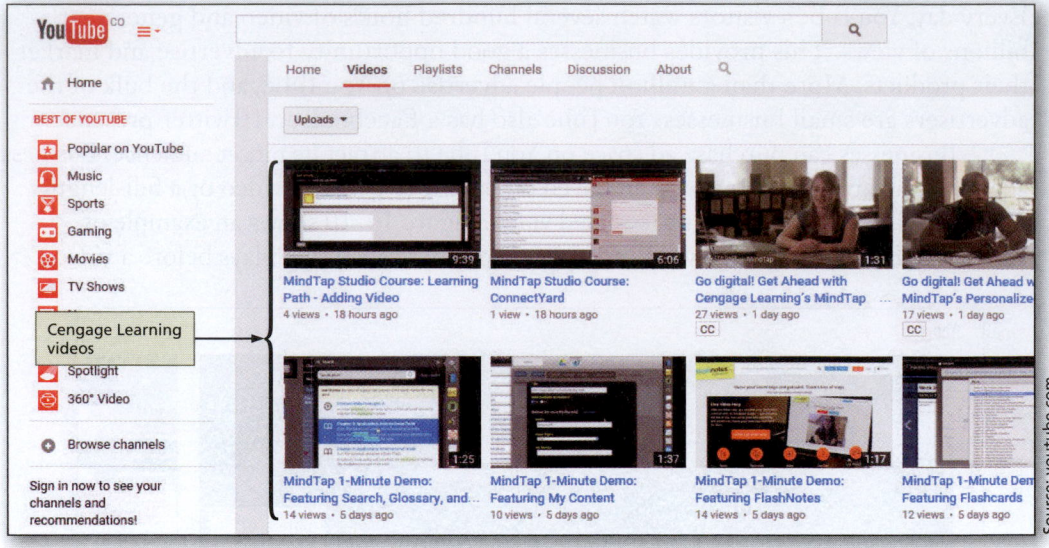

Source: youtube.com

Figure 10–12

The following are several key items to consider when creating and uploading a video to YouTube for your business.

1. Use a clever title to attract your target audience.
2. Use a meaningful name for the video file.
3. Describe your video using keywords to help your customers find your video.
4. Include a call to action and a link to your website.

To Create a YouTube Channel

If you want to create a YouTube channel for your business, use the following steps.

1. Establish a Google account at accounts.google.com.
2. Sign in to YouTube at youtube.com.
3. Tap or click All my channels and then select Create a new channel.
4. Follow the remaining steps to create your YouTube channel.

CONSIDER THIS

What file format do I need to use for my YouTube video?
YouTube accepts the following file formats: .mov, .mpeg4, .mp4, .avi, .wmv, .mpegps, .flv, and .webm.

Instagram

Instagram is a social networking site where members can upload and share photographs, images, and video. Most users view and use Instagram from a mobile device. Instagram is also a free app available at the Apple app store and Google Play. The creators of Instagram wanted to provide users a unique way to connect and express ideas with captivating visual photography. The app allows users to apply various filters that enhance photographs, images, and video to make them look more professional. Many businesses also use Instagram to promote brand awareness. Figure 10–13 shows how McDonald's uses images and video on Instagram to promote its brand.

Source: https://instagram.com/mcdonalds/

Figure 10–13

How do I post a photograph or video to Instagram?
You must first download the Instagram app to your mobile device, create an account, and then use the tools within the app to edit and post a photograph or video on your mobile device.

Pinterest

On **Pinterest**, members browse and "pin" ideas found on the web. Pinterest users search for ideas for just about anything, including recipes, crafts, photography, and do-it-yourself (DIY) projects. Users can follow boards that interest them most and "pin" photos, links, and comments to their own board for future use. Figure 10–14 shows the Pinterest board for Lowe's, which contains several home improvement ideas. Users with an interest in Lowe's content can follow the board and see any new pins made by Lowe's.

BTW
Privacy Policy
Each social networking site has a privacy policy. Be sure to read and review the policy to inform yourself on how each company uses the information you provide on their website.

Source: https://www.pinterest.com/lowes/build-it/

Figure 10–14

CONSIDER THIS

Are photographs required for Pinterest?
To place a pin on a Pinterest board, it must include an image or photograph.

BTW

Social Media Banned in Certain Countries
Although Facebook has more than one billion users, did you know that Facebook and other forms of social media are banned in six countries? These countries are China, Iran, North Korea, Pakistan, Turkey, and Vietnam.

Other Social Media Options

Other social media options for your business to explore include LinkedIn, Quora, Tumblr, StumbleUpon, Flickr, Delicious, Digg, Vimeo, Vine, Foursquare, and many more. The key is to determine which social media outlets are best for your business in attracting new customers. As a business owner, you must also consider the time involved with keeping your social media current and relevant.

Blogs

Many businesses use blogs to promote their business. A **blog** is an online journal, maintained by an individual, group, or a business. The term "blog" is short for a combination of the words web and log. Businesses use a blog to share new information and to keep their customers engaged. Businesses can also use their blog to discuss current trends or changes in the market. Customers can respond to each journal entry to ask questions or provide feedback. Business owners who maintain a blog should respond to customer comments in a timely manner and keep their blog content fresh. The Rocketology blog, one of the many blogs available from NASA, is shown in Figure 10–15.

Figure 10–15

Source: https://blogs.nasa.gov/rocketology/

CONSIDER THIS

How can I start my own blog?
You can use one of many free resources available to start your own blog. If you have a Google account, you can use Google Blogger to create a blog at www.blogger.com. Blog.com and WordPress.com are other popular sources for blogs.

Adding Facebook and Twitter Links to a Website

Businesses that use social media display social media icons and links on their website. The icons let their customers know how to connect with the business on social media. When users click a social media icon, they are redirected to the social media page for the business. Social media links are typically included near the top or bottom of a webpage. Figure 10–16 shows the various social media links near the bottom of the page at Cengage.com.

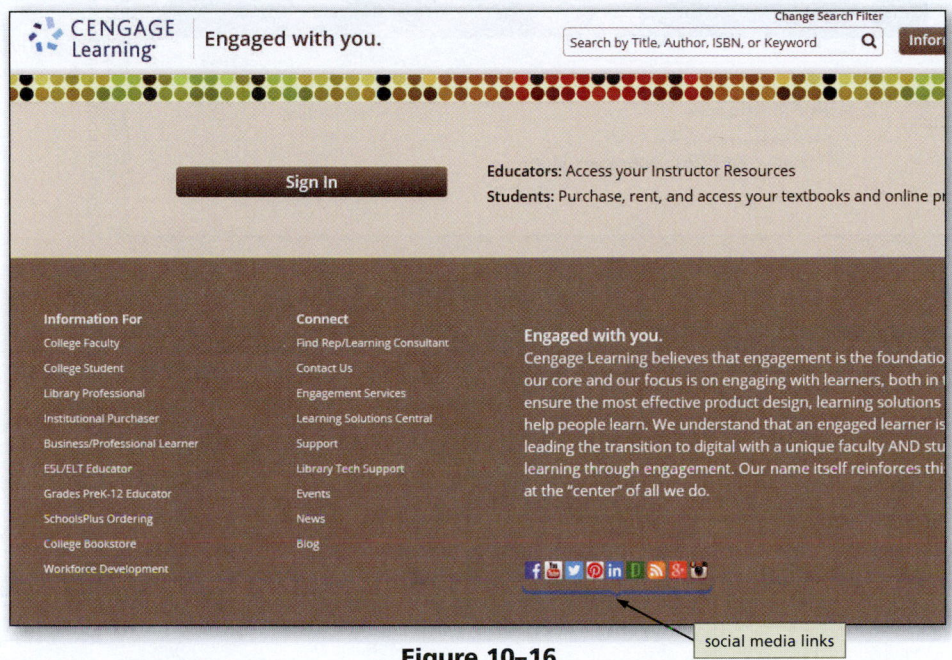

Figure 10–16

The owners of the Forward Fitness Club have decided to promote their business using social media site and created a Facebook page, as shown in Figure 10–17, and a Twitter presence, as shown in Figure 10–18.

Figure 10–17

Figure 10–18

CONSIDER THIS

Where do I obtain social media icons to use on my website?

Each social media source has a brand or brand assets page, which contains information and guidelines for the use of their icons. Most of these pages include logos available for download.

To Add Social Media Icons and Links to the Home Page

1 INSERT SOCIAL MEDIA ICONS & LINKS | 2 STYLE SOCIAL MEDIA ICONS | 3 CREATE JAVASCRIPT ALERT MESSAGE
4 CREATE EXTERNAL JAVASCRIPT FILE MESSAGE | 5 CALL JAVASCRIPT FUNCTIONS

Add Facebook and Twitter icons to the home page for the Forward Fitness Club website. Include a link for the Facebook icon that links to the Forward Fitness Club's Facebook page and include a link for the Twitter icon that links to the Forward Fitness Club's Twitter page. *Why? Connecting with customers on social media allows you to connect and engage with your customers.* The following steps add social media icons and links to the home page.

1

- Copy the image files from the chapter10\fitness\images folder provided with the Data Files for Students to the fitness\images folder.

- Open index.html in your text editor and update the comment with today's date.

Figure 10–19

- Tap or click at the end of Line 79, and then press the ENTER key twice to insert new Lines 80 and 81.

- On Line 81, increase the indent, and then type `<div id="copyright">` to insert a starting div tag.

- Tap or click at the beginning of Line 82, increase the indent, and then type `<p>` to insert a starting paragraph tag.

- Tap or click at the beginning of Line 83 and increase the indent.

- Tap or click at the end of Line 83 and then type `</p>` to insert a closing paragraph tag.

- Press the ENTER key to insert a new Line 84, decrease the indent, and then type `</div>` to insert an ending div tag (Figure 10–19).

Q&A

What is the purpose of the copyright div?

The copyright div contains information that will be formatted in future steps.

2

- Press the ENTER key twice to insert new Lines 85 and 86.

- On Line 86, type `<div id="social">` to insert a starting div tag.

- Press the ENTER key to insert a new Line 87, increase the indent, and then type `<p>Connect with us:</p>` to insert a paragraph element.

```
86    <div id="social">              ← starting div tag
87        <p>Connect with us:</p>
88        <p><a href="https://www.facebook.com/fwdfitclub"><img
          src="images/fblogo.png" alt="Facebook logo"></a>       ← img elements
89        <a href="https://twitter.com/fwdfitclub"><img src="images/twitterlogo.png"
          alt="Twitter logo"></a></p>
90    </div>                          ← ending div tag
```
Line 86 · paragraph elements · anchor elements

Figure 10–20

- Press the ENTER key to insert a new Line 88, and then type `<p><a href="https://www.facebook.com/fwdfitclub"><img src="images/fblogo.png" alt="Facebook logo"></a>` to insert a starting paragraph tag, an anchor element, and an image element.

- Press the ENTER key to insert a new Line 89, and then type `<a href="https://twitter.com/fwdfitclub"><img src="images/twitterlogo.png" alt="Twitter logo"></a></p>` to insert an anchor element, an image element, and ending paragraph tag.

- Press the ENTER key to insert a new Line 90, decrease the indent, and then type `</div>` to insert an ending div tag (Figure 10–20).

Q&A What is the purpose of the social div I just added?
The social div contains the social media icons and links. You will format this div in future steps.

3

- Save your changes, open index.html in your browser, adjust the window to the size of a desktop viewport, and then scroll down to view the social media icons (Figure 10–21).

© Copyright 2015. All Rights Reserved.
forwardfitness@club.net

Connect with us:

Facebook icon · Twitter icon

Figure 10–21

4

- Tap or click the Facebook icon to display the Facebook page for the Forward Fitness Club (Figure 10–22).

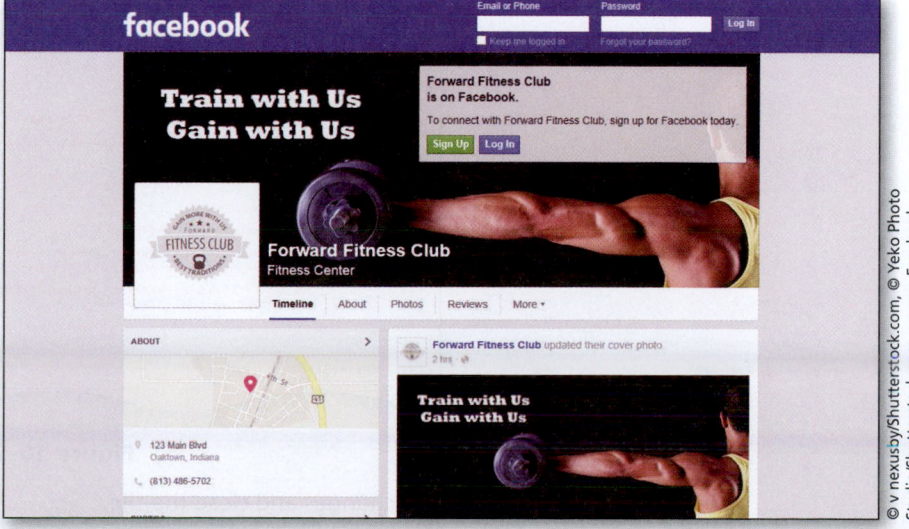

Figure 10–22

5

- Tap or click your browser's Back button to return to the Forward Fitness Club home page.

- Tap or click the Twitter icon to display the Twitter page for the Forward Fitness Club (Figure 10–23).

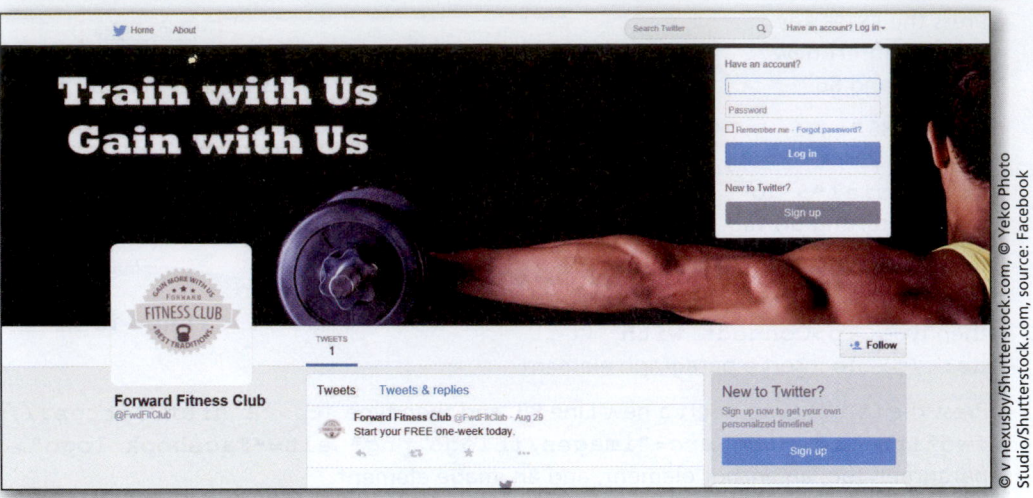

Figure 10–23

To Add Social Media Icons and Links to Webpages

Add Facebook and Twitter icons to all the remaining webpages for the Forward Fitness Club website, including the template. This gives customers access to the social media links from all pages. The following steps add social media icons and links to the About, Classes, Contact, Nutrition, and Fitness template webpages for the Forward Fitness Club.

1 Select Lines 79 through 92 on the index.html page and press CTRL+C to copy the code.

2 Open about.html, select Lines 100 through 103, and then press CTRL+V to paste the code. Save your changes and close the file.

3 Open classes.html, select Lines 111 through 114, and then press CTRL+V to paste the code. Save your changes and close the file.

4 Open contact.html, select Lines 86 through 89, and then press CTRL+V to paste the code. Save your changes and close the file.

5 Open nutrition.html, select Lines 85 through 88, and then press CTRL+V to paste the code. Save your changes and close the file.

6 Open fitness.html, located in the template folder, select Lines 35 through 38, and then press CTRL+V to paste the code (Figure 10–24).

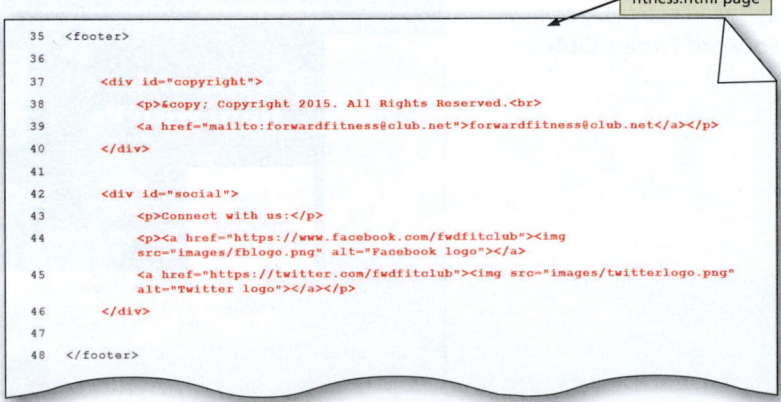

fitness.html page

```
35   <footer>
36
37       <div id="copyright">
38           <p>&copy; Copyright 2015. All Rights Reserved.<br>
39           <a href="mailto:forwardfitness@club.net">forwardfitness@club.net</a></p>
40       </div>
41
42       <div id="social">
43           <p>Connect with us:</p>
44           <p><a href="https://www.facebook.com/fwdfitclub"><img
                 src="images/fblogo.png" alt="Facebook logo"></a>
45           <a href="https://twitter.com/fwdfitclub"><img src="images/twitterlogo.png"
                 alt="Twitter logo"></a></p>
46       </div>
47
48   </footer>
```

Figure 10–24

7 Save your changes and close the file.

To Style the Copyright div Element

You created a copyright **div** element within the footer, which contains the copyright information and the email address and link. Now you must format this **div** to improve its appearance on the webpage. *Why? Style the copyright div to appear to the left of the social div.* Create a new style rule above the media queries to format the copyright **div** to float left, specify a top margin, and specify its width. The following steps add a new style rule for the copyright **div** in the styles.css file.

1

- From the fitness\css folder, open styles.css in your text editor and update the comment with today's date.

`Line 153`   `styles.css file`

- Tap or click at the end of Line 151, and then press the ENTER key twice to insert new Lines 152 and 153.

```
153   /* Style rule for the copyright div */          comment
154   #copyright {
155       float: left;                                style rule for
156       margin-top: 2em;                            #copyright element
157       width: 80%;
158   }
```

Figure 10–25

- On Line 153 type `/* Style rule for the copyright div */` to insert a comment.

- Press the ENTER key to insert a new Line 154, and then type `#copyright {` to insert a new selector.

- Press the ENTER key to insert a new Line 155, increase the indent, and then type `float: left;` to insert a new property and value.

- Press the ENTER key to insert a new Line 156, and then type `margin-top: 2em;` to insert a new property and value.

- Press the ENTER key to insert a new Line 157, and then type `width: 80%;` to insert a new property and value.

- Press the ENTER key to insert a new Line 158, decrease the indent, and then type `}` to insert a closing brace (Figure 10–25).

2

- Save your changes, open index. html in your browser, and then scroll down to view the social media icons (Figure 10–26).

copyright div appears to the left of the social div

Figure 10–26

social div

To Style the Social div Element and Social Media Icons

You created a social **div** element within the footer, which contains the Facebook and Twitter icons and links to social media pages for the Forward Fitness Club. Style the social **div** element to float right and specify a width. Style the images within the social div element by applying padding around the images. *Why? Format the div element and its images to improve their appearance on the webpage.* Once you style the social **div** element and specify a float property, some of the content within the footer area will not be visible. To correct this issue, specify an overflow property with a value of auto for the footer element within the desktop media query, as this will prevent the content within the social div element from overflowing. The following steps create two new style rules for within the styles.css file.

1

- In the styles.css file, tap or click at the end of Line 158, and then press the ENTER key twice to insert new Lines 159 and 160.

- On Line 160 type `/* Style rule for social div */` to insert a comment.

```
160   /* Style rule for social div */    ← comment
161   #social {
162       float: right;                ← style rule for
163       width: 20%;                     #social element
164   }
```
Line 160

Figure 10–27

- Press the ENTER key to insert a new Line 161 and then type `#social {` to insert a new selector.

- Press the ENTER key to insert a new Line 162, increase the indent, and then type `float: right;` to insert a new property and value.

- Press the ENTER key to insert a new Line 163, increase the indent, and then type `width: 20%;` to insert a new property and value.

- Press the ENTER key to insert a new Line 164, decrease the indent, and then type `}` to insert a closing brace (Figure 10–27).

2

- Tap or click at the end of Line 164, and then press the ENTER key twice to insert new Lines 165 and 166.

- On Line 166, type `/* Style rule for social media icons */` to insert a comment.

```
166   /* Style rule for social media icons */    ← comment
167   #social img {
168       padding: 0.5em;                      ← style rule for
169   }                                            social img element
```
Line 166

Figure 10–28

- Press the ENTER key to insert a new Line 167 and then type `#social img {` to insert a new selector.

- Press the ENTER key to insert a new Line 168, increase the indent, and then type `padding: 0.5em;` to insert a new property and value.

- Press the ENTER key to insert a new Line 169, decrease the indent, and then type `}` to insert a closing brace (Figure 10–28).

3

- Save your changes, open index. html in your browser, and then scroll down to view the social media icons (Figure 10–29).

Q&A Why can I not see the social media icons and the copyright div content?

The float property specified within the #social style rule has changed the appearance of the footer content. The solution is to add an overflow property to the footer style rule within the desktop media query.

[Figure 10–29 image: showing "p Fitness", "Meal Plans", "Get Started" navigation with note "new style rules applied, creating a problem to fix with the overflow property" and "Connect with us"]

Figure 10–29

4

- Tap or click at the end of Line 461, and then press the ENTER key once to insert a new Line 462.

- On Line 462 type `overflow: auto;` to insert a new property and value.

- Save your changes and refresh the index.html page in your browser (Figure 10–30).

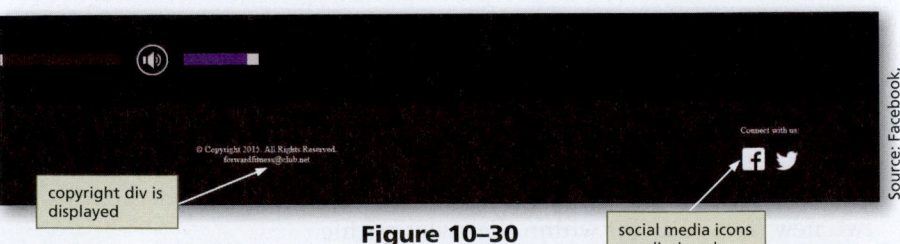

© Copyright 2015. All Rights Reserved.
forwardfitness@club.net

copyright div is displayed

Connect with us:

social media icons are displayed

Figure 10–30

5

- Tap or click the About Us link in the nav area and scroll down to view the social media icons.

- Tap or click each page link in the nav area to view all the webpages and to confirm that the social media icons appear at the bottom of each page.

- Adjust your browser window to a tablet viewport (Figure 10–31).

contact.html page in tablet viewport

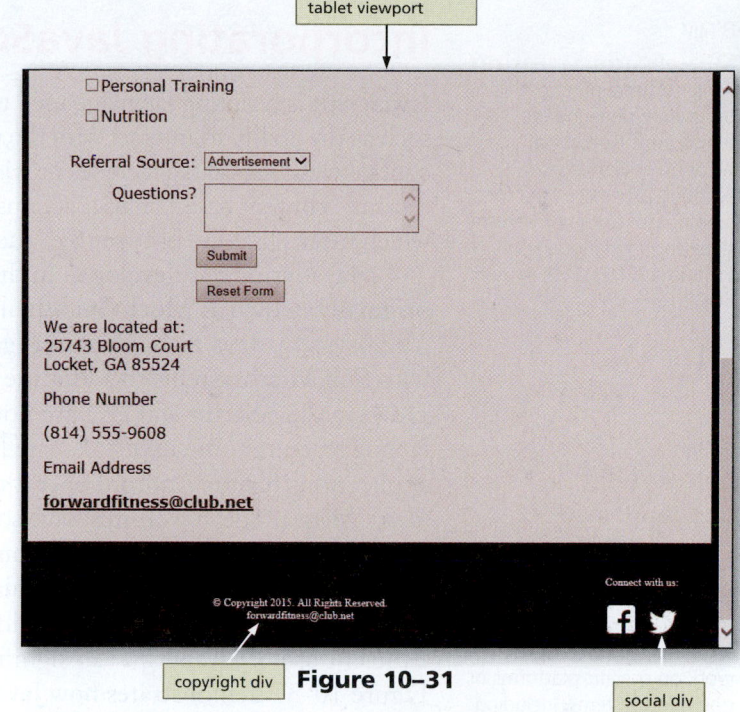

copyright div **Figure 10–31** social div

source: Facebook and Twitter

 6

- Adjust your browser window to a mobile viewport (Figure 10–32).

contact.html page in mobile viewport

copyright div **Figure 10–32** social div

source: Facebook and Twitter

Break Point: If you want to take a break, this is a good place to do so. You can exit the text editor now. To resume at a later time, run your text editor, open index.html, and continue following the steps from this location forward.

Incorporating JavaScript

JavaScript is scripting language used to provide various types of functionality to webpages, such as the ability to interact with the user. Web developers use a scripting language to control webpages. This includes providing user feedback, validating form data, and creating dynamic content based on user actions. JavaScript is a **client-side scripting** language, which means that the browser (i.e., the client) interprets and renders the JavaScript.

JavaScript was developed in the 1990s by Brendan Eich at Netscape and was originally known as Mocha and then LiveScript. During this same period, the Sun Microsystems Java technology was gaining in popularity. A marketing deal was struck with Sun Microsystems to adopt the Java name and change LiveScript to JavaScript. However, JavaScript and Java are not the same. Java is a more complex programming language, commonly used to create large business applications and native mobile applications for the Android operating system.

Most modern websites have some form of JavaScript integrated within their website. JavaScript provides additional interactivity between the webpage and the user. Developers can use JavaScript to validate form information, send an alert to a user, change HTML content, show or hide content, animate elements, and much more. Efficient use of JavaScript can significantly improve and enrich the user experience. Figure 10–33 demonstrates how JavaScript is used to create a slide show on the home page for the University of South Florida.

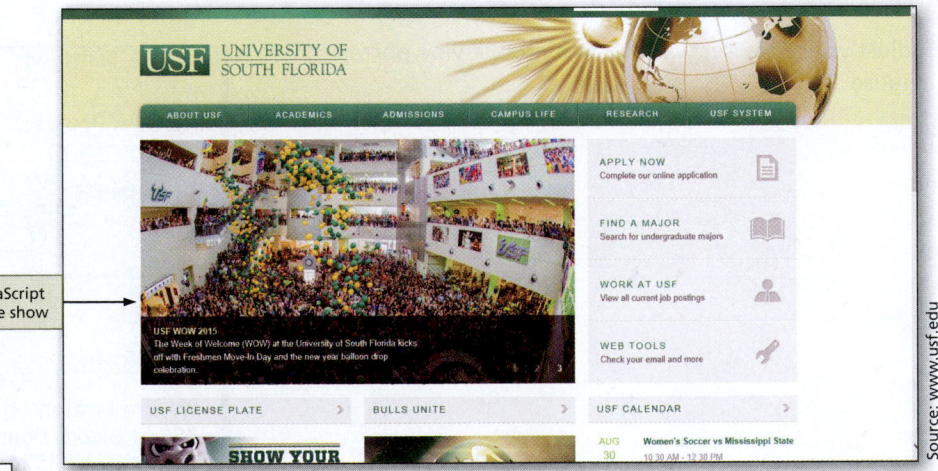

JavaScript slide show

Source: www.usf.edu

Figure 10–33

Many mobile websites integrate an icon commonly called the hamburger icon for use as a menu button. The hamburger icon consists of three, horizontal, parallel lines, as shown in Figure 10–34, and uses JavaScript to display a menu and allow users to select an option.

Figure 10–35 shows how JavaScript is used on the Snap.svg demo page. Users select the type of coffee to make and then watch the animation of the coffee maker. The legend next to the coffee maker lets the user know the ingredients and amounts.

You can integrate JavaScript into webpages in many ways. You must first determine the types of interactivity you want to provide into your website and then determine whether JavaScript is the best approach to accomplish the interactivity.

hamburger icon

Source: w3schools.com

Figure 10–34

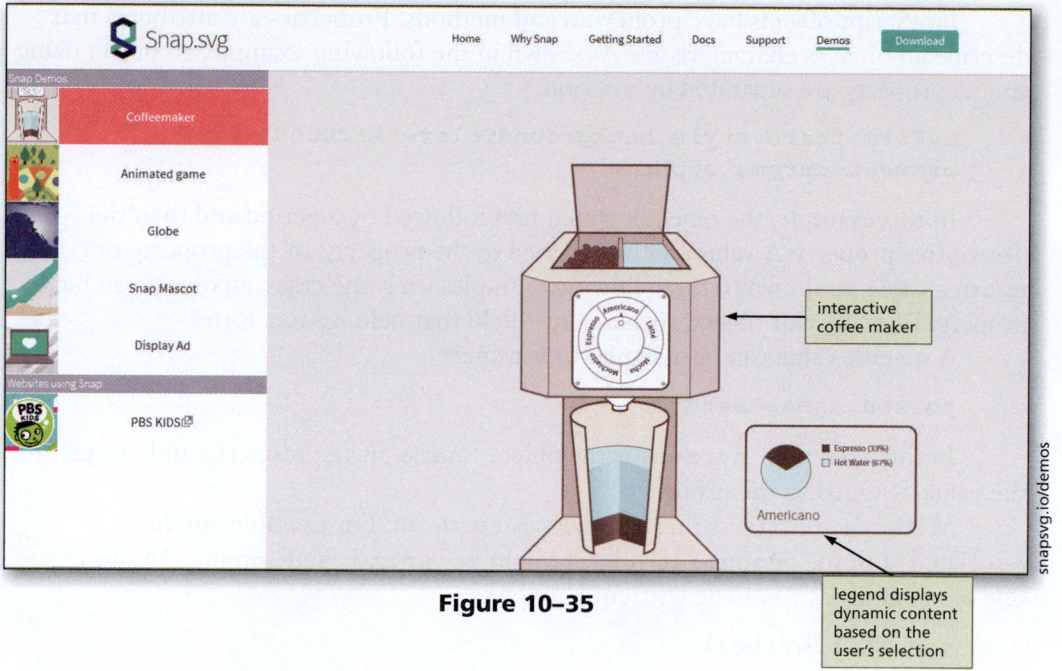

interactive coffee maker

legend displays dynamic content based on the user's selection

snapsvg.io/demos

Figure 10–35

JavaScript Terminology

To use JavaScript effectively, you be familiar with its basic terminology, including objects, properties, methods, arguments, functions, and variables.

An **object** in JavaScript is programming code and data that can be treated as its own entity. For example, a developer might create a validateCard object, used to determine if a credit card number entered by the user is valid. Built-in objects are values that are common to a browser (arrays, dates, and strings, for example) that neither depend on nor belong to another object. Table 10–1 contains a general list of the built-in JavaScript objects common to many browsers. JavaScript developers can create new objects based on the built-in objects, and the new objects inherit properties from the original objects.

Table 10–1 JavaScript Objects

Object	Description
Array	Returns an ordered set of values
Boolean	Converts objects to Boolean values
Date	Accesses the system time and date
Document	Represents the content of a browser's window
DOM	Includes all elements related to the Document Object Model
Function	Accesses information about specific functions
History	Keeps track of webpages visited
Location	Switches to a new webpage
Math	Performs calculations
Navigator	Obtains information about the current web browser
Number	Supports special constants
Object	Creates an Object wrapper
RegExp	Describes patterns of characters
Screen	Gives platform-specific information about the user's screen
String	Represents a set of characters
Window	Represents a browser window

JavaScript objects have properties and methods. Properties are attributes that describe an object's characteristics. As shown in the following example, an object name and its property are separated by a period.

```
myForm.fname.style.backgroundColor="#ff0000"
browser=chrome.appName
```

In this example, the object is stated first followed by a period and then the descriptive property. A value can be assigned to the property, or the property can return a value, as shown in the following examples. In some cases, an object can be a property of a superior object, such as a text field that belongs to a form.

A specific value can be assigned to a property:

```
person.name="Seth"
```

In this example, `person` is the object, `name` is the property, and `Seth` is the value assigned to the property.

Methods are actions that an object can perform. For example, methods associated with the `document` object might be `write` and `open`. An object and one of its methods would be written as follows:

```
document.write()
```

Where `document` is the object and `write` is a method of the `document` object. Methods are followed by parentheses, which may be empty, or may contain an argument.

An **argument** is a value given to a method. Some methods require arguments, and others do not. For example, given a `document` object and the `write()` method, the argument "Good Morning" describes the content to display for the document would be written as:

```
document.write("Good Morning")
```

In this case, the argument "Good Morning" describes the text content to display on the document.

A **function** is a set of JavaScript statements that perform a specific task. For example, you could create a function that calculates the sales tax for items purchased. A function must include a name and statements that specify a task to be performed. An example of a function is shown below.

```
function myFunction () {
    statement 1;
    statement 2;
    statement 3;
}
```

A **variable** is a container that holds a value. JavaScript uses variables to store values temporarily in internal memory. A variable's value can change, depending on the results of an expression or data entered by a user in a form. Variables must have a unique name and must follow the same naming conventions as user-defined functions.

Most JavaScript user-defined functions are called or invoked using event handlers. An event is the result of an action, such as a mouse click or a webpage loading into the browser. An **event handler** is how JavaScript associates an action with a function. JavaScript event handlers make webpages more dynamic and interactive by allowing JavaScript code to execute only in response to a user action, such as a mouse click. Table 10–2 lists common event handlers.

Table 10–2 Event Handlers

Event Handler	Description
onabort	User stopped loading the page
onblur	User left the object
onchange	User changed the object
onclick	User clicked the object
onerror	Script encountered an error
onfocus	User made an object active
onload	Object finished loading
onmouseover	Mouse moved over an object
onmouseout	Mouse moved off an object
onselect	User selected contents of an object
onsubmit	User submitted a form
onunload	User left the page

Writing JavaScript Code

Keep the following syntax rules and guidelines in mind when writing JavaScript code. First, JavaScript is case sensitive, which means that it distinguishes between upper- and lowercase letters. If you create a variable named foodGroup, JavaScript will not recognize this variable if it is written as FoodGroup.

Like HTML and CSS, you can incorporate comments in JavaScript code. Use two slashes for a one-line comment and use the slash and asterisk for multiline comments, as follows:

```
// Single line comment syntax
/* Multiple line
comment syntax */
```

Using semicolons to end JavaScript statements is a common practice by programmers. Though it is not always necessary, it is a good best practice. The only time the semicolon is necessary is when multiple statements appear on the same line. The semicolon is used to separate each statement, similar to how a period separates one sentence from another. The following statements are all valid:

```
foodOne = squash
foodTwo = pepper;
foodOne = squash; foodTwo = pepper;
```

You can write JavaScript within an HTML page or as a separate JavaScript file with the filename extension .js. When JavaScript is written within an HTML page, the code may be within the **head** element or the **body** element, depending upon the developer and the task at hand. The following is an example of how to write a JavaScript statement within an HTML document using the script tags.

```
<script>
    JavaScript statement;
</script>
```

When you create JavaScript as an external .js file, place a script element in the **head** element of the HTML file and specify the external .js file as the file source, as follows:

```
<script src="scripts/myfunction.js"></script>
```

BTW

JavaScript Help
Many websites provide help for JavaScript developers. To find such websites, search using keywords such as "JavaScript Tutorials" or "JavaScript Help" in your search engine.

BTW

JavaScript Advantages and Disadvantages
JavaScript allows for faster response to requests such as form validation. JavaScript code downloads faster than other kinds of applets, such as Flash, and no extra plug-in is needed to execute the JavaScript code. The main disadvantage with JavaScript is that some older browser versions may not execute JavaScript code as intended.

Pop-up Windows

One common and basic use of JavaScript is to create a pop-up window. Pop-up windows are a quick and simple way to add interactivity and capture your user's attention. To add a pop-up window to an HTML page, use the **script** tags and place your JavaScript code within the **script** element.

You can incorporate three types of pop-up windows in a webpage: an alert box, a confirmation box, and a prompt box. Use an **alert box** to display a message. This can be useful if you want to grab the user's attention with information about a special promotion. To create an alert box, use the alert() method. Following is an example of an alert box code:

```
<script>
    alert("Receive a 20% discount today!");
</script>
```

Use a **confirmation box** to confirm the user's action, such as to accept changes or to proceed to another page. To create a confirmation box, use the confirm() method. Following is an example of a confirmation box code:

```
<script>
    if (confirm("Do you wish to proceed?")) {
        alert("You selected OK");
    }
    else {
        alert("You chose to Cancel");
    }
</script>
```

Use a **prompt box** to capture information from a user, such as a name, and then perform an action with the information. To create a prompt box, use the prompt() method. Following is an example of a prompt box code:

```
<script>
    var name = prompt("What is your name?");
    if (name != null) {
        alert("Hello " + name);
    }
    else {
        alert("You did not tell me your name. ");
    }
</script>
```

To Add a Pop-up Window to the Home Page

1 INSERT SOCIAL MEDIA ICONS & LINKS | 2 STYLE SOCIAL MEDIA ICONS | 3 CREATE JAVASCRIPT ALERT MESSAGE
4 CREATE EXTERNAL JAVASCRIPT FILE MESSAGE | 5 CALL JAVASCRIPT FUNCTIONS

The Forward Fitness Club offers a free one-week trial membership. To ensure that potential customers are aware of this special offer, create an alert box pop-up window with information about the promotion. *Why? A pop-up window will grab the user's attention.* Create a function that displays an alert box on the home page two seconds after the page has loaded. Use the setTimeout() method to delay the alert box. The following steps create an alert box in the index.html file.

1

- In the index.html file, tap or click at the end of Line 8, and then press the ENTER key twice to insert new Lines 9 and 10.

- On Line 10 type `<script>` to insert a starting script tag.

- Press the ENTER key to insert a new Line 11, increase the indent, and then type `//Function displays alert box after two seconds` to insert a JavaScript comment.

- Press the ENTER key to insert a new Line 12, and then type `setTimeout (function delay() {` to insert the setTimeout() method.

- Press the ENTER key to insert a new Line 13, and then type `alert("Begin your FREE one-week trial membership today!")` to insert an alert() method.

- Press the ENTER key to insert a new Line 14, and then type `}, 2000);` to complete the statement.

- Press the ENTER key to insert a new Line 15, and then type `</script>` to insert an ending script tag (Figure 10–36).

```
         starting script tag              comment
Line 10  10    <script>
         11        //Function displays alert box after two seconds
         12        setTimeout (function delay() {
         13        alert("Begin your FREE one-week trial membership today!")
         14        }, 2000);
         15    </script>
                                   delay start by 2000        setTimeout
              ending script tag    milliseconds               method
```
alert method

Figure 10–36

Q&A Why is the alert() method placed within the setTimeout() method?
The alert() method is placed within the setTimeout() method because you need to delay the appearance of the alert box.

What does the 2000 represent at the end of the setTimeout statement?
Time is represented in milliseconds in JavaScript. Two seconds is represented as 2000 milliseconds.

2

- Save index.html, open it in your browser, and then, if necessary, adjust the window to a desktop viewport.

- Wait for two seconds to pass to display the alert box (Figure 10–37).

3

- Close your browser.

- Close index.html in your text editor.

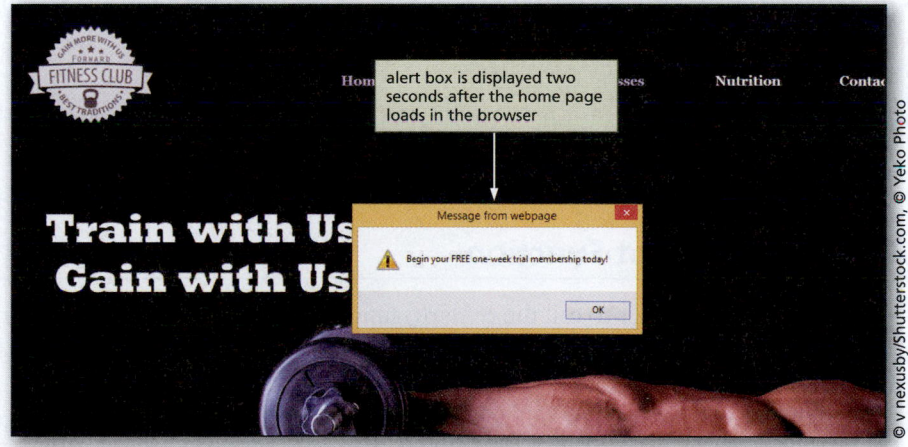

Figure 10–37

© v nexusby/Shutterstock.com, © Yeko Photo Studio/Shutterstock.com

To Create a Function in an External JavaScript File

1 INSERT SOCIAL MEDIA ICONS & LINKS | 2 STYLE SOCIAL MEDIA ICONS | 3 CREATE JAVASCRIPT ALERT MESSAGE
4 CREATE EXTERNAL JAVASCRIPT FILE MESSAGE | 5 CALL JAVASCRIPT FUNCTIONS

Create an external JavaScript file and then create a function that displays an alert box. To keep the JavaScript separate from the HTML, create an external JavaScript file and then use script tags within the head of the contact.html page to reference the JavaScript file. *Why? When scripts are created as an external file, they can be accessed from any page.* Create a function that displays an alert box to thank the customer for their interest. The following steps create an external JavaScript file and a new function.

1

- Copy the scripts folder from the chapter10\fitness folder provided with the Data Files for Students to your fitness folder.

- Use your text editor to create a new document.

- Name the document **myFunctions** and save the file as a JavaScript, .js, file within the fitness\scripts folder.

- On Line 1 type **/* Student's First and Last Name** to insert the first line of a multiline comment.

- Press the ENTER key to insert a new Line 2, and then type today's date to insert the second line of a multiline comment.

- Press the ENTER key to insert a new Line 3, and then type **My Function List** to insert the third line of a multiline comment.

- Press the ENTER key to insert a new Line 4, and then type ***/** to close the multiline comment (Figure 10–38).

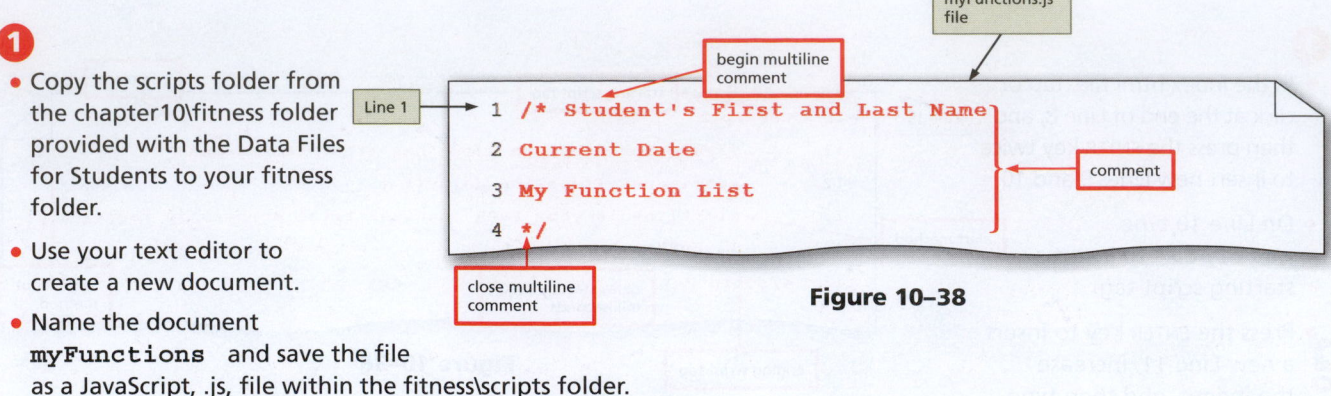

Figure 10–38

2

- Press the ENTER key twice to insert new Lines 5 and 6, and then type **//Thank you alert** to insert a single line comment.

- Press the ENTER key to insert a new Line 7, and then type **function tyAlert() {** to create a new function.

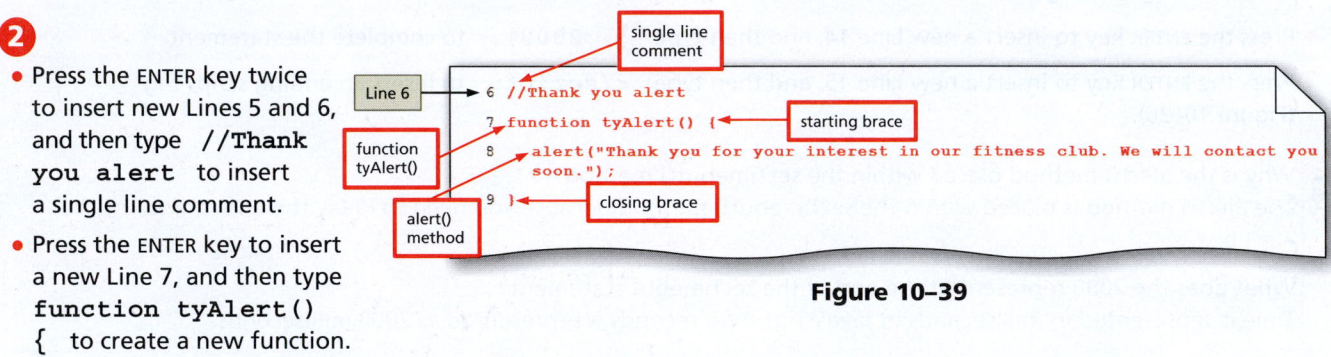

Figure 10–39

- Press the ENTER key to insert a new Line 8, and then type **alert("Thank you for your interest in our fitness club. We will contact you soon.");** to insert an alert method.

- Press the ENTER key to insert a new Line 9, and then type **}** to insert a closing brace and save your changes (Figure 10–39).

◄ | What is the purpose of the tyAlert()?

Q&A | The tyAlert() is the name of the function. You will use an event handler to call this function in future steps.

To Call a JavaScript Function

1 INSERT SOCIAL MEDIA ICONS & LINKS | 2 STYLE SOCIAL MEDIA ICONS | 3 CREATE JAVASCRIPT ALERT MESSAGE

4 CREATE EXTERNAL JAVASCRIPT FILE MESSAGE | **5 CALL JAVASCRIPT FUNCTIONS**

Use an event handler to call the tyAlert() function when a user taps or clicks the Submit button on the Contact Us page. *Why? Using a JavaScript event handler adds* interactivity *to the page.* To keep the JavaScript separate from the HTML, continue using an external JavaScript file and then add script tags within the **head** element of the contact.html page to reference the JavaScript file. The following steps call the tyAlert() function you created in the previous steps.

1

- Open contact.html in your text editor to prepare to modify it.

Figure 10–40

- Tap or click at the end of Line 8 and press the ENTER key to insert a new Line 9.

- On Line 9, type **<script src="scripts/myFunctions.js" type="text/javascript"></script>** to insert a script element (Figure 10–40).

◄ | What is the purpose of this step?

Q&A | This step inserts a script element in the contact.html page that references the myFunctions.js file.

2

- On Line 69, tap or click to the right of the last attribute and value to prepare for adding an onclick event handler.

contact.html file

onclick event handler

Line 69

```
69    <input type="submit" id="submit" value="Submit" class="btn" onclick="tyAlert()">
```

Figure 10–41

- Press the SPACEBAR and then type `onclick="tyAlert()"` to insert an event handler.
- Save your changes (Figure 10–41).

Q&A What is the purpose of this step?
This step inserts an onclick event handler in the code that creates a Submit button. The event handler calls the tyAlert() function when the Submit button is clicked.

3

- Save contact.html, open it in your browser, and then, if necessary, adjust the window to the size of a desktop viewport.

- Tap or click the Submit button to trigger the onclick event handler (Figure 10–42).

4

- Close your browser.

- Close the contact.html file in your text editor.

Figure 10–42

The open() Method

You can use the `open()` method to open a new browser window. This is helpful when you want to provide customers additional information about a product or service. You can specify parameters for the new window, such as the width and height. An example of the open() method is shown below.

```
window.open("http://www.cengage.com", "_blank", "width=400,
    height=400");
```

In this example, a new window opens to the Cengage.com home page. The _blank specifies to open the webpage in a new window. The width and height of the new window are set to 400 pixels. The minimum value for a width and height value is 100 pixels.

Table 10–3 lists commonly used attributes of the open() method, which are used to define pop-up window features.

Table 10–3 open() Method Attributes		
Attribute	**Description**	**Example**
height	States height in pixels	"height=450"
location	Includes address bar	"location=yes"
menubar	Includes menu bar	"menubar=yes"
resize	Allows user to resize	"resizeable=yes"
scrollbars	Includes scroll bars	"scrollbars=yes"
status	Includes status bar	"status=yes"
titlebar	Removes title bar	"titlebar=yes"
toolbar	Includes toolbar	"toolbar=yes"
width	States width in pixels	"width=220"
height	States height in pixels	"height=450"

To Add More Functions to a JavaScript File

Create three more functions in the external myFunctions.js file. Create a function to use the open() method to display examples of the exercises in the description list on the About Us page. *Why? Using the window open() method to display additional content about how to perform an exercise adds value to your website.* First, create a function that opens a window with a video that demonstrates how to perform a burpee. Next, create a function that opens a window with a video that demonstrates how to perform a plank. Finally, create a function that opens a window with a video that demonstrates how to perform a mountain climber. The following steps create three functions within an external JavaScript file.

1

- If necessary, reopen myFunctions.js in your text editor to prepare to modify it.

- Tap or click at the end of Line 9 and press the ENTER key twice to insert new Lines 10 and 11.

Figure 10–43

- On Line 11, type `//Burpees video window` to insert a comment.

- Press the ENTER key to insert a new Line 12, and then type `function burpees() {` to create a new function.

- Press the ENTER key to insert a new Line 13, and then type `window.open("scripts/burpees.html", "_blank", "width=610, height=360");` to insert a window open() method.

- Press the ENTER key to insert a new Line 14, and then type `}` to insert a closing brace (Figure 10–43).

Q&A What does this function do?

This function opens the burpees.html file within a new browser window with the dimensions of 610 × 360 pixels. The burpees.html file contains a video example of how to perform a burpee.

2

- Tap or click at the end of Line 14 and press the ENTER key twice to insert new Lines 15 and 16.

- On Line 16, type `//Plank video window` to insert a comment.

Figure 10–44

- Press the ENTER key to insert a new Line 17, and then type `function plank() {` to create a new function.

- Press the ENTER key to insert a new Line 18, and then type `window.open("scripts/plank.html", "_blank", "width=610, height=360");` to insert a window open() method.

- Press the ENTER key to insert a new Line 19, and then type `}` to insert a closing brace (Figure 10–44).

Q&A What does this function do?

This function opens the plank.html file within a new browser window with the dimensions of 610 × 360 pixels. The plank.html file contains a video example of how to perform a plank.

3

- Tap or click at the end of Line 19 and press the ENTER key twice to insert new Lines 20 and 21.

- On Line 21, type `//Mountain climber video window` to insert a comment.

```
                                    single line
                                    comment

Line 21        21 //Mountain climber video window

function        22  function mtnClimber() {        starting brace
mtnClimber()
               23      window.open("scripts/mtn.html", "_blank", "width=610, height=360");

               24  }

closing brace        window open()
                     method
```

Figure 10–45

- Press the ENTER key to insert a new Line 22, and then type `function mtnClimber() {` to create a new function.

- Press the ENTER key to insert a new Line 23, and then type `window.open("scripts/mtn.html", "_blank", "width=610, height=360");` to insert a window open() method.

- Press the ENTER key to insert a new Line 24, and then type `}` to insert a closing brace (Figure 10–45).

Q&A | What does this function do?
This function opens the mtn.html file within a new browser window with the dimensions of 610 × 360 pixels. The mtn.html file contains a video example of how to perform a mountain climber exercise.

4

- Save your changes and close the myFunctions.js file.

To Call the New Functions

1 INSERT SOCIAL MEDIA ICONS & LINKS | 2 STYLE SOCIAL MEDIA ICONS | 3 CREATE JAVASCRIPT ALERT MESSAGE | 4 CREATE EXTERNAL JAVASCRIPT FILE MESSAGE | **5 CALL JAVASCRIPT FUNCTIONS**

Create buttons on the About Us page that, once clicked, each display a window with a video that demonstrates an exercise. *Why? The video demonstration helps the user understand how to perform the exercise.* First, add a script element within the head element of the about.html file to reference the myFunctions.js file. Next, create a button that uses the onclick event handler to call the burpees() function. Then, create a button that uses the onclick event handler to call the plank() function. Finally, create a button that uses the onclick event handler to call the mtnClimber() function. The following steps create buttons with onclick event handlers on the About Us page.

1

- Open about.html in your text editor to prepare to modify it.

```
                          script element                    about.html file

Line 9    9 <script src="scripts/myFunctions.js" type="text/javascript"></script>
```

Figure 10–46

- Tap or click at the end of Line 8 and press the ENTER key to insert a new Line 9.

- On Line 9, type `<script src="scripts/myFunctions.js" type="text/javascript"></script>` to insert a script element (Figure 10–46).

2

- Tap or click at the end of Line 82 and then type `<br>` to insert a line break.

```
Line 82     82    <dd>Burpees are a great, full body exercise to increase your strength and
                  endurance. Begin in a standing position, drop into a squat and extend your
                  hands forward, kick your feet back and then forward again quickly, and then
                  jump up from a squatted position.<br>              line break

button      83    <button onclick="burpees()">See example</button>
element
            84    </dd>

                         onclick event
                         handler
```

Figure 10–47

- Press the ENTER key to insert a new Line 83, and then type `<button onclick="burpees()">See example</button>` to insert a button element (Figure 10–47).

Q&A | What is the result of this step?
This step adds a button with the onclick event handler. When the button is clicked, a new window displays a video demonstration of how to perform a burpee.

3

- Tap or click at the end of Line 87 and then type `<br>` to insert a line break.

- Press the ENTER key to insert a new Line 88, and then type `<button onclick="plank()">See example</button>` to insert a button element (Figure 10–48).

```
         line break
  87     <dd>Planks build your core strength. To perform a plank, get in a push up
         position and rest your forearms on the floor. Hold the position as long as you
         can.<br>
         <button onclick="plank()">See example</button>
         </dd>
```

button element
onclick event handler
Line 87

Figure 10–48

Q&A | What is the result of this step?

This step also adds a button with the onclick event handler. When the button is clicked, a new window displays a video demonstration of how to perform a plank exercise.

4

- Tap or click at the end of Line 92 and then type `<br>` to insert a line break.

- Press the ENTER key to insert a new Line 93, and then type `<button onclick="mtnClimber()">See example</button>` to insert a button element (Figure 10–49).

```
  92     <dd>Mountain climbers are a good cardio exercise. Place your hands on the floor
         in a push up position, then bring one knee up to your chest and then switch as
         quickly as you can (as though you are climbing a mountain).<br>
  93     <button onclick="mtnClimber()">See example</button>
  94     </dd>
```

Line 92
button element
onclick event handler
line break

Figure 10–49

Q&A | What is the result of this step?

This step adds a third button with the onclick event handler. When the button is clicked, a new window displays a video demonstration of how to perform a mountain climber exercise.

5

- Save your changes, open about. html in your browser, and then, if necessary, adjust the window to the size of a desktop viewport.

- Scroll down to view the buttons within the description list.

- Tap or click the button for the burpees to display a video demonstration of the exercise (Figure 10–50).

onclick event handler calls the burpees() function

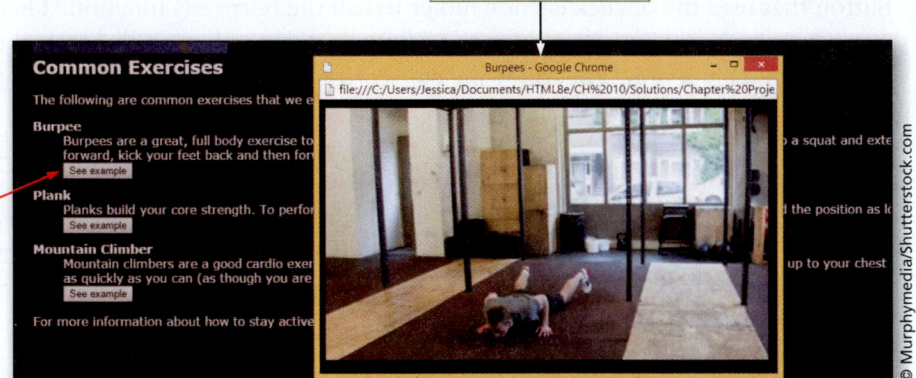

button element for burpee

© Murphymedia/Shutterstock.com

Figure 10–50

6

- Close the new window.

- Tap or click the button for the plank to display a video demonstration of the exercise (Figure 10–51).

onclick event handler calls the plank() function

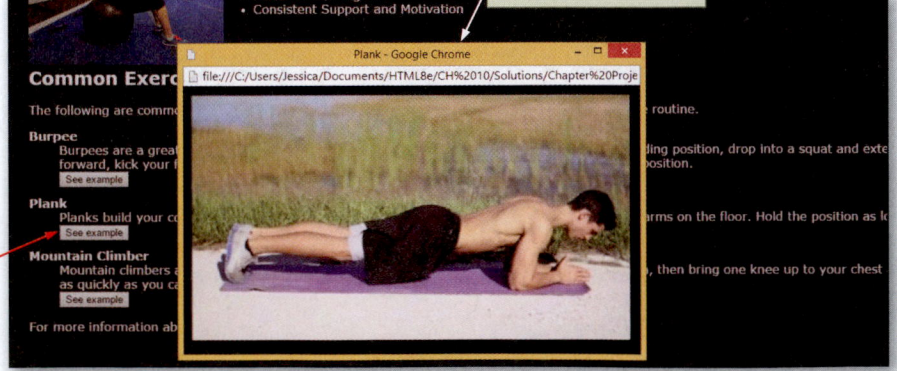

button element for plank

© alexmillos/Shutterstock.com

Figure 10–51

7

- Close the new window.

- Tap or click the button for the mountain climber to display a video demonstration of the exercise (Figure 10–52).

8

- Close your browser and your text editor.

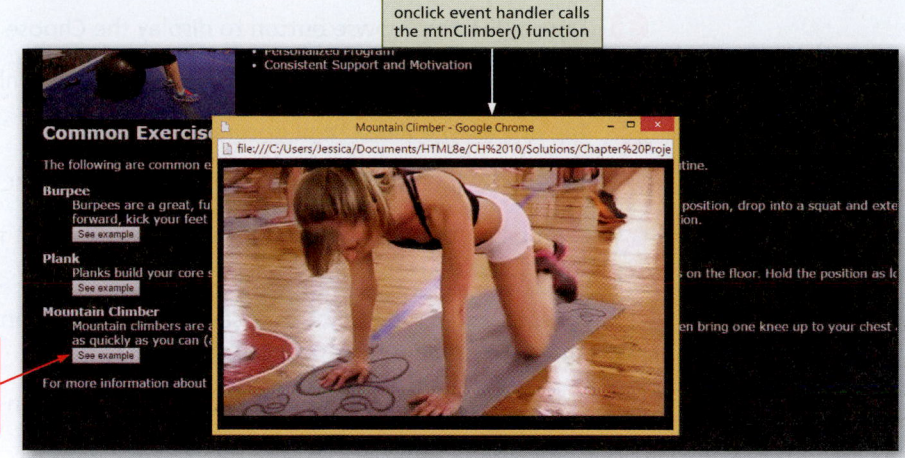

onclick event handler calls the mtnClimber() function

button element for mountain climber

Figure 10–52

To Validate the Style Sheet

Always run your files through W3C's validator to check the document for errors. If the document has any errors, validating gives you a chance to identify and correct them. Validation is also an effective troubleshooting tool during the development process and adds a valuable level of professionalism to your work. The following steps validate a CSS document.

1 Open your browser and type `http://jigsaw.w3.org/css-validator/` in the address bar to display the W3C CSS Validation Service page.

2 Tap or click the By file upload tab to display the Validate by file upload information.

3 Tap or click the Browse button to display the Choose File to Upload dialog box.

4 Navigate to your css folder to find the styles.css file.

5 Tap or click the styles.css document to select it.

6 Tap or click the Open button to upload the selected file to the W3C CSS validator.

7 Tap or click the Check button to send the document through the validator and display the validation results page.

8 If necessary, correct any errors, save your changes, and run through the validator again to revalidate the page.

To Validate the HTML Files

Every time you create a new webpage or modify an existing webpage, run it through W3C's validator to check the document for errors. If any errors exist, you need to correct them. Validation is also an effective troubleshooting tool during the development process and adds a valuable level of professionalism to your work. The following steps validate an HTML document.

1 Open your browser and type `http://validator.w3.org/` in the address bar to display the W3C Markup Validation Service page.

2 Tap or click the Validate by File Upload tab to display the Validate by File Upload information.

3 Tap or click the Browse button to display the Choose File to Upload dialog box.

4 Navigate to your fitness folder to find the index.html file.

5 Tap or click the index.html document to select it.

6 Tap or click the Open button to upload it to the W3C validator.

7 Tap or click the Check button to send the document through the validator and display the validation results page.

8 If necessary, correct any errors, save your changes, and run through the validator again to revalidate the page.

9 Follow these steps to validate all HTML pages within your fitness folder and correct any errors.

Chapter Summary

In this chapter, you learned about the various social media options for a business. You learned how to add social media icons and links to a website. You styled social media icons with CSS. You also learned how to create pop-up windows using JavaScript. You learned how to write JavaScript code within an HTML document. You also learned how to write JavaScript functions in an external JavaScript file and reference the file within an HTML page. The items listed below include all the new skills you have learned in this chapter, with the tasks grouped by activity.

Using Social Media

Add Social Media Icons and Links to the Home
    Page (HTML 478)
Style Copyright div Element (HTML 481)
Style the Social div Element and Social Media
    Icons (HTML 481)

Incorporating JavaScript

Add a Pop-up Window to the Home Page
    (HTML 488)

Create a Function in an External JavaScript File
    (HTML 489)
Call a JavaScript Function (HTML 490)
Add More Functions to a JavaScript File
    (HTML 492)
Call the New Functions (HTML 493)

How will you infuse interactivity within your website?

Use these guidelines as you complete the assignments in this chapter and create your own webpages outside of this class.

1. Determine if social media is ideal to promote your business.

    a) Review the various social media options.

    b) Determine which social media options to implement.

2. Decide how to best integrate JavaScript.

    a) Determine the types of interactivity you wish to use within your website.

    b) Determine what code is needed to accomplish your goal.

3. Decide what pages will use JavaScript.

    a) Determine the whether or not to write the JavaScript code within an HTML page.

    b) Determine if an external JavaScript file is best for your website.

4. Determine other forms of interactivity that JavaScript can provide.

    a) Research how to use JavaScript to validate form information.

    b) Decide if pop-up messages are appropriate for your site.

CONSIDER THIS

Apply Your Knowledge

Reinforce the skills and apply the concepts you learned in this chapter.

Using Social Media and JavaScript

Instructions: In this exercise, you will use your text editor to add social media icons to a webpage. You will also add a pop-up message to the webpage. First, you add Facebook and Twitter icons and include a link to each social media website. Next, use JavaScript to create a pop-up message using the alert() method. Work with the apply10.html file in the apply folder and images files in the apply\images folder from the Data Files for Students. The completed webpage is shown in Figure 10–53. You will also use professional web development practices to indent, space, comment, and validate your code.

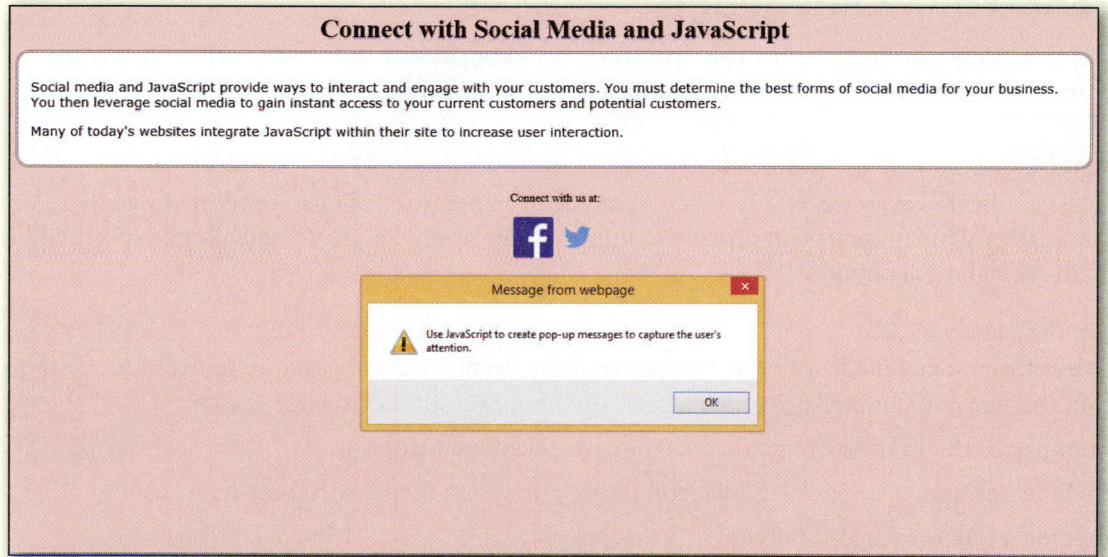

Figure 10–53

Perform the following tasks:

1. Open apply10.html in your text editor, review the page, add a title, modify the comment at the top of the page to include your name and today's date.

2. Update the CSS link within the head element to use the CSS file located within the apply\css folder.

3. Insert a **paragraph** element within the footer element that includes the text, **Connect with us at:**.

4. Insert an **img** element to display the Facebook icon contained within the apply\images folder. Include appropriate alt text.

5. Insert an **anchor** element to link the Facebook icon to facebook.com.

6. Insert an **img** element to display the Twitter icon contained within the apply\images folder. Include appropriate alt text.

Continued >

Apply Your Knowledge *continued*

7. Insert an **anchor** element to link the Twitter icon to twitter.com.

8. Insert a **script** element within the **head** element.

9. Insert a JavaScript comment within the script element that includes the text, **Function displays alert box**.

10. Insert the following JavaScript code below the comment:

```
setTimeout (function message() {
    alert("Use JavaScript to create pop-up messages to capture the
    user's attention.")
    }, 3000);
```

11. Save all of your changes and open the apply10.html in your browser.

12. Validate your HTML document using the W3C validator found at validator.w3.org and fix any errors that are identified.

13. Submit the files in a format specified by your instructor.

14. ❇ In this exercise, you created absolute links to facebook.com and twitter.com. Explain how to update these links so that when selected, they open in a new tab rather than the current window.

Extend Your Knowledge

Extend the skills you learned in this chapter and experiment with new skills. You may need to use additional resources to complete the assignment.

Researching Social Media Brand Information

Instructions: In this exercise, you research brand information for popular social media outlets. You will summarize your findings and provide examples of the available social media logos specified for use by the social media outlet.

Perform the following tasks:

1. Select three social media options and research the brand assets for each. Use the name of the social media and "brand" or "brand assets" or "brand resources" in your search.

2. Summarize the brand asset guidelines for each social media option.

3. Include one approved social media icon or logo provided by the social media website.

4. Include a link for each resource.

5. Submit the document in a format specified by your instructor.

6. ❇ In this exercise, you researched how to use social media brand information. Many social media sites highlight how some select businesses have used the social media site to increase brand awareness. Read one of these business highlights and summarize your findings.

Analyze, Correct, Improve

Analyze a website, correct all errors, and improve it.

Improving a Webpage with JavaScript

Instructions: Work with the analyze10.html file in the analyze folder from the Data Files for Students. The analyze10.html webpage needs pop-up windows to display larger pictures. First, correct the JavaScript syntax errors on the page. Next, use the open() method to display a new window with a picture for the first thumbnail. Then, use the open() method to display a new window with a picture for the second thumbnail and a new window with a picture for the third thumbnail. Finally, create new style rules for the figure and img elements. Use Figure 10–54 as a guide to correct these files.

Figure 10–54

1. Correct

a. Open the analyze10.html file in your text editor from the Data Files for Students. Modify the comment at the top of the page to include your name and today's date and then link the file to analyzestyles10.css. Add a title to the page and add your name to the footer element.

b. Review the JavaScript functions contained within the body element and wrap them in a script element.

c. Move the script element to the head element.

d. Open the analyzestyles10.css file in your text editor from the Data Files for Students and then modify and correct the comment at the top of the document to include your name and today's date.

2. Improve

a. In the analyze10.html file, add an onclick event handler to the first img element that calls the function, cb1.

b. In the analyze10.html file, add an onclick event handler to the second img element that calls the function, cb2.

c. In the analyze10.html file, add an onclick event handler to the third img element that calls the function, cb3.

d. In the analyzestyles10.css file, create a style rule for the figure element to align it center. Include a comment for the style rule.

e. In the analyzstyles10.css file, create a style rule for the img element and specify `1em` of padding. Include a comment for the style rule.

f. Save all of your changes and open the analyze10.html in your browser.

g. Validate your CSS file using the W3C validator found at http://jigsaw.w3.org/css-validator/ and fix any errors that are identified.

h. Validate your HTML webpage using the W3C validator found at validator.w3.org and fix any errors that are identified.

i. ✸ In this exercise, you used JavaScript to view larger images. Use your browser to research how to use JavaScript to create an image gallery and write a summary of your findings.

In the Labs

Labs 1 and 2, which increase in difficulty, require you to create webpages based on what you learned in the chapter; Lab 3 requires you to dive deeper into a topic covered in the chapter.

Lab 1: Determining the Best Social Media Outlets for the New Harvest Food Bank Website

Problem: You volunteer at a local food bank called New Harvest Food Bank that collects community food donations and provides food and other services to those in need. The company has asked you to create a responsive website. You have already created the website but now need to research how to promote the food bank using social media.

Instructions: Perform the following tasks:

1. Research information about the best social media options for a food bank.

2. Determine the top three social media options.

3. Explain why the food bank should use your recommended social media options.

4. Provide a list of pros and cons for each social media site that you recommend.

5. Submit your recommendations in the format specified by your instructor.

6. ✳ In this assignment, you recommended social media options for the food bank. Extend your research to learn more best practices and tips for non-profits to maximize results. Provide a list of the top ten best practices.

Lab 2: Adding Social Media and a Pop-up Message to Steve's Screen Services

Problem: You work for a screening company called Steve's Screen Services that specializes in screening, cleaning, and repairing screened patios. The company has asked you to create a responsive website. You have already created the website, but now need to add social media icons and links. You then need to style the icons and links. Finally, you need to add a pop-up message to the quote. html page. The home page with the social media icons is shown in Figure 10–55. The Quote page with the pop-up message is shown in Figure 10–56.

Instructions: Perform the following tasks:

1. Save the images within the lab2\images folder from the Data Files for Students to your lab2\ images folder.

2. Open the index.html document and update the comment at the top of the page to include today's date.

3. Wrap the content in the footer element within a paragraph element.

4. Wrap the paragraph element you created in the previous step within a div element and assign an id value of `copyright`.

5. Create a new div element below the div you created in the previous step and assign an id value of `social`.

6. Create a new paragraph element within the social div and include the text, `Follow us at:`.

Figure 10–55

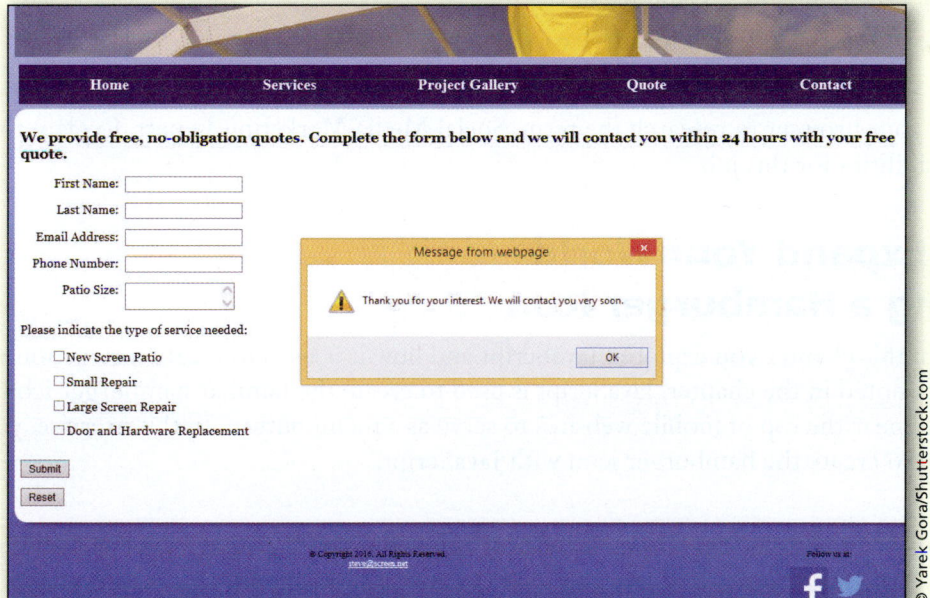

Figure 10–56

7. Insert an img element below the new paragraph and insert the Facebook icon. Include appropriate alt text. Link the img element to facebook.com.

8. Insert an image element below the new paragraph and insert the Twitter icon. Include appropriate alt text. Link the img element to twitter.com.

9. Save your changes, copy the footer element, and then paste it over the footer element on the contact.html page, the gallery.html page, the quote.html page, and the services.html page. Save all of your changes.

10. In the screenstyles.css file, create a new style rule above the media queries for the `#copyright` selector, specify a float property with a value of `left` and then specify a width property with a value of `80%`. Include an appropriate comment for the new style rule.

Continued >

In the Labs *continued*

11. In the screenstyles.css file, create another new style rule above the media queries for the `#social` selector, specify a float property with a value of `right` and then specify a width property with a value of `20%`. Include an appropriate comment for the new style rule.

12. In the screenstyles.css file, in the desktop media query, add the overflow property with a value of `auto` to the existing style rule for the body element.

13. In the screenstyles.css file, in the desktop media query, create a new style rule for anchor elements within the footer element that specifies a color property and a white value. Include an appropriate comment for the new style rule.

14. Save your changes, open the home page in your browser, and compare it to Figure 10–55.

15. Open quote.html in your text editor and update the comment with today's date.

16. Create a script element within the head element.

17. Create a function named thanks within the script element that creates an alert message with the text, **Thank you for your interest. We will contact you very soon.**

18. Add an onclick event handler to the submit button that calls the thanks function.

19. Save your changes, open quote.html in your browser, and then click the Submit button to display the alert message, as shown in Figure 10–56.

20. Validate your HTML code and fix any errors.

21. Validate your CSS code and fix any errors.

22. Submit your assignment in the format specified by your instructor.

23. ✳ Use your browser to research the term, Social Media Marketing Expert. Explain the responsibilities for this job.

Lab 3: Expand Your World
Creating a Hamburger Icon

Problem: In this chapter you explored JavaScript and how it is used to create interaction within a website. As noted in the chapter, JavaScript is used to create the familiar hamburger icon, commonly found near the top of mobile websites to serve as a menu button. In this exercise, you will explore how to create the hamburger icon with JavaScript.

Instructions:

1. Use your browser to search for more information about the hamburger icon and discuss how it is used.

2. Discuss the various ways to create a hamburger icon.

3. Identify three resources that demonstrate how to create a functional hamburger icon and include an example of the code required from at least one resource. Include links to all of your resources.

4. Should mobile websites embrace the hamburger icon? Why or why not? Discuss your findings.

5. Submit your answers in the format specified by your instructor.

6. ✳ In this exercise, you discovered various ways to create a functional hamburger icon. Research and discuss the JavaScript Sidr plugin.

Consider This: Your Turn

Apply your creative thinking and problem-solving skills to design and implement a solution.

1. Using Social Media and Your Personal Portfolio Website

Personal

Part 1: Employers routinely research potential employees. Sometimes, part of the research process involves social media. Potential employers may review the social media page(s) to learn more about the candidate. In this exercise, you research best practices when it comes to using social media and its relationship to gainful employment.

1. Use your browser to research how you can use social media to improve your chances for future employment. Discuss your findings.

2. Use your browser to research things to avoid when it comes to social media and future employment. Discuss your findings.

3. Submit your assignment in the format specified by your instructor.

Part 2: ✳

Discuss the reasons why you should or should not include social media links on your portfolio page.

2. Adding Social Media and JavaScript to the WebDevPros Website

Professional

Part 1: In Chapter 9, you added a video to the WebDevPros website. In this exercise, you update the site to include social media and JavaScript. Update the site as follows:

1. Open the external style sheet you created in Chapter 9 and save it with the name **webdevstyles10.css** in the styles folder within the your_turn_2 folder.

2. Add your name and the current date as a comment to the first line of the webdevstyles10.css file.

3. Open the files you created for WebDevPros in Chapter 9 in your HTML editor and make sure your name and the current date are added as a comment to the first line of all files.

4. Update the HTML files to:

   a. Insert at least two social media icons on all pages.

   b. Include links to the social media home page.

   c. Create an alert message.

5. Update the CSS file to:

   a. Style the social media icons.

   b. Add comments to note all changes and updates.

6. Save and test your files.

7. Validate and correct your HTML and CSS files, and submit your assignment in the format specified by your instructor.

Part 2: ✳ In this exercise, you integrated two social media icons. Identify three other social media resources that you believe would also be good to promote your website.

3. Improving the Design of the Dog Hall of Fame Website

Research and Collaboration

Part 1: In Chapter 9, you added a video to the Dog Hall of Fame website. In this exercise, you update the site to include social media and JavaScript. Do the following activities as a group:

1. Open the external style sheet you created in Chapter 9 and save it with the name **dogstyles10.css** in the styles folder within the your_turn_3 folder.

Continued >

Consider This: Your Turn *continued*

2. Add your names and the current date as a comment to the first line of the dogstyles10.css file.

3. Open the files you created for the Dog Hall of Fame in Chapter 9 in your HTML editor and make sure your names and the current date are added as a comment to the first line of all files.

4. Modify the link to the external style sheet to reference dogstyles10.css.

5. Discuss the best social media options for your website and integrate at least two. At a minimum, update the HTML page to do the following:

   a. Add social media icons to every page.

   b. Include links to the social media home page.

6. Update the CSS file to:

   a. Style the social media icons.

   b. Add comments to note all changes and updates.

7. Create an external JavaScript file and do the following:

   a. Create at least two functions on the page.

   b. Link the page to the appropriate HTML webpage(s).

   c. Call each function from an HTML webpage.

   d. Add comments to note all functions and team members.

8. Save and test your files.

9. Validate and correct your HTML and CSS files, and submit your assignment in the format specified by your instructor.

Part 2: ✳ As a group, research other ways to use JavaScript within your website and summarize your findings.

11 | Publish and Promote a Website

Objectives

You will have mastered the material in this chapter when you can:

- Describe search engines
- Explain search engine optimization (SEO)
- Create description meta tags
- Describe a domain name
- Describe a top-level domain
- Explain the role of a web hosting service

- Describe a File Transfer Protocol (FTP) client
- Connect to a remote server
- Publish a website with an FTP client
- Market a website
- Register a URL with a search engine

11 | Publish and Promote a Website

Introduction

Once a website has been created, validated, and tested, the next step is to publish it on a web server to make it accessible online for customers to access. You can then take appropriate steps to promote your website so potential customers can find it. In this chapter, you will learn how to publish and promote your website. You will learn how to use the `meta` tag to add a description to a webpage, and how to connect to a remote server and publish your website. You will also learn about the many ways to promote and market your website.

Project — Publish a Website

In Chapter 11, you publish and promote the Forward Fitness Club website to establish an online presence for the business. This chapter provides information for publishing webpages and how to promote a website after it is published.

    The project in this chapter adds a description meta tag to the Forward Fitness Club webpages and then publishes the Forward Fitness Club website. To perform these tasks, you first add meta tags to each webpage. Next, you connect to a remote server, and then you use an FTP client to publish your website. Figure 11–1 shows the

```
9    <meta name="description" content="Forward Fitness Club is an elite fitness center
     dedicated to helping our clients achieve their fitness and nutrition goals. We
     provide state-of-the-art fitness equipment, group fitness classes, and nutrition
     planning.">
```

(a) index.html

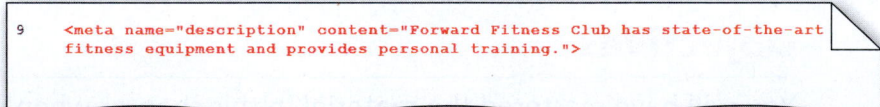

```
9    <meta name="description" content="Forward Fitness Club has state-of-the-art
     fitness equipment and provides personal training.">
```

(b) about.html

```
9    <meta name="description" content="Forward Fitness Club provides a complimentary
     one-week trial membership. Contact us today to learn more.">
```

(c) contact.html

Figure 11–1

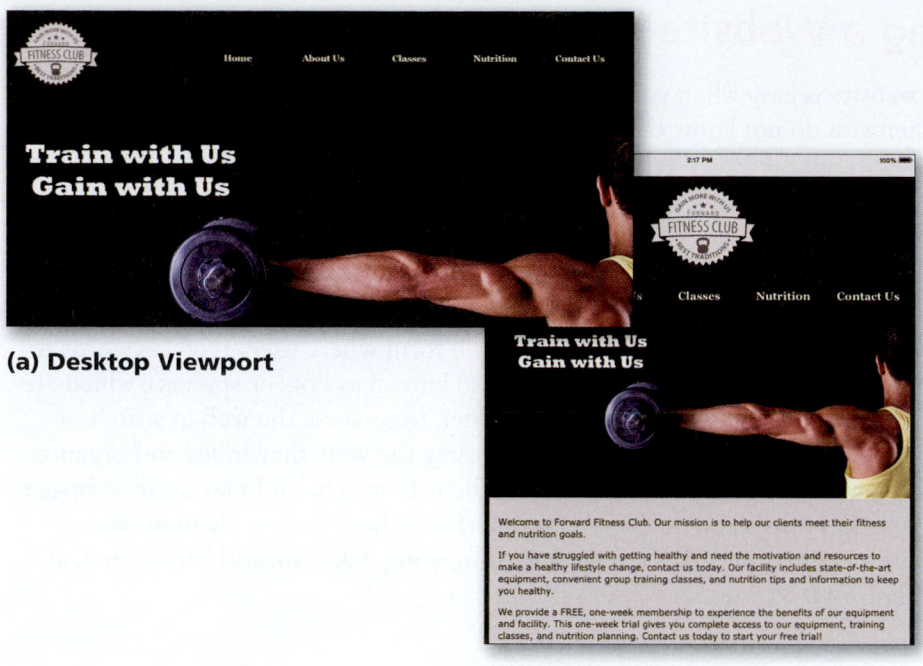

(a) Desktop Viewport

(b) Tablet Viewport

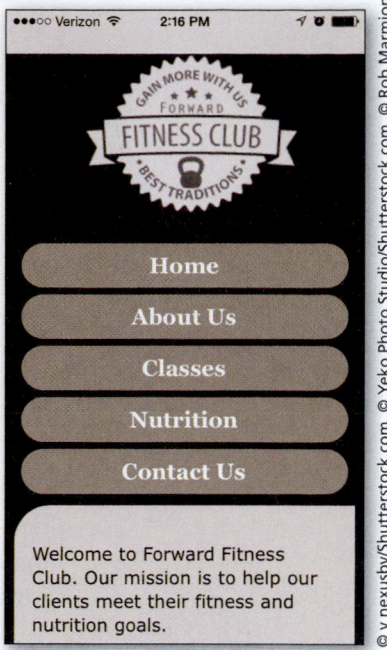

(c) Mobile Viewport

Figure 11–2

description meta tags added to the home page, the About Us page, and the Contact Us page. Figure 11–2a shows the published home page as displayed on a desktop browser. Figure 11–2b shows the published home page as displayed on an iPad. Figure 11-2c shows the published home page as displayed on an iPhone.

Roadmap

In this chapter, you will learn how to create and publish the webpages shown in Figures 11–1 and 11–2. The following roadmap identifies general activities you will perform as you progress through this chapter:

1. INSERT a description META TAG.
2. MODIFY ALT TAGS.
3. CONNECT TO a REMOTE SERVER.
4. UPLOAD FILES TO a REMOTE SERVER.
5. VIEW AND TEST WEBSITE PAGES.

At the beginning of step instructions throughout the chapter, you will see an abbreviated form of this roadmap. The abbreviated roadmap uses colors to indicate chapter progress: gray means the chapter is beyond that activity; blue means the task being shown is covered in that activity; and black means that activity is yet to be covered. For example, the following abbreviated roadmap indicates the chapter would be showing a task in the 4 UPLOAD FILES TO REMOTE SERVER activity.

1 INSERT META TAG | 2 MODIFY ALT TAGS | 3 CONNECT TO REMOTE SERVER

4 UPLOAD FILES TO REMOTE SERVER | 5 VIEW & TEST WEBSITE PAGES

Use the abbreviated roadmap as a progress guide while you read or step through the instructions in this chapter.

Finding a Website

Finding a website is easy when you know the website address. But how do you locate a website when you do not know the URL? The answer is a search engine.

Search Engines

Many people use a **search engine** to find specific businesses or content on the web. A search engine is an online tool that searches for websites based on keywords entered by a user. Search engines provide a search form where users type keywords to use in the search. Search engines use **robots** (also known as bots or spiders), which are programs that run automated tasks on the Internet, to traverse the web in search of the keywords entered by users. As the robots browse the web, they index and organize their findings, which are stored in a database. The robots view and may store webpage titles, meta tag keywords and descriptions, and h1 or other heading element content. Popular search engines include Google.com, Bing.com, Ask.com, and Yahoo.com, as shown in Figure 11–3.

(a) Google

(b) Bing

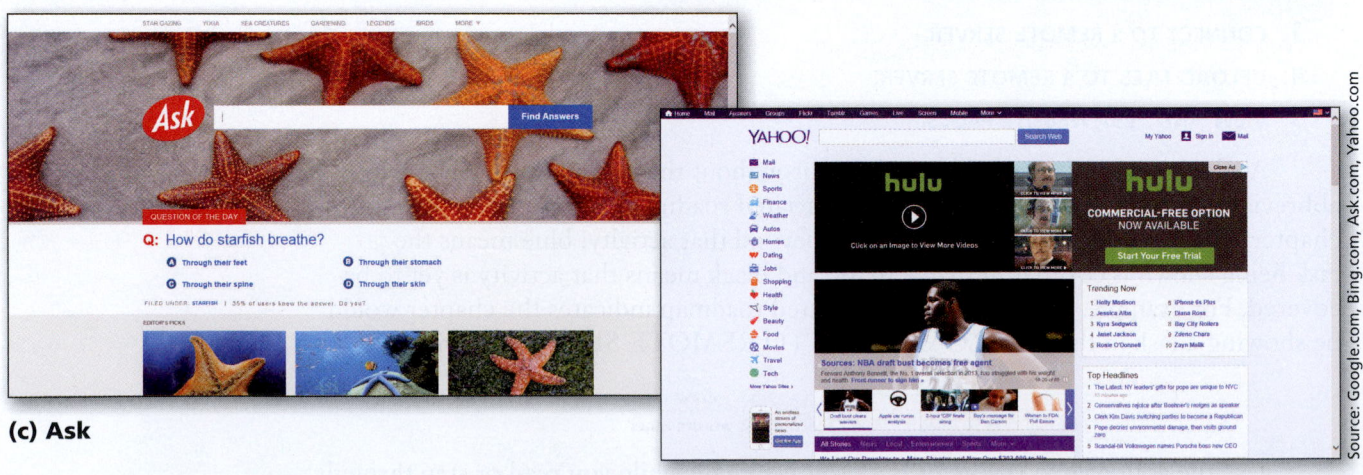

(c) Ask

(d) Yahoo!

Figure 11–3

Source: Google.com, Bing.com, Ask.com, Yahoo.com

Google is the most popular search engine in the world. In fact, according to NetMarketShare, Google has over 67 percent market share when it comes to search engines. Yahoo! is in second place with just over 10 percent market share.

Search Engine Optimization

Search engine optimization (SEO) is the process of improving the amount of traffic to your website by improving the ranking of your site in search engine results pages (SERPs). Your **rank** is the position of your webpage link, as displayed on the SERP. Each time your webpage link appears in a SERP of a related query, it creates what is called an **impression**. The more impressions you have in a SERP, the higher the chances of a user visiting your website. Many business have learned the art of effective SEO and have significantly boosted the amount of traffic to their websites.

Optimizing a website involves editing the content and HTML code in the webpage to increase its relevant keywords and to remove barriers to the page indexing functions of search engines.

Effective SEO involves several key tasks. First, brainstorm keywords that describe your business and write them down. Use these keywords within your domain name, page titles, heading elements, and meta tags. Research your competitors and note their keywords. For example, Forward Fitness Club might brainstorm the keywords fitness, gym, nutrition, fitness equipment, personal training, free trial, and fitness classes. The business should then examine its page titles, heading elements, and meta tags and add these keywords throughout the website pages.

Use the company name within the title element, up to 70 characters. This helps identify the business and is commonly displayed in the SERP. Give focus to two keywords within your meta description and consistently use these keywords within a description meta tag across your webpages. Your description meta tag should not exceed 160 characters. For example, the Forward Fitness Club might use fitness and nutrition as its two keywords and consistently use these words in the meta tags and heading elements throughout the website.

Optimize your images. Because robots cannot read text on images, be sure to use keywords within the alt text of your images. For example, the Forward Fitness Club uses the fitness and nutrition keywords in some alt text, but you can review the current alt text to add more keywords as appropriate.

BTW

Baidu Search Engine
Baidu is a popular search engine in China with over 8 percent market share. Baidu is often referred to as "China's Google."

BTW

Search Engines
Both Google and Yahoo! provide information about optimizing your websites. Review their webmaster guidelines and resources for ideas on registering with their search engines.

How does Google generate its results page?
Google uses an algorithm to generate its search results page. These algorithms are known as Panda, Penguin, and Hummingbird.

CONSIDER THIS

Meta Tags

The `meta` tag name derives from the word, **metadata**, which is information about data. You already included the following `meta` tag in the initial HTML code that you inserted into every webpage:

```
<meta charset="utf-8">
```

You included this element in all webpages throughout the book. As mentioned earlier, this statement declares the character encoding as UTF-8. The Unicode Transformation Format (UTF) is a compressed format that allows computers to display and manipulate text. When the browser encounters this meta tag, it displays the webpage properly, based on the particular UTF-8 encoding embedded in the tag. UTF-8 is the preferred encoding standard for webpages, email, and other applications.

Besides specifying the character encoding, the `meta` tag also allows you to specify the author, a description, and keywords for the webpage through the use of the `name` and `content` attributes. The `name` attribute identifies the type of information in the `content` attribute, and the `content` attribute identifies the specific phrases or words that you want to appear as metadata. You must use these two attributes together; the `content` attribute cannot be defined if the `name` attribute is not defined. The following is an example of an author meta tag:

```
<meta name="author" content="Jordan Wells">
```

In this meta tag example, `author` is the value for the `name` attribute. The `content` attribute specifies the name of the author, in this case, Jordan Wells. The following is an example of a description meta tag:

```
<meta name="description" content="Forward Fitness Club is
an elite fitness center dedicated to helping our clients
achieve their fitness and nutrition goals.">
```

The description is what some search engines add below your webpage URL in the search results to describe the content of the webpage, as shown in a Google search results list in Figure 11–4. Visitors often read the description to determine whether they want to click that particular link (or URL) in the list of URLs in the search engine results. In the description meta tag example, `description` is the value for the `name` attribute. The value of the `content` attribute is a descriptive sentence about the Forward Fitness Club.

Figure 11–4

The following is an example of a keywords meta tag:

```
<meta name="keywords" content="fitness, gym, group fitness,
nutrition">
```

In this meta tag example, `keywords` is the value for the `name` attribute. The `content` attribute specifies keywords that describe the website content, in this case, fitness, gym, group fitness, and nutrition. The keywords meta tag used to be a common standard, but it is not heavily used today. Search engine companies discovered that many websites used keywords that did not pertain to its websites. As a result, many search engines, including Google, have stopped using the keywords meta tag in their search algorithms.

In this project, you will use the description meta tag to provide search engines information about the content of the Forward Fitness Club website.

BTW

Google Search Engine
If you use Google to search for the phrase "search engine," Google does not list itself in the results.

To Add a Description Meta Tag to a Webpage

To help search engines find and index the Forward Fitness Club website, add a description meta tag to the home, About Us, Classes, Nutrition, and Contact Us pages. You place the description meta tag within the head element and should include several keywords to improve SEO. Each description meta tag describes the purpose of a particular page for the Forward Fitness Club website. When description meta tags are used on pages throughout a website and contain consistent keywords, it helps to improve SERP. *Why? Most search engines display the description of a website in its search results.* The following steps add a description meta tag to the Forward Fitness Club webpages.

1

- Open index.html in your text editor and update the comment with today's date.

- Tap or click at the end of Line 8, and then press the ENTER key to insert a new Line 9.

- On Line 9 type `<meta name="description" content="Forward Fitness Club is an elite fitness center dedicated to helping our clients achieve their fitness and nutrition goals. We provide state-of-the-art fitness equipment, group fitness classes, and nutrition planning.">` to insert a new meta tag (Figure 11–5).

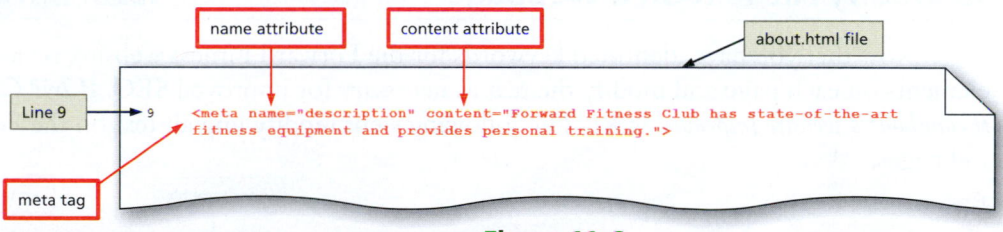

Figure 11–5

2

- Save your changes and close index.html.

- Open about.html in your text editor and update the comment with today's date.

- Tap or click at the end of Line 8, and then press the ENTER key to insert a new Line 9.

- On Line 9 type `<meta name="description" content="Forward Fitness Club has state-of-the-art fitness equipment and provides personal training.">` to insert a new meta tag (Figure 11–6).

Figure 11–6

3

- Save your changes and close about.html.

- Open classes.html in your text editor and update the comment with today's date.

- Tap or click at the end of Line 8, and then press the ENTER key to insert a new Line 9.

- On Line 9 type `<meta name="description" content="Forward Fitness Club has many fitness classes to meet your needs, including boot camp, cardio, kickboxing, spinning, yoga, and zumba.">` to insert a new meta tag (Figure 11–7).

Figure 11–7

4

- Save your changes and close classes.html.

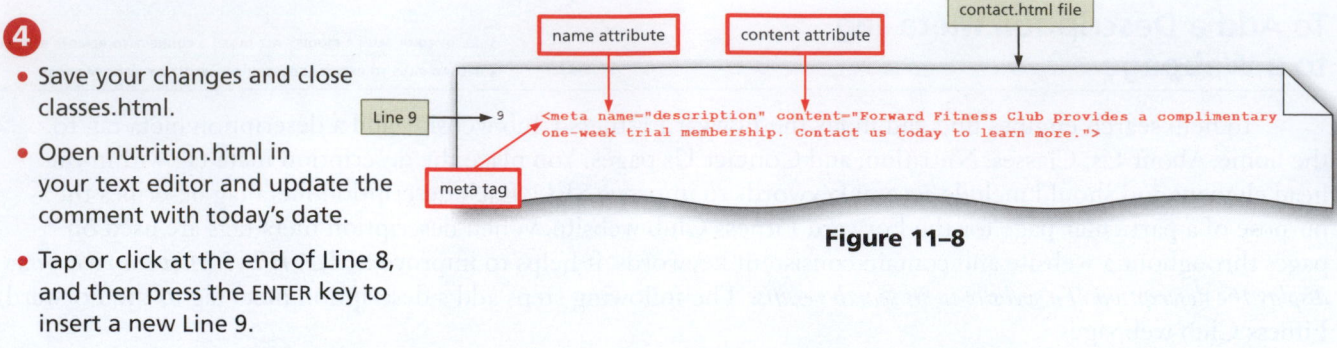

Figure 11–8

- Open nutrition.html in your text editor and update the comment with today's date.

- Tap or click at the end of Line 8, and then press the ENTER key to insert a new Line 9.

- On Line 9 type `<meta name="description" content="Forward Fitness Club provides nutrition guides and meal planning to help you meet your nutrition goals.">` to insert a new meta tag.

- Save your changes and close nutrition.html.

- Open contact.html in your text editor and update the comment with today's date.

- Tap or click at the end of Line 8, and then press the ENTER key to insert a new Line 9.

- On Line 9 type `<meta name="description" content="Forward Fitness Club provides a complimentary one-week trial membership. Contact us today to learn more.">` to insert a new meta tag.

- Save your changes (Figure 11–8).

To Modify Alt Text on a Webpage

1 INSERT META TAG | **2 MODIFY ALT TAGS** | 3 CONNECT TO REMOTE SERVER
4 UPLOAD FILES TO REMOTE SERVER | 5 VIEW & TEST WEBSITE PAGES

Now that you have identified keywords for the Forward Fitness website, review the alt text in the img elements on each page and modify the text as necessary for improved SEO. *Why? Consistent use of keywords throughout a website improves SERP.* The following steps modify img alt text on the Forward Fitness Club webpages.

1

- Open index.html in your text editor to prepare to modify it.

- On Line 45, replace the word "home" in the alt text with **fitness** to include a keyword (Figure 11–9).

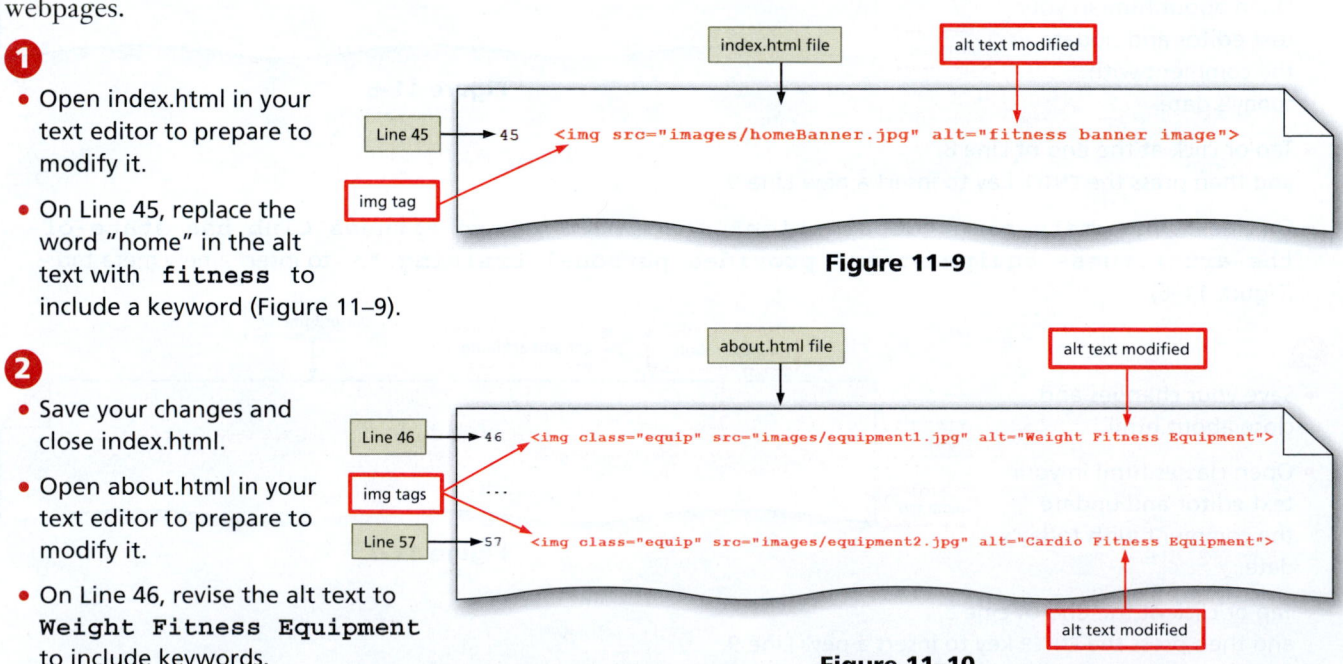

Figure 11–9

2

- Save your changes and close index.html.

- Open about.html in your text editor to prepare to modify it.

- On Line 46, revise the alt text to **Weight Fitness Equipment** to include keywords.

- On Line 57, revise the alt text to **Cardio Fitness Equipment** to include keywords (Figure 11–10).

Figure 11–10

3
- Save your changes and close about.html.
- Open classes.html in your text editor to prepare to modify it.
- On Line 33, revise the alt text to **group fitness classes banner image** to include keywords (Figure 11–11).

| classes.html file | alt text modified |

Line 33 → `33` `<img src="images/classesBanner.jpg" alt="group fitness classes banner image">`

img tag

Figure 11–11

4
- Save your changes and close classes.html.
- Open nutrition.html in your text editor to prepare to modify it.
- On Line 41, revise the alt text to **good nutrition** to include a keyword.
- On Line 51, revise the alt text to **healthy food** to include a keyword.
- On Line 67, revise the alt text to **healthy nutrition meal** to include keywords.
- Save your changes (Figure 11–12).

| nutrition.html file | alt text modified |

img tags

Line 41 → `41` `<img src="images/nutrition1.jpg" alt="good nutrition" class="desktop">`

`...`

alt text modified

Line 51 → `51` `<img src="images/nutrition2.jpg" alt="healthy food" class="desktop">`

`...`

alt text modified

img tag

Line 67 → `67` `<img src="images/nutrition3.jpg" alt="healthy nutrition meal" class="desktop">`

Figure 11–12

Publishing a Website

When you finish developing your website, the next steps are to register a domain name, determine a web hosting strategy, and then publish the website to make it accessible to everyone with an Internet connection. To complete these steps, you need to select and register a domain name, select a web hosting service, and then transfer the website files to the host's server.

Domain Name

A **domain name** is the server name portion of a URL. You can use the domain name of the server on which you publish your webpages together with a path to your specific pages for your webpage address. However, this webpage address option can result in a URL that is long, hard to remember, and not representative of your website or business.

As an alternative, you can register your own domain name on the Internet for minimal cost per year. A unique domain name can make it easier for visitors to find your webpages. The Forward Fitness Club wants to register a unique domain name for their website, as long as you can find a name that is both suitable and available.

When selecting and registering a domain name, make sure it represents your business. Brainstorm and make a list of the top five keywords or phrases that best describe your business. For example, "forward" or "fitness" would be an ideal domain name for the Forward Fitness Club. A short and concise domain name makes it more

BTW

InterNIC

InterNIC contains trusted public information regarding Internet domain name registration services. The InterNIC website includes an FAQ area with information about domain name registrars, as well as links for domain name disputes.

BTW

Top-Level Domains

Many companies have applied for generic top-level domains. For example, Google has applied for the .google and .youtube domain names. The list of requests for new TLDs is very long and can be accessed at https://gtldresult.icann.org. Select Program Status from the top navigation area and then select Current Application Status to view the list.

memorable. Long domain names are more difficult to remember. Avoid the use of hyphens within a domain name, as this make the domain name harder to pronounce and less memorable.

The .com top-level domain (TLD) name is preferred for businesses. Many users assume that business websites end with .com, so using that TLD makes it easier for visitors to find your website. However, you might find that the .com TLD you want has already been taken. In this instance, you could consider several open, top-level domain names. An **open TLD** means that any person or entity can register with the domain name. Furthermore, the .com TLD is not always the best option for every website. For example, most non-profit organizations use the .org TLD. Likewise, most educational institutions use the .edu TLD. Table 11–1 lists common TLDs and their original purpose.

Table 11–1 Common Top-Level Domains	
Name	**Original Purpose**
.com	Commercial
.biz	Business or commercial
.net	Network-related domains
.co	Business or commercial
.org	Non-profit organizations
.edu	Educational institutions
.gov	Restricted use by the United States government
.mil	Restricted use by the United States military
.me	Personal website

To determine if the domain name you are considering is available, you can start your search at InterNIC, www.internic.net. InterNIC is a registered service mark of the U.S. Department of Commerce. The InterNIC website is operated by the Internet Corporation for Assigned Names and Numbers (ICANN) to provide information to the public regarding Internet domain name registration services. ICANN is responsible for managing and coordinating the Domain Name System (DNS) so that every Internet address is unique, and so that all users of the Internet can find valid addresses.

CONSIDER THIS

Do domain names expire?
Yes. Once you purchase a domain name, note the expiration date. If you do not renew the domain name, it may go to an auction to be sold.

Website Hosting

The next step in publishing your website is to find a hosting service. One popular option is to use a company that charges for website hosting services. Of the thousands of companies that provide web hosting services, most charge a monthly fee, but some offer free web hosting in exchange for advertising on your website. Bluehost.com, as shown in Figure 11–13, is one of many web hosting companies.

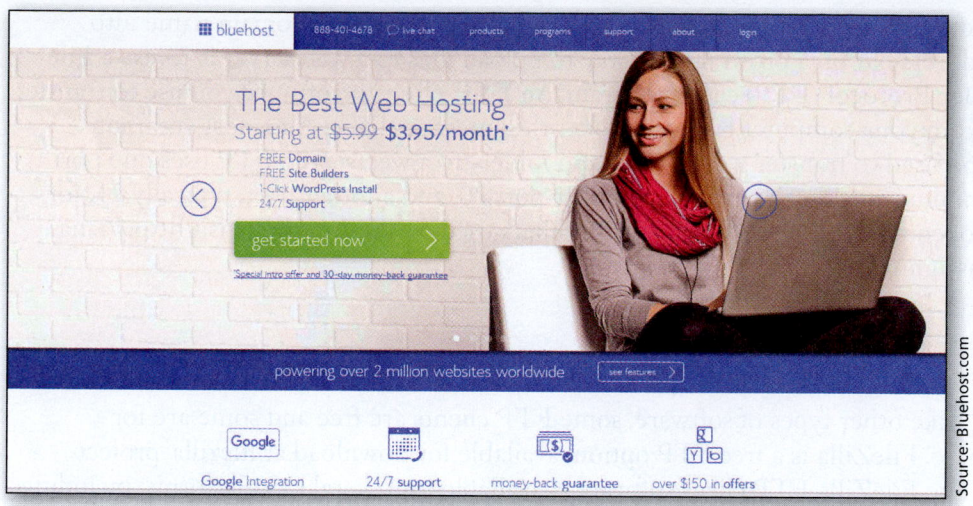

Source: Bluehost.com

Figure 11–13

Another option is to use the Internet service provider (ISP) that you use to connect to the Internet as your website host. ISPs sometimes provide space for their clients to host a website. If you registered your own domain name, you can have your ISP set up a virtual domain, or shared web hosting, on their server with your new domain name. Your ISP's server may be set up to allocate hosting services and bandwidth to more than one website by using a virtual domain. In other words, although you register the domain name, your ISP would host the website on its own web server. Virtual web hosting is a less expensive option because you do not have to pay for a dedicated server to host only your website. You can check with your ISP for details.

A final option is for you to set up and maintain your own web server. You would have to know enough about the technology to set it up and keep it running.

Whether you choose to use your ISP to host your website, to use a web hosting service, or to set up your own web server, you need to answer the following questions:

- What is the total cost? Compare monthly or annual costs; the highest cost may not always provide the best service.

- How much space is available to you? Assess your current needs (i.e., file sizes, number of graphics and other media) and your future needs (i.e., how much more information you will create).

- How fast is the connection speed? The speed of the connection to the Internet determines how efficiently you can serve your visitors.

- How much total bandwidth transfer is available? The number and size of webpages in your website together with the number and size of graphical images is important to consider. Lack of efficient bandwidth can delay the time it takes for a page to load. Pages must load quickly in order to maintain user interest.

- Is technical support provided? You may occasionally need help, especially when you first publish the site.

- Are tracking services provided? Many hosting companies allow you to see how visitors use your website by viewing a tracking log.

After you have selected a web hosting service, you need to transfer your files to the host's server.

Publishing a Website

Once you register a domain name and secure a web hosting strategy, the next step is to publish your website so that it is accessible to the world. When you **publish** your website, you transfer your website files to a web server. After transferring, or uploading, the files, users can access the website by typing the domain name into the Address bar on a browser. One way to upload files to a web server is to use a File Transfer Protocol (FTP) client program. An **FTP client** is software you use to transfer files from your computer to a server over the Internet. This is the most common method used to transfer website files and folders to a web server. FTP uses one port to communicate over a network, typically port 20, and another port, typically 21, for control commands. For a list of port numbers used on the Internet, visit http://iana .org/assignments/port-numbers.

FTP Clients

Like other types of software, some FTP clients are free and some are for purchase. FileZilla is a free FTP option, available for download at filezilla-project .org. The FileZilla FTP client software is available for several OS platforms, including Windows, Mac, and Linux. Figure 11–14 shows the FileZilla FTP client software. Use the Quickconnect bar, located near the top of the FileZilla window, to type the name of the host (your domain name), your username and password, as well as the port number. If you paid for a web hosting service, you establish an FTP username and password through your web hosting service provider. Use the local site directory window, located on the left, to navigate folders and files on your local computer. When you navigate to your website folder, its contents are displayed in the lower-left window, called the local site file list window. The remote site directory window, located on the right, displays the root folder for the website on the remote web server. After you publish the website to a remote web server, its folders and files are displayed in the lower-right window. To publish local files to the remote server, select the local folders and files in the local site file list and then drag them to the remote site file list window or select Transfer on the menu bar.

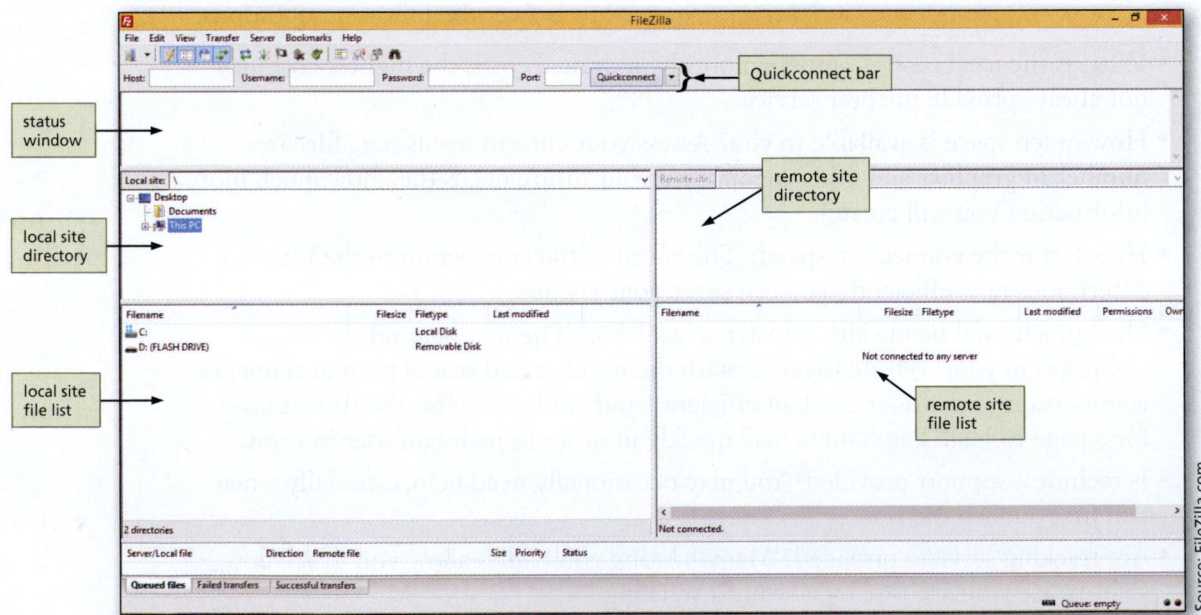

Figure 11–14

Source: FileZilla.com

Another popular free FTP client is SmartFTP, available for download at smartftp.com. SmartFTP is for the Windows platform. CuteFTP, available at cuteftp .com, provides a free trial of its software, with an option to purchase after the trial has expired. CuteFTP is available for both Windows and Mac platforms.

Many webpage editors also provide publishing features. Figure 11–15 shows the built-in FTP tools of Adobe Dreamweaver CC. In Figure 11–15, the remote server files are displayed in the left window and the local site files are displayed in the right window. To publish new or revised content, you select the folders or files from the local site window to publish and then tap or click the up arrow button to transfer the local files to the remote server.

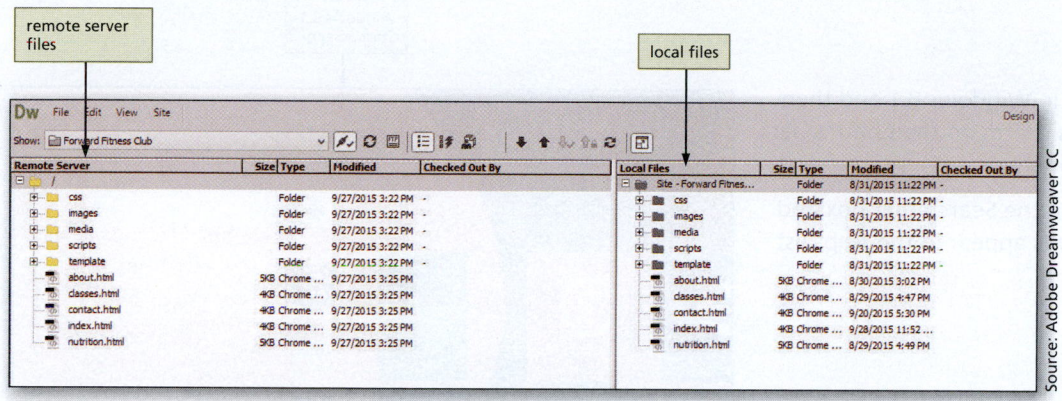

Figure 11–15

To Download and Install an FTP Client

Unless you have direct access to the web hosting server, you will need an FTP client to upload and publish your website files and folders. Ask your instructor if there is a preferred FTP client to use for this course. If no preference is specified, download one of the FTP clients previously discussed. If you wanted to download and install the FileZilla FTP client, you would perform the following steps.

1. Use your browser to access the website for FileZilla at https://filezilla-project .org/.
2. Tap or click the link to download the FileZilla client.
3. Locate the option to install the client for your operating system and then tap or click the appropriate link to download the installation package.
4. When the download is complete, open the downloaded package to begin the install.
5. Follow the instructions within the wizard window to complete the installation.
6. Run FileZilla when finished.

Transferring Files

You need several pieces of information to publish your website, including a URL or domain name, an FTP username and password, and a port number. If you secured a web hosting service provider, contact your provider to obtain this information. Many times you can establish your own FTP username and password by signing into your web hosting service provider's website. Your institution may have web server space available to you as a student. Contact your instructor to request this information. Some web hosting service providers offer free web hosting services. Ask your instructor if there is a preferred, free web hosting service to use.

To Start FileZilla and Connect to a Remote Server

Before you can publish the Forward Fitness Club website, you must use an FTP client to connect to a remote web server. *Why? You need access to a remote server to publish a website.* Before you begin the following steps, ask your instructor if there is a preferred web host for your school and request the login information. The following steps start FileZilla, based on a typical installation in Windows 8.1, and connect to a remote web server.

1

- Open the Charms bar in Windows 8.1 and then tap or click the Search charm on the Charms bar to display the Search menu.

- Type **FileZilla** in the Search text box and watch the Search results appear in the Apps list (Figure 11–16).

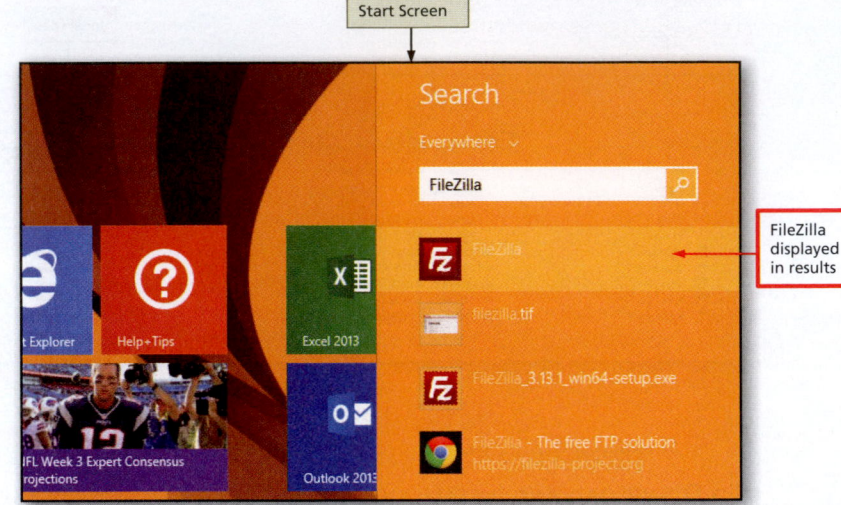

Figure 11–16

2

- Tap or click FileZilla in the search results to start FileZilla.
- In the Host text box on the Quickconnect bar, type the URL of the server to complete the field.
- Type your username in the Username text box to complete the field.
- Type your password in the Password text box to complete the field.
- Type **21** in the Port text box to complete the field (Figure 11–17).

Q&A Where do I obtain the username, password, and port number?
Ask your instructor for this information.

What if I am required to enter different information from that shown in Figure 11–17?
Your information will be different from that shown in Figure 11–17.

Figure 11–17

3

- Tap or click the Quickconnect button on the Quickconnect bar to connect to the remote server.

- Verify that the status shows Connected in the status window to confirm that you have successfully connected to the remote server (Figure 11–18).

Figure 11–18

To Upload Folders and Files to a Remote Server

1 INSERT META TAG | 2 MODIFY ALT TAGS | 3 CONNECT TO REMOTE SERVER

4 UPLOAD FILES TO REMOTE SERVER | 5 VIEW & TEST WEBSITE PAGES

Once you have connected to a remote server, upload your website folders and files to publish your website. *Why? You transfer your website files to a remote server to make it accessible to everyone with an Internet connection.* The following steps upload your website folders and files to a remote web server.

1

- In the Local site pane of the FileZilla window, navigate to your fitness folder and then tap or click it to display the fitness folder contents in the Local site file list.

- Tap or click the css folder in the Local site file list to select the folder and make the lower-left window active.

- Press the CTRL+A keys to select all of the folders and files within the fitness folder (Figure 11–19).

Figure 11–19

2

- Drag the folders and files to the Remote site file list window on the right to upload the folders and files to the remote server (Figure 11–20).

Figure 11–20

To View and Test a Published Website

After successfully publishing your website, view the website on your browser and test all the links. *Why?* *Verify that the website works as designed and confirm that all pages and content are accessible.* The following steps view the published website in a browser.

- Open your browser and type your URL in the address bar to display (Figure 11–21).

Q&A

What is my URL?
If your instructor provided you with the remote site login credentials, ask your instructor for the URL. If you published through another web hosting service, view your account information or contact the web hosting service provider.

Figure 11–21

- Tap or click the About Us link to display the page and to verify the page content.
- Tap or click the Classes link to display the page and to verify the page content.
- Tap or click the Nutrition link to display the page and to verify the page content.
- Tap or click the Contact Us link to display the page and to verify the page content (Figure 11–22).

Q&A

One or more of my pages is not displayed when I click a link. How do I correct this error?
If one or more pages were not displayed, either the page is not published or the link to the page is incorrect. Verify that your pages are published by confirming that the pages appear in the remote file list window. View all of your local site webpage files in your text editor to verify your page links. If you discover and correct a page link, save your changes, and then select the file(s) from the local site file list window and drag it to the remote site file list window to republish your page(s).

None of my images are displayed. How do I correct this problem?
If one or more images are not displayed, upload your images file to the remote site.

Figure 11–22

Marketing a Website

After testing your webpages and correcting any errors, the last step is to market the website location to attract visitors. Develop a comprehensive marketing plan. A website is a passive marketing tool; it serves no purpose if no one knows it is available on the web. To attract customers to your website, take appropriate steps to promote and market your site. You can promote and market your website to reach your target audience in the following ways:

- Add your URL to your business cards, company brochures, stationery, and email signature.

- Advertise your URL in newsletters and print articles.

- Tell people you meet about your website.

- Find and get listed on targeted directories and search engines specific to your industry.

- Buy banner ads.

- Negotiate reciprocal links in which you agree to link to a website if they agree to link to your website.

- Use newsgroups specific to your industry.

BTW
Website Marketing Services
Many businesses handle all marketing aspects of a website, including social media. Use your favorite search engine to research more about website marketing services.

Registering with Search Engines

You are finished entering the meta tags, publishing, and marketing your website. The next step is to register your website with the two most popular search engines, Google and Yahoo! It is also a good idea to register your site with search engines that specialize in subject matter related to your website. To register your website with Google, you could perform the following steps.

1. Open your browser, enter www.google.com/webmasters/tools, and then sign into your Google account. If you do not have a Google account, create one, and then sign in.

2. Enter your URL in the search console text box provided.

After registering your URL with Google, you can use several tools from Google to learn more about user activity on your website. You can review an analysis of user clicks from a Google search. You can request to receive alerts for major errors. You can also verify if Google successfully accessed your content with its robots.

What tool does Google use to test a successful access of website content?
Google provides a tool called Fetch, which is available from their webmaster site. Fetch lets a web developer know how well a Google robot can access a webpage.

CONSIDER THIS

To Validate the HTML Files

Every time you create a new webpage or modify an existing webpage, run it through W3C's validator to check the document for errors. If any errors exist, you need to correct them. Validation is also an effective troubleshooting tool during the development process and adds a valuable level of professionalism to your work. The following steps validate an HTML document.

1. Open your browser and type `http://validator.w3.org/` in the address bar to display the W3C validator page.

2. Tap or click the Validate by File Upload tab to display the Validate by File Upload information.

3. Tap or click the Browse button to display the Choose File to Upload dialog box.

4 Navigate to your fitness folder to find the index.html file.

5 Tap or click the index.html document to select it.

6 Tap or click the Open button to upload it to the W3C validator.

7 Tap or click the Check button to send the document through the validator and display the validation results page.

8 If necessary, correct any errors, save your changes, and run through the validator again to revalidate the page.

9 Follow these steps to validate other pages recently modified and correct any errors.

Chapter Summary

In this chapter, you learned how to add a description meta tag to a webpage. You also learned how to publish and promote a website. You used the meta tag to create a description for a website. You learned how to publish your website with an FTP client. You also learned how to market and promote a website. The items listed below include all the new skills you have learned in this chapter, with the tasks grouped by activity.

Using the Description Meta Tag

Add a Description Meta Tag to a Webpage (HTML 511)

Modify Alt Text on a Webpage (HTML 512)

Publishing a Website

Start FileZilla and Connect to a Remote Server (HTML 518)

Upload Folders and Files to a Remote Server (HTML 519)

View and Test a Published Website (HTML 520)

 How will you promote your website?

CONSIDER THIS

Use these guidelines as you complete the assignments in this chapter and create your own webpages outside of this class.

1. Determine a domain name.

    a) Keep the domain name short and memorable.

    b) Check the domain name availability.

2. Outline a marketing plan for your website.

    a) Make a list of keywords.

    b) Determine your SEO strategy.

3. Determine a web hosting service.

    a) Research and compare web hosting service providers.

    b) Determine the best method for accessing and publishing to your remote site.

 How should you submit solutions to questions in the assignments identified with a **symbol?**

CONSIDER THIS

Every assignment in this book contains one or more questions identified with a symbol. These questions require you to think beyond the assigned presentation. Present your solutions to the questions in the format required by your instructor. Possible formats may include one or more of these options: create a document that contains the answer; present your answer to the class; discuss your answer in a group; record the answer as audio or video using a webcam, smartphone, or portable media player; or post answers on a blog, wiki, or website.

Apply Your Knowledge

Reinforce the skills and apply the concepts you learned in this chapter.

Adding Meta Tags and Publishing a Webpage

Instructions: In this exercise, you will use your text editor to create a webpage. Add a description meta tag to the webpage and then publish the webpage. Work with the apply11styles.css file in the apply\css folder from the Data Files for Students. The completed webpage is shown in Figure 11–23. You will also use professional web development practices to indent, space, comment, and validate your code.

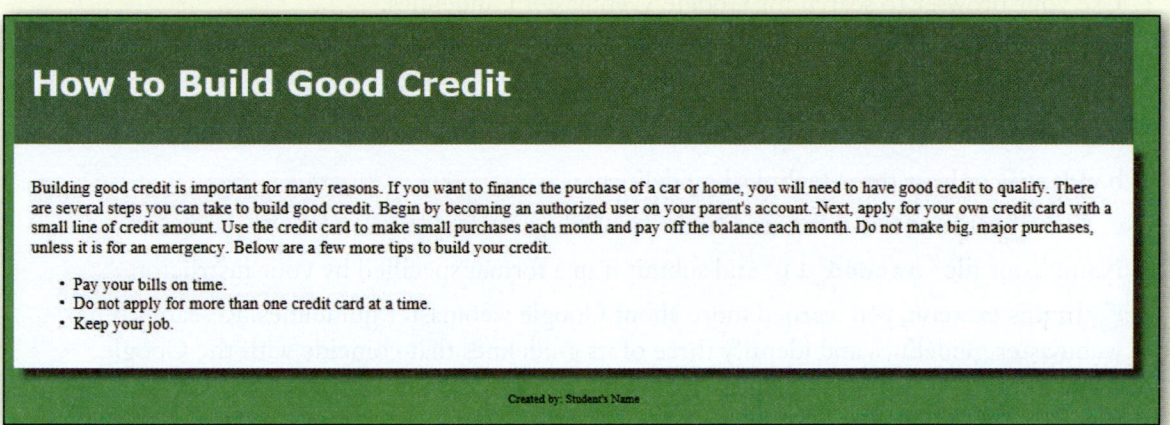

Figure 11–23

Perform the following tasks:

1. Use your text editor to create a new HTML file named apply11.html. Include a comment with your name and today's date.

2. Include all necessary HTML5 elements for a webpage.

3. Create a title for the page and use `Credit` as the webpage title.

4. Insert a description `meta` tag with a content attribute and use `This website provides helpful information about how to build good credit.` as the value.

5. Create a header element.

6. Create an `h1` element within the header element and include the text `How to Build Good Credit` as the heading text.

7. Create a `main` element.

8. Use your browser to research ways to build good credit. Summarize your findings within a paragraph element within the `main` element.

9. Create an unordered list of at least three steps one should take to build credit. Place the unordered list below the paragraph element, but within the `main` element.

10. Create a footer element that contains your name.

11. Save your changes.

12. Publish the website files to a remote server.

13. View your published website in your browser.

14. Submit the project in a format specified by your instructor.

15. ✸ In this exercise, you researched information about how to build good credit. Return to one of the websites you used to conduct your research and view the page's source file. View the source file and identify the meta tags used for the webpage.

Extend Your Knowledge

Extend the skills you learned in this chapter and experiment with new skills. You may need to use additional resources to complete the assignment.

Learning More About Google Webmaster Guidelines

Instructions: In this exercise, you research information about Google webmaster guidelines and summarize your findings.

Perform the following tasks:

1. Use your browser to search for Google Webmaster Guidelines.
2. Read the information and use your word processor to summarize your findings.
3. Include the following information in your response.
   a. Identify at least three design guidelines.
   b. Identify at least three technical guidelines.
   c. Identify at least five things to avoid.
4. Name your file **extend_11** and submit it in a format specified by your instructor.
5. ✺ In this exercise, you learned more about Google webmaster guidelines. Research Bing webmaster guidelines and identify three of its guidelines that coincide with the Google guidelines.

Analyze, Correct, Improve

Analyze a website, correct all errors, and improve it.

Improving SEO for a Webpage

Instructions: Work with the analyze11.html file in the analyze folder and the analyze11styles.css file from analyze/css folder from the Data Files for Students. The analyze11.html webpage needs a page title, a meta description, and an h1 tag. The alt text on the page also needs to be improved. Use Figure 11–24 as a guide to correct these files.

Figure 11–24

Photos courtesy of Jessica Minnick

1. Correct

a. Open the analyze11.html file in your text editor from the Data Files for Students. Modify the comment at the top of the page to include your name and today's date and then link the file to analyze11styles.css.

b. Review the webpage content and insert an appropriate title for this page.

2. Improve

a. In the analyze11.html file, wrap the header element content within an h1 element.

b. Review the img tag alt text and modify it for SEO.

c. Save all of your changes and open the analyze11.html in your browser.

d. Create a style rule for the h1 element you added and specify a color. Include a comment for the new style rule.

e. Specify a color for the footer style rule.

f. Save all of your changes and refresh analyze11.html in your browser.

g. Validate your HTML webpage using the W3C validator found at validator.w3.org and fix any errors that are identified.

h. ✳ Research why Google no longer supports the keywords meta tag and summarize your findings.

In the Labs

Labs 1 and 2, which increase in difficulty, require you to create webpages based on what you learned in the chapter; Lab 3 requires you to dive deeper into a topic covered in the chapter.

Lab 1: **Publishing the New Harvest Food Bank Website**

Problem: You volunteer at a local food bank called New Harvest Food Bank that collects community food donations and provides food and other services to those in need. You have created a website for the food bank and now need to add a description meta tag and publish it. Figure 11–25 shows the published website, as displayed in a desktop browser.

Figure 11–25

Continued >

In the Labs *continued*

Instructions: Perform the following tasks:

1. Open your text editor and then open the index.html document in the lab1 folder and update the comment at the top of the page to include today's date.

2. Insert a description `meta` tag with a content value of **"New Harvest Food Bank is a non-profit organization, dedicated to supporting our local community."**

3. Save your changes.

4. Publish the website files to a remote server.

5. View your published website in your browser and verify that all webpages and website content is published.

6. Submit the project in a format specified by your instructor.

7. ✺ Research domain name ideas for this website and provide a list of three available domain name options.

Lab 2: **Publishing the Steve's Screen Services Website**

Problem: You work for a screening company called Steve's Screen Services that specializes in screening, cleaning, and repairing screened patios. You have created a website for the business and now need to add a description meta tag and publish it. Figure 11–26 shows the published website, as displayed in a desktop browser.

Figure 11–26

Instructions: Perform the following tasks:

1. Open your text editor and then open the index.html document in the lab2 folder and update the comment at the top of the page to include today's date.

2. Insert a description `meta` tag with an appropriate content value.

3. Insert another `meta` tag that identifies the author.

4. Save your changes.

5. Publish the website files to a remote server.

6. View your published website in your browser and verify that all webpages and website content is published.

7. Submit the project in a format specified by your instructor.

8. ✳ Research how you can stop a robot from indexing a page. Discuss how and why you would do this.

Lab 3: Expand Your World
Exploring Web Hosting Providers

Problem: In this chapter you learned that you have many options for hosting a website. In this exercise, you will research web hosting service providers and list your findings.

Instructions:

1. Search the Internet for web hosting service providers.

2. Select three providers and compare their services and costs.

3. Identify which provider you would select and why.

4. Submit your answers in the format specified by your instructor.

5. ✳ Use your browser to research an SEO company and provide a list of their services and costs.

Consider This: Your Turn

Apply your creative thinking and problem-solving skills to design and implement a solution.

1. Publishing Your Personal Portfolio Website Design

Personal

Part 1: You have completed your portfolio website. In this exercise, you update the page as follows:

1. Open the external style sheet you created in Chapter 10 and save it with the name **portfoliostyles11.css** in the styles folder within the your_turn_1 folder.

2. Add your name and the current date as a comment to the first line of the portfoliostyles11.css file.

3. In your HTML editor, open the files you created for your portfolio website in Chapter 10 and make sure your name and the current date are added as a comment to the first line of all files.

   a. Update the HTML files to modify the link to the external style sheet to reference portfoliostyles11.css.

   b. Create a description meta tag for the home page.

4. Save your files.

5. Publish your website.

6. Test your website to verify that all pages and content are published.

7. Submit your assignment in the format specified by your instructor.

Part 2: ✳ Use your browser to research the software needed to host your own web server and summarize your findings.

Continued >

Consider This: Your Turn *continued*

2. Publishing the WebDevPros Website

Professional

Part 1: You have completed the website for WebDevPros. In this exercise, you update the site as follows:

1. Open the external style sheet you created in Chapter 10 and save it with the name **webdevstyles11.css** in the styles folder within the your_turn_2 folder.

2. Add your name and the current date as a comment to the first line of the webdevstyles11.css file.

3. Open the files you created for WebDevPros in Chapter 10 in your HTML editor and make sure your name and the current date are added as a comment to the first line of all files.

4. Update the HTML files to:

    a. Modify the link to the external style sheet to reference webdevstyles11.css.

    b. Create a description meta tag for the home page.

    c. Create an author meta tag.

5. Save your files.

6. Publish your website.

7. Test your website to verify that all pages and content are published.

8. Submit your assignment in the format specified by your instructor.

Part 2: ✳ Create a marketing plan with at least five steps you can take to market this website.

3. Publishing the Dog Hall of Fame Website

Research and Collaboration

Part 1: You have completed the Dog Hall of Fame website. Do the following activities as a group:

1. Open the external style sheet you created in Chapter 10 and save it with the name **dogstyles11.css** in the styles folder within the your_turn_3 folder.

2. Add your names and the current date as a comment to the first line of the dogstyles11.css file.

3. Open the files you created for the Dog Hall of Fame in Chapter 10 in your HTML editor and make sure your names and the current date are added as a comment to the first line of all files.

4. Modify the link to the external style sheet to reference dogstyles11.css.

5. Insert a description meta tag on the home page.

6. Insert an author meta tag on all pages.

7. Save your files.

8. Publish your website.

9. Test your website to verify that all pages and content are published.

10. Submit your assignment in the format specified by your instructor.

Part 2: ✳ As a group, research how to create an HTML site map for Google. Use your findings to create a site map.

12 | Maintaining a Website

Rob Marmion/Shutterstock.com; Milleflore Images/Shutterstock.com; Faysal/Shutterstock.com; Nexusby/Shutterstock.com; Yeko Photo Studio/Shutterstock.com; source: Facebook; source: Twitter

Objectives

You will have mastered the material in this chapter when you can:

- Describe a website development life cycle
- Outline project management for a website
- Define copyright

- Develop a website maintenance plan
- Explain the purpose of a content management system
- Describe web frameworks
- Explain the basics of e-commerce

12 | Maintaining a Website

Introduction

After a website is designed, developed, and launched, the next phase of the website development begins: maintenance. A well-polished website demands continuous maintenance. As changes take place within a company and within an industry, a web developer must work closely with a project team to ensure that a business website stays fresh and stands out from its competition. Likewise, a web developer must keep up with emerging trends in technology and new ways to reach a target audience.

In this chapter, you will learn about the development life cycle of a website. To keep a website current, you will examine the steps in project management, including content and design updates, and develop a maintenance plan for a business website. You will also learn about copyright law as it pertains to text and media. After reviewing several content management systems, you will explore frameworks within a website. Finally, you will learn more about electronic commerce (e-commerce) websites.

Project — Performing Website Maintenance

In Chapter 12, you review webpage content for the Forward Fitness Club website and make improvements or update the content to keep it fresh. You will also consider each page to determine whether it needs design improvements.

This chapter provides an overview of the website development life cycle, as well as website project management, which should be ongoing when working with very large websites. This chapter also provides a basic introduction to content management systems, frameworks, and e-commerce.

The project in this chapter improves a website by updating content on the home page, the About Us page, and the Classes page. You also update the CSS file. To perform these tasks, you first make content adjustments and add new content to the home page. Next, you modify the **video** element on the About Us page and update content on the Classes page. In the style sheet, you add a style rule to format the **checkbox** elements within the form for tablet and desktop viewports. Figure 12–1 shows the home page with the updated content. Figure 12–2 shows the updated video on the About Us page. Figure 12–3 shows the updated table content on the Classes page. Figure 12–4 shows the style updates to the **checkbox** elements on the Contact Us page.

Figure 12-1

Figure 12-2

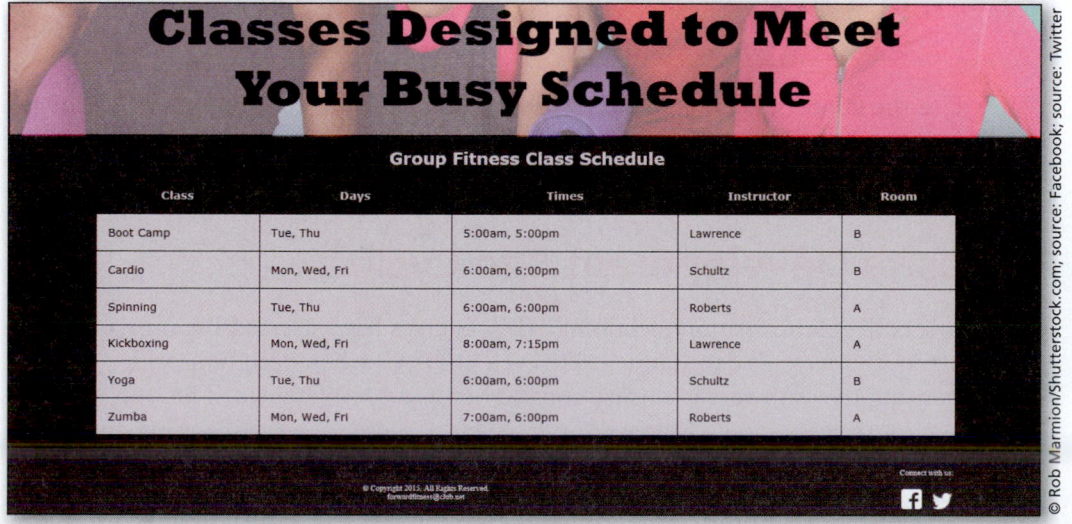

Figure 12-3

Figure 12–4

Roadmap

In this chapter, you will learn how to create the webpages shown in Figures 12–1, 12–2, 12–3, and 12–4. The following roadmap identifies general activities you will perform as you progress through this chapter:

1. IMPROVE the HOME PAGE.
2. IMPROVE the ABOUT US PAGE.
3. UPDATE the CLASSES PAGE.
4. UPDATE the CSS FILE.

At the beginning of step instructions throughout the chapter, you will see an abbreviated form of this roadmap. The abbreviated roadmap uses colors to indicate chapter progress: gray means the chapter is beyond that activity; blue means the task being shown is covered in that activity; and black means that activity is yet to be covered. For example, the following abbreviated roadmap indicates the chapter would be showing a task in the 2 IMPROVE ABOUT US PAGE activity.

1 IMPROVE HOME PAGE | 2 IMPROVE ABOUT US PAGE

3 UPDATE CLASSES PAGE | 4 UPDATE CSS FILE

Use the abbreviated roadmap as a progress guide while you read or step through the instructions in this chapter.

Website Development Life Cycle

For years, college information technology (IT) courses have stressed the importance of following the systems development life cycle (SDLC) when designing and implementing new software to ensure consistency and completeness. The web development process should follow a similar cycle. Comprehensive planning and analysis ensure that developers will provide what the users want. If you start to code your webpages without thorough planning and analysis, you run the risk of missing pertinent information. It is much less expensive to make corrections to a website in the early phases of project development than it is to alter webpages that are completed.

The web development life cycle outlined in this section is one that can be used for any type or size of web development project. The **web development life cycle** is a process that can be used for developing webpages at any level of complexity. As shown in Figure 12–5, the web development life cycle includes the following phases: planning, analysis, design and development, testing, implementation, and maintenance. Table 12–1 lists several questions that should be asked during each phase in the web development life cycle.

Figure 12–5 Web Development Life Cycle

Table 12–1 Web Development Life Cycle	
Web Development Phase	**Questions to Ask**
Planning	What is the purpose of this website?
	Who will use this website?
	What are the users' computing environments?
	Who owns and authors the information on the website?
	Who decides if and where the information belongs on the website?
Analysis	What tasks do the users need to perform?
	What information is useful to the users?
	What process considerations must be made?
Design and Development	How many webpages will be included in the website?
	How will the webpages be organized?
	What type of website structure is appropriate for the content?
	How can I best present the content for ease of use?
	What file naming convention will be employed for this website?
	What folder structure will be used for the webpage files?
	How do I apply standards throughout the development process?
	What forms of multimedia contribute positively to the website?
	How can accessibility issues be addressed without limiting usability?
	Does the website have an international audience?
Testing	Do the webpages pass the World Wide Web Consortium (W3C) validation process as HTML5 compliant?
	Is the website content correct?
	Does the website function correctly?
	Are users able to find the information they need to complete desired tasks?
	Is navigation clear and easy to use?
Implementation	How is the website published?
	How can users be attracted to visit and revisit the website?
Maintenance	How is the website updated?
	Who is responsible for content updates?
	Who is responsible for structure updates?
	How will users be notified about updates to the website?
	Will the website be monitored?

Website Planning

Website planning is the first phase of the web development life cycle. As you learned in Chapter 1, it involves identifying the goals or purpose of the website. The first step in the website planning phase is to answer the question "What is the purpose of this website?" As you have learned, individuals and groups design and publish websites for a variety of purposes. People develop websites to share their hobbies, to post résumés, or to share ideas on personal interests. Organizations create websites to keep members informed of upcoming events or to recruit new members. Businesses create websites to advertise and sell products and services or to give their customers 24-hour online support. Instructors publish websites or add information to their courses using a school's online learning management system to inform students of course policies, assignments, due dates, and course requirements. Until you can adequately identify the intended purpose of the website, you should not proceed with the web development project.

In addition to understanding the website's purpose, you should also analyze who will use the website and identify the computing environments of most of the users. Knowing the makeup of your target audience, including age, gender, general demographic background, and level of computer literacy, will help you design a website appropriate for likely visitors. Understanding users' computing environments will determine what types of web technologies to use. For example, if most users have low-speed Internet connections, you would not want to create pages with large graphics or multimedia elements.

A final aspect to the website planning phase is to identify the content owners and authors. To determine this, you need to ask the following questions:

- Who owns and authors the information on the website?
- Who decides content placement on the website?

After you identify who will provide and authorize the website content, you can include those stakeholders in all aspects of the web development project.

Website Analysis

During the analysis phase, you make decisions about the website content and functionality. To help define the appropriate website content and functionality, you should first identify the tasks that users need to perform. Identifying the tasks allows you to define the controls users need to perform the tasks and determine useful information for the users. Extraneous content that does not serve any purpose should be eliminated from the website.

In the analysis phase, also consider the procedures required to support website features. For example, if you determine that users should be able to order products through the website, then you also need to define the actions to perform each time an order is submitted. For instance, how will an order travel from one back-office business application to another such as inventory control and accounts payable? Will users receive email confirmations with details about their orders? Clearly understanding and defining the desired content and functionality of the website will direct the type of website that you design and reduce changes during website development.

Website Design and Development

After determining the purpose of the website and defining the content and functionality, you need to consider the website's design. Some key considerations in website design are defining the organization for webpage content, selecting the appropriate website structure, determining how to use multimedia, addressing accessibility issues, and designing pages for an international audience. During this phase, you also determine the best way to provide navigation on the website. Recall that the navigation design can make or break a website. If users cannot easily find the information they are seeking, they will not return to your website.

You can organize a webpage in many ways. Choose an organization that makes sense for the purpose and audience of the website. Table 12–2 lists some organizational standards for creating a webpage that is easy to read and navigate.

Table 12–2 Webpage Organizational Standards

Element	Organizational Standard	Reason
Titles	Use simple titles that clearly explain the purpose of the page.	Titles help users understand the purpose of the page; a good title explains the page in the search engine results lists.
Headings	Use headings to separate main topics.	Headings make a webpage easier to read; simple headings clearly explain the purpose of the page.
Paragraphs	Use paragraphs to help divide large amounts of text.	Paragraphs provide shorter, more readable sections of text.
Lists	Use bulleted or numbered lists when appropriate.	Lists provide organized, easy-to-read text that readers can scan.
Page length	Maintain suitable webpage lengths.	Web users do not always scroll to view information on longer pages; appropriate page lengths increase the likelihood that users will view key information.
Content	Emphasize the most important information by placing it at the top of a webpage.	Web users are quick to peruse a page; placing critical information at the top of the page increases the likelihood that users will view key information.
Contact information	Provide contact information such as an email address on the home page.	Email addresses give users a way to contact a business with questions.

As discussed in Chapter 1, websites can use several types of structures, including linear, hierarchical, and webbed. Each structure connects the webpages in a different way to define how users navigate the site and view the webpages. You should select a structure for the website based on how users will navigate the site and view the website content.

As a web developer, you must select an appropriate structure for the website and work to balance breadth and depth. Users go to a website looking for information to complete a task. Good design provides ease of navigation, allowing users to find content quickly and easily. In addition to planning the design of the website itself, a web developer should plan the specifics of the file naming and storage conventions early on in the design phase. For instance, saving your webpages with names such as page1.html and page2.html does not indicate the purpose of those webpages, making them difficult to maintain. A better option would be to use file names that reflect the webpage content such as about.html, contact.html, and services.html. These file names tell the developer, as well as future developers maintaining the website, the purpose of the webpages.

The same principle applies to the folder structure that you use in your web development. It is a best practice to place images in an images folder, audio/video in a media folder, css in a css folder, and so on. Larger, more complex websites might also require a folder for webpages pertaining to specific departments. Where you store the files will affect how you access those files in your HTML code. Determining a logical folder structure in the planning phase of the web development life cycle simplifies creating and updating the pages.

During the design and development phase, consider what, if any, types of multimedia could contribute positively to the website experience. For instance, adding a video message from the company CEO might be useful, but if the computing environment of your users cannot accommodate video playback, then the video serves no purpose. In general, do not use advanced multimedia technologies in a website unless they make a positive contribution to the website experience. Today, websites increasingly are using audio and video content. Adding multimedia can enhance the overall purpose of the website, but it sometimes detracts from the message.

Finally, consider accessibility issues and **localization**, adapting a website to meet the needs of a particular language or culture. A practical approach is to design for viewing by a diverse audience, including physically impaired and global users. Consider the software that physically impaired people use when visiting websites. For instance, if you use graphics on the website, include alternative text for each graphic so that screen readers can recite the alternative text to people with low vision. To support an international audience, use generic icons that can be understood globally, avoid slang expressions in the content, and build simple pages that load quickly over lower-speed connections.

Website Testing

Test your website at various stages of the web design and development processes. The testing process should be comprehensive and include a review of webpage content, functionality, and usability. Websites with broken links, missing graphics, and incorrect content create a poor impression on visitors. You want to attract users to your website and maintain their interest. If visitors find that features of your website do not work as intended, they will be less likely to return. Having people return to your website determines whether it is successful. After all, you cannot get your message out if users do not frequently visit the website. The following are basic steps to test content and functionality:

- Validate each webpage by running it through the W3C markup validation service.
- Proofread webpage content and titles for accurate spelling and grammar.
- Check links to make sure they are not broken and use the correct targets.
- Review graphics to confirm they are displayed properly and are linked correctly.
- Ensure that accessibility and internationalization issues are addressed.
- Fill out forms and use other interactive page elements the way that visitors will use them.
- Test pages to make sure they load quickly, even over low-speed connections.
- Print each page to check its printed appearance.

Usability is the measure of how well a product, such as a website, allows a user to accomplish his or her goals. **Usability testing** is a method by which users of a website or other product are asked to perform certain tasks in an effort to measure the product's ease of use and the user's perception of the experience. Usability testing for a website should focus on three parts of the site: content, navigation, and presentation.

One effective way to conduct usability testing is to directly observe users interacting with the website. As you observe users, you can track the links they click and record their actions and comments. Ask the users to explain what tasks they were trying to accomplish while navigating the site and whether they succeeded or failed. The information gained by observing users can help you identify potential problem areas in the website and then resolve them. For example, if you observe that users have difficulty finding the webpage that lists store locations and hours of operation, you may want to clarify the link descriptions or make the links more prominent on the home page.

Another way to conduct usability testing is to give users a specific task to complete, such as finding a product price list, and then observe how they navigate the site to complete the task. If possible, ask them to explain why they selected certain links. Direct observation reveals valuable information, but does require access to users.

If you cannot work directly with users, you can perform usability testing with a questionnaire or survey. Be sure to write open-ended or scaled survey questions to elicit information. For instance, asking the yes or no question, "Is the website visually appealing?" will not gather especially useful information. If a user answers no to that question, you do not know how to improve the site to make it more appealing. Even if a user answers yes, you do not know how much appeal the website has. If you change that question to use a scaled response, such as "Rate the visual appeal of this website, using a scale of 1 for low and 5 for high," you can get more valuable input from the users. Make sure, however, that the scale itself is clear and understandable to the users. If you intend that a selection of 1 equates to a "low" rating, but the users think 1 means "high," then your survey results are questionable. Another way to ask for design feedback is to list parts of the site, such as graphics, sidebars, and navigation, and ask users to select the parts that are appealing to them. In addition, provide space on the usability testing questionnaire where users can write comments.

Table 12–3 provides an example of a usability testing questionnaire.

Table 12–3 Usability Testing Questionnaire

Statement	Strongly Agree	Agree	Neutral	Disagree	Strongly Disagree
The website is easy to navigate.					
The graphics on the website are visually appealing.					
I would recommend this website to family and friends.					
I was able to find what I was looking for.					
The website is intuitive and user-friendly.					
The information on the website is clearly organized.					

The following are additional examples of the types of open-ended questions to include in a website usability testing questionnaire.

- If you could change one thing about the website, what would it be?
- What do you like best about the website?
- What do you like least about the website?

In addition to content, functionality, and usability testing, you can conduct other types of testing. For a newly implemented or maintained website, use two other types of tests: compatibility testing and stress testing. **Compatibility testing** verifies that the website works with a variety of browsers and browser versions. Initially, test using the browsers that your audience is most likely to use. Each browser displays some aspects of webpages differently, so you must test webpages in several browsers to verify the pages appear correctly. If you have used technologies that are not supported by older browsers or that require plug-ins, consider changing the content or providing alternative webpages for viewing in older browsers. If your audience uses Windows, Mac, and Android devices, you need to test the webpages using browsers on all platforms. You may also want to test the webpages in several versions of the same browser (usually the two most recent versions), in case users have not upgraded to the most recent version.

Stress testing determines what happens on your website when many users access the site. When 120 users access a website simultaneously, for example, the performance might not suffer. However, when thousands of users access the website at the same time, it may respond at an unacceptably slow speed. Stress testing verifies that a website runs at an acceptable speed with many users. For websites published without effective stress testing, the results have been disastrous, with websites locking up when too many users tried to access the same website function. Websites used for e-commerce must stay online to sell products or services; otherwise, the company stands to suffer a loss of reputation and profit.

CONSIDER THIS

How can I test my website on multiple browsers?
You can download and install multiple browsers to view and test your website. Several resources also are available online to test websites across multiple browsers, such as browsershots.org.

Website Implementation

Implement, or publish, a website after completing the testing phase and making any required changes. Implementing a website involves the actual publishing of the webpages to a web server. As discussed in Chapter 11, many HTML editors and WYSIWYG editors provide publishing capabilities. You can also use FTP software, such as FileZilla, to publish your webpages to a web server. After you publish a website, you should test the webpages again to confirm no obvious errors have been introduced such as broken links or missing graphics.

Website Maintenance

Before you publish your website, develop a process to maintain the website. Maintenance begins the day you publish the site. Employees within the business will undoubtedly request changes and timely content will require updates. If it is a large website, the webmaster should meet with webpage content authors to discuss ongoing updates and circulate the maintenance plan for the website. A maintenance plan includes refreshing content, updating the design, adding marketing promotions, and checking links. As you make these updates, test again to avoid compromising the site's integrity and consistency. For example, if several people are updating various webpages on a large website, they need guidance to maintain a consistent look on pages across the website. Update the site maps, wireframes, and templates and provide them to everyone working on the website.

Plan to update your website on a regular basis to keep content up-to-date. This could mean hourly, daily, weekly, or less often, depending on the site's purpose. Do not allow your content to become stale, outdated, or include broken links to webpages that no longer exist.

To help manage the task of website maintenance, first determine who is responsible for updates to content, structure, functionality, and other elements. Limit update responsibilities to specific users. Be sure the implementation is controlled by one or more web developers who can verify that the webpages are tested thoroughly before they are published.

Depending on how large the website is, you may need to create a form for employees to complete when requesting a change to the website. Figure 12–6 shows an example of a website maintenance request form.

Website Maintenance Request Form			
Employee Name:			
Employee Email:			
Today's Date:			
Priority Level:	High	Medium	Low
Date Needed by:			
Detailed Change Requested:			

Figure 12–6

As updates and changes are made to a website, consider notifying users through social media and an announcement on the home page, explaining any new features and how the features will benefit them. This technique not only keeps users informed but also encourages them to come back to the website to see what is new.

Finally, monitor the website and its visitors. Usually, the web servers that host websites keep logs of information about website usage. A **log** is the file that lists all of the webpages that have been requested from the website. Analyze the logs to determine the number of visitors, browser types and versions, connection speeds, pages most commonly requested, and usage patterns. With this information, you can design a website that is effective for your target audience, providing visitors with a rich and rewarding experience.

Reviewing Websites

As you embark on your web development career, one useful practice is to be an observant web user. You probably use the web several times a day (or more often) to complete your daily tasks. As you do, review the webpages that you access with an eye on functionality and design. You can bookmark websites you find effective or ineffective, appealing or unappealing, and use them as references for your own web development efforts. Watch for trends on the web as you search for information or make online purchases. For example, blinking text and patterned backgrounds were once popular on websites, but were replaced by other design techniques. Being an observant web user can help you become a more effective web developer.

Updating Websites

After publishing the website for the Forward Fitness Club, you conducted a survey to solicit user feedback. Most users found the audio and the alert message on the home page to be distracting. Additionally, most users commented that they would prefer to start the video on the About Us page rather than have the video play automatically when the page loads. After reviewing the user feedback, you have decided to implement these changes. Owners of the Forward Fitness Club also informed you that a new instructor is teaching the Boot Camp class. Besides making this change, you also want to format the check boxes on the Contact Us page by increasing the left margin for an improved appearance.

To Update the Home Page

**1 IMPROVE HOME PAGE | 2 IMPROVE ABOUT US PAGE
3 UPDATE CLASSES PAGE | 4 UPDATE CSS FILE**

Update the home page by removing the audio element and JavaScript alert message. In a recent survey, users commented that both of these items were distracting. After removing these items, insert an h1 element to highlight the free trial membership. The following steps remove the script element and audio element on the home page and add an h1 element.

1 Open index.html, select Lines 11 through 16, and then press the DELETE key to delete the script element.

2 Press the DELETE key as many times as necessary to place the closing head tag on Line 10.

3 Select Lines 70 through 75, and then press the DELETE key to delete the audio element.

4 Press the DELETE key as many times as necessary to place the closing main tag on Line 70.

5 Tap or click at the end of Line 58 and press the ENTER key twice to insert new Lines 59 and 60.

6 On Line 60, type **FREE Trial Membership** to insert an h1 element.

7 Save your changes and open the file in your browser to view the changes (Figure 12–7).

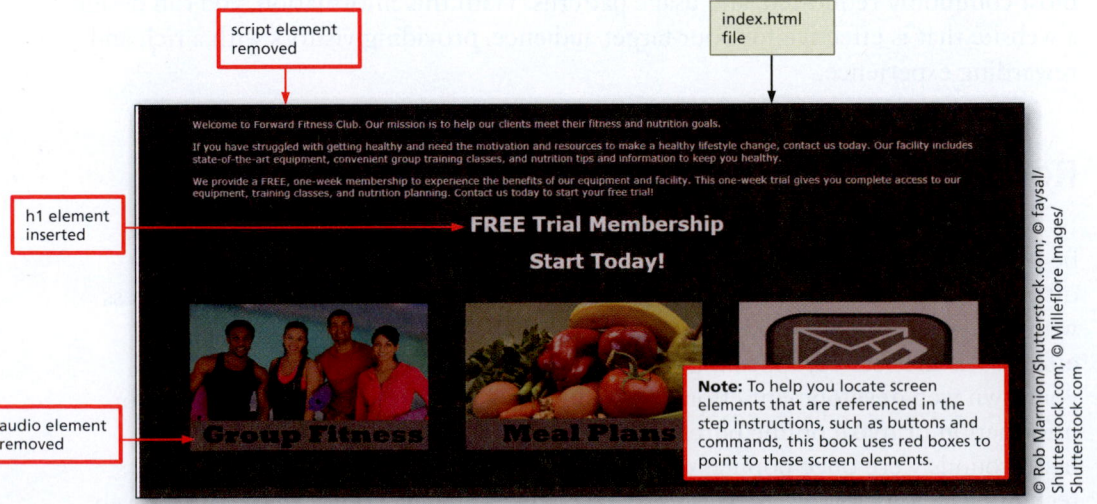

Figure 12–7

To Update the About Us Page

1 IMPROVE HOME PAGE | 2 IMPROVE ABOUT US PAGE
3 UPDATE CLASSES PAGE | 4 UPDATE CSS FILE

Update the About Us page by removing the autoplay attribute from the video element and add a poster attribute that displays an image before the video is played. In a recent survey, users commented that they wanted control over whether to play the video. Because the video will not play automatically when the page opens, use a poster attribute to display an image for the video element rather than displaying a blank frame. The following steps remove the autoplay attribute from the video element and add a poster attribute to the video element on the About Us page.

1 Open about.html in your text editor, and then scroll to Line 36.

2 Delete the autoplay attribute from the starting video tag to remove it.

3 Tap or click after the controls attribute within the starting video tag element, insert a space, and then type `poster="images/homeBanner.jpg"` to insert a poster attribute and value.

4 Save your changes and open the file in your browser to view the changes (Figure 12–8).

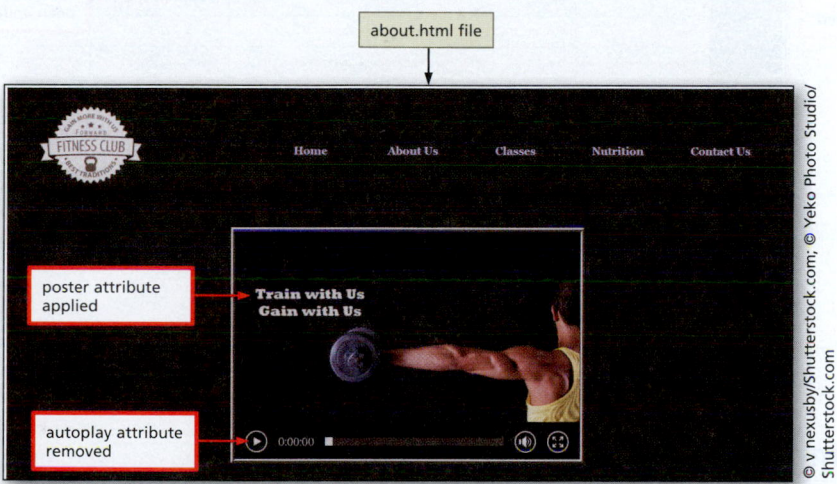

about.html file

poster attribute applied

Train with Us
Gain with Us

autoplay attribute removed

© v nexusby/Shutterstock.com; © Yeko Photo Studio/ Shutterstock.com

Figure 12–8

To Update the Classes Page

1 IMPROVE HOME PAGE | 2 IMPROVE ABOUT US PAGE
3 UPDATE CLASSES PAGE | 4 UPDATE CSS FILE

Update the Classes page by modifying the class information. List the Boot Camp class in the second row and list the Cardio class in the third row. The Boot Camp class instructor recently moved out of the area, so you need to update the instructor information. The following steps update the table information on the Classes page.

1 Open classes.html in your text editor, select Lines 63 through 67, and then press the CTRL+X keys to cut the code. Be sure to leave a blank line on Line 63.

2 Tap or click before the table data element on Line 66 and then press the ENTER key to place the first table element on Line 67.

3 On Line 66, press the CTRL+V keys to paste the code within Row 3.

4 Select Lines 71 through 75 and then press the CTRL+X keys to cut the code.

5 Tap or click on Line 63 and then press the CTRL+V keys to paste the code.

6 If necessary, tap or click Line 75 and press the BACKSPACE key as many times as necessary to move the ending table row tag up to Line 75.

7 On Line 66, replace the text within the table data element with `Lawrence` to update the instructor information.

8 Save your changes and open the file in your browser to view the changes (Figure 12–9).

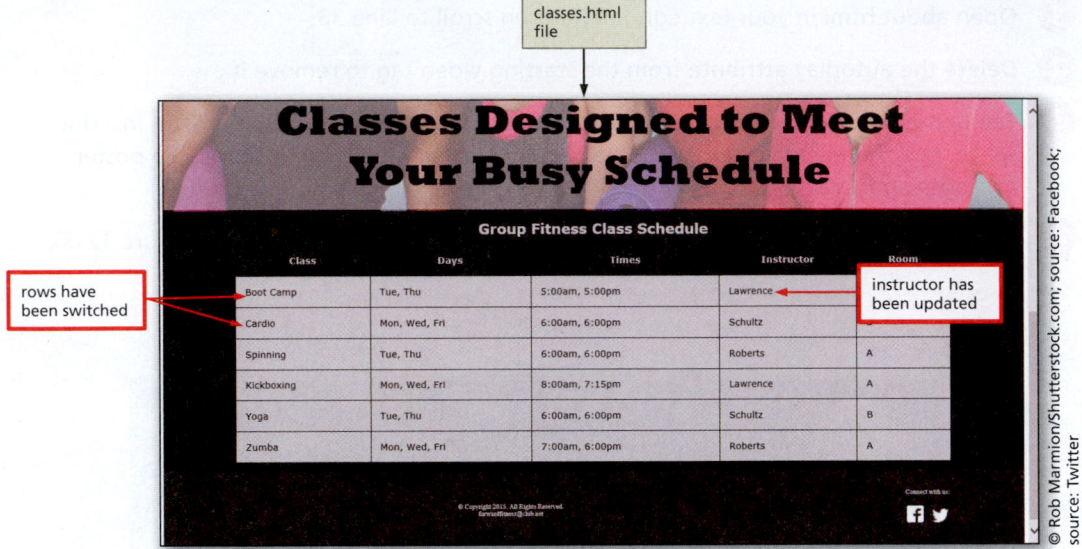

Figure 12–9

To Improve the Contact Us Page

1 IMPROVE HOME PAGE | 2 IMPROVE ABOUT US PAGE
3 UPDATE CLASSES PAGE | 4 UPDATE CSS FILE

Improve the Contact Us page by applying a left margin to the check boxes within the form. The check boxes are contained within an unordered list element. You create a new style rule in the tablet media query that applies a left margin to the unordered list within the form. The following steps create a new style rule within the tablet media query.

1 Open styles.css in your text editor, tap or click at the end of Line 360, and then press the ENTER key twice to insert new Lines 361 and 362.

2 On Line 362, type `/* Style rule for form unordered list element */` to insert a comment.

3 Press the ENTER key to insert a new Line 363 and then type `form ul {` to begin a new style rule.

4 Press the ENTER key to insert a new Line 364, increase the indent, and then type `margin-left: 2em;` to insert a property and value.

5 Press the ENTER key to insert a new Line 365, decrease the indent, and then type `}` to insert a closing brace (Figure 12–10).

Figure 12–10

6 Open contact.html in your text editor, delete the script element on Line 10, and then delete the blank line so that the closing head element appears on Line 10.

7 Save your changes, open contact.html in your browser to view the changes, and then resize the window to tablet width (Figure 12–11).

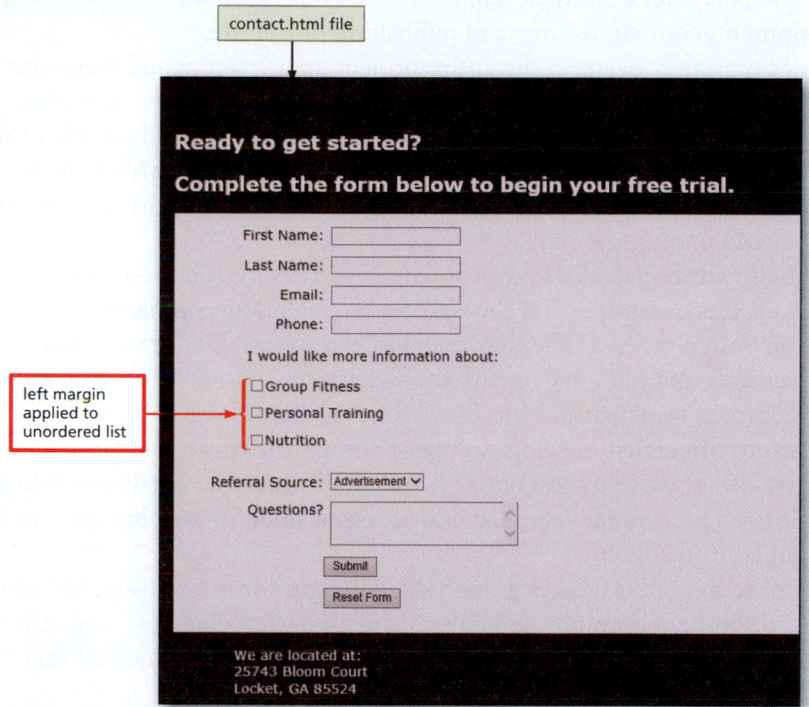

Figure 12–11

Project Management

If you are working with a large website, such as the National Park Service website at nps.gov, you must manage website updates efficiently to keep the site current and working online. Figure 12–12 shows a site map for the National Park Service website.

This website contains numerous pages and information about parks all around the United States. One person alone could not design, develop, monitor, and update this website. A project team must manage a large website such as the National Park Service website. Project team members include a project manager, website strategist,

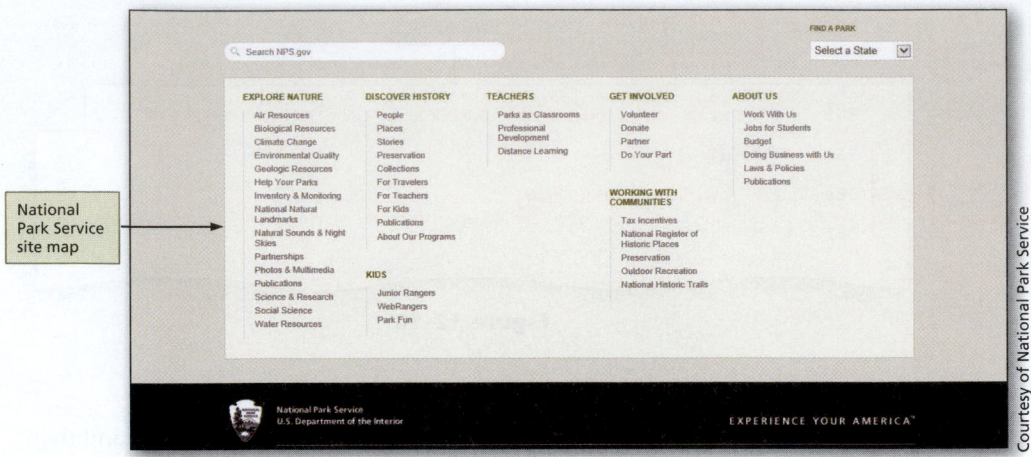

National Park Service site map

Figure 12–12

content specialist, graphic designer, website designer, website developer, marketing professional, and a network administrator. **Project management** of a website involves delegating and supervising website development activities, including the planning, design, development, content, testing, and publishing of the site.

A **project manager** oversees the entire project management and maintains a timeline of project tasks and goals. The project manager creates a project plan, which includes a schedule and project deliverables, and then tracks all aspects of the project, delegates tasks, and evaluates the website against high standards to make sure it meets its goals and serves its audience. The project manager must have exceptional communication and managerial skills.

The **website strategist**, also known as a user interface (UI) or user experience (UX) architect, creates the strategy for the web design, including completing the planning phase of the web design process. The web strategist is responsible for researching competitors' websites, analyzing the organization's current website, identifying the target audience, and creating a sitemap and wireframe for the new website.

The **content specialist** develops webpage content to attract the target audience through creative use of written messages. The person in this role needs experience in persuasive writing. The content specialist is also responsible for keeping content fresh and writing and editing content.

The **graphic designer** creates graphics and images for the website, including business logos, digital photography and enhancement, design elements, and other graphic images. The graphic designer should be well-versed in graphics-editing software and optimizing graphics for web use.

The **website designer** takes the wireframes created by the website strategist and creates mock-up webpages. The designer's role is to create site concepts for the team to review. After a concept is approved, it is given to the website developer.

The **website developer** develops the webpages for the website. This project team member uses the mock-up webpage concepts to create the actual webpages. The website developer uses HTML, CSS, and other web programming languages to develop the desired webpages. The website developer works closely with the website designer, the content specialist, and the graphic designer.

The **marketing professional** designs a market campaign to drive traffic to the website. This person may be someone within the organization's marketing department or a consultant hired to provide marketing services. The marketing professional works closely with the content specialist.

The **network administrator** sets up and maintains the web server that will house the website. The network administrator may be someone within the organization's IT department or a member of a different company. The person in this role ensures that the website is accessible via the Internet. The network administrator is also responsible for the hardware, software, and security needed to keep the website running smoothly.

Who puts a website project team together?
The project manager is typically the person in charge of delegating website tasks. The project manager should use experienced team members and carefully review each team member's portfolio, education, and past experience.

Content Updates

Updating website content is an ongoing process. When a business launches a new product or service, its website content must be updated to reflect the changes. Updating a website regularly can help increase search engine results and improve SEO. The following is a list of tips to keep your content updated and fresh.

- When you have a new product or service, add an image or video to your website to showcase it.
- If your company submits press releases on a regular basis, create a page for press releases, as this shows that your business is active and busy.
- Consider a page for client testimonials to spur potential sales.
- Update your social media on regular basis.

Copyright Law

You may find images, audio, and video online that fit the needs of your website, but think twice before downloading media to use on your website. The person or business who created the media is the owner of the media. You cannot legally use media content created by someone else without permission. You must be granted permission to use the media on your website. This includes photographs, illustrations, audio, video, and other webpage content.

At times, it is acceptable to use media created by another source on your website. Students and educators may use online media for educational purposes, such as an academic project. This is known as **fair use**. To qualify for fair use, the media must not be used for any type of commercial business.

Use of a **Creative Commons license** lets media content authors share their work with others, while maintaining ownership of their work. The Creative Commons license specifies appropriate use of the media. For more information about the Creative Commons license, visit creativecommons.org.

BTW
U.S. Copyright Law
For more information about U.S. copyright law, visit copyright.gov.

Can I purchase media for use on my website?
Yes. Several online resources provide images, audio, and video for a fee. Some examples of online media resources include gettyimages.com, istockphoto.com, and shutterstock.com.

Content Management Systems

Content management systems (CMSs) have become increasingly popular with many online businesses. A **CMS** is an online system used to manage website content. A typical CMS consists of a content management application (CMA) and a content delivery application (CDA). Using a CMA, a webpage author can add, remove, and update content without knowing HTML. After the author makes the necessary modifications, the CDA compiles the changes and writes the underlying code "behind the scenes." With a CMS, a web developer can create and preserve, or lock, a design so that webpage authors can only update content and not the design. Locking a design is especially helpful when novice users are updating webpage content. A CMS also allows multiple authors to update their pages as necessary. It also provides peace of mind to the webmaster, knowing that the website design cannot be undone by an inexperienced webpage author. Popular CMSs include WordPress, Joomla, and Drupal.

Figure 12–13 shows the home page for WordPress. Several businesses use WordPress for their websites and blogs. Nearly 25 percent of all websites use WordPress, making it one of the top-ranked CMSs with over 50 percent market share, according to w3techs.com.

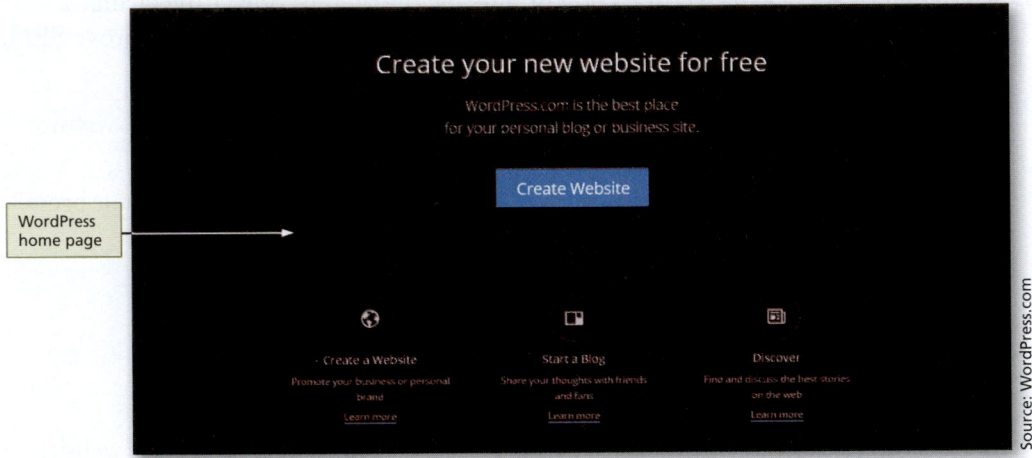

Figure 12–13

WordPress offers web developers many tools for building a website. They also provide support and functionality for high-traffic e-commerce websites. *Forbes* is a popular source for business news and financial information and uses WordPress for its website. The *Forbes* home page is shown in Figure 12–14.

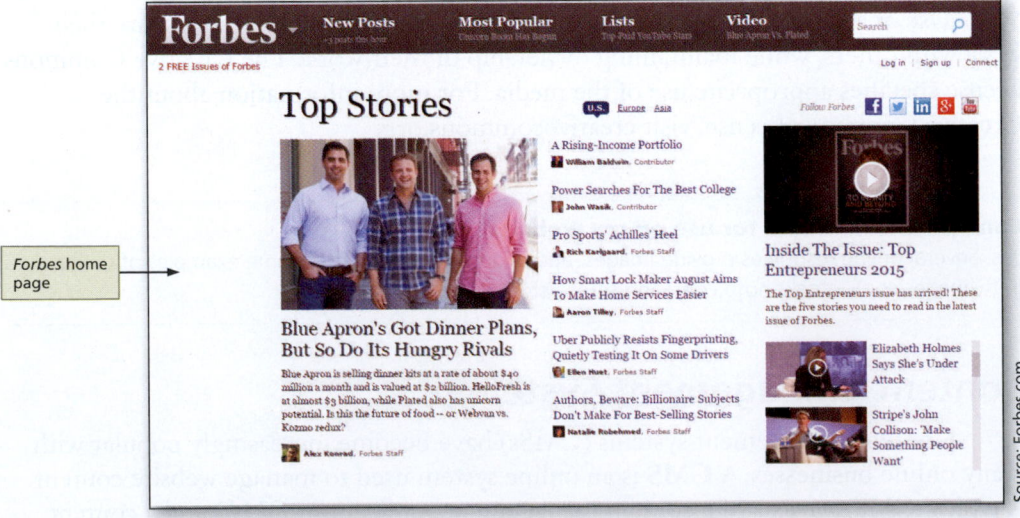

Figure 12–14

Figure 12–15 shows the home page for Joomla. Joomla is an open-source CMS, ideal for experienced web developers who enjoy coding.

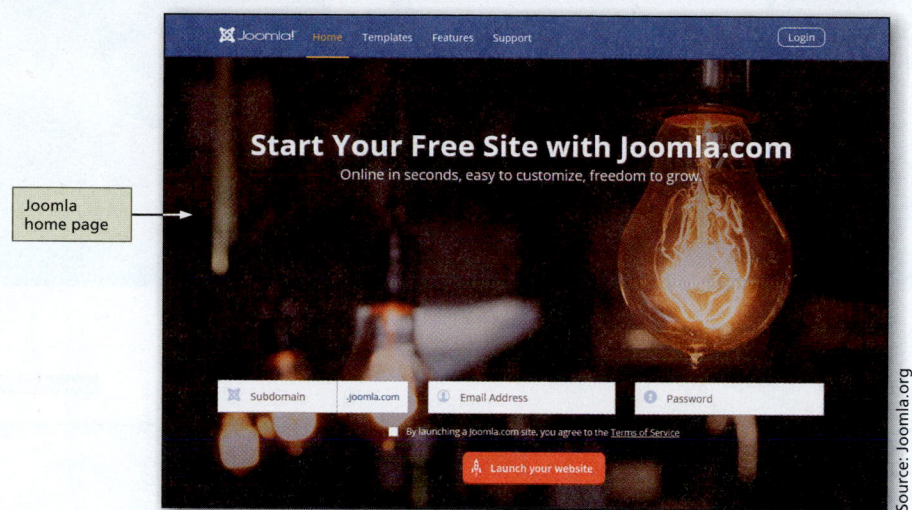

Figure 12–15

Joomla offers many of the same tools as WordPress for developing a website. E-commerce, nonprofit, and government websites are some of those using Joomla for their CMS. For example, Outdoor Photographer uses Joomla for its online magazine. The home page for Outdoor Photographer is shown in Figure 12–16.

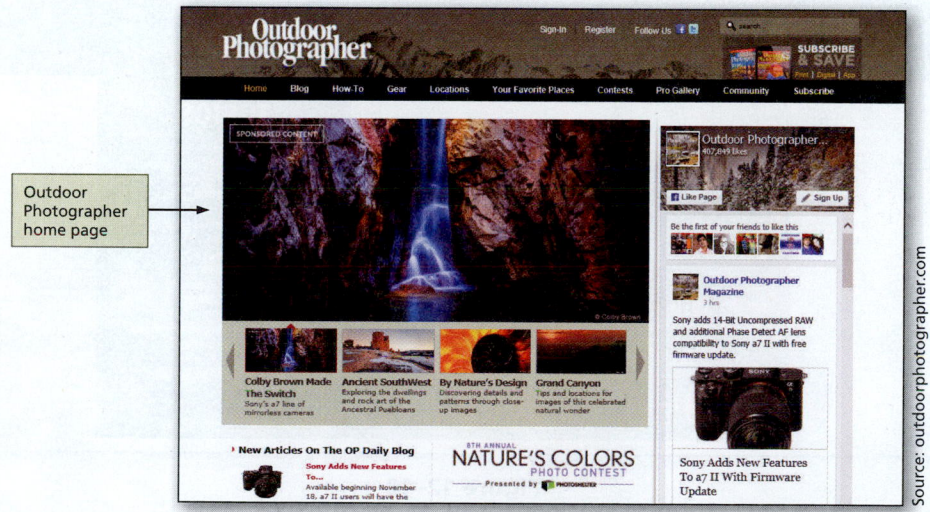

Figure 12–16

Figure 12–17 shows the home page for Drupal, another open-source CMS, distributed under the GNU General Public License.

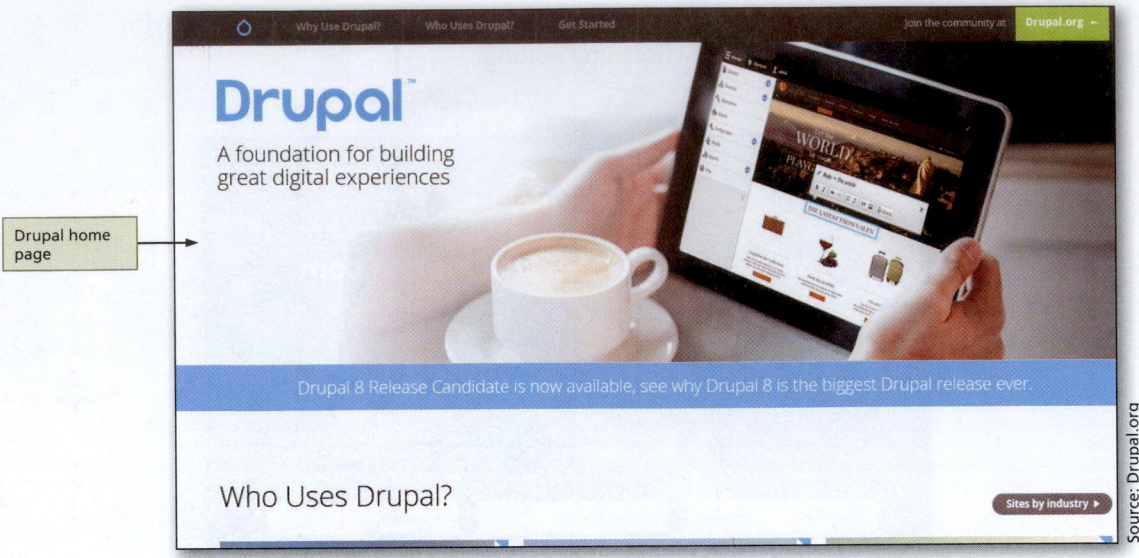

Source: Drupal.org

Figure 12–17

Georgia.gov is a government agency that uses Drupal for its website. Its home page is shown in Figure 12–18.

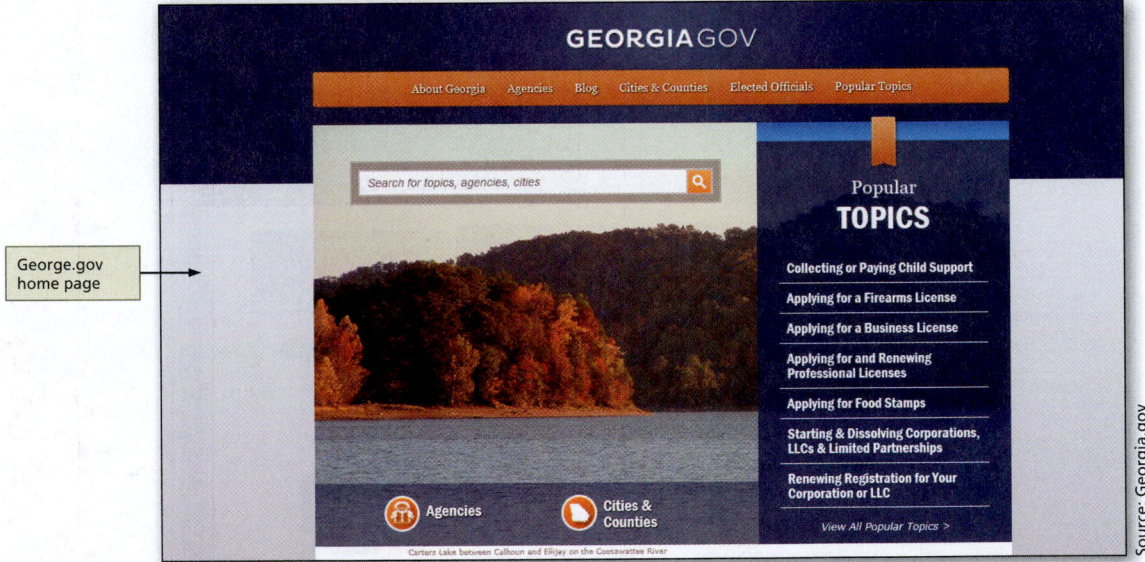

Source: Georgia.gov

Figure 12–18

Web Frameworks

A **web framework** is software that allows a web developer to use a collection of tools to build a web application, which simplifies the website building process. Web frameworks provide a website additional functionality, such as a database, session management, and cookies. Using a web framework can save web developers a significant amount of time coding a website. Popular frameworks include Django, Bootstrap, Ruby on Rails, CakePHP, and Fusebox. Django is shown in Figure 12–19 and Bootstrap is shown in Figure 12–20.

Source: djangoproject.com

Figure 12–19

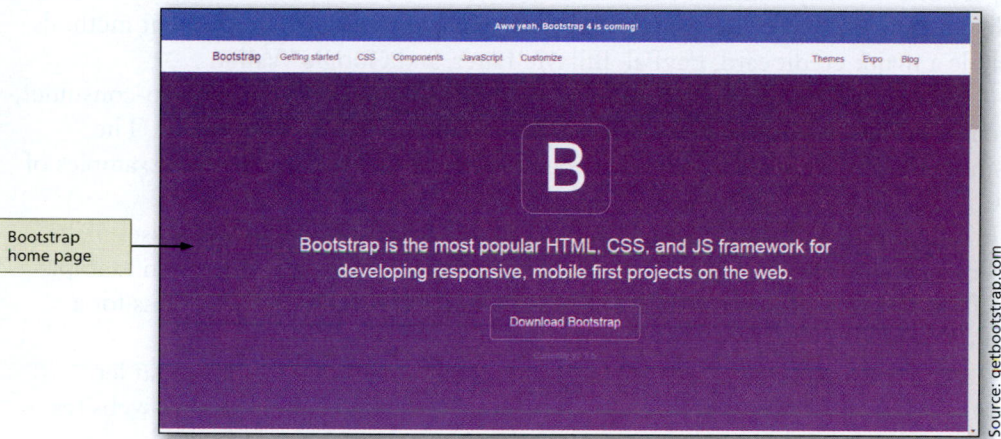

Source: getbootstrap.com

Figure 12–20

E-Commerce

The term electronic commerce, or **e-commerce**, refers to businesses that conduct transactions online, including large retail websites that sell products to consumers. Amazon, shown in Figure 12–21, is a popular e-commerce website that sells an array of products to consumers.

Source: Amazon.com

Figure 12–21

BTW

Transport Layer Security

Transport Layer Security (TLS) was created to replace SSL. It blocks any third party from capturing data as it is transferred from one machine to another, such as a client device to a server.

E-commerce is a booming business. Having an online store open around the clock allows businesses to sell products anytime. Online customers enjoy the convenience of finding, reviewing, and purchasing products at e-commerce sites.

E-commerce also has drawbacks. With the rise in identity theft and fraud, some consumers hesitate to make purchases online. An e-commerce business must invest time and money into securing their systems. For enhanced security, an e-commerce site should implement secure socket layer (SSL) technology to encrypt sensitive customer information.

E-commerce websites must also consider what happens if a server fails and the site is not accessible to customers. These websites must ensure their connections, create and maintain several backups, and have a plan in place to deal with potential technology issues that may arise.

E-commerce websites must also have a proven and tested interface to handle orders, which usually takes the form of electronic shopping carts. Website developers can use one of many online tools to create and maintain shopping carts. E-commerce website must also be able to efficiently handle payments. Common payment methods include a major credit card, PayPal, Bill Me Later, and Google Wallet.

E-commerce websites use four common business models: business-to-consumer, business-to-business, consumer-to-consumer, and business-to-government. The business-to-consumer (B2C) model is the most common business model. Examples of B2C e-commerce websites include Amazon and Wayfair.

The business-to-business (B2B) business model is used when businesses make purchases from other businesses, such as supplies required by a business. An example of a B2B business model is a wholesale glass manufacturer that supplies glass for a window company.

The consumer-to-consumer (C2C) business model is for websites that let consumers buy from and sell to each other. Examples of C2C e-commerce websites include eBay and Etsy.

The business-to-government (B2G) business model occurs when government makes online purchases from a business. An example of a B2G business model may include a government agency purchasing software from an online vendor.

To Validate the Style Sheet

Always run your files through W3C's validator to check the document for errors. If the document has any errors, validating gives you a chance to identify and correct them. Validation is also an effective troubleshooting tool during the development process and adds a valuable level of professionalism to your work. The following steps validate a CSS document.

1 Open your browser and type `http://jigsaw.w3.org/css-validator/` in the address bar to display the W3C CSS Validation Service page.

2 Tap or click the By file upload tab to display the Validate by file upload information.

3 Tap or click the Browse button to display the Choose File to Upload dialog box.

4 Navigate to your css folder to find, select, and upload the styles.css file to the W3C CSS validator.

5 Tap or click the Check button to send the document through the validator and display the validation results page.

6 If necessary, correct any errors, save your changes, and run through the validator again to revalidate the page.

To Validate the HTML Files

Every time you create a new webpage or modify an existing webpage, run it through W3C's validator to check the document for errors. If any errors exist, you need to correct them. Validation is also an effective troubleshooting tool during the development process and adds a valuable level of professionalism to your work. The following steps validate an HTML document.

1 Open your browser and type `validator.w3.org` in the address bar to display the W3C HTML validator page.

2 If necessary, tap or click the Validate By File Upload tab.

3 Tap or click the Browse button to display the Choose File to Upload dialog box.

4 Navigate to your fitness folder to find, select, and upload the index.html file to the W3C validator.

5 Tap or click the Check button to send the document through the validator and display the validation results page.

6 If necessary, correct any errors, save your changes, and run through the validator again to revalidate the page.

7 Follow these steps to validate all HTML pages within your fitness folder and correct any errors.

Chapter Summary

In this chapter, you learned about the website development life cycle. You learned about website project management and the team members needed to support the website project. You learned about website maintenance and content updates. You also learned about content management systems. You also learned about e-commerce and frameworks. The items listed below include all the new skills you have learned in this chapter, with the tasks grouped by activity.

Website Development Life Cycle
Website Planning (HTML 534)
Website Analysis (HTML 534)
Website Design and Development (HTML 534)
Website Testing (HTML 536)
Website Implementation (HTML 538)
Website Maintenance (HTML 538)

Reviewing Websites (HTML 539)
Updating Websites (HTML 540)

Project Management
Content Updates (HTML 545)
Copyright Law (HTML 545)
Content Management Systems (HTML 545)
Web Frameworks (HTML 548)

How will you develop your project team and maintenance plan?
Use these guidelines as you complete the assignments in this chapter and create your own webpages outside of this class.

1. Determine project team members.

   a) Conduct internal interviews for potential team members.

   b) Externally advertise positions.

2. Decide how to handle maintenance and update requests.

   a) Determine who will have access to update website content.

   b) Determine how you will manage content update requests.

CONSIDER THIS

3. Decide if you should use a content management system.

    a) Determine if a content management system is best for your business.

    b) Determine which content management system to use.

4. Determine if you should use web frameworks.

    a) Review web framework options.

    b) Learn how to develop a website using web frameworks.

CONSIDER THIS

How should you submit solutions to questions in the assignments identified with a symbol?

Every assignment in this book contains one or more questions identified with a ✹ symbol. These questions require you to think beyond the assigned presentation. Present your solutions to the questions in the format required by your instructor. Possible formats may include one or more of these options: create a document that contains the answer; present your answer to the class; discuss your answer in a group; record the answer as audio or video using a webcam, smartphone, or portable media player; or post answers on a blog, wiki, or website.

Apply Your Knowledge

Reinforce the skills and apply the concepts you learned in this chapter.

Updating a Webpage

Instructions: In this exercise, you review a webpage, update its content, and improve its appearance. Work with the apply12.html file in the apply folder, image files in the apply\images folder, and applystyles12.css file in the apply\css folder from the Data Files for Students. The completed webpage is shown in Figure 12–22. You will also use professional web development practices to indent, space, comment, and validate your code.

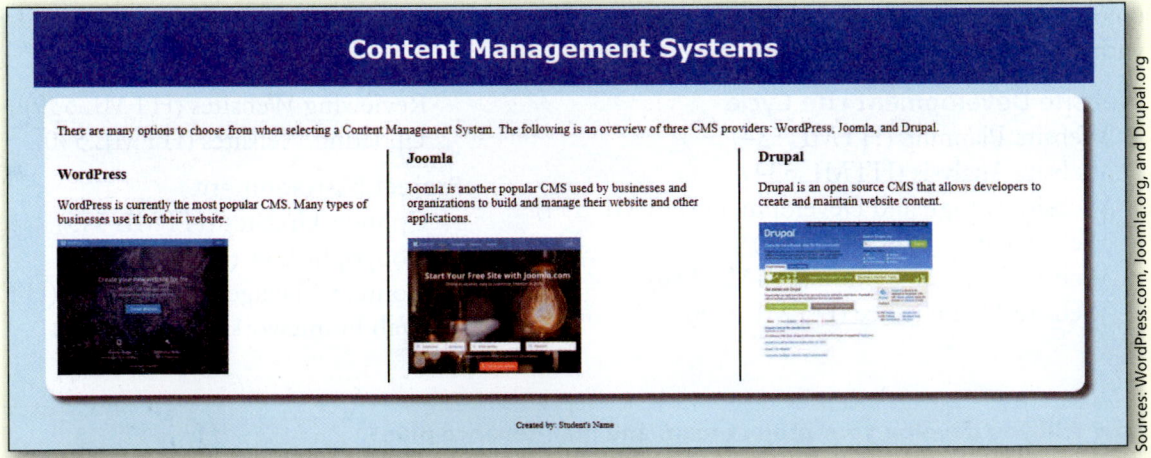

Figure 12–22

Perform the following tasks:

1. Create a new folder named apply12 and copy the apply12.html file and the css and images folders from the Data Files for Students to the apply12 folder.

2. Open apply12.html in your text editor, review the page, add a title, modify the comment at the top of the page to include your name and today's date, and a paragraph element with your name in the footer element.

3. Insert a paragraph element below each **h3** element and include one to two sentences about each content management system.

4. Insert an **img** element after each paragraph element that uses the appropriate image from the apply\images folder. Include appropriate alt text, a width attribute, and a height attribute.

5. Link each image to the respective website (WordPress, Joomla, and Drupal).

6. Rename the CSS file within the css folder to applystyles12.css and update the CSS file link in the apply12.html file.

7. Open applystyles12.css in your text editor and add the following properties and values to the header style rule:

```
background-color: #1427A6;

color: #FFFFFF;
```

8. Create a new style rule for the h1 element that center aligns text. Include a comment above the new style rule.

9. Update the main style rule to specify a white background color.

10. Create a new style rule for the article element that specifies the following properties:

```
column-count: 3;

-webkit-column-count: 3; /* Chrome, Safari, Opera */

-moz-column-count: 3; /* Firefox */

column-gap: 3em;

-webkit-column-gap: 3em; /* Chrome, Safari, Opera */

-moz-column-gap: 3em; /* Firefox */

column-rule-style: solid;

-webkit-column-rule-style: solid; /* Chrome, Safari, Opera */

-moz-column-rule-style: solid; /* Firefox */
```

11. Add a comment to the article style rule.

12. Update the footer style rule to specify top margin with a value of 3em.

13. Save all of your changes and open the apply12.html in your browser.

14. Validate your HTML document and CSS file and fix any errors that are identified.

15. Submit the files in a format specified by your instructor.

16. ✹ Research an online ticketing system to handle website maintenance requests and discuss how you could implement this type of system for your website.

Extend Your Knowledge

Extend the skills you learned in this chapter and experiment with new skills. You may need to use additional resources to complete the assignment.

Copyright Law

Instructions: In this exercise, you research more information about copyright law as it pertains to websites. You will summarize your findings and provide examples of what you may do and what you may not do when it comes to copyright law and website media content.

Perform the following tasks:

1. Use your browser to research copyright law as it pertains to the Internet.

2. Create a webpage with a summary of your findings and include at least three links to helpful resources.

Continued >

Extend Your Knowledge *continued*

3. Find and list at least two resources for media options with a Creative Commons license.

4. Submit the document in a format specified by your instructor.

5. ✹ Research more information about fair use and discuss how a student should document their media sources within a website.

Analyze, Correct, Improve

Analyze a website, correct all errors, and improve it.

Correcting and Improving Website Content

Instructions: Review the analyze12.html file in the analyze folder from the Data Files for Students. Display the page in a web browser and note the improvements you would make for this webpage. First, correct the hyperlinks. Next, update the webpage content. Then, improve the appearance of the webpage by updating the CSS file. Finally, review your changes and validate your files. Use Figure 12–23 as a guide to correct these files.

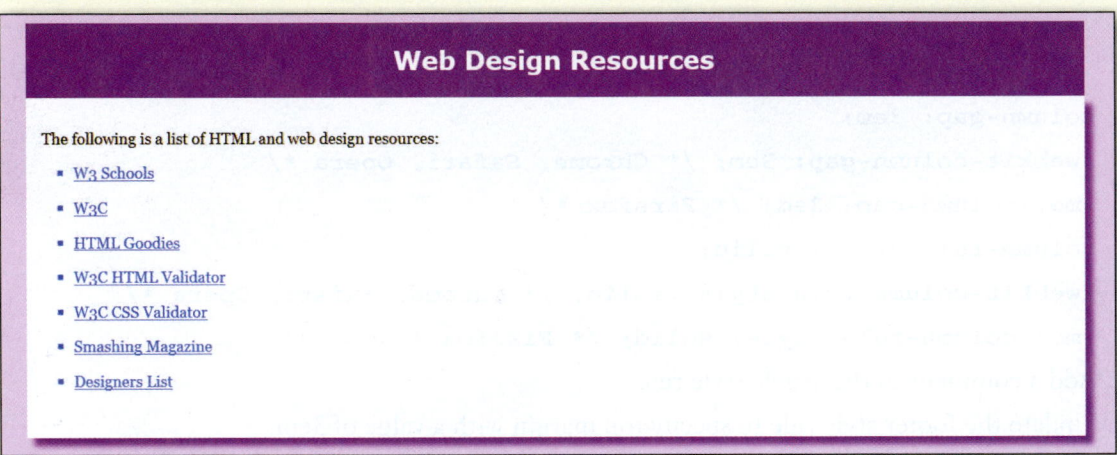

Figure 12–23

1. Correct

a. Open the analyze12.html file in your text editor from the Data Files for Students. Modify the comment at the top of the page to include your name and today's date and then link the file to analyzestyles12.css.

b. Open the analyzestyles12.css file in your text editor from the Data Files for Students and then modify and correct the comment at the top of the document to include your name and today's date.

c. Open analyze12.html in your web browser and test the hyperlinks. Note the hyperlinks to be corrected.

d. Return to analyze12.html in your text editor and correct the hyperlinks.

e. Add a paragraph element to the footer element that contains your first and last name.

2. Improve

a. Add three more HTML5 resources to the unordered list and include links for each.

b. Update the analyzestyles12.css file to be consistent with Figure 12–23.

c. Save all of your changes and open the analyze12.html in your browser.

d. Validate your CSS file using the W3C validator found at http://jigsaw.w3.org/css-validator/ and fix any errors that are identified.

e. Validate your HTML webpage using the W3C validator found at validator.w3.org and fix any errors that are identified.

f. ✷ Research content strategy ideas and discuss your findings.

In the Labs

Labs 1 and 2, which increase in difficulty, require you to create webpages based on what you learned in the chapter; Lab 3 requires you to dive deeper into a topic covered in the chapter.

Lab 1: Updating and Improving the New Harvest Food Bank Website

Problem: You volunteer at a local food bank called New Harvest Food Bank that collects community food donations and provides food and other services to those in need. You have already created a responsive website and recently conducted a user survey. The survey results indicate that users would prefer to start the video located on the home page instead of having the video play automatically. Mobile users note that they prefer to see a list of immediate needs instead of the video. In addition, you also reviewed the website and determined a number of improvements to make to the style sheet to improve the appearance of the website. The updated mobile home page is shown in Figure 12–24. The updated desktop home page is shown in Figure 12–25. The updated desktop About page is shown in Figure 12–26. The updated desktop Volunteer page is shown in Figure 12–27.

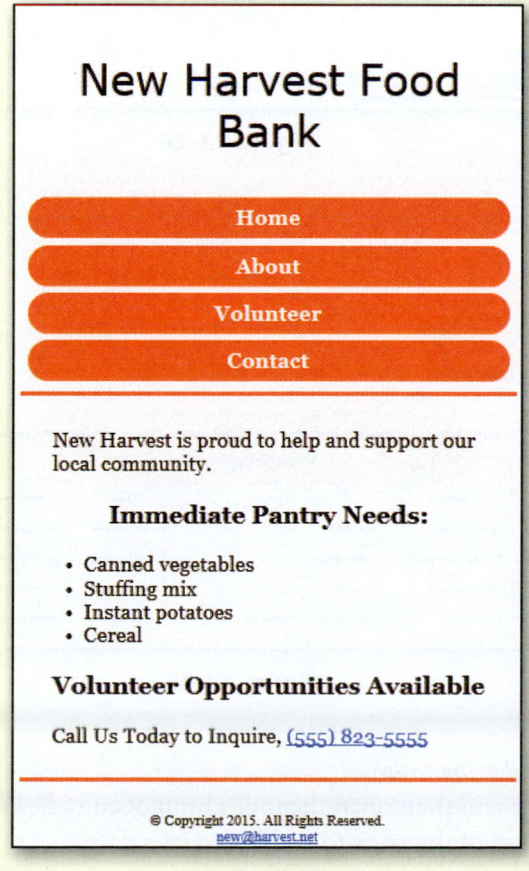

Figure 12–24

Continued >

In the Labs *continued*

Figure 12–25

Figure 12–26

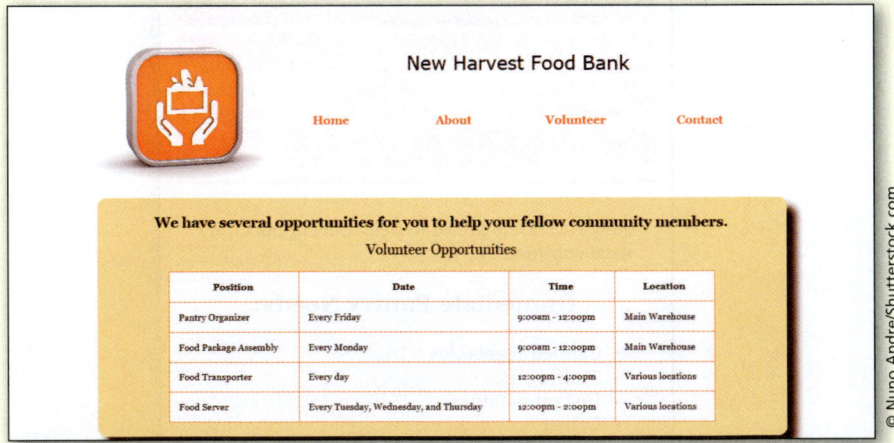

Figure 12–27

Instructions: Perform the following tasks:

1. Open your text editor and then open the index.html document in the lab1 folder and update the comment at the top of the page to include today's date.

2. Remove the autoplay attribute from the video element.

3. Add the poster attribute to the video element and use `images/logo.jpg` as the value.

4. Move the div class="video" element to the div class="desktop" element and place it above the first paragraph element within the div desktop class.

5. Add an h3 element below the first paragraph element within the div class="mobile" element and add `Immediate Pantry Needs:` as the text.

6. Create an unordered list below the h3 element with the following four list items: `Canned vegetables, Stuffing mix, Instant potatoes, Cereal`.

7. Open fbstyles.css in your text editor and create the following new comment and style rule above the media queries.

```
/* Style rule for h2 and h3 elements */
h2, h3 {
text-align: center;
}
```

8. Update the main style rule within the desktop media query by adding a background color property with `#FAE5A0` as the value.

9. Update the section style rule within the desktop media query by adding a background color property with `transparent` as the value.

10. Update the table style rule within the desktop media query by adding a background color property with `#FFFFFF` as the value.

11. Save all of your changes and review each page within the website in all three viewports.

12. Validate your HTML code and fix any errors.

13. Validate your CSS code and fix any errors.

14. Submit your assignment in the format specified by your instructor.

15. ✳ In this chapter, you learned about the various team members needed to create a website. Select one of the roles for a team member, research more about the role, and summarize your findings.

Lab 2: Updating and Improving the Steve's Screen Services Website

Problem: You work for a screening company called Steve's Screen Services that specializes in screening, cleaning, and repairing screened patios. You have created a responsive website for the business, but now need to update and improve the website. You update content on the home page. Then you update the style sheet to improve the website. The updated home page is shown in Figure 12–28. The updated services page is shown in Figure 12–29. The updated desktop gallery page is shown in Figure 12–30.

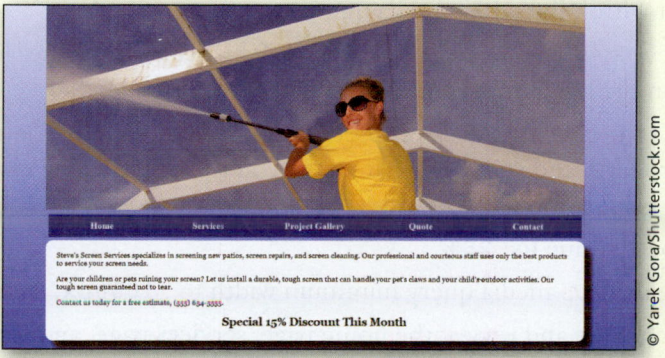

Figure 12–28

Continued >

In the Labs *continued*

Figure 12–29

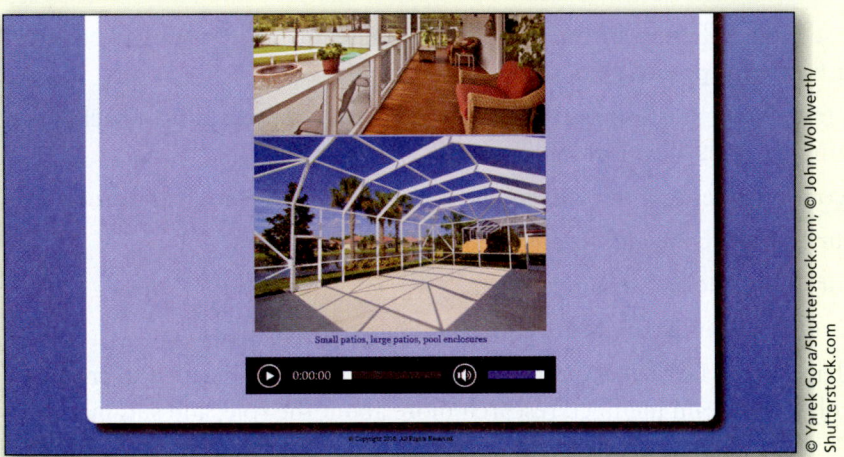

Figure 12–30

Instructions: Perform the following tasks:

1. Open the index.html document and update the comment at the top of the page to include today's date.

2. Insert an h2 element below the last paragraph element within the desktop div class and include the text, `Special 15% Discount This Month`, within the h2 element.

3. Open gallery.html in your text editor and remove the autoplay attribute from the audio tag.

4. Open screenstyles.css in your text editor and create a new style rule for the h2 element that centers text within the tablet media query.

5. Create a new style rule for main paragraph elements that specifies left and right padding of `1em` within the tablet media query.

6. Locate the style rule for the hover pseudo class within the desktop media query and remove the font size property and style and change the color property value to `#9DBDF5`.

7. Locate the style rule for the section element within the desktop media query and update the width property value to `25%`.

8. Update the desktop media query minimum width to `1050px`.

9. Save your changes and review the home page, services page, and the gallery page in a desktop viewport.

10. Validate your HTML code and fix any errors.

11. Validate your CSS code and fix any errors.

12. Submit your assignment in the format specified by your instructor.

13. ✴ In this chapter, you learned about browser compatibility testing. Research the web for an online resource that can test a webpage in multiple browsers and summarize your findings.

Lab 3: Expand Your World
Getting Started with Bootstrap

Problem: In this chapter you learned about website frameworks. In this exercise, you will research more about Bootstrap to learn more about how to use it.

Instructions:

1. Use your browser to visit getbootstrap.com and review the information on the website.

2. Summarize your findings.

3. Outline the steps to download and use Bootstrap.

4. Identify hardware and software requirements for Bootstrap.

5. Submit your answers in the format specified by your instructor.

6. ✴ In this exercise, you discovered more about Bootstrap, a web framework. Research other web frameworks and list at least three others that you found and the URL for each.

Consider This: Your Turn

Apply your creative thinking and problem-solving skills to design and implement a solution.

1. Improving and Updating Your Personal Portfolio Website
Personal

Part 1: As you have learned in Chapter 12, updating and maintaining a website is a continuous process. In this exercise, you review your personal portfolio website and determine ways to improve its design and update its content.

1. Review each page and determine ways to improve the website.

2. Review the content on each page and update it as necessary.

3. Update your CSS file and include comments for all changes.

4. Update your HTML pages and include comments for all changes.

5. Submit your assignment in the format specified by your instructor.

Part 2: ✴ Discuss how you would create a webpage that showcases examples of your website design skills.

2. Improving and Updating the WebDevPros Website
Professional

Part 1: In this exercise, you review the WebDevPros website and determine ways to improve the site's appearance and update its content. Update the site as follows:

1. Review each webpage and determine how you will improve the website.

2. Review each webpage and determine content updates.

3. Update your CSS file name to `webdevstyles12.css` in the styles folder within the your_turn_2 folder.

Continued >

Consider This: Your Turn *continued*

4. Update the current date within the comment area at the top of the webdevstyles12.css file.

5. Open the HTML files from Chapter 11 in your HTML editor and add the current date to the comment near the top of the page.

6. Modify the link to the external style sheet to reference webdevstyles12.css.

7. Determine the content updates for each page. At a minimum, update the HTML page to do the following:

   a. Update content on at least two pages.

   b. Include comments to note all changes.

8. Update the CSS file to:

   a. Implement desired changes and improvements.

   b. Add comments to note all changes and updates.

9. Save and test your files.

10. Validate and correct your HTML and CSS files, and submit your assignment in the format specified by your instructor.

Part 2: ✳ Research more information about web frameworks and determine which framework you would consider implementing for the WebDevPros website.

3. Improving and Updating the Design of the Dog Hall of Fame Website

Research and Collaboration

Part 1: In this exercise, you review the website as a team and decide how you will improve the website and update the website content. Do the following activities as a group:

1. Review each webpage and discuss ways to improve the website.

2. Review each webpage and discuss content updates.

3. Create a user survey and obtain feedback from at least ten users.

4. Review the user feedback and note other areas of improvement.

5. Update your CSS file name to **dogstyles12.css** in the styles folder within the your_turn_3 folder.

6. Add your names and the current date as a comment to the first line of the dogstyles12.css file.

7. Open the files you created for the Dog Hall of Fame in Chapter 11 in your HTML editor and make sure your names and the current date are added as a comment to the first line of all files.

8. Modify the link to the external style sheet to reference dogstyles12.css.

9. Discuss the content updates for each page. At a minimum, update the HTML page to do the following:

   a. Update content on each page.

   b. Include comments to note all changes.

10. Update the CSS file to:

    a. Implement the discussed changes.

    b. Add comments to note all changes and updates.

11. Save and test your files.

12. Validate and correct your HTML and CSS files, and submit your assignment in the format specified by your instructor.

Part 2: ✳ As a group, discuss ideas to expand the website and note a new webpage that could be added to the website.

HTML Quick Reference

Common HTML Elements

HTML uses tags such as <h1> and <p> to structure content into headings, paragraphs, lists, hypertext links, and so on. Many HTML tags have attributes that further structure and describe the content of the element. For example, the height and width attributes in the <img> tag describe the size of the image.

The W3C continually updates the HTML specifications by adding, deleting, and replacing HTML tags and attributes. Table A–1 lists HTML tags and their associated attributes. The default value for each attribute is indicated by bold text in the Description column. The ⬛ icon indicates tags or attributes that are new with HTML5.

Global attributes can be used with most HTML tags. Table A–2 lists global attributes for HTML, including those new to HTML5.

As a web developer, you will most likely inherit a website developed by someone else. Carefully view the code to find **deprecated elements**, elements that are no longer supported in HTML5. Table A–3 lists deprecated elements. Attribute values in italic are value placeholders.

For a comprehensive list of HTML tags and attributes, more thorough descriptions, examples of HTML tags, and coding standards, visit the W3C website at w3.org.

Table A–1 Common HTML Elements and Attributes

New to HTML5	HTML Tags	Common Attributes	Values	Description
	<!DOCTYPE>	None		Indicates the version of HTML used
	<!-- Comments here -->	None		Inserts comments that are ignored by browsers
	<a> ... </a>	Global attributes		Anchor; creates a hyperlink or fragment identifier
⬛		download	*filename*	Sets the target to be downloaded
		href	*URL*	Hyperlink reference that specifies the target URL
		hreflang	*language_code*	Specifies the language of the linked document
⬛		media	*media_query*	Specifies the media or device the target URL is optimized for
		id	*text*	Specifies an id for enclosed text, allowing it to be the target of a hyperlink

Table A–1 Common HTML Elements and Attributes (continued)

New to HTML5	HTML Tags	Common Attributes	Values	Description
		rel	alternate author bookmark help license next nofollow noreferrer prefetch prev search tag	Indicates the relationship from the current page to the target
		target	_blank _self _parent _top *framename*	Defines the name of the window or frame in which the linked resource will appear
		type	*media_type*	Specifies the media type of the target URL
	<abbr> …. </abbr>	Global attributes		Specifies an abbreviation or acronym
	<address> ... </address>	Global attributes		Used for information such as author name, email address, or street address; enclosed text appears italicized and indented in some browsers
	<area> ... </area>	Global attributes		Creates a hotspot (an area that can be tapped or clicked) on a client-side image map
		alt	*text*	Specifies alternate text for the area
		coords	*coordinates*	Specifies the coordinates that define the edges of the hotspot; a comma-delimited list of values
5		download	*filename*	Sets the target to be downloaded
		href	*URL*	Hyperlink reference that specifies the target URL
5		hreflang	*language_code*	Specifies the language of the target URL
5		media	*media query*	Specifies the media or device the target URL is optimized for
		rel	alternate author bookmark help license next nofollow noreferrer prefetch prev search tag	Specifies the relationship between the current page and the target URL

Table A–1 Common HTML Elements and Attributes (continued)

New to HTML5	HTML Tags	Common Attributes	Values	Description
		shape	default rect circle poly	Identifies the shape of the area
		target	_blank _self _parent _top *framename*	Defines the name of the window or frame in which the linked resource will appear
5		type	*media_type*	Specifies the media type of the target URL
5	\<article\> ... \</article\>	Global attributes		Defines an article
5	\<aside\> ... \</aside\>	Global attributes		Defines content aside from the main page content
5	\<audio\> ... \</audio\>			Defines sound content
		autoplay	autoplay	Specifies that the audio should start playing as soon as it is ready
		controls	controls	Specifies that playback controls should be displayed
		loop	loop	Specifies that the audio should start over when it is finished
		muted	muted	Specifies that the audio output should be muted
		preload	auto metadata none	Specifies whether the audio should be loaded when the page loads
		src	*URL*	Specifies the URL of the audio to play
	\<b\> ... \</b\>	Global attributes		Specifies text to appear in bold However, W3C recommends using CSS to bold text rather than using the \<b\> element
	\<base\>	Global attributes		Identifies the base in all relative URLs in the document Empty tag
		href	*URL*	Specifies the absolute URL used to resolve all relative URLs in the document
		target	_blank _self _parent _top *framename*	Defines the name for the default window (or frame*) in which the hyperlinked pages are displayed
	\<blockquote\> ... \</blockquote\>	Global attributes		Sets enclosed text to appear as a quotation, indented on the right and left
		cite	*URL*	Specifies the source of the quotation
	\<body\> ... \</body\>	Global attributes		Defines the start and end of the webpage content

Table A–1 Common HTML Elements and Attributes *(continued)*

New to HTML5	HTML Tags	Common Attributes	Values	Description
	` `	Global attributes		Inserts a line break Empty tag
5	`<canvas> ... </canvas>`	Global attributes		Defines graphics
		height	*pixels*	Specifies the height of the canvas
		width	*pixels*	Specifies the width of the canvas
	`<caption> ... </caption>`	Global attributes		Creates a caption for a table
	`<cite> ... </cite>`	Global attributes		Indicates that the enclosed text is a citation; text is usually displayed in italics
	`<code> ... </code>`	Global attributes		Indicates that the enclosed text is a code sample from a program; text is usually displayed in fixed-width font such as Courier
	`<col> ... </col>`	Global attributes		Organizes columns in a table into column groups to share attribute values
		span	*number*	Sets the number of columns that span the `<col>` element
	`<colgroup> ... </colgroup>`	Global attributes		Encloses a group of `<col>` tags and groups the columns to set properties
		span	*number*	Sets the number of columns the `<col>` element spans
5	`<datalist> ... </datalist>`	Global attributes		Defines a drop-down list
	`<dd> ... </dd>`	Global attributes		Indicates that the enclosed text is a definition in the definition list
5	`<details> ... </details>`	Global attributes		Defines details of an element
		open	open	Specifies that the details should be visible (open) to the user
5	`<dialog> .... </dialog>`	Global attributes		Specifies a dialog box
		open	open	Specifies that the dialog element is active and that the user can interact with it
	`<div> ... </div>`	Global attributes		Defines a block-level structure or division in the HTML document
	`<dl> ... </dl>`	Global attributes		Creates a definition list
	`<dt> ... </dt>`	Global attributes		Indicates that the enclosed text is a term in the definition list
	`<em> ... </em>`	Global attributes		Indicates that the enclosed text should be emphasized; usually appears in italics
5	`<embed> ... </embed>`	Global attributes		Defines external interactive content or plug-in
		height	*pixels*	Specifies the height of the embedded content
		src	*URL*	Specifies the URL of the embedded content

Table A–1 Common HTML Elements and Attributes *(continued)*

New to HTML5	HTML Tags	Common Attributes	Values	Description
		type	*media_type*	Specifies the media type of the embedded content
		width	*pixels*	Specifies the width of the embedded content
	<fieldset> ... </fieldset>	Global attributes		Groups related form controls and labels
		disabled	*disabled*	Specifies that a fieldset should be disabled
		form	*form_id*	Specifies one or more forms that a fieldset belongs to
		name	*text*	Specifies the name of the fieldset
5	<figcaption> ... </figcaption>	Global attributes		Defines the caption of a figure element
5	<figure> ... </figure>	Global attributes		Defines a group of media content and its caption
5	<footer> ... </footer>	Global attributes		Defines a footer for a section or page
	<form> ... </form>	Global attributes		Marks the start and end of a webpage form
		action	*URL*	Specifies the URL of the application that will process the form; required attribute
5		*autocomplete*	*on* *off*	Specifies whether the form should have autocomplete enabled
		enctype	*encoding*	Specifies how the form element values will be encoded
		method	get post	Specifies the method used to pass form parameters (data) to the server
		name= "form_name"		Specifies the name for a form
5		novalidate	novalidate	Indicates the form should not be validated when submitted
		target	_blank _self _parent _top *framename*	Specifies the frame or window that displays the form's results
	<head> ... </head>	Global attributes		Delimits the start and end of the HTML document's head
5	<header> ... </header>	Global attributes		Defines a header for a section or page
5	<hgroup> ... </hgroup>	Global attributes		Defines information about a section in a document
	<h*n*> ... </h*n*>	Global attributes		Defines a header level *n*, ranging from the largest (h1) to the smallest (h6)
	<hr>	Global attributes		Inserts a horizontal rule
	<html> ... </html>	Global attributes		Indicates the start and the end of the HTML document
5		manifest	*URL*	Specifies the URL of the document's cache manifest

Table A–1 Common HTML Elements and Attributes *(continued)*

New to HTML5	HTML Tags	Common Attributes	Values	Description
	`<i> ... </i>`	Global attributes		Sets enclosed text to appear in italics; W3C recommends using CSS to apply italic to text rather than using the `<i>` element
	`<iframe> ... </iframe>`	Global attributes		Creates an inline frame, also called a floating frame or subwindow, within an HTML document
		height	*pixels*	Sets the frame height to a value in pixels
		name	*text*	Specifies the name of the iframe
5		sandbox	allow-option	Specifies restrictions to the iframe content
5		seamless	seamless	Specifies that the iframe should be seamlessly integrated
		src	*URL*	Defines the URL of the source document displayed in the frame
5		srcdoc	*HTML_code*	Specifies the HTML code of the source document
		width	*pixels*	Sets the frame width to a value in pixels
	`<img> ... </img>`	Global attributes		Inserts an image into the current webpage
		alt	*text*	Provides a text description of an image if the browser cannot display the image; should always be used
		height	*pixels*	Sets the height of the image to a value in pixels (not percentages); should always be used
		src	*URL*	Specifies the URL of the image to be displayed; required
		usemap	*#mapname*	Specifies the map of coordinates and links that defines the href within this image
		width	*pixels*	Sets the width of the image to a value in pixels (not percentages); should always be used
	`<input> ... </input>`	Global attributes		Defines controls used in forms
		alt	*text*	Provides a short description of the control or image button
5		autocomplete	on off	Specifies whether the input field should display autocompletion options when a user starts to type in the field
5		autofocus	autofocus	Specifies that the input field should have focus on page load
		checked	checked	Sets option buttons and check boxes to the checked state
		disabled	disabled	Disables the control
5		form	*form_id*	Specifies one or more forms the input element belongs to

Table A–1 Common HTML Elements and Attributes *(continued)*

New to HTML5	HTML Tags	Common Attributes	Values	Description
5		formaction	*URL*	Overrides the form's action attribute; defines where to send the data when the form is submitted (for type="submit" and type="image")
5		formenctype	*encoding*	Overrides the form's enctype attribute; defines how form data should be encoded before sending it to the server (for type="submit" and type="image")
5		formmethod	get post	Overrides the form's method attribute; defines the HTTP method for sending data to the action URL (for type="submit" and type="image")
5		formnovalidate	formnovalidate	Overrides the form's novalidate attribute; defines that the input element should not be validated when submitted
		formtarget	_blank _self _parent _top *framename*	Overrides the form's target attribute; defines the target window to use when the form is submitted (for type="submit" and type="image")
5		height	*pixels*	Sets the height of an input element (for type="image")
5		list	*datalist_id*	Refers to a datalist that contains predefined options for the input element
5		max	*number* *date*	Specifies a maximum value for an input field
		maxlength	*number*	Sets a value for the maximum number of characters allowed as input for a text or password control
		multiple	*multiple*	Allows the user to enter more than one value
		name	*text*	Assigns a name to the control
5		pattern	*regexp*	Specifies a pattern or format for the input field's value
5		placeholder	*text*	Specifies a hint to help users fill out the input field
		readonly	readonly	Prevents changes to the control
5		required	required	Indicates that the input field's value is required in order to submit the form
		size	*number*	Sets the initial size of the control to a value in characters
5		step	*number*	Specifies the legal number of intervals for the input field
		src	*URL*	Identifies the location of the image if the control is set to an image
		type	*type*	Defines the type of control
		value	*value*	Sets the initial value of the control

Table A–1 Common HTML Elements and Attributes *(continued)*

New to HTML5	HTML Tags	Common Attributes	Values	Description
	<ins> ... </ins>	Global attributes		Identifies and displays text as having been inserted in the document in relation to a previous version
		cite	*URL*	Specifies the URL of a document that has more information on the inserted text
		datetime	*datetime*	Indicates the date and time of a change
	<kbd> ... </kbd>	Global attributes		Displays enclosed text as keyboard-like input
5	<keygen> ... </keygen>	Global attributes		Defines a generated key in a form
		autofocus	autofocus	Sets the focus on the input field on page load
		challenge	challenge	Specifies that the value of the keygen is set to be challenged when submitted
		disabled	disabled	Disables the keygen field
		form	*form_id*	Defines one or more forms the input field belongs to
		keytype	rsa dsa ec	Specifies the security algorithm of the key (for example, rsa generates an RSA key)
		name	*text*	Defines a unique name for the input element; the name attribute is used to collect the field's value when submitted
	<label> ... </label>	Global attributes		Creates a label for a form control
		for	*element_id*	Indicates the name or ID of the element to which the label is applied
		form	*form_id*	Specifies one or more forms the label field belongs to
	<legend> ... </legend>	Global attributes		Assigns a caption to a fieldset element, as defined by the <fieldset> tags
	<li> ... </li>	Global attributes		Defines the enclosed text as a list item in a list
		value	*value*	Inserts or restarts counting with value
	<link>	Global attributes		Establishes a link between the HTML document and another document, such as an external style sheet
		href	*URL*	Defines the URL of the linked document
		name	*text*	Names the current anchor so that it can be the destination for other links
		rel	*relationship*	Indicates the relationship from the current page to the target
5		sizes	any *heightxwidth*	Specifies sizes (height and width) of the linked resource
		type	*media_type*	Indicates the data or media type of the linked document
5	<main> ... </main>	Global attributes		Specifies the main content area of the page

Table A–1 Common HTML Elements and Attributes *(continued)*

New to HTML5	HTML Tags	Common Attributes	Values	Description
	\<map\> ... \</map\>	Global attributes		Specifies a client-side image map; must enclose \<area\> tags
		name	*text*	Assigns a name to the image map
5	\<mark\> ... \</mark\>	Global attributes		Defines marked text
	\<meta\>			Provides additional data (metadata) about an HTML document Empty tag
5		charset	*character_set*	Specifies the character encoding for the HTML document
		content	*text*	Specifies the value for the \<meta\> information; required
		http-equiv	*content-type* *default-style* *refresh*	Specifies the HTTP-equivalent name for metadata; tells the server to include that name and content in the HTTP header when the HTML document is sent to the client
		name	*text*	Assigns a name to metadata
5	\<meter\> ... \</meter\>	Global attributes		Defines measurement within a predefined range
		form	*form_id*	Specifies which form this meter belongs to
		high	*number*	Specifies at which point the measurement's value is considered a high value
		low	*number*	Specifies at which point the measurement's value is considered a low value
		max	*number*	Specifies the maximum value; default value is 1.0
		min	*number*	Specifies the minimum value; default value is 0
		optimum	*number*	Specifies which measurement's value is the best value
		value	*number*	Required; specifies the measurement's current or "measured" value
5	\<nav\> ... \</nav\>	Global attributes		Defines area for navigation links
	\<object\> ... \</object\>	Global attributes		Includes an external object in the HTML document such as an image, a Java applet, or other external object
		data	*URL*	Identifies the location of the object's data
5		form	*form_id*	Specifies one or more forms the object belongs to
		height	*pixels*	Sets the height of the object to a value in pixels
		name	*text*	Assigns a control name to the object for use in forms
		type	*media_type*	Specifies the content or media type of the object

Table A–1 Common HTML Elements and Attributes (continued)

New to HTML5	HTML Tags	Common Attributes	Values	Description
		usemap	#mapname	Associates an image map as defined by the <map> element
		width	pixels	Sets the width of the object to a value in pixels
	<ol> ... </ol>	Global attributes		Defines an ordered list that contains numbered list item elements (<li>)
5		reversed	reversed	Specifies that the list order should be descending
		start	start	Specifies the start value of an ordered list
		type	option	Sets or resets the numbering format for the list
5	<optgroup> ... </optgroup>	Global attributes		Defines an option group
		disabled	disabled	Specifies that an option group should be disabled
		label	text	Specifies a label for the option group
	<option> ... </option>	Global attributes		Defines individual options in a selection list, as defined by the <select> element
		disabled	disabled	Disables the option items
		label	text	Provides a shorter label for the option than that specified in its content
		selected	selected	Sets the option to be the default or the selected option in a list
		value	text	Sets a value returned to the server when the user selects the option
5	<output> ... </output>	Global attributes		Defines some types of output
		for	element_id	Specifies one or more elements the output field relates to
		form	form_id	Specifies one or more forms the output field belongs to
		name	text	Specifies a name for the object (to use when a form is submitted)
	<p> ... </p>	Global attributes		Delimits a paragraph; automatically inserts a blank line between text
	<param> ... </param>	Global attributes		Passes a parameter to an object or applet, as defined by the <object>
		name	text	Defines the name of the parameter required by an object
		value	value	Sets the value of the parameter
	<pre> ... </pre>	Global attributes		Preserves the original format of the enclosed text; keeps line breaks and spacing the same as the original
5	<progress> ... </progress>	Global attributes		Defines progress of a task of any kind
		max	number	Defines the value of completion

Table A–1 Common HTML Elements and Attributes *(continued)*

New to HTML5	HTML Tags	Common Attributes	Values	Description
		value	*number*	Defines the current value of the progress
	<q> ... </q>	Global attributes		Sets enclosed text as a short quotation
		cite	*URL*	Specifies the source URL of the quotation
5	<rp> ... </rp>	Global attributes		Used in ruby annotations to define what to show if a browser does not support the ruby element
5	<rt> ... </rt>	Global attributes		Defines explanation to ruby annotations
5	<ruby> ... </ruby>	Global attributes		Defines ruby annotations, which are used for East Asian typography
	<s> ... </s>	Global attributes		Defines text that is no longer correct, accurate, or relevant
	<samp> ... </samp>	Global attributes		Sets enclosed text to appear as sample output from a computer program or script; usually appears in a monospace font
	<script> ... </script>	Global attributes		Inserts a client-side script into an HTML document
5		async	async	Defines whether the script should be executed asynchronously
		charset	*charset*	Specifies the character encoding used in an external script file
		defer	defer	Indicates that the browser should defer executing the script
		src	*URL*	Identifies the location of an external script
		type	*media_type*	Specifies the media type of the script
5	<section> ... </section>	Global attributes		Defines a section
	<select> ... </select>	Global attributes		Defines a form control to create a multiple-choice menu or scrolling list; encloses a set of <option> tags to define one or more options
5		autofocus	autofocus	Sets the focus on the select field on page load
		disabled	disabled	Disables the selection list
		form	*form_id*	Defines one or more forms the select field belongs to
		multiple	multiple	Sets the list to allow multiple selections
		name	*text*	Assigns a name to the selection list
		size	*number*	Sets the number of visible options in the list
	<small> ... </small>	Global attributes		Sets enclosed text to appear in a smaller typeface
5	<source> ... </source>	Global attributes		Defines media resources
		media	*media_query* all	Specifies the media or device the media resource is optimized for; default value: all

Table A–1 Common HTML Elements and Attributes (continued)

New to HTML5	HTML Tags	Common Attributes	Values	Description
		src	*URL*	Specifies the URL of the media
		type	*media_type*	Specifies the media type of the media resource
	`<span> ... </span>`	Global attributes		Creates a user-defined container to add inline structure to the HTML document
	`<strong> ... </strong>`	Global attributes		Sets enclosed text to appear with strong emphasis; usually displayed as bold text W3C recommends using CSS instead of the `<strong>` element
	`<style> ... </style>`	Global attributes		Encloses embedded style sheet rules for use in the HTML document
		media	*media_query*	Identifies the intended medium of the style
5		scoped	*scoped*	Indicates the styles should only apply to this element's parent element and its child elements
		type	text/css	Specifies the media type of the style sheet
	`<sub> ... </sub>`	Global attributes		Sets enclosed text to appear in subscript
5	`<summary> ... </summary>`	Global attributes		Defines the header of a "detail" element
	`<sup> ... </sup>`	Global attributes		Sets enclosed text to appear in superscript
	`<table> ... </table>`	Global attributes		Marks the start and end of a data table
		sortable	sortable	Specifies that the table can be sorted
	`<tbody> ... </tbody>`	Global attributes		Defines a group of rows in a table body
	`<td> ... </td>`	Global attributes		Defines a data cell in a table; contents are left-aligned and normal text by default
		colspan	*number*	Defines the number of adjacent columns spanned by the cell
		headers	*header_id*	Defines the list of header cells for the current cell
		rowspan	*number*	Defines the number of adjacent rows spanned by the cell
	`<textarea> ... </textarea>`	Global attributes		Creates a multiline text input area within a form
5		autofocus	autofocus	Specifies that the text area field should have focus on page load
		cols	*number*	Defines the number of columns in the text input area
		disabled	disabled	Disables the element
5		form	*form_id*	Specifies one or more forms the text area belongs to
5		maxlength	*number*	Specifies the maximum number of characters allowed in the text area
		name	*text*	Assigns a name to the text area

Table A–1 Common HTML Elements and Attributes *(continued)*

New to HTML5	HTML Tags	Common Attributes	Values	Description
5		placeholder	*text*	Specifies a hint to help users fill out the input field
		readonly	readonly	Prevents the user from editing content in the text area
5		required	*required*	Indicates that the input field's value is required in order to submit the form
		rows	*number*	Defines the number of rows in the text input area
5		wrap	hard soft	Specifies how the text in the text area is wrapped, and if it should be wrapped when submitted in a form
	\<tfoot> ... \</tfoot>	Global attributes		Identifies and groups rows into a table footer
	\<th> ... \</th>	Global attributes		Defines a table header cell; contents are bold and center-aligned by default
		abbr	*text*	Specifies an abbreviated version of the content in a header cell
		colspan	*number*	Defines the number of adjacent columns spanned by the cell
5		headers	*header_id*	Specifies one or more header cells a cell is related to
		rowspan	*number*	Defines the number of adjacent rows spanned by the cell
		scope	col colgroup row rowgroup	Specifies whether a header cell is a header for a column, row, or group of columns or rows
	\<thead> ... \</thead>	Global attributes		Identifies and groups rows into a table header
5	\<time> ... \</time>	Global attributes		Defines a date or time
		datetime	*datetime*	Specifies the date or time for the \<time> element; this attribute is used if no date or time is specified in the element's content
	\<title> ... \</title>	Global attributes		Defines the title for the HTML document; should always be used
	\<tr> ... \</tr>	Global attributes		Defines a row of cells within a table
	\<ul> ... \</ul>	Global attributes		Defines an unordered list that contains bulleted list item elements (\<li>)
	\<var> ... \</var>	Global attributes		Indicates the enclosed text is a variable's name; used to mark up variables or program arguments
5	\<video> ... \</video>	Global attributes		Defines a video
		autoplay	autoplay	Sets the video to start playing as soon as it is ready
		controls	controls	Displays controls such as a play button
		height	*pixels*	Sets the height of the video player in pixels

Table A–1 Common HTML Elements and Attributes *(continued)*

New to HTML5	HTML Tags	Common Attributes	Values	Description
		loop	loop	Starts playing the video every time it is finished
		muted	muted	Specifies the default state of the audio; currently, only "muted" is allowed
		poster	*URL*	Specifies the URL of an image representing the video
		preload	auto metadata none	Specifies whether the video should be loaded when the page loads
		src	*URL*	Provides the URL of the video to play
		width	*pixels*	Sets the width of the video player in pixels
5	<wbr> ... </wbr>	Global attributes		Defines a possible line break

Table A–2 Global Attributes

New to HTML5	Attribute	Values	Example	Description
	accesskey	*character*	accesskey="s"	Specifies a shortcut key to access an element
	class	*classname*	class="intro"	Refers to a class specified in a style sheet
5	contenteditable	true false inherit	contenteditable= "false"	Specifies whether a user can edit the content of an element
5	contextmenu	*menu_id*	contextmenu= "mymenu"	Specifies a context menu for an element; the value must be the id of a <menu> element
	dir	ltr rtl auto	dir="rtl"	Specifies the text direction for the content in an element
5	draggable	true false auto	draggable="true"	Specifies whether a user is allowed to drag an element
5	dropzone	copy move link	dropzone="move"	Specifies what happens when dragged items/data are dropped in the element
5	hidden	hidden	hidden="hidden"	Specifies that an element should be hidden
	id	*id*	id="hoursOpen"	Specifies a unique id for an element
	lang	*language_code*	lang="en"	Specifies the language of the element's content
5	spellcheck	true false	spellcheck="false"	Specifies if the element must have its spelling and grammar checked
	style	*style_definitions*	style="color: red;"	Specifies an inline style for an element
	tabindex	*number*	tabindex="2"	Specifies the tab order of an element
	title	*text*	title="Product Information"	Specifies extra information about an element
5	translate	yes no	translate="no"	Specifies whether content should be translated

Table A–3 Deprecated Elements	
Element	**Replace with**
<acronym>	<abbr>
<applet>	<object>
<basefront>	CSS style
<big>	CSS style
<center>	CSS style
<dir>	<ul>
<font>	CSS style
<frame>	no replacement
<frameset>	no replacement
<noframes>	no replacement
<s>	CSS style
<strike>	CSS style
<tt>	CSS style
<u>	CSS style
<xmp>	<pre>

Appendix B
CSS Quick Reference

This appendix provides a brief review of Cascading Style Sheets (CSS) concepts and terminology, and lists CSS level 1, 2, and 3 properties and values. CSS3 uses a modularized approach to style sheets, which allows CSS to be updated in a more timely and flexible manner. Many of the new properties are not supported by all modern browsers as of yet. Like HTML5, CSS3 is a moving target. Browsers adapt new properties on an ongoing basis and will continue to do so.

For a more comprehensive list of CSS properties and values, visit the World Wide Web Consortium at www.w3.org. In addition to an abundance of information about CSS levels 1 and 2, the W3C site also has extensive information about CSS3, from its history to its use with browsers today. The website also includes many online tutorials for learning CSS levels 1 and 2 as well as CSS3.

CSS Properties

Table B–1 shows units of measurement for web development. Tables B–2 through B–16 show the property names, descriptions, and valid values for various categories of CSS properties. Values listed in bold are the defaults.

Table B–1 Units of Measurement

Property Name	Description	Values
color	Keyword or a numerical hexadecimal, RGB, RGBA, HSL, or HSLA color specification	[keyword] [#rrggbb] [rgb(r,g,b)]
length	Indicates both relative (em, ex, px) and absolute (in, cm, mm, pt, pc) lengths	em — relative to size of capital M of browser default font ex — relative to small x of browser default font px — represents 1 pixel, smallest unit of measure in — 1 inch cm — 1 centimeter mm — 1 millimeter pt — 1/72 of an inch pc — 1/12 of an inch
percentage	Values are always relative to another value	percentage of width or height of parent element; if only one value is given, the second is set to "auto"

Table B–2 Animation Properties

Property Name	Description	Values	CSS
@keyframes	Specifies the animation	[animationname] [keyframes-selector] [css-styles]	3
animation	Shorthand property for all the other animation properties, except the animation-play-state property		3
animation-delay	Specifies when the animation starts	[time] initial inherit	3
animation-direction	Specifies whether the animation should play in reverse on alternate cycles	**normal** alternate	3
animation-duration	Specifies how many seconds or milliseconds an animation takes to complete one cycle	[time]	3
animation-fill-mode	Specifies values applied by the animation separate from the time it is executing	none forwards backwards both initial inherit	3
animation-iteration-count	Specifies the number of times an animation should be played	[n] infinite	3
animation-name	Specifies a name for the @keyframes animation	[keyframename] **none**	3
animation-play-state	Specifies whether the animation is running or paused	paused **running**	3
animation-timing-function	Specifies the speed curve of the animation	**ease** ease-in ease-out ease-in-out cubic-bezier linear	3

Table B–3 Background Properties

Property Name	Description	Values	CSS
background	Shorthand property for setting the individual background properties		1
background-attachment	Sets the background image to be fixed or to scroll with the page	scroll fixed	1
background-clip	Specifies the painting area of the background	border-box content-box padding-box	3
background-color	Sets the background color of an element	transparent [color]	1
background-image	Sets an image as the background	**none** [URL]	1
background-origin	Specifies the positioning area of the background images	border-box content-box padding-box	3

Table B–3 Background Properties *(continued)*

Property Name	Description	Values	CSS
background-position	Sets the starting position of a background image	[length] [percentage] bottom center left right top	1
background-repeat	Sets whether or how a background image is repeated	**repeat** repeat-x repeat-y no-repeat inherit	1
background-size	Specifies the size of the background images	auto contain cover length percentage	3

Table B–4 Border Properties

Property Name	Description	Values	CSS
border	Sets all the border properties in one declaration		1
border-color	Shorthand property for setting the color of the four borders in one declaration; can have from one to four colors	[color] transparent	1
border-top-color border-right-color border-bottom-color border-left-color	Sets the respective color of the top, right, bottom, and left borders individually	[color]	1
border-image	Shorthand property for setting all the border-image-*n* properties		3
border-image-outset	Specifies the amount by which the border image area extends beyond the border box	[length] [number]	3
border-image-repeat	Specifies whether the image-border should be repeated, rounded, or stretched	**stretch** repeat round	3
border-image-slice	Specifies the inward offsets of the image-border	[number] [percentage] fill	3
border-image-source	Specifies an image to be used as a border	**none** [image]	3
border-image-width	Specifies the widths of the image-border	[number] [percentage] auto	3
border-radius	Shorthand property for setting all the four border-*n*-radius properties		3
border-bottom-left-radius border-bottom-right-radius border-top-left-radius border-top-right-radius	Sets the shape of the border of the bottom-left, bottom-right, top-left, and top-right corners individually	[percentage] [length]	3

Table B–4 Border Properties (continued)

Property Name	Description	Values	CSS
border-style	Shorthand property for setting the style of the four borders in one declaration; can have from one to four styles	**none** dashed dotted double groove inset outset ridge solid	1
border-top-style border-right-style border-bottom-style border-left-style	Sets the respective style of the top, right, bottom, and left borders individually	**none** dashed dotted double groove inset outset ridge solid	1
border-width	Shorthand property for setting the width of the four borders in one declaration; can have from one to four values	**medium** [length] thick thin	1
border-top-width border-right-width border-bottom-width border-left-width	Sets the respective width of the top, right, bottom, and left borders individually	**medium** [length] thick thin	1

Table B–5 Basic Box Properties

Property Name	Description	Values	CSS
box-decoration-break	Sets the behavior of the background and border of an element at page-break, or at line-break for inline elements		3
box-shadow	Attaches one or more drop-shadows to the box	[h-shadow] [v-shadow] [blur] [spread] [color] inset none	3
overflow	Specifies what happens if content overflows into a box element's area	auto hidden scroll visible	2
overflow-x	Specifies whether to clip the left or right edges of the content, if it overflows the element's content area	**visible** hidden scroll auto no-display no-content	3
overflow-y	Specifies whether to clip the top or bottom edges of the content, if it overflows the element's content area	visible hidden scroll auto no-display no-content	3

Table B–6 Classification Properties

Property Name	Description	Values	CSS
display	Describes whether or how an element is displayed on the canvas, which may be on a printed page or a computer monitor, for example	block inline list-item none	1
white-space	Declares how white-space inside the element is handled: the 'normal' way (where white-space is collapsed), as pre (which behaves like the \<pre\> element in HTML) or as nowrap (where wrapping is done only through \<br\> elements)	**normal** pre nowrap	1

Table B–7 Color Properties

Property Name	Description	Values	CSS
color	Sets the color of text	[value]	1
opacity	Sets the opacity level for an element	[value] inherit	3

Table B–8 Dimension Properties

Property Name	Description	Values	CSS
height	Sets the height of an element	**auto** [length] [percentage] inherit	1
max-height	Sets the maximum height of an element	**none** [length] [percentage] inherit	2
max-width	Sets the maximum width of an element	**none** [length] [percentage] inherit	2
min-height	Sets the minimum height of an element	[length] [percentage] inherit	2
min-width	Sets the minimum width of an element	[length] [percentage] inherit	2
width	Sets the width of an element	**auto** [length] [percentage] inherit	1

Table B–9 Flexible Box Properties

Property Name	Description	Values	CSS
align-content	Specifies alignment between lines inside flexible container when items do not use all available space	center flex-end flex-start space-around space-between stretch	3
align-items	Specifies alignment for items inside flexible container	baseline center flex-end flex-start stretch	3
align-self	Specifies alignment for specific elements inside flexible container	auto baseline center flex-end flex-start	3
flex	Specifies the length of an element, relative to the other elements	auto none	3
flex-basis	Specifies initial length of a flexible element	auto	3
flex-direction	Specifies direction of the flexible elements	column column-reverse row row-reverse	3
flex-flow	Shorthand property of flex-direction and flex-wrap properties		3
flex-grow	Specifies how much an element can grow relative to the other elements	[number]	3
flex-shrink	Specifies how much an element can shrink relative to the other elements	[number]	3
flex-wrap	Specifies whether flexible elements can wrap	nowrap wrap wrap-reverse	3
justify-content	Specifies the alignment between elements inside a flexible container when the elements do not use all available space	center flex-end flex-start space-around space-between	3
order	Sets the order of the flexible element, relative to the other elements	[number]	3

Table B–10 Font Properties

Property Name	Description	Values	CSS
font	Shorthand property for setting font properties		1
@font-face	Rule that allows websites to download and use fonts other than the "web-safe" fonts		3
font-family	Prioritized list of font-family names and/or generic family names for an element	[family-name] cursive fantasy monospace sans-serif serif	1

Table B–10 Font Properties *(continued)*

Property Name	Description	Values	CSS
font-size	Sets the size of a font	[length] [percentage] large larger **medium** small smaller x-large x-small xx-large xx-small inherit	1
font-size-adjust	Preserves the readability of text when font fallback occurs	[number] none inherit	3
font-stretch	Selects a normal, condensed, or expanded face from a font family		3
font-style	Sets the style of a font	**normal** italic oblique	1
font-variant	Displays text in a small-caps font or a normal font	**normal** small-caps	1
font-weight	Sets the weight of a font	**normal** bold bolder lighter	1

Table B–11 List Properties

Property Name	Description	Values	CSS
list-style	Shorthand property for setting list-style-image, list-style-position, and list-style-type in one declaration		1
list-style-image	Sets an image as the list-item marker	**none** [URL]	1
list-style-position	Indents or extends a list-item marker with respect to the item's content	**outside** inside	1
list-style-type	Sets the type of list-item marker	**disc** circle square decimal lower-alpha lower-roman upper-alpha upper-roman	1

Table B–12 Margin and Padding Properties

Property Name	Description	Values	CSS
margin	Shorthand property for setting margin properties		1
margin-top margin-right margin-bottom margin-left	Sets the top, right, bottom, and left margin of an element individually	[length] [percentage] auto inherit	1
padding	Shorthand property for setting padding properties in one declaration		1
padding-top padding-right padding-bottom padding-left	Sets the top, right, bottom, and left padding of an element individually	[length] [percentage] inherit	1

Table B–13 Positioning Properties

Property Name	Description	Values	CSS
bottom	Specifies the bottom position of a positioned element	**auto** [length] [percentage] inherit	2
clear	Specifies the sides of an element where other floating elements are not allowed	left right both **none** inherit	1
clip	Clips an absolutely positioned element	[shape] **auto** inherit	2
cursor	Specifies the type of cursor to display	[URL] auto crosshair default e-resize help move n-resize ne-resize nw-resize pointer progress s-resize se-resize sw-resize text w-resize wait inherit	2

Table B–13 Positioning Properties *(continued)*

Property Name	Description	Values	CSS
display	Specifies the type of box an element should generate	none block inline inline-block inline-table list-item run-in table table-caption table-cell table-column table-column-group table-footer-group table-header-group table-row table-row-group inherit	1
float	Specifies whether a box should float	left right **none** inherit	1
left	Specifies the left position of a positioned element	**auto** [length] [percentage] inherit	2
overflow	Specifies what happens if content overflows an element's box	**visible** hidden scroll auto inherit	2
position	Specifies the type of positioning method used for an element (static, relative, absolute, or fixed)	**static** absolute fixed relative inherit	2
right	Specifies the right position of a positioned element	**auto** [length] [percentage] inherit	2
top	Specifies the top position of a positioned element	auto [length] [percentage] inherit	2
visibility	Specifies whether an element is visible	visible hidden collapse inherit	2
z-index	Sets the stack order of a positioned element	auto [number] inherit	2

Table B–14 Table Properties

Property Name	Description	Values	CSS
border-collapse	Specifies whether table borders should be collapsed	collapse **separate** inherit	2
border-spacing	Specifies the distance between the borders of adjacent cells	[length] inherit	2
caption-side	Specifies the placement of a table caption	**top** bottom inherit	2
empty-cells	Specifies whether to display borders and background on empty cells in a table	hide **show** inherit	2
table-layout	Sets the layout algorithm to be used for a table	**auto** fixed inherit	2

Table B–15 Text Properties

Property Name	Description	Values	CSS
color	Sets the color of text	[color] inherit	1
direction	Specifies the text or writing direction	ltr rtl inherit	2
hanging-punctuation	Specifies whether a punctuation character may be placed outside the line box	none first last allow-end force-end	3
letter-spacing	Increases or decreases the space between characters	**normal** [length] inherit	1
line-height	Sets the line height	**normal** [length] [number] [percentage] inherit	1
punctuation-trim	Specifies whether a punctuation character should be trimmed	none start end allow-end adjacent	3
text-align	Specifies the horizontal alignment of text	left right center justify inherit	1
text-align-last	Describes how the last line of a block or a line right before a forced line break is aligned when text-align is "justify"		3
text-decoration	Adds decoration to text	**none** blink line-through overline underline inherit	1

Table B–15 Text Properties *(continued)*

Property Name	Description	Values	CSS
text-indent	Indents the first line of text in an element	[length] [percentage] inherit	1
text-justify	Specifies the justification method used when text-align is "justify"	auto interword interideograph intercluster distribute kashida none	3
text-overflow	Specifies what should happen when text overflows the containing element	clip ellipsis [string]	3
text-shadow	Adds shadow to text	[h-shadow] [v-shadow] [blur] [color]	3
text-transform	Controls text capitalization	**none** capitalize lowercase uppercase inherit	1
text-wrap	Specifies line breaking rules for text	normal none unrestricted suppress	3
vertical-align	Sets the vertical positioning of text	baseline [length] [percentage] bottom middle sub super text-bottom text-top top inherit	1
white-space	Specifies how white-space inside an element is handled	normal nowrap pre preline prewrap inherit	1
word-break	Specifies the line breaking rules for non-CJK scripts	normal break-all hyphenate	3
word-spacing	Increases or decreases the space between words	**normal** [length] inherit	1
word-wrap	Allows long, unbreakable words to be broken and wrap to the next line	normal break-word	3

Table B–16 Transition Properties

Property Name	Description	Values	CSS
transition	Shorthand property for setting the four transition properties		3
transition-delay	Specifies when the transition effect starts	[time]	3
transition-duration	Specifies how many seconds or milliseconds a transition effect takes to complete	[time]	3
transition-property	Specifies the name of the CSS property the transition effect is for	none **all** property	3
transition-timing-function	Specifies the speed curve of the transition effect	linear ease ease-in ease-in-out ease-out cubic-bezier	3

Appendix C
Color Reference Palette

Color Reference

Three hardware components help deliver color to a computer user: the processor, the video card, and the monitor. Because these components vary widely, the color quality that users see can vary. The software on a user's computer, specifically the web browser, also affects the way that color is displayed on a screen. It is very difficult, if not impossible, to plan for all possible color variations created by a web browser. In the past, web developers had to make sure that they used browser-safe colors. These browser-safe colors restricted the number of colors used on a webpage and minimized the impact of color variations. The trend for screens today is to display "true color," which means that any of 16 million colors can be displayed on the monitor. Few people use 8-bit monitors anymore, so you generally do not have to limit yourself to browser-safe colors.

A total of 216 browser-safe colors appear the same on different monitors, operating systems, and browsers — including Windows and Macintosh operating systems and Internet Explorer, Apple Safari, Google Chrome, and Mozilla Firefox browsers. When using color on your website, keep in mind that using only the 216 browser-safe colors can be very restrictive. On 8-bit monitors, only the browser-safe colors will be displayed. If you decide to use a non-browser-safe color, the browser will try to create the color by combining (a process called dithering) any number of the 216 acceptable colors. The resulting color could be slightly different from the color you had intended. Figure C–1 shows the original 216 browser-safe colors.

Figure C–1

000000	000033	000066	000099	0000CC	0000FF	003300	003333	003366	003399	0033CC	0033FF
006600	006633	006666	006699	0066CC	0066FF	009900	009933	009966	009999	0099CC	0099FF
00CC00	00CC33	00CC66	00CC99	00CCCC	00CCFF	00FF00	00FF33	00FF66	00FF99	00FFCC	00FFFF
330000	330033	330066	330099	3300CC	3300FF	333300	333333	333366	333399	3333CC	3333FF
336600	336633	336666	336699	3366CC	3366FF	339900	339933	339966	339999	3399CC	3399FF
33CC00	33CC33	33CC66	33CC99	33CCCC	33CCFF	33FF00	33FF33	33FF66	33FF99	33FFCC	33FFFF
660000	660033	660066	660099	6600CC	6600FF	663300	663333	663366	663399	6633CC	6633FF
666600	666633	666666	666699	6666CC	6666FF	669900	669933	669966	669999	6699CC	6699FF
66CC00	66CC33	66CC66	66CC99	66CCCC	66CCFF	66FF00	66FF33	66FF66	66FF99	66FFCC	66FFFF
990000	990033	990066	990099	9900CC	9900FF	993300	993333	993366	993399	9933CC	9933FF
996600	996633	996666	996699	9966CC	9966FF	999900	999933	999966	999999	9999CC	9999FF
99CC00	99CC33	99CC66	99CC99	99CCCC	99CCFF	99FF00	99FF33	99FF66	99FF99	99FFCC	99FFFF
CC0000	CC0033	CC0066	CC0099	CC00CC	CC00FF	CC3300	CC3333	CC3366	CC3399	CC33CC	CC33FF
CC6600	CC6633	CC6666	CC6699	CC66CC	CC66FF	CC9900	CC9933	CC9966	CC9999	CC99CC	CC99FF
CCCC00	CCCC33	CCCC66	CCCC99	CCCCCC	CCCCFF	CCFF00	CCFF33	CCFF66	CCFF99	CCFFCC	CCFFFF
FF0000	FF0033	FF0066	FF0099	FF00CC	FF00FF	FF3300	FF3333	FF3366	FF3399	FF33CC	FF33FF
FF6600	FF6633	FF6666	FF6699	FF66CC	FF66FF	FF9900	FF9933	FF9966	FF9999	FF99CC	FF99FF
FFCC00	FFCC33	FFCC66	FFCC99	FFCCCC	FFCCFF	FFFF00	FFFF33	FFFF66	FFFF99	FFFFCC	FFFFFF

With today's displays, you are not limited to these colors. To view additional color options, visit any of the following websites:

1. W3Schools: www.w3schools.com/tags/ref_colorpicker.asp
2. CSS Portal: www.cssportal.com/css3-color-names/
3. Color Picker: www.colorpicker.com/
4. HTML Color Codes: http://html-color-codes.info/

Appendix D
Accessibility Standards for Webpage Developers

Making the Web Accessible

According to the W3C, the goal of the web is to be accessible to all people, including those with a disability that limits their ability to perform computer tasks. The U.S. Congress passed the Rehabilitation Act in 1973, which prohibits discrimination for those with disabilities. In 1998, Congress amended this Act to reflect the latest changes in information technology. Section 508 requires that any electronic information developed, procured, maintained, or used by the federal government be accessible to people with disabilities. Disabilities that inhibit a person's ability to use the web fall into four main categories: visual, hearing, motor, and cognitive. This amendment has had a profound effect on how webpages are designed and developed.

The summary of Section 508 §1194.22 states, "The criteria for web-based technology and information are based on access guidelines developed by the Web Accessibility Initiative of the World Wide Web Consortium." The guidelines help to include everyone as a — potential user of your website, including those with disabilities. The Web Accessibility Initiative (WAI) develops guidelines and support materials for accessibility standards. These guidelines are known as the Web Content Accessibility Guidelines (WCAG) 2.0.

Section 508 Guidelines

Every federal government website must follow the Section 508 guidelines. Section 508 § 1194.22 refers to web-based intranet and internet information and applications and includes the following 16 rules.

(a) A text equivalent for every non-text element shall be provided (e.g., via "alt," "longdesc," or in element content).

(b) Equivalent alternatives for any multimedia presentation shall be synchronized with the presentation.

(c) Web pages shall be designed so that all information conveyed with color is also available without color, for example from context or markup.

(d) Documents shall be organized so they are readable without requiring an associated style sheet.

(e) Redundant text links shall be provided for each active region of a server-side image map.

(f) Client-side image maps shall be provided instead of server-side image maps except where the regions cannot be defined with an available geometric shape.

(g) Row and column headers shall be identified for data tables.

(h) Markup shall be used to associate data cells and header cells for data tables that have two or more logical levels of row or column headers.

(i) Frames shall be titled with text that facilitates frame identification and navigation.

(j) Pages shall be designed to avoid causing the screen to flicker with a frequency greater than 2 Hz and lower than 55 Hz.

(k) A text-only page, with equivalent information or functionality, shall be provided to make a web site comply with the provisions of this part, when compliance cannot be accomplished in any other way. The content of the text-only page shall be updated whenever the primary page changes.

(l) When pages utilize scripting languages to display content, or to create interface elements, the information provided by the script shall be identified with functional text that can be read by assistive technology.

(m) When a web page requires that an applet, plug-in or other application be present on the client system to interpret page content, the page must provide a link to a plug-in or applet that complies with §1194.21(a) through (l).

(n) When electronic forms are designed to be completed on-line, the form shall allow people using assistive technology to access the information, field elements, and functionality required for completion and submission of the form, including all directions and cues.

(o) A method shall be provided that permits users to skip repetitive navigation links.

(p) When a timed response is required, the user shall be alerted and given sufficient time to indicate more time is required.

For more detailed information about these rules, please visit www.section508.gov.

Web Content Accessibility Guidelines

The WAI identifies 12 guidelines for web developers, known as Web Content Accessibility Guidelines (WCAG) 2.0. The WCAG specifies how to make web content more accessible to people with disabilities. **Web content** generally refers to the information in a web. Page or web application, including text, images, forms, and sounds. All web developers should review the information at the official website at w3.org/WAI/intro/wcag.php for complete information on these guidelines, and should apply the guidelines to their webpage development.

The 12 WCAG 2.0 guidelines are organized under four principles: perceivable, operable, understandable, and robust. Anyone who wants to use the web must have content that is:

Perceivable: Information and user interface components must be presentable to users in ways they can perceive. Users must be able to perceive the information being presented (it can't be invisible to all of their senses).

Operable: User interface components and navigation must be operable. Users must be able to operate the interface (the interface cannot require interaction that a user cannot perform).

Understandable: Information and the operation of the user interface must be understandable. Users must be able to understand the information as well as the operation of the user interface (the content or operation cannot be beyond their understanding).

Robust: Content must be robust enough that it can be interpreted reliably by a wide variety of user agents, including assistive technologies. Users must be able to access the content as technologies advance (as technologies and user agents evolve, the content should remain accessible).

If any of these are not true, users with disabilities will not be able to use the web.

For each guideline, there are testable success criteria, which are at three levels: A, AA, and AAA. In order for a web page to conform to WCAG 2.0, all of the following conformance requirements must be satisfied:

- **Level A:** For Level A conformance (the minimum level of conformance), the web page satisfies all the Level A Success Criteria, or a conforming alternate version is provided.

- **Level AA:** For Level AA conformance, the web page satisfies all the Level A and Level AA Success Criteria, or a Level AA conforming alternate version is provided.

- **Level AAA:** For Level AAA conformance, the web page satisfies all the Level A, Level AA, and Level AAA Success Criteria, or a Level AAA conforming alternate version is provided.

Table D–1 contains a summary of the WCAG 2.0 guidelines and the corresponding level of conformance.

Table D–1 WCAG 2.0 Guidelines

Item	Level
Principle 1: Perceivable — Information and user interface components must be presentable to users in ways they can perceive.	
Guideline 1.1 Text Alternatives: Provide text alternatives for any non-text content so that it can be changed into other forms people need, such as large print, braille, speech, symbols or simpler language.	
1.1.1 Nontext Content: All nontext content that is presented to the user has a text alternative that serves the equivalent purpose.	A
Guideline 1.2 Time Based Media: Provide alternatives for time-based media.	
1.2.1 Audio-only and Video-only (Prerecorded): An alternative for time-based media is provided that presents equivalent information for prerecorded audio-only or video-only content.	A
1.2.2 Captions (Prerecorded): Captions are provided for all prerecorded audio content in synchronized media, except when the media is a media alternative for text and is clearly labeled as such.	A
1.2.3 Audio Description or Media Alternative (Prerecorded): An alternative for time-based media or audio description of the prerecorded video content is provided for synchronized media, except when the media is a media alternative for text and is clearly labeled as such.	A
1.2.4 Captions (Live): Captions are provided for all live audio content in synchronized media.	AA
1.2.5 Audio Description (Prerecorded): Audio description is provided for all prerecorded video content in synchronized media.	AA
1.2.6 Sign Language (Prerecorded): Sign language interpretation is provided for all prerecorded audio content in synchronized media.	AAA
1.2.7 Extended Audio Description (Prerecorded): Where pauses in foreground audio are insufficient to allow audio descriptions to convey the sense of the video, extended audio description is provided for all prerecorded video content in synchronized media.	AAA

Table D–1 WCAG 2.0 Guidelines *(continued)*

Item	Level
1.2.8 Media Alternative (Prerecorded): An alternative for time-based media is provided for all prerecorded synchronized media and for all prerecorded video-only media.	AAA
1.2.9 Audio-only (Live): An alternative for time-based media that presents equivalent information for live audio-only content is provided.	AAA
Guideline 1.3 Adaptable: Create content that can be presented in different ways (for example simpler layout) without losing information or structure.	
1.3.1 Info and Relationships: Information, structure, and relationships conveyed through presentation can be programmatically determined or are available in text.	A
1.3.2 Meaningful Sequence: When the sequence in which content is presented affects its meaning, a correct reading sequence can be programmatically determined.	A
1.3.3 Sensory Characteristics: Instructions provided for understanding and operating content do not rely solely on sensory characteristics of components such as shape, size, visual location, orientation, or sound.	A
Guideline 1.4 Distinguishable: Make it easier for users to see and hear content including separating foreground from background.	
1.4.1 Use of Color: Color is not used as the only visual means of conveying information, indicating an action, prompting a response, or distinguishing a visual element.	A
1.4.2 Audio Control: If any audio on a web page plays automatically for more than 3 seconds, either a mechanism is available to pause or stop the audio, or a mechanism is available to control the audio volume independently from the overall system volume level.	A
1.4.3 Contrast (Minimum): The visual presentation of text and images of text has a contrast ratio of at least 4.5:1 (for specific exceptions, refer to w3.org/TR/WCAG).	AA
1.4.4 Resize text: Except for captions and images of text, text can be resized without assistive technology up to 200 percent without loss of content or functionality.	AA
1.4.5 Images of Text: If the technologies being used can achieve the visual presentation, text is used to convey information rather than images of (for specific exceptions, refer to w3.org/TR/WCAG).	AA
1.4.6 Contrast (Enhanced): The visual presentation of text and images of text has a contrast ratio of at least 7:1 (for specific exceptions, refer to w3.org/TR/WCAG).	AAA
1.4.7 Low or No Background Audio: For prerecorded audio-only content in which 1) the audio does not contain background sounds, 2) the background sounds can be turned off, or 3) the background sounds are at least 20 decibels lower than the foreground speech content.	AAA
1.4.8 Visual Presentation: For the visual presentation of blocks of text, a mechanism is available to manipulate the look of the page (e.g., background colors, text size) easily.	AAA
1.4.9 Images of Text (No Exception): Images of text are only used for pure decoration or where a particular presentation of text is essential to the information being conveyed.	AAA
Principle 2: Operable — User interface components and navigation must be operable.	
Guideline 2.1 Keyboard Accessible: Make all functionality available from the keyboard.	
2.1.1 Keyboard: All functionality of the content is operable through a keyboard interface without requiring specific timings for individual keystrokes, except where the underlying function requires input that depends on the path of the user's movement and not just the endpoints.	A
2.1.2 No Keyboard Trap: If keyboard focus can be moved to a component of the page using a keyboard interface, then focus can be moved away from that component using only a keyboard interface, and, if it requires more than unmodified arrow or tab keys or other standard exit methods, the user is advised of the method for moving focus away.	A
2.1.3 Keyboard (No Exception): All functionality of the content is operable through a keyboard interface without requiring specific timings for individual keystrokes.	AAA
Guideline 2.2 Enough Time: Provide users enough time to read and use content.	
2.2.1 Timing Adjustable: The user should be able to easily change each time limit that is set by the content.	A

Table D–1 WCAG 2.0 Guidelines (continued)

Item	Level
2.2.2 Pause, Stop, Hide: The user should be able to pause, stop, or hide moving, blinking, scrolling, or auto-updating information.	A
2.2.3 No Timing: Timing is not an essential part of the event or activity presented by the content, except for noninteractive synchronized media and real-time events.	AAA
2.2.4 Interruptions: Interruptions can be postponed or suppressed by the user, except interruptions involving an emergency.	AAA
2.2.5 Re-authenticating: When an authenticated session expires, the user can continue the activity without loss of data after re-authenticating.	AAA
Guideline 2.3 Seizures: Do not design content in a way that is known to cause seizures.	
2.3.1 Three Flashes or Below Threshold: web pages do not contain anything that flashes more than three times in any one second period, or the flash is below the general flash and red flash thresholds.	A
2.3.2 Three Flashes: web pages do not contain anything that flashes more than three times in any one second period.	AAA
Guideline 2.4 Navigable: Provide ways to help users navigate, find content, and determine where they are.	
2.4.1 Bypass Blocks: A mechanism is available to bypass blocks of content that are repeated on multiple web pages.	A
2.4.2 Page Titled: web pages have titles that describe topic or purpose.	A
2.4.3 Focus Order: If a web page can be navigated sequentially and the navigation sequences affect meaning or operation, focusable components receive focus in an order that preserves meaning and operability.	A
2.4.4 Link Purpose (In Context): The purpose of each link can be determined from the link text alone or from the link text together with its programmatically determined link context, except where the purpose of the link would be ambiguous to users in general.	A
2.4.5 Multiple Ways: More than one way is available to locate a web page within a set of web pages except where the web Page is the result of, or a step in, a process.	AA
2.4.6 Headings and Labels: Headings and labels describe topic or purpose.	AA
2.4.7 Focus Visible: Any keyboard operable user interface has a mode of operation where the keyboard focus indicator is visible.	AA
2.4.8 Location: Information about the user's location within a set of web pages is available.	AAA
2.4.9 Link Purpose (Link Only): A mechanism is available to allow the purpose of each link to be identified from link text alone, except where the purpose of the link would be ambiguous to users in general.	AAA
2.4.10 Section Headings: Section headings are used to organize the content.	AAA
Principle 3: Understandable—Information and the operation of user interface must be understandable.	
Guideline 3.1 Readable: Make text content readable and understandable.	
3.1.1 Language of Page: The default human language of each web page can be programmatically determined.	A
3.1.2 Language of Parts: The human language of each passage or phrase in the content can be programmatically determined except for proper names, technical terms, words of indeterminate language, and words or phrases that have become part of the vernacular of the immediately surrounding text.	AA
3.1.3 Unusual Words: A mechanism is available for identifying specific definitions of words or phrases used in an unusual or restricted way, including idioms and jargon.	AAA
3.1.4 Abbreviations: A mechanism for identifying the expanded form or meaning of abbreviations is available.	AAA

Table D–1 WCAG 2.0 Guidelines *(continued)*	
Item	**Level**
3.1.5 Reading Level: When text requires reading ability more advanced than the lower secondary education level after removal of proper names and titles, supplemental content, or a version that does not require reading ability more advanced than the lower secondary education level, is available.	AAA
3.1.6 Pronunciation: A mechanism is available for identifying specific pronunciation of words where the meaning of the words, in context, is ambiguous without knowing the pronunciation.	AAA
Guideline 3.2 Predictable: Make web pages appear and operate in predictable ways.	
3.2.1 On Focus: When any component receives focus, it does not initiate a change of context.	A
3.2.2 On Input: Changing the setting of any user interface component does not automatically cause a change of context unless the user has been advised of the behavior before using the component.	A
3.2.3 Consistent Navigation: Navigational mechanisms that are repeated on multiple web pages within a set of web pages occur in the same relative order each time they are repeated, unless a change is initiated by the user.	AA
3.2.4 Consistent Identification: Components that have the same functionality within a set of web pages are identified consistently.	AA
3.2.5 Change on Request: Changes of context are initiated only by user request or a mechanism is available to turn off such changes.	AAA
Guideline 3.3 Input Assistance: Help users avoid and correct mistakes.	
3.3.1 Error Identification: If an input error is automatically detected, the item that is in error is identified and the error is described to the user in text.	A
3.3.2 Labels or Instructions: Labels or instructions are provided when content requires user input.	A
3.3.3 Error Suggestion: If an input error is automatically detected and suggestions for its correction are known, then the suggestions are provided to the user, unless it would jeopardize the security or purpose of the content.	AA
3.3.4 Error Prevention (Legal, Financial, Data): For web pages that cause legal commitments or financial transactions for the user to occur, that modify or delete user-controllable data in data storage systems, or that submit user test responses, a mechanism is available for reviewing, confirming, and correcting information before finalizing the submission.	AA
3.3.5 Help: Context-sensitive help is available.	AAA
3.3.6 Error Prevention (All): For web pages that require the user to submit information, a mechanism is available for reviewing, confirming, and correcting information before finalizing the submission.	AAA
Principle 4: Robust — Content must be robust enough that it can be interpreted reliably by a wide variety of user agents, including assistive technologies.	
Guideline 4.1 Compatible: Maximize compatibility with current and future user agents, including assistive technologies.	
4.1.1 Parsing: In content implemented using markup languages, elements have complete start and end tags, elements are nested according to their specifications, elements do not contain duplicate attributes, and any IDs are unique, except where the specifications allow these features.	A
4.1.2 Name, Role, Value: For all user interface components (including but not limited to: form elements, links, and components generated by scripts), the name and role can be programmatically determined; states, properties, and values that can be set by the user can be programmatically set; and notification of changes to these items is available to user agents, including assistive technologies.	A

Source of data: w3.org

Appendix E
Symbols and Characters Quick Reference

Using Symbols and Special Characters

At times you may want to insert a symbol such as an arrow or other symbol such as a copyright symbol — a character not found on most keyboards — on a webpage. These characters are called **character references** or **symbol entities** and are summarized in Tables E–1 through E–3.

The table references below are for English characters. If you need characters for other languages, visit the Unicode Consortium at unicode.org. The Unicode Consortium allows everyone around the world to use computers in their native language. You can visit their website to find characters for many languages. You can also search the web for many other Unicode character map resources.

Table E–1 Commonly Used Characters

Symbol	Character Reference	Description
&	&	Ampersand
¦	¦	Broken vertical bar
¢	¢	Cent sign
©	©	Copyright sign
¤	¤	Currency sign
†	†	Dagger
‡	‡	Double dagger
€	€	Euro
>	>	Greater-than sign
«	«	Left-pointing double angle quotation mark
<	<	Less-than sign
—	—	Em dash
		Nonbreaking space
–	–	En dash
¬	¬	Not sign
¶	¶	Paragraph sign
£	£	Pound
"	"	Quotation mark = APL quote
®	®	Registered mark sign
»	»	Right-pointing double angle quotation mark
§	§	Section sign
™	™	Trademark sign
¥	¥	Yen

Table E–2 Mathematical and Technical Characters

Symbol	Character Reference	Description
∧	&and;	Logical and
∠	&ang;	Angle
≈	&asymp;	Almost equal to
∩	&cap;	Intersection
∪	&cup;	Union
°	&deg;	Degree sign
÷	&divide;	Division sign
≡	&equiv;	Identical to
∃	&exist;	There exists
ƒ	&fnof;	Function
∀	&forall;	For all
½	&frac12;	Fraction one half
¼	&frac14;	Fraction one quarter
¾	&frac34;	Fraction three quarters
≥	&ge;	Greater-than or equal to
∞	&infin;	Infinity
∫	&int;	Integral
∈	&isin;	Element of
≤	&le;	Less-than or equal to
µ	&micro;	Micro sign
∇	&nabla;	Backward difference
≠	&ne;	Not equal to
∋	&ni;	Contains as a member
∂	&part;	Partial differential
⊥	&perp;	Perpendicular
±	&plusmn;	Plus-minus sign
∏	&prod;	n-ary product
∏	&prop;	Proportional to
√	&radic;	Square root
~	&sim;	Tilde
Σ	&sum;	n-ary summation
∴	&there4;	Therefore

Table E–3 Arrow Characters

Symbol	Character Reference	Description
↓	↓	Downward arrow
↔	↔	Left right arrow
←	←	Leftward arrow
→	→	Rightward arrow
↑	↑	Upward arrow

Index

Note:

- Page numbers in bold type indicate definitions.
- Page numbers followed by "t" indicate tables.
- Page numbers followed by "btw" indicate margin notes.
- Page numbers followed by "+t" or "+btw" indicate discussions plus tables or margin notes.

Symbols